KU-713-741

For
Sonia, Miranda, Nicholas,
Rosalind and Ophelia

Social Interaction

MICHAEL ARGYLE

*Reader in Social Psychology University of Oxford
and fellow of Wolfson College*

TAVISTOCK PUBLICATIONS

First published 1969
by Methuen and Co Ltd

©1969 Michael Argyle

First published as a Social Science Paperback
in 1973 by Tavistock Publications Ltd
11 New Fetter Lane, London EC4P 4EE
Reprinted twice
Reprinted 1978

ISBN 0 422 75480 3

Printed and bound in Great Britain by
J. W. Arrowsmith Ltd, Bristol

This paperback edition is sold subject to the condition that it shall not, by way of trade or otherwise,
be lent, resold, hired out, or otherwise circulated
without the publisher's prior consent in any form
of binding or cover other than that in which it is
published and without a similar condition including
this condition being imposed on the subsequent
purchaser.

THE CITY OF LIVERPOOL COLLEGE
OF HIGHER EDUCATION
LIBRARY

301·15

181 840

Contents

Analysis of the behaviour of an interactor
Dyads as social systems
Forming the relationship

Preface

This book is intended as a textbook for students of social psychology and other social sciences. It covers some of the same ground as *The Psychology of Interpersonal Behaviour* but in considerably more detail.

The approach of this book differs from that of other books about social behaviour in two main ways. Firstly it analyses social behaviour in terms of the basic elements of interaction – bodily contact, proximity, orientation, gestures, facial expression, eye-movements, the verbal and non-verbal aspects of speech. Secondly it relates social interaction to its biological roots, and to the surrounding culture.

I have drawn freely from the writings of researchers in interpersonal psychiatry, primate ethology, anthropology, developmental psychology, organisational psychology, as well as those in experimental social psychology. I am particularly indebted to the pioneers of research into interaction and non-verbal communication – E. D. Chapple, J. R. Davitz, Paul Ekman, E. H. Erikson, Ralph Exline, Erving Goffman, E. T. Hall, Sidney Jourard, Albert Scheflen and T. R. Sarbin.

I am indebted to past and present members of the Oxford social psychology research group, who have collaborated on research reported here and commented on the MS – Nigel Armistead, Nicholas Bateson, Bridget Bryant, Peter Collett, Mark Cook, Janet Dean, Roger Ingham, Adam Kendon, Barbara Lalljee, Mansur Lalljee, Brian Little, Mary Lydall, Robert McHenry, Peter McPhail, Hilary Nicholson, Euan Porter, Veronica Salter, Mary Sissons, Jerry Tognoli, Ederyn Williams, and Marylin Williams.

We are grateful to Professor Albert Cherns, Hilary Clay and the Social Science Research Council for making grants to support this research, and to Douglas Seymour and Joyce Clarke who acted as consultants. Elizabeth Sidney and the staff of the Careers Research and Advisory Centre collaborated over the development of training methods. Ann McKendry typed the MS.

MICHAEL ARGYLE

Institute of Experimental Psychology,
Oxford
May 1968

Acknowledgements

The author and publishers would like to thank the following for permission to use figures from the sources given below:

The Editors, *British Journal of Social and Clinical Psychology*, for Figure 3.1 from 'An Exploratory Study of Body-Accessibility' by S. M. Jourard, Figure 3.4 from 'The Effects of Dependency and Social Reinforcement upon Visual Behaviour during an Interview' by R. V. Exline and D. Messick and Figure 3.6 from 'Anxiety, Speech Disturbance and Speech Rate' by M. Cook; The Editor, *Human Relations*, for Figure 3.2 from 'The Directions of Activity and Communication in a Departmental Executive Group' by T. Burns and Figure 7.1 from 'A Mathematical Model for Structural Role Theory' by O. A. Oeser and F. Harary; Oxford University Press, N.Y., for Figure 3.7 from *Principles and Methods of Social Psychology* by E. P. Hollander; *Journal of Experimental Psychology*, for Figure 3.8 from 'The Description of Facial Expression in Terms of Two Dimension' by H. Schlosberg © 1952 American Psychological Association; Addison-Wesley Publishing Co. Inc. for Figure 4.1 from T. R. Sarbin in *Handbook of Social Psychology*, ed. G. Lindzey and E. Aronson; Penguin Books Ltd for Figures 5.1 and 7.5 from *The Psychology of Interpersonal Behaviour* by M. Argyle; John Wiley & Sons Inc. for Figures 5.5 and 5.6 from *Foundations of Social Psychology* by E. E. Jones and H. B. Gerard; The Author for Figure 5.8 from 'Some Aspects of the Development of Interpersonal Relationship' by D. A. Taylor; The Editor, *American Sociological Review*, for Figure 6.1 from 'Channels of Communication in Small Groups' by R. F. Bales *et al.*; McGraw-Hill Publishing Co. Ltd for Figures 7.2 and 7.3 from *New Patterns of Management* by R. Likert; *Journal of Abnormal and Social Psychology*, for Figure 7.4 from 'Some Effects of Certain Communication Patterns' by H. J. Leavitt © 1951 American Psychological Association; *Journal of Personality and Social Psychology* for Figure 8.2 from 'Expansion of the Interpersonal Behaviour Circle' by M. Lorr and D. McNair © 1965 American Psychological Association; The Editor, *Sociometry*, for Figure 9.1 from 'Self-Conception and the Reactions of Others' by R. Videbeck; Stanford University Press for Figure 10.4 from *Insight v. Desensitization in Psychotherapy* by G. L. Paul.

I

Introduction

A NEW LOOK AT THE STUDY OF SOCIAL BEHAVIOUR

There seems to be widespread support for the view that man's achievements in the physical sciences and technology have outstripped his powers to control them, and that it is up to the biological and social sciences to provide the necessary understanding of human nature. It may be argued that the most pressing social problems are concerned with the relationships between people, and that these are an essential and central part of human nature. Human beings are reared in families, on which they are at first completely dependent, and in which they acquire most of their learnt behaviour. The death of a close relative is a deeply disturbing experience (Gorer, 1965) and can permanently impair the personality of other members. In all communities there is work to be done, to provide food and shelter, and to satisfy other needs; this work is always performed by cooperative working groups. Outside family and work, human beings at most stages of life seek the company and support of friends. Much individual unhappiness, including that caused by mental disorder, is associated with a breakdown of relationships with other people. Most social problems consist of the breakdown of communication, interaction and cooperation between different races or classes, or between groups at work.

For many years very little was known about the process of social interaction – there were no concepts to describe it or methods to study it. During the last few years several different groups of research workers have started to look at social behaviour in a new way. They have focused their attention on the sequence of events taking place during social interaction – at the level of bodily contact and proximity, facial expression, bodily posture and gesture, head movements and direction of gaze, the verbal and non-verbal contents of speech. They looked at what happens in social encounters in more detail, and in a more concrete way than had been attempted before. We now know how these different elements function in social behaviour. The research has been carried out by workers in a number of different fields – experimental social psychology, psychotherapy research, anthropology, linguistics and animal behaviour. The advances in each of these fields are in some cases closely related, though the investigators were working quite independently. For example the research by experimental social psychologists on 'non-verbal communication' was carried out in ignorance of the work on signalling in non-human primates. Other groups have been in contact for some time. The link between work on human verbal communication and on non-verbal behaviour has hardly been made at all.

This work constitutes something of a 'new look' in the study of social behaviour. Parts of it have sometimes been referred to as 'human ethology', 'interpersonal psychiatry', 'kinesics' and 'paralinguistics'. In view of its interdisciplinary character, and since it is based on concrete interpersonal events, it is possible that it may contribute towards the integration of the biological and social sciences. Kuhn, in his account of *The Structure of Scientific Revolutions* (1962), points out that scientific advances are rarely produced by the refutation of earlier theories, but are brought about by groups of scientists working out alternative ways of studying or conceptualising the problems in question.

Social behaviour is often thought to be the special province of social psychology, yet some of the main advances have come from outside this field by workers in the other disciplines mentioned. It is the view of the present author that social psychology has become too isolated from other behavioural sciences, and has suffered by restricting itself too narrowly to 'social psychology' experiments and theories. A great impetus was given to social psychology by the development of experimental techniques for studying small social groups, and the early results were very interesting (cf. Cartwright and Zander, 1959; Hare, Borgatta and Bales, 1955). However, there are signs that this vein has been worked out. 'Cohesiveness' for example is a central variable here, and much of the research on small groups has been concerned with its causes and effects. Lott and Lott (1965) have produced a comprehensive review of it, from which it seems to this author that (a) little remains to be done, and (b) nothing very exciting has been found out. Mann (1967) comments:

Ask a group therapist, a trainer, or a teacher what use he can make of the voluminous outpouring of empirical research on small groups. The unhappy fact is that many, if not most, of the potential consumers of such work feel that such research is constantly asking the wrong questions in the wrong ways and that it is at best irrelevant and at worst inaccurate and misleading (p. 7).

Recent textbooks of social psychology take a very different approach from the 'new look' approach. They use rather abstract terms such as 'frequency of interaction' (regardless of what is said or done), and 'small social group' (regardless of whether this is a family, a work-group, etc.). Little is said about the actual behaviour taking place in social encounters. Contrasted with the new look approach they place most emphasis on laboratory experiments, often under highly artificial conditions.

Social behaviour occurs in animals and has evolutionary origins. Ethologists have been making careful, descriptive studies of animal behaviour for some time. Since about 1960 the earlier work of Tinbergen (1951) and Lorenz has been extended into field studies of the social behaviour of monkeys and apes (DeVore, 1965). The findings of this research are closely parallel to findings of new look research carried out on humans during the same period – for example showing the importance of non-verbal signals in regulating interpersonal relationships. The link with ethology is an important part of the new perspective – it draws attention to the evolutionary and instinctive roots of social behaviour, the sensory channels and methods of signalling used, and the biological and other drives which produce social interaction. It is this similarity which has led to the new look research being described as 'human ethology'. In so far as it involves the careful descriptive study of human interaction in more or less natural habitats, this is an accurate description, but it also includes a range of experimentation some of which would not be acceptable to ethologists proper.

There is one striking difference between the social behaviour of men and that of apes and monkeys – we use language, where they can only emit a small range of grunts, signalling emotion and interpersonal attitudes. Most human behaviour involves speech, but students of social behaviour until very recently have paid very little attention to the content of what is said, and have simply measured how long utterances lasted. Linguists on the other hand have paid no attention to the social setting of speech. New look research has been concerned with the two main channels used in human social interaction – hearing and vision – and the ways in which these are linked. Verbal communication depends in a number of ways on the accompanying non-verbal signals – for example to control the timing of utterances and to obtain feedback on what is being said.

Ethologists maintain that animals should be studied in their natural habitats; however, much recent work in social psychology has used highly artificial laboratory situations which are unlike anything in the outside world. There is a particular objection to this for the study of human social behaviour: we learn to interact in a number of different kinds of social situation – in the family, at school, with friends, etc. – in each of which there are definite rules and role-relationships between the interactors. For this reason it is essential to study social behaviour in specific cultural settings. Sociology and anthropology have been concerned mainly with such uniformities of social behaviour, and these consist basically of interaction patterns. A social structure consists of regularities of social behaviour between people occupying different positions.

Psychologists, of various kinds, are concerned with human behaviour; social interaction is one of the most important kinds of human behaviour and must depend on the same neurophysiological and cognitive processes as other behaviour. Earlier approaches in psychology, emphasising rather elementary learning processes, were not very helpful to the study of social behaviour. However, certain advances in experimental psychology have provided a model of human behaviour that can embrace some, though not all, of the phenomena of interaction. One of the most important developments in recent years has been the rediscovery of the importance of cognitive processes in behaviour, for example of the verbal mediation of behaviour. Other developments of importance for the study of social interaction have been the study of motor skill and the physiological basis of motivation. Developmental psychologists have been interested in the childhood origin of social behaviour for some time; there have been important advances in this area, as well as links with animal behaviour (Foss, 1961–5).

Psychiatrists have become increasingly aware that mental disorder has interpersonal as well as biological origins, that many of the symptoms are in the sphere of interaction, and that various kinds of social treatment can be useful (Argyle, 1964b). Psychotherapy may or may not cure patients; it is however a dyadic situation which it has been possible to study in great detail and which has added enormously to our understanding of social interaction.

One of the main achievements of the new research has been to establish the basic elements of social behaviour, such as the different kinds of bodily posture and looking; these are described, together with the processes producing them, in Chapter III. The study of person perception has been held back by a failure to take account of the interactional content – of what people are trying to find out and the cues which they use, in different social situations; this is discussed in Chapter IV. Much of the new look research has been carried out so far in 2-person interaction, and even here the sheer quantity of data soon becomes unmanageable; the work is reviewed in Chapter V. The impact of the new look on small social groups has been small so far; we have concentrated attention on non-laboratory groups and the main types of group in the outside world (Chapter VI). Much remains to be done too in the field of social organisations; the main developments have been concerned with interaction associated with leadership and role conflict (Chapter VII). Individual differences have been found in social interaction between different personalities, normal and abnormal, making a somewhat unexpected contribution to the study of personality – for example in producing some new dimensions which are needed to deal with interpersonal behaviour (Chapter VIII). Interaction is also affected in special ways by identity and self-image (Chapter IX). Some of the main practical applications of social interaction research are in the development of methods of training for professional social skill, for social competence in mental patients, and training schoolchildren to perform competently in everyday social situations (Chapter X).

DILEMMA OF EXPERIMENTAL RESEARCH

Experiments are devised in order to test hypotheses which cannot be tested in ordinary situations. This usually results in constructing a situation which is in some way simplified or stripped down, which may lack some essential features of the original situation, and which may produce types of behaviour that would not normally occur. Bannister (1966) protested against experiments in human experimental psychology:

> Experimental psychology presents one aspect of our paradox in its sharpest form. In order to behave like scientists we must construct situations in which our subjects are totally controlled, manipulated and measured. We must cut our subjects down to size. We construct situations in which they can behave as little like human beings as possible and we do this in order to allow ourselves to make statements about the nature of their humanity.
>
> It may be that an imprisoned, minuscule man is all we are capable of studying but let us acknowledge that we do miserable experiments because we lack the imagination to do better ones, not claim that these are scientifically ideal because they are simple minded (p. 24).

Research in experimental social psychology has sometimes gone even further – it has compelled people to behave not only like rats but like *solitary* rats. In order to eliminate interfering variables, subjects may be placed in separate cubicles and have to communicate by pressing buttons or passing notes. A visitor to a new laboratory which consisted largely of such cubicles said 'but I thought this was supposed to be a *social* psychology laboratory'. In several areas of research in social psychology there has been a gradual shift to ever more stripped-down kinds of experiment as investigators have tried to hold constant supposedly extraneous variables, by eliminating them. How does one find out what the essential elements are? Clearly not by experimental methods. Psychoanalysts and clinical psychologists have made important contributions to psychology in the past because their detailed descriptive studies have thrown light on important phenomena, which were later studied more rigorously by experiments. Anthropologists and ethologists have played a similar role in the study of social behaviour; their data is rich and detailed, whereas experiments restrict the variables and processes operating, and prevent things happening which fall outside the conceptual scheme of the experimenter. On the other hand experimental research clearly does have certain crucial advantages – experiments can show that variable X affects Y, rather than vice versa, or both being an effect of Z; experiments can disentangle which of several possible variables or processes is most important, by holding the others constant; and experiments can show the strength of relationships, their mathematical form, and the range of conditions under which they operate.

We shall discuss three ways in which the results of experimental research can be misleading or actually wrong, and then consider how hypothesis-testing research can be conducted to escape from the dilemma described above.

1. *Key elements and processes may be omitted*. The 'stripped-down' kind of experiment has a certain appeal – it seems to enable the testing of hypotheses in a highly controlled manner, where the experimental variable operates without the interference of other features of the situation. An example is experiments on the 'minimal social situation', where two subjects are placed in cubicles unaware of the existence of each other. Each can press two buttons of which one gives the other subject a shock and the second switches a red light on for the other subject, and gives him a point. The task is to get as large a score as possible (p. 193 f). Another example is experiments with game-playing tasks in which subjects are asked to make as much money as possible, but are not

allowed to communicate with the other player (p. 196 f). There is a similarity between these experiments and those in which human subjects are asked to learn finger-mazes blindfold, or to learn nonsense syllables: because the forms of learning found in rats are used by subjects in the experiments, it does not follow that these processes operate under normal conditions. The social experiments referred to above exclude the following components of social behaviour: verbal and most non-verbal communication, the arousal of the usual social drives, perception of the other person, role-relationships, most aspects of the cultural background. Research of this kind has added some of these elements, one at a time – for example permitting some communication, or providing information about the other person (p. 197). Interesting results have certainly been obtained using these procedures, for example about reciprocity and helping behaviour (p. 171 ff), but there is a great danger that key elements and processes may be left out of account. The procedures described do not lend themselves however to the study of the process of interaction.

2. *The results may be exaggerated.* A good example comes from studies of the effects of mass communications. Hovland (1959) observed that in laboratory experiments the percentage of subjects showing attitude change is typically 30–50%, while in field situations it is only 5%. The reason for the discrepancy is that in the field situation a number of other factors operate to reduce the effects of the communications, such as selective exposure and the restraining influence of group norms. Similar considerations apply to interaction research. Person perception studies using photographs or brief exposure of the stimulus person have commonly found that spectacles, lipstick and untidy hair have a great effect on judgements of intelligence and other traits. It is suggested later that these results are probably an exaggeration of any effects that might occur when more information about a person is available (p. 135).

3. *The results may be wrong.* A number of experiments have been repeated under artificial and more natural conditions and have obtained quite different results. Laboratory experiments on operant verbal conditioning on the whole suggest that learning without awareness does not occur, and that the process involved is one of verbalised concept-formation (Spielberger, 1965). However, experiments carried out under naturalistic conditions appear to support a different conclusion (p. 176 ff).

There is a more general way in which laboratory research can produce the wrong results. When a subject steps inside a psychological laboratory he steps out of culture, and all the normal rules and conventions are temporarily discarded and replaced by the single rule of laboratory culture – 'do what the experimenter says, no matter how absurd or unethical it may be'. This is shown by the results of experiments in which subjects comply with instructions to give other subjects very large electric shocks (e.g. Milgram, 1963).

Research on the social behaviour of animals in captivity has notoriously obtained misleading results. DeVore (1968) comments: 'From the perspective of modern field studies, the conclusions based on the behavior of primates in captivity bore as little relation to the behavior of free-ranging groups as would a monograph on middle-class society based solely on a study of inmates in a maximum-security prison' (p. 358). There are a number of other ways in which the results of experiments may be wrong or misleading, but these can usually be avoided by skilful techniques. The experimenter may confirm his hypotheses by giving subtle hints to subjects about what he wants them to do (Rosenthal, 1966); subjects may guess, rightly or wrongly, the point of the experiment and try to help the experimenter confirm the hypotheses; the experimental manipulation may have a different effect on the subject than that intended, and more than one process may be taking place (Aronson and Carlsmith, 1968). Experiments should be designed to make proper use of control groups, and to minimise the effects of practice, repeated testing, etc. (Campbell and Stanley, 1963).

Having seen the shortcomings of some kinds of experimental research, we must now consider how to escape from the dilemma which we posed originally – how to test hypotheses without creating situations which produce the wrong results. We are not concerned here so much with the details of different experimental designs, but with the general strategy or art of research; the same experimental design can be used successfully or unsuccessfully. We stressed above the importance of clinical and observational studies: here we shall be concerned only with hypothesis-testing designs.

1. *Natural experiments* and 'ex post facto' studies are the traditional solution to the problem (Argyle, 1957a), and a number of studies with groups and organisations have been of this form. However, our present concern is with the details of interaction processes, which cannot be studied after the event, so that this method is of rather limited value.

2. *Experiments on unsuspecting subjects.* Members of the public who are walking down the street or sitting in libraries are approached by trained

confederates, and the subject's behaviour is recorded either by the confederate or by another person. An example of this kind of research is Feldman's study (1968) of helpfulness to strangers in different cultures, in which confederates asked people the way or asked for help with posting a letter. The experiment on operant verbal conditioning by Verplanck (1955) is another example; experimenters held quite natural conversations with friends in their rooms or homes, but varied the pattern of reinforcement given for the expression of opinions, and recorded how many were expressed. This kind of research is really restricted to the study of one-way influences, and there are practical difficulties of recording the responses, but otherwise the method is most valuable.

3. *Laboratory experiments which re-create real-life situations.* In some studies subjects do not realise that they are taking part in an experiment – they may be studied while in the 'waiting-room' for example. In others they are asked to take part in a replica of a kind of encounter with which they are familiar, such as an interview. This serves to arouse the social conventions and some of the motivation present in real-life encounters, and the subjects may be friends, relations, or strangers. It is possible to create all kinds of experimental manipulations and still keep the situation fairly normal and conventional. The dilemma of experimental research becomes really acute when the experimenter wants to interfere with the situation to test some kinds of hypothesis. It is not clear whether the dilemma can in fact be resolved in some cases.

4. *Projective and mock-up methods.* Experimental problems are sometimes translated into projective and schematic situations. Thayer and Schiff (1967) constructed pairs of schematic faces where the elements of facial expression were varied; the pattern of motion between the pairs was also varied, and subjects were asked to infer interpersonal attitudes from the combination of facial and movement cues. This experiment shows another aspect of the original dilemma – the technique has the great advantage of eliminating 'interfering factors', but it remains to be seen whether too much has been stripped off, and whether the same results are obtained under more realistic conditions. Another example is an experiment by Tognoli (1968), who tested hypotheses about proximity by means of cardboard cut-outs. Cut-out A was moved nearer or further from cut-out B, and subjects were asked to show how they would expect B to respond. He was able to incorporate variations in status, sex, and situation, and test a number of hypotheses (p. 175).

Rather similar is the technique of providing a written description of some situation to subjects and asking how they would respond, as used by McPhail (1967) in studies of adolescent social behaviour (p. 398 ff). A difficulty with these techniques is that people are not aware of such variables as proximity, or bodily posture, and do not know how they would actually behave.

5. *The intensive analysis of sequences of normal interaction.* Very useful work can be done by making audio-, video- or interaction recordings of natural sequences of interaction, and then subjecting them to detailed statistical analysis. Kendon (1967) did this for conversations between people invited to 'get acquainted', and Scheflen (1965) did the same for psychotherapy interviews. The method can provide information about the correlation and sequence of different elements of interaction, but does not enable hypotheses to be tested so clearly as experimental designs do. It is possible to make causal inferences however; Kendon (op. cit.) showed for example that the absence of a terminal look at the end of an utterance resulted in a long pause before the other person replied. This method has mainly been applied to psychotherapy sessions and laboratory groups. It would be most valuable to have similar material on sequences of interaction in families, work-groups, etc.

There has been a growing interest in training groups (T-groups) because an extensive body of data can be collected over a series of meetings (see p. 260 ff). Mann (1967) succeeded in making a statistical analysis of the pattern of role-differentiation in these groups (p. 264 f). The difficulty with T-groups however is that they are quite unlike any other kind of small social group, and the results obtained will probably not be applicable to other groups – except perhaps in a very general sense, e.g. showing that there *is* role-differentiation in groups.

T-group practitioners maintain that investigators should take subjects fully into their confidence and discuss the empirical material with them. In experiments this is often impossible, since if subjects knew that, for example, their posture or eye-movements were being studied, they would behave differently. The author agrees with Jourard (1964) that subjects should be told as much as possible, treated as collaborators, and should normally be 'de-briefed' after the experiment. It is usually unnecessary to mislead subjects, and the author's practice is simply to tell them that this is a study of what happens in conversations (or groups, etc.), and that the specific hypotheses will be explained later.

In this book we shall give priority to investigations of the kinds just described. We shall also refer to more artificial investigations, where these are the only ones available on a given problem, but we shall try to bear in mind their limitations.

THEORIES OF SOCIAL BEHAVIOUR

There are three reasons for having theories in science. Firstly they integrate diverse findings in a coherent and economical form. Secondly, they provide a frame of reference for looking at phenomena, suggest the variables to be studied and they make concrete predictions for further research. Thirdly, they give a satisfying feeling of 'explanation' which makes the phenomena seem less perplexing.

1. *Integrating diverse findings.* Current theories of social behaviour are based on a small body of empirical data, and then used to 're-interpret' a few other highly selected studies. For example 'exchange theory' appears to have been based originally on a small number of (non-experimental) studies, such as Blau's study of a bureaucracy (1955) and the reformatory study by Jennings (1950). A large number of further studies have been re-interpreted in exchange theory terms, by re-labelling some of the variables (e.g. by Secord and Backman, 1964). A similar account could be given of other theories in this area. The data accommodated by theories of social behaviour tends to be restricted to small groups of experiments carried out by workers in a particular tradition, and to have little application to familiar real-life phenomena. Bannister (1966) observes of theories in experimental psychology: 'It may be that psychology is the only science which has been able to produce concepts of its subject which are clearly more mean, more miserable, and more limited than lay concepts' (p. 26). The same is even more true of theories of social behaviour, and it must be concluded that the power of these theories to integrate existing findings is extremely weak.

2. *Providing the basis for research.* Most theories in this area have however generated research. But since the theories have usually been formulated in terms of simple, abstract concepts, the resulting research has often been of a greatly over-simplified, 'stripped-down', variety. Learning theory and games-theory result in experiments which exclude some of the essential factors in social behaviour – language, culture, a biological basis, and social interaction itself. It may be argued that if a theory generates experiments in which the crucial elements are lacking, then there is something missing from the theory. It is interesting that many of the most interesting experiments in social interaction have

either been very loosely linked to theory, or quite unconnected with theory.

3. *Giving a feeling of explanation.* This is perhaps the least important feature of theorising, from a scientific point of view. Furthermore, theories which are later found to be mistaken can provide this feeling as well as or better than the theories that replace them – Newton's account of gravitation seems better than Einstein's from this point of view. The author has noticed that psychologists tend to become satisfied by simply translating phenomena into the terminology of their favourite theory – introversion and extroversion, reward and punishment, super-ego and id, information flow and so on.

We would like to argue that theorising in the field of social behaviour is premature: theories have been constructed before the basic empirical phenomena in the field were discovered. In an attempt to provide a systematic way of describing the phenomena, they in fact say less than what everyone knows already. What is needed first is a working picture of what is going on in social situations. This means mapping the sensory channels of communication, listing the biological and other drives, and describing the basic sequences of behaviour which make up social inter-action. This task has been most successfully achieved so far in the area of dyadic interaction.

II

The Biological and Cultural Roots of Interaction

This chapter is intended to provide an account of the biological and cultural background to social interaction. These topics will be treated relatively briefly, focusing on those aspects of them that are most relevant to the study of social interaction. It is believed that these matters are essential for an understanding of social behaviour.

Social interaction is to a great extent pre-programmed by innate neural structures which result from natural selection, and by cultural norms, which represent past collective solutions to the problems of interaction. In lower animals social interaction is largely governed by the innate programme; the sequence of interaction leading to copulation in pigeons for example is stereotyped (Fabricius and Jansson, 1963), and has presumably emerged from the process of natural selection because it has survival value. In the higher mammals infants are born with more 'open' instinctive programmes, that remain to be completed by early experiences in the family, which depend on instinctive patterns of rearing by the mother. Field studies of animals have shown how their social behaviour is related to basic biological needs – for food, shelter, defence against predators, reproduction and care of young. Recent studies of apes and monkeys have shown that there are remarkable parallels with the social behaviour of humans – in the types of social relationships that are formed and the ways of establishing these relationships by non-verbal signals. This work has provided a fresh perspective on human social interaction, showing in particular that interaction serves biological needs and has instinctive roots.

Human social interaction is pre-programmed in a second way: patterns of interaction have been worked out by earlier members of the society, embodied in cultural rules and norms, and are taught to the young. Each of these rules or patterns has been retained because it has been found to be a useful way of handling some situation, and the rules can take rather different forms in different cultures. It is not always easy to find out which is the origin of a particular programme; for example hand-shaking or something like it is found in apes, and appears to have an innate basis, but in humans the particular method and occasion is defined by the culture.

Human infants are socialised in two ways – they acquire the basic drives of sex, affiliation, dominance, etc., which have an innate basis, but need completion through socialisation. They also learn the basic patterns of interaction and rules governing different social situations in their society. Furthermore, they learn a language, and this makes their subsequent behaviour very different from that of animals; their social interaction thereafter consists partly of speech, and they are able to learn, modify and pass on the contents of the culture.

THE SOCIAL BEHAVIOUR OF NON-HUMAN PRIMATES

Man is a branch of the primates that has evolved in a different way from the various species of apes (chimpanzees, gorillas, etc.) and monkeys (macaques, baboons, etc.). Chimpanzees are most similar to man in intelligence. The main differences are probably the power of language, the growth of culture, and the longer period of dependence on the family in humans. Men also eat other animals, stand upright, and use weapons and tools. Learning from the environment is more important for the non-human primates than for animals lower in the evolutionary scale; nevertheless primate social behaviour is species specific and clearly has a strong innate, instinctive basis.

It is not generally recognised by social psychologists that social behaviour has any innate origins. An important part of the social signalling system is the expression of emotions and interpersonal attitudes by postures and facial expression. Darwin (1872) argued that the pattern of emotional expression in animals and men is innate and reflects the biological structure of the autonomic system – producing weeping, baring of teeth, blushing, pupil expansion, hair erection, etc. He argued that these expressions appear in young children, are mainly outside voluntary control (and hence could not be learned), are found in the blind, in different races, and are very similar in men and animals. He recognised that this was less true of other signals such as head nodding and shaking. Darwin and later zoologists have been concerned with the evolutionary processes which have led up to such innate patterns of emotional response. Ethological research has used the same approach for the study of behaviour. Experiments with animals reared in isolation have confirmed the existence of innate patterns of social behaviour. For example Sackett (1965) found that rhesus monkeys reared alone in closed cages responded to pictures of monkeys threatening and pictures of infant monkeys, by increased play, exploration, vocalisation and disturbance, and would operate a lever to expose these two pictures.

The study of animal behaviour by ethological methods began with the work of Tinbergen, Lorenz and their students, mainly on birds and fish. The ethological method is to carry out detailed field observations of the behaviour patterns of a species, to carry out laboratory experiments which are closely related to the normal life of the animal, and to interpret the results in relation to the biological needs met by behaviour, and the evolutionary processes leading up to it. Since about 1960 there has been a considerable amount of ethological research on monkeys and apes, both in the field and in the laboratory. The field studies have provided important information about the social behaviour of primates under natural conditions.

Field studies have been carried out of a number of species of primates (DeVore, 1965). There is some variation in the social behaviour of different species but it is possible to generalise about it to some extent (Mason, 1965a; Schrier, Harlow and Stollnitz, 1965). This work has been carried out during the same period as, and totally independently of, the work on human social interaction to be described later, and it is likely that ideas and findings from each field will stimulate work in the other. For example there is little primate research on the role of eye-contact in socialisation, on patterns of maternal behaviour, or on the social skills of dominance.

We can see how basic biological processes require patterns of social behaviour, which must have become selected in the course of evolution for this purpose. Hunger, thirst, reproduction, and care of young need patterns of behaviour in which (1) adult males cooperate in the defence of territory and group, (2) opposite-sex pairs mate, (3) mothers look after children. In addition there are (4) patterns of cooperative play apart from work, which may serve the function of restraining aggression and holding the group together.

Territory

Nearly all animals live in groups that inhabit a territory. The territory provides for the basic biological needs of hunger and thirst. Wynne-Edwards (1962) proposed the theory that there is a homeostatic mechanism to attain the ideal numbers and dispersion of animals in relation to the food available. When the density is perceived to be too great there is migration and fighting, when the density is too small the breeding rate goes up. A different view was put forward by Ardrey (1967) who suggested that there is an innate disposition to occupy territory as a group and to defend it against invasion.

Monkeys and apes live in groups, or troops, of fixed membership, which may be as high as 750. Unlike many other animals however they do not have a permanent nest or hole, but wander over their territory, usually sleeping in temporary nests in the trees. The territory may be as large as 15 square miles (chimpanzees, gorillas, baboons) or as small as $\frac{1}{10}$ of a square mile (gibbons). Within these territories are core areas used exclusively by one group and containing trees for sleeping, and sources of food and water. Outside the core areas there may be considerable overlap of territories, but different troops keep apart and avoid fighting by hearing each other's calls. Under overcrowded conditions as for macaques in Indian cities, there is frequent fighting between the males of same and different groups. While some kinds of monkeys will drive off other groups with great ferocity, chimpanzees do not defend their territory, but they do not have groups of fixed membership either (Goodall, 1965; Jay, 1965a).

Aggression

Primates, like other animals, fight members of other species when competing for the same source of food, when hunting, and when attacked. They will also attack members of their own species if their territory is invaded, or if there is a severe shortage of food. It is necessary, for the survival of species and group, that aggression should take place to defend the sources of food and water.

They may also fight members of their own troop, but not with the intention of killing. Intra-group aggression is thought to serve four purposes, and to have evolved for these reasons. (1) It leads to members of the group spreading out evenly over the food-producing area. (2) Fighting between males for females results in the stronger males reproducing themselves (this can have useless consequences, such as the stag's antlers). (3) Fighting is useful in the defence of the young. (4) It leads to the formation of a stable dominance hierarchy; while preventing further fighting, this enables the older and stronger males to assume leadership of the group (Lorenz, 1963: Tinbergen, 1953).

When two males are going to fight they begin by making threatening gestures – 'The contestants circle one another in a characteristically stilted fashion, their bodies tense and stiff. They may bow, nod, shake, shiver, swing rhythmically from side to side, or make repeated short, stylized runs. They paw the ground, arch their backs, or lower their heads' (Morris, 1967). This pattern of threat behaviour is partly the result of a conflict between the drives to attack and to flee; the conflict generates 'displacement activities', such as scratching, cleaning, yawning or stretching. The result is a somewhat ritualized pattern of threat behaviour. It is against the interests of the species for the fight to actually take place, and generally it does not; attacks on other animals are quite rare. The animal which has been threatened or attacked may react in three main ways. (1) It may run away, screeching, urinating and looking over its shoulder. (2) It may threaten or attack the first animal; eventually one submits or there may be an actual fight; however, most of these conflicts are resolved by bluff in the form of threat displays. (3) It may appease the aggressor, by cowering, curling up, holding out a hand, facing away, and lowering the eyes. In addition the submitting animal may try to re-motivate the other by trying to arouse a different drive: it may present its hindquarters (even if male) to arouse sex, beg for food like a child, or invite grooming by smacking its lips together (Morris, 1967; Lorenz, op. cit.).

Aggression between males for females is aroused only during the breeding season. Territorial aggression is aroused when an intruder invades the home territory. The aggressive response is particularly released by the sight or smell of a male of the same species. Apes and monkeys, like humans, become angry if frustrated from obtaining some expected satisfaction. It seems likely that aggression is the innate response to these releasing stimuli and situations. Some scientists have argued that aggression is also a positive appetite or drive, and can appear without external stimulation. It is true that the threshold for release of aggression falls when the organism is in certain internal states, but it probably needs *some* external stimulus (Tinbergen, 1968). It is certainly the case that much social play consists of a kind of aggression, though this is different from real aggression. On the other hand there are various social mechanisms, such as ritualisation, dominance hierarchy, and avoidance of other troops, which prevent aggression taking place.

Aggression depends partly on socialisation experiences in childhood. Harlow and Harlow (1965) report that the strength of aggression is affected by the presence or absence of mother or peers during childhood; probably it is the affiliative *restraints* on aggression which are most affected. Aggression may be the result of learning experiences with other animals of different degrees of aggressiveness. Mason (1965b) reports that animals reared in isolation lack the 'social skills' of dominating others by the use of threatening gestures alone.

Sexual behaviour

Monkeys and apes live in groups whose membership is fairly stable. The relations between males and females within the group are usually much less long-lasting. The gibbon lives in a permanent family group of an adult male and female and their children, but this is an exception. A similar long-lasting and intense relationship is found in geese. Lorenz (1963) suggests that this bond is created by the 'triumph ceremony', which consists of displaced aggressive responses that have the effect of appeasing and enabling habituation to overcome fear. A more common arrangement among the non-human primates is for a couple to consort together while the female is in oestrus for periods varying between a few hours and a few days. There may be a poly-gynous family consisting of one male, several females, and their children, as with patas monkeys. Or there may be a fairly high degree of promis-cuity, with the dominant males having most access to females – females seek out the dominant males, and the latter prevent lesser males from copulating with their females.

Male sexual behaviour in the form of penile erection and thrusting is found shortly after birth; homosexual behaviour occurs in childhood; heterosexual intercourse occurs during adolescence, and the correct position is gradually acquired. Goodall (1965) reports that in-experienced chimpanzees are unable to copulate successfully, but that they watch their mothers in the act, and are later able to perform properly. One infant 'reached out one hand and felt in the region where the penis was inserted'. Those reared in isolation do not usually engage in sexual behaviour at all, though it is not yet known which are the crucial childhood experiences (Harlow and Harlow, op. cit.). The sexual instinct therefore is 'open' and needs certain environmental experiences for it to appear.

Females will normally copulate only when in oestrus, usually about a week of their monthly cycle. In addition some species have an annual cycle, and are receptive only during the mating season (Lancaster and Lee, 1965). Female chimpanzees are receptive for 6–7 days out of a monthly cycle of 35 days, for 4 months of the year (Goodall, op. cit.) It is observed that females are more responsive to some males than to others. Males continue to display sexual behaviour after castration; it seems that in apes and monkeys sexual behaviour is less dependent on hormone concentration in the blood and more under cortical control than in lower mammals (Ford and Beach, 1952).

Females signal their readiness for copulation by their bodily colouring and swellings, and by presenting to the male. The male may also give a display – including erection of hair and penis, and gaze-fixation at the female; the female runs and is chased, and then presents. Copulation in monkeys and apes is very quick: there is very little foreplay, the male mounts, gives a few thrusts, and dismounts, the whole process lasting a few seconds. It may be repeated with the same female several times at short intervals.

Presenting and mounting may take place under other conditions as well. Both males and females may mount other animals, sometimes with intromission, as part of a dominance relationship; the other animal presents as an appeasement gesture (Wickler, 1967). Presenting is often used in greeting, probably to appease aggression on the part of the other animal. It is also a regular feature of social play, though it is less common than fighting.

Affiliation

Animals in a group constantly compete for food and females; this arouses aggression yet there is very little fighting between them. On the contrary there is a high degree of cooperation between them, in collective defence against predators and other groups, in seeking food and water, and in care of young. It seems likely that affiliative social bonds have survival value for the group and that innate affiliative patterns of behaviour have evolved. Relations between members of a group can be seen as an equilibrium between aggressive and affiliative processes: the affiliative forces hold the aggressive ones in check. It has been observed that a monkey or ape which leaves the group is usually unable to survive by itself – social cooperation is biologically necessary. Herbert Spencer (1904) regarded this as the biological basis for ethics – morals are innate because they have survival value for the group. There are other social bonds in primate groups, such as sex and the links between parents and children. It is now clear that sex is not the basis for primate cooperation – because females are available only at certain periods. Familial bonds are specifically directed towards children or parents, and are clearly a separate kind of affectional system.

Affiliative behaviour has been observed to follow a regular pattern of development; Harlow and Harlow (1965) suggest that there are four main stages for rhesus monkeys. (1) In the reflex stage infant monkeys maintain close physical proximity to each other; it is suggested that this is due to orienting reflexes. (2) In the exploratory stage there is oral and manual exploration of all objects present. There is interest in moving objects, and particularly in other animals. Young primates seek more and more responsiveness until the others develop aggressive reactions. (3) Rough-and-tumble play, is described below and is followed by (4) aggressive play, in the course of which stable relationships are formed.

Affiliative behaviour is affected by socialisation experiences in the family, though the only variables to have been studied so far are the sheer presence or absence of mother or peers; nothing is known about the effects of different styles of maternal behaviour for example. Nor do the findings enable us to decide between the two main theories about the origins of affiliative behaviour: one hypothesis is that affiliative behaviour is due to generalisation of positive responses towards the mother (Mason, 1965a); the other is that affiliative responses are partly innate but develop through experience with the peer group (Harlow and Harlow, op. cit.). Studies of primates reared in total isolation, both from mother and peers, demonstrate the importance of early experience but do not show whether the mother or the peers are most important. A number of such studies show that after 6 months of total isolation for rhesus monkeys, or after 21 months for chimpanzees, no affiliative attachment ever develops and there is no clinging. Infants reared with other infants but without a mother cling together, and patterns of play are retarded, but eventually their social behaviour becomes normal (Sackett, 1967). Infants reared with their mother but without peers are more cautious and aggressive with peers later; Harlow and Harlow (op. cit.) suggest that this is because they have failed to form positive attachments with peers which would act as restraints for aggression. In the present state of research it appears that experiences both with peers and with the mother play a role in the development of affiliative behaviour.

Affiliative behaviour takes several forms. We shall consider greeting, play, grooming, cooperation and sympathy. When two animals meet, they often engage in lip-smacking and touch each other; one may present and the other mount, regardless of their sex; a chimpanzee may hold out a hand and touch the other on the top of the head, the shoulder, groin, thigh or genital area; baboons smell one another's genitals and nose; a friendly pair may embrace each other enthusiastically. Lorenz (1963) describes the ritualised greeting ceremonies observed in geese and other species, and considers that their purpose is the prevention of aggression. It will be shown below that lip-smacking is the usual way of inviting grooming, and that it reassures a subordinate animal and appeases a dominant one.

Young primates spend most of their time playing, and chimpanzees are the most playful. Their play consists mainly of approach and withdrawal in mock attack, wrestling and tumbling in mock fighting. They also engage in presenting and mounting. An invitation to play is made by various playful postures and gestures, and by the playface. The tempo of a play-chase or play fighting is different from the real thing – it is gentler and more relaxed, and is accompanied by the playface. Play begins in the early months of life, and is the main activity of the young. As they get older the play becomes rougher, and eventually leads to the formation of a dominance hierarchy. Play is thought to serve the functions of providing practice for adult life, of developing social skills, establishing positive bonds and enabling young animals to find their niche in society. Adult females also play with their young; adults play with each other to some extent, though they spend more time grooming (Loizos, 1967). It may be suggested that play is an expression of various kinds of positive social motivation.

Non-human primates spend a great deal of time grooming themselves and each other, sometimes alternately or simultaneously. One animal explores another's fur with its fingers, extracts small pieces of dried skin or foreign matter, conveys them to the mouth, and eats or tastes them. It is accompanied by rhythmic lip-smacking and the lip-smacking face. The groomee may invite grooming by lip-smacking, rolling on its side, or sitting sideways in front of the other animal, looking away from it and displaying part of its body. The groomer may initiate grooming by lip-smacking. Grooming occurs under several conditions. (1) Parents, especially mothers, groom their young; childless females may try to groom the young of other females. (2) Oestrous females and males may groom each other in the intervals between copulating. (3) Adults may groom each other; subordinate members of the hierarchy tend to groom more dominant members, young animals groom older, females groom males. This is interesting since being groomed means adopting a submissive posture. It has been suggested that a dominant animal will offer himself for grooming in order to reassure another – to prevent him from being frightened or running away. Similarly a subordinate animal may offer itself for grooming as an appeasement gesture. Grooming tends to be more prevalent in species with a steep dominance hierarchy. It looks as if grooming, and its lip-smacking signal, is a means of establishing an affiliative bond (Sparks, 1967). While play takes place under conditions of high arousal, such as when there is a tense relation between two animals, grooming appeases the aggression. Under intense fear animals will cling together in close bodily contact.

A further manifestation of affiliative motivation is cooperation. Threat from predators or other groups leads to a fierce, and coordinated defence of the group and its territory (Ardrey, 1967). There is also cooperation over food-gathering. Studies in the laboratory have shown that two chimpanzees will cooperate to manipulate laboratory apparatus to gain a food reward (Hebb and Thompson, 1954). There is evidence that chimpanzees are concerned for each other's welfare – what is called 'sympathy' in the case of humans. Nissen and Crawford (1936) studied the behaviour of pairs of chimpanzees in adjacent cages where only one of them had food. The animal without food begged for food and was given it, or the other would pass food without being asked. When two animals were in the same cage, the food was divided up fairly. In the wild, group cooperation is brought about by a form of group structure and leadership that varies for different species; it is described in the next section.

Group behaviour

Innate tendencies towards affiliation do more than create positive social bonds, they prescribe the form of group life for each species. The basic social unit of monkeys or apes is not the family but the group, or troop. The size of group varies from species to species: for gorillas 15–20, chimpanzees 30–60, baboons 5–750. For most species these groups are very stable in composition; it is very rare for an animal to change groups, and once it has left a group it is very hard to be readmitted (Jay, 1965a). The main exception to this is the chimpanzee – chimpanzee bands may change by the hour (Goodall, 1965). Groups contain a number of sub-groups of adult males, groups of children, of adult and adolescent females and infants, and pairs of males and oestrous females. These sub-groups are held together by the affiliative, familial and sexual bonds described above. In addition to these positive social forces another major motivation is operative – the struggle for dominance.

The phenomenon of the 'pecking order' was first observed in chickens; it is also found in primates and most other species. It is in the biological interests of an individual male animal to be dominant since it takes precedence over access to food and to females. Dominance may be of advantage to the group because it prevents internal aggression, provides leadership by the strongest males, and ensures that the strongest members will survive during a food shortage. The dominance hierarchy is strongest in ground-dwelling species, that are most liable to be attacked. The relative status of two males may be settled by fighting, but in the great majority of cases it is settled by a ritualised threat display, after which one submits. It is probably advantageous for the survival of the species for members of the group not to fight. Once the dominance order of two animals has been decided it remains fixed for ever afterwards. Dominance conveys a greater degree of satisfaction of bodily needs, in particular hunger and sex; dominance also entails control of territory, which is 'chiefly a licence to feed and mate' (Brown, 1965, p. 19). Since dominant males have preferential access to females, and are indeed sought out by them, they are the fathers of most of the children; presumably successive generations should evolve in the direction of whatever properties convey dominance. It is not known what these qualities are, but it is likely that size, strength and fighting ability are involved (Jay, 1965a).

The leadership and control of primate groups take a variety of forms.

1. Baboons and macaques live on the ground in open country in large troops; there is an oligarchy of dominant males, with a sharp pecking order between them, who share a harem of females and keep authoritarian control of the troop.

2. Gorillas, langurs and others live in thick forests in troops with a very relaxed hierarchy; one male assumes leadership but there is no monopolising of females by high-status males, and no fiercely established pecking order.

3. Hamadryas baboons and some other kinds of monkey live in smaller troops consisting of one male, his harem, and the children.

4. Gibbons and others live in families consisting of one male, one female and children.

5. Chimpanzees also live in the forests, in smaller groups of rapidly changing membership and with no dominance hierarchy (cf. DeVore, 1968; Morris and Morris, 1966).

The most common arrangement is for a number of dominant males to share degrees of social influence. A dominant male in the first four cases will direct the movements of the group, will decide whether food or water is satisfactory, and will stop quarrels within the group. His relations with the other males, once their social standing has been settled, is that others present while he mounts, and others groom him. It is interesting that the others are strongly attracted to him (Chance, 1955); this is more likely with a dominant male who only threatens without actually aggressing. Adult females when oestrous seek out dominant males and present for them. This results in a temporary rise in status for a female. Dominant males protect children, both from out-side predators, and from larger children in the group.

The dominance and leadership hierarchy is often associated with a particular spatial arrangement. Where attacks from predators are fre-quent, the adult males arrange themselves on the periphery of the group. In baboons, sentinels are placed at the periphery of the group, but inside there are a series of concentric circles with the most dominant animals at the middle. This pattern has been observed in langurs and macaques also (Chance, 1967). In this kind of group an animal will approach only to a certain distance from a more dominant male, depending on the social distance. His posture and gait reflect this – he will not put his tail up until he is a suitable distance away. The most dominant animals in a group have the most erect posture. Chance (op. cit.) observes that the lesser animals focus their attention on more dominant ones, in a chain. This enables them to follow the lead of more dominant animals and is, he suggests, the reason for the concentric spatial arrangement.

Interaction between parents and children

We have seen that there are elaborate patterns of primate social be-haviour which appear to be the result of evolutionary processes. A most important evolutionary development has been the opening of innate tendencies so that environmental experiences are needed to supplement and complete them. The period of dependence on the family has lengthened, as has the learning capacity of organisms. It is now neces-sary for there to be a series of behaviour patterns, partly innate, which produce appropriate behaviour of infants to parents, and parents to infants. As we shall see, this too is partly learnt.

It is biologically necessary for parents to provide food, shelter and protection from predators for their young. In the absence of a per-manent nest it is necessary for the young to be carried – infant chim-panzees are carried for $2\frac{1}{2}$–3 years; in the absence of any permanent family the larger group helps with these tasks. The infant shortly after birth has a number of innate reflexes which enable it to respond to the mother – finding and sucking the nipple, upward climbing, clinging and grasping the mother so that it can be carried. There is evidence that infants are very interested in the mother's face. They become condi-tioned to the mother and can discriminate her from other animals. Infants then go through a period (10 weeks for rhesus) in which they derive comfort from physical contact and feeding from the mother. External stress produces intense clinging to the mother; clinging is produced by arousal and is able to reduce arousal (Mason, 1965b). During a further period the presence of the mother provides security in the presence of unfamiliar and frightening objects. Finally there is a degree of separation from the mother, although the bond is extremely long-lasting (Harlow and Harlow, 1962). In his well-known experiments on cloth and wire mothers, Harlow (1959) has thrown considerable light on the development of the infant–mother bond. The most important finding is that infants spent much longer clinging to the cloth mother than to the wire mother (15 hours per day *v.* $2\frac{1}{2}$), and that it made little difference whether milk was supplied by the cloth or the wire mother. The cloth mother also provided more security: infants clung to her when frightened, and were then able to explore frightening objects. The usual interpretation of these experiments is that there is an innate response to fur, and that this is more important than food reinforcement in the development of the infant–mother bond. It may be pointed out however that there was a second difference between the cloth and the wire mothers – the face of the wire mother was less like a monkey face than that of the cloth mother. The role of the mother's face and eyes in socialisation remains to be studied, for the non-human primates.

It is also biologically necessary for there to be a bond from parents to infants, if the latter are to be properly cared for rather than neglected or attacked. Shortly after birth the mother produces the maternal responses of cradling, feeding and grooming the infant, and retrieving it if it escapes. As the infant gets older, increasing freedom of movement is allowed, but the mother continues to protect the infant. Similar behaviour is extended to other infants; female primates all show a great interest in infants. When the child is older the mother becomes ambivalent and starts to punish the child; finally there is a degree of separation and rejection of the child, especially when the next baby is born. Maternal behaviour is thought to be stimulated by the infant's clinging and sucking; monkeys reared without mothers themselves show no affection for infants and treat them very harshly. The behaviour of fathers is rather different: 'Male monkeys in the wild should be regarded as generalised fathers: they show affectional responses to members of their social group but do not show them differentially to their own or other children' (Harlow and Harlow, op. cit., p. 330). Adult males protect children as described above.

We have seen that experiences in the family affect the development of later affiliative, sexual and maternal behaviour. In other words family experiences are necessary for the normal development of these basic patterns of primate behaviour. In addition animals learn the particular behaviour pattern of their troop. Studies with Japanese monkeys have found that new elements of behaviour may be acquired by the whole troop and persist over a 10-year period. Examples are eating caramels, washing sweet potatoes, and separating grains of wheat from sand by washing in the sea. New habits were picked up most readily by younger, adolescent monkeys, and by males (Tsumori, 1967).

The elements of social interaction

We shall anticipate the next chapter of this book, on the elements of human social interaction, by considering the elements used or responded to by apes and monkeys.

Olfactory. Apes and monkeys make little use of taste and smell compared with most other mammals, though it probably plays some role in sexual arousal. Many species use olfactory markers to mark out territory; dogs for example use urine in this way; apes and monkeys however are very mobile and do not need to do this (Marler, 1965).

Tactile. The main form of tactile behaviour is grooming, which is done mainly by use of the hands, helped by the teeth, tongue and nose; it may be reciprocal. Aggressive bodily contacts are biting, striking and pulling the fur. Presentation, mounting and embracing occur not only between sexual partners, but in connection with dominance and appeasement. Clinging takes place when an animal is frightened. Greetings involve a wide variety of bodily contacts – genital and stomach nuzzling, kissing, embracing and grooming. These bodily contacts may take a variety of forms depending on the social relationship between two animals; biting may be aggressive or playful, grooming may last for a longer or shorter time (Hall, 1962).

Visible

(1) Bodily changes. Females in oestrus are marked by bright blue or red areas of skin and swellings, in baboons and other species; when presenting, the female turns the coloured area to the male, and it acts as a releaser for sexual activity (Wickler, 1967). Sexual arousal in the male is shown by erection; aggressive arousal is accompanied by the hair on the neck bristling.

(2) Posture. A threatening posture consists of an arched back and lowered head; submission is shown by crouching, curling up, or by presenting. The tail is raised by a dominant animal, in proportion to its status in the immediate group. Gorillas adopt a strutting walk when in a

dominant position. Other postures are used to invite grooming; the presenting position is the prelude to copulation. A gorilla leader may signal departure by standing motionless and facing in the direction to be taken.

(3) Gestures. Aggression is signalled by various threatening gestures such as fist-shaking and stamping, waving things about and banging them. A friendly approach may be indicated by holding out a hand, or putting hands on the head.

(4) Proximity. Following another primate can be a friendly overture, or an aggressive chase; the difference is seen from the way it is done. A dominant male allows other males to approach only up to a certain distance. A langur will force another to move by going close to him, a gesture of dominance (Jay, 1965b).

(5) Facial expression. Unlike most lower animals, apes and monkeys have a series of facial expressions, corresponding to their emotional state. There are about 13 different facial expressions, and these are similar in different species. The playface is an open-mouthed smile with teeth covered; it occurs during play. The lip-smacking face has lips together and protruded; it indicates desire to approach and goes with grooming. The pout face is rather similar and is shown by children who want to be with their mother. When an animal wants to attack it bares its teeth, and frowns. When about to flee the eyebrows are raised, the forehead wrinkles, the mouth corners are pulled back, baring the teeth (Van Hooff, 1967; Morris, 1967).

(6) Eye-movements. The direct gaze is widely used as a threat signal. Chance (1962) observed that if there is a 'cut-off' of mutual gaze by one animal, the other will not attack. It is postulated that mutual gaze is highly arousing, and aggression can be averted by cutting it off. A number of forms of cut-off have been observed in different species, including averting the gaze, shielding the face with a hand, lowering the eyes, and turning the head (Vine, 1969). Looking away can be regarded as an act of submission or appeasement. There may also be lowering or fluttering of the eyelids for the same purpose. Lesser animals watch the more dominant ones and are thus able to follow their leadership. Apart from this, not much is yet known about gaze-direction or eye-contact in non-human primates. It is interesting that some moths have evolved wing patterns that look like giant eyes, which are used as threat displays.

Auditory. Different kinds of monkeys and apes can make between 7 and 25 different vocal sounds. The most common are as follows: bark and growl (when attacking), scream and shriek (being attacked and giving alarm), soft grunt (when grooming, and for keeping in touch in the

jungle), clicking and chittering (by young animals). These sounds cannot be regarded as intended to communicate – they are emotional
reactions which are audible to others. The sounds are furthermore continuous noises rather than words – similar to human groans rather than
grammatical sequences. Motivational information however is conveyed
with some precision, by small variations in the intensity, speed and pitch
of the noises emitted (Marler, 1965). Attempts have been made to teach
chimpanzees to speak. Hayes (1952) taught a female chimpanzee to use
the words 'papa', 'cup' and 'mamma' by rewarding her with milk. It was
thought that the word 'cup' came to mean 'I want a drink', but normally animal sounds are highly stereotyped responses conditioned to the
original learning situation; they are not intended to communicate. When
apes and other animals respond to human speech they are responding to
the physical sounds, not to their meaning (de Haan, 1929).

Combinations of signals. The elements of social behaviour, olfactory,
tactile, visual and auditory, which act as signals, do not occur alone.
There are a number of regular combinations. Threat, for example, includes the bared teeth, staring eyes, lowered eyebrows, a tense posture
with head lowered and forelegs bent, hair bristling, and is accompanied
by barking or grunting. There are several basic patterns like this,
associated with attack, withdrawal, appeasement, grooming, copulation,
group coordination and care of young. The signals are therefore highly
redundant, but are very efficient for communicating motivational states.
Visual signals are far more effective than auditory, and appear to be
designed to convey information at short range. 'By far the greatest part
of the whole system of communication seems to be devoted to the organisation of social behaviour of the group, to dominance and sub-
ordination, the maintenance of peace and cohesion of the group, reproduction and care of the young' (Marler, op. cit., p. 584).

THE DEVELOPMENT OF HUMAN SOCIAL DRIVES

The psychology of motivation

Behaviour does not consist just of learned responses to stimuli; it is
energised through the physiological arousal of the autonomic system. It
is goal-directed in that instinctively defined or environmentally acquired
goals are pursued with varied patterns of response. The same individual
will be differently aroused on different occasions, and there are individual differences both in levels of arousal and in the goals which are
sought.

The commonsense alternative to the postulation of drives is to explain behaviour in terms of conscious desires and intentions. The objection to this is that conscious experiences are now known to be partial and sometimes inaccurate representations of what is probably happening; psychoanalysis and experiments with post-hypnotic suggestion have shown that the reasons people give themselves for their actions are sometimes rationalisations, i.e. cognitive constructions that are more acceptable than the true motivation – for example a religious young man may be very concerned about the beliefs or spiritual state of an attractive young woman.

We have just discussed the social behaviour of non-human primates in terms of basic drives. These are clearly related to basic biological processes, and it is easy to see how they have evolved to preserve the species. Hunger and thirst provide for basic bodily needs; sex continues the species; aggression defends the group against predators and rivals for food; parent–child forces ensure that infants are looked after while dependent; the affiliative drive acts as a social bond to restrain aggression, and forms the basis for cooperation over defence and food-gathering; dominance creates social order and leadership inside the group, and is in the direct biological interests of the most dominant. This set of partly innate drives brings about a pattern of behaviour, including social behaviour, that enables individuals and groups to survive. All of these drives appear in humans too. The differences are that there is greater scope for environmental learning, assisted by the larger brain, the longer period of dependence in the family, and the existence of elaborate cultural patterns.

When we speak of a drive, we refer to a pattern of goal-directed behaviour, energised by autonomic arousal, and released by certain internal and external conditions. The drives found in non-human primates are all partly innate, partly learnt. Some of them can be regarded as needs, others not. Hunger and thirst are needs in the sense that they are aroused by deprivation, and satiated by eating and drinking. We shall show that sex, in the case of humans, is not a need in this sense; it is certainly a drive since sexual activity is energised by autonomic arousal. We shall not distinguish between 'primary' and 'secondary' drives, corresponding to innate versus learnt, or biological versus social drives. There are however certain other 'cultural' drives found in humans which are less directly associated with biological processes, and more associated with cultural products and social structures. Achievement motivation, the need for money, and commitment to ethical or ideological values and to organisational goals, are examples of this.

Probably they are made possible by language and associated symbolic processes. Is it correct to speak of these as 'drives' at all? They are similar to more basic drives in that goal-directed activity is released, and that autonomic arousal is produced; they are dissimilar in that there is no instinctive basis for them. It is also impossible to satiate cultural drives – when a person has made some money he wants to make more money; indeed these drives appear to follow a reinforcement rather than a satiation model.

The physiological basis of motivation is the activity of the autonomic nervous system, as controlled by the hypothalamus. Neural messages from the hypothalamus set off sympathetic or parasympathetic arousal. Sympathetic arousal consists of a discharge of adrenalin from the adrenal glands; this in turn produces an increase in heart-rate, of blood-pressure and of perspiration, thus preparing the organism for action. There are individual differences in the physiological pattern of response. Parasympathetic activity is related to the digestive processes, and to hunger and thirst. Sympathetic arousal results in greater effective effort, but only up to a point, after which over-arousal produces anxiety and disorganisation of response. Arousal can be produced directly by injecting adrenalin into the bloodstream, or by other physiological conditions such as hunger; arousal depends also on external stimuli, both innate releasing stimuli and other stimuli which become sources of arousal as a result of learning. Environmental stimuli have a dual effect when motivation is aroused: they lead to particular responses, and they lead to diffuse autonomic activity, which has an energising role.

For lower animals motivation is largely instinctive. That is to say there are innate sequences of motor response which are released by particular stimuli when there is an internal state of physiological readiness. In man and higher animals the state of arousal is much the same, but it is aroused under new conditions, and new patterns of associated behaviour are acquired. The releasing stimuli are not only such things as the blue bottoms of baboons, but clothes of fashionable design; more abstract drives are aroused by such stimuli as the national flag and religious symbols. The form of sympathetic arousal is probably very similar, even though different action patterns are being set off, as Schachter (1964) showed in an interesting experiment. Some subjects were given an injection of adrenalin, while others had neutral injections of salt solution. Some of each group of subjects were placed in the company of a confederate of the experimenter, who generally behaved in a wild and crazy manner. Further subjects were subjected to an insulting interview, in the company of a confederate, who became very angry with the interviewer. The main finding was that the adrenalin-injected subjects became very euphoric in the first situation, and aggressive in the second – more so than those injected with salt solution. Thus the form of arousal, the emotions and drives experienced, and the goals sought, depend on the nature of the arousing situation.

The patterns of behaviour which are set off in an aroused organism may be innate, as in the food-seeking behaviour of insects. There are similar innate patterns in humans, for example some of the responses of infants to mothers (p. 47 ff), and some features of sexual behaviour (Morris, 1967). More important however are the general innate tendencies towards dependent, sexual and affiliative behaviour, which require environmental experience for them to develop. In animals special forms of learning, during critical periods, are involved (Thorpe, 1962). As in other areas of behaviour, genetics and environment play complementary roles, and neither can operate without the other. Twin studies have shown that broad dimensions of personality depend upon both, and that their relative weight varies between different traits – schizophrenia being more dependent on inheritance than neurosis for example (Shields and Slater, 1960).

Some of these drives are commonly restrained either by other drives, or by anxiety. In the non-human primates we saw that aggression within the group is restrained by affiliation. In human society aggression and sex are associated with internalised restraints, often leading to the suppression of the normal goal responses or to their replacement by substitute or 'displaced' alternatives. Miller's theory of approach-avoidance conflict (1944) predicts that there will be an equilibrium degree of approach to the original goal, and that this will be nearer to the goal if the avoidance forces are weakened, for example by alcohol.

Hunger and thirst

Hunger and thirst have a direct effect on many aspects of primate social behaviour and group life – the collective gathering and eating of food, the feeding of young, the occupation and defence of food-bearing territory. The same is true to a considerable extent of human primitive societies, but in more advanced societies the links are less direct. In addition, when people are rarely hungry, and meals are eaten out of habit, hunger ceases to operate as a major drive. It may still affect social behaviour however: Schachter (1959) found that the majority of subjects who had been without food for 20 hours chose to take part in experiments where they would be together with other subjects, while the reverse was the case for non-hungry subjects. It is possible that the universal human trait of eating in the company of others is due to this link with affiliative behaviour. Experience suggests that eating together has the result of increasing the social bonds between people. The hunger and thirst drives themselves we shall not discuss here. They are different from most other drives in that arousal depends on the contents of the bloodstream; they are unlike all other drives in that they are aroused by deficit, and operate in a homeostatic manner. The needs themselves are innate, together with the elementary feeding responses of the infant; apart from this, what is eaten, and how it is eaten depends on the culture; this is to some extent true of monkeys too (p. 38).

Sex

Sexual motivation is biologically necessary for the preservation of the species, though not for the survival of the individual, and it has widespread effects on social behaviour. Compared with monkeys and apes, humans are much less promiscuous, and family arrangements are longer lasting – though in some societies adolescents are allowed to be promiscuous, and the one man–one woman family is not the only arrangement, though it is the commonest. The more permanent family enables children to have a longer period under parental care, and they have a father as well as a mother. In many societies there are restraints on sexuality, in order to prevent premarital or extramarital copulation, and such restraints become internalised during socialisation. Sears, Maccoby and Levin (1957) found that American mothers usually punish small children for early sexual behaviour, such as playing with the genitals.

Sexual motivation is aroused in lower animals by the concentration of sex hormones in the bloodstream, and by releasing stimuli from members of the opposite sex. Sexual behaviour proper begins at puberty, when sex hormones are produced. Unlike hunger there is no physiological deficit, and deprivation does not increase the strength of drive. In lower animals female sexual behaviour can only occur during oestrus, while hormonal injections have a great effect on sexual activity. In apes this is less true, and with humans scarcely true at all: castration and ovary removal do not produce much loss of sexual drive, and hormone injections have little effect (Ford and Beach, 1952). On the other hand removal of large areas of the cortex, even in rats, but especially in males, has the effect of eliminating sexual activity entirely. This evidence suggests that sexual motivation in higher mammals becomes controlled by cortical structures rather than by hormones, and that this is particularly true of males. Thus learning can have a greater effect, and cultural factors may be very influential (Cofer and Appley, 1964).

There are however clear innate response patterns – erection in infants, and the intromission-ejaculation sequence; indeed the whole interaction sequence making up copulation takes a very similar form in most human societies (Morris, 1967). On the other hand sexual behaviour does not develop in monkeys reared in isolation, and it has been suggested that for human infants bodily contact with the mother is a source of later sexual behaviour (Walters and Parke, 1965). Chimpanzees need to observe others in the act before they can perform properly (p. 30); humans appear to need books of instruction. In addition elaborate cultural patterns of etiquette and social skills for handling the opposite sex are acquired. Among the non-human primates sexual motivation mainly results in copulation; among humans there is frequent sexual arousal, but internal and external restraints prevent copulation occurring, except under very restricted conditions. The result is that sexual motivation has a widespread impact on social behaviour, where the end-product is conversation, proximity and eye-contact, and more rarely bodily contact, rather than copulation. Such intermediate levels of intimacy can be regarded as equilibria brought about by conflict between sexual motivation and restraining forces. The intermediate steps are far more widely attained than is copulation, and become sub-goals which are sources of gratification for the sexual drive. This interpretation is supported by an experiment by Clark and Sensibar (1955) in which it was found that stories told to TAT cards following sexual arousal contained overt sexual themes if subjects were drunk, but contained only covert, symbolic themes if the subjects were sober. The result of the greater dependence of sex on cortical and learnt processes in man, combined with internalised restraints on copulation, has been to convert sex into a generalised drive of social approach.

Aggression

We have seen that aggression in animals is biologically useful for the group – in defending territory, resisting predators, and spreading the group out over the territory; it is useful to the individual in giving priority over food and access to females. Aggression inside the group is restrained by affiliative forces. Humans are far more aggressive than the other primates. We differ in eating meat, as lions and tigers do; we use weapons, which now kill people at a distance, so that the appeasement signals of victims are inoperative; and we are becoming very over-crowded (Lorenz, 1963). Aggression within the group is most often of a new, and relatively harmless kind however – verbal aggression. This does not inflict direct biological damage, but it affects self-esteem (which can have somatic consequences). We may distinguish different types of aggression, according to the conditions that arouse it. (a) Aggression often results when an individual is attacked by another, or when self-esteem is attacked. Frustration may also result in aggression, but only if the frustration is seen as arbitrary or unnecessary – and we can regard this as a kind of attack. (b) Aggression can be instrumental to other needs, such as food or sex; much animal aggression is due to competition for biological satisfactions. Aggression of this kind in humans is not 'angry', as the first kind is. Struggles for dominance can also lead to aggression (see p. 28 f). (c) There may be spontaneous aggression which is not caused either by attack or by biological needs; this has been observed in male mice reared in isolation, and it is possible that fighting is instinctively related to competition for females. On the whole the evidence does not support the idea that there is an aggressive need in higher mammals that can act as a source of spontaneous aggression (Berkowitz, 1962; Buss, 1961).

Aggression is however a drive in that certain stimuli (e.g. attack) release patterns of response (e.g. fighting), which are accompanied by autonomic arousal. The vigour of response is furthermore affected by the internal physiological state of the organism: it is stronger in the presence of male hormones, in people of muscular physique, and in those with a high level of noradrenalin (Funkenstein *et al.*, 1957). The aggressive response to frustration or attack appears to be innate in lower animals and partly innate in man. Infants use such forms of aggression as screaming, and kicking, though these become modified by experience (Goodenough, 1931).

Learning is also important, and even animals have to learn the appropriate targets for attack. Socialisation studies of humans have shown that aggression is strongest when children have been (1) frustrated, by rejection or in other ways, (2) frequently punished, especially by physical punishment, (3) exposed to aggressive models, including the mere presence of a male parent in the family. Sears (1961) found that anti-social aggression was stronger at age 5 in children who had received punitive discipline; however, at age 12 such aggression correlated with earlier permissiveness and *low* punishment, though pro-social aggression correlated with punishment. Sears suggests that early punishment has the effect of displacing aggression into socially acceptable channels.

Aggression is frequently aroused, in animals and men, but rarely occurs. In non-human primates it is thought that affiliative feelings towards the group restrain aggression. Physiological studies show that parts of the cortex act as suppressors of aggression in monkeys. Socialisation studies of humans show how these restraints are acquired in childhood. Aggression is lowest in those who have had warm relations with parents, and where parents have discouraged the use of aggression, and used love-oriented methods of discipline and reasoning; cognitive processes can also restrain aggression, when it is thought to be morally wrong (Berkowitz, op. cit.).

When aggression is aroused, the restraining processes are activated too. The conflict thus created results in the suppression of the immediate response, and its replacement by a substitute or displaced form of aggression, in exactly the same way as sex. A number of experiments have shown that the degree of displacement, to different objects or less direct forms of aggression, is related to the strength of restraints (Buss, op. cit.). As a result, aggression of an indirect, verbal kind is a common feature of social behaviour, though physical violence is not.

The relation between aggression and dominance is far from clear. Our view is that dominance is both a need in itself and instrumental to biological needs, and in man to self-esteem; a dominant position is established by actual or threatened fighting, i.e. aggression of a competitive, instrumental kind; attacks are not made on stronger people through fear of the consequences, while attacks on weaker individuals are restrained by their giving way or appeasing.

Dependency

It is biologically necessary for infants to have dependent responses towards their mothers while in need of food and protection. As the period of family care and childhood learning has lengthened, these dependent reactions have become even more necessary. We saw that young monkeys and apes have instinctive responses to seize the mother's hair and to seek the nipple; attachment to the mother is increased during the period of childhood play and early family life; the child then becomes increasingly independent and is eventually rejected by the mother (p. 37). Dependent behaviour in human children includes such behaviour as touching and holding a parent, being near, seeking attention or reassurance, and seeking affection or need satisfaction, though the correlation between these elements is low, especially for boys (Sears, 1963). Such behaviour continues during later childhood, and is often punished or discouraged by parents (Sears, Maccoby and Levin, 1957). Children break out of this dependent relationship during adolescence, and boys try to do so earlier, since it is not an approved pattern of behaviour for boys (Kagan and Moss, 1962). There is a correlation of about ·30 between dependency or passivity before the age of 3, and dependency on a love object in adulthood, or dependency on parents, for girls only. This was not true of later dependence on friends (Kagan and Moss, op. cit.). Children and adults who are strong in dependency are more susceptible to social influence (Walters and Parke, 1964). Gewirtz (1961) regards it as a learnt drive, and reports experiments in which 20 minutes of isolation made children more susceptible to social influence. Walters and Parke (1965) argue that these results could be due to anxiety aroused rather than isolation; Walters and Ray (1960) manipulated both arousal and isolation and found that arousal was the crucial variable affecting social learning. The effects of isolation are more marked for younger children, for whom it might be expected to create more anxiety. It is unfortunately difficult to create arousal without anxiety, or arousal without social rejection. The outcome is unclear, and it seems likely that both isolation and anxiety can arouse dependent behaviour. The dependent activity also serves to reduce the arousal – as when a human or monkey infant clings to its mother.

Dependence has certain innate motor components that appear immediately after birth in monkeys; there is sucking in human infants, but reaching and grasping appear later – the 5th to 6th month. Infants show a preference for the human face, or for masks resembling it by the 4th week of life; smiling in response to the face reaches a peak at 11th–14th week, after which infants can discriminate the mother from strangers (Spitz, 1946; Ambrose, 1961). Infants prefer a female face, a female voice, and like the sound of heart-beats. It is not known how far these phenomena are due to innate neural patterns, and how far they are due to early learning. Coss (1965) found that pairs of circular stimuli placed side by side (i.e. resembling two eyes) produced more arousal in subjects than one or three such stimuli or when one circle was above the other, and that there was more arousal if solid black circles were placed inside the circles (i.e. like pupils); this suggests but does not prove that response to eyes may be innate. Walters and Parke (1965) suggest that the innate orienting and following response leads to exploration, and attending to the mother. Schaffer and Emerson (1964a) conclude from their longitudinal study of 60 infants that infants seek proximity with people during the first 6 months of life, but that this is a nonspecific attachment to certain stimuli; during the period 6–9 months attachment to particular individuals develops. Children reared in institutions shortly after birth are apathetic towards adults and do not show a dependent response (Yarrow, 1964).

Recent research has caused older ideas on the learning of dependency to be revised. It was previously believed that feeding by the mother reinforced dependency, which then became a secondary drive. Harlow's experiments showed that this was not true for monkeys (p. 37); human studies found similarly that early dependent attachments are formed to people who had taken no part in feeding (Schaffer and Emerson, 1964a), and that dependence has no correlation with maternal feeding methods (Sears, Maccoby and Levin, op. cit.). Harlow's work suggested a second variable – innate attraction to the mother's skin, which is a source of anxiety-reduction. However, Schaffer and Emerson (1964b) found that some infants resist physical contact involving restraint ('non-cuddlers'), and obtain comfort from looking at the mother, or holding her skirt. Walters and Parke (1965) suggest a third source of early dependence – the stimulation of the distance receptors of vision and sound but not by specific stimuli. Ambrose (1961) and others found that a face elicited a smile more readily if it was moving, but also if there was eye-contact. Walters and Parke (op. cit.) suggest that while sexual motivation is partly based on bodily contact with the mother, 'the formation of psychological attachment is primarily fostered by distance-receptor experiences'.

Robson (1967) and others have suggested that the amount of eye-contact between infant and mother may be a crucial determinant of dependence. Eye-contact of a sort takes place at 4 weeks; this means nothing to the infant but is highly rewarding to the mother who then becomes more attached to the child and plays with it more (Wolff, 1963). It is suggested by Robson that this an instinctive response for the *mother* with the biological value of appeasing hostility due to the frustrations of child-rearing. By 4 months the child may seek out eye-contact, though this varies with the extent to which the mother has sought or avoided eye-contact, and possibly with the extent to which eye-contact occurred during feeding or was followed by other rewarding reactions.

A further factor in the growth of dependence is the social interaction between mother and infant. Schaffer and Emerson (1964a) found that dependence was strongest when the mother had been most responsive to the child's crying, and when there had been a lot of interaction between them. The use of crying and smiling to elicit a maternal response could be regarded as the earliest form of social behaviour. Infant and mother are able to remain in social contact at a distance by the means of such visual and vocal messages. Interaction between them during the pre-verbal period takes a number of forms, such as making imitative noises and play. Appell and David (1965) report that at 13 months the infant–mother relation may take various forms, from mutual satisfaction to mutual frustration.

While an infant has a great deal of maternal attention during the first two years of life, this attention is liable to decline, especially if another child is born. The change is greatest for a first-born child, who previously had its mother's undivided attention. Thus there are grounds for supposing that first-born children would be high in dependence, but also high in independence, since they are expected to take a dominant role in the family. Sampson (1965) suggests that first-born children suffer from a resultant dependency conflict. The style of maternal behaviour during childhood affects the development of dependence, though the results of different studies are rather inconsistent. One agreed result is that dependence is not valued for males in Western society; it is regarded as a failure to develop normally (Sears, op. cit.; Kagan and Moss, op. cit.).

Affiliation

We saw that in groups of primates there is affiliative behaviour in the form of playing and grooming, and that affiliative forces appear to restrain aggression to other members of the group. In humans there is similar affiliative behaviour, which takes the form of joint activities at work, play, or conversation, and consists of such elements as physical proximity, eye-contact, and friendly styles of verbal and non-verbal behaviour. There are considerable individual differences in the strength of affiliative tendencies; for example some members of groups are found to be more concerned with being accepted by other members, and with establishing friendly relations in the group, as opposed to getting on with the task. Some psychologists conceptualise this behaviour in terms of a need for affiliation (Atkinson, 1958), others in terms of learnt habits, or traits such as extraversion. Sex, dependency and affiliation are all approach tendencies directed towards social objects, though with somewhat different goal responses; sex and affiliation are indeed sometimes difficult to distinguish. We saw that animals cannot survive alone, and that these drives have survival value for the group, and thus for its members.

In the case of monkeys there are two current theories about the environmental experiences needed for affiliative behaviour to develop – that it depends on relations with the mother or with other infants. In the case of humans most workers have assumed that experiences with the mother, of one kind or another, are the crucial factor, and that affiliation is derived from dependence. Studies of maternal deprivation and separation on the whole confirm this view. Children in institutions have the company of other children, but are separated from their own mothers, and often have impersonal and inadequate mothering from the staff. Spitz (1946) observed that institutionalised children showed a marked deterioration in behaviour during the period 8–12 months, and that some simply sat staring expressionlessly into space. Later studies have confirmed that institutionalisation particularly affects language and social responsiveness. Goldfarb (1955) found that children who had spent the first three years of their life in institutions were unable to form close interpersonal relationships, as well as having deficient control of impulses. Studies by Bowlby (1952) and others confirm that being reared without a mother, though with other children, often results in a lack of dependent and affiliative tendencies; the effects are minimised if there is adequate mothering in the institution, and varies with the inherited constitution of the child (Yarrow, 1964). There may in fact be advantages in multiple mothering, inside or outside the family, so that there is adequate contact with nurturant adults, but an avoidance of over-intense emotional relationships (Mussen *et al*, 1963).

There is however a difficulty with the dependence–affiliation theory – that it is hard to see why a dependent response to an adult should generalise to an affiliative response to other small children. Generalisation should take place from responding to a child's mother to responding to another child's mother, not to another child. It remains to be shown how this transition takes place. Rheingold (1956) found that experimental social contacts with institutionalised children over an 8-week period generated greater social responsiveness than that exhibited by control children, and that this generalised to other adults – but other children were not used as stimuli here. McGinn *et al*. (1965) found that individuals who reported their parents as encouraging dependency were stronger in affiliative behaviour.

A case can be made for the theory that affiliative motivation develops partly at least as a result of contacts with peers, rather than contacts with mother. Harlow and Harlow (1965) proposed this theory for monkeys – there is an instinctive peer affectional system which develops if there is early contact with other infants. It has been found that human first-born children are somewhat lower in affiliative motivation than are later-born; on the other hand they are not completely lacking in affiliative behaviour as this theory would predict (Sampson, 1965). A number of studies however show that children who are strong in dependency are unpopular with their peers (McCandless and Marshall, 1957), suggesting that dependence and affiliation are incompatible patterns of behaviour.

Some light can be thrown on the problem by studying the early development of affiliative behaviour with peers. As we describe below (p. 57 f), peer interaction begins much later than interaction with the mother; there is some form of interaction at 8–9 months, which develops into interaction and cooperative behaviour during the next two years. However, this interaction takes a rather different form from interaction with the mother – parallel and cooperative play rather than seeking comfort – which gives some support for the theory that affiliation is separate from dependency.

The best-known version of the dependence–affiliation theory is that of Schachter (1959), who suggested that mothers reduce anxiety in young children, so that social contact becomes associated with anxiety-reduction. He found that female students made anxious by the expectation of receiving electric shocks from a 'Dr Zilstein', preferred to wait with other subjects rather than alone; the social choice was made more often when the anxiety level was high and when subjects had been first-born or only children. (This does not contradict the results on birth-order given above; we are here concerned with the affiliative response to anxiety, not affiliative behaviour in general.) They also preferred to wait in the company of other subjects, rather than with other people, and it made no difference whether they could talk or not. Sarnoff and Zimbardo (1961) aroused 'Freudian' anxiety, i.e. from fear of the return of repressed impulses, e.g. the expectation of sucking a baby's bottle; their subjects did *not* seek the company of other subjects. This result is probably due to embarrassment rather than to the other processes under discussion (Cofer and Appley, 1964). The explanation offered for the birth-order difference is that early-born children are handled in such a way that dependency is greater and contacts with others are associated with anxiety-reduction. The social response to anxiety is explained in terms of (a) children learning that social situations reduce anxiety and (b) a need for self-evaluation. (The main evidence for the latter acting as an affiliative force is an experiment in which there was conformity over level of anxiety: however, the fact that belonging to a group has certain effects does not show that these effects were sought by the group members in the first place.)

Argyle and Dean (1965) suggested that affiliative motivation has both approach and avoidance components – motives to approach and withdraw from others, probably acquired as a result of rewarding and punishing experiences with people. This theory suggests that the amount of intimacy sought with another person is at an equilibrium level based on the relative strengths of the approach and avoidance forces aroused (cf. p. 107 f).

Dominance

This is one of the main drives in monkeys, and is thought to have the biological value of providing leaders who can keep order in the group, and repel enemies. It is stronger in males, is increased by male sex hormones, and is one of the main sources of aggressive behaviour. Dominance is one of the main dimensions of human social behaviour, and is in some ways the opposite of dependence, or of submission (Foa, 1961). Dominant people try to become task leaders, want to have power and status, to talk most and to have their ideas attended to. From the biological evidence it seems likely that there is a genetic basis to this pattern of behaviour, and that individual differences are partly innate.

The socialisation origins of dominance are not known. Dominance, as opposed to passivity and dependence, is part of the male sex-role, which is acquired through identification with the father or other available male models (Kagan, 1964). It would be expected that dominant behaviour would be acquired when the conditions for such identification are met – a dominant father, who is visibly successful and who is rewarding to his son. Dominance may also be acquired through instrumental learning if it is found to lead to getting a bigger share-out of the food or sweets, for example. In this case it would be expected that large and strong children would acquire most dominance. Anderson (1939) distinguished between 'dominative' and 'integrative' behaviour in pre-school children; the former is a direct attempt to satisfy needs at the expense of others, the latter is a pursuit of common purposes. Dominant behaviour in the pre-school period is an unskilled form of behaviour. At a slightly later age dominance requires greater skill: Jack (1934) was able to increase dominance in 7–8-year-olds by training in task skills, just as it has been possible to train adults in leadership skills (Chap. X). Authoritarianism is a combination of dominance with subordinates and submissiveness with superiors. It has been found that parents of authoritarians were strict, rigid and punitive as parents (Frenkel-Brunswik, 1954). It is possible that authoritarians imitate their parents when themselves in a dominant position, but persist in a child role when someone else is in charge. This is an example of a failure to develop a personality that is integrated and independent of parents (Marcia, 1966).

Nothing is known in detail about the conditions under which dominance is aroused. In primates the presence of other males, especially in the presence of receptive females, is such a condition. It is likely that dominance is aroused in many people simply by the presence of individuals or of a group of peers, or near-peers. Dominance over others is the preferred relationship. While arousal is clearly associated with dominance, there is no evidence that the latter is a need that requires regular satisfaction.

Self-esteem

This motivational system is discussed in Chapter IX. Self-esteem depends on receiving the right responses from others. The behaviour which is used to produce these is called 'self-presentation', and is rather different from behaviour associated with dominance. As far as is known animals do not seek self-esteem. This pattern of behaviour is a result of the cognitive structure known as the 'self-image', which presumably animals do not have.

Cultural drives

There are other human behaviour patterns which are wholly acquired from the culture, but which can usefully be regarded as drives, since they are accompanied by autonomic arousal, and are goal-directed. One of these is achievement motivation. It is found that members of work-groups or committees who are high on achievement motivation are more concerned with the task than with social relations in the group, and tend to become task leaders (McClelland *et al.*, 1953). An interesting feature of this drive is that it is never satiated by any level of achievement – the goal is progressively revised upwards. Money is another goal associated with arousal, so that the need for money can be looked at as an acquired drive – though it is not known how far there is an autonomous need for money for its own sake, and how much the goal is what money will buy. These drives lead to cooperative or competitive behaviour in relation to others. Much group and organisational behaviour is concerned with carrying out tasks linked to such drives, and over which the members cooperate to some extent.

Motivational arousal can become associated with more abstract goals than achievement and money. Human powers of cognition enable very remote goals to assume drive properties, and to become energisers of behaviour by supplying arousal. Members of a social group or organisation for example can become committed to the welfare and goals of the group; this is an important source of motivation in organisations (p. 289). People become attached to political parties and churches, and to their country; they are aroused to action by flags, anthems, and other symbolic objects. Ideologies and morals acquire motivating force, and they may affect interpersonal behaviour – as when a person believes that he should love his neighbour, or believes that he should be humble and meek.

SOCIAL INTERACTION IN CHILDREN

Interaction in the family

We described above how a dependent bond with the mother develops during the first year of life. The strength of this bond varies with the mother's behaviour, but as long as she is actually present and interacts with the child a bond is formed, and continues to develop during the following years. At the same time the child becomes increasingly mobile, adventurous and independent. During middle childhood children appear to prefer independence combined with love and protection. Factorial studies of maternal behaviour show that there are two main dimensions of variation in maternal behaviour – love *v.* hostility, and overcontrol *v.* granting autonomy (e.g. Schaefer, 1959). Parental love and warmth lead to a stronger relationship with the child, and friendly, cooperative and attentive behaviour on the part of the child (Schaefer and Bayley, 1963). Granting autonomy leads to greater independence and self-confidence. The combination of rejection and overcontrol is very disturbing and is probably a cause of mental disorder (cf. p. 340). The relationship that is established with the parents persists until adolescence; at about 12 there is a suddenly increased desire on the part of the child to break out of its dependent relationship with the parents and to become more independent. The social behaviour of adolescents is described later (p. 246 ff).

Children often identify with their parents, i.e. take them as models for imitation. This is more likely to happen when parents are warm and nurturant, and have an easy-going relationship with the child. Children usually identify more with the same-sexed parent, partly because of the perceived similarity, partly because of social pressures and rewards for

doing things with that parent. There is also some evidence that identification with parents depends on a parent's importance in the child's
life, his ability to control rewards and punishments (Mussen, 1967).
Boys identify with fathers more often than daughters with mothers,
perhaps because the father is an attractive model for both sexes
(Emmerich, 1959). By the age of 5 most children have a clear feeling of
being a boy or a girl, and prefer the appropriate toys and activities for
their sex. The acquisition of the sex-role is partly the result of identifying with the same-sex parent, partly of direct encouragement and
rewards. It is found, in American studies, that boys acquire their sex
role earlier than girls, perhaps because sissy behaviour in boys is less
acceptable than tomboy behaviour in girls, in addition to the differences
in identification with the same-sex parent noted above (cf. Mussen,
Conger and Kagan, 1963). Sex-role is affected also by family composition: girls with older brothers are more aggressive and masculine, while
boys with older sisters are less masculine (Koch, 1956). In addition to
imitating parents, children acquire internalised 'moral' restraints from
them. These are strongest when parents are warm and strict. The precise
learning process involved is not known; the present author produced
evidence that it is due to introjection of parental behaviour in the course
of interaction (Argyle, 1964a; p. 365). These moral restraints influence
social behaviour in ways that are discussed below (p. 87 ff).

Later social behaviour is affected by position in the family in several
ways. (1) Relations with people in authority are most affected by relations with parents: rejection or neglect by parents leads to dependence
on the peer-group and hostility to adults, as in 'pseudo-social delinquents' (Hewitt and Jenkins, 1946). An intense and strict relationship
creates authoritarian submission (Adorno *et al.*, 1950); warm and democratic management produces a more cooperative and positive attitude to
adults (Mussen *et al.*, 1963). The simplest explanation of these findings
is that children generalise from parents to other older people. It is also
found that first-born males submit more than later-born to people in
authority, though the reverse is true for females (Sampson, 1965).
Second-born males and first-born females make more use of 'machiavellian' strategies for dealing with people in authority (Singer, 1964). The
explanation of these results is not known. (2) Relations with the peer-
group are affected by experiences in the family. When children have had
a warm relationship with their parents, they seek warm relationships
with peers (Schutz, 1958); when they had little contact with parents
during the first year of life they are low in affiliative motivation (p. 51);
when children have acquired a relationship with parents and later been

rejected they become extremely dependent on the peer-group. These results can be accounted for partly in terms of the dependence–affiliation hypothesis, partly by supposing that the peer-group acts as a substitute for the parents. Later-born children, especially boys, are more competitive and aggressive than first-born or only children; this presumably derives from the experience of attempting to compete with older siblings. Later-born children are also more socially outgoing, and have been found to be stronger in measures of sympathy or empathy – they can understand others' problems better, perhaps because of their own experience of being in an inferior position (Sampson, 1965). (3) Relations with subordinates. As mentioned above, authoritarians are found to have been reared in a strict and punitive manner; we suggested that identification with parents was involved here, together with resumption of the child role when with superiors. Older siblings have experience with subordinates in the family, and it would be expected that they would continue in a similar style, and perhaps be more skilled than others without this experience. (4) Relations with the opposite sex. It is found that when parents quarrel the children are less likely to make a successful marriage (Terman, 1938), and are also more likely to be neurotic (Langner and Michael, 1963). This suggests another source of learning about social behaviour – observing it at close quarters in the family and copying it.

Parsons and Bales (1955) maintain that the family is a 4-role system which is learnt and internalised by children. In fact the role-structure of the family is more complex than this, and typical role patterns are discussed later (p. 240 ff). It seems likely however that a child will acquire a role in the family and tend to behave in this way in later groups. He will also learn the other roles in the family, and perhaps be able to play these too. If two or more members of the family are in conflict, the child may learn two conflicting roles. Psychoanalysts explain the emotionally disturbing effects of quarrelling parents in terms of a conflict between 'internalised objects'; if parents can be introjected as moral standards that are internalised this is possible; another possibility is that the child tries to play one or other of these roles later but does so in a way that generates a conflict similar to that between his parents.

Dyadic interaction with peers

The first development of social performance is in the area of perceptual discrimination. Children do not distinguish between people and things until about 2 months, after which they smile more at the sight of a face or the sound of a voice. They can distinguish delight and distress by 3 months, and anger, fear and disgust by 6 months (Bridges, 1932). By the end of the first year they can discriminate between different members of the family, and can tell them from strangers (Gesell and Thompson, 1934). Ability to distinguish between different emotions increases at least up to the age of 12, when such states as 'surprise' and 'scorn' can be recognised (Gates, 1923). Three-year-olds can tell boys from girls by their clothes and hair; 6-year-olds can do this from bodily features alone. In inter-racial communities children can distinguish between whites, negroes, orientals, etc. by 4 or 5 (Clark and Clark, 1940), but learning the difference between Jew and Gentiles is more difficult, and indeed may never be learnt since the visible differences are so small. Similarly class differences are learnt, probably at a rather later age (Munn, 1965).

The first social communications towards peers take place from 8–9 months onwards. Social behaviour is entirely non-verbal at this age and a repertoire of non-verbal signals is used during the first two years, as shown in Table 2.1. In addition to making these communications, infants from 10–11 months onwards seek responses from others, and try to attract the attention of another child. Interaction during the second year of life is mainly in relation to toys: an infant of 8–9 months may offer a toy to another, later they will fight over a toy, and by the end of the second year they will play together cooperatively with toys.

Conflict over toys is one of the earliest forms of social interaction. Jersild and Markey (1935) found that such conflicts were very common in nursery schools; they found that there were attempts to remove toys by force, attacks on other children, verbal demands and threats, and emotional displays. Competitive behaviour is rather different – trying to do better than other children. This is a pattern of behaviour that varies between individuals and between cultures, and is clearly a product of social learning processes. In Western culture it is probably encouraged by the sibling situation at home and, experiences at school. Experiments in which pairs of infants are given similar tasks to perform, such as building with bricks, show that competitive behaviour is absent before 3, but increases from 3 at least to the age of 7 (Greenberg, 1932).

Cooperation is a more sophisticated kind of social behaviour than ego-centric or competitive behaviour – it results in both social acceptance and the attainment of group goals (p. 220 f). Mandry and Nekula (1939) found that the percentage of time two children cooperated when in a play-pen rose to 25% by the age of 2. They play with each other, at games which consist of various forms of bodily contact and eye-contact, such as pat-a-cake and peek-a-boo, and make imitative noises. Parten (1933) made time-sampled observations of 42 children aged between 2 and 5. There was a decline with age of solitary play, onlooking, and parallel play; there was a slow increase in 'associative group play' in which children played at the same thing, in borrowing and lending,

TABLE 2.1 *Non-verbal communication in infants* (from Carroll, 1944)

Non-linguistic responses	Conventionalised sign-vehicles
Respiratory processes:	
Breathing	Sigh (of grief, of boredom)
Blowing through nose	Snort (scorn)
Coughing	'Ahem'
Hiccough	Deliberate suggestion or imitation of intoxication
Facial movements:	
Blinking of eyes	Blink of surprise
Wrinkling of brows	Deliberate suggestion of puzzlement
Emotion, etc.:	
Laughter	Forced 'ha-ha-ha'
Crying	'Boo-hoo' – imitation of crying: crying for a reward, sympathy, etc.
Fainting	A conventionalised response of the Victorian woman
Postural movements:	
Searching	Peering (to suggest careful scrutiny)
Autistic gestures:	
Drumming with fingers	Deliberate suggestion of boredom or of impatience
Nail-biting	Playful suggestion of shyness, remorse
Pulling at beard	Pulling at chin – a good-natured affection of wisdom

though they still essentially played individually; there was an increase after the age of 3 in 'cooperative play', in which there is a shared goal, division of labour with complementary roles, and control of the group by one or two members.

Speech begins during the second year of life and the vocabulary increases rapidly between 2 and 4. Children's social behaviour increasingly involves speech to ask for things, convey information and establish social relations. The development of language is discussed below (p. 67ff).

At first infants treat others as physical objects; by the end of the first year they treat them as other people, whose attention is sought and who can be played with. At a later stage they develop a concern for others, usually described as 'sympathy' or 'altruism'. Murphy (1937) studied 2–5-year-olds, and observed that they would comfort each other when upset, by pats, embraces or speech, and would help another against a third child. A child would however abandon sympathetic behaviour in favour of egocentric behaviour if the second child's activities interfered with his own interests. The capacity to engage in such sympathetic behaviour has been thought to depend on development of the cognitive capacity to 'take the role of the other', or 'decentre' (p. 188 ff), yet it appears that sympathetic behaviour occurs rather earlier than would be expected on this basis.

Not much is known about the acquisition of interaction skills during childhood. As with other capacities it probably depends both on maturation, for example of the cognitive ability to take the role of the other, and also on learning experiences. Parents reward and punish various kinds of social response; they also act as models for imitation. They may give children verbal instruction about social behaviour, they tell them which behaviour is desirable and undesirable, so that the children acquire verbalised rules of behaviour. Parents may also give instructions about *how* to interact effectively. It has been found that the parents of clinical psychologists make a practice of giving verbalised interpretations of behaviour, thus giving greater insight and understanding.

Interaction in the peer-group

At the age of 2 children can interact with only one other child at a time; at 3 and 4 groups of three are common (Bühler, 1933). At this age, and on entering school, peer-group contacts are increased, and the amount of time spent with the peer-group increases continuously up to adolescence, when there may be a further sharp increase in time spent with peers as opposed to parents (Musgrove, 1963). Attachments to friends become stronger and more long-lasting, and the pressures exerted by groups of peers increase. During childhood, and especially from 7 onwards up to adolescence, there is segregation between boys and girls; their interests are different, girls preferring social activities while boys like rough and competitive sports and games; pressures are exerted to conform to such norms, and this helps to establish male and female sex-roles (Campbell, 1964). There is also segregation by age, though children will play inside the family with siblings of a different age.

Peer-groups of children exist in all known societies; in some societies they are more salient than others; in some they are organised by adults, while in others they are spontaneous. In America and Europe there are formal groups at school, under the close control of teachers, and informal groups outside school. It has often been observed that in America children take part in and become influenced by the peer-group at an earlier age than in Europe (Riesman *et al.*, 1950), where they are kept at home and are more closely supervised by parents. The present author has tried to rear children in England and the USA and has been struck by the difference. The informal peer-group becomes most salient during adolescence. In some other countries deliberate use is made of peer-groups, both in and out of school, to socialise children. In Russian schools competition is encouraged not between individuals but between groups, while cooperative helping and internalisation of standards is encouraged within groups (Bronfenbrenner, 1962). In Israeli kibbutzim infants spend much of their time in groups from the age of 6 months onwards. Strong in-group feelings are generated, and there is mutual help, sharing and taking turns; as in Russia there is no emphasis on individual achievement, but here there is no group competition either; social control is performed by the group, especially by the older members, and the deviant is shamed by appeal to ideology (Spiro, 1958).

As children get older they spend more time with peers outside the family, and these friends become increasingly important to them. The amount of time spent in this way varies between different cultures, as shown above. It also varies with the parental style of child-rearing. Thus democratic or permissive parents, and fathers working in large organisations, tend to encourage peer-group activities more than strict or authoritarian parents, or fathers in entrepreneurial jobs (Miller and Swanson, 1960). There can be conflict between the pressures exerted by parents and by peer-group, though this is partly avoided by children accepting parental ideas about which friends or groups are acceptable. There are individual differences in whether the ideas of family or friends are followed, depending mainly on the strength of attachment to parents. However, by the age of 11 most children prefer the company of peers, and pressure from this source is very influential. As described later (p. 246 ff), the company of friends during adolesence is used to work out an independent identity and to acquire social skills of dealing with adults on a more equal basis.

The peer-group can be regarded as an agent of socialisation, in addition to the family. Children spend time with the group because they enjoy it, and because it satisfies affiliative needs, but this experience has a permanent effect on them. (a) It affects their attitudes, beliefs and values.

Numerous studies show that children's groups have norms of their own, to which members usually conform. The sources of such norms are the families of other members, teachers and other adults connected with the group, and the mass media, which influence a group via its opinion leaders. Sex-roles are examples of such norms. (b) Members of groups take up particular roles in their groups, and others react to them in a distinctive way. This is one of the most important origins of the self-image, and is a major constituent of the final identity (p. 363 ff). (c) Children learn the social skills of cooperation, making friends and influencing people, both by trial and error and by observing other members of the group. In the Russian and Israeli groups described above the emphasis on cooperation and mutual help probably affects behaviour in later life. It is said that the importance of informal groups in the USA is a cause of the development of other-directed personality (Riesman *et al.*, op. cit.).

Children's friendship choices have been studied extensively by socio-metric methods (p. 236 ff). Choices of young children change rapidly, and the duration of friendships increases with age, at least up to 18. Young children quarrel a lot, both because of their lack of sensitivity and social skills, and also because they can't find more satisfactory companions. Indeed they may quarrel almost continuously (Thompson, 1962). The basis for choice is similar to that among adults (p. 209 f) – frequency of interaction, similar interests, similar age, class, IQ, etc. Popular children in the USA are found to be either talkative, enthusiastic and daring, or happy and friendly (Bonney, 1943), and to be conforming and cooperative, intelligent, of high social status, and sensitive to others. Unpopular children are found to be socially retiring, uninterested in others, or socially annoying (Northway, 1944). On the other hand the attributes leading to popularity are somewhat different for boys and for girls, among children of different ages, and in different social class or cultural areas – to be popular a child must conform to the norms of his particular group. Most children are keen to be accepted by the peer group. Phillips *et al.* (1951) introduced four 6- and 7-year-old children, one at a time, to well-established play groups of three children of the same age. The new children made great efforts to become a part of the group; they had to take the initiative, and used social techniques such as imitating the behaviour of the most active member, and sought help from the adult in charge.

In all groups there are differences between the power and influence of different members. Lippitt, Polansky and Rosen (1952) found that there was a definite power structure among boys at a summer camp, that the powerful boys made more attempts to influence others, and succeeded in doing so. Children use a variety of techniques of social influence or ascendance, some more acceptable to adults, and more effective with peers, than others. Anderson and Anderson (1954) distinguished between 'dominative' and 'integrative' behaviour: dominative behaviour is aimed at the satisfaction of the child's own needs regardless of others, or at the expense of others; integrative behaviour seeks activities which are satisfying to self and others. Integrative behaviour involves both more concern for others, and a higher level of social skill; it is an essential part of successful leadership. Hanfmann (1935) studied the leadership hierarchy in a group of 10 kindergarten boys: two were gladly followed by the others, one because he initiated constructive group play, the other because he was primarily concerned with good social relationships – an example of the task and socio-emotional leaders often found in adult groups (p. 232). Children also try to exert influence by less skilled methods – physical force for example, which may produce unwilling submission. In groups of working-class boys there is a lot of fighting, and this is a factor in establishing the dominance hierarchy. In other groups the most influential children are those who are older, more intelligent, independent of adults, possess athletic prowess or whatever skills are most valued by the group, and are known to be fair and good at controlling deviants (Campbell, 1964).

Children's groups like other groups have norms, and these are developed and maintained in much the same way as elsewhere (p. 224 f). The pressures used to make deviates conform are less subtle than in groups of older people, and one of the most common is ridicule, creating a feeling of shame in the offending member.

LANGUAGE

Introduction

The capacity to communicate by means of language is probably the crucial difference between men and the non-human primates. It is a biological capacity which has evolved only in man; Pavlov (1927) referred to it as 'the second signalling system' – whereby we respond to stimuli in terms of their symbolic meaning rather than to their physical attributes. It is assumed that this capacity evolved in primitive man because of the biological survival value of being able to communicate in this way, though it is not known what the early stages of this development were, since there is a total gap between men and animals in this respect. Although language probably arose out of social interaction, its possession had other important consequences – linguistic processes became important in the control and coordination of individual behaviour, and in the development and transmission of culture.

Human social behaviour consists primarily of the exchange of verbal utterances, but until recently there has been little contact between the work of social psychologists and linguists. Social psychologists have overlooked the detailed contents and organisation of utterances, as causes and effects of behaviour. Linguists on the other hand have considered speech in isolation from its interpersonal setting, and have paid little attention to whether utterances are intended to convey information, produce action or express feelings, or to differences due to the method of communication, e.g. face-to-face, telephone, writing (Moscovici, 1967). When language is spoken, it is inevitably accompanied by non-verbal signals in the 'audio-vocal' channel, and usually by further signals in the 'visual-gestural' channel (Diebold, 1967). The verbal utterances proper are closely dependent on non-verbal signals, which keep the speaker and listener attending properly to each other, sustain the smooth alternation of speaking and listening, and add further information to the literal messages transmitted (Argyle and Kendon, 1967).

A verbal utterance is a piece of social behaviour; like other social acts it may be initiated by more-or-less conscious intentions, themselves partly verbalised in character. The utterance itself has the same hierarchical structure that other skilled social performances have, with paragraphs, sentences, words, morphemes and phonemes as the levels, each level being governed by elaborate rules. An utterance differs from other social acts in that it is intended to communicate a message; words differ from other physical stimuli in that they have agreed meanings, and in that they can be combined in many ways to convey information.

The universal structure of languages

There are hundreds of different human languages, but they all have a common structure, which will be specified below. While many species of animals can communicate with one another, none of them can do so by means of symbols. Some people suffer from 'language disability', i.e. poor speech, reading difficulties, etc.; family studies show that this is transmitted by a dominant gene, and that it is unrelated to intelligence. This suggests that the ability to acquire language depends on 'specific modes of internal organisation of neurophysiological processes', rather than on general cognitive abilities (Lenneberg, 1964). Speech also depends on the necessary anatomical developments for both speaking and listening, and the successful use of it depends on general intelligence.

Human infants are born with the innate capacity to use language, and succeed in learning it at much the same early age, even when handicapped by blindness, or by gross neglect. They can learn any language to which they are exposed, while no animal can be taught a language. The actual language learnt is the one which has developed, over a long period of cultural development, in the child's culture. The rate of learning depends on such factors as the amount of contact with adults.

All human languages have a certain common structure. Use is made of up to 45 basic sounds or 'phonemes', most of which have no meaning in themselves. The phonemes are combined two, three or more at a time, to make up to 100,000 'morphemes', the basis stems of words, which have agreed symbolic meanings in the culture. Morphemes are made into words by adding various inflexions; in English this includes the formation of verbs and adding 's' for plurals; this is a more important matter in languages like Latin and German.

A word is quite different from any noise made by a parrot or a chimpanzee. It is an arbitrary symbol for an object, activity, etc., which need not be present. It is usually a symbol for a whole class of rather different objects – as 'cat' stands for cats in general. It represents a categorisation of numerous objects or events into a number of discrete classes, all of whose members can be treated alike. Thus 'green' is a range of wavelengths in the spectrum which it has been agreed to group together, though this range is divided into two or more colour-groupings in other cultures. Learning to use a word is an example of concept-formation: the child slowly learns the common features of all the concrete examples which its parents call by this word (Brown, 1965).

In every language words are combined together in sentences, and every language has rules of grammar, or syntax, prescribing how this should be done. Learning theorists at one time regarded language as a kind of learnt skill consisting of chains of responses, each associated with referents in the outside world. Chomsky (1957) and others have argued that there are 'linguistic universals', that there is a similar structure to all languages; it is assumed that this structure has a biological basis. 'Although language families are so different, one from the other, that we cannot find any historical connection between them, every language, without exception, is based on the same *universal principles* of semantics, syntax and phonology. All languages have words for relations, objects, feelings, and qualities . . .' (Lenneberg, op. cit.). Chomsky

(1957) suggested that the basic element of speech is a simple, positive 'kernel' sentence, which can then produce, via a series of transformations, passive, negative and other complex sentences. The rules for making these transformations vary in detail, but in no language is a proposition turned into a question by reversing the order of words, for example. Children learn to use the syntactic categories of nouns, verbs, adjectives, adverbs etc.; in word association tests subjects tend to produce associations in the same category as the stimulus word (Ervin, 1961). Once a person knows a language he can generate an infinite number of new, grammatical and meaningful sentences; he has not learnt a series of messages, he has learnt the underlying structure of the language, even though he could not formulate its rules.

Sentences communicate because they consist of combinations of words, which have meanings. The study of meanings is known as 'semantics'. What meaning consists of is still not entirely understood. Words sometimes evoke images, including blurred, generic images; e.g. of 'cat' or 'horse'; but some people just do not have visual images. Words sometimes evoke motor responses, or implicit motor responses, which have been associated with them; Osgood (1953) suggests that a word elicits a 'mediating response', i.e. a fraction of the responses to the object which is detached from it; however, there is little evidence for the occurrence of such responses. Brown (1958) suggests that the meaning of a word consists of neurophysiological processes associated with it, giving the user the ability to name objects, and to react to words as signs for objects.

Words also have meaning in terms of other words to which they are related. Groups of words form closely related systems; for example the kinship words, son, nephew, brother, etc., are related in this way, and can be reduced to simpler elements. Definitions of words in dictionaries are of course in terms of further words. Words for physical objects may be learned by a process of concept-formation: Lewis (1959) describes how his son learned to use the word 'Fa Fa', meaning for him 'flowers', between the ages of 16 and 22 months, in the course of a series of conversations with his father in the presence of different specimens of flowers. More abstract terms are learnt by means of verbal instruction and experience of the relevant events – which give understanding of such abstract terms as 'guilt', 'fairness', 'democracy' and so on. There can be agreed meanings for words which represent nothing in the real world – 'unicorn' for example. Human conceptual and linguistic powers enable us to generate and use highly abstract scientific and philosophical terms whose relation to observable events can be extremely remote.

The meaning of a word also depends on the sentence of which it is a part – as with words like 'can', 'will', 'stand', etc. When words are combined, further aspects of meaning occur – a 'Venetian blind' is not the same as a 'blind Venetian'; meaning depends on the grouping of words – 'they are hunting dogs' has two possible meanings (Miller, 1965). Combinations of words can be meaningful although no referent exists – 'a big, red, rock-eating dog'; others are meaningless, such as 'a green square-root', because a rule has been broken. Sentences have meanings too, but in terms of information about objects, or requests for such, or attempts to influence the behaviour of the hearer.

The early development of language

The earliest noises made by children consist of babbling, and other kinds of non-verbal sounds, some of which are used to attract attention, to engage in imitative play, and to take part in games like 'pat-a-cake', during the second year of life. The vocabulary grows slowly at first – at 12 months the average child has a vocabulary of 2–3 words, at 24 months it has 154, and at 6 it knows 2,500 words (Smith, 1926). At the same time children are learning to combine words into grammatical sentences, and are building up a structure of meanings in which the words are related. The meanings of words are at first very vague and inaccurate, but greater elaboration and depth of meaning develops with time and as a result of asking questions. Language develops slowly for children in institutions, perhaps because they are rewarded less for using it, and more rapidly for only children, probably because of their greater contact with adults; learning is faster for the children of more educated parents. Irwin (1960) arranged for working-class children to be read to for 15 minutes per day, and found superior production of speech sounds compared with controls by the age of 18 months.

Much early speech takes the form of monologues, accompanying action, and helping to control behaviour. This is most common at ages 4–5 (Ervin-Tripp, 1966). A great deal of speech when others are present is 'egocentric' – the child does not put himself in the position of the listener, or worry too much about whether the message is being received. At some point in middle childhood speech becomes more 'sociocentric' – the child 'addresses his hearer, considers his point of view, and tries to influence him, or actually exchange ideas with him' (Piaget, 1926). An example of egocentric conversation between two $3\frac{1}{2}$-year-old girls is reported by Mussen *et al.* (1963) – 'the first said "my sister has a birth-day today", to which the second replied, "my doggie wet the bed last night" ' (p. 246). Piaget (1924) obtained evidence about this by asking children to explain things to other children. Brown (1965) observes that their explanations fail to take account of the informational needs of the hearer in three ways – (1) failure to define terms, e.g. what is meant by 'door' when describing how a tap works, (2) being very approximate, as in saying 'there', and (3) unclear use of pronouns such as 'it'. Flavell (cited by Brown) devised situations which reveal how much account a child takes of the other's situation: the hearer may be blindfolded, or may be able to obtain information from a third party. McCarthy (1929) found that egocentricity of speech varied with the situation, and was higher when with other children than with adults.

A great deal of children's speech consists of questions, especially when they are with adults. At ages 4–6 they ask about all kinds of things, such as the causes of events, classification, and social relations; they have an immense curiosity, and are trying to classify and understand the outside world (Thompson, 1962). Small children often seem to ask questions, not primarily because they want to know the answers, but in order to keep the attention of adults, i.e. to sustain a social relationship. We shall discuss later the phenomenon of 'informal' conversation, in which the amount of information exchanged is small, but in which social relationships are established and maintained (p. 118 f). The content of the conversation here is unimportant, but an opportunity is provided for communication at a non-verbal level.

Language is used to convey information to others, and this is probably the original purpose for which it was developed by primitive men. In addition to conveying information about facts it can be used to make suggestions about the solutions to problems and to offer opinions. In these ways it plays an important part in enabling two or more people to work together at a joint task, discuss problems and take decisions. The value of language in making cooperation possible is demonstrated in an interesting experiment by Wolfle and Wolfle (1939). Pairs of pre-school children, and monkeys, were placed in cages so that one could reach for food in a cup by using a lever, but only the other subject could see which cup had food in it. The children solved this by use of speech, and even made bargains, while the monkeys were unable to solve it. Clearly it is very rewarding to be able to communicate by means of language in these ways; it is found that twins and triplets learn more slowly than others, probably because they can understand each other's non-verbal signals so well (McCarthy, 1954).

Speech is also used to influence the behaviour of others. Children ask for help, for example with games or dressing, and for objects, such as toys or food. Adults give instructions, suggestions or orders to others. These include instructions about behaviour in the social situation itself, as when an interviewer or psychotherapist tells the client what to do. It also includes various kinds of persuasion and propaganda, where the hearer is induced to do something he doesn't really want to do. One technique for doing this is to arouse some emotional or motivational state, and then to suggest a way of satisfying it – a method much used by advertisers. Propagandists often make use of words with heavy emotional leadings, and they may use words which force the hearer to look at the problem in terms of certain concepts, so that certain conclusions follow inevitably – for example the use of legal, religious or military vocabularies.

Speech *can* be used for expression of emotions, attitudes to the others present, and for self-presentation. We shall show later that speech is an unsatisfactory medium for these kinds of messages, and that nonverbal communication is more effective.

Most human social interaction consists partly of conversation, which is usually a mixture of problem-solving and information-conveying on the one hand, and sustaining social relationships and enjoying social interaction on the other. The topic of conversation reflects the shared interests of those conversing, and this can be quite instructive; Moore (1922) overheard conversations in Broadway at 7.30 on a number of evenings and found that for male–male conversations 48% were about money or business and 8% about females, while in female–female conversations, 3% were about money or business and 44% about males.

Emotional meaning

Words often carry further information in addition to their descriptive meanings as described above. The terms 'yid', 'nigger', etc. do more than refer to racial groups, they also indicate that the speaker is hostile to these groups. Efforts are sometimes made to improve the images of social groups by giving them honorific new titles – 'senior citizen', the 'hard of hearing', for example. A systematic method for measuring the emotional meanings of words was devised by Osgood *et al.* (1957) in the Semantic Differential. Subjects fill in a series of 7-point scales such as:

Cold — — — — — — Warm

This indicates their feelings about a verbalised concept. The results can be expressed as a profile of scores, or in terms of three dimensions: Evaluation, Potency and Activity. Of these the Evaluation dimension is

the most familiar and most important. These dimensions correspond to
Wundt's dimensions of feeling, i.e. pleasantness, strain and excitement; it
has been suggested that the three dimensions are basic responses to the
environment – approach-avoidance, strength and rate.

The variation between words in their emotional meaning is closely
parallel to the effects of non-verbal signals accompanying speech. For
example the total impact of the word 'nigger' can be created by saying
'negro' in a certain tone of voice.

A speaker may indicate by his choice of words attitudes to people or
things discussed. Wiener and Mehrabian (1968) found that different
words are chosen depending on the amount of positive feeling a communicator has towards the people or objects he is speaking about. They
have constructed a scale of 'non-immediacy' and have found that
speakers with a negative attitude have a higher score, and that readers
of such communications could identify the attitudes correctly. The full
scale is shown in Table 2.2. In other studies it has been found that the
words 'I' and 'we' indicate the extent to which a person feels himself to
be a member of a cohesive group, and the rate of 'we's' to 'I's' has been
used as a measure of group cohesiveness. In each of these examples the
main verbal message is communicated equally well by either version,
but the secondary message is different.

Sentences, as well as words, can convey secondary meanings. Since
the same message can be sent by means of a variety of different sentences, it is possible to listen 'with the third ear' for latent messages,
which are often unintended by the speaker. Brown (1965) gives the
example of a young academic who said, during a conversation about
Nigeria, 'That's a place I've not been to', thus producing a rather crude
and unacceptably direct piece of self-presentation (see p. 384 f). A skilled
speaker carefully controls his utterances for such latent messages, and
may send them deliberately. A speaker may use a whole vocabulary, just
as he may put on a particular accent, which modifies the impact of what
is said. He might for example use the vocabulary of teenage slang,
international politics, or psychoanalysis in this way.

The role of non-verbal communication in conversation

Some of the most important findings in the field of social interaction are
about the ways that verbal interaction needs the support of non-verbal
communications. Human communication by speech depends on specialised use of the audio-vocal channel. However, this channel also carries
messages in the paralinguistic area ('how it is said' as opposed to 'what

TABLE 2.2 *Linguistic cover for immediacy* (from Mehrabian, 1966).

Type I

SPEAKER A: I liked the *party*.
SPEAKER B: I liked the food at the *party*.
SPEAKER B: I am concerned about X.
SPEAKER A: I am concerned about X's personality.
SPEAKER A: I hope *you* are successful.
SPEAKER B: I hope your career is successful.

Type II

SPEAKER B: X is my neighbor.
SPEAKER A: X and I live in the same neighborhood.
SPEAKER A: X and I live together.
SPEAKER B: X and I live in the same room.
SPEAKER A: X is my teammate.
SPEAKER B: X and I are on the same team.

Type III

SPEAKER A: I know X.
SPEAKER B: Our group knows X.
SPEAKER B: I am looking at X.
SPEAKER A: I am looking at them (including X).
SPEAKER B: I used to meet X.

Type IV

SPEAKER A: I visited X.
SPEAKER B: I visited X's house.
SPEAKER B: I like X.
SPEAKER A: I like X's children.
SPEAKER A: I saw X.
SPEAKER B: I saw X's car.

Type V

SPEAKER B: *Negroes* have many problems; these people need our help.
SPEAKER A: *Negroes* have many problems; these people need help.
SPEAKER B: I should help X.
SPEAKER A: Someone should help X.
SPEAKER A: Do you remember what we decided the other day?
SPEAKER B: Do you remember what was decided the other day?

is said'). Under most conditions of conversation the visual-gestural channel is simultaneously in use; conversation depends on a subtle combination of signals in these two channels (Diebold, 1967).

There are a number of ways in which non-verbal signals make verbal exchanges possible, and these are discussed below. I am indebted to Ekman and Friesen (1967b), though the present account is somewhat different from theirs.

(*a*) *Mutual attention and responsiveness.* For two people to engage in conversation there must be continuous evidence that each is attending and responding to the other. The conversation is usually initiated by two people taking up positions so that they are sufficiently close together and oriented towards each other, and by making eye-contact. There must be continuous evidence during the encounter that the other is attending and responding; this is done by eye-movements, head-nods and gestural reciprocity (p. 170f); the encounter is terminated by a withdrawal of these cues and changes in position or orientation. The origins of this pattern of behaviour probably lie in the experience of early relations with the mother. The non-verbal signals are uncoded, in the sense that they are in themselves acts of attending and responding. Interactors are highly aware of signals of this kind emitted by others but may not realise what signals they are sending themselves.

(*b*) *Channel control.* Interactors have to take it in turns to speak and listen, and speech itself cannot be used to decide who shall speak or for how long. We shall see later that channel control is effected by small non-verbal signals, mainly head-nods and eye-movements (p. 201 f). These signals are presumably learnt; Ekman and Friesen (1967b) suggest that there are class and cultural differences in their use, and that use of unfamiliar methods is regarded as rudeness. The coding of these signals appears to be partly arbitrary – for example a steady glance at the other indicates the end of an utterance. Interactors do not appear to be aware of making or receiving these signals.

(*c*) *Interpersonal attitudes.* Non-human primates indicate their attitudes and intentions towards one another by means of facial and postural cues – for threat, appeasement, sexual desire, etc. It is most important for interactors to have this information; verbal messages are so polite and so carefully controlled that these attitudes and intentions are concealed; however, the significance of the verbal message may depend on the interpersonal attitude accompanying it. Also in this category can be included self-presentation – indicating how an interactor sees himself and how he would like to be treated. The cues used include spatial proximity, posture, hand and leg movements, and tones of voice, indicating approach or withdrawal, dominance and submission, sexual advances and so on. The origins of this behaviour may lie in instinct, as in primates, or may be learnt during childhood. Such signals are not really coded, they are fragments of actual aggressive, sexual or intimate behaviour. There is partial awareness of the cues that are being used.

(d) *Illustrations*. Speech is often accompanied by a flow of gestural movements, mainly of the hands, which accompany and illustrate what is being said. Ekman and Friesen (loc. cit.) suggest that they can do this in six ways:

batons, movements which time out, accent or emphasize a particular word or phrase, 'beat the tempo of mental locomotion'; *ideographs*, movements which sketch a path or direction of thought, 'tracing the itinerary of a logical journey'; *deictic* movements, pointing to a present object; *spatial* movements depicting a spatial relationship; or *kinetographs*, movements which depict a bodily action. A last type of illustrator, would be *pictographs*, which draw a picture of their referent.

These illustrations are probably learned by watching other people; the style of gestural accompaniment is quite different in different cultures, and it is sometimes taught for public-speaking purposes. The coding is mainly 'iconic', in the sense that the gestures resemble what they symbolise. There is some degree of awareness of the gestures being made.

(e) *Feedback*. A speaker needs to know how his utterances are received – whether the other person understands, believes or disbelieves, is surprised, agrees or disagrees, is pleased or annoyed. Without this information the speaker does not know how to plan the next utterance. The relevant information is mainly obtained by studying the other's face: raised eyebrows signal surprise or disbelief, while the mouth and eyes show pleasure and displeasure. The communication of emotion is partly innate but is overlaid by cultural habits and rules. Interactors are partly aware of the emotional cues which they emit and in many cultures control their facial expressions very carefully; tone of voice is less well controlled.

(*f*) A sixth type of non-verbal signal is the 'emblem' (Efron, 1941): emblems are gestures used in the place of words by deaf people and people who do not speak the same language. Emblems are little used in normal interaction: an example is head shaking, which like other emblems is an arbitrary symbol. Language can be replaced by a non-verbal signalling system when speech is impossible, for example by the deaf, tic-tac men and under water swimmers. Such signals are also used during ordinary discourse in some cultures, e.g. in Greece and the Arab countries (Brun, 1969). We shall suggest later that the physical symptoms of psychosomatic patients act as non-verbal signals in a similar way.

Language developed so that men could communicate with one another; since language is symbolic it may be supposed that they wanted to communicate about things such as food, people or events, which were not immediately present – otherwise pointing would be sufficient. Language is not necessary for showing emotions, or for indicating interpersonal attitudes – primates can do this perfectly well in other ways. The unique sphere of language, it may be suggested, was communication about absent objects and distant events. Language has of course been extended to deal with more immediate events, but it seems to be a relatively ineffective means of doing so.

Non-verbal signals are used both by human and non-human primates to communicate about the immediate social situation, in the ways listed above. We will consider some examples from this sphere.

Interpersonal attitudes. We describe later experiments by the author and others in which the relative impacts of verbal and non-verbal signals for communicating positive and negative, superior and inferior attitudes are compared. The non-verbal cues have considerably more impact than the verbal (p. 142 f); this is a puzzling finding in view of the far greater richness of the verbal code. Probably the main reason for this is that non-verbal signals create an immediate emotive response based on the innate, instinctive structure of the organism. Language appears to have evolved as a specialised means of communication, but it is used to negotiate the matters being discussed, not the relation between speakers. As a result interpersonal relations lie at the background of consciousness and are negotiated by the 'silent language', the non-verbal code. This code has an advantage over language, it is rather vague, and does not commit an interactor to an explicit degree of intimacy or inferiority in relation to another. Further, it is usually assumed that non-verbal signals are spontaneous and unmanipulated and so can be trusted more than speech can. Lastly it is confusing to talk and talk about the talk in the same breath, as in the remark 'there's an awkward pause, isn't there?'

Emotional reactions. Verbal and non-verbal signals function in a very similar way here. An interactor could say 'I feel happy' in a flat, deadpan voice, and with an expressionless face, but he would not be believed; the non-verbal signals must match and confirm the verbal ones. However, if he simply sounded and looked happy (while talking of something else) the message would be received, as experiments to be reviewed later show (p.136 f): therefore the verbal statement 'I am happy' is a totally ineffective communication and is unnecessary.

Self-presentation. As we show later, self-presentation is normally carried out by the non-verbal cues of dress and manner, though very indirect verbal techniques can also be used (p. 384 f). In Britain and many other cultures there is a strong cultural taboo on verbal self-presentation.

Some of the differences between verbal and non-verbal communications may be summarised: (a) Language is most useful for discussing objects and other people; non-verbal signals are better for communicating emotions, interpersonal attitudes, and about other aspects of the immediate interaction. (b) Language is carefully managed; non-verbal signals are more spontaneous, though this varies between different kinds. Study and training in the field of social interaction makes them less spontaneous, more under conscious control. (c) Language is produced by specialised parts of the central nervous system; most non-verbal communication is governed by lower, autonomic and instinctive levels of the organism. (d) Language is arbitrarily coded; non-verbal signals are mostly iconic (fragments of the real things) or uncoded (i.e. are themselves the emotions or acts indicated).

We may conclude this section by observing that most human communication consists of combinations of verbal and non-verbal signals. The form of this integration is discussed further below (p. 119 f).

Coding and interaction

For two people to communicate by means of language, it is necessary for them to use words in the same way; they also need to be able to refer to objects quickly. Zipf (1935) has shown, for several languages, that the more frequently a word is used the shorter it is. Brown (1965) argues that the direction of causation here is from frequency to shortness, in view of the changes in the terms used for a number of new inventions which became household objects – ending up as 'TV', 'car', 'bus', etc. Much time would be wasted during interaction if the longer originals were used. Within particular social groups there are private codes which refer to the most common objects, events and people that have to be discussed; nicknames are one example of this. Zazzo (1960) found in a large sample of twins that private languages developed for 48% of identicals, and for a lower percentage of fraternals, often preceding normal speech. Everstine and Crossman (1966) found that two subjects who could only send each other eight symbols could devise a code to communicate simple messages about objects.

It is easier to refer to some objects or events than others. First, it depends on whether or not the culture or social group has developed a specific word for it. The large number of words for snow used by Eskimos or for scones in Scotland make it easy for those peoples to specify particular kinds of snow or scone. Second, it depends on how many similar objects the thing in question has to be distinguished from – it is easier to refer to a zebra in a herd of elephants than in a herd of zebras (Brown, op. cit.). Third, it depends on how good the speaker is at coding and the listener at decoding.

It also depends on how well the coder can estimate the needs of the decoder: he may give too much information or not enough. Brown (op. cit.) gives an example of a visitor from Ceylon asking the way to Harvard Square and being told, 'Take the drive to Madison Bridge, then turn right and keep going till you see the Yard.' As we reported above, the speech of children below the age of 7–8 tends to be egocentric, and there is often little real attempt to communicate. This is an example of the need to 'take the role of the other' in social behaviour, which will be discussed further below (p. 188 ff).

There may be failure of verbal communication between people for several reasons. (a) They may be using words representing different categories of objects. This is particularly likely when the words are used to categorise objects that vary continuously, as in the cases of colour or size. People may differ in what they understand by a 'large' university, or a 'good' student. (b) Two people may differ in the emotional meanings attached to words. This is common when they belong to groups with different ideologies. For example the words 'socialism' and 'worker' have very different emotional associations in different groups. (c) Interactors may fail to communicate because some of the words they are using are embedded in different intellectual frameworks and thus carry different theoretical meanings. Psychologists may have difficulties with words such as 'arousal' and 'self' in this way. Quite a lot of verbal interaction is spent in trying to disentangle failures of communications of these three kinds. Children try to find out how adults are using words, and students try to discover the full significance of technical terms. At international meetings there are acute problems of finding exact equivalents in one language for words in another. Political and ideological differences are sustained by such differences of usage. When a right-wing politician speaks of a 'capitalist' he is thinking of a large group of people, including a proportion of poor people, who finance and encourage industrial progress by risking some of their own money. A left-wing politician thinks of a small number of absentee owners of firms, who do no work but absorb the profits. The two senses differ in each of the three ways described above.

Further consequences of language for behaviour

Although it may be assumed that language was originally developed in order to help men to communicate with one another, it has further consequences for human behaviour which are of great importance. Brown and Lenneberg (1954) found that colours could be recognised better if they were easily codable into words, as compared with colours such as 'yellow-green' which are not, and that this effect increased with longer time intervals. It is advantageous, therefore, on the input side to code stimuli in words. It is also advantageous to code responses in terms of words. Luria (1961) found that children of 4 could perform better in a discrimination task if they said 'now' or 'press' for a red light, and 'don't' for a blue light, for example. Luria suggests that children go through three stages here: (1) the verbal response acts as a trigger for the motor response but the actual words are meaningless; (2) the meanings of the words are responded to; (3) the speech becomes silent. Later research has shown that verbal mediation increases with age, and improves performance in a number of tasks (Ervin-Tripp, 1966), but there is disagreement about whether silent speech takes place (Brown, 1965). Verbal mediation also helps with serial motor tasks, such as temporal alternation, and it is likely that the same is true of all motor skills, including social interaction (p. 185). The performance of a skilled task is made easier by verbal instructions of the kind 'take the first turning to the right, the second to the left, and the third to the right' (when finding the way), or 'when people talk too little, ask open-ended questions and reinforce them' (when interviewing). The conscious control of skilled performance usually takes a verbalised form. Language also makes possible the formulation of complex and abstract principles, which in turn are used to think about and to control behaviour, as in the case of moral principles and the psychological analysis of social behaviour. Other examples of verbal mediation are the conscience, which consists partly of internalised commands to the self (Argyle, 1964a), and the self-image, which consists mainly of verbalised self-definitions which must be maintained (p. 363 ff).

Language also plays a crucial part in the transmission and building up of culture. Not only can individuals remember things better if they are coded in words, they can also make written notes to aid their memory. They can teach others by means of speech or writing, so that knowledge becomes transmitted through the group and to the next generation. Language also helps in problem-solving, by individuals and groups, thus speeding up the growth of new cultural solutions to problems. While these processes are occurring, language itself changes, to provide the necessary means of communication. New words are invented for new sub-categories or new phenomena, commonly used words become shorter, and private in-group languages are devised, partly for technical reasons and also to promote group solidarity, as for example among soldiers (Elkin, 1946).

CULTURE

Human infants are born with basic biological needs, but much remains to be acquired by learning. Compared with animals, humans are born with less instinctive equipment, but with greater powers of learning, and have a correspondingly longer period of dependence in the family. As a result of the evolution of the power of language, human beings can communicate their solutions of problems to one another, and to the next generation, and can add continuously to this heritage of skills and knowledge. Different societies, over long periods of time, develop different ways of completing the instinctive equipment and satisfying biological drives. These alternative solutions are called cultures. Culture includes (i) a shared language, which symbolises and categorises events; (ii) a shared way of perceiving and thinking about the world; (iii) agreed forms of non-verbal communication and social interaction, which makes cooperation possible; (iv) rules and conventions about what shall be done in different situations; (v) agreed moral and other values, and a system of religious and allied beliefs; (vi) technology and material culture. Societies all differ in two other ways: (i) the kinds of personality which are most prevalent, and the relative strength of drives such as aggression and achievement; (ii) the form of social organisation in the society as a whole and in its sub-groups. Some aspects of the culture are openly stated and acknowledged, but many aspects are not consciously appreciated at all. Members of a culture do not realise how their cognitive world is affected by their language, how their values differ from the values of other societies, or how the process of social interaction is different. Large modern states have a shared culture that permeates the whole society – the language and technology for example; there are also sub-cultures, corresponding to different social classes and geographical regions. These too can be subdivided, down to the smallest unit – the norms of small social groups.

Some behaviour is much the same in all cultures. Sexual intercourse is performed in a very similar way in nearly all parts of the world (Morris, 1967). People eat, drink, rear children, live in families, communicate by language, work in cooperative groups, defend their territory and have religious beliefs in all cultures, but the details of these processes vary (Kluckhohn, 1954). The basic human problems and the general lines of their solution are the same, but the difference in the life and experience of a New York businessman and an African peasant are nevertheless very great.

The study of cultural difference is of interest for several reasons – it shows something of the range of solutions to human problems, that human nature can take very varied forms, and that there may be better solutions to some of these problems than those in one's own culture. It is also important to know how far the results of experiments conducted in one country are universally valid, and how far they depend on the local culture. It is unfortunate for our purposes that most anthropological studies have paid little attention to questions of social interaction, so that we still know very little about cross-cultural variations in the subtler aspects of social behaviour.

Culture and language
Most human societies have their own language; sub-groupings of class, region or occupation use special versions of the language of the surrounding society. While the possession of language and speech is universal, languages are quite distinct and vary in the ways in which they conceptualise the world. Whorf (1956) and others have suggested that the language of a culture embodies and perpetuates a certain world view, and determines the perception, thought and action of its users. The best studied aspect of this problem is the effect of different labelling of continua such as hot–cold, and the colour spectrum. Brown and Lenneberg (1954) repeated their colour-memory experiment among the

Zuni Indians; here different colours were remembered better – because the Zunis divide up the spectrum in a different way from us; for example orange and yellow have the same name so that these colours were often confused in memory.

Whorf (op. cit.) suggested that grammar also may affect cognition and behaviour. There is some support for this from the study of American Indian languages. For example Wintu verbs are conjugated for the evidence (e.g. hearsay, or seeing) rather than for the time, while Navaho verbs must specify clearly whether the action is in progress or just about to stop (Brown, 1958). However, later studies have thrown doubt on the Whorfian hypothesis. When a language has a small number of words for snow or rice, it is still possible to talk about the sub-varieties: it just takes more words. Secondly, it seems that the direction of causation is partly in the reverse direction – when a distinction is important in the culture different words are devised to make it. Lastly, it is doubtful whether language has any effect on the philosophy or world-view of the speaker (Triandis, 1964).

However, language can affect social behaviour in at least one important way: languages differ in the number of alternative personal pronouns available. In French there are two words *tu* and *vous* for different degrees of intimacy, where in English there is now only one; some Far Eastern languages have up to 12 such divisions of pronouns. These usages may also communicate status: *tu* conveys either intimacy or a difference of status, in the same way that the use of Christian names does. A younger or subordinate person may be addressed in these ways without it being reciprocated.

It has been suggested by Bernstein (1959) that English middle- and working-class speakers use linguistic codes that are different both in grammar and words: working-class people use a 'restricted' code, middle-class people an 'elaborated' code. He suggested that the differences are that the restricted code has the following features:

1. Short, grammatically simple sentences, often unfinished, with syntactically poor construction.
2. Simple and repetitive use of small number of conjunctions (so, and, then, because).
3. Rigid and limited use of adjectives and adverbs.
4. Frequent use of personal pronouns (we, you) as subjects, rather than impersonal pronouns (one, it).
5. Frequent use of statements formulated as implicit questions which set up a sympathetic circularity ('It's only natural, isn't it?').

6. Frequent tendency for reason and conclusion to be confounded to produce a categoric statement ('Do as I tell you').
7. Frequent use of traditional, idiomatic phrases.
8. Implicit meaning, failing to explain the background, assumption and implication of remarks.

Robinson and Rackstraw (1967) subsequently carried out a careful comparison of the speech of English mothers from different social classes; their results in general support Bernstein's hypothesis, and the differences were still found with intelligence held constant. Klein (1965) suggested that these differences would be expected to give middle-class children an advantage in the verbalised control of behaviour, and that differences in speech explain why middle-class children engage in more planning for long-term goals, and have higher achievement motivation. Bernstein and Henderson (1969) have recently found that middle-class mothers make greater use of language for discussing topics such as helping children to work things out for themselves, discipline, morals, and emotional states.

The presence in a language of certain abstract terms may influence behaviour in other ways. De Madariaga (1928) suggested that 'fair play' in English, 'le droit' in French, and 'el honor' in Spanish are key expressions providing a key to the three cultures. There are differences of meaning in the sense that the words are embedded in different sets of ideas; they may generate different processes and thus modify behaviour.

Culture and personality

People may behave differently in two cultures because of differences of personality. This is much less clear-cut than differences of language – all Frenchmen speak French and all Englishmen speak English, but if there are any differences of personality between the English and French there will be considerable overlap between the two populations. Differences within either population will be greater than any differences between them. By 'personality traits' we mean general patterns of behaviour which are manifested in a wide range of situations – like aggressiveness, conformity, extraversion; more specific differences may be due to cultural rules rather than to personality. It is very difficult to establish that there are differences in the distribution of traits in two populations – this requires extensive sampling of the populations concerned as well as tests that are valid in both. There are probably no studies that meet both criteria: social surveys have good samples but do not tap personality traits or social behaviour, more intensive studies fail to include representative samples. However, several studies have provided data that is of interest. Cultural differences in personality are mainly caused by different patterns of child-rearing, as statistical comparisons of primitive societies have shown (e.g. Whiting and Child, 1953). Since personality traits are also partly inherited it is possible that natural selection has led to changes in the genetic composition of different populations. Morris (1967) suggests that aggression may have developed in some American Indian tribes in this way.

We will consider evidence for cultural differences in some of the traits most closely linked with social behaviour.

Authoritarianism. Melikian (1959) administered the F-scale to large samples of schoolchildren and students in Egypt and found that they scored considerably higher than similar groups in the USA. McClelland (1961) assessed motivational themes in popular children's reading books: in countries with totalitarian regimes such as Russia, Spain, Iraq and Argentina, the stories had high scores for power motivation, low scores for affiliative motivation. Germany showed this same pattern both for the 1925 and 1950 reading books. Rabbie (1965) compared child-rearing methods in the USA and Germany by questioning students who had lived in similar families in both countries. American parents were less strict and gave more autonomy; German parents were more punitive, and the parental roles were more differentiated, the father being stricter and the mother warmer.

Affiliation. The Maudsley Personality Inventory has been administered to large numbers of students in several countries: American and Australian students score considerably more extroverted than British students (Eysenck, 1959). It is a common experience that it is easier to get to know people in some countries than in others; this is sometimes described as 'accessibility' (p. 362); it is not known quite how it is related to affiliation. It has often been observed that the Swedes are more difficult to get to know than the British, and the British more difficult than Americans. It has been found that British emigrants to Australia dislike the 'excessive familiarity' of Australians in using Christian names after very brief acquaintance (Richardson, 1961).

Conformity. There appear to be cultural differences in the amount of conformity in groups. Milgram (1961) found that Norwegian students conformed more than French students, in a series of different conformity experiments; he interpreted this in terms of the cohesiveness of

Norwegian society and the tradition of dissent and argument in France. Riesman *et al.* (1950) suggest that Americans have become 'other-directed' and conformist, as opposed to the 'inner-directed' Europeans, and they relate this to the importance of the peer-group in American child-rearing. Lipset (1961) argues that there has always been an emphasis on conformity in the USA, and that there has been no historical change, as Riesman suggested; he postulates that accepting group norms can be combined with developing greater individual autonomy. In a study of American students it was indeed found that those who were most concerned about group norms also had the most strongly internalised values of their own (Riley, Riley and Moore, 1961).

Other personality dimensions. Cultural differences have been found in a number of other personality dimensions which are relevant to social behaviour. McClelland (1961) measured differences in achievement motivation, and found that they were related to the rate of economic growth. Whiting and Child (1953) found differences in aggression, and also differences in the direction of aggression (e.g. overt *v.* fantasy) in different societies. Mead (1937) reported differences in cooperation and competition in different primitive societies.

Social conventions

Every culture has its rules and conventions – the equivalent of norms in smaller groups. In fact the entire content of a culture, the ways in which it differs from other cultures, could be described in terms of such norms; however it is more useful to describe some of these differences in terms of the distribution of personality traits, as above. The two processes probably overlap – some norms exist because of the kinds of people in the cultural group: rules favouring fighting and warfare would be more common in a society containing aggressive personalities. Other norms are residues of solutions to earlier problems and are not so directly related to personality needs – the Jewish and Moslem rules about eating, for example.

We are most concerned with the rules governing social situations. Some of these rules are universal and apply to nearly all encounters in the culture. Hall (1966) has drawn attention to different rules about proximity in different cultures: Arabs and Latin Americans stand considerably closer than Europeans or Americans. Other rules apply to particular situations – to behaviour at meals, or with subordinates. Swedes and Arabs have distinctive rules about behaviour at meals for example. Sitting down together to eat is a situation that occurs in all cultures, but other situations are unique to the culture, and simply do not exist in other cultures, though there may be approximate equivalents. Members of the culture, or sub-culture, must learn what these situations are, and what the rules are for each.

Barker and Wright (1954) listed the standard 'behaviour settings' which were publicly recognised by the occupants of a small town in Kansas. They found a total of 2,030, including such events as church services, school classes, baby showers, and visiting the barber. For each setting there was a standard pattern of behaviour, including the appropriate emotional state. Such a list of situations, with the amount of time different sections of the population spend in them, gives a total picture of social interaction in the community.

In different communities the behaviour settings and their rules are quite different. Newcomers to Oxford University for example have to become familiar with 'collections', 'tutorials', 'commem balls', 'vivas', 'bump suppers', 'dessert', and so on. The same two people may interact in a limited number of standard situations, each with their own rules. At Oxford University, for example, a faculty member can meet students at lectures, tutorials, discussion classes, or to give personal advice and guidance. He can meet his friends at sherry parties, dinner, 'coffee', etc. In each of these situations it is generally understood how long the encounter will last (for some the actual time of day is fixed), what clothes shall be worn (e.g. whether a gown, suit, etc.), how much of the time each person will talk, whether they stand or sit, and so on. This pattern of conventions varies sharply between different cultures, and sub-cultures, and certain types of encounter may be unique to a particular culture. Visitors to the USA may have to learn what happens at a pyjama party, a bull session, a picnic, a baby shower, and may have to learn the elaborate rules which surround dating. When visiting someone to ask a favour in West Africa it is assumed that a gift will be presented – not as a bribe, but as the traditional exchange of gifts. The rules governing selling vary in different parts of the world, and the procedure will involve more or less bargaining, and take more or less time accordingly. If one party breaks the cultural rules this creates anger and consternation among the others involved; we shall show later that part of the shock produced by T-group training is due to the failure of the trainer to conform to cultural expectations about his role (p. 260 ff). In some social skills it is necessary to teach clients the new cultural tradition – as with subjects of motivation research interviews, or patients undergoing psychotherapy. It seems to be usual to create the impression that there is a stable tradition, which the newcomer hasn't heard about. A peculiarity of research in psychology is that subjects are placed in very unusual situations – but even here there has come to be a tradition, governing how long it shall take, how much subjects are paid, how much they are told, and so on. New words are created to cover new situations, which become added to the cultural store. If a person does not know the word he will be unlikely to distinguish the situation or to know about the rules. New situations in our own culture include the 'T-group', the 'demonstration', and the 'teach-in'; while others have disappeared – such as the reading party and the social breakfast (Argyle, 1967).

Goffman (1963a) has analysed the rules governing some of the main types of social encounter in the USA. He has shown that these rules penetrate to the key processes of social interaction and non-verbal communication – such things as the pattern of eye-movements and of bodily movements. This elaborate pattern of unverbalised rules, of which we are only dimly aware, creates regular patterns of interaction, so that the behaviour of other people is predictable, and social encounters proceed smoothly. If a person does not keep to the rules, interaction is disrupted, others are disturbed, and the offender will be branded as eccentric or even mad. When the rules are formulated they are known as etiquette. Sometimes rather elaborate rules are built up for social situations – so that the behaviour of participants is partly programmed for them. Etiquette soon takes over a secondary role – embarrassing and excluding those who don't know the rules, and thus preserving the status of those who do. Etiquette is most highly developed in connection with entertaining guests to meals, and with occasions on which individuals of different status are present. The Swedish rules about 'skolling' prescribe at whom a person shall look each time he drinks from his wineglass; at Bostonian dinner parties it was prescribed whether each person should talk to the person on his left or right for each course of the meal. Although some cultures are often described as more formal and etiquette-ridden than others, there appears to be little consistency: while the Japanese are very formal in traditional social situations, this is not true of getting onto trains or buses. While it is sometimes said that formality characterises older, more ossified, sub-cultures, this not wholly true: there is a great deal of etiquette in connection with sport, committee meetings and TV programmes.

Social interaction

Cultures differ in the verbal means of communication; they also differ in their non-verbal signals, and to some extent in the actual processes of social interaction. Firstly there are differences in the way language is used. We have seen that the number of personal pronouns available makes it more or less possible to indicate intimacy and status by the choice of pronoun. There are conventions about the amount of politeness and understatement which should be used. The Japanese are elaborately polite; Arabs use a great deal of exaggeration: 'If an Arab says what he means without the expected exaggeration, other Arabs may think that he means the opposite' (Shouby, 1951). Thus an Arab will continue to pursue a girl who does not rebuff him vigorously enough, and will assume that a visitor really wants to eat more unless he refuses three times. This is an interesting example of speech needing to be supported not only by non-verbal signals but in addition by further verbal ones.

It has long been appreciated by modern language teachers that it is necessary to teach the paralinguistic elements as well as what is read or written. Only recently has it been appreciated that the visible elements of gesture and facial expression also need to be learnt if a speaker is to be able to communicate effectively with native speakers of the language (Hayes, 1964). The same non-verbal signals may have quite different meanings in two cultures, and thus lead to confusion if used wrongly. Sticking out the tongue means an apology in parts of China, the evil eye in parts of India, deference in Tibet, negation in the Marquesans (La Barre, 1964), and is a rude sign used by children in England. Hissing is used in Japan to show deference to superiors, but is a way of expressing disdain in England. Facial expressions have a certain variation; in many places a smile does not indicate that its wearer is happy.

It is important to know how far the processes of social interaction, as described in this book, are different in cultures outside Europe and the USA. Unfortunately there is little evidence on this point, but a number of findings are of interest. (*a*) *Sensory channels used.* In parts of Africa and Asia it is normal for two interactors to be in bodily contact, by holding hands, having a hand on knee, or legs intertwined; this creates an extra channel of communication. Hall (1966) suggests that Arabs stand close together in order to smell one another's breath. (*b*) *Channel control.* It is likely, as Ekman and Friesen (1967b) suggest, that different cues are used for negotiating the alternation of speaking and listening. Poor meshing is common between people from different cultures; the author has noticed that English people are sometimes unable to stop French delegates at conferences from talking all the time. (*c*) *Use of gesture.* Italians and Greeks make far more use of gesture than people from other cultures, and they have a more elaborate gesture language.

Efron (1941) found that Jewish immigrants to the USA used batons (emphasising words) and ideographs (sketching the direction of thought), while Italian immigrants used kinetographs (depicting a bodily action) and pictographs (drawing pictures of objects). (*d*) *Self-presentation.* While self-presentation occurs in all cultures, it is of greater importance in some. In most of the East there is great anxiety about losing 'face', so that self-presentation is of great importance. The way it is done also varies; in England there is a taboo on overt self-presentation in words, and a misleading modesty is approved of – it must be done in a less direct way. In the USA this is less true, and in India and Japan it is quite normal to speak highly of oneself. In England and the USA it is conventional to provide praiseworthy motives for one's actions; candidates being interviewed, if asked why they want the job, are supposed to speak of the contribution they could make to the organisation; candidates from other countries sometimes shock English interviewers by saying that they want to make more money. (*e*) *Proximity, and the use of space.* Hall (1966) suggests that there are cultural differences in proximity and other aspects of spatial positioning. He observes that Arabs in public places recognise no zone of privacy round persons or groups and will stand in physical contact with a stranger or try to push him aside. He thinks that a cultural adaptation to population pressures has resulted in forms of social interaction involving greater proximity, more bodily contact and eye-contact than elsewhere. Watson and Graves (1966) carried out observational laboratory studies of Arabs and Americans, each from 4 geographical areas. The Arabs faced each other more directly, sat closer to each other (within body contact distance), touched each other more, looked each other more in the eye, and talked more loudly than the Americans. In Germany Hall observes that if a person looks at another person or group he is regarded as intruding, as spatial separation is not enough to create social separation. There is also a taboo in changing spatial position during an encounter, for example by moving a chair. These observations, and those on the other cultures discussed, must be regarded as hypotheses rather than conclusions, but clearly there are differences between cultures in the use of space.

Morals and values

Moral and other values affect behaviour both by becoming internalised and forming part of the cognitive control system, and by being embodied in social norms which enforce conformity by threat of rejection or punishment. Social behaviour is one of the main objects of these in-

fluences. At the lowest level of generality there are specific moral rules –
thou shalt not lie, steal, commit adultery, etc. Something like the Ten
Commandments is fairly universal through all human societies, though
the extent to which they are followed varies. Anderson and Anderson
(1962) asked children and teachers to complete stories, in which a child
in the story could get out of trouble by telling a lie. The majority of
Mexican subjects thought that the child would lie, the majority of
American subjects thought the child would tell the truth, while subjects
in Rio de Janeiro were intermediate; the teachers gave similar answers to
the children. There are also differences in moral regulations, especially
those regulating sexual behaviour. Premarital intercourse is approved,
under certain conditions, in Scandinavian countries and in many primitive societies; the permitted number of wives or husbands is greater
than one in a number of societies.

As guides to conduct some of these rules are unsatisfactory – there are
situations when most people could regard lying as morally correct.
Moral values may accordingly be embodied in more abstract general
principles such as, love thy neighbour as thyself, treat people as ends in
themselves, seek the greatest happiness of the greatest number. In fact
these formulations vary somewhat in the kinds of behaviour they
recommend. Rettig and Pasamanick (1962) for example found that
Koreans had a 'personal welfare' and Americans a 'puritanical morality'
factor in their sets of moral ideas. In totalitarian countries there is a
greater willingness to allow individuals to suffer for the common good.
There are differences in the extent to which people have a feeling of
responsibility for other people and take part in community affairs.
Berkowitz and Lutterman (1964) devised a scale for measuring 'social
responsibility', and found that middle-class respondents scored considerably higher than working-class respondents in American samples.
Berkowitz and Friedman (1967) suggest that for American and British
middle-class people there is a cultural norm that a person should help
those who depend on him or need his help; in other cultural groups
helpfulness is a function more of reciprocity – i.e. what the other person
does in exchange (p. 174). Feldman (1967) carried out some naturalistic
field studies to find out how residents of an area reacted to strangers
who asked for help, with finding the way and with posting a letter. On
asking the way, foreigners were treated worse than compatriots in Paris
and Athens, but not in Boston, and the Bostonians were more helpful
to both.

Cultures emphasise certain values and goals at the expense of others:
it is in this sense that cultures are most clearly seen as alternative solu-

tions to life's problems. While developed countries value economic achievement and hard work, other societies prefer other values – such as the 'African personality' which is spontaneous, relaxed and happy (Mphahlele, 1962). While capitalist countries value political freedom, communist countries think that this is less important than 'freedom to eat'. Value is also placed on different interpersonal styles, and this is embodied more clearly in individuals than in abstract rules. Such styles are seen in revered models like the Cowboy of 1890 vintage, and the English Gentleman of the same era.

Social structure

Societies have distinctive social structures, rather like large social organisations. The structure consists of the main roles in the society, and the patterns of social interaction between the occupants of these roles. This includes relations between males and females, young and old, different castes or classes, different racial and religious groups, between members of families, and between neighbours. We shall discuss briefly one aspect of social structure – the class system.

All societies have classes, and many sociologists believe that stratification has positive functions, such as providing an incentive system and stable leadership. Social classes are groups within the society, where the 'higher' groups have more money and property, and greater access to rewards generally, and are also more powerful. There are certain universal features of the pattern of social interaction in class systems – there is greater ease of interaction within than between classes; it is generally agreed that the members of higher classes are in some vague sense 'superior', those of lower classes 'inferior'; when members of different classes interact, the member of the lower class is usually deferential.

There are many differences between the class systems in different societies – in the qualities which convey status (e.g. economic, military or religious prowess), the extent of social inequality, the amount of social mobility (Davis and Moore, 1945). However, sociologists have paid little attention to the character of social interaction within different class systems, and we will describe four rather different kinds of social stratification from this point of view.

(a) *Castes*. The Indian caste system provides the best example, though it is now largely breaking down. There are two key features of the Indian system. Firstly it was almost impossible for a person to move from the caste into which he was born. Secondly there was virtually no social interaction at all between one caste, the untouchables, who comprise up to 25% of the population in some areas, and the rest. Racial minority groups are often in the position of castes, and under conditions of apartheid, or extreme prejudice, are in a similar position to members of the lower Indian castes.

(b) *Feudal and paternalistic systems.* In feudal Europe, and the American Southern States, there was a paternalistic system, in which the 'lower orders' accepted their place in society, and in turn were looked after by their social superiors. This kind of relationship can still be found in the country in England, though it is rare in the cities. The easy social interaction, and mutual positive feelings in a context of inequality, are of interest – both sides accepted their roles and took part in an exchange of rewards. The relationship was excellently caricatured by P. G. Wodehouse in the Bertie Wooster–Jeeves stories.

(c) *European industrial society.* With the growth of industry and cities, the feudal system dissolved and social mobility greatly increased. Social contact between different classes was greatly restricted and confined to work situations. The 'social distance' between classes was greater, in the sense that communication became more difficult, and the growth of political divisions created hostility between social classes. The education of children at different kinds of school perpetuated the differences. In England since the war the economic status and material conditions of many members of the working class have become very similar to those of many middle-class people. However, there is still a considerable cultural difference – in values and way of life, and there is very little social contact between these two classes (Goldthorpe and Lockwood, 1962). There is also a relatively high degree of visibility of class, in terms of different clothes, accent, cars, etc.

(d) *Modern American society.* In the USA there has always been an emphasis on equal opportunity, and on the basic equality of people, despite great actual differences in wealth. Interaction between different classes is easier than in Europe, and visibility of class is less, while social mobility is much the same. The shift from feudalism is greater than in Europe in that a person's class depends more on his own achievements than on his family background (Lipset, 1961).

III

The Elements of Social Behaviour

In this chapter we begin the detailed analysis of social interaction, by considering the elements of behaviour which are relevant. When two or more people are engaged in interaction, each one emits a variety of visible and audible signals, some intentional, others not, which may affect the others present. This is true whether the interaction is primarily verbal – as in a conversation – or is mainly non-verbal – as when people are dancing, playing an outdoor game, or working together at a manual task. In this chapter we shall consider the main categories of behaviour which are displayed by people in social situations, discuss their causes and the roles they play in social interaction. In the next chapter we shall take up the ways in which other people perceive, synthesise and interpret these cues.

While it would be absurd to analyse in great detail behaviour which is clearly invisible and inaudible, it is difficult to know *a priori* what can and cannot be responded to. There is the famous case of the horse Clever Hans who could apparently do arithmetic, and gave answers by tapping his foot on the ground, but who was really responding to the bodily posture of the questioner, which told him when to stop tapping his foot (Pfungst, 1911). Similarly it has been found that experimenters may unwittingly influence the behaviour of their subjects so as to confirm hypotheses, by minor variations in their verbal or non-verbal behaviour (Rosenthal, 1966). It has been found that the amount E looks at S, the time E takes over the instructions, and his stress on certain words can function in this way, and that male E's behave very differently towards male and female S's (Friedman, 1967).

Speech is important in most human social behaviour, and it is what most distinguishes our social activities from those of animals; however, even when an encounter is primarily conversational, non-verbal cues of various kinds play an essential role in the process as we have seen. We now know, as a result of quite recent research, what the key elements of social behaviour are, and we have a good idea of what they communicate

91

during social encounters. Later in the chapter we shall consider how verbal and non-verbal communications are combined, and how they may substitute for each other.

The elements of social behaviour used by humans are very similar to those used by animals, especially the primates. Certain elements used by animals are used rather less by humans. The autonomic responses of hair erection, and changes of colour of the face and other parts of the body, occur less in humans, and are to some extent deliberately restrained. We also make little use of smell; perspiration can result from and signal emotional arousal, and the breath is affected by what has been eaten or drunk; however, in the West these odours are restrained, and other interactors do not usually get close enough to smell them.

NON-VERBAL COMMUNICATION: TACTILE AND VISUAL

Bodily contact

This is the most basic type of social behaviour; relations between an infant and other people consist at first entirely of patterns of physical contact. Later these are largely replaced by the visual cues of facial and gestural expression, and the auditory cues of speech. However, much of the meaning of these signals is in terms of bodily contacts which they have replaced, especially in so far as they refer to interpersonal relationships (Frank, 1957). The clearest instance of this process is in the development of infant-mother relationship, as was shown earlier (p. 47ff). A relation of bodily contact becomes transformed into a similar relationship which is mediated almost entirely by vision, and later by speech.

Bodily contact can occur in a very wide variety of ways, though some may not be used in any one culture. Different parts of the body can be touched in many different ways, but the main ways of touching another can be divided into a few broad types, as follows:

(a) Hitting another person, as an act of aggression, is usually done in a way defined by the culture, e.g. punching on the jaw or spanking on the bottom.

(b) Stroking, caressing or holding occur in parental, sexual and other nurturant behaviour, as well as in dancing and other indoor and outdoor games. Grooming is one of the main forms of affiliative activity in primates, but is rare in humans (p. 33 f). Play in young humans and primates involves a good deal of bodily contact, but it decreases with age.

(c) Greetings and farewells may involve shaking hands, kissing, or more elaborate processes of striking or stroking: '. . . the Copper Eskimo welcome strangers with a buffet on the head and shoulders with the fist

. . . An Ainu, meeting his sister, grasped her hands in his for a few seconds, suddenly released his hold, grasped her by both ears . . . then they stroked each other down the face and shoulders' (La Barre, 1964). (d) Holding can be used for communication and companionship, as when two people remain in bodily contact during a whole period of interaction, by holding hands, keeping a hand on a knee, and so on. There can be said to be a 'language' of bodily contact, though it is not a very elaborate one. Different degrees of pressure, and different points of contact can signal emotional states such as fear, or interpersonal attitudes such as desire for intimacy. When two people are in contact there is a two-way system of interaction, because the other can reciprocate or withdraw to keep the interpersonal system as he or she wants it. (e) Guiding another's movements may entail leading by the hand, steering by the elbow, or be combined with aggression, as in pushing and pulling. Touch is used to guide skilled motor responses, and bodily contact with another is important in teaching such skills.

It is possible to study which parts of the body are touched. Jourard (1966) has studied this question by asking subjects to indicate who had touched them on which areas of their anatomy. He found that students were touched most by their mothers and by friends of the opposite sex; for many of them their fathers touched no more than hands. The details are given in Fig. 3.1.

The extent to which bodily contact occurs between people depends very much on their age and the relation between them. There is a great deal of contact between mothers and infants, which declines as the child gets older. There is a certain amount between pre-adolescent children of the same sex, and rather more between adolescent and older opposite-sex couples; it is fairly extensive between husbands and wives. Otherwise there is virtually a taboo in our society on bodily contact, apart from greetings and farewells. In Cambridge (England) it used to be the custom that one shook hands only at the beginning and end of term.

There are however great cultural variations in the extent of bodily contact and the forms which it takes – as is shown by the variations in methods of greeting described above. Even aggressive and sexual contact follows conventional forms – in some parts of the world the 'missionary position' is never used (Kinsey *et al.*, 1948). Jourard (1966) counted the frequency of contact of couples in cafés in cities in different countries and reports the following contacts per hour: San Juan (Puerto Rico) 180; Paris 110; Gainesville (Florida) 2; London 0. It has been observed that physical contact is very extensive in some primitive societies; in some places it is common to hold hands while having a conversation.

The common element running through most kinds of bodily contact is an increased intensity of involvement with the other person – often of a sexual, affiliative or allied kind. Bodily contact of a non-painful type indicates intimacy. Rougher kinds of bodily contact of course go with aggression and coercion.

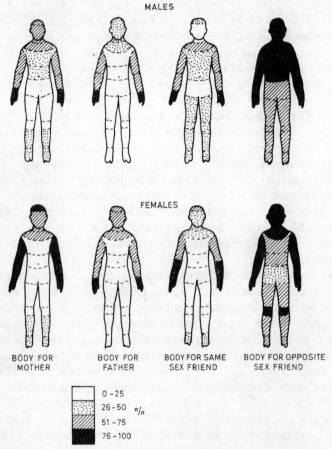

Figure 3.1. Areas of the body involved in bodily contact (Jourard, 1966)

Proximity

Whenever two people engage in a social encounter they must choose some degree of physical proximity. The lower limit equals bodily contact; the upper limit is set by factors of visibility and audibility. Hall (1963) has suggested a four-point classification of degrees of proximity, which he calls 'Intimate', 'Casual-personal', 'Social-consultative', and

'Public'. Each of these differs from the others in that different sets of senses predominate. At the Casual-personal distance (about 5 feet) vision and hearing are used, but in the Intimate range smell, touch and even taste play a part, and vision becomes less useful. (See p. 83 f on proximity among Arabs.) What determines how close a person will come to another? Factors of sight, sound, smell, etc., are clearly important, as mentioned already. Greater proximity will be sought by a person who is deaf or short-sighted for example. This is intertwined with cultural factors – such as whether smell is sought or avoided.

The usual method in studies of this problem is to ask a subject to go and hold a conversation with a confederate, and the distance between them is measured. Mehrabian (1968) asked subjects to go and stand so as to talk to a hat-rack imagined as being a person with certain properties. Little (1965) asked subjects to place cardboard cut-outs at appropriate distances for different descriptions of the situation. Porter, Argyle and Salter (1969), as well as other investigators, have found that individuals are highly consistent in the proximities they adopt in different situations, and that experimental manipulations produce modest effects of 3–6 inches at a distance of 4–7 feet. However, it is not yet known what personality variables control proximity. Introverts have been found to prefer slightly greater distances, but only when the most intimate situations are involved, e.g. they do not like dancing cheek to cheek (Williams, 1963). Porter *et al.* (op. cit.) found no consistent correlation with extroversion in interviews and informal conversations.

Argyle and Dean (1965) proposed an approach-avoidance theory of proximity. It is supposed that a person is both attracted and repelled by another, and takes up a position corresponding to the equilibrium position (see p. 107 f). In experiments in which pairs of subjects were placed 2, 6 and 10 feet apart it was found that at 2 feet subjects leant backwards, while at 10 feet they leant forwards – as if trying to get to their normal equilibrium point. If two people like one another, according to this theory, the approach forces would be stronger and greater proximity results. It was also postulated that proximity is one among a number of ways of establishing intimacy, and that one signal could compensate for another.

$$\text{Intimacy} = f \begin{cases} \text{proximity} \\ \text{eye-contact} \\ \text{smiling} \\ \text{personal topics of conversation, etc.} \end{cases}$$

It follows if one of these variables is manipulated, one or more of the others should move in a direction to compensate for the change in level of intimacy. This generates a large number of predictions about complementary relationships between the variables concerned. The theory was confirmed by the finding that people come closer to someone whose eyes are shut; this effect was greatest for males approaching females, coming 13·2 inches closer in the eyes-shut condition (Porter *et al.*, op. cit.). Subjects also stand closer to an inanimate object. The theory postulates that proximity depends on the balance of approach and avoidance forces. It was found by Mehrabian (1968) that subjects stand closer to someone they like (6½ inches), and by Campbell *et al.* (1966) that they move closer to members of preferred racial groups. Porter *et al.* also found that females stood closer than males to a same-sex target (5·3 inches).

Proximity varies with the social setting. At a crowded party people stand close together, partly in order to hear one another speak, partly to signal whom they are interacting with; in a sitting-room people may sit 8-10 feet apart, though 5½ feet is more common for discussions in the work situation (Sommer, 1961, 1967). There are probably implicit cultural rules about these matters, which in turn are the result of factors of the kind already discussed. Porter *et al.* (op. cit.) found some evidence that subjects stood at one of certain standard positions, 2–4 or 9–12 feet but rarely between, perhaps corresponding to different definitions of the situation, and the adoption of different rules.

Proximity can be considered in conjunction with another element – orientation. The closer degrees of proximity are usually combined with a shift of orientation away from head-on to side-by-side. Intimacy can be maintained at the same level, since there is a progressive loss of eye-contact as the body is turned. Sommer (1965) and Cook (1968b) have studied these phenomena in experiments in which a subject is asked to go and sit at a table with a second subject, or to indicate on a diagram where two people would sit under certain conditions. The following seating positions are commonly found:

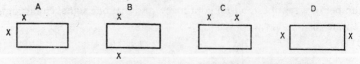

A is most common for a conversation, B for competition (USA), C for cooperation, D for competition (GB). Close friends of same or opposite sex choose C. Extroverts tend to choose the positions B and D. Orientation depends on the situation – in pubs position C is common, with backs to the wall, while in restaurants B is more usual. When there are more than two people, a person tends to position himself opposite those to whom he will talk most. A person who is going to give a lecture or take the chair orients himself so that he faces as many people as possible (Sommer, 1961). In general it can be said that the relationships between people are reflected in the way they are positioned and oriented – as can be seen in a courtroom or a debating hall.

Research with animals reveals a further source of proximity behaviour. Wynne Edwards (1962) has shown that there are instinctive biological mechanisms to maintain the right population density in relation to factors such as the food supply (p. 27 f). Every species of animals has its own characteristic separation distance (Hediger, 1955). Hutt and Vaizey (1966) found a possibly similar process operating in children, in an experiment in which they varied the density of children in a playroom. Normal and brain-damaged children became more aggressive as density increased, but this was not the case with autistic children.

Posture

Posture can be classified into several main varieties – standing, sitting, lying on face or back, kneeling, etc. Each of these can be further subdivided according to the manner in which it is done, for example how relaxed different parts of the body are, whether arms or legs are crossed, and so on. A person can sit at attention, with feet on desk, with legs crossed, slumped in chair, or with knees apart (males and females considered separately).

What decides the posture which a person will adopt on a particular occasion? It is partly a matter of the cultural conventions governing a situation – as in a church service for example. A newcomer here would be explicitly told about such things. One of the main sources of variation is a person's attitude to the others present. Mehrabian (1968), in his hat-rack experiment, found that subjects adopted different postures to those they liked or disliked: subjects adopted an arms-akimbo position with people they disliked, and females had a more open arms posture with males they liked. Scheflen (1965) analysed films of group therapy sessions and found that people would vary their posture to be congruent or non-congruent with others present. Sometimes in a group one person can be seen in a contrasted posture; this might be equivalent to facing away from the group or placing himself at some distance from it.

Posture can also reflect status – or rather the way a person perceives his status in relation to the others. Goffman (1961) has observed how,

D

at the staff meetings of a psychiatric hospital, the high-status people, such as the psychiatrists, would sit in relaxed postures, putting their feet on the table, and lying slumped in their seats. (They would also sit in front, a matter of spatial position.) The junior people would sit more formally (and further back). Mehrabian (op. cit.) found similarly that with a low-status person subjects were more relaxed, faced him less directly, were more likely to have arms akimbo, and had a less open arm or leg position.

Posture reflects a person's emotional state; as will be shown later there is considerable agreement among judges as to which emotion a given posture expresses. Similarly posture can be regarded as an aspect of personality, since individuals have their characteristic styles of expressive movement. In so far as the style is deliberately chosen, it will reflect a person's self-image, and show the cultural models to which he aspires. Here is an acute piece of description of styles of walking seen in London:

> In a street market I watched a working class mum and her daughter. The mother waddled as if her feet were playing her up. Outside a Knightsbridge Hotel I watched an upper class mum and her daughter come out from a wedding reception and walk towards Hyde Park Corner, the mother on very thin legs slightly bowed as though she had wet herself. She controlled her body as if it might snap if moved too impulsively. Both daughters walked identically (Melly, 1965).

The way people stand or sit, and the ways they move about, are partly a matter of cultural conventions, and reflect the relative status of those concerned. Hutte and Cohen in Holland made silent films of managers entering the offices of other managers. It was quite clear from the posture and movements of the two men what their respective status was (Burns, 1964).

Physical appearance

One of the main ways in which one person impinges on another is via his sheer physical appearance. We will confine ourselves to outlining the main variables, and to suggesting some of the most likely determinants. The general physical attractiveness, rated on an 8-point scale by the experimenters, of 752 students was found to be the most important predictor of how often they were asked out by members of the opposite sex; surprisingly this was nearly as true of male students as of females (Walster *et al.*, 1966). The components out of which attractiveness and other perceptions are based are clothes, physique, face, hair and hands. The specific perceptual inferences which are made about personality traits, or social grouping, will be considered in the next chapter.

Most of the body is hidden by clothes, at least in the colder and more civilised cultures, so that the clothes themselves are a major element in appearance. Furthermore clothes are entirely a matter of personal choice, so that wearing of clothes can be regarded as a piece of social

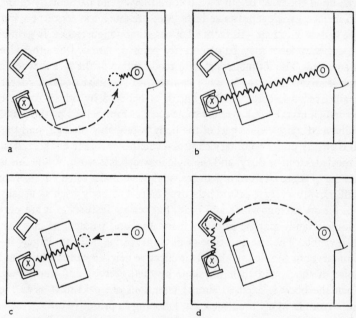

Figure 3.2. Key movements between men in an office indicating their social separation (from Burns, 1964)

behaviour. Clothes are meaningful only within a cultural setting; they can be more or less in fashion, and can be the clothes associated with a particular social group – students, country gentlemen, bohemians, farmers, or bankers, for example. To this extent they resemble uniforms – where the insignia show clearly the rank and branch of the wearer. In each case quite small cues can be commonly discriminated by those concerned. Clothes may be worn well or in a slovenly way, they may be dramatic or drab; in these ways they reflect the personality of the wearer.

As will be shown later, people look mainly at each other's faces, so the face is the most important item to be considered. Some aspects of the face are not under voluntary control at all, though they may be the basis of another's reactions – such as the distance between the eyes, and the shape and length of nose. Facial tension, smiling and so on, will be considered later in connection with the faster-moving elements of emotional expression. Some aspects of the face are almost completely under voluntary control and so can be regarded as elements of social behaviour. Women in most cultures pay a great deal of attention to the make-up of the face. In our own culture they attend particularly to the skin surface, eyes, eyebrows and lips. Men are much less concerned, but have to deal with hair – the control of beards and moustaches. In primitive societies faces may be elaborately painted, tattooed or otherwise ornamented. The ultimate degree of modification of the face is when a mask is worn. This too is more common in primitive society. Masks usually resemble some animal, and it is believed by others that the person behind the mask is really some spirit as represented by the mask.

The next most visible part of the body is probably the hair, and this too is largely under voluntary control – whether it is long or short, neat or tousled, clean or dirty, and the style in which it is worn. While this is a matter of more concern to females, adolescent males often have severe conflicts with parents or teachers over hair. The body itself is usually invisible apart from hands and head, but certain features of it are perceptible. Hands may be carefully manicured and painted, as may feet when visible. The size and type of physique of the body are largely involuntary, but people can alter their effective height by their stance and choice of shoes, and their physique by diet, exercise and underwear. When the body is exposed similar attentions are paid to it as to the face – sun-tan in civilised societies, tattooing in primitive ones.

It seems that the aspects of physical appearance that are fairly constant during an encounter (i.e. excluding emotional expression) are partly biologically given and unchangeable, and partly under voluntary control. What are the determinants of this voluntary manipulation of physical appearance? Several general hypotheses may be presented briefly. (1) As has been assumed throughout, social norms in the form of cultural fashions are extremely important. To seek prestige leads to quite different manipulations in different cultural settings. (2) People indicate by their appearance the social group to which they belong. A good example of this is in the 'uniform' and hair style of teenagers. More generally, by their appearance people present a self-image (see Chapter IX), which includes also their social status, and their emotional state – as shown by the drabness or brightness of their clothes. There are however great variations in the extent to which people are concerned about their appearance, varying from some mental patients who are totally unconcerned, to women who cannot appear in public without spending two hours in front of a mirror, and trying on several different appearances first. (3) The appearance of young women is dominated by consideration of sexual attractiveness. To be attractive involves being up to date, and fashions for this purpose move extremely fast.

Facial and gestural movements

So far we have been dealing with aspects of behaviour which remain unchanged during a whole period of interaction. We come now to the faster-moving elements, and we can consider units of behaviour of different sizes. Scheflen (1965) has proposed three such sizes – 'presentations', 'positions' and 'points'. These units were devised for the analysis of verbal encounters – psychotherapy interviews. The units of bodily movement accompany corresponding units of speech, so that for example a *presentation* is a complete encounter: the bodily movements here are those involved in entering and leaving the situation, while the verbal unit is the sum total of the conversation.

A *position* is a phase of an encounter, distinguished by the context of what is said, and often by changes in posture. A psychotherapist was found to lean towards the patient when he was giving an interpretation, but lean back while the patient was free-associating. *Points* are smaller units of corresponding to single sentences, and are often marked by changes in head position, facial expression or by hand movements. Kendon (1967) analysed films of 2-person conversations; one person was found to cock her head in a different way when speaking of each of her brothers and sisters. It is with this level of facial and bodily movement that this section is concerned.

One of the most expressive areas of the body is the face. In man the face is a specialised area of communication, and visual acuity is sufficient to perceive it; the same is true of the non-human primates (Vine, 1969). The face is the area which is most closely observed during interaction; infants have an innate interest in faces, which develops during early social experience (p. 57 f). The face signals interpersonal attitudes, and comments on utterances, such as puzzlement or surprise. The possible facial expressions can be categorised in various ways. (a) The main messages can be listed; these are probably happiness, surprise, sadness, fear, anger, disgust/contempt, and interest (Ekman and Friesen, 1967b). (b) Responses to facial expressions can be factor analysed: Osgood (1966) found three dimensions – Pleasantness, Activation and Control – though he also suggests that 7–10 basic regions can be distinguished by cluster analysis, which may correspond to the previous list (cf. p. 136). (c) An alternative approach is to analyse the basic physical movements of the face (and body). Birdwhistell (1968) now suggests that there are 4 eyebrow positions, 4 eyelid positions, 7 mouth positions, and so on, 33 in all. A similar scheme developed by Kendon (1965) at Oxford is given in the Appendix to this chapter. These lists are less finely structured than previous formulations, which included 9 degrees of eyebrow raising for example. However the Nandikéśvara theatre in India uses 6 formalised eyebrow positions, as well as 28 eye-positions and 60 hand-positions (Vine, 1969), so Birdwhistell's later version probably does not exaggerate what may be discriminated and responded to.

Emotional expression is innate in apes and monkeys, who have about 13 facial expressions (p. 39). It seems likely that emotional expressions have been selected as means of communication, though originally based on parts of a directly adaptive response, such as preparing to bite in the case of anger. In man some emotions are expressed identically in all cultures, can be recognised in members of other cultural groups, and appear in blind children, e.g. smiling for joy, weeping for sorrow (Vine, op. cit.); on the other hand there is also a certain amount of cultural learning, for example to restrain emotional expressions and to smile politely. The most innate aspects of facial expression are those connected with the autonomic system – blushing, turning white, weeping, and pupil-expansion. The first three of these are relatively rare, though they do occur and are very hard to control. Hess (1965) has shown that the pupils do expand as a result of emotional arousal, but it is not known how far people notice it, or how close they have to be to see it. Rate of blinking is also related to level of arousal – when a person is attentive to objects in the environment or when thinking is taking place the blink rate goes down (Ponder and Kennedy, 1927). Facial expressions may be of very short duration – 'micromomentary expressions'. Haggard and Isaacs (1966) observed that brief grimaces, for example, could be seen on slow motion films, and that there were bursts of such expressions during periods of general inexpressiveness. Ekman (personal communication) has found that mental nurses are able to perceive these brief expressions though most observers are not.

Facial expression plays several roles in human social interaction. (a) It shows the emotional state of an interactor, though he may try to conceal this. (b) It provides continuous feedback on whether he understands, is surprised, agrees, etc., with what is being said. Facial expression is the main second channel used at the same time as speech. (c) It indicates attitudes to others. Rosenfeld (1966) asked subjects to seek or avoid another's approval: approval-seeking subjects smiled more (as well as using more head-nods and gesticulations). (d) Facial expression can act as a meta-communication, modifying or commenting on what is being said or done at the time. Chimpanzees (Loizos, 1967) and small children (Blurton-Jones, 1967) signal whether they are playing or fighting in this way, and speakers indicate how seriously their remarks should be taken.

Next to the face the hands are the most visible and expressive part of the body, though they are attended to much less than the face is. There is no agreed set of categories for hand positions and movements, and there are a large number of these – note the 60 formal movements in the Nandikésvara theatre. Individuals have different hand movements from one another, and what communicative significance they have is highly variable. Ekman and Friesen (1967a) have made films of the hands of individual patients. In the case of one patient they found 20 kinds of hand act in her admission interview. Examples of these movements are – 'hands toss' (one or two hands are thrown up to shoulder or head area space, and fall or bang down; palms partly open), 'hand shrug rotation', 'chair arm rub', etc. It is not known whether there are any innate hand positions; clenching the fists in anger, showing the palms of the hands in submission, gripping the hands together in anxiety are possible cases. Learning is a more important source; deaf people learn elaborate systems of hand signalling, and it is likely that others do the same, to a lesser degree. Considerable use is made of gestures in some cultural areas, like Italy and Greece; these gestures are illustrations of what is being said at the time (Efron, 1941).

Hand movements play a quite different role from facial expression in social interaction. (a) Their principal function is as illustrators, accompanying speech, and augmenting it when verbal skills are inadequate. The gestures here are 'iconically' coded, i.e. resemble what is being represented (Ekman and Friesen, 1967b, p. 72 f). (b) Gestures can replace speech, as in deaf-and-dumb language, and similar codes: here the gestures are given arbitrary meanings. (c) Hand movements show emotional states, though this is usually unintentional. Nervous interviewees clasp their hands tightly together or fiddle with small objects. More specific emotions may also be unintentionally revealed. Ekman and Friesen (1967a) found that one patient covered her eyes with a hand when discussing things of which she was ashamed, and pulled her skirt up when talking of her relationship to the therapist; the significance of each act was quite clear to observers of films of the therapy sessions. Krout (1954a and b) elicited hand movements by an interesting technique: he asked subjects personal questions designed to arouse different emotional and motivational states; subjects were asked to delay their reply until signalled – the signal being given when a gesture had appeared. 5,238 gestures were produced in this way from 100 subjects, and wide variation in hand movements was found for each stimulus. There were some statistical regularities however, e.g. fear – hand to nose; aggression – fist gestures; shame – finger at lips; frustration – open hand dangling between legs. There are various difficulties with this experiment from our point of view – the gestures were aroused by *conflicting* verbal stimuli, e.g. sexual desire and rejection, and the gestures did not accompany speech, but really replaced it – and were probably reinforced during the experiment. Dittman (1962) found that high degrees of emotional arousal are associated with a lot of bodily movement, most of it otherwise communicating nothing. (d) Many hand movements are concerned with self-grooming – nose-picking, bottom-scratching, etc. These movements are restrained during social encounters. Ekman and Friesen (1967b) report that there is a lot of hand–face contact among disturbed patients, and suggest that various forms of grooming may have a generally understood meaning – scratching or picking is attacking the self, rubbing is giving reassurance, the forehead is wiped for tiredness, etc.

Head positions and head movements are highly visible, but the amount of information they can convey is limited. The head can be in a raised or lowered position, and can be turned into a frontal or sideways position. Similarly the head may be nodded or shaken. Animals when threatened turn their body or head so that they cannot see their opponent; this both 'cuts off' the arousing stimuli and gives an appeasement signal (Chance, 1962). Head-lowering in primates is part of the threat posture (p. 29). There may therefore be innate factors in head positions. Mehrabian (1968) found that a subject would raise his head more when speaking to a high-status person (in his hat-rack experiment), especially for a high-status male, for male subjects. Argyle *et al.* (1969) found that a raised head position was adopted by confederates acting a superior role, and a lowered head by those taking an inferior role. Turning the head sideways is done to attend to a third person, or to avoid intensity of eye-contact; in either case the result is to cut off visual signals from the original interactor. Head *movements* on the other hand mean totally different things in different cultures and must be learnt. Head-nods play a distinctive and important part in verbal interaction: a head-nod gives another person permission to carry on speaking, and can act as a reinforcer of some behaviour during interaction (p. 176 ff). Head-shaking has the reverse effect. Rosenfeld (1966) found approval-seeking subjects nodded, while approval-avoiders did more head-shaking.

Foot movements are less visible and less expressive than head or hand movement, and there is no gesture language for feet. Ekman and Friesen (1967a) have taken films of foot movements, and found such units as 'one foot floor slide' (forward and/or back), 'foot swing up and slight sole show', etc. Again no common categories have yet been found.

Direction of gaze

The patterning of eye-movements is one of the most important aspects of social interaction, and some of the most interesting recent advances in the study of interaction have been concerned with the role of vision. Since direction of gaze shows direction of attention, it is important to A whether B is looking at him, at some object with which they are both concerned, or at other people or objects. When A looks at B, B may also be looking at A, in which case there is mutual gaze or 'eye-contact'. From A's point of view, the main dimension here is how much B looks at him, as a percentage of the time available. Secondly A is concerned with the expression on B's face when he looks – since the significance of a look depends on whether the facial expression is friendly, hostile, that of a clinical observer, etc. A will also be affected by the timing of B's looks – whether he looks while A is talking or while B is talking for example. B may also look at A peripherally, receiving information but avoiding eye-contact – as may be done by waiters or chairmen who do not want their eyes to be caught. A may be influenced by whether B's eyes are wide-open or narrowed slits, and by whether B's pupils are dilated or contracted. Laboratory arrangements for studying direction of gaze are shown in Fig. 3.3. A typical record of eye-movements in relation to speech is shown in Fig. 3.4.

The typical pattern of eye-movements during a 2-person conversation, in Western culture, can be described, on the basis of studies by Nielsen (1962, Denmark), Exline and Winters (1965, USA) and Kendon (1967, England). Interaction is often started by a period of eye-contact, which seems to signal that each is ready to interact with the other (Goffman, 1963a). Once under way each person looks at the other in the region of the eyes intermittently, in glances of varying length, usually between 1 and 10 seconds. The proportion of time each person looks at the other may vary from 0 to 100%, though more typically it lies between 25 and 75%. The proportion of time spent in eye-contact is,

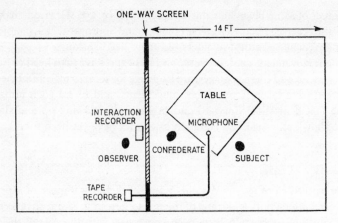

Figure 3.3. Laboratory arrangements for studying direction of gaze

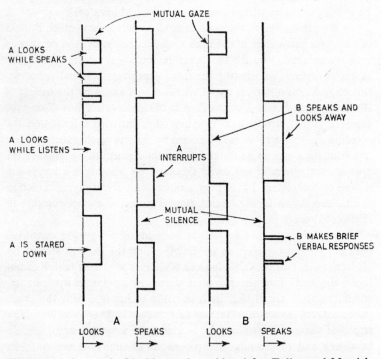

Figure 3.4. A record of looking and speaking (after Exline and Messick, 1967)

however, much less than the proportion of time spent looking by either subject. The person listening gives longer glances than the one talking, and tends to look considerably more. There may be more or less eye-contact than would be expected from the amount each interactor looks. Strongman and Champness (1968) used the formula

$$\frac{\text{A's looking time} \times \text{B's looking time}}{\text{total time}}$$

to obtain an expected level of eye-contact. Their subjects engaged in more than the expected amount, Kendon's (1967) in less.

Several different processes seem to be involved in gaze-direction, which is a result of complex interactions between these processes. In the first place A may look at B to try to establish a relationship, and will look more if he wants to establish a closer relationship of some kind. In this case eye-contact is sought, but too much of it creates anxiety. This suggests that both approach and avoidance motivation are involved: Argyle and Dean (1965) postulated that there should be an equilibrium level for eye-contact, combined with physical proximity and other aspects of intimacy. This is supported by their finding that eye-contact is greatly reduced when two people are placed closer together (see Fig. 3.5). The theory is supported by some findings by Exline, at the University of Delaware. Exline and Winters (1965) found that a person would look more at a person whom he liked – for whom the relative strength of the approach motivation would be expected to be stronger. Similarly Exline (1963) and Exline, Gray and Schuette (1965) found that people high in affiliative motivation look more, at any rate in a non-competitive interview or discussion. In the latter study it was found that there was less eye-contact when subjects were interviewed on more intimate topics – as would be expected from the equilibrium theory.

Secondly, looking at the other can be used to establish a particular kind of relationship.

(a) In the last paragraph we confined discussion to affiliative motivation, which is probably the most common occasion for eye-contact in humans. To communicate this the gazer should also smile.

(b) A sexual relationship can also be suggested by looking – 'making eyes'; the smile is softer and the pupils more dilated, and those involved are usually of opposite sexes.

(c) In primates and other animals looking, especially with wide eyes, is usually a threat signal. In humans too staring can be used to establish a dominant relationship. Strongman and Champness (1968) used the frequency of looking away first from eye-contact as a measure of submission; they observed 10 subjects interacting in all combinations of 2, and found a highly consistent dominance hierarchy. However, since a speaker looks away when starting to talk, and looks less while talking,

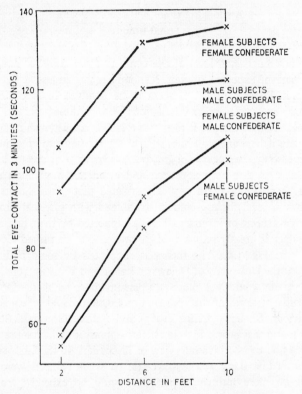

Figure 3.5. Eye-contact as a function of distance (from Argyle and Dean, 1965)

this measure of 'visual dominance' would be improved by a correction for the amount each person speaks.

(d) Looking can be used, with a different facial expression, to establish a dependent relation. Exline and Messick (1967) found that dependent subjects who were given *low* verbal reinforcement for looking, looked more at the interviewer.

A third process which affects gaze-direction is the need for feedback about the reactions of others – an implication of the motor skill model of social behaviour (see p. 180 ff). A wants to know whether B is still attending – B's direction of gaze shows if he is asleep, or looking at someone else. A also wants to know how his last message was received – whether B understood, agreed, thought it was funny. This may be partly learnt from B's speech, but A cannot obtain much information via this channel while he is speaking himself, and in any case the eyes and face are extremely expressive and can convey a lot of additional information. Once A looks in this area it is difficult for him not to focus on the eyes – for instinctive reasons which were discussed earlier (p. 48). Kendon (1967) has found, from the analysis of films of 2-person inter-actions, that people look up at or just before the end of long utterances – this is the point at which they need the feedback. Argyle, Lalljee and Cook (1968) found that it is the face rather than the eyes which needs to be seen for feedback purposes (p. 186 ff).

A fourth function of eye-movements is in channel control; together with head-nods they are the main form of signalling here. The details are discussed later (p. 201 f). In the Argyle, Lalljee and Cook experiment it was found that there were longer pauses and more interruptions when both subjects wore dark glasses, confirming that eye-movements are an important cue.

People look more when what they see is rewarding. Efran and Broughton (1966) found that a subject looked more at a confederate with whom he had previously had a friendly conversation than at a second confederate. In a second experiment, Efran (1968) found that subjects looked more at a confederate who smiled and nodded at them, especially if the confederate was of higher status.

In addition to these positive motives for looking at another person there appear to be avoidance forces – too much eye-contact is experienced as unpleasant and embarrassing. There are a number of such sources of avoidance of gaze.

(a) Animals, when threatened, 'cut-off' the aggressor from view (Chance, 1962). Humans do the same to lower their level of arousal by seeking a less intense relationship, of whatever kind. This occurs in an extreme form in autistic children and other mental patients, as will be shown later (p. 342). Exline *et al.* (1961) found that subjects looked less when they had been implicated in deception – unless they were 'Machia-vellian' personalities. Perhaps the increased intensity of involvement created by mutual gaze makes deception more difficult: it is easier to avoid such intimacy.

(b) Feedback may be reduced under certain conditions. There is aversion of gaze at the beginning of long utterances, during hesitating and unfluent passages (Kendon, 1967), and during the discussion of cognitively difficult material (Exline, 1966). In all of these conditions the speaker seeks to avoid the distraction of further inputs of information.

NON-VERBAL ASPECTS OF SPEECH

A tape-recording of the sounds made during a conversation contains a good deal more than a typist would normally put down on paper. The verbal contents proper we shall deal with in the following section: here we are concerned with the non-verbal, or paralinguistic elements. Much of the communication involved in speech in fact goes on at a non-verbal level – *how* it is said rather than *what* is said. A very interesting analysis of these elements is given in the study of *The First Five Minutes* of a psychotherapy interview by Pittenger, Hockett and Danehy (1960).

We shall deal separately with some of the main non-verbal components of speech – the timing of speech, emotional tone, speech errors, and accent.

The timing of speech

This has been extensively studied by Chapple (1956) and his colleagues. Conversations are recorded on the interaction chronograph, which simply shows duration of utterances of those present. Numerous measures and derived indices can be obtained. The main ones are the length, frequency and total amount of acts (utterances), and silences, length of pauses before replying, frequency of interruptions, response to interruption, and smoothness of synchronising. A further development is the 'standard interview' (Chapple, 1953) in which the interviewer systematically interrupts in a standard way in one phase of the interview, and leaves long silences in another part; the subject's reactions to the various treatments are analysed in terms of the variables listed before.

Studies of the same individual in a series of encounters show that there is considerable consistency in the timing of speech for a given person. In other words the timing of speech is to some extent a function of personality. Some people tend to talk more than others, and this correlates with manic and extroverted tendencies. Others speak little, and give long pauses before replying. Further discussion of the relations between personality and style of social interaction will be given in, Chapter VIII. However, the same person does to some extent vary his timing when interacting with different people. The processes of mutual accommodation whereby two or more individuals may work out a harmonious pattern of interaction are dealt with in Chapter V. If A asks B open-ended questions, B will talk more than if asked closed questions or if A gives his own opinions. If A interrupts, B will do the same. In these and other ways, A's timing and kind of utterances affect B's.

The emotional tone of speech

This is one of the most primitive aspects of speech; animals communicate their emotional states by sounds, and so in effect do humans. This is not the main conscious purpose of speech, in adults at least, but it is an important part of the message that gets across. The range of noises that can be made may be described in terms of physical dimensions of sound such as speech, pitch and loudness. This can be elaborated to include frequency distribution, voice quality (e.g. resonant, breathy, quavery, articulation control), drawling and clipping, and the inhalation or exhalation of breath. Frequency distributions of the speech of mental patients are discussed in Chapter VIII.

What are the determinants of the emotional qualities of speech? In some languages variations of meaning are communicated by changes of pitch. This does not happen with European languages, but modifications of the verbal content are often conveyed paralinguistically. 'Yes' can be pronounced to mean 'no', to take an extreme case; reluctance, enthusiasm, or other qualifying comments can certainly be communicated in this way. The most important determinant of emotional tone is of course the emotion of the speaker. One aspect of this problem which has been investigated is the emotional basis of rate of speech. The results are rather conflicting, but two of the best-controlled studies have found that people who are normally anxious talk slower under experimentally induced anxiety, while those normally not anxious speak faster (Paivio, 1963; Cook, 1969). There is some evidence that speech rate is generally higher for people who are anxious by temperament, as well as in those who are intelligent and extroverted (e.g. Carment, Miles and Cervin, 1965).

Psychologists have hoped and assumed that it would be possible to construct a kind of dictionary to translate emotions into non-verbal cues. This has proved to be difficult – because the same emotion is expressed differently by different people, and at different times. An attempt to produce some translations was made by Eldred and Price (1958) by comparing responses of judges with physical measures:

suppressed anger: high pitch, loud, fast, break-up.
overt anger: high pitch, loud, fast, little break-up.

suppressed depression: low pitch, soft, slow, increased break-up.
overt depression: low pitch, soft, slow, little break-up.
anxiety: increased break-up (rapid pattern).

Other workers have added to this dictionary, by suggesting, for example, that anxiety is associated also with 'breathiness', and rapid, incoherent speech. Clearly much more could be done, to describe adequately the speech patterns of, for example, a Shakespearean actor, a 'bright' hostess, a surly adolescent, a dreamy TV commercial, etc.

People vary greatly in their ability to express different emotions by quality of speech. Davitz (1964) asked subjects to read neutral passages to convey fourteen different emotional states; they varied considerably in their ability to do so, and those that could do it well were also good at recognising emotions in the speech of others.

Speech errors

Speech errors of various kinds occur continuously while people are speaking. Kasl and Mahl (1965) distinguished eight main kinds; these are shown in Table 3.1, together with frequencies and examples obtained in Oxford by Cook (1969). Categories 2–8 together are usually

TABLE 3.1 *Speech disturbance categories, with examples, and % frequencies of each* (from Cook, 1969)

Category	% of total	Example
1. 'Er', 'Ah', or 'Um'	40·5	Well . . . er . . . when I go home
2. Sentence change	25·3	I have a book which . . . the book I need for Finals.
3. Repetition	19·2	I often . . . often work at night.
4. Stutter	7·8	It sort of l . . . l . . . leaves me.
5. Omission (i.e. leaving out a word or leaving it unfinished)	4·5	I went to the lib . . . the Bod.
6. Sentence incompletion	1·2	He said the reason was . . . anyway I couldn't go.
7. Tongue slip	0·7	I haven't much term (*i.e. time*) these days.
8. Intruding incoherent sound	1·2	I don't really know why . . . dh . . . I went

known as 'non-ah' disturbances. The distinction between ah and non-ah speech errors has turned out to be important, since their causes and functions are quite different. Cook (1969) and other workers have found that non-ah errors increase with induced anxiety, while ah-errors do not, as shown in Fig. 3.6. Other studies have shown that non-ah errors have some correlation with anxiety as a personality trait, but ah-errors do not (Mahl and Schulze, 1964). It looks as if non-ah errors

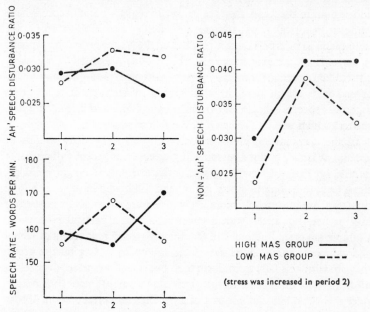

Figure 3.6. Speech disturbance, speech rate and anxiety (from Cook, 1969)

can be regarded as disturbances of speech due to anxiety. Ah-errors on the other hand increase when the talking-task is more difficult, with or without an audience (Paivio, 1965) and seem to represent 'thinking time'. Maclay and Osgood (1959) suggest that ahs have the function of keeping the floor during a conversation while a speaker thinks.

However, the direct impact of emotion upon speech is often concealed by other influences. There may be a convention that emotions, or certain emotions like anger, are not expressed – though people may not be aware that they *are* expressing such emotions. Feedback of speech is very indirect, via the bones in the head, so that people do not know how they sound to others unless they have access to a tape-recorder. There may be norms or conventions about speech, and a person may be influenced by admired models, which results in a certain style of expression.

Accent

In every community there are a number of alternative accents with which people commonly speak. In Britain these reflect both social class and region, in the USA they are primarily regional. Such accents have complex historical roots: the current middle-class English accent for example is to a large extent a product of the Victorian public schools. A person's accent may thus reflect his national, regional, social class, educational or occupational background. Although we are primarily concerned with accent here, it is difficult to disentangle it from other aspects of speech – the use of particular expressions and linguistic styles, matters which will be discussed in the following section.

In the classification above we have indicated the main origins of accents. Whether or not a person will pick up a new accent will probably depend on the usual conditions of social learning. Younger children, those keen to belong to a new group, and those who have spent a long time in it, are presumably more likely to acquire a new accent. A person may or may not speak with a given accent on a particular occasion. Children are often 'bilingual' in that they use a different accent at school and at home. Some adults vary their accent depending on the group they are with – usually to conform to it, but sometimes to set themselves off from it, as in the case of the 'professional Englishman' in America. Accent is thus, like clothes, part of a person's self-presentation. Under stress however people are liable to regress to using an earlier accent or dialect, as was found by Bender and Mahl (1960) in a study of students from the Southern States.

VERBAL BEHAVIOUR

Human social behaviour resembles that of the non-human primates in a number of ways, especially the use of non-verbal communication to signal emotions and interpersonal attitudes. The main difference is that humans can also communicate by means of language. It is important therefore to treat verbal behaviour not as an abstract entity, but as one of the main forms of social behaviour.

For our purposes the unit of verbal behaviour is the 'utterance', which may consist of a sentence or its equivalent in informal speech, since the grammatical structure of spoken language tends to be highly irregular, to say the least. Scheflen (1965) found that each 'point' of behaviour, corresponding roughly to a sentence, is generally accompanied by a particular position of head and hands. This enables us to locate units of utterance in a lecture or other monologue. The smallest utterances consist of grunts, which may sound like 'mhm-hmm', or 'uh-huh'. (The paralinguistic accompaniments of the latter can turn it into either 'yes' or 'no', at any rate in American English.)

The majority of social psychologists have been content to measure the number or length of utterances; recently however some workers have begun to make use of linguistic analyses of utterances (Moscovici, 1967).

Types of utterance

It is possible to categorise utterances in many different ways. We shall mention some which are relevant from our point of view – the impact of the utterance on others. We shall not in this section consider the determinants of utterances – utterances are generated by other utterances, together with present motivation and past learning of the performers.
(a) We listed previously the main purposes of speech: egocentric utterances, questions, influencing the behaviour of others, conveying information (about facts or opinions), and to establish and sustain social relationships (p. 67 ff). A distinction can be made between utterances about events external to the interactors, and utterances about the interactors or the interaction (Lennard and Bernstein, 1960). Different classes of utterance have specific effects on subsequent interaction: questions lead to answers, orders may lead to action, and information may have varied consequences as a result of adding to the data available to others. Questions may be closed or open-ended: the second kind, in requiring a long answer, has the effect of getting another to talk more.
(b) Rewards and punishments. Utterances can be rewarding – when a person agrees, encourages, praises, etc. – or they can be punishing. This aspect of utterance is important for future behaviour by the other, since he will produce either more or less of whatever was reinforced. This principle has been used in experiments on operant verbal conditioning, together with such non-linguistic rewards as eye-contact, smiling, etc., and punishments such as looking bored, cross, or out of the window (p. 176 ff).

The Bales (1950) method of interaction recording uses 12 categories of verbal utterances, though the non-verbal accompaniments are also taken into account. The distribution of acts into these categories in a contented and discontented group are shown in Fig. 3.7. The Bales system has subsequently been revised by Borgatta (1962) into an 18-category system, in which some of the original categories have been dropped or subdivided.

(c) The topic of conversation. This can affect interaction in a number of ways. The topic can be impersonal, remote and abstract, or it can be

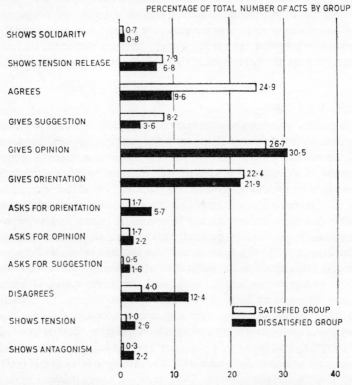

PERCENTAGE OF TOTAL NUMBER OF ACTS BY GROUP

Category	Satisfied	Dissatisfied
SHOWS SOLIDARITY	0.7	0.8
SHOWS TENSION RELEASE	7.9	6.8
AGREES	24.9	9.6
GIVES SUGGESTION	8.2	3.6
GIVES OPINION	26.7	30.5
GIVES ORIENTATION	22.4	21.9
ASKS FOR ORIENTATION	1.7	5.7
ASKS FOR OPINION	1.7	2.2
ASKS FOR SUGGESTION	0.5	1.6
DISAGREES	4.0	12.4
SHOWS TENSION	1.0	2.6
SHOWS ANTAGONISM	0.3	2.2

SATISFIED GROUP
DISSATISFIED GROUP

Figure 3.7. Distribution of interactions in terms of the Bales categories in two groups (Hollander, 1967, p. 353, from data in Bales, 1952)

highly personal. Conversation on more personal topics creates intimacy – so that it may be compensated for by reduction of eye-contact, as Exline has found (Exline, Gray and Schuette, 1965). If one speaker reveals intimate things about himself this encourages the other to do the same – an example of 'reciprocity' (see p. 173 f). The topic may be cognitively easy or difficult, which will affect paralinguistic variables such as rate of speech and number of speech errors. It may be concerned with matters external to the speakers, or it may be about the interaction itself – 'there is an awkward silence, isn't there'. Goffman (1957) has observed that such second-order utterances can be very disruptive, and this is an important example of the limits of verbal communication (cf. p. 75). The topic of conversation may be very interesting to the other – in which case he will be keen to talk about it, or uninteresting, embarrassing or in other ways displeasing to him.

(d) In specialised kinds of interaction particular kinds of utterances may be important. In psychotherapy research for example the distinction between 'interpretation' and 'reflection' is crucial, since the former is associated with Freudian psychoanalysis, the latter with Rogerian non-directive therapy. Again, in the personnel interview, in which a subordinate is disciplined, 'inviting the other to give his point of view' may be a crucial move.

(e) Speeches may have latent meanings. Sometimes these are unintentional, as when a speaker reveals things he hadn't meant to reveal; psychiatrists speak of 'listening with the third ear' to such messages. Sometimes they are partly or unthinkingly intended, as with the person who said that Nigeria was 'a place I've not been to' (p. 70). Sometimes the latent message is the real message, as in the 'games' played by Berne's patients (1966, and cf. p. 348). It has been observed by McPhail that such games are also played by schoolchildren on teachers – 'Please, sir, the bell's gone' (when it hasn't), 'Please, miss, the board's shining', 'Please, sir, what did you do in the war?' (P. McPhail, personal communication). In these cases the speaker is trying to control or disrupt the hearer's behaviour, and uses a message whose manifest content is untrue or misleading.

(f) Jokes are rather infrequent in laboratory discussion groups, but common in families and groups of friends. They serve to create a feeling of cohesion and euphoria in the group, and are an example of informal discourse, which is concerned with establishing and enjoying interaction, as opposed to serious problem-solving or persuasion.

The linguistic structure of utterances

Krauss and Weinheimer, in a number of experiments, have studied the conditions under which long or short phrases are used to refer to objects (cited by Moscovici, 1967). When an object is in the midst of similar objects a longer phrase is used: it becomes less easily codable. Unfamiliar, infrequently occurring objects needed longer phrases, though these became shorter with repeated use: a simplified code was being arrived at. When there is feedback, and when this indicates that the correct objects are being referred to, the messages become shorter:

Moscovici (loc. cit.) interprets this as example of shorter 'distance' between the communicators.

Under some conditions, messages have more repetition of words, measured by the type/token ratio, or by the number of new words introduced during periods of discussion. Moscovici (loc. cit.) found that there was more repetition when speakers were under pressure to reach a conclusion, probably because they needed to arrive at a common code in order to reach an agreement. It is suggested that the relatively repetitive 'restricted code' found among working-class people by Bernstein (1959) is the result of such pressures; for middle-class people reduced pressure makes possible the diversification of words used, by drawing on other sources outside the immediate conversation. In another experiment it was found that a greater variety of words was used when discussing the parts of a car with a specialist than with a friend, and that more technical words were used (Moscovici, loc. cit.).

In the experiments referred to above no changes were produced in the grammatical structure. Such differences are however found if spoken and written messages are compared: spoken language is 'generally less redundant, less elaborate, less well organised syntactically, and employs more verbs' (Moscovici, loc. cit., p. 256). In an experiment by Moscovici and Plon (1966) it was found that pairs of subjects sitting back-to-back or side-by-side spoke more in the written style, compared with subjects sitting face-to-face or screened. It is surprising that the screened situation was not like the back-to-back in this respect, and the authors explain their results in terms of unfamiliarity, rather than lack of vision, in the first two conditions. Back and Strickland (Back, 1961) found that when groups of three subjects were given group tasks, and had to communicate by written messages, the latter contained more nouns and adjectives (i.e. more like 'writing') if emphasis was placed on work efficiency and formal organisation.

The differences between speaking and writing give us a dimension of 'formality' of linguistic style. Formal speech is similar to writing, and appears in purest form when someone reads out a carefully prepared speech. Writing also varies in formality, from scientific papers and business letters to love-letters and letters between adolescents. In addition to having a different grammatical structure, the second kind of letter contains a lot of paralinguistic information, such as underlinings and exclamation marks. Informal speech occurs on relaxed and intimate occasions between friends and in families, and is found to be ungrammatical, repetitive, full of slang words and private abbreviations, and is extremely redundant and inefficient as far as conveying information is concerned. However, the main purpose of such conversation is probably not to convey information at all in the usual sense, but to establish and sustain social relationships between people. Joos (1962) distinguished five degrees of formality, which he suggested were used on different sorts of occasions – intimate, casual-personal, social-consultative, formal and frozen.

There are also individual styles of speech. Sanford (1942) gives samples from the speech of two students. The speech of one of them was 'complex, perseverative, thorough, uncoordinated, cautious, static, highly definitive, and stimulus bound . . . we might conceive of his whole style as defensive and deferent . . . [it] seems to reflect a desire to avoid blame or disapproval'. The speech of the other was 'colourful, varied, emphatic, direct, active, progressing always in a forward direction . . . His speech is confident, definite and independent . . . to express his personality and to impress the auditor'.

THE ORGANISATION OF VERBAL AND NON-VERBAL ELEMENTS

The links between verbal and non-verbal elements

When a person speaks to another, he inevitably emits non-verbal signals as well; we showed earlier that verbal communication depends on the non-verbal background in several ways. (a) Each interactor must signal continuously his attentiveness and responsiveness to the others; (b) there must be continuous regulation of speaking and listening; (c) interactors must signal their attitudes and intentions towards the others; (d) gestures accompany speech to illustrate it in various ways; (e) speakers need continuous feedback about how their utterances are being received (p. 72 f). A person who stood staring into space, with expressionless face, would not succeed in communicating with anyone.

In general, the non-verbal elements should be supportive of the verbal. A person delivering bad news should sound gloomy, and not roar with laughter. A person giving a subordinate the sack should not sit side-by-side in close physical proximity. Since verbal elements are easier to control than non-verbal ones there is sometimes a failure of the latter to confirm the former. A public speaker who is very nervous may manage to smile and sound relaxed, but shakes from head to foot and perspires visibly. Ekman and Friesen (1967a) observed that hand and foot movements sometimes signal messages that are quite inconsistent with the utterances being produced – such as the patient's flirtatious leg display when talking about her attitude to the therapist.

The best-known example of such inconsistent behaviour is the 'double-bind'. Bateson and his group (1956) suggested that the origin of schizophrenia was to be found in the way parents, and especially mothers, communicate with their children. The mothers of schizophrenics, it is suggested, send messages which are inconsistent in one way or another. Examples which have been given are (a) 'Of course I love you', spoken in an angry voice; (b) a mother who stiffened when her son put his arm round her shoulders, but who said 'Don't you love me any more?'; (c) communications that in effect order the child to disobey. Subsequent research however has failed to confirm the hypothesis that this is the origin of schizophrenia (Schuham, 1967), though Argyle *et al.* (1969) found that when verbal and non-verbal cues conflicted (for being 'hostile' or 'friendly') the total signal was found to be disturbing and confusing, though this did not happen when they conflicted for being superior or inferior.

Verbal and non-verbal signals as alternatives

Language is normally used to discuss facts, opinions and problems; non-verbal signals are used to express emotions and interpersonal attitudes (p. 75). However, each can substitute for the other, to a limited extent, under certain conditions.

An interactor may resort to speech when non-verbal methods have failed. This may be necessary with schizophrenics or others who are insensitive to non-verbal cues. When verbal signals fail there is withdrawal or aggression. For example if a young women wants a young man to be less amorous, she first acts in a cool, distant way. If this does not have the desired result she says, 'Please let's just be good friends', etc.; if this is no good she slaps his face and departs. Or a person whose efforts at impressive self-presentation have failed might say, 'Look here, young man, I've written more books about this than you've read'. If this produces mirth or derision, the self-presenter will depart and try to present himself to someone else.

Non-verbal signals can, to a rather limited extent, take over the functions of words. Words may fail because two people don't speak the same language; they may fail because of noise, distance or deafness, and special gesture languages grow up to deal with these situations. They may fail because of lack of verbal skill, and illustrative gestures can be particularly helpful – as when a person is asked to 'describe a spiral'. Non-verbal cues really only work when a sign language exists or when gestures can illustrate, otherwise their power to substitute for language is very small.

Words can be used in place of non-verbal cues in several ways. They are more successful when used in a subtle and indirect way. We discuss later how self-presentation can be carried out successfully by means of words (p. 384 f). Emotive sounds can be replaced by emotive words. Intimate auditory and visible signals can be replaced by the discussion of intimate topics. These forms of words are more effective than bald, direct statements of the form 'I am very clever', 'I don't believe you', 'Please stop talking to me, I want to talk to someone else'. There are certain people whose job it is to put into words what is normally signalled non-verbally. Chairmen at lectures, and public relations officers engage in presentation of the merits of others, though not of themselves. Poets are skilled at putting emotions into words. Psychotherapists and social skill trainers are experts at commenting on the social performance of others: it is an established part of their role, which makes it more acceptable, and they do it in an extremely delicate and tactful manner, which is constructive and inoffensive.

Patterns and groups of elements

Social interaction consists entirely of the verbal and non-verbal elements which have been described. It is necessary however to consider groupings of elements, which constitute higher-order units with a new significance of their own. An example is 'warmth', which consists of a combination of facial expression, direction of gaze, posture, proximity, orientation, tone of voice, and content of speech, all sustained over a period of time. Such a pattern of elements is generated by a single interpersonal attitude, and may be consciously controlled as a unitary style of behaviour. The perceiver may not be aware of the separate elements, but integrates them and interprets the total pattern as a single unit.

We shall come across several kinds of higher-order groupings of elements. (1) The factor analysis of interaction in groups commonly yields two dimensions of interaction style – dominance and affiliation (Foa, 1961). These styles also occur in combination as shown in Fig. 3.8. When a person persistently behaves in a certain manner in different situations he is said to possess the corresponding personality trait – of dominance, extraversion, rewardingness, social anxiety, etc. (2) Interviewers, supervisors, psychotherapists, and other professional social skill practitioners have complex patterns and sequences of social responses for dealing with their clients. The skilled performer emits higher-order groupings – e.g. a morse sender sends 'words' rather than letters. (3) The relations between members of a dyad or small social group can usefully be analysed in terms of the roles adopted by those present; they must agree on the roles to be played in the group, e.g. who is the leader, and also on the identities presented by the members. These roles and identities are negotiated at the level of the elements of which they consist (p. 203).

	dominance		
	analyses	advises	
	criticises	coordinates	
	disapproves	directs	
	judges	leads	
low	resists	initiates	high
affiliation	evades	acquiesces	affiliation
	concedes	agrees	
	relinquishes	assists	
	retreats	cooperates	
	withdraws	obliges	
	dependency		

Figure 3.8. Combinations of dominant and affiliative techniques (Gough, 1957)

Strategies

Sometimes an interactor produces a number of responses in a planned sequence in order to elicit some reaction from others. For example a person telling a joke may build up some expectation in his hearers of how the story will end, and then suddenly produce a quite unexpected ending. The personnel interview, for dealing with unsatisfactory subordinates, may consist of eight definite stages in a particular order (p. 304 f).

A second aspect of strategies is that they usually involve taking account of the other person's reactions at earlier points in the series. This may follow the general principles of continuous correction in responses to feedback from the other, as described in Chapter V. There may also be special ways of dealing with the main types of reaction which the other may show. For example a salesman may first show an article of intermediate cost, and then produce more or less expensive alternatives depending on the customer's reaction. The skilled interviewer knows how to deal with the various kinds of awkward respondent that he may encounter. An interesting feature of strategies is that they usually enable the performer to control the interaction – unless the others are aware of the strategies in hand and can take independent action.

A Notation for Facial Postures and Bodily Position

ADAM KENDON AND J. EX.

A. Eyes

Under this aspect the modes are distinguished in terms of the way the lids are disposed around the eyes. The modes are as follows:

1.	e	Normal, or baseline position. Eyes open, lids relaxed.
2.	⊻	Half-closed. Upper lid falling relaxedly over the eyeball.
3.	⌄⌃	'Tight eyes'. Upper lid drawn forwards over eyeball, lower lid tightened, drawn upwards.
4.	米	'Screwed eyes'. Both lids drawn tightly together usually with accompanying contraction of zygomatic musculature.
5.	>	'Laughing eyes'. Eyes narrowed or closed by contraction of zygomatic and levator musculature, but eyelids relaxed.
6.	⟍	'Frowning eyes'. Eyebrows lowered over eyes, partially closing them.
7.	◯	'Widened eyes'. Both lids drawn back from eyeball.

B. Brows (including forehead)

1.	Ϭ	Normal, or baseline position.
2.	⌒⌒	Raised brows.
3.	⟋⟍	Sloping brows. The brows are drawn upwards and together.
4.	W	Knitted brows. The brows are drawn together over the nose as in a frown.
5.	⋜	The brows are drawn downwards over the nose, with transverse wrinkling above nose bridge.

123

C. Mouth

1. _____ Normal or inexpressive mouth.

2. Normal or inexpressive mouth, open.

3. Mouth with slight smile at corners.

4. Smiling mouth.

5. Smiling, mouth open.

6. Smiling mouth, lips parted to expose teeth.

7. Smiling mouth, open, lips drawn back to expose teeth.

8. t __ t Mouth with corners slightly tightened.

9. Lips drawn tightly together.

10. Lips rolled inwards into the mouth.

11. Lips pushed outwards, closed. 'Pouting'.

12. Lips pushed outwards, open.

13. Lips pushed outwards, pressed together. 'Pursed'.

14. Corners of the mouth drawn downwards.

15. Lips together, tongue protruding.

16. Lower lips protruding. 'Half-pout'.

D. Position of the head

Any description of the position of the head must include three dimensions of change. The head can rotate on a vertical axis, it can tilt forwards or backwards, it can 'wag' from side to side. Here the position of the head is described in reference to its deviation from an erect position, the face facing directly frontwards. Degrees and points of a degree of deviation from this position are noted in the same way as for the modes for the face, for each of the three dimensions separately.

1. Head erect, face pointing forwards.

2. Head turned to left.

3. Head turned to right.

4. Head 'wagged' to left.

5. Head 'wagged' to right.

6. Head tilted backwards.

7. Head tilted forwards.

Associated with changes in head position are changes in the neck. In the film we have so far examined, we have observed an extension or a contraction of the neck.

1. ↑ Neck extended.

2. ↓ Neck retracted.

E. Hands and arms

No set of positions which can be easily distinguished have been developed for the hands and arms. Resort was had to stylised drawings to indicate their pose. A few examples illustrate.

 Elbows on table, hands clasped.

 Right elbow on table, hand touching head. Left hand placed on table.

 Elbows and forearms resting on table, hands clasped.

F. Positions of shoulders and trunk

1. L Trunk erect.

2. ⊣L Leaning to left.

3. Ŀ Leaning to right.

4. ∠ Leaning forwards.

5. ∖_ Leaning backwards.

6. Γ Shoulders hunched forwards. ⎫

7. ⅂ Shoulders hunched backwards. ⎬ These signs for shoulder position are added to the pictograph for the trunk. Thus:

8. Y Shoulders raised.

9. ↑ Shoulders lowered. ⎭

Γ̲ Leaning right,
L shoulders forwards.

G. Direction of gaze

1. ○ p looking at q, that is looking at his eyes, or looking at that point where he would meet q's eyes if q looked up at him.

2. ○̧ p looking down.

3. ‑o p looking to left.

4. o‑ p looking right.

5. ♂ p looking upwards.

For the downwards and upwards positions, numerical subscripts may be used to indicate the degree to which p is looking in one or other of these directions.

IV

Perception of the other during Interaction

INTRODUCTION AND METHODS

Person perception has been extensively studied in recent years, and several good accounts of this work are available (e.g. Tagiuri, 1969; Smith, 1967). Much of the research has taken person perception as a primarily cognitive problem, rather akin to concept-formation or problem-solving – and of course these processes are important here. In this chapter we will look instead at person perception as something that happens during social interaction, and which is a very important part of such interaction. Thus we shall be concerned with what perceptual information is needed by an interactor, how it is obtained, and the fact that the 'judge' is simultaneously being perceived by the other person. We shall also broaden the range of perceptual data beyond facial expression, which has often been the object of research in this field, to include tones of voice, and the whole range of verbal and non-verbal behaviour discussed in the last chapter. The term 'perception' is used here in somewhat different sense from the way it is used in experimental psychology. We are not concerned with whether A perceives B to be short or tall, dark or fair, but with A's inferences about B's personality, emotional state, attitudes to himself, and so on. In other words we are concerned with inferences about another person based on his visible or audible behaviour.

The perception of persons is a more complex matter than the perception of other physical objects, since the sensory inputs are normally obtained as part of the process of interaction; there are two main channels of information, visual and auditory, and both are open intermittently – the other speaks for only part of the time, emitting verbal and non-verbal noises, and the judge can look for relatively short intervals. Inferences are made because they are needed by each interactor, and the kind of inferences made depend on the situation and the relationship between the interactors. The other person is seen, not only

127

as an object of perception, but as another centre of conscious experiences and intentions and as a perceiver himself.

An emphasis on cognitive processes in much past research has resulted in highly inadequate methods from the point of view of social interaction. We discussed earlier the danger, in experimental research, of stripping off crucial aspects of the phenomenon. This is precisely what has happened in the field of person perception, so that a great deal of the work in this area has little relevance to real social behaviour. (a) In many studies of person perception no social interaction takes place between judges and subjects. In the well-known experiments by Asch (1946), for example, subjects were given lists of words like 'intelligent', 'skilful', 'industrious', 'warm', 'determined', 'practical', 'cautious', and were led to believe that these words referred to a real person, and asked to give a description of this person. It may be objected that cues about other people are rarely received in this verbalised manner, so that this does not at all represent what goes on in real-life person perceptions – apart from reading testimonials. The fact that a series of experiments with interesting results has been reported does not alter this conclusion: the results refer to a very special laboratory situation which is more akin to a word-association test than to any kind of social behaviour. (b) Similar criticisms can be made of another popular technique in this area – showing subjects photographs and asking them to judge the emotions or personality traits of the person photographed; or a target person may be shown very briefly to the judges. So little data is presented to the judges that what is presented has an exaggerated effect. Thornton (1944) found that a person seen briefly while wearing his spectacles was judged as more intelligent than when seen not wearing them; however, this effect is eliminated by seeing 5 minutes conversation on the part of the target person (p. 135). The alleged effects on judgements of untidy hair, lipstick, and even race, may be inflated by the absence of true social interaction in the experiments. (c) In real life people who are angry do not usually adopt gorilla-like expressions, like the people in the photographs which are often used. On the contrary they try to conceal their feelings. Coleman (1949) found that emotions could be perceived from the mouth region of actors portraying emotions, but not from photographs of naturally expressed feelings. Similarly people do not normally announce that they are 'cold, unintelligent and bad-tempered' as in the word-list experiments. On the contrary they try to present a more favourable impression of themselves. An interviewer has to outwit the interviewee and penetrate his misleading behaviour. (d) On the other hand people do display a wide range of facial expression during encounters, but these are not due to sudden changes of emotion or of personality. Kendon (1967) observed such changes during quiet conversations between pairs of people who were asked to 'get acquainted'. He observed that many of these expressions are simply parts of larger units of interaction – a smile is part of greeting and saying farewell, a frown is part of trying to understand, or a sign of concentration, and so on. (e) The kinds of questions which an interactor may ask, and the extent to which he can scrutinise another, depend on the nature of the situation and its rules. A clinical psychologist can ask a patient intimate questions, but the patient cannot do the same. Experiments using word-lists have often presented judges with conflicting data to be reconciled. In practice the judge would solve this problem by collecting further data – which is one of the main purposes of the assessment interview. (f) In real encounters, people are able to look at the other person for only part of the time, which may be as low as 0–10%. Hence the actual input of visual information may be very low. (g) It may be very misleading to ask subjects to judge stimulus persons in terms of the experimenter's categories and dimensions. A given subject might for example not normally discriminate between people who are 'extroverted' or 'introverted'; he would not treat them differently and would not know what cues to use, and he would thus appear to be very 'insensitive'. The same person might however be an expert on social class differences. We shall describe later experiments showing that people give more extreme judgements on dimensions which are important to them (p. 154 f). Hastorf, Richardson and Dornbusch (1958) argue that psychologists should be less concerned with accuracy, and more concerned with which categories are used by judges. There has indeed been a shift towards using free descriptions as a research method.

To understand the process of person perception as it functions during interaction therefore we shall be cautious about adopting the results of much of the published work on the subject. What research methods then are acceptable in this field? We can consider separately (1) the stimulus materials, (2) the recording of responses, and (3) the manipulation of variables.

(1) *Stimulus materials.* We shall emphasise studies in which there is some interaction between judges and subjects. The judge may interview the subjects, or they may work together at a joint task, or interact in some other way. Slightly less satisfactory are studies using filmed or taped interviews as stimulus materials. Least satisfactory are still

photographs, and lists of attributes said to be possessed by the subjects. In real interaction the judge observes while he is interacting, and is able to seek further information, for instance by asking questions.

(2) *Recording the response.* New techniques of recording the perceptual response have been accompanied by corresponding advances in conceptualisation. The earliest studies used rating scales, such as:

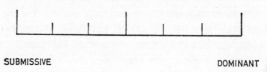

SUBMISSIVE   DOMINANT

Such scales force subjects to use them, whether they normally use the dimensions or not. It should be noted however that the use of rating scales in personnel assessment is extremely advantageous – it makes assessors decide what they are looking for, and it increases the comparability of their assessments. They should focus on these dimensions so that the latter become salient to them.

Research in person perception took a big step forward when a different method was introduced – simply asking people to write free descriptions of those they had seen. (Paradoxically, it corresponds to an older method in personnel selection.) This method makes it possible to discover which dimensions are *salient* to a person: if he consistently refers first to, for example, the social class of those observed, it is deduced that this dimension is important, or salient for him. Research on salience will be reviewed later.

A third basic method of studying perceptual responses was introduced by Kelly (1955) – the 'repertory grid'. There are three steps: (1) Subjects are asked to fill in the names of people occupying certain roles in their lives (such as 'a teacher you liked', 'a friend of the same sex', etc.). From 10 to 15 names are usually elicited in this way. (2) Subjects are asked to compare these names, three at a time; out of each triad they are asked which pair is most alike, and in what way this pair differs from the third. (3) After sorting individuals in triads, subjects are then asked to sort the remaining people in the grid in terms of the construct they have used for the three selected individuals. By this technique the dimensions a person uses can be discovered, as well as such derivative measures as his cognitive complexity – i.e. the number of independent dimensions he uses, and the statistical relations between dimensions (Bieri *et al.*, 1966, Bannister and Mair, 1968).

(3) *Manipulation of variables.* Given satisfactory means of presenting the stimulus and recording the perceptual response, all that remains is to manipulate the necessary experimental variables. Examples of such manipulation will be given later – the motivation of the judge, the relations between judge and subject, the personality of the judges, and so on.

INTERPRETATION OF THE ELEMENTS OF INTERACTION

In Chapter. III we presented the elements of behaviour, verbal and non-verbal, that are used in social encounters. We are now concerned with how these are received and interpreted by others in the situation. It is interesting that the same item of behaviour can be the basis of several distinct kinds of inference. If a person smiles, for example, this may be interpreted in terms of personality (e.g. he is well adjusted), or as an emotion (he is pleased), or as an attitude to others (he likes me), and so on. In this section we shall consider the main kinds of perceptual inference about others, and the ways in which they are made.

Interpretation as personality

One of the main ways in which another's behaviour may be interpreted is to suppose that he possesses a certain kind of personality. In a clinical or assessment interview, the interviewer is mainly concerned with such perceptual goals. A person meeting someone else for the first time will be concerned with the permanent features of the other, in order to predict his future behaviour, and in order to select an appropriate style of social behaviour to deal with him.

Thus perception of B results both in A behaving towards B in a certain way, and in A constructing a cognitive model of B's personality. Most research in this area has concentrated on the cognitive model rather than on the behaviour, and it has been assumed that cognitions mediate between stimuli and behaviour. However, people respond during interaction to stimuli of which they are not consciously aware – such as the other's eye-movements and bodily posture – so we shall have to allow for the possibility of intervening cognitions being 'unconscious'. The way in which cognitions mediate between stimuli and behaviour may be illustrated by the following example – if B has a long nose A may conceivably perceive him as Jewish, Egyptian, Lebanese or Roman; which interpretation A makes will depend on his past learning experiences with noses; his behaviour will depend on the interpretation he makes. In a real interaction situation, as opposed to looking at a photograph, A will seek further information on this point, if racial origins are important to him.

Under what conditions will the other person's behaviour be interpreted in terms of permanent personality traits? Heider (1958) pointed out that whereas we perceive other environmental events as part of the impersonal causal network of the natural world, the actions of people are seen as *intentional*, as consciously willed, and as acts for which they are *responsible*. However, there is often some ambiguity about another's motivations, in particular when his actions have more than one consequence. In these cases we may not interpret them in terms of personality in the usual way. Another example Heider gives is when a person is seen to fail through lack of ability rather than because he didn't try. Several experiments have been carried out within this framework of ideas, and have carried the matter further. Thibaut and Riecken (1955) found that high-status yielders were seen as doing so more voluntarily than low-status yielders. Jones (1964) found that high-status flatterers were seen as more sincere than low-status ones. These experiments are discussed further below. There are other cues to a person's sincerity. Exline *et al.* (1961) found that if A looks B in the eye, A is seen as being more sincere. This is to some extent justified, since Exline has found that when a person had been implicated in cheating he looked an interviewer in the eye less. This was not the case however for subjects scoring high in Machiavellianism.

In another experiment Jones *et al.* (1961) played tape-recordings of job interviews to subjects. In these recordings the experimenter described the ideal submariner as very gregarious and other-directed, or the ideal astronaut as strong in inner resources and very inner-directed. Candidates were listened to who either displayed the ideal requirements for the job, or the reverse ones. Subjects then rated the 'candidates'. The results showed that when a candidate behaved in-role he was perceived as moderately affiliative and moderately independent. Candidates who behaved out of role however were seen as very high on affiliation (for the astronaut-other), or independence (for the submarine-inner). Ratings were made with far more confidence in the out-of-role cases. Thus the behaviour of a person who conforms to a stated role or norm is much less informative than the behaviour of a deviate.

In practice people take some account of the situation when making inferences about personality. A person seen laughing is not necessarily regarded as permanently happy, extroverted and well adjusted – if for example he has just been told a good joke at which everyone else is laughing too. However, there is one feature of the situation which it is rather difficult to make allowances for – the presence of the perceiver himself. A only sees B when A is present himself – unless he is an expert in the use of disguises, one-way screens, etc. A tutor finds it hard to imagine his polite and submissive pupils as they are when he is not there – taking part in militant demonstrations, at drunken and promiscuous parties, etc. It is found that the interview has rather low reliability, i.e. interviewers often form different impressions of the same candidate. Part of the reason for this is that the candidate actually behaves differently with the different interviewers.

One of the main processes involved in person perception is the assignment of people to categories, and the application of the relevant stereotypes. This is clearly important for interaction purposes – most people for example behave differently towards males and females, so that it is important to know the sex of the people they are dealing with. A given person will probably vary his interaction style with some dimensions of individual difference, but not with others, e.g. he may respond differently to people of different sex and age, but not according to their social class, or whether they are Jewish or not.

Stereotypes have been studied mainly by means of verbal methods. There are the classic findings by Katz and Braly (1933) about the stereotypes attributed by Princeton students to various ethnic groups, which seemed to show a high degree of agreement within that population – 84% thought Negroes were superstitious, 79% thought Jews were shrewd, and 78% thought Germans were scientifically minded, for example. It is interesting to note that in a later study of Princeton students by Gilbert (1951), it was found that these stereotypes had become considerably weaker; the three percentages quoted above had dropped to 41%, 47% and 62% respectively. It may be objected that the method used – asking which of 84 words applied most to each group – is open to the criticism that it encourages subjects to express stereotyped judgements, and that their behaviour with real members of the groups mentioned might not be affected. The apparent decline in stereotypes could simply be because it is no longer intellectually respectable to hold these views. It is possible however that a prejudiced person might be influenced during interaction by expectations that a person would fit the stereotype, and it might take a long time for it to be overcome.

But how is the assignment of people to categories performed? Ultimately it depends on inferences from particular physical cues, such as grey hair and wrinkles (for age), accent and clothes (for class), facial features (for race). Lambert *et al.* (1960) demonstrated the effects of accent on person perception in Montreal by asking subjects to judge tape-recordings of speakers who were able to speak English both in a Canadian and a French-Canadian accent. English-speaking subjects gave more favourable judgements to speakers when they were using their Canadian accent – in height, good looks, intelligence, dependability, kindness, ambition and character.

There is also a more direct way of making inferences about personality – by going straight from physical cues to inferred traits. A number of investigators have studied the inferences made by Americans. Here is Allport's summary of the findings (1961):

1. to ascribe to dark-skinned people attributes of unfriendliness, hostility, lack of humor.
2. to ascribe to blondes various favorable qualities. One study shows that fiction tends to make its heroes blond, its villains swarthy and dark.
3. to see faces with wrinkles at eye corners as friendly, humorous, easygoing.
4. to see older males as more distinguished, responsible, and refined than younger males.
5. to see older women as motherly.
6. to perceive people wearing eyeglasses or with high foreheads as more intelligent, dependable, industrious.
7. to perceive smiling faces as more intelligent. (The moral here is that if you are applying for a job submit a smiling photograph; if you are an employer pay no attention to it!)
8. to perceive women with thicker than average lips as sexy, and those with thin lips as asexual.
9. to consider bowed lips as indicating conceit, demandingness, even immorality.
10. to attribute to any Negro face the stereotypes of superstition, religiosity, easygoingness.
11. to see faces that are average in size of nose, hair grooming, set of jaw, and so on, as having more favorable traits than faces that deviate, e.g. by having prominent or receding features. Apparently we feel safer with someone who does not depart far from the cultural norm.

Similar inferences can come from a person's speech, clothes, bodily movements, and so on. Research on judgements of personality from speech show that it is easier to judge occupation than personality traits (Kramer, 1963), though other studies show that different kinds of mental patients do have characteristic ways of speaking (Ostwald, 1965). However, these results were obtained from studies of the kind criticised above – they used photographs or very brief exposure, which tends to exaggerate the effects of any data presented to subjects. Some experiments have shown this quantitatively; for example Brunswik (1945) found that judgements of IQ correlated ·25 with the height of the person judged, but actual IQ correlated only ·10. Argyle and McHenry found that target persons were judged as 13 points of IQ more intelligent when wearing spectacles and when seen for 15 seconds; however, if they were seen during 5 minutes of conversation spectacles made no difference.

How are these inferences from bodily appearance and speech to personality made? Secord (1958) suggests that analogy or metaphor may be involved. For example a person with a coarse skin is seen as coarse. Inferences may be based on functional qualities – a girl with full lips is seen as highly sexed, a person with spectacles as intelligent. There may also be generalisation from the personalities from similar people who have been known in the past. Sometimes the origins of these inferences are rather obscure; why should people who wear spectacles be seen as intelligent, for example? It used to be thought that this was due to an inference that spectacle wearers could read; it has recently been found by Jahoda (1963) that short-sighted people *are* on average more intelligent than normals.

How far can personality traits be perceived with accuracy during interaction? There has been considerable controversy over the validity of the interview for personnel selection and clinical diagnosis. At the present time it appears that good interviewers are probably as good as available tests in certain areas, such as motivation, interpersonal skills, traits like neuroticism and authoritarianism, and some aspects of cognitive functioning, e.g. creativity and practical judgement (cf. Ulrich and Trumbo, 1965). There are however very great individual differences between interviewers. The assessment of such traits can be based to a limited extent on a candidate's or client's performance in the interview itself; more useful however is questioning directed to his behaviour in relevant situations in the past. In order to assess neuroticism for example an interviewer can enquire about the other's reactions to various stressful situations, about what situations or people upset him, and about head-aches, fatigue, and other stress reactions.

Interpretation as emotions

Another person's behaviour may be categorised not as a constant feature of his personality, but as an emotion he is undergoing temporarily. Sometimes both inferences are made – a person seen smiling may be judged both as being in a happy state, and also as being well adjusted. We will consider separately the interpretation of emotions from facial expression, bodily movements and posture, and the tone and context of speech. In practice information from all these sources is received simultaneously.

Many early experiments on facial expression were concerned with the recognition of emotions from photographs, often of actors displaying exaggerated poses; under these conditions there was a rather poor degree of recognition by judges – typically 60%. However in other studies subjects were provided with information about the situation which the target person was in: here the success rate was considerably higher (Vine, 1969). Schlosberg (1952) found that discriminations could be made if very different emotions are compared, and he constructed a scale along which emotions can be arranged in a circle, corresponding to variation along two dimensions pleasant–unpleasant and attention–rejection. Emotions which lie next to one another on the circle are harder to discriminate between than those which are further apart – for example surprise and happiness would be confused more easily than surprise and disgust. Fig. 4.1 (Schlosberg, 1952).

A recent contribution to this problem has been made by Stringer (1967), who asked subjects to group photographs together; he then performed a cluster analysis and found the following groupings: worry, disgust, thoughtfulness and happiness. Other studies have been concerned with the effects of specific facial cues. It has been found by Tagiuri (1968) that surprise and fear are recognised from cues in the top part of the face, while laughing and smiling are seen in the bottom half. Harrison (1965) presented subjects with drawings of faces in which eyebrows, eyelids and mouth were systematically varied. He found that raised brows were seen as surprise, half-raised brows as worry, and a single raised brow as disbelief; wide-open eyes were seen as alertness, half-closed eyes as boredom; an up-curved mouth showed happiness, a down-curved mouth as distress. Facial elements are seen in combinations: Thayer and Schiff (1967), in a rather similar study, found that lowered brows and upturned mouth together were seen as 'fiendish'. Facial movements are also important, for example rapid blinking is seen as anxiety. It is interesting to note that the labels given to facial expressions include a number which are not strictly emotions, such as 'surprise' and 'disbelief'. These are comments on the on-going situation, usually on what has just been said. Hess (1965) found that male students preferred photographs of females whose pupils had been enlarged in the photos – presumably because pupil enlargement is a signal for arousal; this is an interesting example of a facial cue which is responded to without awareness.

More recently research has been extended into cues other than facial expression. Ekman and Friesen (1967a) showed judges silent films of the

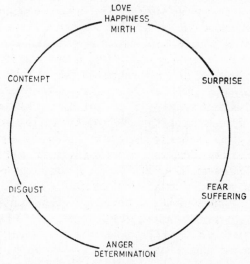

Figure 4.1. The dimensions of facial·expression (from Schlosberg, 1952)

hand and foot movements of patients in psychotherapy interviews. There was considerable agreement on the emotions which the judges thought were being expressed. For example 'hands toss' was seen as uncertainty or defensiveness, and 'hand shrug rotation' was seen as frustration or exasperated anger. Sarbin and Hardyck (1953) prepared a set of stick figures and asked subjects to describe the emotions represented by the various postures. Examples of their findings are given in Fig. 4.2. Compared with facial expression, bodily postures and gestures are a relatively poor channel of communication. Ekman and Friesen (1967c) conclude that the body can communicate whether the emotional state is generally positive or negative, and also how intense the emotion is, but cannot usually convey the specific emotion.

Non-verbal aspects of speech have been studied to find out how

emotions are transmitted. Davitz (1964) prepared tape-recordings of
actors reading a neutral passage, and asked subjects to judge the emotions being expressed; the following emotions were portrayed:

> admiration, affection, amusement, anger, boredom, cheerfulness,
> despair, disgust, fear, impatience, joy, satisfaction and surprise.

Stable individual differences were found in sensitivity to the emotional

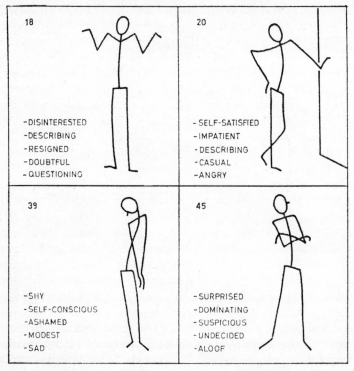

Figure 4.2. Emotional states communicated by posture (from Sarbin and
Hardyck, 1953)

aspects of speech, which were found to be correlated with sensitivity to
facial expressions, and the ability to express emotions. Differences were
also found in the extent to which people attended to emotional aspects
of speech: blind people were found to be high on this, but not on
sensitivity. Schizophrenics however were low on sensitivity. Lalljee
(1967), working at Oxford, recently completed a study of some of the
physical cues involved in judging emotion from speech. Speech was

judged as most *anxious* when of medium speed and with many speech disturbances, least anxious when it was fast and fluent. It was judged as contemptuous when slow with non-ah disturbances.

There are certain basic problems about the perception of emotion. One is that there is considerable variability in the way in which an emotion may be expressed. Indeed the same person may use different modes of expression on different occasions. There are also differences between individuals, and there are differences between cultures and social classes. Furthermore, as mentioned above, emotions cannot be judged accurately unless the context of the visible expression is known. While this may be a criticism of studies using photographs, interaction studies provide much more contextual information. They may not on the other hand provide much of a 'base-line' concerning the normal state of the subject being observed. If a person was normally extremely gay and euphoric, but on a particular occasion was rather quiet, those who know him well would interpret this differently from those who hadn't seen him before.

The face appears to be the main region for communicating emotions; it is the area that is looked at during interaction, it signals emotion fairly clearly, and there are innate patterns of expression. The innate expressions are however overlaid with cultural modifications – mainly restraining the expression of strong feelings. Chinese girls are instructed not to smile easily and not to show their teeth when they smile; this leads to the same expression being seen as sly or blank by Westerners and happy by Orientals. In the West, on the other hand, people are encouraged to smile a lot. Facial expression is to a large extent under deliberate control and is used to communicate with others; of all forms of non-verbal communication it is the least spontaneous. It is therefore very difficult to penetrate polite smiles and other forms of controlled self-presentation, to estimate the emotion behind them, since the perceiver tends to respond automatically to the expression. Bodily posture and gesture, on the other hand, while less informative than facial expression, are also less carefully controlled. Ekman and Friesen (1967a) suggest that there is a 'leakage' of the true emotional state into such uncontrolled bodily movements – a nervous interviewee may smile but tremble for example. Tones of voice communicate more clearly than bodily movements, but may be more controlled.

There are also individual differences in awareness and control of these cues for emotion. Bodily posture and gestures, and to a lesser degree tones of voice, tend not to be noticed, except by those who are unusually sensitive, have a special interest in these things, or have been specially trained. On the other hand people seem to respond to more than they are aware of perceiving, such as pupillary expansion, or head-nods.

Interpretation as interpersonal attitudes

When A observes B's behaviour he may interpret it in terms of B's attitudes towards himself, or B's attitudes to other people, C and D. The cues and processes involved in the two cases are similar, though they are experienced differently. We shall consider here the two main dimensions of B's attitudes towards others – the extent of liking versus rejecting, and feelings of dominance versus submission.

What are the cues for perceiving whether B likes someone or not? As we showed in the last chapter, such attitudes are not usually expressed in words, and can better be signalled by the various kinds of non-verbal communication. If B likes A, he may show this by looking him in the eye with a friendly facial expression, bodily contact and proximity, sitting side-by-side, and so on. This behaviour may or may not be intentional on B's part, but in either case A may be sensitive to such cues and able to perceive correctly what B's attitude is.

Facial expression is probably the clearest signal for liking and disliking. Thayer and Schiff (1967) varied facial expression and movements towards and away, using animated faces, and found that facial expression was much the stronger cue for judgements of friendly–hostile. How does the observer know that facial expression indicates an interpersonal attitude rather than an emotional state? This is not yet known, but two factors seem likely: firstly there is the immediate behavioural or verbal context, secondly A will interpret B's expression interpersonally if B looks A in the eye and orients himself towards B at the same time.

As we showed before (p. 107), a high level of gaze-direction is interpreted as an attempt to establish a more intimate relationship; combined with a smile this will be seen as a friendly approach. Mehrabian (1966c) carried out an experiment in which an interviewer talked to two subjects, but looked at A more than at B while orienting his body towards B rather than A. The subject looked at most thought that the interviewer liked him more; direction of gaze was found to outweigh the effects of bodily orientation. Kendon (1967) found that subjects thought that an interviewer who did not look at them for part of the interview had 'lost interest' in what they were saying.

Bodily posture is a third cue to interpersonal attitude. Mehrabian

(1968) showed photographs of people in experimentally varied bodily postures. He found that they were seen as friendly when sitting in a relaxed posture, leaning forwards, with an open posture (females) or closed posture (males); females were seen as more friendly than males. A side-by-side orientation combined with proximity is seen as friendly, otherwise a direct orientation usually indicates a positive attitude (Mehrabian, op. cit.). Bodily contact often indicates a friendly attitude, and the precise way in which an act of contact is performed may signal the way the other person sees the relationship, in particular the degree of intimacy he desires. There is a sense in which such moments of bodily contact are dramatic indicators of one party's attitude to the other. The perceived significance of these events depends of course on the situation and the relationship in question. Being shaken by the hand in a reception line means precisely nothing; *not* being shaken by the hand would mean a great deal. Being kissed by an aunt is different from being kissed for the first time by an attractive member of the opposite sex.

Attitudes of dominance and submission are expressed by other variations on the same themes. They can be perceived from facial expression, patterns of eye-movement, bodily posture, and so on. Dominance is signalled by a 'haughty', unsmiling expression with raised head; submission is shown by a nervous apologetic smile and lowered head. Dominance can be established by staring another person down. In a group situation however Weisbrod (1965) found that those individuals who were looked at most by speakers in the group, saw themselves, and were seen by other members, as being more powerful in the group than those who were looked at less. Dominance and submission are perhaps most clearly conveyed by tone of voice: dominance is conveyed by a loud 'confident' style, submission by a softer, nervous tone of voice.

There are also verbal cues to dominance–submission; in an experiment to be described below, subjects were addressed in different ways.

[1] It is probably quite a good thing for you subjects to come along to help in these experiments because it gives you a small glimpse of what psychological research is about. In fact the whole process is far more complex than you would be able to appreciate without a considerable training in research methods, paralinguistics and kinesic analysis, and so on.

[2] These experiments must seem rather silly to you and I'm afraid they are not really concerned with anything very interesting

and important. We'd be very glad if you could spare us a few moments afterwards to tell us how we could improve the experiment. We feel that we are not making a very good job of it, and feel rather guilty about wasting the time of busy people like yourself.

Argyle, Salter, Nicholson, Williams and Burgess (1970) carried out an experiment to study the relative impact of verbal and non-verbal cues for dominance–submission. Three verbal contents were used – dominant, equal and neutral (two are given above); three non-verbal styles were used consisting of different tones of voice, facial expressions

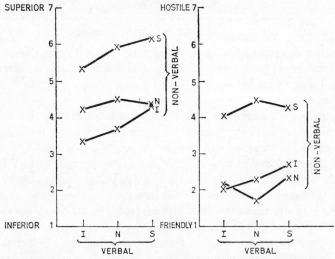

Figure 4.3. Effects of inferior, neutral and superior verbal and non-verbal signals on semantic rating (from Argyle *et al.*, 1969)

and head-orientations. Video-tapes were prepared and the speakers were shown, life-size, on a TV monitor. Ratings on two of the dimensions are shown in Fig. 4.3. As can be seen, the non-verbal cues had a greater effect than the verbal had. When the superior non-verbal style was used, verbal content had almost no effect.

Mehrabian and Wiener (1967) carried out a rather similar experiment in which single words were heard from a tape-recorder; three classes of words were used, conveying positive, neutral and negative affect; speakers conveyed positive neutral and negative affect by tone of voice. In a later experiment by Mehrabian and Ferris (1967) vocal and facial expressions were varied independently. The combined results of these two studies show that non-verbal cues had much more impact on subjects' reactions than the actual words used, and the following equation was derived.

Perceived attitude $= \cdot 07$ (verbal) $+ \cdot 38$ (tone) $+ \cdot 55$ (face)

In the Argyle *et al.* study the verbal and non-verbal components were initially presented separately and equated in strength; when combined the non-verbal signals had about four and a half times the effect of the verbal ones.

How accurate are perceptions of the interpersonal attitudes of others? Tagiuri (1958) studied the perception of preferences in 60 groups of well-acquainted people, varying from 6 to 35 in number of members. Subjects made few major errors about who accepted them and who rejected them – 4% of choices were seen as rejections and 9% of rejections were seen as choices, but most errors consisted of mistaking choices or rejections for omissions. Acceptance was perceived considerably more accurately than rejection – probably because overt cues for rejection are inhibited in polite Western society. Perception of choices between others, and the popularity of others were also judged with considerable accuracy.

While an interviewer is trying to assess the interviewee, the latter does not try to assess the interviewer – he is more concerned with how the interviewer perceives *him*. In other words A is trying to perceive how B perceives A – what Laing *et al.* (1966) call the 'meta-perspective'. We shall consider later the various conditions under which the meta-perspective becomes dominant, and when interactions are primarily concerned with imagining how the other person sees things (p. 374 ff). Laing *et al.* (op. cit.) go a step further – into A's perception of B's perception of A's perception of B. They call this the meta-meta-perspective, and they provide evidence that such perceptions are less accurate within disturbed marriages than in happy marriages. This variable is perhaps most familiar in a situation where B dislikes, or thinks ill of, A, but does not want A to know this; B will then be concerned with A's perception of how B sees A.

PERCEPTION DURING INTERACTION

The goals of perception in interaction

As was shown in Chapter II, social interaction can be motivated by a number of different drives. Motivation will affect the perceptual activity that takes place. The social situation which is most similar to the looking-at-photographs kind of experiment is when A sees B at a party, or in some other open setting, and is deciding whether or not to interact with B. The problem here is one of *predicting* B's behaviour – will B be a sufficiently entertaining and agreeable person to talk to? Is he likely to be able to tell A the way? etc. The prediction here is about behaviour which is relevant to A's goals in this particular situation, and whether B is likely to be able to help him to realise those goals.

If A decides to initiate an encounter with B, A's initial problem is to select an appropriate interaction style from his repertoire that is suitable for B. If A behaves differently to others of different sex, age and social class (as everyone in fact does), he needs to be able to categorise B in terms of these variables, and whatever others are salient for him. At this stage then A is concerned with certain demographic and personality variables in B; once this is done that particular perceptual task is over, though some revision may be made in the light of further experience of B.

During the encounter itself, A is concerned with eliciting certain responses from B, or with establishing and maintaining some relationship with B. In order to do this, A needs continuous information about B's reactions to his own behaviour, so that he can modify it if necessary. A may simply want B to like him, or he may have other quite personal motivations with regard to B, or A may want B to learn, buy, vote, or respond in terms of mainly professional goals which A has. In either case A needs to know what progress he is making with B. He may be concerned with B's attitude towards himself, with B's emotional state, with B's degree of understanding, or with other aspects of B's response.

In some situations A's main concern is with B's opinions, attitudes, beliefs or values. This is obviously true of social survey interviews, but in many more informal situations people want to find out how far their own attitudes have social support from others, and how far their ideas about the outside world are correct.

In other situations, for example interviews for personnel selection and personality assessment, the main object may be to assess personality, either in order to understand its clinical origins, or to decide upon its suitability for a given job. In other situations, such as law courts, or interviews with administrators, it is more a matter of deciding what sanctions to apply; here the personality is matched against some social norm of the behaviour that is required (Jones and Thibaut, 1958).

These are some of the motivations that govern social interaction, and the perceptual activities to which they give rise. It is clear that perception becomes focused on different cues in each case. Furthermore the actual judgements made may also be affected. Jones and de Charms

(1957) asked subjects to work on a series of problems in groups: some were going to be rewarded for their individual performances, for others the whole group had to succeed for any member to be rewarded. The second condition was intended to arouse inter-personal motivations of a cooperative kind. In each group a confederate failed by prior arrangement; he was seen as less dependable when his failure affected the group; this was especially true when the tasks were presented as tests of motivation rather than of intelligence – as motivation is more under intentional control than intelligence.

Perception in different types of interaction

The process of perception also varies with the kind of social interaction which is taking place. We shall follow here the typology first proposed by Jones and Thibaut (1958) and Sarbin, Taft and Bailey (1960), adding to it considerations put forward by Argyle and Kendon (1967).

Firstly there are various kinds of *non-reciprocal* social situation – i.e. A's behaviour is not affected by B's, and vice versa: there is no true social interaction at all. This covers the experimental situations in which person perception has often been studied, and which were criticised above. It also includes watching someone on TV, and observing other people from a distance. Other instances have been described as 'pseudo-reciprocal', for example participants in military and religious ceremonies, and actors in plays; in these cases each player knows his complete part, and is affected by the others only in respect of the timing of his responses. Finally there is 'parallel' behaviour, for example when two people are talking but when neither is really listening to what the other has to say. This may occur with mothers telling each other about their children; the author recalls such behaviour among RAF air crews returned from a flight. A more extreme case of parallel behaviour is conversation by schizophrenics – who talk regardless of whether the other person is speaking or not, and on totally unrelated topics (see p. 337 ff). In the observation-at-a-distance case there may be no need for any perceptual information at all, unless the judge is wondering whether to interact with the subject, or whether to vote for him, etc. In most of the other cases mentioned the only perceptual information needed is about the timing of the other's responses.

A second kind of interaction is *reciprocal but asymmetrical*; i.e. A's responses depend on B's, but B's do not depend on A's. Most interaction is asymmetrical to some degree, but this is the extreme case. Here B can do as he likes, and follows a predetermined plan of action, while

A's behaviour is contingent on B's. One example is when B is an interviewer, who is using a set schedule of questions (ana makes little use of
follow-up probes). In fact all 'social skill' performers are to some extent
in this position – leaders, teachers, therapists, etc.; their behaviour is
however partly determined by clients, since special controlling and
correction techniques have to be resorted to in order to deal with them.
Another example of asymmetrical interaction is the social psychology
experiment in which there is a carefully programmed confederate. The
perceptual requirements in the case for example of interviewer and
respondent will be rather different. The interviewer, if he is using a
fixed schedule of questions, will not need any information about the
respondent's interaction, but only about his answers to the questions –
he is interested in building up a cognitive model, not in choosing an
interaction style. The respondent may be aware that the interviewer has
a fixed plan of action, in which case he will try to discover what it is.
If he is not aware that the other is behaving in a programmed manner
he may interpret the programme in terms of personality. It is only
possible to make correct deductions if one has extensive experience with
other operators of the programme, or performers of the role. In most
asymmetrical situations the performer does need continuous information
about the other's response for interaction purposes. He will want to
know whether his socially skilled activities are being successful, or
whether some modification is needed in his performance. An interviewer is in a strong position for gathering perceptual information if he
wants it: besides merely observing the other's behaviour he can probe
for further information, and can even vary his own style of interaction
deliberately to see how the other responds – as in the stress interview
and the 'standard interview' (p. 110).

Thirdly, there may be *symmetrically reciprocal* interaction between A
and B – neither has more of a predetermined programme than the other,
and the course of the encounter is the outcome of a genuine two-way
interaction between them. This can of course be extended to situations
involving more than two people. Each interactor requires continuous
perceptual information about the reactions of the other, in order to
make his own future responses as effectively as possible. As Jones and
Thibaut (1958) suggest, there is a conflict here between obtaining perceptual information, and the planning of future responses; in other
words perceptual input may become distracting. We shall show in the
next section how this conflict is in fact resolved through strategies of
perceptual activity during interaction. Each interactor may, like the
interviewer, probe for further information about the other. This is

likely to happen at first meeting, especially if the other presents himself unclearly. The process is however severely restricted by conventions about how far it is socially acceptable to ask personal questions.

Several experiments have compared the effects of different kinds of social interaction on the resultant perceptions. For example it is found that leaders judge followers more accurately than followers judge leaders. (Foa, 1958), and Sarbin *et al.* (1960) report that in asymmetrical interaction the programmed person can judge better than the other person can judge him, as would be expected from the analysis above. It is also found that peer or 'buddy' ratings are more accurate predictors of future behaviour than are ratings by superiors, i.e. symmetrically reciprocal behaviour leads to better perceptions than asymmetrical. Although a superior officer etc., can probe more, he sees a more artificial, more carefully controlled sample of behaviour than do members of the peer-group.

The pattern of perceptual activity during interaction

Before any interaction takes place at all A may have quite a lot of information about B – from what others have told him. This will give A more or less precise expectations about how B is likely to behave, and how he needs to be handled. It may sensitise him to certain aspects of B's behaviour. They may meet through introduction, by belonging to the same group, through professional dealings, at a party, etc. In each case A will manœuvre himself into an appropriate spatial position, with a certain proximity and orientation. This spatial positioning will be selected partly on grounds of intimacy, and interpersonal attitudes, as was shown in the last chapter. It will also be affected by perceptual considerations; A will want to be able to see and hear B as well as possible, and may or may not want B to see him. At a noisy gathering they will have to stand close together in order to hear, and this will entail standing side-by-side or at an angle. As was shown in the last chapter, the choices of spatial positioning and orientation are partly the result of visual and auditory accessibility. In formal situations these are often far from satisfactory. As Michael Frayn (1967) points out,

... the position of the seats at a banquet is a particularly irritating arrangement, because one's neighbours to the left and right, whom one can hear but not see, are usually women, and thus may well be more rewarding to see than to hear; while the figure opposite, who can be seen but not heard, is almost certainly a man, a species in my experience more agreeable to hear than to see.

If A is interviewing B he will probably put B in a good light and may put himself in a weaker one. (This practice is not being recommended, but it is commonly used.) A person may sit with his back to the wall, or in the back row at a lecture, so that he can see others, and cannot be observed by people whom he can't see. The last two examples are due to people preferring to be 'observers' rather than 'observed' in social situations, a phenomenon which is discussed later (p. 374 ff). Human social interaction normally uses two perceptual channels – hearing and vision – and the two are closely linked. Both are open intermittently: interactors look at the other between 25% and 75% of the time; they look all the time if behind a one-way screen, but are prevented from doing so in normal interaction because of the high level of eye-contact generated. Hearing is intermittent since people usually take turns to speak and listen. These two channels are linked in that people look over twice as much while listening than while speaking and because the visual channel is used to help the verbal-auditory channel in a number of ways (p. 72 ff).

When several people are speaking at once audition can be selective – the hearer can tune in to a particular voice. He is also especially sensitive to certain sounds – such as his own name being mentioned – this has been described as the 'cocktail party problem'. Hearers are almost certain to hear the verbal content of speech, if it is loud enough, and if there is little distraction; they will not necessarily receive the non-verbal aspects, such as emotional tone. Another peculiarity of audition is that speakers hear themselves – whereas they do not usually see, feel or smell themselves. The sound they hear is of course rather different from the sound heard by others, owing to the conduction of sound through the bones as well as through the air. A tape-recording of one's voice gives a more accurate impression of what it sounds like to others. Many people must be extremely insensitive to their own non-verbal emissions, or they probably would not sound as bad-tempered or bored as they do.

The pattern of visual perception during interaction can now be described. In our experiments on this we have always found more looking at the other's face during the early stages of an encounter. This is probably because A needs predictive information about B – his personality, his emotional state, etc. Probably there is more attention to B's clothes and general appearance also. If A knows B well this period of perceptual activity can be cut fairly short, though A will notice any deviations from past performance. Kendon (1967) has made detailed studies of the pattern of perceptual activity during conversations. He finds that A looks away when he starts to speak, probably because he is planning and organising the utterance and does not want distracting input. He looks B in the face at grammatical breaks, probably to make sure that B is still listening and following, and that he is willing to let A continue talking. B will probably nod his head and say 'uh-huh' or something similar; at a hesitating passage, or speech errors, A will look away, presumably so that he can reorganise the utterance. Just before ending the utterance A looks up, in order to get feedback on how B is reacting to it – whether he agrees, thinks it funny, etc. By this intermittent scanning, interactors are able to resolve the conflict described by Jones and Thibaut (1958) – between studying the reactions of the other, and planning the next response. We also know something about *where* people look during interaction. They look either at the other's face, in the region of the eyes, or they look right away, at the surrounding furniture or scenery. They may observe hand movements, but foot movements and bodily posture are probably noticed much less.

Compared with vision and hearing, the other senses of smell, touch, taste, and awareness of warmth, are unimportant for most kinds of social interaction. In Western culture it is unusual to smell people, and it is only when scent, perspiration or the smell of breath are unusually strong that smell operates at all. Perspiration may be a useful cue since it indicates a high degree of arousal, for example in an interviewee.

In addition to the sensory activity described above, A can add to his information about B by asking questions. This happens when people first meet and throughout an interview for personality assessment. The answers to such questions may or may not be revealing. In a personnel selection interview most note is taken of 'negative information' – it is as if the interviewer is looking for evidence against the candidate, and the candidate is trying to conceal it.

INTERPERSONAL RELATIONS AND PERSON PERCEPTION

The effect of interpersonal attitudes

If A knows B well he will have already formed a detailed impression of B, and knows which styles of behaviour to use with him. He will notice any deviation from B's normal behaviour, and interpret it as a temporary state or mood. Similarly A will be able to interpret B's behaviour better – he will know when B is anxious or cross better than could someone who has not met B before. Generally speaking the better A knows B the more accurate his judgements of B's personality are. This is not always so, since A and B become involved in an intricate relationship, and A's judgement can become highly distorted. This was found in the disturbed marriages studied by Laing *et al.* (1967), and can be found with tense relationships between colleagues at work – each of whom may believe that the others are no good at the job. In a complex and emotional relationship, interpersonal perception can be regarded as part of the system.

If A likes or dislikes B, his judgements of B become systematically affected. If he likes B he will perceive B as liking A, more than he actually does. As Tagiuri (1958) observes, 'interestingly enough, although there is actually greater mutuality of choice than there is of rejection, members feel just as reciprocated in their dislikes as in their preferences'. This is a case of cognitions tending to organise themselves in consistent systems, as Heider (1958) has argued. In this case there is congruence between A's attitudes to B and to himself, and B's attitude to A. If all are positive or two negative, the system is balanced. If A likes B, he also tends to see B in a favourable light, and bias all judgements in a socially desirable direction (Pastore, 1960). This may be the result of interaction: if A likes B he will behave more pleasantly towards B, and elicit more favourable behaviour from B.

If A likes B he will see B as more like himself and having more similar attitudes than is really the case; this was clearly shown in a study by Newcomb (1961) in which students were experimentally assigned to rooms in a hostel. The effect is called assimilation, or simple projection; it would be expected that if A and B are really alike, A's judgements will be more accurate, and this is found to be so (Halpern, 1955). This kind of projection is quite different from the Freudian kind – in which people fail to see their shortcomings in themselves, and instead believe that other people suffer from them. This was demonstrated by Sears (1936), in relation to the trait of stinginess, but later workers including the present author have consistently failed to find it operating and we may conclude that it must be a rare mechanism or one that operates only under special conditions.

When there is an intense emotional relation between A and B, B may be perceived clearly as a physical object, regardless of the effects of the surrounding perceptual setting. Ittelson and Slack (1958) studied perception of others using a distorting room. Accuracy of size judgements was greater when the other person was a marital partner, a superior officer or an amputee. These results cannot be explained in terms of familiarity.

The effect of role-relations

If A is senior to B, and especially if B is dependent on A, then B's behaviour becomes highly ambiguous as far as A is concerned. If B shows friendly, helpful behaviour to A, is this because he really likes A and wishes him well, or is it because he is seeking A's help and support? As Jones (1964) has pointed out, 'ingratiation' is ambiguous, though of course hostile behaviour is very clear. Jones carried out several experiments with members of university OTC units. Older and younger cadets exchanged written messages, and in some cases the younger person was presented as dependent on the older's approval. Observers and senior members of these pairs perceived positive, supporting messages from the younger members as more sincere when they were not dependent in this way. When subjects were dependent, they were better liked and seen as having more positive characteristics when they did not agree too closely with the senior partner. There is a further ambiguity about ingratiation: it is very likely that the dependent person really does have strong positive feelings towards his superior, at any rate at the time of the ingratiating behaviour; it would be highly dissonant for him if he did not. If B is senior to A, A will see his behaviour as more autonomous. Thibaut and Riecken (1955) carried out an experiment in which subjects tried to influence another person, who was in fact a confederate and eventually gave way. When the stooge was presented as a faculty member he was seen by the subjects as having changed his mind 'voluntarily'. If he was presented as of low status he was seen as changing as the result of social pressure. In other experiments Pepitone (1958) found that higher-status people are seen as being responsible for their actions, possessing good intentions and being justified in their actions.

If B behaves aggressively towards A, this affects A's perception of B in an interesting way. The immediate effect is for B to be seen as aggressive, and to be judged unfavourably in other ways. However, this effect may be mitigated when the causes of B's aggressive behaviour can readily be seen. This is an excellent example of the shift from personal to impersonal causation. If A thinks that he has done badly on a task, for which B could reasonably blame him, he will feel less negative towards B (Jones and Davis, 1966).

The effects of set

A person's previous information, whether true or not, will affect his perception of another. An early demonstration of this effect was produced by Kelley (1950). He gave brief character sketches to judges before they met the subjects; some of the descriptions included the word 'warm', others included the word 'cold'. The observers who were given the warm set perceived subjects as having other favourable traits as well. Such a result is probably due to several distinct processes, which we can now disentangle in the light of later research. (1) The set can sensitise the observer to certain cues – he expects them and looks for them, so can perceive them more readily. Or he may misconstrue what he sees, or see things that are not there at all. (2) The set has an effect on the observer's own behaviour; the 'warm' set is likely to induce friendly behaviour on his part, which in turn elicits warm behaviour from the target person. Such instructions have indeed been used to create group cohesiveness experimentally, and are successful in bringing about what has been described as 'autistic friendship'. (3) The set acts as part of the input of information, and affects judgements as a result of cognitive pressures towards consistency. Asch (1946) found that 'warm' and 'cold' functioned in this way when subjects were asked to form an impression of a person from a list of words. (4) The set may help to overcome the resistance of judges to making judgements about others; some people are very reluctant to do this.

However, a set may act in rather a different way as well – by giving a frame of reference against which later information may be compared. Berkowitz (1960) created the impression that a second person was very hostile; when his initial behaviour showed that he really liked the subject, this first impression was soon changed. The direction in which another person's behaviour changes has similar effects. Aronson and Linder (1965) performed an experiment in which subjects heard a series of tape-recorded remarks about themselves; if these became derogatory, subjects liked the speaker less than when they were derogatory all the time. This is reminiscent of the advice sometimes given to teachers – 'never smile before Christmas'; this may give rise to comments of the kind 'she's really very nice once you get to know her'.

The effects of motivation and emotion on perception

Probably the main way in which the state of the observer affects his perception is by simple projection. Leuba and Lucas (1945) hypnotised subjects and put them into the moods happy, anxious and aggressive. When shown vague pictures, their interpretations clearly reflected their mood. This has of course been the basis for the assessment of achievement motivation and other drives by means of TAT-type methods

(Atkinson, 1958). Feshbach and Singer (1957) found that subjects who had been put in a state of fear by electric shocks judged photographs as more fearful and more aggressive.

Another effect of the perceiver's motivational state is that he may see things in a wish-fulfilling manner. An illustration of this is provided by an experiment by Pepitone (1950). Schoolboys were interviewed about their ideas on athletics by three judges, who were to decide whether or not the boys qualified for free tickets to a baseball game. Some boys were made more highly motivated in that they were told that the tickets were for a very desirable game; these boys saw the judges as more approving than did the less highly motivated boys. Another example perhaps is the tendency for A to see B as liking A if A likes B, which is usually regarded as a case of consonant cognitions. It is not yet known how general such wish-fulfilling distortion is. It is possible that the reverse may sometimes occur, in a defensive manner.

More complex distortions take place in psychotic patients. Distortion of perception is a regular feature of psychosis, and this includes the perception of persons. Liggett (1957) constructed a test consisting of a series of photographs which the subject is asked to describe. Very different and eccentric interpretations are made – the object of the same photograph is described as a killer, a parasite, or sexual. Paranoids both with photographs and in real-life situations tend to force people into roles related to their fantasies – courtiers, secretaries, spies, etc. This and other aspects of the social behaviour of mental patients will be discussed in Chapter VIII.

COGNITIVE PROCESSES IN PERSON PERCEPTION

Between the perception of physical cues and the interpretations which are made of other people lie various cognitive processes.

The search process

A very large amount of perceptual data is potentially available in an interaction situation, but only a small proportion of it is actually used. Perception is highly selective and is focused on certain areas of information which are thought to be most useful. Different observers may observe different things: a doctor might notice a person's pupils, the way he walks, or the quality of his skin; a phonetician, a tailor, a barber, or a psychiatrist would probably notice different things. In the last chapter it was shown that there are a wide range of non-verbal cues, which carry more or less standard meanings. It follows that there is considerable scope for training in sensitivity to such cues.

It was argued earlier in this chapter that the initial purpose of person perception is to know how, or whether, to interact with a person. This may lead to the establishment of a cognitive model of the person, possibly described in verbal terms, and probably in terms of some implicit set of personality dimensions or types. The process of person perception can be characterised as a search process, directed towards making certain decisions. A clinical or personnel psychologist may be asked to settle certain problems about a patient or candidate. If it is suspected that a candidate is an authoritarian personality for example, the interviewer may ask him about relations with teachers, tutors, clergymen and police, and about how he has handled positions of authority himself, e.g. as a school prefect. In less formal situations it may not be possible to collect data with such dogged persistence, but an ear is kept open for relevant data.

For different observers, different dimensions will be salient. If perception is for interaction, and different interaction styles are needed for different categories of people, then perception will be directed towards making this categorisation. Which dimensions or categories are relevant will depend on the culture, the situation, and the motivations of the perceiver. Soldiers may first perceive another's rank, members of a primitive society will be more concerned with family relations and whether a woman is sexually taboo, a religious enthusiast wants to know if people are saved or not saved, a political enthusiast which side they are on, a snob which social class they are, and so on. Professional role will lead to an interest in certain dimensions – psychiatrists categorise people in terms of mental abnormalities, educationalists in terms of abilities, doctors in terms of biological and health variables, and so on. The usual method of discovering which dimensions are salient for a person is to ask him to write descriptions of a number of different people, and to see which areas he writes about first in each case.

Some of the effects of salience have already been described. When a dimension is salient, the following things will happen. (1) Perception is focused initially on cues relevant to this dimension, so that the other person can be categorised. (2) The relevant pattern of interaction, or social relationship is adopted. This is clearest in an organisational setting, like a hospital, where behaviour will vary depending on whether the other person is a patient, doctor, nurse, visitor, etc. (3) There will be increased discrimination along salient dimensions: Tajfel and Wilkes (1964) found that a wider scatter of ratings was made for dimensions previously found to be salient for judges. (4) It seems likely that greater expertise in interpretation will be acquired for salient traits. The evidence on whether anti-semitic people are better at identifying Jews is rather complex: anti-semitic subjects do recognise Jews more often, but this is partly because they simply classify more people as Jewish – they make this categorisation on the basis of less evidence (Tajfel, 1968). Nancy Mitford (Ross *et al.*, 1956) maintains that upper-class people in England use different words for a number of common objects – 'greatcoat' for 'overcoat', 'chimney breast' for 'mantelpiece', and so on. If this is true, experts at social class can make use of these cues, which should help them to place people correctly.

There are systematic individual differences in what sort of categories are salient. Men tend to use task- and achievement-oriented categories such as occupation and income; women use personality and inter-personal behaviour traits. Such individual differences are probably closely related to the personality structure and motivations of the perceiver – he will make salient those dimensions of people which are most important to him, and which result in his treating people differently. Rommetveit (1960) found that ratings of the desirability of others as friends for some judges correlated highly with intelligence, but for others with good looks or honesty. As Tagiuri (1969) points out, quite different qualities are looked for in friends, parents or children.

The combination of data

Persons are seen as highly integrated unities, with conscious experiences and intentions that make sense of their observed behaviour. The achievement of such perceptions involves cognitive processes whereby the stimulus material is integrated, and a concept or schema of the other is constructed. As Bartlett (1932) said, there is an 'effort after meaning' in perception. Heider (1958) described the tendency to achieve balanced states of cognition, and we gave an example of this in the perception of other's perceptions (p. 150). In the field of person perception the most familiar example of the process is 'halo effect', whereby the ratings of judges are found to be more highly correlated than are objective measures of the properties in question, when these are socially desirable. For example, Brunswik (1945) found that judgements of intelligence and energy correlated ·84, whereas objective measures of these two variables correlated only ·28. The tendencies towards simplicity and consonance are usually regarded as purely cognitive in origin; it is possible that they are also due to the process of planning interactions with people, when a definite decision must be reached about how to interact with them.

When two or more items of information about a person are presented, one effect may be for the meaning of one or other item to be altered, i.e. there is a new interpretation of it. This may be a way of reconciling otherwise puzzling and conflicting information. Jahoda (1962) carried out an experiment in which subjects were asked to write a personality description from a list of attributes. For some subjects the list includes 'owns a large country home', where other lists instead had 'owns a semi-detached house', 'lives in a council house', or 'lives in a crowded tenement': the other attributes were quite differently interpreted according to this indicator of social class, e.g. for 'enjoys pictures' and 'is keen on sport'.

When two or more items conflict, for example when they are of very different degrees of social desirability, or when they do not belong in the same social stereotype, a problem is created for the judge. Haire and Grunes (1950) created such a situation experimentally by asking subjects to write personality descriptions from a list of traits: most of the traits described a manual worker, with the exception of the word 'intelligent'. Some dealt with this cognitive problem by simply omitting this part of the information, others modified it to explain why he was only a worker, others said he was really a foreman, while others recognised the incongruity while reasserting their belief that most workers are not intelligent. In the first of the studies of this type, Asch (1952) found that some items carried more weight than others – 'warm' and 'cold' in his experiment. It seems very likely that these words would be important for many people from the point of view of planning behaviour. However, Wishner (1960) found that the centrality of an item depends on the other traits which are being inferred or predicted. Wishner argued that it depended on the single correlations between items and traits. He found that 'warm' correlated with judgements of 'sociable' at ·70, but with 'serious' at only ·02, so that warm–cold should have little effect on the latter. Bruner, Shapiro and Tagiuri (1958) used the same approach to study the effect of two conflicting items – 'intelligent' and 'inconsiderate' on trait inferences. For example 'intelligent' suggests 'honest', while inconsiderate suggests 'dishonest'. However, the latter link is stronger, so that most subjects are influenced more by 'inconsiderate' here.

Two reservations should be made about studies of this type. In the first place, in most real-life situations when an interactor is confronted by conflicting data he can collect further information to resolve the problem. As mentioned before this is a typical procedure in an assessment interview; little is known about what happens in other kinds of situation. Secondly, the information to be combined is partly mediated by verbal processes and partly not. A judge may categorise a piece of behaviour as 'serious' or 'sociable'; however, other elements such as bodily postures and eye-movements are not verbally labelled by most people, but have been found to affect judgements and must operate at a sub-verbal level.

Data has to be combined when judging emotions too. The main data here are the other's facial expression, his tone of voice, and the nature of the situation. Usually these all point in the same direction, so that the information is redundant. Fernberger (1928), using photographs, found that if there was conflict between facial expression and situation, judges followed the situation. Ekman and Friesen (1967b) suggest that there can be 'leakage' of emotion, when facial expression is controlled, but bodily behaviour is not; in this case it would be normal to infer emotion from bodily behaviour only.

Further evidence on how conflicting data is combined comes from studies of interpersonal attitudes. Thayer and Schiff (1967) presented subjects with schematic faces varying in expression and movement pattern. In some presentation there was conflict between cues, for example a smiling face and withdrawal when a second person approached. There was no averaging of stimuli, and mainly extreme judgements were made; subjects either discounted one cue, or perceived it as in line with the other, or re-interpreted one of the cues. A judge may arrive at some explanation for the dissonance. For example if A sees B laughing at C's misfortune, A would probably deduce that B didn't like C, or that B was sadistic or otherwise emotionally disturbed.

The order in which items of information are received is also important. Luchins (1957a) found that earlier items were more influential: if subjects first read a paragraph describing a person Jim as extroverted and later a paragraph describing him as introverted, 71% thought he would be friendly, as opposed to 54% for those who read the paragraphs in the reversed order. Subjects reconciled the conflicting information by explaining the second set of data in terms of external events. However, Luchins (1957b) found that the primacy effect was almost completely overcome if subjects were first warned about the danger of first impressions and advised to suspend judgement. If a time interval was given between the two sets of data, the second set became more influential, i.e. there was a 'recency' effect. Anderson (1965) also obtained a recency effect by asking subjects to make a fresh judgement after each piece of information had been given. However, all of these results were obtained under highly artificial conditions, and it is not known how important first impressions are in real interaction. It is quite possible that they create an initial set which affects the subsequent behaviour of the judge. Newcomb (1947) suggested that a circular process of autistic friendship to hostility can recur: if A initially behaves pleasantly, B like him and behaves in similar style, eliciting more friendly behaviour from A, and vice versa.

In the case of emotions, the order in which stimuli are received affects the interpretation made: a smiling face following a tense one is seen as 'relief', while a sudden smile after a period without expression is seen perhaps as 'pleasant surprise' (Tagiuri, 1968).

INDIVIDUAL DIFFERENCES IN PERSON PERCEPTION
The effect of the perceiver's cognitive structure

Different perceivers will handle incoming perceptual data in widely differing ways. We have already considered individual differences for which dimensions are salient; these will affect the cognitive search, and will also affect the way items are weighted. Another way in which perceivers differ is in what is called 'implicit personality theory'. Psychologists have more or less *explicit* personality theories, which lead them to have expectations about the correlation of traits, which categories or dimensions are useful, which items should be heavily weighted, and so on. A psychoanalyst for example would use categories such as 'anal' and 'oral', and would attach particular importance to sexual adjustment. In fact everyone has implicit assumptions of a similar sort. Chelsea (1965) asked five girls to rate ten others on a number of traits. All the judges assumed that boldness and extroversion were correlated (median $r = \cdot 88$); one thought that boldness and calmness correlated $\cdot 59$, another that they correlated $-\cdot 30$. Studies of the correlation between objective measures of these traits showed no significant correlation between them, showing that the girls' implicit theories were wrong (Smith, 1967). Similarly if a person was familiar with the statistical study of attitudes it would be surprising for him to encounter a person who was prejudiced against racial minority groups but who also had liberal views on the treatment of criminals.

We discussed above the stereotyped ideas that individuals may have about national groups, and other categories of people (p. 133 f). Triandis (1964) devised a method of finding the effects of race, nationality, religion and occupation on social distance. Subjects are asked to express their willingness to enter into various kinds of social relationship with persons with different combinations of these variables. In Illinois most variance was due to race (77%), while for Greeks religion was most important, and for Arabs nationality. People also place one another into further categories such as 'teenagers', 'public school types', and numerous other mythical groupings. Language plays an important role here: once a kind of person has been given a label in this way people are likely to use it as part of their classification system in person perception. Similarly elements and styles of behaviour may become labelled, as when behaviour is regarded as 'aggressive', 'rude', 'cooperative', showing 'presence', and so on. These classifications may be in terms of wider or narrower categories. Fiedler (1958b) developed a measure of how similarly leaders perceived the best co-worker and the poorest co-worker using 6-point rating scales, which shows how much importance a leader pays to task performance in assessing his subordinates.

Cognitive complexity

Various measures have been proposed of 'cognitive complexity' – the number of words or dimensions a person uses to categorise events. Crockett (1965) uses the number of different words used to describe other people. Bieri *et al.* (1966) use the number of independent dimensions which can be extracted from a repertory grid (or the reverse of the explanatory power of the first factor). Little (1968) and others have found that these two measures are uncorrelated, and that they relate to other variables in quite different ways. A number of studies have been carried out to study the process of person perception as a function of these variables. It has been found that complex perceivers (in the first sense) use both favourable and unfavourable items in describing their friends, and can accommodate unbalanced items, e.g. by integrating them under a higher-level construct giving a united impression. Little has also devised a questionnaire scale to measure 'person specialism' and 'thing specialism' – interest in persons versus interest in things. He found that person specialists use a lot of words but few dimensions to describe people – they are complex in one sense but not in the other. He also found that if a person likes someone, and feels comfortable with him, he uses many words but few dimensions; this may be because people feel uncomfortable with those that cannot be easily categorised, and who present conflicting cues. Person specialists had parents in person-oriented occupations, thing specialists had parents who worked with things. There are interesting sex differences in this area. If subjects are asked to write descriptions of other people, women are found to use personality and interpersonal traits, where men make more use of roles, achievement and physical characteristics. The only exception to this is that adolescent girls make a lot of use of physical characteristics, such as hair colour and height (Little, 1967). Females are found to be person specialists and to use more words, but use fewer dimensions for people.

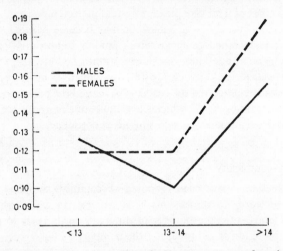

Figure 4.4. Proportions of psychological constructs as a function of age and sex (from Little, 1967)

Males who are person specialists and are verbally complex for people, are found to go far beyond the data in impression formation studies, and to invent characteristics for which no evidence has been supplied. This may explain some earlier findings to the effect that psychology students make less accurate judgements of personality than other students. Person specialists were found to make more use of non-verbal than of verbal data in an experiment using the repertory test triad method (Little, 1969).

The components of accuracy

By the accuracy of person perception is meant the degree of correspondence between, for example, ratings of the intelligence of persons seen, and objective measures of intelligence. Alternatively subjects are asked to predict how other people would answer a questionnaire. Cline and Richards made sound films of interviews, and asked subjects to make a number of predictions about how the people seen would behave in everyday life, would describe themselves, and would complete sentences. The actual behaviour of those seen was studied and used as the criterion (Cline, 1964).

Cronbach (1955) pointed out that a judge could obtain an 'accurate' score in several different ways, and he suggested that accuracy should be split up into four components, which operate in rather different ways. We will use his components here.

(1) *Constant error, or 'level'.* A judge who is estimating the IQ's of a series of subjects might give an average IQ of 107, whereas the average of their measured IQ's was 118. This judge would have a constant error of -11, and is using the scale wrongly, in relation to level. The phenomenon is usually discussed in respect of such evaluative dimensions but could operate for others, such as introversion–extraversion. The judgements of a judge who erred *only* in this respect are shown in Fig. 4.5.

Such variations in level appear to be fairly general for a given judge, and can have an important effect on whether he makes accurate ratings. High levellers are people who are outgoing, warm, and considerate of others, while low levellers are rigid and introverted, and do not form strong ties with other people (Smith, 1967). It is possible to eliminate this source of error by asking judges to make paired comparisons, or to place subjects in rank order.

(2) *Variability or 'spread'.* The author recalls an examination in which one examiner gave marks ranging from 45 to 65 out of 100, while another's marks ranged from 0 to 105; their averages were much the same. Fig. 4.5 shows some hypothetical judgements made by a judge with a high spread, i.e. high in relation to the true distribution of the quality rated. As shown above, spread is greater for dimensions that are salient for the judge. Spread is greater for more confident and experienced judges, but also for people who are cognitively simple and make rapid closure on cognitive problems (Smith, op. cit.). As Cronbach (op. cit.) has shown, the lower the correlation between judgements and criterion, the lower the spread that should be used, to achieve the smallest errors: if a judge knows nothing at all about the subjects he should give them all the same score. Thus the spread of ratings should normally be smaller than the spread of the actual behaviour.

(3) *Stereotype accuracy.* A judge may achieve accurate results not because he has perceived carefully the individuals before him, but because

F

he is well informed about the population to which they belong. Stone, Leavitt and Gage (1957) asked judges to predict the questionnaire responses of subjects, who were described as simply 'students'. Later the judges actually met the subjects and made a second set of predictions. The second set proved to be *less* accurate than the first: the judges had an accurate stereotype about students, and failed to make any good

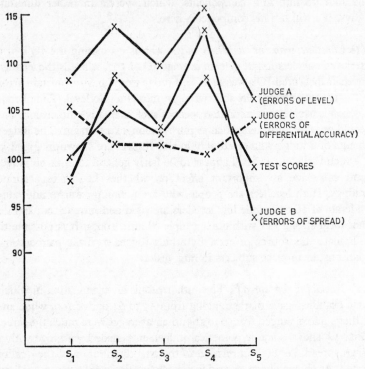

Figure 4.5. Errors of judgement

use of their perceptions of these particular students. As Brown (1965) points out, in real life stereotype accuracy may be more useful than the differential perception of individuals (see (4) below), unless one is interested in how a person will behave in ways which are not part of his role, such as a bank clerk doing a favour. Stereotype accuracy is not however perceptual, except in so far as correct identification of another's cultural role is concerned; the knowledge concerned may be based on experience, but it may also be derived from the study of social survey data, or other literary sources. At one time it was common to warn judges and interviewers against the use of stereotypes. Perhaps this could be restated: they should make sure that their stereotypes are correct, and that they are prepared to meet exceptions who do not fit the stereotype.

(4) *Differential accuracy*. In Fig. 4.5 are shown the ratings made by a judge whose level and spread are correct, but who has assessed the individuals wrongly in relation to each other: he would be described as low in differential accuracy. When there is a high correlation between judgements and criterion there may be accuracy of this kind, though the level and spread may still be wrong, so that absolute errors can be considerable. Grossman (1963) devised a means of measuring differential accuracy: judges were asked to match verbal statements to subjects seen in films – this eliminates level and spread; as all subjects were male there was little scope for the operation of stereotypes. Judges high in differential accuracy were tough-minded, empirical and nonconforming.

This component of accuracy is probably the one most closely related to our postulated personality dimension of 'perceptual sensitivity' (p. 328 f). This dimension is primarily concerned with sensitivity to on-going cues, especially non-verbal cues during interaction, but some of these will be relevant to the perception of personality traits. Bronfenbrenner, Harding and Gallwey (1958) obtained measures of differential accuracy for 72 students, and correlated these in turn with ratings of the judges. The ratings varied with sex of judge and sex of person observed.

Males		Females	
Sensitive to: males	females	males	females
resourceful	tact	submissive	submissive
dominant	tolerance	reasonable	insecure
outgoing	timidity	accepting	inhibited

For all subjects and judgements combined, differential accuracy was associated with being hesitant and passive towards others, and lacking in 'creative expression and leadership'. Thus high differential accuracy, in this age-group, is not consistently related to social competence.

In a number of early studies correlations were found between the ratings of judges or interviewers, and more objective indices of the personality or performance of those judged. Such a measure does not eliminate the other sources of judgemental error, but probably comes closest to differential accuracy. With this procedure, the most accurate judgements are made of those who are similar to the judge in cultural background, age and personality, and who are introverted and detached, well adjusted and intelligent; females do slightly better than males. From studies cited above it follows that a judge should be cognitively complex for people, should not have incorrect implicit personality theories, and should be salient for the dimensions being assessed. He should be sensitive to minor verbal and non-verbal cues. There is evidence that training in interviewing skills and in sensitivity can improve accuracy; appropriate training methods are discussed in Chapter X.

V

Two-Person Interaction

Concepts and models

We now know the elements of social interaction which need to be studied, but we also need conceptual models to integrate findings and direct research. In fact research in this area has been very much held up for this reason; models of human behaviour devised for other fields of psychology simply failed to apply in this field. It is almost a classic case of the phenomena seeming incomprehensible until the right conceptual tools were devised to deal with them.

We have already introduced the main background to dyadic inter-action. Each person comes to the encounter as a result of motivations which can be satisfied by happenings in the encounter; motivation can be looked at here in terms of the goals an individual is trying to attain, which consist either of behaviour on the part of the other (e.g. admiration, buying something), or of a pattern of dyadic interaction (e.g. intimacy, excitement). Each interactor emits verbal and non-verbal signals of the kinds described previously; non-verbal communication plays several essential roles, such as controlling timing of speech and expressing interpersonal attitudes. Interactors perceive the behaviour of the other, mainly through the two channels of hearing and vision, each of which operates intermittently; eye-movements play several closely related functions – the other person cannot be observed without looking at him, but to look is also to send a signal. The two interactors meet in one of a limited class of situations defined by the culture, such as an interview or a friendly chat, which has definite rules and prescribes role-relationships between the interactors: their behaviour is partly programmed in advance. We are concerned in this chapter with the detailed sequences of interaction occurring in dyads.

One early approach to the subject can be called the S–R model.

Interaction is seen as a series of alternating responses on the part of those involved, and can be looked at as a stochastic process. This approach has been extended by considering both verbal and non-verbal responses, and the links between them. Two sequences are of particular interest – the effect of reinforcement, and the phenomena of imitation and reciprocity.

A second approach is to consider as a whole the pattern of behaviour emitted by one interactor. We shall develop the social skill model, which interprets social interaction as a serial motor skill. This will be supplemented by an account of certain cognitive processes which may be involved, such as taking the role of the other. As well as trying to manipulate the other, interactors 'take the role of the other' both cognitively and by sharing the other's emotional state.

However, it is not possible to provide a complete account of dyadic interaction by considering only one person at a time. We have to study how two personalities may be compatible or incompatible, and what happens when they meet. The conceptual model which we shall use is that of a system in equilibrium. For interaction to occur there must be a certain degree of coordination and meshing between the two interactors; this may develop into a stable pattern of interaction; the character of this pattern constitutes the relationship between them.

Taken together, these models throw a great deal of light on the process of interaction in a dyad. The theoretical task is not complete by any means. There is still no conceptual scheme that can handle and predict the detailed development of a long sequence of interaction, for example.

Research methods

General problems of research methods were discussed earlier (p. 20f); here we shall be concerned with the particular problem of research with dyads.

(a) *Statistical analysis of normal interaction sequences.* Pittenger, Hockett and Danehy (1960) carried out an exhaustive analysis of the verbal and paralinguistic contents of the first five minutes of a psychotherapy interview. Later workers have used interaction recording (Lennard and Bernstein, 1960) or films (Condon and Ogston, 1966) for longer sequences of behaviour in the same situation, and have carried out statistical analyses of the data. There is an advantage in using one-way screens and concealed cameras for this kind of work, otherwise the dyadic situation is likely to become transformed into a triadic one.

(*b*) *Experimental techniques using real interaction in which one interactor is a confederate.* Numerous experiments have used this design. For example a subject may be interviewed by an experimenter who systematically rewards or punishes certain kinds of behaviour – as in 'operant verbal conditioning'. Or an interviewer may follow a set pattern of timing for his responses, as in the 'standard interview', devised by Chapple (1956) (cf. p. 110). In other experiments a confederate, pretending to be a subject, may stare continuously at the subject or follow some other pattern of visual behaviour. It is possible to use this strategy in highly realistic field experiments. Blake (1958) for example studied imitation by planting a stooge next to an intended subject in the library. A second stooge approached the first for a contribution to charity, then going on to the subject – whose behaviour was found to be influenced by that of the first stooge. The limitation of such procedures is that they do not allow for the occurrences of genuine interaction – they can show how the subject's behaviour is affected by the confederate, but they cannot show the emergence of interaction, in which each person has to react and accommodate to the other.

(*c*) *Experimental techniques using real interaction and two subjects.* Many experiments have been conducted in which both interactors were real subjects. In such experiments the experimental variable may be the task, the motivations aroused by the instructions, the degree of visibility or audibility of the subjects, and so on. A rather different version of this design is where experimentally controlled combinations of people are brought together, in order to test predictions about compatibility, relative dominance, and so on. In many ways this approach is the best in that there is genuine two-way interaction. On the other hand it must be recognised that as an experiment it quickly gets outside the experimenter's control, so that his dependent variable is really the entire situation and relationship that develops, rather than any particular responses.

(*d*) *Techniques which eliminate interaction* were criticised earlier. An interesting and extreme version of this approach which has been used for dyads is the 'minimal social situation', in which subjects sit in cubicles and are not aware of the existence of other subjects, although in fact they control one another's rewards. Experiments with this situation are discussed later.

(*e*) *Projective methods* have been used with some success in this area, but are open to the limitations mentioned earlier.

RESPONSE SEQUENCES

S–R models

One early way of conceiving interaction was as a chain of responses, each interactor reacting to the other's most recent social act.

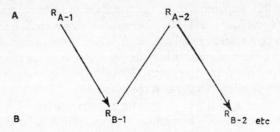

This model assumes that each social act is determined by the last act of the other: it leads to the study of simple empirical sequences of social acts.

An example of such research is the analysis by Bales (1953) of sequences of responses as observed in 16 meetings of 5-man groups. (Similar information on dyads is not available.) In Table 5.1 below we give only the main types of response for each of the 12 Bales categories.

TABLE 5.1 *Response probabilities for the Bales categories* (from Bales, 1950)

	1	2	3	4	5	6	7	8	9	10	11	12
1. Shows solidarity	28%				15%							
2. Shows tension release		68%										
3. Agrees			16%		41%	21%						
4. Gives suggestions			46%									
5. Gives opinion			49%		19%							
6. Gives orientation			35%		15%	24%						
7. Asks for orientation						74%						
8. Asks for opinion					46%							
9. Asks for suggestion			36%		28%							
10. Disagrees					25%				24%			
11. Shows tension					39%	23%						
12. Shows antagonism												36%

These findings show that the model has a considerable degree of fit with what actually happens, in that quite a high degree of prediction can be made of the next act if the last one is known. In theory it should be possible to programme a computer to simulate social interaction, or to interact with a real person. The main practical difficulty is on the person perception side – a device is needed to decide how to categorise a particular act in terms of the categories used. In the MAD Doctor computer programme at MIT something like this has been done (Weizenbaum, 1967). The 'patient' types at a console, and the computer's reply is typed underneath; here is an example of what happens:

HOW DO YOU DO. I AM THE DOCTOR. PLEASE SIT DOWN AT THE
TYPEWRITER AND TELL ME YOUR PROBLEM.
I am unhappy.
I AM SORRY TO HEAR YOU ARE UNHAPPY.
What shall I do about it?
WHY DO YOU ASK?
I don't like being unhappy.
YOU SAY YOU DON'T LIKE BEING UNHAPPY.
Yes, I don't like it.
YOU SEEM QUITE POSITIVE.
Of course I am.
IS IT BECAUSE YOU ARE THAT YOU CAME TO ME?
Because I am what?

As can be seen, the computer has been programmed along the lines of non-directive therapy, and uses the technique of reflecting the emotion expressed by the patient and encouraging the patient to say more about it. This is an extremely ingenious programme in that it is able to respond to and to produce grammatical speech as well as produce socially appropriate responses. During the course of this chapter we shall list a number of other sequential principles that need to be added to simple S–R processes if real-life social interaction is to be reproduced successfully.

Within the verbal content of utterances a number of regular sequences are found.

Topic. If A makes a remark about a particular topic, B will probably reply by speaking on the same topic. If he does not, and fails to explain why not ('to change the subject . . .'), there will be a discontinuity of interaction, and indeed social interaction will have broken down. *Type of utterance.* If A asks a question, B will probably answer it (cf. Table 5.1); if A gives orders or instructions, B will probably carry them out or explain why not. If A asks open-ended questions on a specific topic, B will give longer replies, and this is one way of getting another person to talk more. *Timing of speech* covers such things as lengths of utterances and pauses, tendency to interrupt, response to interruption, and rate of speech. People have characteristic styles of speech in all these respects, but also adjust to one another. For example an interruption virtually forces a person to stop speaking. There are also strong elements of imitation involved, for example if A interrupts B, B will interrupt A.

S–R sequences can also be studied between non-verbal elements. A number of investigators have suggested that there is commonly a 'gestural dance' between interactors, in that they continuously respond to each other's bodily movements. Condon and Ogston (1966, 1967) have made very detailed analyses of films of psychotherapy, and produced evidence for 'interactional synchrony' between speaker and listener, in terms of small movements of hands, head, eyes, etc., over periods of time corresponding to sentences and even words. Kendon (1968) has confirmed this finding from the analysis of a short film of a discussion in a London hotel stimulated by Birdwhistell; the film was taken at 24 frames per second and portions of it were subjected to frame-by-frame analysis. Kendon distinguishes the following sequences. (1) *Movement mirroring*, which can be detected by the naked eye, consists of the copying of another's movements, and was particularly found in listeners, and as interaction between two people began. (2) *Listening behaviour*. The listener gives a continuous kinesic commentary on the speaker's performance, consisting of head-nods and changes of facial expression. (3) *Speech analogous movement*. The listener acts out features of the speaker's utterances, sometimes giving an exaggerated version of the speaker's movements. It was found that people present but not immediately involved in the dyadic conversation showed gross changes of position when there were changes in who was speaking, and that these changes triggered off similar movements by others. It is suggested that these changes are more tightly synchronised in an attentive group.

We can also consider S–R sequences where one R is verbal, the other not. We discuss later the non-verbal signalling whereby channel control is negotiated (p. 201 f). For example a head-nod results in more speech, a frown in less. The problem is made more difficult by the fact that verbal and non-verbal signals occur together in more-or-less integrated units. A further complication that has emerged from the study of sequences of social responses is that there may be more than one series taking place at once, but at different speeds. In the following section we discuss the twin phenomena of reciprocity and imitation – two ways in which A may respond to B with a similar or equivalent response. We shall conclude that the two depend on quite different psychological processes, and that they proceed at different speeds. The faster one (imitation) depends on more automatic, habitual processes, the slower one (reciprocity) on more reflective, cognitive processes.

Let us go on now to consider some of the ways in which the S–R model needs to be supplemented. We have already extended it by thinking of a stochastic series containing both verbal and non-verbal elements. The main addition is the motivation of each interactor, which leads to his not simply responding to the other, but initiating an integrated series of social acts himself. Secondly we need to add the pre-programmed rules of the situation, and the role-relations between the participants. However, an S–R analysis still gives little understanding of the psychological processes involved. We turn now to theories about what these processes may be.

Response Matching: Imitation and Reciprocity

During social interaction it is very common for an act by A to be followed by a similar act from B. This we will call 'response matching', and we will not for the moment be concerned with the psychological process involved. Here are some of the main ways in which response matching has been found to occur.

Length of utterances. In many situations, if A is instructed to make long utterances, B makes long ones too, and similarly for short utterances. Psychotherapists commonly speak one-fifth or one-sixth as much as their patients, but if a psychotherapist doubles or halves the length of his utterances, the patient does likewise (Matarazzo, 1965). There are also conditions however, such as shortage of available time, when an inverse relationship is found between utterance lengths (Argyle and Kendon, 1967).

Interruptions and silences. In the Chapple 'standard interview', the interviewer at different parts of the interview pauses for 15 seconds before replying, or persistently interrupts the interviewee. It is found that the interviewee is likely to respond by also pausing or interrupting (Argyle and Kendon, op. cit.).

Kind of utterance. From the results of the Bales study (1950) shown in Table 5.1, it can be seen that jokes lead to jokes (68%), and that there is response matching for showing solidarity (28%), giving opinions (19%), giving orientation (24%), and disagreeing (24%). It is also found that questions, once answered, lead to more questions.

Words used. In studies of psychotherapy sessions, Jaffe (1964) found that there was a positive correlation between therapist and patient use of such words as 'I', 'you', 'the', 'a', and so on.

Gesture and posture. Rosenfeld (1967) found that if an interviewer responded to each of a subject's utterances by a smile or a head-nod, the subject's rate of smiling and nodding was much greater than when this was not done. Scheflen (1965) has analysed films of psychotherapy sessions and found that the pairs involved often adopted congruent postures. It has been observed that this is more common when two people have a favourable attitude to one another.

Information about self. In a number of studies (e.g. Taylor, 1965) it has been found that if one interactor is programmed to reveal more about himself, the other person will do the same.

Other areas. It is very likely that similar response matching takes place with regard to emotional state ('emotional contagion'), bodily contact and other elements of social behaviour.

Response matching evidently occurs in dyads, for a number of different kinds of response. Two different processes could be responsible for it – imitation and reciprocity. We will give a fairly brief account of imitation as it has been dealt with extensively elsewhere (Bandura, 1962). Imitation is usually taken to refer to the situation in which A copies some response of B's to the same or a similar situation. It has not hitherto been used to include the case where the response by B is towards A, as in the examples listed above.

A good example is the study by Blake (1958) of people crossing a road when a 'wait' sign was showing. An experimental confederate crossed at this point, and was found to be followed by a number of those waiting; if the confederate was smartly dressed, more people followed than when he was badly dressed. Numerous studies of imitation have shown that it occurs under the following main conditions: (a) when the follower is rewarded for this behaviour, especially (b) if he is rewarded by the model, (c) if the model is of high power or status, (d) if the model is seen to be rewarded for the behaviour in question, (e) if the follower is similar to the model, and (f) if there are no other clear guides to the follower's behaviour.

A number of theories have been put forward about the psychological processes that may be involved, but it is not very clear how any of them

apply to the interaction situation. In any case imitation during interaction might be something of a special case governed by different
processes, in that the following behaviour is both visible to and directed
towards the model. Imitation is a learnt process, and it is more complex
than responses produced by simple conditioning. On the other hand
other fairly elementary learning mechanisms, such as secondary reinforcement (by the model), may be all that is involved. If simple
imitation experiments are set up for humans they may fail to produce
the expected behaviour because subjects regard this as 'cheating', i.e. a
more complex cognitive process may interfere with the relatively elementary imitation response. Wheeler and Arrowood (1966) showed that
these restraints against imitation could be experimentally reduced: out
of 4 subjects in an ESP experiment, if S4 always imitated S3, then S2
was more likely to imitate S1.

Reciprocity was first observed by anthropologists as a feature of life
in primitive society; if A does something for B, B usually responds by
the performance of some equivalent act for A. This sequence differs
from imitation, as conceptualised above, in a number of ways. (1) The
reciprocity act is not necessarily similar to the original, but is equivalent
in reward value; (2) reciprocity is not an immediate, unthinking response, but is carefully calculated and follows after an appropriate
interval of time; (3) conscious awareness of what is happening inhibits
imitation, but makes reciprocity more probable; (4) reciprocation is *less*
likely when the other is of higher status, not more likely as with imitation.

There is widespread evidence for the occurrence of reciprocity in
primitive societies, and it has been reviewed by Sahlins (1965). This
writer makes a useful distinction between three degrees of reciprocity.
(1) 'Generalised' (altruistic) reciprocity where A gives to B without
thought of future rewards from B; (2) 'balanced' or 'economic' reciprocity where A and B give one another exactly equivalent rewards; (3) 'negative' reciprocity where each person tries to get more than he gives.
Sahlins further suggests that the degree of reciprocity that takes place
depends on the degree of intimacy between the two people concerned:

Type of relationship	*Type of reciprocity*
close kinship, common residence	generalised (altruistic)
non-kin, but in same tribe	balanced
intertribal	negative

In other words, the closer the relationship, the more altruistic the form
of reciprocity observed. Within the family, or between intimates, help
is freely given and resources freely shared. Outside such close relation-

ships, balanced reciprocity is found, which is of a more formal and less personal character.

Berkowitz (1968) and his colleagues have carried out a series of laboratory experiments on reciprocity. A subject is (or is not) helped by a second (unseen) subject, and later has the opportunity to help the other; in general it was found that if A had helped B, then B was more likely to help A. However, the phenomenon varied considerably between different cultural and social class groups. (1) Altruistic reciprocity was strongest among middle-class subjects in Wisconsin and Oxford who had fathers in bureaucratic occupations; (2) economic reciprocity was shown by middle-class Wisconsin subjects from entrepreneurial backgrounds, and by Oxford working-class subjects; (3) very little reciprocity was shown by Wisconsin working-class subjects. It seems likely that altruistic reciprocity (what Berkowitz calls 'social responsibility') is stronger in developed societies, as is the concept of professional duty, which should be carried out without assistance from bribes or other releasers of reciprocity.

To demonstrate that reciprocity can take place independently of imitation, we can cite a study in which the response was quite different from the original, and so could not be classified as imitation. Schopler (1968) interviewed female students and tried to persuade them to wash a blouse a number of times, as part of a product-testing exercise. In half the cases he gave them a flower at the beginning of the interview. In this condition the girls agreed to wash the blouse on average a larger number of times than when no flower was given. However, the effect only worked when relations between the two were established on an 'informal' basis, i.e. with no defined power or status relations between them. Although somewhat fantastic, this experiment does demonstrate the occurrence of reciprocity in the absence of imitation.

Having established that reciprocity does take place, we shall now list the conditions under which it is most likely to occur.

Intimacy of relationship was postulated by Sahlins as a major determinant, and it seems very likely that altruistic reciprocity will occur most in an intimate relationship. Berkowitz (1968) found that English working-class boys were less likely to reciprocate if their partner came from a different social class.

Relative status. It has been observed that there is less reciprocation by the person of lower status. This may be because he simply lacks the resources to do so. If a rich man gives a beggar some money, how can the beggar reciprocate? One answer is that he responds by deference, and this is part of the analysis given by Homans (1961). He postulates that if A gives B more than B gives A, then B will give A social approval.

Voluntariness of each act. Goranson and Berkowitz (1966) found that there was more reciprocation of help when the original helping act had been voluntary than when it had been part of their instructions. Schopler (1966) found reciprocity only when the relationship was informal.

What is the explanation of reciprocity? We have seen that it is different from imitation. Gouldner (1960) argued that there is simply a social norm which demands reciprocity. This is supported by the observation that when the events are made salient, reciprocation is made more likely – and imitation less likely. The cultural differences mentioned above can then be looked at as variations in the strength of the norm. If such a norm becomes internalised there should be reciprocity regardless of any possible subsequent gains by the agent. Evidence for this was found in an experiment by Tognoli (1968). In this experiment subjects were instructed to make as much money as possible: they were told that by giving the other a small sum he would receive several times as much as this. Subjects played against confederates who were either consistently generous or consistently mean. It was found that if the stooge was generous, the subject became more generous; this was true also of the last trial, which could not in turn be reciprocated by the stooge.

A second line of explanation is in terms of the future rewards each participant hopes to receive from the other. In the 'exchange theory' formulation of Thibaut and Kelley (1959) and Homans (1961), for a relationship to be sustained each party must get sufficient out of it, and will produce acts which are calculated to benefit him in the future. Clearly this theory cannot account for the kind of behaviour observed in Tognoli's experiment, or for Sahlins' 'altruistic reciprocity'. It could however explain what Sahlins called 'balanced reciprocity'.

How can altruistic reciprocity be explained? It could be due to a norm of reciprocity, but it involves a further degree of generosity and spontaneity. Perhaps it is more appropriately regarded simply as part of an intimate social relationship, in which it is natural for each person to do things for the other 'without counting the cost', because he wants to do so. Indeed if he reciprocates too soon, or with behaviour that is too similar to the original, or too equal in value, this will make it seem less spontaneous, and possibly end the relationship by paying off the original debt. The causes of altruistic behaviour are discussed later (p. 192 f).

What part does reciprocity play in social interaction? We have suggested that it operates at a relatively slow and reflective level, as contrasted with the faster and more automatic process of imitation. Referring back to the various kinds of response matching which were listed earlier (p. 171 f), how many of these would be affected by reciprocity? Self-disclosure is perhaps the most likely candidate, though lengths of utterances and use of interruptions certainly may operate at a slow and reflective level. On the other hand, matching of bodily posture and use of particular kinds of words are clearly responses of an automatic and unreflective kind. It may be suggested that general patterns of behaviour related to major dimensions of relationship, such as intimacy and dominance, are the most likely to be governed by reciprocity. We shall see later however that intimacy is also governed by another principle – equilibrium maintenance, which may oppose and outweigh reciprocity.

The effects of reinforcement

One of the most extensively studied sequences of events during interaction is the effect of A consistently rewarding or punishing some aspect of B's behaviour. The effect was first studied by Greenspoon (1955) in an experiment in which subjects were reinforced while producing a series of individual words, and was later demonstrated by Verplanck (1955) in real conversations, where subjects were not aware that an experiment was in progress. In this experiment 24 subjects had conversations with experimenters; in the first of three 10-minute periods there was normal conversation, in the second period expressions of opinion by the subject were reinforced by agreement or paraphrasing, in the third period they were followed by disagreement or no-response. Frequencies of opinion-giving were unobtrusively recorded by doodling. The percentages of utterances expressing opinion were 32%, 56% and 33% in the three periods. Much of the later work has supposed that the phenomenon was one of operant conditioning, and use has been made of experimental procedures that are rather far removed from social interaction. Subjects are asked to produce lists of words, to complete sentences, to tell stories, to talk about themselves, or to answer tests or questionnaires. The responses reinforced are such things as plural nouns, the word 'I', or other classes of words; the reinforcers used are 'good', 'mhmm-hmm', or a flashing light. We shall distinguish here between such laboratory studies and reinforcement in true social situations, such as the Verplanck experiment. Later experiments of this kind have reinforced various categories of social response, and have often made use of non-verbal reinforcers, such as smiling, nodding the head and leaning forwards. In different experiments the following kinds of behaviour have been influenced in this way: (1) amount of speech, (2) opinions, information, etc., (3) speech on selected topics, (4) non-delusional speech, (5) favourable self references, and (6) leader activity. (See Krasner, 1958; Greenspoon, 1962; Williams, 1964).

However, some doubt has been thrown on what is actually happening in these experiments – are subjects being influenced without awareness or are they simply finding out what pleases the experimenter? Is it a case of operant conditioning or of cognitive learning assisted by the verbalisation of hypotheses? It has been assumed that the crucial issue is whether or not learning takes place without awareness – for cognitive theory there should be no learning without awareness – if awareness can be regarded as a valid index of the presence of central cognitive processes. In the early experiments about 3% of subjects were aware of what was being done to them, as ascertained in subsequent interviews or question-naires. However, if questioned at greater length a rather larger number come to be classified as 'aware'. Several studies have shown that rein-forcement has a greater effect for aware subjects. The question is does reinforcement have any effect at all on the non-aware subjects? Here the evidence is conflicting, but it suggests that if there is any effect for these subjects, it is relatively slight. Another approach to the problem is to manipulate awareness experimentally – by the nature of the in-structions, by previous instruction about the phenomenon, or by simply asking subjects to get the interviewer to say 'good'. Normally subjects who have been made aware in these ways are more affected by reinforce-ment (Spielberger, 1965). These results have been obtained in the laboratory type of experiment, in which subjects are asked to produce lists of words. It has been observed by Greenspoon (1962) and Dulaney (1961) that subjects in these experiments formulate a series of verbalised hypotheses about what they should say. The behaviour in question looks exactly like concept-formation as assisted by verbalised mediation processes.

On the other hand the experiments conducted under natural condi-tions, usually with non-verbal reinforcers, may be cases of operant conditioning. Subjects in the Verplanck experiment and in the similar study by Centers (1963) did not know it was an experiment. Hildum and Brown (1956) carried out an 'attitude survey' by telephone, and were able to influence the opinions expressed by 'good', though not by 'mmhmm'; subjects claimed not to have been influenced and were not aware of what was happening. Subjects do not become aware of the reinforcement pattern in these studies either because they are not aware that they are taking part in an experiment, or because the reinforcements used are the less obvious non-verbal ones. It is reported that the students of one of the early workers in this field succeeded in moving him to the extreme left-hand end of his lecture platform by means of smiles and nods versus frowns and head-shakes delivered by an attractive female student sitting in the front row.

Azrin *et al.* (1961) however found some difficulties in repeating Verplanck's experiment. They found experimenters unable to perform the interview *without* giving additional non-verbal reinforcements such as nodding and smiling. They also found that if interviewers were led to expect that agreement would have a cathartic effect and lead to a reduced rate of interaction, this is what happened; otherwise agreement led to an *increased* rate of interaction. This looks like another example of Rosenthal's finding (1966) that experimenters can unwittingly elicit the desired behaviour from their subjects, but how do they do it? Presumably the 'cathartic' interviewers agreed in a different style to the others – perhaps saying 'yes' with a downward note, rather than 'yes-yes' as if to say 'tell me more'. It suggests that what is happening may not be simply reinforcement. Perhaps a second process is operating in that the relevant feature of the 'reinforcing' response is the extent to which it encourages further speech. As Bandura pointed out, 'If the experimenter simply asked subjects politely to emit personal pronouns, it is a safe prediction that these responses would reach asymptotic level almost instantaneously' (Bandura, 1962).

The conditions under which this form of influence is greatest have been studied in a number of experiments, most of them unfortunately of the laboratory type.

The reinforcer used. As far as can be seen, non-verbal reinforcements such as smiling, nodding, leaning forward and looking interested, are more effective than verbal reinforcers such as 'good', 'right', 'mhmmm-hmm', used by themselves. It is doubtful in most experiments whether the latter are used by themselves.

Status and sex of interviewer. Many studies show that a high-status male, or a young and attractive female interviewer, produce the best results, at any rate for male college students.

Personality of subjects. There are considerable individual differences in the response to reinforcement in these situations. The greatest effects have been found in subjects who are anxious, have a high need for approval, who are easily hypnotisable, and who are low in independence. Several studies have failed to find any relationship with extraversion. Schizophrenics, especially chronics and those with a poor prognosis, do not respond to reinforcement – partly because they have such a low verbal output anyway. The effect of reinforcement is greater in subjects who have been isolated, or who have been aroused in other ways.

It may be concluded that operant conditioning of verbal behaviour, and probably of other behaviour too, is an important process of influence in dyadic encounters. The effect is rapid, and can occur without the awareness of the person influenced. It may also occur without the knowledge of the influencer, so that both parties are constantly influencing one another in the direction of producing the desired behaviour.

We shall show later in this chapter that social interaction can usefully be looked at as the operation of a serial motor skill, in which each interactor is trying to manipulate the others in order to elicit certain desired responses. Suppose that A wants B to produce responses of type R, whether this is connected with his professional goals or private motivation. When B emits such a response A probably responds with approval – whether or not he is consciously aware of the value of such reinforcers. One of B's goals is almost certainly to get A to produce responses of approval, liking or social acceptance, so he is reinforced and the rate of production of response R goes up. It is possible for interactors to become aware of this form of influence, and to use it to control the behaviour of others. Interviewers for example can control the amount of talk of those who initially talk too much or too little. It has also been observed that patients undergoing psychotherapy are influenced in this way, and it has been suggested that reinforcements could produce changes in verbal behaviour, which in turn would operate to direct and control other behaviour.

ANALYSIS OF THE BEHAVIOUR OF AN INTERACTOR

The social skill model

At the end of the section on S–R models we concluded that the S–R approach was inadequate because it is necessary to take account of the related and purposive sequence of social responses emitted by each interactor. If it is recognised that an interactor is pursuing certain goals, and that he takes corrective action dependent on the effects of his actions on the other, then we are saying that his behaviour has some of the features of a motor skill. A model of interaction as a kind of motor skill was developed by Argyle and Kendon (1967), and Argyle (1967), from which the following account is taken.

A 'skill' may be defined as an organised, coordinated activity in relation to an object or a situation, which involves a whole chain of sensory, central and motor mechanisms. One of its main characteristics is that the performance, or stream of action, is continuously under the control of the sensory input. This input derives in part from the object or situation at which the performance may be said to be directed, and it controls the performance in the sense that the outcomes of actions are continuously matched against some criterion of achievement or degree of approach to a goal, and the performance is nicely adapted to its occasion (Bartlett, 1943; Welford, 1958).

Here we suggest that an individual engaged in interaction is engaged in a performance that is more or less skilled. His behaviour here, as when he is driving a car, is directed, adaptive, and far from automatic, though it may be seen to be built up of elements that are automatised. And here, too, we have an individual carrying out a series of actions which are related to consequences that he has in mind to bring about: in order to do this he has to match his output with the input available to him and to correct his output in the light of this matching process. Thus he may be discussing current affairs with an acquaintance, and be concerned perhaps merely to sustain a pleasant flow of talk. He must be on the watch then for signs of emotional disturbance in his acquaintance, which might signal that he had said something which might provoke an argument. At another level, he must be on the lookout for signals that his acquaintance is ready for him to talk, or for him to listen. He must make sure his tone of voice and choice of words, his gestures, and the level of involvement in what he is saying, are appropriate for the kind of occasion of the encounter.

In the treatment of human performance as developed by such workers as Welford (1958) and Crossman (1964), a distinction is drawn between the perceptual input, the central translation processes, and the motor output, or performance. We will discuss the various elements of the model in more detail.

(1) *The goals of skilled performance.* The motor skill operator has quite definite immediate goals – to screw a nut on to a bolt, to guide a car along the road by turning the steering wheel, and so on. He also has further

goals, under which the immediate ones are subsumed: to make a bridge, or to drive to Aberdeen. He knows when each goal is attained by the appearance of certain physical stimuli. These goals in turn are linked to basic motivations; for example, he may be paid for each unit of work

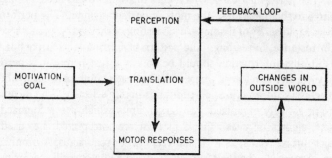

Figure 5.1. Motor skill model (from Argyle, 1967)

completed. In much the same way, a 'social skill' operator may have quite definite goals, for example:

conveying knowledge, information or understanding (teaching)
obtaining information (interviewing)
changing attitudes, behaviour or beliefs (salesmanship, canvassing, disciplinary action)
changing the emotional state of another (telling jokes, dealing with hostile person)
changing another's personality (psychotherapy, child-rearing)
working at a cooperative task (most industrial work)
supervising the activities of another (nursing)
supervision and coordination of a group (chairmanship, foremanship, arbitration)

These aims are linked in turn to more basic motivations in the performer, connected with his work. In everyday non-professional social situations the actors are motivated too, but this time simply by basic social motivations of the kind discussed in Chapter II. Each person wants the other person to respond in an affiliative, submissive or dominant manner, according to his own motivational structure. In professional situations the social skill operator will, in fact, be motivated by a combination of professional and social motivations – he may for example want the client both to learn and to be impressed by his knowledge. Like the motor skill performer, he will also pursue a series of sub-goals in turn. The interviewer first establishes rapport, collects personal data, obtains the answers to a series of questions, and then closes the interview.

(2) *The selective perception of cues* is an essential element in serial motor skills. The performer learns which cues to attend to and becomes highly sensitive to them. Vision is the most important channel. The performer makes a rapid series of fixations, each lasting perhaps ·25–·35 of a second as, for instance, in reading. The pattern of fixation is itself part of the skill; ideally, information should be collected just before it is needed. The performer also learns where to look at each point, in order to obtain the necessary information: perception is highly selective. The incoming data are actively organized into larger units which are recognized as objects, signals or cues. These in turn are interpreted, i.e. used to predict future events, as with dial-readings or road signs. A number of other perceptual channels are used by the motor skill performer – hearing, touch and signals from the muscles (kinaesthesis) about the position of the limbs and body. It is common for more use to be made of touch and kinaesthesis when the skill is well learnt: vision is reserved for the cues which cannot be dealt with by the other senses, and for cues at a distance. It is found that as learning proceeds less use is made of external cues. An experienced motorist concentrates his attention on certain stimuli: outside the car he attends to the movement of other traffic and the position of the edge of the road, rather than the architecture of the houses; while inside he is aware of the speedometer rather than the upholstery of the seats. He knows where to look for the cues, and what they mean; he can interpret road signs and can anticipate what is going to happen next. Part of the training for some industrial skills consists in teaching performers to make finer discriminations, to learn the significance of cues, concentrating on particular cues and suppressing irrelevant ones.

During the course of social interaction each participant receives a stream of visual and auditory information about the other. In Chapter IV it was shown how people learn to perceive and interpret the relevant cues, and how some people are more sensitive than others, especially in areas about which they are personally concerned. In Chapter X methods of training in social sensitivity will be described, and in Chapter VIII it will be shown that some kinds of mental patient are seriously deficient in it.

The motor skill performer gets quite a lot of information from perceiving his own movements, either by sound, vision or by kinaesthetic sensations. Do social interactors receive any direct feedback in a similar way? As we shall show in Chapter IX, people are very interested in the image they are projecting: one of the goals of interaction is to present oneself in a certain light to others. The main source of direct feedback is the sound of one's own voice. Some people are said to be very fond of this sound, but the sound they hear is quite different from what other people hear, since they hear the sound as transmitted through bones. Many people fail to recognise tape-recordings of their voices, and are very startled the first time they hear one. People are often quite unaware of the emotive paralinguistic aspects of their speech. They may also be unaware of the timing aspects of their speech – such as how often they interrupt. Posture, gestures and facial expression cannot be perceived visually by the actor: it is very difficult to see ourselves as others see us. The only way to do this is to have a lot of mirrors, or to study films of oneself. There are however kinaesthetic, muscular cues to bodily movements. People have a fairly definite body image, and do have some idea of their posture.

(3) *Central 'translation' processes.* Information gathered by the receptor systems is transferred to more central regions of the brain and is converted into an appropriate plan of action. If someone is steering a boat he must learn which way to turn the rudder to go in the desired direction. There has to be some central store of 'translation' processes in the brain, which prescribe what to do about any particular perceptual information. This may be in the form of verbalised information, e.g. 'pull the rope on the side you want to turn towards', in the case of the rudder. Often the translation processes are completely unverbalised and lead to automatic sequences of behaviour with little conscious awareness – as in riding a bicycle. Or they may start as conscious rules and deliberate decisions but become automatic later, as with changing gear in a car. A curious feature of the central system is that it can only handle one piece of information at a time – it has limited capacity. The output from it consists of a plan, i.e. the decision to make a particular series of motor responses, which has been selected from a range of possible alternatives. This involves some prediction about how external events are likely to develop while the response is being organised – as when a tennis or squash player, while he is shaping his shot, anticipates exactly where the ball will be.

We can see how the skill model is able to take account of the differing levels of organisation involved in behaviour, from the most automatic to the most reflective. It also takes account of the fact that the same pattern of behaviour can be more or less automatic at different points in time. Social interaction also depends on the existence of a learnt store of central translation processes. In the course of socialisation people learn which social techniques will elicit affiliative or other responses from those they encounter. Research has shown how these can be improved upon in many cases. For example, to get another person to talk more the best techniques are (1) to talk less, (2) to ask open-ended questions, (3) to talk about things he is interested in, and (4) to reward anything he does say. The effects of limited channel capacity are seen in social interaction as in motor skill performance: during periods of hesitating and unfluent speech speakers do not scan the faces of the others present – presumably to avoid overloading the system.

(4) *Motor responses*. Commands go from the central translation system to the muscles, producing a pattern of movements. In fact, there is a hierarchy of goals, consisting of progressively smaller groups of muscular responses. There is also a series of sub-goals: when one sub-goal has been reached the sequence leading to the next sub-goal begins, until the main goal is attained. Driving a car from A to B involves the sub-goals of getting the engine started, getting the car moving in top gear, and getting to the intermediate points X, Y and Z. One of the interesting findings about motor skill is that the series of responses leading to sub-goals become more or less automatic, and can be regarded as larger response units; for example, words rather than letters become the units for morse or typing (cf. Miller, Galanter and Pribram, 1966).

While the essence of the central processes is to *plan*, the essence of the response system is to initiate and control; the desired responses are set in motion and steered with the help of perceptual guidance. As well as learning the perceptual cues and translation processes, it is necessary to learn to perform these patterns of motor response smoothly and accurately. When a motor skill has been perfected, it is faster, movements are eliminated, conscious awareness is much reduced, tension is reduced or sometimes focused at points of difficulty, and there is less need for feedback and some danger of becoming rather mechanical. There are broader aspects of response such as the styles of psychotherapy, foremanship, etc., which have been found to be most effective. These entail rather subtle and complex combinations of social responses, consisting of integrated patterns of social techniques. Establishing rapport, building up a relation of dominance and reducing another's anxiety, are all examples of such higher units of social behaviour, and are probably unitary and automatic sequences of behaviour for many people. Another example is establishing and negotiating relationships and identities in an encounter. These are larger units, composed of smaller units, but interactors are consciously aware of the larger units rather than the smaller ones, and relationships are partly established in terms of the interlocking of these larger units, e.g. relationship between roles.

In considering a performance in this way, we note how it may be said to be made up of a combination of elements, though what we refer to as an 'element' will depend upon the level in the hierarchy we are discussing. It may be noted that 'elements' can be recombined in a fairly flexible way, and it is this that makes a skill so adaptive. On the other hand, once a particular combination of elements achieves, for the performer, an acceptable level of success, and provided the sequence of sensory input is stable upon subsequent occasions when the skill is used, it is found that many sequences of actions in the performance become 'automatised', that is freed from the continuous sensory control. The smaller, lower-level units in the hierarchy are more habitual and automatic than the larger, higher-level units. Feedback operates at each level, so that at the higher levels corrective action involves bringing whole lower-level units into play. More conscious attention is given to the performance of the larger units; their strategy is carefully planned where the lower levels are run off unthinkingly. It seems likely that a similar phenomenon of automatisation occurs with social skills. Thus lecturers and interviewers, for instance, who make use of a fairly standard social technique on repeated occasions, may be able to run off long sequences of actions automatically. An experienced interviewer might give considerable thought to the overall strategy of an interview, but much less to particular questions, and none at all to particular words. Museum guides offer a notorious example, where automatisation has gone too far. Lecturers have occasionally reported on this process in themselves. Thus Lashley (1951) mentions a colleague who reported to him that 'he had reached a stage where he could arise before an audience, turn his mouth loose, and go to sleep' (p. 184). It is found that speech is accompanied by continuous shifts of head, hands and body, and that these bodily movements are also arranged hierarchically, so that a head position may accompany a sentence, a bodily position a paragraph (Scheflen, 1965). However, these shifts do not appear to be under conscious control at all, except for those who have learnt about these phenomena.

(5) *Feedback and corrective action.* The motor skill performer uses perceptual cues to take corrective action. He can thus correct a continuous

action, like steering a car, when it shows signs of going wrong, or correct later performances in the light of earlier ones, as when firing a rifle at a target. It is in a continuous skill or 'tracking' task that this can be seen most clearly. A beginner motorist tries to steer the car down the road; he sees that he is about to hit the kerb, so he corrects the steering to the right. When he is more competent the same process takes place with greater speed and accuracy. Feedback provides information for correct-ive action, which makes allowances for variation in the conditions or materials and for error in the initial plan of response. The social skill performer corrects in a similar way. A teacher who sees that her pupils have not understood the point will repeat it slowly in another way; a person who realises that he is annoying someone by his behaviour will usually change his style of behaviour. The experiments on 'operant verbal conditioning' can be looked at as demonstrations of the effect of feedback – working at two different levels of psychological functioning.

The model is of course only a starting point: it provides a language for talking about interaction, and it is suggestive in a number of ways. We shall have to elaborate it in two main ways, (1) to take account of some of the special cognitive processes taking place during interaction, such as 'taking the role of the other', and (2) to take account of the fact that other interactors are playing the same game, and that there must be a meaning-ful sequence of responses for social interaction to take place. The model as expounded so far has however been useful in showing the various points at which social skill training may be needed, and in providing a classification of the ways in which social competence may fail, in mental patients and others. These points will be pursued further later in this book.

Several experiments on the effect of feedback have been stimulated by the model. An earlier experiment by Leavitt and Mueller (1951) showed that one subject could verbally communicate a complex design to another more quickly and accurately if he had feedback from the other. Kendon (1967) analysed films of bodily movements in dyads, and found that people look up at the ends of their utterance. It is at this point presumably that feedback is required, i.e. on how the utterance has been received by the other (Fig. 5.2). The speaker's terminal look acts at the same time as a signal to the other that the speaker is about to stop speaking. If he fails to look, the other fails to reply or there is a long pause. In a later experiment Argyle, Lalljee and Cook (1968) varied the amount that one interactor could see of another, by means of masks, dark glasses and a one-way screen. Dark glasses had little effect on ease of communication, but when the other was masked or behind a one-way

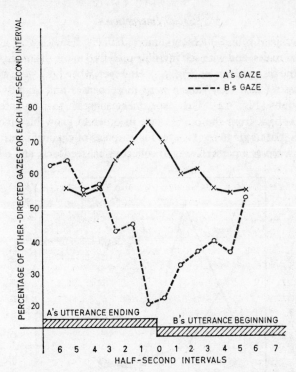

Figure 5.2. Direction of gaze at the beginning and end of long utterances (from Kendon, 1965)

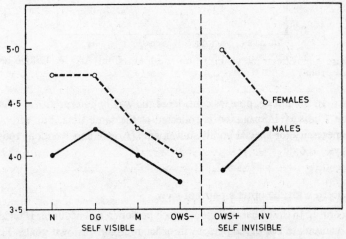

Figure 5.3. Effects of visibility of others on ease of interaction (from Argyle, Lalljee and Cook, 1968). N = Normal, M = Mask, NV = No Vision. OWS + = one-way screen from see through side. OWS − = one-way screen from other side.

screen, subjects found interaction more difficult; females were affected more than males, and with self invisible preferred to see the other, which was not the case with males (Fig. 5.3). However, when both were wearing dark glasses ('face only') there were more pauses and slightly more interruptions (Fig. 5.4). This experiment suggests that an interactor needs feedback from the other's face in order to know his emotional reactions, but needs to see his eyes for purposes of channel control. We now know *where* a person looks to collect visual feedback, and *when* he

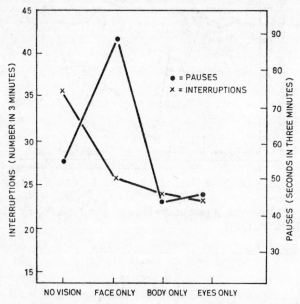

Figure 5.4. Effects of visibility on meshing (from Argyle, Lalljee and Cook, 1968)

looks. In the last chapter we considered the way he interprets the visual data. Auditory information is collected at the same time, but without the necessity for special bodily movements (Argyle and Kendon, 1967; Argyle, 1967).

Concern with the other's point of view

According to the social skill model, each person in an encounter is trying to manipulate the other person, in order to attain his own goals. The model likens dealing with people to the manipulation of a machine – which is probably how psychopaths deal with people, but this doesn't quite fit the social behaviour and experience of normal people. The model can be extended in two ways to make it less psychopathic. (1) An interactor's immediate goals may be for the other to benefit in some way – as in the case of teachers and psychotherapists for example. (2) During social behaviour we are usually aware of being the object of intentions, perceptions and attitudes on the part of the others present. This can be brought within the skill model to some extent by saying that one of the goals of interaction is self-presentation, that is to create certain impressions for others. However, in order to take account of concern with the other's point of view, this use of an imaginative cognitive model of the other, some addition seems necessary to the social skill model itself, perhaps as an extra loop at the 'translation' stage.

According to exchange theory each interactor is trying to maximise his own rewards, regardless of what happens to the other. Experiments in this tradition have shown how cooperation can develop out of pure self-interest (Sidowski *et al.*, 1956 and p 194); however an interactor often has to pay *some* attention to the rewards of the other, or the latter will simply leave the situation, or fail to cooperate. Again the model could be extended by supposing that it can be rewarding to obtain rewards for another under certain conditions. In this section we are concerned with the additional processes which are missing from both of these models in their basic form.

One formulation of the missing process is to postulate that interactors in a cognitive sense 'take the role of the other'. G. H. Mead (1934) was the first person to put forward the idea that interactors in some sense see the encounter from the point of view of the other person. Sarbin has developed this in his analysis of social behaviour as 'role enactment', and sees social behaviour as the playing of parts for an audience (Sarbin and Allen, 1968). Goffman (1956a) has developed the theme of self-presentation during encounters. The difference between the social skill model and the present one is brought out by Turner (1956). He contrasts taking the role of the other in the sense of 'identifying with his standpoint', and in the sense of taking account of his role but keeping at a distance from it, as a salesman might do. Turner lists a third way – taking the point of view of a third party, or of the generalised other, as when a social norm is salient.

There are no ways of assessing whether someone is actually taking the role of the other on a particular occasion, but there are several measures of ability to do it. The earliest method was to see how well A could predict B's (and C's) responses to a questionnaire; this technique is open to a number of statistical difficulties which were discussed before

(p. 161 f). Sarbin and Jones (1956) devised the 'as-if' test, in which subjects are asked to describe how their life would have been different if (1) they had been born a member of the opposite sex, and (2) if they had been born a Russian. This measures the imaginative aspect of taking the role of the other. Another kind of measure is the stick-figure test devised by Sarbin and Hardyck (1955) (cf. p. 137f); subjects are asked to identify the emotions portrayed by the 43 stick figures; this is a measure of 'empathy' in the emotional or postural sense.

Do people interact more effectively if they take the role of the other? It seems likely that if A takes the role of B he should be able to predict B's responses better. Feffer suggested that in order to engage in effective social interaction a person should be able to consider simultaneously his own point of view, and that of others. Feffer and Gourevitch (1960) devised a role-taking test of social decentering – subjects are asked to retell their own projection test stories from the points of view of other people in the pictures. Scores at this correlated with several Piaget tests for simultaneous perceptual decentring, and both scores increased with age between 6 and 13. Feffer and Suchotliff (1966) found that people who did well at the role-taking test also did well in a test of skill in social interaction. The test of interaction was a situation in which subjects had to communicate a password by one-word clues, and the findings may not apply to other kinds of social skill.

Ability to take the role of another would be expected to depend on who the other person is. If A has never experienced B's position it might be more difficult – as when B is of a different sex, race or class for example. The other person might 'see' the situation quite differently, in the sense that different motivations and goals, different rules, different group pressures are operating. There may be a difference of cognitive structure, so that events are categorised differently. Even to speak to another person involves considering what he can understand and is interested in; we discussed earlier experiments showing how people beyond the stage of egocentric speech adapted their uttterances to the listener (p. 118). Triandis (1964) found that dyads were more effective if the members had similar cognitive structures. It might be expected that an older person should be able to deal with a younger one, as he has experienced this role (though cultural changes may and do alter it), but a younger person would have difficulty in dealing with an older one. Knowledge of another role may be obtained by having experienced it at second hand, for example through literary sources or other mass media. It may be suggested that one of the causes of difficulty in interaction with members of other classes, races or national groups is difficulty in taking the role of the other. Some attempts have been made to train people for behaviour in other cultures by means of programmed instruction in the cognitive world of the other culture (p. 418). It is well known that interaction at close quarters over a period of time can remove racial prejudice (cf. Harding *et al.*, 1954); the reason may be that the point of view of the other is learnt under these conditions.

However, taking the role of the other does not necessarily lead to a better social performance. Consider the case of a nervous performer in front of an audience. From the skill model it follows that he should attend to whether or not the audience can understand him and agrees with him, but not with what the audience thinks about him, or whether the audience likes him. The latter will lead to undue 'self-consciousness' and anxiety, and thus to deterioration in his performance. It may not be necessary to take all aspects of another's role, and the right balance between attending to the two points of view should be maintained; Feffer adds that they should be considered simultaneously and integrated. Sarbin and Allen (1969) point out that if the interests of the other are opposed, for example if he is a soldier on the other side, effectiveness may be diminished by taking his point of view too vigorously; here the most effective solution might be to take his point of view only as a detached outsider.

Several phenomena to be discussed later depend on taking the role of the other.

(*a*) *Self-presentation.* Everyone has some concern with what other people think of them, and this affects their behaviour. These phenomena are discussed in Chapter IX.

(*b*) *Observer or observed.* In situations such as appearing in front of an audience or being interviewed individuals become more concerned with how others see them than with their own appraisal of the others. In other words the extent to which people take the role of the other varies; it has been found to be a function of personality as well as of the situation (p. 379).

(*c*) *Taking roles.* When a person occupies a position in a social structure, the other members will have certain expectations of how he should behave. His perceptions of these role-expectations is one of the determinants of his behaviour.

As Turner suggests (1956), there is a difference between taking the role of another as a detached onlooker, and 'identifying with his standpoint'. When a person shares the feelings of another, this is called 'empathy'; when the feelings involved are of distress, it is called 'sympathy'. A may perceive B's behaviour, and find that he is adopting B's postural state, and sharing what he thinks are B's emotions. He may perceive B's reactions incorrectly, but may still empathise with what he thinks is B's response. Lipps (1907) thought that the copying of the other's postural movements came first; Sarbin, Taft and Bailey (1960) thought that cognitive processes are primary and spill over into action. An interesting technique for measuring empathy was used by Stotland and Walsh (1963): subjects heard tape-recordings of good and bad demonstrators teaching a class, and measures were taken of the perceived anxiety of the demonstrator and of the subjective anxiety and PGR of the subjects. Lenrow (1965) also played tape-recordings to subjects; the tapes described the situation of an individual in conflict where to help someone would infringe an impersonal rule, e.g. 'Guards are held hostage by rioting prisoners and threatened with death unless Warden yields. He doesn't.' The measure of sympathy was obtained from analysis of free written responses.

Several factors are responsible for empathy. (1) The ability to take the role of the other cognitively is no doubt important. (2) The arousal of some form of interpersonal motivation is probably necessary – affiliation, sex and nurturance in particular. (3) When a person has been in a similar situation himself he is better able to appreciate and share the state another is in. Lenrow (1966) found a greater sympathetic response to seven tape-recorded descriptions of individuals in difficulty for subjects who had role-played the part of a distressed person and where a partner had responded in a friendly, reassuring way. Lenrow suggests that sympathy develops in children as a result of experiencing distress themselves and through concern for close friends.

Lastly we shall discuss helping behaviour – where concern for another person leads to action. A number of writers have supposed that helping can be accounted for in terms of an exchange of rewards; however, it is clear from numerous field studies and laboratory experiments that people commonly help others without expectation of reward, and that some social behaviour is not oriented towards expected return from others. There are three psychological processes which may be responsible for altruism.

(1) We saw previously that a young chimpanzee will give food to another, spontaneously or in response to begging (p. 34), and that children of 3–5 will help others in distress (p. 60). Hebb (1966) con-

cludes from the animal studies that 'altruism is a product of evolution and not something that must be beaten into the growing human child because of the needs of society' (p. 248). This may be the basis for a cultural norm that a person should help others, especially if they are dependent on him, as Berkowitz and Daniels (1964) suggest. They found that subjects would give more help to subjects who were believed to be dependent on them. (2) A further factor in helping is probably taking the role of the person who needs help. In an experiment using a projective, puppet situation, Lenrow (1966) found that children would help more (a) if they had frequently been in a state of distress themselves, and (b) if they had been successful themselves in the past in taking the action required. (3) Finally altruism may be due to more familiar social processes – such as reciprocation of help and imitation of altruism in others (Berkowitz, 1968a).

DYADS AS SOCIAL SYSTEMS

So far we have considered 2-person interaction from the point of view of one person at a time. However, each person is simultaneously trying to communicate with and influence the other. We turn now to the patterns or systems of interaction developing in a dyad.

Game theory models of dyads

A number of investigators have constructed theoretical models of the reward–cost exchanges active in dyads, and have then incorporated them in rather stripped-down experiments, often in terms of games. In these experiments all that is reproduced from real dyadic interaction is the reward–cost exchange. All other elements and processes are omitted.

The first experiment in this tradition was by Sidowski, Wycoff and Tabory (1956), who devised the 'minimal social situation'. It was found that something resembling 'cooperation' developed between two subjects who did not know of each other's existence, but who could press two buttons which in fact gave rewards or punishments to the other. Cooperation developed faster if strong shocks were used, and it took about 5 minutes for cooperation to be established. The experiment has been thought to show that cooperative social behaviour is due to each member of a dyad seeking his own rewards, without concern for the welfare or point of view of the other. Jones and Gerard (1967) show why cooperation developed in this experiment: if it is assumed that a subject sticks to his previous button to press when rewarded, and shifts when punished, it follows that cooperation will develop through one of three

G

different routes (see Fig. 5.5). In a similar experiment, Sidowsky (1967) informed half of the subjects of the nature of the situation; here co-operation developed more rapidly – suggesting that knowledge of the role of the other can help cooperation to develop. In another experiment Kelley *et al.* (1962) found that most of the subjects thought that the other would stick to his response if rewarded. These experiments how-ever are open to criticisms made earlier (p. 17 ff). The main processes of

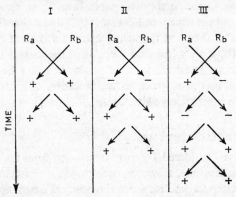

Figure 5.5. Routes leading to mutual rewards in a minimal social situation (from Jones and Gerard, 1967, p. 552)

interaction are prevented from occurring, and subjects are forced into using forms of behaviour which may not occur under normal conditions.

Thibaut and Kelley (1959) were the first to analyse social situations in terms of pay-off matrices. Homans (1961) devised a similar scheme, and made some further derivations about status. Thibaut and Kelley see a social encounter, or each part of an encounter, as a choice for each person between several possible social acts, every combination of which has a pay-off for each person. The following method of representation is commonly used:

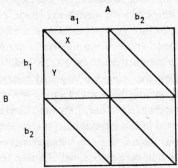

In the cells are entered the pay-offs for each person for that combination of moves. Thus X is A's pay-off for a_1b_1, while Y is B's pay-off.

What these authors have done is to abstract one element of social encounters, which they believe to be the most important. They are then enabled to give representations of social situations, from which the resultant behaviour is predictable. Their model of human behaviour is a rational, or economic one; people act in order to maximise their pay-offs.

Thibaut and Kelley suppose that a person's behaviour will be determined by his subjective pay-off matrix. It is not shown how this matrix can be discovered; in most of the experiments it is simply provided by the experimenter. An outcome is compared with a person's 'comparison level' – what a person thinks he deserves, or considers normal; if an outcome is less than that it is felt to be unsatisfying and unattractive. Outcomes are also compared with the 'comparison level for alternatives' – the values of the best available alternatives open to him. Thus a person might stay in a social relationship, although the reward-value was low, because it was the best option open to him. Although there is an 'exchange of rewards', one person may receive more than the other. The Homans treatment is somewhat similar, but includes further predictions about status. If one person receives more rewards than the other, he becomes rewarded by receiving greater deference. It follows that if a low-status person is able to reward a high-status person, the former should be less deferential.

One way of pursuing these ideas in the field of social interaction is to classify social acts in terms of the amount and type of reward involved; an interaction recording system in these terms was devised by Longabaugh (1963). The three main types of reward he considered are information, freedom and support. This approach could be extended by taking account of the motivations of the actors, and the extent to which these are satisfied or frustrated by particular acts. People may also be concerned about pay-offs of the others involved – when they are behaving altruistically, cooperatively or maliciously.

This approach is quite different from the approach being put forward in this book – it uses abstract variables such as 'reward' rather than the elements of social behaviour involved; it is concerned either with single moves or overall relationships, not with interaction; and it tends to lead to stripped-down experiments in which there is no interaction but subjects play games with fixed pay-off notices. Nevertheless a lot of research has been generated by the exchange theory approach, and we can learn something about interaction from it.

(1) *The development of cooperation and trust.* It follows from exchange theory that people seek and remain in social situations because of the rewards which they receive. Social situations therefore contain a co-operative element – each person depends on rewards mediated by the other. This assumption has been built into 'non zero-sum' games, of which the most widely studied has been the 'Prisoner's Dilemma' game. This is based on the dilemma of two mythical prisoners where each has the choice of confessing to their joint crime or of not confessing. If A confesses and B does not, A is let off lightly and B is heavily punished; if B confesses too they both receive fairly severe sentences; if A does not confess he is lightly treated, on condition that B does not confess either.

The pay-off matrix can be represented as in Fig. 5.6.

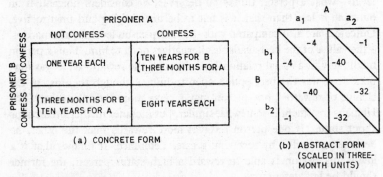

(a) CONCRETE FORM

(b) ABSTRACT FORM (SCALED IN THREE-MONTH UNITS)

Figure 5.6. Two representations of the prisoner's delemma (from Jones and Gerard, 1967)

The particular interest of this kind of game is that the best joint solu-tion is a_1b_1, yet this involves a risk for each player – A has to trust B not to make move b_2.

A more realistic kind of cooperative game was devised by Deutsch and Krauss (1960) in which two players try to move their trucks to destina-tions, and where the shortest route is a one-lane road. They have an economic incentive for arriving at the destination as quickly as possible. The best solution is for the players to take turns to use the one-way road first, and this solution developed during the course of the game for some pairs. In some conditions one or both players could operate a gate to prevent the other truck from reaching its goal; in these conditions there was much less cooperation, and lower pay-offs were received. This situation aroused very real interpersonal feelings and in some cases con-siderable aggression. Deutsch has used this game with marital partners, who are said to be given insight into their mutual feelings.

Experiments of this kind have provided information about some of the conditions under which mutual trust can develop.

(a) If some communication is allowed between players, greater trust and cooperation developed. Loomis (1959) allowed five levels of communication and found that trust increased from 50% of subjects to 83% in the high communication conditions.

(b) Deutsch (1960) found that cooperation developed if a subject was asked to be interested in the partner's welfare and was told that the partner was interested in his. If subjects were told that the only purpose of the game was to make money, non-cooperative behaviour increased with successive trials. Jones and Gerard (op. cit.) comment, 'Without communication the game provides no mechanism for breaking the vicious circle that begins when one non-cooperative choice leads to retaliation by the other' (p. 567).

(c) As shown previously (p. 175) cooperative strategies tend to be reciprocated. It also depends on changes in the other's strategy: if his level of cooperation increases, a subject's cooperative responses are maximised (Bixenstine and Wilson, 1963).

(d) If the partner is said to be humble rather than egotistical, more cooperation occurs (Marlowe *et al.*, 1966).

(2) *Interpersonal strategies.* According to exchange theory the pay-off to each interactor depends on the combination of moves made. This has led to experimental games where both players move simultaneously and have no information about what the other will do. (In real interaction alternation and the opportunity for rapid corrective action make the situation rather different.) Given this situation, which move does a player make, and how similar are the strategies used to the mathematically derived best strategy? In 'zero-sum' games, what one player wins the other loses: there is no cooperation. An example of a pay-off matrix is given in Fig. 5.7. How does a player decide which is the best move to make? Von Neumann and Morgenstern (1944) showed that the best solution is for A to adopt the 'minimax' strategy, when there is a 'saddle-point' – i.e. a combination of moves such that each player gets the best outcome for the worst conditions which the other can create. In Fig. 5.7 the saddlepoint is at a_2b_1, so that B should make move b_1. Where there is no saddlepoint the best strategy is to employ a random sequence of moves mixed in proportion to the average gains corresponding to each move (Jones and Gerard, 1967). But do people actually behave in this way? Rapoport and Orwant (1962), reviewing the results of these games, conclude that American students move towards the saddlepoint, when

there is one, and the game is fairly simple. When there is no saddlepoint they do not adopt the optimum strategy, and when the game is too complex they lack the necessary memory, logical facility or 'computational facility' to work out the best strategy.

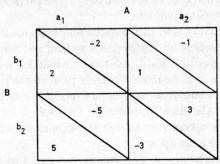

Figure 5.7. Pay-off matrix for zero-sum game with saddlepoint at a_2b_1

(3) *Exchange of rewards leading to influence.* If A wants B to reward him in some way, he should provide equivalent rewards for B. Experiments on reciprocity have shown that if A helps B, then B is more likely to help A. However, we saw that between close friends and relations 'altruistic reciprocity' develops, which does not require any balancing of rewards – there is a high degree of trust, and the relationship is more important than the rewards.

If A wants B to help him, he could offer B quite different rewards. Rosen and Bielefeld (1967) obtained some evidence that a person who behaved more deferentially received more help; Schopler and Bateson (1965) found that more help was given if the costs to the helper were small. However, other results show that helping cannot always be explained in terms of exchange theory, and that other concepts such as a norm of social responsibility or a sympathetic taking of the role of the other must be postulated (p. 188 f). Another kind of influence is known as 'ingratiation', where A influences B by making himself agreeable. In a series of experiments Jones (1964) found that if a low-power person A was motivated to influence a high-power person B he would make himself attractive to B, avoid disagreeing, and flatter B. These tactics were only successful however if their motivation was concealed, and performed with some degree of subtlety. The low-power person A increases his power by ingratiation in two ways: (1) he is in a position to withdraw rewards from B, (2) B becomes more concerned with A's welfare and will suffer by not rewarding A. The second point incorporates the effects of taking the role of the other on B's rewards.

Exchange theory emphasises an important feature of social inter-action – the role of reinforcements. This is useful in several areas: (a) For A to stay in a social situation, B must make it sufficiently reward-ing for him. This will also depend on other factors, such as rules – which have the effect of creating large 'costs' for those who break them. (b) The extent that A will like B depends on B's rewardingness; this is the key to popularity, and we propose it later as an important dimension of per-sonality (p. 326 f). (c) B's power to influence A depends on the rewards and costs which he can provide for A; the ramifications of power are developed later (p. 286 ff).

It is our view however that the conceptual model of exchange theory does not *fit* the phenomenon of social interaction. Social interaction consists of a continuous flow of verbal and non-verbal signals by both parties; the verbal signals are not simultaneous but alternate; the effects of moves are not fully known in advance but depend on trial and error; social behaviour is emitted at two levels, the more global, cognitively controlled components consisting of smaller elements, many of them unconscious and non-verbal; the streams of behaviour emitted by the interactors have to synchronise; interactors are cognitively con-cerned not only with their own gratification, but also with the point of view and condition of others. These features are encompassed by the account given above, but cannot be analysed in terms of exchange theory.

The account of several kinds of interaction given by exchange theory appears to be incomplete and misleading. We mentioned above the cases of reciprocity and helping behaviour. Some social behaviour is governed by factors in addition to the seeking of rewards from others.

Equilibrium processes in dyads

In some of the experimental games discussed above it was found that dyads would discover a stable pattern of behaviour which was satis-factory to both – for example the saddlepoint in a zero-sum game and alternation in the trucking game. We now consider the growth of such cooperative relationships when the whole pattern of interaction is taken into account. To begin with there is an even more basic task – to achieve interaction at all. For anything approaching social interaction to occur there must be a considerable amount of 'coordination', 'meshing' or 'synchronising' of the two patterns of behaviour. If each person acts quite independently, as small children and some schizophrenics do, there is no real social interaction. The author was once interviewing a schizophrenic; while the former was in the middle of a sentence about the hospital football team the patient suddenly said 'they've taken my railings away', thus failing to mesh either with regard to timing, or with regard to subject-matter (and incidentally referring to an event 26 years earlier). It is like a game in which one person is playing squash and the other is playing chess. In all these cases two people are together, are trying to communicate with or to influence one another, but they are not accommodating sufficiently to one another for either to be able to elicit any of the desired responses from the other.

Let us list some of the ways in which coordination seems to be necessary for interaction to be possible.

(1) *The content of interaction.* There must be agreement on the game being played, the dance being danced, the topic of conversation, or the nature of the activity in other respects. Garfinkel (1963) arranged demonstrations to study the effect of breaking this rule: for example a player moves his opponent's piece, or deliberately moves out of turn. The effect is deeply disturbing and disruptive.

(2) *Dimensions of relationships – I. Role-relations.* Two people must agree on the role-relations between them – if one is a teacher, the other must be a pupil, if one is an interviewer the other should be an interviewee. Another way of putting this is to say that they must agree on the definition of the situation, and be prepared to play socially defined parts in it. American hippies, 'acidheads' and teenagers have evolved a social style known as the 'put-on', which consists of refusing to accept normal role-relationships by adopting deliberately non-meshing responses, which prevent any proper interaction taking place, and make the other person look an idiot. The role-relationship offered is ridiculed, so that no valid communication can take place. Brackman (1967) cites the following example from an interview in *Playboy*:

PLAYBOY: How do you get your kicks these days?

DYLAN: I hire people to look into my eyes, and then I have them kick me.

PLAYBOY: And that's the way you get your kicks?

DYLAN: No. Then I forgive them, that's where my kicks come in.

PLAYBOY: Did you ever have the standard boyhood dream of growing up to be President?

DYLAN: No. When I was a boy, Harry Truman was President. Who'd want to be Harry Truman?

PLAYBOY: Well, let's suppose that you were the President. What would you accomplish during your first thousand days?

DYLAN: Well, just for laughs so long as you insist, the first thing I'd do is probably move the White House. Instead of being in Texas, it'd be on the East Side of New York. McGeorge Bundy would definitely have to change his name, and General McNamara would be forced to wear a coonskin cap and shades.

As Brackman points out, this technique 'is invoked when the moment of reconciliation is in sight, at the point when dialogue might begin – to prevent dialogue, to guarantee continued estrangement . . . '.

(3) *Dimensions of relationship – II. Intimacy.* If two people seek different degrees of intimacy there will be incongruity and awkwardness, and a compromise must be adopted. If A uses social techniques such as standing nearer, looking more and smiling, to a greater extent than B, B will feel that A is intrusive and over-familiar, while A will feel that B is cold and standoffish. Clearly A is seeking an affiliative response from B: it is not enough for him to be able to look B in the eye – B must look back and with the right kind of facial expression. The Argyle and Dean (1965) model postulates that each person tries to maintain his own equilibrium level of intimacy; in addition the two members of a dyad would have to compromise on a joint level, more or less agreeable to each. Altman and Haythorn (1967) studied the behaviour of dyads who spent ten days in an isolation room together. There was an increase in territorial behaviour, each progressively keeping to his own bed, chair and side of the table; this was accompanied by progressive social withdrawal and was most marked in dyads that were incompatible for dominance or affiliation.

(4) *Dimensions of relationships – III. Dominance.* Two people may have different ideas about which is most important, entitled to most deference, allowed to talk most, and take the decisions. The commonest source of conflict is where each wants to dominate. We will discuss later the question of how far the outcome can be predicted.

(5) *Timing of speech.* There must be smooth synchronising of speech in a conversation, so that most of the time is occupied, and there are no long silences, and there are also no interruptions. The two members of the dyad have to agree on how long each shall speak, and the rate at which

the conversation proceeds, and they must be able to coordinate their utterances to avoid silences and interruptions. Kendon (1967) by the detailed analysis of films of conversations has shown the techniques by means of which 'floor-holding' and 'floor-apportionment' are achieved. This is partly done by purely verbal methods: a speaker can continue to hold the floor by carrying on talking, and by not pausing between sentences; the other can seize the floor by making noises indicative of desire to speak or by simply interrupting. There is a certain skill in smoothly and politely, but firmly, taking the floor as the other comes to a grammatical break. Floor-apportionment is also requested by eye-movements which act as signals of a speaker's intentions. A speaker looks away as he starts to speak and looks up as he is about to stop. He also looks up at grammatical breaks, to make sure that the other is willing for him to carry on. At these points a third element appears – the listener may or may not give a head-nod and say 'uh-huh', or words to that effect. By these means two speakers will work out a joint pattern of floor-holding. Short utterances are used in several different ways: accompaniment signals, indicating that the listener is attending, are accompanied by looking; agreement signals, laughter and other signs of affective unity, are not; attempted interruptions, in which there is a struggle for the floor, are accompanied by a steady gaze.

(6) *Sequences of behaviour*. Each response of A's must be followed by a response of B's which is 'appropriate' in terms of the various sequential principles described earlier. In a conversation, question should lead to answer, jokes to laughter, for example.

(7) *Non-verbal responsiveness*. Each interactor should continuously signal his attentiveness to the other, by adopting an appropriate distance, orientation and bodily posture, and by a stream of small movements of head, hands and face in response to verbal and non-verbal acts of the other (cf. p. 170).

(8) *Emotional tone*. While interaction *can* proceed between two people who are in different emotional states, this is not a stable state of affairs: probably interaction will cease, or a change of emotional state will take place.

When the above conditions are satisfied, social interaction may be said to take place, as opposed to two people acting independently.

The equilibrium can be described at two different levels of analysis.

(1) There are the details of timing, and synchronising of speech, and the accompanying bodily movements. (2) There are also higher-order units such as 'dominance', 'intimacy' and 'role-relationship'. A social relationship is usually thought of in terms of the second level, but it is negotiated by moves at the first level.

> The innovation is broached in such a manner as to elicit from others reactions suggesting their receptivity; ... at the same time the innovation occurs by increments so small, tentative and ambiguous as to permit the actor to retreat, if the signs be unfavourable. ... Perhaps all social actions have, in addition to their instrumental, communicative and expressive functions, this quality of being *exploratory gestures* ... (Cohen, 1955, pp. 60–1).

At the same time relationships and identities function as high-level cognitive elements, and are handled at this level by performers. It may take some time to establish a steady state, and the ways in which this is done will be described in the next section. When it *has* been established, it appears to have some of the properties of a system in equilibrium. A system is said to be in equilibrium if it remains in a steady state and if deviations are met with forces to restore conditions to normal.

The idea that a stable equilibrium may develop in dyads and larger groups has guided a certain amount of research. Lennard and Bernstein (1960) analysed interaction between psychotherapist–patient pairs over long series of sessions. They found that after the initial sessions each pair settled down to a particular pattern of interaction which then remained constant for the rest of the series. For example the percentage of time taken up by the patient's conversation was very stable, and fluctuated very little between sessions. If the patient spoke less than usual the therapist corrected this by making statements containing more specific information, which had the effect of reducing anxiety.

Jaffe (1964) also studied psychotherapy sessions, and analysed the 40,000 words produced in a series of nine sessions. He found a convergence of vocabulary – therapist and patient learnt 'to speak each other's language'; they showed related fluctuations in sentence length – if one used longer sentences during a session, so did the other; however, these fluctuations diminished and they settled down with the therapist using sentences ·80 as long as the patient's; the same was true of utterance length, where the corresponding figure was ·40; there was differentiation in the use of 'I' and 'you', the former being most used by the patient, the latter by the therapist.

Goffman (1955) showed how group members act to restore equilibrium after it has been disturbed through someone losing face. For example the offending person is given a chance to correct things – his behaviour was perhaps unintentional, or intended as a joke. He may be helped to re-establish himself in the group, in a somewhat modified role. These cases of corrective action contrast with the unstable *positive* feedback which may occur in the early phases of group-formation. For example interaction leads to liking which leads to more interaction, and so on up to some limiting point.

The studies of computer simulation of interaction by Loehlin (1965) showed a similar process operating. Some pairs of computerised 'personalities' never established a stable relationship, but simply withdrew in fear or anger. Others moved towards a final equilibrium state, in the course of 20–30 interaction sequences, during which learning occurred. This final state was not obtained in a steady manner, but evolved through a series of phases. It was found that such positive relations were difficult to bring about but that they were very stable once they had been established.

A number of experiments have been carried out in which compatible and incompatible pairs of people have been put together. Two main kinds of incompatibility have been used – combining people who differ in strength of affiliative needs, or who are both high in dominance, for example on the Schutz (1958) scales. There are three results of incompatibility – meshing is poor, the interactors do not enjoy the interaction or like each other, and task performance is poor. Sapolsky (1965) found that patients recovered faster if they were compatible with their therapist in the Schutz sense. Smelser (1961) found that dyads were least effective at a laboratory task if given roles in conflict with their personalities – the more dominant person was given a submissive role.

For an equilibrium to develop from the spontaneous behaviour of two or more interactors, someone will usually have to modify his behaviour. It seems likely that this will be the person most dependent on the relationship, and also perhaps the person who is most flexible, and who has the larger repertoire of social skills. The more a person gives way on the other hand, the less he is likely to enjoy the interaction. When two 'incompatible' people meet, they are in effect faced by a problem – how to reconcile their respective personalities and styles of interaction. With sufficient time and effort they may be able to solve the problem with the equivalent of a 'creative' solution. They may do this by a kind of collective trial and error, in which most of the moves are of a subtle nonverbal variety. There is very rarely any discussion of the relationship itself, partly because people are only dimly aware of what is happening, partly because, as we have seen, it is embarrassing to talk about these things.

How far is it possible to predict the way in which two people will interact? We shall not be concerned here with the prediction of the actual sequence of responses, which is not yet possible, but with the general relationship, the state of equilibrium that develops. Some degree of prediction can be made of an individual's behaviour on the basis of personality traits, or from observation of his behaviour in other situations. A person who is anxious, tries to dominate, or interrupts in one social situation is likely to do the same in other social situations; it is this consistency which makes it possible to use the notion of 'personality' and 'personality trait'. Chapple (1956) devised a method of scoring a number of interpersonal response traits from a person's performance in his 'standard' interview' (p. 110). These scores have been used to predict interaction in other social settings, and for the selection of sales personnel for different selling situations (Chapple and Donald, 1947). A number of studies have found correlations between aspects of social interaction and scores on personality tests, such as extraversion and neuroticism. These findings will be reviewed in Chapter VIII.

However, people also behave somewhat differently in different situations. Behaviour is a function of both person and environment –

$$beh. = f(P.E.)$$

There is still consistency: if X is more anxious than Y, he will be more anxious than Y in situation E_1 (being held up by a gangster) and in situation E_2 (drinking morning coffee), though both X and Y are far more anxious in E_1. For present purposes the most important part of E to be considered is the other person: so X will behave differently with different Y's, depending on their sex, age, social class, intelligence, and other aspects of their personality. Block (1953) studied the relationships between nine members of a laboratory, including secretaries and technicians. Each person did a Q-sort to describe his relationship with each of the others. It was found that people varied their behaviour considerably according to the age and sex of the other person, but that some people varied their behaviour more than others. It is a familiar observation that some people vary their behaviour very greatly in this way – a young man may be relaxed with men, but terrified with women, or aggressive and competitive with men, but very amorous and at ease with women. Such patterns of behaviour are presumably learnt over the years in the course of interaction with parents and male and female members of the peer-group.

The prediction issue can be taken further by considering the personalities of both members of a dyad. The pattern of interaction that two people evolve is a product of the personalities of each of them. Several studies have shown how predictions can be made of the outcome in this way. We have already considered the conditions under which two people will be compatible. Other studies have been concerned with the question of which will be dominant. Breer (1960) calculated an ascendance index for each person, based on the assumption that subjects of greater age, higher intelligence and social class, and males as opposed to females, would be more dominant. There was also a questionnaire measure of dominance. X's dominance could be predicted to some extent from his own score, or inversely from Y's, but the best prediction was made by subtracting Y's score from X's. Carment, Miles and Cervin (1965) paired subjects who differed in intelligence or extraversion, and who were known to disagree on some topic. It was found that the more intelligent and extroverted subjects were most likely to persuade the other to change their mind, possibly because the intelligent and extroverted subjects talked sooner, and more than the others.

A's behaviour is a function of fixed aspects of B, like age and sex; it is also a function of variable aspects of B, such as his 'personality', as manifested by his actual behaviour towards A. Each person has a variety of styles of behaviour, or sub-personalities, A_1, A_2, etc. If, for some reason, A produces personality A_3, this may elicit B_2, whereas A_4 might elicit B_1. Back (1951) introduced pairs of subjects who were to carry out a joint task; members of some pairs were told that they would find the other person very agreeable and easy to get on with, while other subjects were told the reverse. If A thinks that B is friendly, this elicits friendly behaviour in B – what has been described as 'autistic friendship' (though it can lead to real friendship later). The opposite information results in cautious and suspicious behaviour, and mutual withdrawal – 'autistic hostility'. It is therefore possible for two people to relate to one another in more than one way: there is more than one solution to the problem of discovering compatible, synchronising interaction styles from the sub-personalities available.

A	B
A_1	B_1
A_2	B_2
A_3	B_3
A_h	B_h

A's behaviour is a function of other aspects of the situation besides B – such as the task, the physical environment, and the social norms operating. It is largely this which produces further variations in the behaviour of each. It is thus possible that there are a number of different equilibria for any dyad, depending on the situation, and that there may be greater compatibility in some situations than others.

FORMING THE RELATIONSHIP

First meeting, and the growth of relationships

When two people first meet they proceed cautiously. They may start by going through one of the standard conversational routines that are commonly used in their culture. Here is an American example:

'Hi!'
'Hi!'
'Warm enough forya?'
'Sure is. Looks like rain, though.'
'Well take cara yourself.'
'I'll be seeing you.'
'So long.'
'So long.' (Berne, 1966, p. 37).

Conversation about the weather, or similar vacuous topics, can be kept going for quite a long time. No information is exchanged at a verbal level, but the opportunity is created for non-verbal signals to be exchanged and some progress is made towards establishing an equilibrium. The crucial point is that each person reveals very little about himself, and that no attempts are made to transact any 'business'. Furthermore, they are likely to act with formality and constraint, and reveal little about their social personalities. With friends on the other hand it is possible to be oneself, without fear of rejection by the other. There are cultural conventions about how long these initial moves should last – for old-fashioned Arab chiefs three days was the prescribed period. An interesting exception is found in certain kinds of social survey interviews. Interviewers, who will never be seen again, can capitalise on their 'stranger value' and be told things that would never be revealed to the neighbours.

Such initial meetings may develop into social relationships, of varying degrees of intimacy, and of a number of different kinds. For this to happen there must be interaction over a period of time, and some kind of 'fit' between the personalities and needs of the two people concerned.

Their proximity in the physical environment, and their relationships in the organisational structure are also very important. The dynamic processes involved will be explored in the next section. Here we are concerned with the characteristics of a close social relationship.

(1) A smooth pattern of interaction develops. Meshing improves up to a point, where the best available equilibrium is discovered. Thibaut and Kelley (1959) interpret the early stages of interaction as a process of exploring the outcomes available in the relationship. The account we gave above placed the emphasis more on joint problem-solving, and an effort to find the pattern of interaction most satisfactory to both members of the dyad. The interaction pattern is found to change slowly with time, for different kinds of dyad. For example Lennard and Bernstein (1960), in their study of patient–therapist interaction, found that therapist instructions on how to behave in the situation decreased, his evaluations increased, and both talked more about emotional matters. Rather more is known about stages in the development of small group social systems and these will be discussed in Chapter VI.

(2) The role-relationship between the two interactors is clear. They agree on the definition of the situation and its rules, and they accept the self-image presented by the other. It is rare for all of a person's identities to be involved in a single relationship, and 'an interpersonal relationship is actually a relationship between two "personas", which do not include . . . the entire selves of the respective individuals but merely biased samples' (McCall and Simmons, 1966, p. 189). As the relationship develops however the areas included increase.

(3) Each comes to see the other and the link between them in a special way – the relation is felt to have a unique quality, the other is seen as a special person, and as part of the individual's self system by virtue of his complementary and interlocking role.

(4) As people interact over a period of time, they disclose more and more to each other. Taylor (1965) studied pairs of students who shared rooms at college; the amount disclosed increased during the first nine weeks and then levelled off – but at rather different levels for different pairs, as shown in Figure 5.8.

Greater amounts of disclosure are possible as people come to 'trust' each other more; that is they know that the other will not laugh at or reject the revealer, nor pass it on to others, nor use it to his advantage (Naegele, 1956). A trusting relationship is a cooperative one. In the prisoner's dilemma experiments the other person may be trusted not to take sudden advantage, and to keep to the jointly most advantageous strategy.

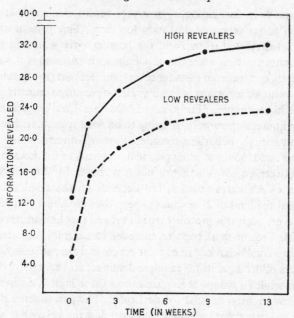

Figure 5.8. Amount of disclosure over time of high- and low-revealing dyads (from Taylor, 1965)

(5) The pair come to function as a social unit or team, when dealing with other people, and others may treat them as such.

Determinants of friendship

The development of friendship can be accounted for in terms of the approach put forward in this chapter. Two people will like one another if interaction with the other is rewarding; the rewards may come from each of two sources – the satisfaction of social drives during interaction, and the existence of a cooperative rather than a conflicting relationship in connection with outside events.

Helen Jennings (1950) studied popular and unpopular girls in a reformatory; her results show clearly how a person who is socially rewarding comes to be liked. The popular girls helped and protected others, encouraged, cheered them up, made them feel accepted and wanted, controlled their own moods so as not to inflict anxiety or depression on others, were able to establish rapport quickly, and won the confidence of a wide variety of other personalities, and were concerned with the feelings and needs of others. The unpopular girls on the other hand were dominating, aggressive, boastful, demanded attention, and tried to get others to do things for them. This pattern has been generally interpreted in terms of the popular girls providing rewards and minimising costs, while the unpopular girls tried to get rewards for themselves, and incurred costs for others. As Homans (1961) points out, the girls who were popular with other girls were not necessarily popular with the housemothers. The kinds of behaviour liked by girls but disliked by housemothers were 'refusing to do what is requested by a person in authority', 'behaviour considered too self-directive and too self-confident', and 'does not bring personal problems to the housemother'. Even between equals, whether or not A is chosen by B is not simply a function of A's characteristics, but depends on the relation between them, and the kind of interaction pattern they are able to establish.

However, while it is probably true in general that individuals who are rewarding become more popular, there are considerable differences between the actual behaviour of popular people in different kinds of group. In groups of delinquents for example dominant and aggressive boys are popular, while in groups of English nurses those high in deference and abasement are most popular (Miller, 1967). The personalities of members in the two groups are very different, and the behaviour which is most valued is different.

Friendship between two people usually requires more than an exchange of rewards through interaction. Two people are said to be in a *cooperative* relationship if they have some common goal which cannot easily be attained by either alone, and where each will benefit from its attainment. Catching an elephant, building a house, playing golf or playing a duet, carrying out research and rearing a family would all be examples of this. Laboratory experiments have been carried out in which a cooperative relation has been created in the laboratory. Deutsch (1949) set up groups which would share the rewards of success equally, and others where the best performer would receive the reward. In this and other experiments it was found that in the cooperative groups members came to like one another more than in the competitive groups. Another kind of cooperation is the *coalition*, where two or more members of a larger group combine together against the rest of the group since they find it is in their interest to do so (cf. p. 239). Cooperative relations need not be symmetrical; the goals may be different for the two partners. MacAndrew and Edgerton (1966) describes a close friendship between two boys in a colony for mental defectives; one was blind, the other crippled – the blind boy pushed the cripple about; the cripple prevented others from stealing the blind boy's food.

Frequency of interaction

If two people never interact they cannot become friends, indeed they are unlikely to have any attitude at all to one another. Physical proximity, creating greater frequency of interaction, leads to the polarising of inter-personal attitudes, and they are more likely to become favourable than unfavourable. Festinger, Schachter and Back (1950) found that socio-metric choices in a student housing estate were closely linked to spatial proximity – those living in the next room or house were the most likely to be chosen, followed by those next-door but one, and so on. Warr (1965) studied the effect of living in the same hostel on the sociometric choices of students. He found that both choices and rejections increased when students had lived in the same hall, but the effect was much greater for positive choices. These findings can be accounted for in terms of the two hypotheses given earlier. Firstly, if two people are able to interact over a longer period they have more opportunity to establish a mutually satisfactory pattern of interaction. If they do establish one, further interaction is rewarding, so they come to like each other more; if they don't succeed, interaction is punishing so that the more they have to interact the more they will dislike one another. At the same time, people who live or work near to one another are very likely to have certain common interests, so that a cooperative relationship is likely to develop. It is also possible that conflicts may develop, in which case interaction leads to negative relationships.

The effect of proximity is greater when a number of people first assemble, and in the early history of a group. Loomis and Beegle (1950), in a study of a new farming community, found that while initial clique-formation was largely based on proximity, this was much less true two years later. As people get to know each other better, and as deeper levels of intimacy develop, personal compatibility becomes of greater impor-tance. In the next section it will be shown that similarity is effective in friendship choice at a later stage in the relationship.

Interaction leads to liking, but it is very probable that liking leads to interaction – which gives an unstable positive feedback system. It follows that once two people have met they should become inseparable. This does sometimes happen, but usually it does not – the frequency of interaction and the intensity of liking both stop short of this point. The explanation is probably that as frequency of interaction increases the difficulties of synchronising increase, and greater and greater accom-modations have to be made to the ways of the other. As intimacy and amount of interaction increase there are more things to disagree about;

if it is possible to agree over them, the relationship becomes even more rewarding. Frequency of interaction is also limited by the fact that people have other things to do.

Similarity

Studies of friends have often found that they are similar in attitudes, personality and in demographic characteristics. Two studies of similarity of attitudes will be mentioned first, illustrating rather different research procedures. Newcomb (1961) arranged for two groups of students to live in a hostel. It was found that friendship choices developed over a 16-week period between people with attitudes that were similar. It took some weeks for this pattern to emerge, presumably because it took the students some time to discover what one another's attitudes were. If more basic attitudes are more important, and if these are not readily disclosed, it would be expected that friendship-formation would be a slow process. Byrne (1962) has used a rather different technique: he first measured the attitudes of subjects as expressed on a number of 7-point scales, and then asked their feelings towards mythical individuals said to hold various combinations of the same attitudes. He found that liking was closely connected with similarity of attitudes, and that this effect was stronger for subjects high in need for affiliation. Byrne and Nelson (1965) found that attraction was a linear function of the *proportion* of similar attitudes.

The effect of similarity of personality traits, and of motivation, on sociometric choice is less straightforward. Some recent studies have thrown doubt on the importance of similarity in this sphere. Miller *et al.* (1966) carried out a careful study of 95 pairs of female friends and 90 pairs of male friends. They found a general, though rather weak, tendency for pairs of friends to have similar traits, as measured by *reputation* – the average correlation was ·20 for females, ·14 for males, over 28 traits. There was however no correlation between *self-descriptions*. Rychlak (1965) studied the development of interpersonal preferences in 96 management trainees, who were working in groups of 6. He found no evidence of preference for others with similar needs. Hoffman and Maier (1966) similarly found no greater interpersonal attraction in homogeneous compared with heterogeneous laboratory groups of 4. The explanation of these negative results may be that it takes some time for attraction to develop along lines of similarity – as the Newcomb study showed. On the other hand it may be that similarity is less important in work-groups than in settings primarily devoted to sociable purposes, such as colleges and hostels.

Winch (1958) put forward the very different view, that people are attracted to one another if they have *complementary* needs, such as dominance and submission, or nurturance and dependence. He obtained some support for this theory in his study of 25 married couples. Rychlak (op. cit.) found limited evidence for complementarity: e.g. those high in nurturance chose others high in succorance. We have already seen that two very dominant people are incompatible, whereas one dominant and one submissive person are compatible (p. 204 ff). What are the conditions under which complementarity rather than similarity leads to friendship? (a) Complementarity operates particularly for dominance-submission and nurturance–succorance, while similarity works for demographic variables, interests, values and other personality traits. (b) Complementary persons may be preferred for some kinds of role-relationships, e.g. to work at a task where a range of abilities or interests are needed. Even friends should not be exactly similar, or the relationship would become rather boring (Jones and Gerard, 1967).

Why does similarity lead to friendship? If two people have similar interests and a similar life situation they are in something of a cooperative relationship – they want to talk about and do the same things, and are in a position to help one another. If they have similar beliefs and values they provide social support for each other's views (Newcomb, 1961). There is however no particular reason why people with similar personalities should be able to help one another. Whether or not interaction will be easier depends on the personality trait in question. It seems very probable that two people will interact more easily if their usual emotional states are similar, and if they are of similar intelligence, and possibly neuroticism. On the other hand it is easy to see why they will be able to interact more easily if they differ in dominance, exhibitionism or nurturance. It is in the realm of personality and motivation that complementarity operates for certain traits, which demand asymmetrical relationships.

It should be mentioned that friendship is not the only kind of positive social relationship between two people. Marriage is discussed in the next section. Family relationships in general are rather different from friendships in that there is less emphasis on common interests and attitudes, while the relationship is more long-lasting, and accompanied by a feeling of positive concern and obligation (Adams, 1967). Relationships at work are also different, being based primarily on the cooperative nature of the situation and interlocking role-relationships. These matters are discussed further in the following two chapters. Of these different kinds of two-person relationship, those between family members are the most intense, as is shown by the distress commonly created when they are broken. The ways in which the personality is maintained by intense social relationships remain to be explored.

Love and marriage

So far we have been dealing mainly with friendships between young people of the same sex. When we consider people of the opposite sex, further interesting things happen. Adolescents become very interested in and excited by the opposite sex, but for some time they only establish very casual and impermanent relationships. There is very little sexual behaviour at first. Erikson (1950) reports that they 'would rather converse, and settle matters of mutual identification'. Perhaps until the ego-identity is established it is difficult to enter into an intimate relationship outside the home; alternatively a young person does not know which kind of mate to choose until he has made certain basic decisions about himself. The intense kind of relationship involved in romantic love is a recent and largely Western phenomenon; it does not occur in most primitive societies. It has been suggested (B. A. Farrell, personal communication) that this kind of relationship is only possible where there has been experience of a similar intense relationship with parents, and it does not occur when there is a more diffuse family system, each child being reared by a number of adults. Falling in love means that A is very strongly rewarded by B in the sexual sphere, with the result that A likes B very much, and becomes dependent on B for further rewards. On the other hand A incurs costs – through loss of independence and the difficulties of synchronising; thus he is in an approach-avoidance conflict, and this is confirmed by the common phenomenon of lovers repeatedly breaking off and then coming together again. Waller and Hill (1951) stress the pains of dependence; we are more inclined to stress the difficulties of meshing, and of reconciling conflicts. It could be said that without sex, marriage would be impossible – there would not be the incentive to make the necessary adjustments.

The progress of love is marked by two public rituals – engagement and marriage. The usual purpose of such rites of passage is to proclaim publicly a change of state, in this case the relationship between two people. A further interesting ritual is the honeymoon. Rapoport and Rapoport (1964) suggest that there are two main interpersonal tasks to be completed during the honeymoon – to work out mutually satisfactory ways of regulating sexual behaviour, and of living together at closer quarters. A working agreement has to be arrived at over a huge range of interpersonal issues, and towards many outside situations. In other words a new level of equilibrium has to be worked out, with synchronising at a greater level of intimacy, and a higher rate of interaction. Rapoport and Rapoport (op. cit.) report that in the USA this new level of intimacy is often found stressful, and that honeymoon couples seek the company of other honeymoon couples and often go home earlier than was planned. The honeymoon does however ease the change of relationship with family and friends which must take place with marriage. This sequence of events may be compared favourably with the change in relationship with parents which adolescents have to make.

After marriage the couple have to settle down to a way of life in which there is usually some degree of division of labour. The pattern of life, and of social interaction, which they adopt is very much a function of the surrounding culture, and varies considerably between different times and places, with varying degrees of role-differentiation (p. 241 f).

If sexual relationships are so rewarding, why do so many marriages end in divorce – about one in ten in Britain? Two theoretical reasons are suggested by the previous analysis. Firstly, when the level of sexual reinforcement declines, the balance of the approach-avoidance conflict may shift; this would be expected to happen if a synchronising system had been established with difficulty, involving costs to both sides. Continued intimacy would then become on balance punishing rather than rewarding. Secondly, the situation which the dyad is in changes with time – with the addition of children to the family, and changes in the domestic or work situation. These may all elicit changed styles of behaviour in one partner or in both, and are further possible sources of conflict.

When marriage does succeed, there is a pattern of dyadic behaviour rather different from that discussed so far. There is a high degree of meshing, great similarity of outlook, and there are also changes in identity in which the other is seen not so much as a separate person, but as a regular part of the immediate social environment, and becomes in some ways a part of the self-image.

VI

Small Social Groups

THE STUDY OF SMALL GROUPS AS INTERACTION SYSTEMS

Concepts and methods

A great deal of social interaction takes place in small social groups. Monkeys and apes live in groups, within which children are procreated and reared with various family structures. The work of gathering food and drink and arranging shelter is performed, leisurely social activities occur, and defence against predators is organised (p. 27 ff). This is presumably an instinctive pattern of behaviour, which has evolved through the survival of those groups and their members that adopted it. Human life is similar: children are reared in families, go out to play with groups of friends, are educated in groups at school; later they work in cooperative groups, and live in families of their own, which form communities, and they pursue common interests in various societies and clubs. Just as the two members of a dyad work out a pattern of interaction and a social relationship, so the members of small groups work out a pattern of interaction in which all of the members are related as members of the group.

Since 1950 there has been a great deal of research on small groups, mainly in the form of laboratory experiments, much of it carried out with great skill. The implicit strategy of research has been to assume that all kinds of small groups follow the same empirical laws, and that these can best be studied under controlled laboratory conditions, where confusing environmental variables are absent. The result is that there is now an extensive literature about small social groups of students engaged mainly in problem-solving or allied tasks, and we really do not know very much about real groups in the outside world. One of the things I have tried to do in this chapter is to describe the patterns of interaction in some of the main kinds of small group. It will be apparent that what happens is startlingly different from the behaviour in any experimental group so far studied. This is a further demonstration of the danger of stripped-down laboratory experiments, in which the only variables

216

included are those the experimenter knows about. Perhaps the most pressing need at the present time is for detailed studies of small groups in the field.

Some of the work on small social groups furthermore has been of the very artificial kind, where actual interaction is eliminated, that was criticised previously (p. 17 ff). There are experiments on conformity in which 'group members' cannot see or hear one another, but only see what are alleged to be judgements made by other members, and there are experiments on coalitions in which the interaction taking place is restricted to moves in a dice game. Such experiments may throw light on the effect of social processes on cognitive or decision processes, but they tell us nothing at all about interaction – and very little about conformity or coalitions.

Most experimental groups have the disadvantage of lasting for about half an hour; it is now recognised that the most important group phenomena will not appear under these conditions, and experimenters have started to keep their subjects for longer – for 10 days in isolation in one experiment (Altman and Haythorn, 1967). Even this is rather short, in view of the finding that it takes about 9 weeks for room-mates to settle down into a stable pattern of interaction (Taylor, 1965). A number of small group researchers have turned to the study of T-groups, since these groups last over a period of time. T-groups however have the considerable disadvantage of being totally unlike any kind of naturally existing group.

Most research on small social groups has so far been at a less detailed and concrete level of analysis than the work on dyads. This is partly for the historical reason that small group research was originally inspired by Lewin (1952) and has made use of his field theory concepts. There is also the practical reason that those interested in the details of interaction have mainly confined themselves to dyads because of the enormous amount of data produced by small groups. Another pressing need in this area then is the study of small groups at the level of analysis of the elements of social behaviour. Meanwhile what has been discovered, albeit at a relatively macroscopic level, is of great interest from the point of view of interaction, and will be reviewed selectively in this chapter.

The formation of social groups

Different kinds of group come together in different ways: leisure and interest groups through common interests and some degree of mutual compatibility, work and educational groups mainly in order to work and as organised by administrators. The balance of task and interpersonal motivations, and the degree of external direction is different in these two main types of group. Although groups in laboratory experiments may endure for only 30 minutes, most groups in real life last for very much longer, and some of the main phenomena of group-formation can be seen only in groups which persist over some weeks or months. Most studies of such groups have been of therapy groups or of T-groups, though in fact the stages of development are similar in groups of a number of kinds. Most observers of groups have reported that they progress through a number of developmental stages. Tuckman (1965), after reviewing a large number of studies, suggested that there are four main phases, and that both group structure and task activity develop in parallel ways. His scheme is as follows:

	Group structure	Task activity
1. *Forming*	There is anxiety, dependence on a leader, testing to find out the nature of the situation and what behaviour is acceptable.	Members find out what the task is, what the rules are, what methods are appropriate.
2. *Storming*	Conflict between sub-groups, rebellion against leader, opinions are polarised, resistance to control by group; conflicts over intimacy.	Emotional resistance to demands of task.
3. *Norming*	Development of group cohesion, norms emerge, resistance overcome and conflicts patched up, mutual support and development of group feeling.	Open exchange of views and feelings: cooperation develops.
4. *Performing*	Interpersonal problems are resolved, interpersonal structure is the tool of task activity, roles are flexible and functional.	Emergence of solutions to problems, constructive attempts at task completion, energy is now available for effective work; this is major work period.

It is recognised that these stages may take quite different amounts of time in different kinds of group. For example laboratory discussion groups have been found to go through these stages in a few hours, while therapy groups might take a year of meetings. In most groups new members are added from time to time, sometimes replacing previous members. Mills (1967) suggests that a new member goes through a series of stages: (1) he is concerned with the satisfaction of the basic needs which bring him to the group, (2) he conforms to group norms, (3) he is concerned with the pattern of social interaction in the group, and the pursuit of group goals, (4) he takes part in leadership of the group and consideration of its long-term aims. In the early stages of a group, the problem is that of attaining an equilibrium pattern of inter-action and relationships, which is sufficiently acceptable to all members. This is the equivalent of the process of trial and error that takes place in dyads.

For some groups a mutually satisfactory equilibrium may not exist: the members are simply incompatible. Schutz (1953) set up experi-mental groups which were high and low in compatibility. Incompatible groups were put together by including more than one person who was very high in dominance, or members with very different levels of affiliative motivation. These groups were ineffective at tasks requiring cooperation. Haythorn *et al.* (1956) set up groups of four, where one was designated the leader, and with different combinations of authori-tarian and non-authoritarian leaders and followers. When there was an authoritarian leader and democratic followers, or vice versa, there was observed to be lower morale, less effective communication, more con-flict and worse cooperation. Bales (1953) supposes that there must be a preponderance of positive, rewarding responses for equilibrium to be maintained. Negative reactions would act to inhibit the preceding act, so that trial and error towards a more stable pattern can take place. On the other hand attempts at influence and direction may very often lead to negative reactions, though they are an essential part of much inter-action. Social skills may be developed which avert such responses, for example the persuasive–consultative style of leadership.

Once equilibrium has been established the group will persist in a stable condition. However, further slow developments will occur, because the group will have to adjust to changes in the outside world, and because members of the group may try to introduce changes in group activities and goals. The history of a group ends with its dissolution: Mann (1967) observes how this stage is marked by a nostalgic pre-occupation with the earlier phases of the group, preparation for re-entry into the 'outside world', and plans for reunions. Although we have written of groups as autonomous entities which have some kind of life of their own, all group actions consist of the behaviour of individuals, and all changes are initiated by individuals.

Members of a group come together, motivated both by interpersonal needs and by concern for the task; they are in a cultural and organisational setting which requires certain kinds of behaviour. What emerges from these given elements is a pattern of group activity which both gets the job done and which satisfies interpersonal needs. Homans (1951) distinguished between the 'primary system' of activity concerned with the task, and the 'secondary system' of additional social interaction for purely social purposes. A group may start meeting to do a job, and then carry on meeting because the members like one another. Group development is the process of working out, largely by trial and error, an interaction pattern and set of relationships that are adequate to both problems. Three main aspects of this social system will be discussed below: (1) the norms of behaviour, representing agreed solutions to task and interpersonal problems; (2) the hierarchical structure of leadership, power and social influence; (3) the affective, or sociometric, structure of liking and disliking, corresponding also to frequencies of interaction or communication between members. Each of these three aspects of the social system have been observed to emerge in developmental studies. As in the case of dyadic interaction, once an agreed social system has emerged it tends to persist in a state of stable equilibrium, resisting change. Again, it is a matter of degree how far such a system may develop in different groups. The affective structure develops greater or lesser degrees of cohesiveness; there may be varying degrees of consensus about the status hierarchy; there may be various amounts of conformity to norms about matters of central importance to the group.

A group can hardly be regarded as a group, as opposed to a collection of individuals, unless there is some minimal degree of attraction to the group. The overall level of attraction towards the group, 'cohesiveness', is one of the most important dimensions of social groups, and can be equated with 'loyalty'; 'cohesiveness' can be measured by indices such as the percentage of in-group choices, the 'we/I' ratio, the turnover rate, or the number of supportive interactions. There have been numerous investigations of the conditions under which cohesiveness develops, in both laboratory and field settings (cf. Lott and Lott, 1965; Cartwright and Zander, 1959). Members may be attracted by the other members, or by the group task; the attraction to members can be measured by sociometric methods. The sources of cohesiveness can be summarised under these two headings – satisfaction of interpersonal needs and satisfaction of needs related to the task.

Interpersonal needs are satisfied when the conditions for friendship-formation are present – frequent interaction and similarity of members (cf. p. 209 ff). Members will be drawn towards the group if they are valued, popular and prestigeful in the group – those who are lowest in these respects are the most likely to leave it. Certain kinds of group behaviour are more satisfying and produce cohesion – democratic leadership, and cooperation rather than competition. Mutual compatibility of members, making for a smooth meshing social system, is important – there should not be too many very dominant members. A skilful leader can help to produce meshing – by integrating newcomers and isolates, by smoothing out and resolving conflicts, and by trying to maximise interpersonal satisfactions. Psychopaths, schizoids and other mentally disturbed personalities can have a very disrupting influence – they produce an atmosphere of unease and tension, and may deliberately create conflicts between others. External threat can lead to an increase of group cohesiveness, especially if it is thought that cooperative action is the best means of dealing with the threat (Lott and Lott, 1965).

Satisfaction of needs related to the task also generates group cohesiveness. Shared success in group tasks, especially if this leads to an increase of status or other rewards, acts in this way, as a number of laboratory experiments show. Attraction to the group may be based on the prestige of belonging to it, the economic benefits incurred, or the opportunities for work or play, rather than the interpersonal attractions of membership, in the first place (e.g. Ross and Zander, 1957).

In order for a group to develop to the state in which the external task is effectively performed and interpersonal problems are solved, it is necessary for it to become a cooperative group, in which the members are committed to agreed group goals. These may be openly stated goals, though it has been suggested that groups may pursue collective goals of which the members are not consciously aware – such as avoidance of the task or rebellion against the leader in T-groups and therapy groups (see p. 260 ff.). The group's task goals are linked more or less closely to the individual goals of members, as when members of a research group stand to gain professional rewards from the successful completion of a research project. There may be some disagreement among the members as to what the group goal should be, but unless members suppress their individual preferences to some extent the group will not function effectively, and there will be no satisfaction of task-related needs. It is for this reason that most groups are in a state of mixed cooperation and competition (Cartwright and Zander, 1959; Thibaut and Kelley, 1969). However, in addition to needs which are linked to the external task, members also have interpersonal needs which they seek to satisfy in the course of social interaction. Again if members do not suppress their personal preferences about how they should behave in the group, there will not be a smoothly synchronising group, or it may not have the optimal structure for task performance – as for example when the least competent member is too influential over decisions.

Clearly it is most satisfactory if group goals are closely compatible with individual needs. Members can however become committed to group goals in a number of ways. An interesting demonstration that group goals can become internalised was produced by Lewis (1944). She found that in cooperative groups tension for task completion was discharged by another member completing the task, as measured by the Zeigarnik effect – enhanced memory for uncompleted tasks.

How can members be induced to accept group goals? (1) Thomas (1957) found that by creating a division of labour in which members performed complementary roles a cooperative relation was established between them: there was greater cohesiveness, greater effort, more work and greater feeling of responsibility. The same principle may produce cooperation over social tasks, e.g. on committees and other groups where task and social interaction coincide: if members can work out complementary, i.e. synchronising, role-relationships there will be a cooperative group. (2) Cooperation can be induced by the reward-structure imposed on the group. Deutsch (1949) offered shared grades to be based on the overall group performance, and found that this induced more cooperation than when grades were offered for individual performance. In the cooperative groups, members saw themselves as interdependent, coordinated their efforts, were more strongly motivated, communicated more with one another, got more work done, and were more friendly to one another. (3) When members of the group participate in setting the group goals, they become more strongly committed to them. This may come about through the practice of group decision, in which the leader steers the group to make a decision about its goals. A number of studies have demonstrated the effectiveness of this procedure (cf. Argyle, 1957a). A leader may also consult members individually. These techniques will be discussed further in relation to effective styles of leadership (p. 299 ff.). (4) Group members may be more or less cooperative as a result of personality or cultural background. Margaret Mead (1937) showed that whole cultures can be placed along a cooperative-competitive dimension. (5) Cooperation over social tasks can be induced by creating satisfactory conditions for synchronising and complementary role-differentiation. Exline and Ziller

(1959) created *un*cooperative groups by setting up incongruence between status, voting power and ability. (6) Coalitions may develop among some or all members of a group if they see that this increases the probability of need satisfaction. This topic will be taken up later (p. 239).

Some of the effects of cooperation on group interaction and task performance have been reported already. The *task* is more effectively and rapidly completed by a cooperative group, if it is a group task, requiring coordination of individual efforts, as was shown in the Deutsch experiment. In a study of 72 actual committees, Fouriezos, Hutt and Guetzkow (1950) found that the committees in which members were rated lowest on self-oriented needs get through more business. If each person is working independently however, competitive motivation has a stronger motivating effect, as various studies of subjects turning crank-handles, and copying newspaper material with rubber stamps, showed (e.g. Whittemore, 1925). The reason for the superiority of cooperative groups is that the group is a more effectively organised unit for coordinating individual effort, in the ways that the Deutsch study showed. In particular there is fuller and more effective exchange of information – while in a competitive group information tends either to be concealed or not received. Zander and Wolfe (1964) found that under more cooperative conditions there was greater providing of information and a greater desire for information.

The *social interaction* in the group also differs under cooperation. There are more positive, friendly and trusting relations between members, as compared with hostile and suspicious relations in competitive groups. The reason is that efforts by a member towards the shared goal are also contributing directly to the satisfaction of others – members are mutually rewarding. In work situations cooperative or competitive relations may be set up by the use of group or individual incentives. When salesmen in shops are paid by individual bonus this may create deadly warfare between them, including such strategies as hiding the goods, keeping control of keys, and stealing wealthy-looking customers. In addition members are in a tenser emotional state in a competitive group, where the mutual distrust and hostility, and frantic competing for scarce resources can induce great emotional disturbance. Mintz (1951) was able to generate a simulated panic situation by creating a situation in which competing group members all tried to pull their corks out of a large bottle at the same time. A cooperative group can be regarded as providing a secure and calming social environment. Finally members of cooperative groups enjoy the group meetings more, as many of these studies show.

BASIC PROCESSES OF INTERACTION IN SMALL GROUPS

Social norms

Members of a group will have much in common from the beginning, but it is also found that there is convergence towards shared ways of perceiving and judging, of communication and interaction, shared attitudes and beliefs, and shared ways of doing whatever the group does. The phenomenon has been extensively studied in laboratory experiments, and there are several excellent reviews of the literature (Allen, 1965; Hollander and Willis, 1967; Secord and Backman, 1964). Much of this work has been concerned with perception or cognition, and many experiments have involved no social interaction at all (e.g. Crutchfield 1955) – although the behaviour in question is learned and normally functions in a setting of social interaction. We shall concentrate on the processes of interaction connected with conformity. Most research has concentrated on the causes of conformity, and it has often been assumed that conformity is rather discreditable. It could be argued that for a group to function at all there must be some degree of agreement over how things shall be done, but that there must also be innovators who suggest new ways of doing them, and thus enable the group to develop and to keep up to date.

Probably the single most important and widely confirmed generalisation about social groups is that they form norms. Our first interest is in why they do this – the functions served by norms and the processes leading to their being formed. The matter is more complex than was at one time realised, and at least four different processes seem to be involved, though they could be condensed to a single formula: shared patterns of behaviour are adopted by group members because this enables them to attain group goals and satisfy interpersonal needs.

(1) Most groups have some task to perform and goals to attain. Norms are formed particularly about matters which are relevant to the task; the norms represent shared solutions to problems, and cooperation is easier if all are working on the same lines. Failure to conform may threaten the attainment of the group goal; in work-groups for example there are strongly enforced norms about not working too hard since this could lead to reduction in piecework rates (Roethlisberger and Dickson, 1939); among professional thieves there are strong pressures on matters like punctuality, where deviation might lead to arrest of the gang (Sutherland, 1937).

(2) Groups have internal problems too – the regulation of interaction in the group. Newcomb *et al.* (1965) stress the need for shared means of

communication; group members usually have the same language, but they also develop additional private and slang terminology. The requirements of meshing produce conformity – of mood and content of interaction. The existence of rules makes life easier – decisions don't have to be taken, and the behaviour of others is predictable – as with norms about the times of meals. Sherif and Sherif (1964) describe the norms of adolescent groups, which include such things as 'going with a new girl is permissible so long as it is announced to the group in case there are any objections'; clearly such norms enable conflicts to be avoided. Thibaut and Faucheux (1965) found there was a special kind of norm-formation – the making of contracts – in a game-playing situation when members had unequal power and one was worried about the division of outcomes; it is argued that norms are formed as an impersonal means of ensuring fair distribution.

(3) Norms are also formed about opinions, attitudes and beliefs. When there is no means of checking such ideas against physical reality, individuals may turn to 'social reality' instead (Festinger, 1950). Where the others are known to be well informed this may be a very reasonable procedure.

(4) Norms are formed about clothes, other aspects of physical appearance, and behaviour whose main purpose is to identify the actor as a member of the group. Such shared behaviour indicates to members of the group and to others who the members are, and also functions as part of the self-presentation of an individual (p. 384 f). This behaviour is particularly noticeable in adolescent groups (p. 246 ff). It is probable that groups will bring pressures to bear about the appearance of members when the latter is likely to bring the group into disrepute, and that such pressures will occur more in groups that are uncertain of their social standing.

Norms begin as a kind of working agreement among the original members of the group. New members may share the norm behaviour from the outset (and may have joined for this reason); if they do not share it, group processes are set into operation which often result in their conforming. Halla Beloff (1958) distinguished between people simply agreeing and actually moving towards the norm. To the members the norms seem to have some kind of independent existence exterior to the group, and to have a moral quality. Thibaut and Kelley (1959) suggest that the basis of this may be that parents have in the past laid down the rules and arbitrated between siblings.

The newcomer to the group may later move beyond *overt compliance*, in the presence of other members, to *internalisation* of the norms. Whereas

H

previously he would only conform when the group was looking, now he will always do it, will believe it is right, and be prepared to influence or convert deviating members. Criteria such as these are used in Chinese thought reform centres to decide when a person has been indoctrinated (Lifton, 1961). It has been suggested by Kelman (1961) that there is a third level of conformity between compliance and internalisation which he calls 'identification': this is where there is an attitude change which is sustained by the relationship with the influencing agent, as in brainwashing and religious conversion. The processes of social learning involved in internalisation may include introjection of the reactions of group members (Argyle, 1964a), and a shift of self-image resulting from taking group members as models (p. 368 f).

We now consider nonconforming behaviour. Willis (1963) suggested that anti-conformity (movement away from group norms) is different from independence (behaviour not influenced by group norm). Willis and Hollander (1964) carried out an experiment in which these two patterns of behaviour were produced experimentally. Anti-conformity appeared when the partner was initially seen to be 90% incorrect, when flexibility was encouraged, and subjects were rewarded if they did better than their partner. Independence was produced when the subject initially found himself to be correct 90% of the time, when consistency was encouraged, and subjects were rewarded for being right regardless of what the partner did (the independent variable was a combination of these conditions).

We have argued that groups need innovators to supply new ideas. It has been suggested that deviates play a second important role in groups – they make norms more explicit and show other members what happens to those who break them (Mills, 1967). Deviates are also a major topic of conversation in groups and seem to add interest and variety to group life.

But why should an individual deviate, and what does he gain from it?

(1) He may be more influenced by the norms of a second group which is more important to him – he is 'marching to a more distant drummer'. In this way he may function as an opinion leader, providing a channel of communication for the flow of ideas through the community.

(2) He may have strong personality needs which prevent him from accepting the norm – for example a very aggressive person might be resistant to norms about pacifism. Such individuals may leave the group, or the norm may change if it does not meet the needs of enough members.

(3) A member may arrive at new ideas about how to tackle the group's internal or external problems: such new ideas may have various sources, including some original problem-solving. But how can the

deviate persuade the group to accept his ideas instead of rejecting him as a deviate? It has been observed that new members start by conforming, and when sufficiently accepted start to introduce innovation. Hollander (1958) suggested that members acquire 'idiosyncrasy credit', i.e. permission to deviate, by virtue of their past good behaviour – conformity and contribution to group goals. Deviation is now seen as potentially valuable to the group rather than otherwise. If a member is, or feels himself to be, an expert upon some matter, he has greater confidence in his ideas in this sphere, and will be more persistent. This was seen in the Willis and Hollander (1964) experiment.

(4) Sometimes a member will deviate for no better reason than that he wants to challenge the leader.

When a member deviates, a characteristic sequence of interactions follows. Firstly there is 'norm-sending', i.e. leading members of the group indicate what the norms are. This may be done by the example of their own behaviour; in this case the relevant influence process is one of identification and imitation. They may explain verbally what behaviour is expected, and what the acceptable limits are (Thibaut and Kelley, 1959). When a member has deviated this may be responded to in a variety of ways. There may be minor non-verbal signals – the raised eyebrow or frown. There may be verbal communication, either of a persuasive or threatening kind; it is found that communication to a deviate increases unless he is seen as a hopeless case (Festinger, 1950). There may be total social rejection and exclusion from the group, or physical violence. The deviate may now conform if he is keen to be accepted by the group. Walker and Heyns (1962) found that there was more conformity in cohesive groups if subjects had been led to believe that conformity was instrumental to being liked, not if they were informed otherwise. Schachter (1951) showed that deviates are rejected, particularly in cohesive groups and on topics relevant to group goals.

Some aspects of conformity must be looked at in terms of cognitive processes. Deutsch and Gerard (1955) showed that people sometimes conform because they think that the rest of the group are right – and not just to avoid being rejected. Deviates may regard the other group members as sources of expert advice, or of factual information, which may be useful for solving external problems. The amount of conformity will depend on the perceived expertise or competence of the other members.

We will now consider some of the main variables governing the conformity behaviour of deviates, and the basis for the findings in interaction.

(1) *Relation to the group*. People conform most to the norms of groups to which they are keen to belong – known as 'reference groups' (New-comb, 1943). This has been confirmed in laboratory experiments in which groups are made to appear more or less attractive (e.g. Back, 1951). It may be through processes of identification with group members, because acceptance by the group is a desirable goal, or because the group is regarded as a reliable source of information. Status in the group should affect conformity, as predicted by Hollander's theory. The results are somewhat contradictory (see Allen op. cit.): some of the better studies suggest that the relationship is curvilinear – the greatest conformity is shown by those of medium status (Dittes and Kelley, 1956). There is much less conformity when a deviate is supported by even one other person than when he is alone. This was found for example in a very realistic experiment by Milgram (1965): subjects were instructed by the experimenter to give large electric shocks to another person, but were more able to refuse if others refused also.

(2) *Personality of subject*. A number of studies have tried to find out which subjects conform most. In laboratory situations, usually involving little or no interaction, it is found that conformers are female, unintelligent, authoritarian, and lacking in self-confidence (Crutchfield, 1955; Mann, 1959). However, whether a person will conform also depends on situational factors: although women conform more on judgemental tasks and McDavid (1965) found that women conformed more on 'male' issues, it was found that they did not do so on matters that were either sex-free or feminine. Hollander and Willis (1967) have suggested that conformity is no more of a personality trait than is leadership – both depend very much on the group and the situation. As with leadership there is evidence for a rather small degree of consistency between one conformity situation and another (Vaughan, 1964). Furthermore the correlation between conformity and personality depends on the nature of the situation. For example whereas authoritarians conform more if the other people are more powerful or of higher status, it is people with low confidence and strong affiliation needs who respond most to peer-group pressures. Different personalities also react differently depending on their competence in the situation, as will be shown below.

There may be cross-cultural differences in conformity to norms. Milgram (1961) found that Norwegians conformed more than comparable French subjects in the Crutchfield situation, and Riesman *et al.* (1950) have argued that conformity is stronger in the USA than in more inner-directed cultures such as Europe. It is our impression that there are great differences in conformity between different sub-populations within each of these countries – British teenagers conform, American writers do not.

(3) *Nature of the situation.* There is more conformity when the behaviour in question is public rather than private, as an experiment by the author showed (Argyle, 1957). The more surveillance there is by the group, the greater the likelihood of sanctions for deviance. Conformity is greatest if a person feels that the other people have greater competence or knowledge of the situation – so that he will conform to quite different extents in different situations. This has been demonstrated by experiments in which subjects are given preliminary trials in which feedback indicates they are good or bad at a judging task. The more difficult the topic or task, the more a person conforms (Allen, 1965).

Hierarchical structure and role-differentiation

Although groups form norms, the members do not all behave identically. This is partly because there are different tasks to be done in a group, partly because members have different personalities. We saw earlier that in groups of primates a hierarchical order develops in which the dominant animals direct the group activity, provide defence against predators, and see that young animals are protected against larger ones (p. 34 ff). The emergence of a leadership hierarchy is characteristic of human groups too, but there are other kinds of role-differentiation as well. It is found that a clear leadership structure is more likely to appear under some conditions than others – these are the conditions in which a leader is required to direct and coordinate group activities.

(1) Bales *et al.* (1951) found a more unequal distribution of verbal acts in larger groups, and Hemphill (1950) found that in groups over 30 in size leader-centred direction was more acceptable; without firm leadership in a large group there is chaos.

(2) When decisions must be made quickly, an ineffective leader will quickly be replaced by another person, and a leader is allowed to be more influential (Hamblin, 1958). On the other hand trivial decisions are also delegated to a leader, so perhaps equalitarian and democratic processes flourish only for problems of intermediate urgency or importance (Jones and Gerard, 1967), or when there is enough time.

(3) When the task to be performed is complex, and when there are diverse persons or roles to be coordinated, there is probably greater need for an effective leader.

The emergence of a leadership hierarchy seems to be a universal feature of human groups. It may partly be arrived at by trial and error, as the best way of getting the task done. Perhaps the family provides a model, which is unwittingly copied in all other groups. There is also a cultural tradition in different societies, and experience in one group will generalise to others.

We are primarily concerned here with *informal* groups, i.e. groups where there are no *formal* ranks, titles or offices: formal organisations will be considered in Chapter VII. (We shall however deal with the family in this chapter since it is more like a small group than like a social organisation.) Although all members may be equal in age or social class, nevertheless some acquire greater power or status than the others. By leadership or power is meant a person's capacity to influence other members of the group. By status is meant the admiration or esteem which a person enjoys in the group.

There are some human groups where leadership is based on the physical size and fighting power of members, as is the case with primates. Apart from groups of small boys and juvenile delinquents, leadership in human groups is decided more on the basis of conversation and contribution to the group's problems. Bales has studied the pattern of verbal interaction in problem-solving groups of 3 to 8. Fig. 6.1 gives the totals of a number of groups, where each member has been ranked in order of number of communications sent. These results show clearly that some people communicate much more than others; the distribution is usually J-shaped, with the majority of members saying little. The larger the group, and the more unequal the status or competence of members, the more unequal are the rates of contribution. It was found that the people who say most are also addressed most, and they address the groups as a whole most, which is rarely done by the low contributors. The lows communicate upwards, highs to the group. The pattern of interaction is furthermore different for high and low contributors. The highs contribute more attempted solutions and information, lows agree or disagree and ask for information (Bales, 1953).

How does this J-shaped, hierarchical pattern of behaviour develop? It seems likely that people communicate as much as the rest of the group wants and permits them to, and that non-verbal reinforcements by the group control the rates. Banta and Nelson (1964) found that frequency of offering opinions in problem-solving groups could be increased or reduced by experimentally controlled agreement–disagreement. Differences in interaction rates may indeed increase within the group until checked, when an equilibrium level of differentiation has been reached

(Bales, 1953). Thus a person's final level of interaction is jointly determined by his motivation to talk and the value the others place upon it.
The process does not work perfectly, since some people are insensitive
to negative reactions, so that their rate of contribution may be high in
relation to their perceived value to the group. It takes time for a hierarchical structure to settle down to a stable pattern, and there is usually
a struggle for status in the early life of a group. There tends to be

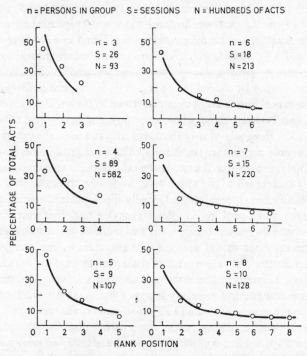

Figure 6.1. The distribution of participation in groups of different sizes
(from Bales *et al.*, 1951)

oscillation between attending to these interpersonal problems and
getting on with the group's work; until the internal problems have been
solved, work will be ineffective, and there will be wrangling and polar-
isation of opinion over trivial issues, reflecting disagreements over social
relationships (Bales, 1953; Tuckman, 1965).

Group members differ not only in the total amount of their contributions, but also in their style of social behaviour. We have already noted
the difference between highs and lows. These differences are often

referred to as the adoption of different 'roles' in the group, by which is meant that there are a limited number of alternative styles commonly adopted. Slater (1955) studied 20 discussion groups of 3–7 men, and found that there were varying degrees of role-differentiation; a common pattern was for there to be an ideas man and a best-liked man. The ideas man communicated a lot, particularly in the task area, while the best-liked man was high on showing solidarity, tension release, agreeing and asking questions. In similar studies of 5-man groups, Bales (1953) found that the person rated highest in 'guidance' and 'best ideas' was the highest interactor, but was disliked most and only third in positive choices. A rather similar differentiation was found in a study of 'Great Books' clubs by Davis (1961). He found that the roles of providing 'fuel' for discussion, putting the 'threads' together, and clarification, were often performed by the same person, while joking and making tactful remarks to heal hurt feelings were performed by others. Group members distinguish between those whose company they enjoy and choose as friends, and those whom they think can help to realise the group goals. Can the same person carry both roles? The Bales group report not, but Turk (1961) reports that the two leaders can coincide when members are strongly committed to the group task. As will be shown later, it is not only possible but essential that a formally appointed leader should carry both task and social roles. Slater (1955) found that there was a close social relationship between the two kinds of leader in his groups. It is certainly not always the case that two clear leaders emerge in a group. It is true that there are two main jobs to be done – organising the group to perform the external task, and resolving interpersonal problems and keeping members happy. On the other hand these two activities are closely related and a formal leader cannot perform the first effectively without at the same time performing the second. The democratic-persuasive-consultative style of leadership does both simul-taneously (p. 299 ff). Perhaps the subjects used in these experiments did not have the necessary social skills, or perhaps it is more difficult for an informal leader to use these techniques. Males and females often play their characteristic roles – males are task-oriented and dominant, females are socially oriented and submissive.

We can analyse group hierarchies in terms of the different amounts of power, influence or leadership which each member can exercise. This may be defined as the extent to which a member can and does influence others, and it can be assessed by observation of influence attempts. Lippitt *et al.* (1952) counted the numbers of attempts at influence made by 127 boys at two camps, and also the percentages of successful influence attempts. Power can be assessed from ratings made by group members about 'who is best at getting others to do what he wants them to do?', as used in the study above. Many of the earlier studies in this area used the term 'leadership' rather than power, and tried to find the person or persons who had most influence on the group, using observations or ratings (Gibb, 1969). A person can be said to have power or influence over one person, or a group, and the internal power structure of a group can be analysed.

Many studies were carried out to find the personality correlates of leadership. Rather small correlations were found between leadership in general and personality traits. In any particular group and situation however leadership depends entirely on the personal attributes of those present – but which these are varies greatly between different situations and groups. The situation – the external task – calls for someone who is an expert on the task in question and can help the group towards its goals; leadership is found to rotate if a group is confronted by a series of different tasks or situations (Carter and Nixon, 1949). Leadership and influence in an informal group are a matter of degree – there is no clear separation of leader and led as there is in groups with appointed leaders. Furthermore *all* group members have some influence on the group. Hollander and Webb (1955) found that group members nominated much the same people as followers as they would for leaders – but they did not nominate them as friends. Leaders, like followers, are chosen because they are good at the job.

The group – the internal task – calls for someone who can synchronise with the rest of the group in a rewarding relationship and maintain cohesion. Haythorn *et al.* (1965) found that authoritarian groups get on best with authoritarian leaders; it has often been found that there is some correlation between informal leadership and intelligence, extraversion, adjustment and social sensitivity (Mann, 1959; Gibb, 1969). It is not only a matter of social skill, though this is important; it is necessary to have the kind of personality that fits into the group in the right way. Whether or not a person becomes a leader also depends on his motivation – his involvement in the group and its goals, his motivation to lead, and hence the amount of time and effort he is prepared to put in. Some are motivated to lead, others to be dependent, others to establish affiliative relations – the latter will become the socio-emotional leaders.

The various sources of power are discussed in the next chapter (p. 286 ff). How is power related to social interaction? By definition powerful individuals are able to exert greater influence; the Lippitt *et al.* (1952)

study shows how those rated as powerful tried to influence others more often, and were more often successful. Bandura *et al.* (1963) found that there was also more voluntary imitation of powerful confederates. Powerful people can influence the group, including the change of group norms; this is partly achieved through the powerful person having greater freedom of action, or permission to deviate (see p. 227). How successful a person will be also depends on his social skill – how skilfully he persuades and manipulates the others.

The powerful person will contribute more in group discussion – Bass (1949) found a correlation between interaction rate and ratings of leadership in 10-man groups. He also enjoys the interaction more. There is some truth in the theory that there is an 'exchange of rewards', and that the more powerful people are given power by the other members because they are useful. On the other hand the most powerful members receive more rewards, and there are usually others who would like to have more influence than they do.

The hierarchical structure of groups can be analysed in terms of *status* differences. We will define a person's status as the extent to which he is esteemed, admired or approved by other members of the group. This is distinct from his popularity – based on affection, and his power – based on his ability to influence. Groups develop stable status structures, in which the placement of members is fairly well agreed. Feelings of subjective status also correspond fairly well with status awarded by others. Status is based on factors such as excellence of performance, to be discussed shortly. It is associated with objective rewards, such as higher rank or pay, and is indicated by visible status symbols, such as clothes, size of desks and thickness of carpet.

Status appears to be based on conformity to group norms, superior attainment in directions valued by the group, contribution of effort and other costs expended in group affairs. Homans (1961) sees status primarily as recognition by the group in exchange for rewarding services received. This principle does not hold when status is awarded to people of higher social class, or some other external kind of rank. (In the wider society social classes develop from equivalent levels of various hierarchies; a person's position in this system becomes recognisable through the cultural differences between classes.) Excellence of performance in different spheres, status awarded by the group, and tangible rewards may get out of step, and this is called 'status incongruence'. Several studies show that the individuals concerned feel uncomfortable, the group is ineffective, and that changes will occur in the group to improve the alignment of the different aspects of status (Benoit-Smullyan, 1944;

Trow and Herschdorfer, 1965). The explanation for this phenomenon may lie in reduction of cognitive dissonance or the difficulty of predicting behaviour and interacting when there are conflicting indices of status. People strive to increase their status, and to make maximum use of dimensions on which their status is highest. This is an important aspect of self-presentation. Status symbols are both used by individuals for this purpose, and awarded by the group to them. There can be violent rivalry for status, especially when two people are in a similar position and the treatment they receive is highly visible – as in the case of sibling rivalry (Thibaut and Kelley, 1959).

How do status differences affect social interaction in a group? No detailed evidence appears to be available, but the phenomena are fairly familiar. The high-status person is treated with respect and deference; not only may he receive higher pay or other material benefits, but he is rewarded interpersonally as well – which seems to go against exchange-theory expectations. On the other hand he will not receive affiliative rewards since lower-status individuals find his presence makes them nervous and uneasy, and there may not be reciprocity of his efforts for others (see p. 174 f). Around the man who has just been to the moon, or made some great discovery, there is a kind of almost holy atmosphere. His company is sought, since sheer association with him confers status on others. While others are nervous and excited, he is genial and relaxed, secure in his position in the group, and conveying rewards to others at little cost to himself.

In addition to differences of power or status, role-differentiation of other kinds appears within groups. We have discussed the emergence of task and socio-emotional leaders above. It is found that members of problem-solving groups specialise in different aspects of the task – a kind of division of labour; this is more likely to happen in larger groups (Thomas and Fink, 1963). In every kind of group some kind of role-differentiation takes place, but the roles which appear are different, as will be shown below. Three possible explanations may be suggested for the appearance of different roles in a group.

(1) There may be a number of definite jobs to be done in the group. The emergence of two kinds of leaders in discussion groups is an example of this. It would be expected that different kinds of groups would have rather different tasks – a committee needs a secretary, a coffee-group needs someone to make the coffee. On this theory if the person who usually fills the role is absent, another person should step into it. The experimental removal of individuals from groups would therefore show whether a role was essential or not.

(2) There is extensive evidence that individuals with different personalities behave differently in groups (Chapter VIII). The observed differences in behaviour could simply be due to personality factors. Clearly this is not the whole story, since there can only be one task leader, and other dominant individuals would have to find somewhat different parts to play. If there is a choice of roles, people try to take the one which is most congenial. Mann (1967) found that there are seven common roles in T-groups (p. 269 f); Bossard and Boll (1956) found eight common roles for the children of large families (p. 244 f). It is not known how far these roles represent group tasks, or how far they represent the main preferences by different personalities. The two leader roles are probably roles that have to be done by someone, but the same may not be true of the others.

(3) A third possible source of role-differentiation is the desire of members to present themselves as unique individuals. It is found that there is greater specialisation in different aspects of the group task in larger groups (Thomas and Fink, 1963), though this could be accounted for by the first theory. On the individuation hypothesis, if a number of very similar personalities are put together in a group, there should be divergence of behaviour.

The affective structure

There are three main kinds of human group – family, work and friendship groups. Friendship groups exist entirely because the members like one another (there are attitudes of liking and disliking in the other kinds of group too). Primates spend much of their time playing with or grooming their friends. Friendship groups are composed largely of peers, and it has been suggested that they have a function in society of integrating families and organisations and providing channels of communication, as well as satisfying various social needs for individuals. At different phases in the life-cycle individuals spend different amounts of their time with the three kinds of group. The most accessible subjects for research purposes – students – are at a time of life when friendship groups are the most important, and research on affective structure has been mainly concerned with these groups.

One way of analysing the internal structure of a small social group is in terms of likings and dislikings, attractions and repulsions, between pairs of members. The most widely used technique for measuring these is that of *sociometry*, devised by Moreno (1953). Each member is simply asked which other members he would choose (or reject) as companions for some joint activity. Moreno's rules, which have not always been followed, are that (1) the choice should be made from a limited group, (2) subjects should be given an unlimited number of choices or rejections (in practice they are often given from 1 to 3), (3) choices are made in terms of specific activities, (4) the results of the sociometric survey are actually used to rearrange the group (often omitted in research studies), (5) choices are private, and (6) members should understand the question. The 'criteria', or activities used, are usually of three main kinds: choosing the other for (a) leisure-time activities, (b) work or (c) leadership. Leadership nominations have been considered above. Leisure and work choices correspond to the two main aspects of groups distinguished previously – socio-emotional and task. Socio-emotional choices correspond to the satisfaction of affiliative and other interpersonal needs, while task choices reflect achievement and other task

Figure 6.2

motivations, and the other's capacity to contribute to the group task. Factor analyses of interpersonal attitudes have confirmed the value of this approach: three dimensions commonly appear – influence and initiative, task competence, and like–dislike (Tagiuri, 1958). While leisure or socio-emotional choices reflect the third, work and leadership reflect the other two.

The total set of choices between members can be plotted to form a sociogram, as in Fig. 6.2. Some of the main structural features which may be found in a sociogram can be seen here. C is popular (a 'star'); E is not chosen by anyone (an 'isolate'); XYZ is a triangle, and ABCF is a larger clique; there is a 'cleavage' between XYZ and the rest; there is mutual choice between A and B and several other pairs. When rejections are plotted as well, the plot thickens. A number of quantitative indices have been devised for summarising sociometric data; the most useful is that for *cohesiveness*, taken as the percentage of total choices made to other members of a particular sub-group.

When a group first forms, members choose the same people for all activities; as they get to know each other they choose different people for leisure, work and other criteria. More of the leisure choices are reciprocated – 70% versus 35% for work choices – and leisure choices are more evenly distributed through the group (Jennings, 1950). Mutuality is more common for choices such as 'sit next to' than for leadership or achievement-oriented criteria (Criswell, 1949).

There is no doubt that this simple technique provides a very valuable method of studying groups, and it is often used by teachers and administrators for selecting sub-groups, and for finding out what is happening (Lindzey and Borgatta, 1954). There are several criticisms that could be made. Firstly, the sociometric method fails to bring out the immense differences between different types of 'choice' – between husband and wife, committee member and chairman, adolescent friends, etc. These relationships will be discussed later in the chapter. Secondly like all measures and indices, it abstracts certain things and overlooks the rest: whether or not A chooses B as a companion for some activity does not tell us much about the relationship – even though this is one of the most important dimensions of interpersonal attitudes. The complexities of interaction between two people are very great, as we have seen, and it may be doubted how far these simple attitudinal variables are adequate. Thirdly, sociometry treats a group as the sum of a number of dyadic relationships; however, this is only part of the story – A's relation to B may be quite changed if C is going to be there too.

When a number of people are present in a social situation, the group often divides up into smaller groups. Even in groups of three, a sub-group of two may separate off. Mills (1953) studied 48 3-man groups which were asked to produce a single story from three TAT pictures. He found that most communications were exchanged between the two most active members, and that the third was virtually isolated. Robson (1967) repeated this study using different sex-combinations. He found that in mixed-sex triads the two members of the same sex competed to form a liaison with the other member. In 3-female triads there was more mutual support than in 3-male groups; there were coalitions, but the least active female received the most support of any member. These results are consistent with other findings to the effect that females are more affiliative, more concerned with socio-emotional problems, and less competitive than males.

One reason for the formation of sub-groups is that in larger groups there is a highly skewed distribution of participation; many members cannot participate as much as they would like to, and they have little say in decisions. For many purposes a group size of about 5 is preferred – members can talk as much as they like and there is sufficient variety of interests and diversity of talents in the group (Hare

1962). Sub-groups may form because of common interests, or because there is an 'in-group' of people with something in common.

A group may in time divide permanently into sub-groups. Such sub-grouping comes about in much the same way as friendship choices and group-formation – frequency of interaction, similar attributes, etc. In work settings sub-groups may divide because they are doing different work, or are differently located (Roethlisberger and Dickson, 1939); in leisure groups it may be more a matter of mutual compatibility and similarity of interests. Sub-groups may divide vertically or horizontally. It is common for a miniature class system to develop, most interaction taking place between people of equal status. On the other hand both communications and sociometric choices are skewed slightly upwards, i.e. are directed to people slightly more popular (Riecken and Homans, 1954) or powerful (Mulder *et al.*, 1964). There is a difference between a sub-group forming because of common interests, for example business or political interests, and a sub-group forming temporarily because interaction is more congenial that way – although ease of interaction is certainly one basis for permanent association.

A *coalition* is a number of people who act jointly to improve their outcomes at the expense of the other members. Gamson (1964) argues that the experiments by Mills and Robson are not strictly studies of coalitions since it is not clear that outcomes were affected – though it could be argued that a mutually supportive sub-group is a coalition by virtue of the interpersonal rewards involved. Experimental analyses of coalitions have been set up, mostly consisting of dice-throwing games, where different players multiply their scores by different weights. As in other experimental games, all interaction was excluded. (This research is reviewed by Gamson, op. cit.) It is found that if A has a weight of 2, B of 2, and C of 3, then A and B will form a coalition against C (Vinacke and Arkoff, 1957). It may be suggested that this kind of experiment is very far removed from social interaction. However, the behaviour observed in the dice-game experiments is not entirely without interest to social psychologists. While male subjects behave in a Machiavellian manner to maximise their own gains, female subjects do not; Bond and Vinacke (1961) conclude that females try to arrive at a fair and just division of outcomes and avoid competition. Males are 'exploitive' and females are 'accommodative'. Furthermore such anti-competitive behaviour was found to pay off in the course of a long series of games, since mutual trust was established.

How is the sociometric structure related to social interaction? The most important link is simply that there is more interaction between people who choose each other; interaction leads to liking, and liking leads to interaction, and they are two aspects of the same relationship (p. 211 f). The nature of the interaction almost certainly varies too, with sociometric choice, and between work and leisure choices, and between single and mutual choices, but this has not as yet been documented. It has however been found that more aggression can occur when there are stronger sociometric links, probably because there is less fear of disrupting the relationship. In cohesive groups there is less absenteeism and labour turnover – people are less likely to leave a group when sociometric links are strong. Conformity pressures are stronger, and it is usually found that more conformity occurs in cohesive groups (Lott and Lott, 1965).

FIVE KINDS OF SMALL SOCIAL GROUP

The concentration of research on laboratory groups has diverted attention away from the very varied kinds of interaction taking place in real-life groups. We shall describe interaction in the three most important types of group – the family, work-groups and groups of friends (we shall concentrate on adolescent friendship groups). In addition an account will be given of some other kinds of group which have been extensively studied – committees, T-groups and therapy groups. We shall describe the environmental settings of these groups, the motivation of members, the task, the social structure, and the special patterns of interaction found in them. To do this we draw on descriptive sociological and clinical studies, some of them not particularly rigorous, and we shall not shrink from stating the obvious. Recent books about groups have overlooked the obvious but extremely important differences between these different kinds of group.

The family as a small group

There is something like a family in all species of mammals: the mother has to care for the young, and the father often provides food and protection during this period. Only in humans does the father become an enduring member of the family, and only in humans is there a life-long link between children and parents. What is probably the most important kind of small group in human society is often overlooked by small group researchers – and consequently there are important features of the family group which have never been embodied in small group experiments or theorising.

The nuclear family consists of two parents, sons and daughters, and can thus be regarded as a four-role system, divided by generation and sex (Parsons and Bales, 1955). There are also characteristic relations between older and younger brothers, and between older and younger sisters, so that it may be better to see the family as potentially a six-role system, though not all the positions may be filled (Murdock, 1949). The basic features of the relationship between each pair of positions are much the same in all human societies. For example between older and younger brothers there is a 'relationship of playmates, developing into that of comrades; economic co-operation under leadership of elder; moderate responsibility of elder for instruction and discipline of younger' (Murdock, op. cit.). The family has some of the features of a formal organisation – a set of positions, each associated with a role, including patterns of interaction with occupants of other positions (see Chapter VII).

There are considerable cross-cultural variations in the composition of the family unit. There are variations in the number of wives or husbands, in the role of uncles, aunts and grandparents, and in the living arrangements. In rural Ghana for example the domestic unit consists of a compound presided over by a grandmother, with sheds or huts for her daughters and their families. It is common in primitive societies for the domestic unit to be larger than in Western society, and for extended kinship ties to assume greater importance. In Western society these relationships are generally more important in the working class, and are taken more seriously by women.

The parents are drawn together by a combination of sexual and other motivations; they have protective and nurturant motivations towards the children, the children have dependent motivations towards the parents, at least until adolescence. The parents join up voluntarily, in most societies; the children do not, indeed their mode of entry to the group is rather unusual; it is also very difficult for members of the family group to leave it. The relations between family members depend not only on their personalities, but also on their positions in a role-structure, and possession of different degrees of power. In this respect the family resembles a formal organisation, like a school or hospital, rather than an informal group of equals with no appointed leader. The pattern of this role-structure, the prescribed relationship between family members, and their relative power, vary greatly between societies, social classes and historical periods. Herbst (1952) studied the roles of husband and wife by asking children who did what; he found that activities could be ordered from wife's (e.g. ironing) to husband's (e.g.

paying for holidays), and that there was most conflict over activities in the middle; if a husband dealt with any one area, he would deal with all those below it in the list, as in a Guttman scale. Blood and Wolfe (1960) did a field study of 731 wives in Detroit; they too found that husbands and wives controlled different domains, and also that husbands were more likely to be dominant if they were economically successful, the wife did not have a job, the wife needed love and affection, and if the wife was younger. Strodtbeck (1951) created disagreements experimentally between husbands and wives from different cultures and found that among Mormons the husband usually won, among Navaho Indians the wife did, while Texans were intermediate. The detailed analysis of culture variations in kinship relationships has been a major preoccupation of anthropologists. The traditional British working-class family had a rigid division between the husband who was the wage-earner, was given the best food and was waited on by the female members, and the wife who had to manage the home and the children with what money the husband gave her. This pattern has been changing in the direction of the middle-class family with less rigid role division, more shared interests and more cooperation over running the home (McGregor and Rowntree, 1962). This role-differentiation corresponds to the 'task' and 'maintenance' functions found in leaders of other kinds of small group. Zelditch (1955) has found that it exists in most societies, though the differentiation of father and mother roles is least in the American middle class.

The power relations of family members are greatly dependent on money – the main wage-earner generally has the most power. The control of parents over children is in addition strengthened by the law, so that they can call in external authorities to help deal with the children if necessary.

Unlike groups of friends, family members have tasks to perform. In primitive societies these are mainly the growing and preparation of food, the rearing and education of children, and maintenance of the house. In modern society some of these activities are performed by outside agencies, but there are still the domestic jobs connected with eating, sleeping and the care of young children. In addition there are leisure activities such as TV, gardening, games and family outings. Some of these are like activities of friends in that they are performed because of the interaction involved. Interaction in the family is closely connected with these joint activities – eating, watching or playing together. Interaction is also brought about through the members pursuing their private goals under conditions of physical proximity, and where their joint activities have to be more or less closely coordinated – this is an extension of the necessity for meshing. The physical environment and technology have an important effect on family life. Overcrowding of other animals results in aggression, and the murder rate is greater in overcrowded areas (Henry and Short, 1954). The family tasks include looking after one another, in particular caring for the bodily needs of members: in addition to close physical proximity there is also intimacy and interdependence.

Family groups are linked to other groups. There are relations, who are peripheral members of the family group and who may live nearby and be the people most frequently seen. This is common in primitive society, and has also been found among working-class British families (Young and Wilmott, 1957). Members of the family group belong to other groups – of friends and neighbours, and at work and school, in which they lead a second life, with more emphasis on self-presentation and, for the last two, on task activities. Elizabeth Bott (1957) found that these links make up a network rather than a social group, except in small closed communities. She also found some evidence that families with greater segregation of marital roles were more involved with the network of social links outside the family.

What goes on inside the family is private and not readily subject to external control. Models of how families should behave are however provided by magazines and TV, and by the previous families of the parents. The actual elements of interaction of which family life consists differ from all other groups, in that greater intimacy, aggression, affection and emotional violence occurs. Family members see each other undressed, or naked, and there is almost no attempt at self-presentation; they know each other's weaknesses and understand each other extremely well; family life is very much 'off-stage', in Goffman's terminology (1956a). There is physical aggression, mainly of parents towards children, but also between children; there is aggression between parents, but it is mainly verbal. Affection is equally violent and often takes the form of bodily contact, between parents, and between parents and children until they 'get too old for it'. Members of laboratory groups do not usually take their clothes off, laugh uproariously, cry, attack or kiss each other, or crawl all over each other, as members of families commonly do. Interaction in the family is more complex and subtle than most other interaction because of the intense and complex relationships between members, and their long history of previous interaction. Spiegel (1956) describes cases of tense mother–daughter interaction, and suggests that various unconscious fantasies and projections are taking place in addition to what seems to be occurring. This is similar to the inter-personal behaviour found in some neurotics (p. 348). The subtler non-verbal communications may be very important – as in the possible effect of 'double-bind' parents in making children schizophrenic (p. 340 f). The dimensions of parent behaviour which have the greatest effect on children however are probably warmth *v*. rejection, strictness *v*. permissiveness, and type of discipline (Sears, Maccoby and Levin, 1957).

The family group is in a state of some degree of equilibrium much of the time, but there are continual crises – illness, difficulties with the children, financial and so on. With each crisis there is a temporary period of dislocation, followed by a gradual return to the previous equilibrium or a shift to a new one (Waller and Hill, 1951). Sometimes it is impossible to re-establish equilibrium: a common result is that one member of the family leaves the home, temporarily or permanently. The family group displays the structural features of other kinds of groups, but in special ways. The hierarchical structure of power and influence depends mainly on cultural roles, but there can be variations depending on attributes of the members. Koos (1946) found among New York tenement families that the father could lose his position of dominance if he failed to deal with an emergency, and that the mother or even a child would replace him. The sibling hierarchy is fairly rigid, though inequalities of intelligence, earning power or other kinds of competence can change it. We showed above that role-differentiation occurs between fathers and mothers, in a way similar to other small groups. There may also be role-differentiation between the children. Bossard and Boll (1956) studied 100 families with six or more children and found that the following roles were most common, in this order: (1) *responsible*, looks after others (often oldest daughter), (2) *most popular* (often second-born), (3) *socially ambitious*, social butterfly (usually later-born daughter), (4) *studious*, (5) *self-centred isolate* (often the only one of a sex), (6) *irresponsible*, (7) *not well*, (8) *spoiled* (often the last-born). Most of them are not roles in the sense that someone has to play them, though in a large family the first two may be like this – corresponding to the task and socio-emotional leaders of other groups.

The sociometric structure of the family group differs from that of all other groups in the quality and intensity of the bonds. The two parents were initially drawn together by sexual desire and the other complex dyadic processes making up romantic love (p. 214 f). The parents see their children as part of themselves, and the children are closely dependent on them – both bonds are extremely strong affectional ties. Parents and children may not 'like' one another particularly but there is still a powerful bond. It is found that parents never really recover from the death of a child (Gorer, 1965), and the death of a parent is highly damaging to the later mental health of a child (p. 344). Relations between siblings are rather different: their essentially competitive relationship can produce intense hostility, and the links in later life can be weak. Adams (1967) points out that kinship relations are quite different from friendship outside the family: there is a feeling of obligation and concern for the other, the link is very long-lasting, and there is a feeling both of responsibility for the other and of sharing in his activities. Adams suggests that the early intimacy and shared emotional experience create this kind of social bond. There may however be a similar feeling for relations outside the nuclear family – the so-called 'blood-tie'. There may be a feeling of shared identity with a person who carries the same name or who has some of the same physical features.

The family is usually divided into two sub-groups – the parents and the children. The older children may cross the line into the parental group, and the grouping may cut across generations, especially in an incestuous way, and this is associated with later schizophrenia in the children (p. 340). Families have norms about a very wide range of matters. The parents usually decide how everything shall be done, set the style of life, and have a shared outlook on life. This is all picked up by the children, so that by 11–12 they have accepted and learnt the parental ways. During adolescence there is an attempt to become independent of the family, and some or most of these conventions are rejected, for a time at least. Families also develop 'rituals', especially about what happens at meals, on holidays, at anniversaries and during leisure time. These are particularly marked when there are young children, and in middle-class families. Bossard and Boll (1950) maintain that rituals serve the functions of binding the family together, keeping discipline, maintaining traditional values and promoting a feeling of social well-being.

Parsons and Bales (1955) argue that the family group is like other small groups, such as laboratory discussion groups, in showing the same kind of role-differentiation, etc. There are however a number of features of family groups which are absent from most other kinds of small group. (1) There is a formal role-structure, whose pattern is defined by the culture. (2) There is little self-presentation, while there is greater intimacy and intensity of interpersonal feelings, both of love and hate. (3) The links between members have extra qualities lacking in other groups – romantic love, parent–child relations and the 'blood-tie'; these go beyond the bases for sociometric choice considered so far. (4) The

family group lasts, in a changing form, for a great many years; the bonds
are very long-lasting.

Adolescent groups

Friendship groups are one of the basic forms of social grouping in animals
and men; they are distinguished by the fact that members are brought
together primarily through interpersonal motivations and attractions,
not through concern with any task. Of all friendship groups, adolescent
groups are the most interesting. During adolescence work and family
attachments are weak and the strongest attachments are to friends.
These groups are formed of young people between the ages of 11–12 up
to 21–23, when the members marry and settle down in jobs, and other
kinds of group become more important to them. The motivations of
members are partly to engage in various joint activities, but more
important are interpersonal needs – sexual, affiliative, and the establishment of identity. It has been suggested that there are certain 'developmental tasks' during this period of life to develop an identity independent of the family, and to establish a changed relation with adults
(Erikson, 1956; Muuss, 1962). The environmental setting of adolescent
groups tends to be public places such as coffee-bars, clubs and dance-
halls, and to a lesser extent schools and the homes of members. Adolescent social activity is often thought to fill a gap which exists in modern
societies between the world of children in families and school, and the
world of work and the establishment of another family some years later
(Sherif and Cantril, 1947). Adolescent groups are established *outside* the
regular institutions of family life and work. They are also established
independently of the influence of adults: adolescents are trying first to
become independent of parents and other adults, and then to meet them
on terms of equality; it is in groups of other adolescents that this independence is established. Sometimes young adults can play a role in these
groups – as club leaders for example – if they behave as sympathetic
older members of the group.

   These phenomena vary with the cultural setting: there is no gap
between childhood and adulthood in most primitive societies, and a
rapid transition is assisted by initiation rites. Teenage culture appeared
in the USA shortly before World War II, and has since spread to many
other countries. In Great Britain the evolution of teenage society has
been one of the greatest social changes since 1950, and is thought to be
responsible for the increase in crime over this period (Argyle, 1964b).
The mass media play an important role in the diffusion of styles of teen-

age behaviour (Riesman *et al.*, 1950), and opinion leaders in these groups pass on the latest ideas. Advertisements aimed at teenagers have had a big effect by creating a demand for clothes, records, scooters and so on, and have thus helped to develop a special teenage culture. Eugene Gilbert in the USA made a fortune from developing advertising techniques directed towards teenagers (Macdonald, 1958).

The activities of adolescent groups vary with the culture: in the USA groups of boys are concerned with cars, entertainment, sport and girls (Sherif and Sherif, 1964). There is avoidance of the tasks of home and school. Many group activities are invented, whose chief point is the social interaction involved – such as dancing, listening to records, and drinking coffee. The forms of social interaction involved are rather different from those in other groups – there is more bodily contact, joking, aggressive horseplay, and just being together, less problem-centred discussion. Schmuck and Lohman (1965) observe that 'adolescents in a group often engage in infantile behaviour and pranks, while giggling and laughing hilariously; and are encouraged to feel silly together, and to withhold evaluation from such experiences' (p. 27). They suggest that this behavioural abandon has a regressive element. There is an easy intimacy and social acceptance of those who wear the right uniform. Conversation is mainly about other adolescents, parents, interpersonal feelings and social interaction. These are probably the only natural groups that discuss social interaction (T-groups do it too). Such topics are discussed because adolescents have problems to solve in this area – as well as working out an identity and establishing a changed relationship with adults, they have to acquire the social skills of dealing with the opposite sex, to come to terms with the difficulty of playing different roles on different occasions, and having relationships of different degrees of intimacy with different people (Fleming, 1963).

Adolescent groups show the three main forms of social structure which have been discussed – informal hierarchy, sociometric structure and norms – but in special ways. There is no marked hierarchy of power or leadership, since there is no central task activity. There are leaders for particular activities and leadership is found to rotate as the group does different things, such as football and crime in the case of delinquent groups, the person best at each activity becoming temporarily the leader. There are also opinion leaders, whose guidance is accepted on such matters as clothes, or films (Katz and Lazarsfeld, 1955). More important is the sociometric structure. Adolescent groups are small – often three to six in size, and the friendships are intense, more so than those formed later in life. Thus an important aspect of the structure of adolescent group concerns who is in and who is out. Adults, children and other kinds of adolescent – e.g. mods *v.* rockers *v.* hippies, etc., are 'out' and can instantly be seen to be out by their appearance. Social acceptance is a matter of great concern, and most adolescents are concerned with it. Sub-groups and opposite-sex pairs make up the internal structure of the group. Sociometric choice is partly determined by similarity and proximity. Popularity goes to those who realise the adolescent values most fully; Coleman (1963) in his study of American high schools found that boys who were athletic and girls who were beautiful were most popular, those who were brainy not quite so popular. Conformity to norms is one of the most striking features of these groups. The norms of adults or of the outside world may be violently rejected, and replaced by various kinds of informality, deviance or even criminality, but the norms of the group are slavishly conformed to. Sherif and Sherif (op. cit.) observe that members do not conform through fear of sanctions but willingly commit themselves to the norms because they belong to the group and the group is very important to them; sanctions are used however if a member's deviation threatens the existence of the group. There are norms in three main areas. (1) Those regulating interpersonal matters, such as dating (p. 224 f); interpersonal behaviour, sexual and affiliative, is the main purpose of these groups, and norms are needed to regulate it. (2) Those relating to group activities such as dancing, sport or pop music. (3) There are strong norms about clothes and hair, probably because they define who belongs to the group and thus convey identity. Adolescents are often worried about their physical appearance – 31% of boys and 41% of girls think at some time during adolescence that their bodies are inadequate in some way (Stolz and Stolz, 1944). Appropriate clothes are part of the solution to this problem. Adolescents are very self-conscious, and fear rejection by the group and collapse of identity if their appearance is wrong (Garrison, 1951).

Adolescent groups are of interest to us because a number of special processes can be seen, which are not present in laboratory groups. (1) There is no specific task, but joint activities are devised which entail the kinds of interaction which meet the needs of members (2). One of these needs is the establishing of an ego-identity, independent of the family of origin (Erikson, 1956). This explains the emphasis on clothes, the great self-consciousness, and the concern about acceptance by members of these groups. (3) Sexual motivation is a major factor in adolescent groups, and is partly responsible for the intensity of attraction to the groups, and for their pairing structure. (4) There is a group task of acquiring together the social skills of dealing with the opposite sex and dealing with adults.

Work-groups

In groups of animals the work of gathering food and building homes is often carried out by males. In ants it is a specialised and highly organised group activity. In primitive society this work may be carried out by males or females, and follows a seasonal cycle. In modern communities work outside the home has become a highly specialised activity, mainly performed by adult males, for financial reward, and is done in special social organisations. Work is performed in groups for several reasons – (1) One man alone may not be able to perform the task; in primitive societies this is the case with hunting and building; (2) there can be division of labour, so that different people can use or develop specialised skills; this is a central feature of work in modern communities; (3) people prefer to work together because of their social motivations; (4) another factor is social facilitation; the presence of others is arousing, so more work is done. Even ants work harder when there is more than one of them on the job (Zajonc, 1965).

Work-groups are at the opposite pole from adolescent groups in that their primary concern is with carrying out a task. They are the other main kind of group outside the family in which adults spend most of their time. They are not so well defined as the other two kinds, and often have no clear membership. It is sometimes difficult, in a factory for example, to decide which are the group – all that can be seen are a lot of people, some of whom collaborate over work or interact informally from time to time. Such groups can be defined in terms of the formal organisation – having the same supervisor or being paid jointly, or in terms of informal group-formation – sociometric cliques, or people who think of themselves as a group. Much research in this area has been on groups of manual workers – gangs of men engaged in the maintenance of railway track, men on assembly lines. There has also been research on the more technically skilled men in charge of automated plant, and recently attention has turned to the work of engineers, accountants, scientists and managers. In these latter cases much of the social interaction is between people two at a time, so there is a network rather than a group. They may also meet in committees and similar talking and decision-taking groups, which will be discussed separately in the following section. In this section we are concerned with groups which have a definite task to do, and where the social interaction arises out of the task activity.

The members of work-groups are usually adults, and the majority of them are male, apart from secretaries and other occupants of female roles. The organisation exists to complete certain tasks, and members are partly motivated by task-related motivations – such as the need for money and achievement motivation. In addition members bring to the work situation a number of social needs: Schein (1965) suggests that these are the needs for affiliation, for identity and self-esteem, to check attitudes and perceptions against social reality, for security and power, and for mutual help, e.g. when tired or ill. The behaviour of work-groups is thus a joint product of task-related and purely social motivation, and consists of extra social interaction superimposed on the formal interaction necessary for the job.

Work-groups exist in a complex environmental setting, only part of which will be dealt with here. There is usually a formally appointed leader, or supervisor; the effects of appointed leaders on groups will be considered in the next chapter. The nature of the task, and its physical layout, will affect interaction between members (p. 306 ff). Task activity is the primary purpose of work-groups, and most research has been with the social conditions for maximum productivity. The Hawthorne experiment, in which five girls in a test room showed large increases in output over a five-year period, produced high hopes for the effects of various social factors on output (Roethlisberger and Dickson, 1939). The results of that experiment could however be accounted for entirely in terms of uncontrolled factors, such as the changed incentive arrangements, the replacement of the two slowest girls by two faster ones, and the reduced variety of work done (Argyle, 1953). Although fallacious in its conclusions this experiment was nevertheless of great historical importance. Another part of the Hawthorne studies is also interesting: workers in the Bank Wiring Observation Room developed strong norms of output restriction. Numerous studies have shown that work-groups can develop goals which are opposed to those of the organisation, and that cohesive work-groups can enforce relevant behaviour on members. It has been argued that industrial organisations often fail to satisfy the affiliative and other motivations of their members (Argyris, 1957); where this is so, groups are liable to devise means of satisfying them. Examples of this are social interaction where this entails leaving the work-place, and output restriction. When social needs are satisfied job satisfaction is greater. Studies of manual workers show that those who belong to small and cohesive work-groups are more satisfied. Furthermore, when workers are higher in job satisfaction their labour turnover and voluntary absenteeism are reduced (Argyle, 1957a).

However, Herzberg *et al.* (1959) have produced evidence to show that engineers, accountants and a variety of other workers receive most positive satisfaction from achievement and recognition – social factors, they say, only produce dissatisfaction.

It is often found that cohesive groups have more favourable attitudes towards the supervisor and the company, higher output, and higher job satisfaction, lower absenteeism and labour turnover (Lott and Lott, 1965; Likert, 1961). The term 'morale' is sometimes used to refer to one or some combination of these variables, but we think it better to use this term to refer to a 'positive attitude to the goals of the organisation' (Argyle, 1964c). However, cohesive groups do not always do more work; if the task prevents social interaction cohesive groups may do less work as a result of stopping work to talk. When the work requires inter-action, as in groups of bricklayers, cohesive groups do more work (Van Zelst, 1952) – here the task activity satisfies social needs. Cohesive groups do show strong conformity to norms, and there may be a norm of high productivity or for output restriction. Sayles (1958) found four main kinds of work-groups in a car factory, cohesiveness being one of the key variables. (1) *Apathetic groups* – low cohesion and no clear leadership, no strong grievances but low output found among men doing jobs with low pay and skills, for example on long assembly lines. (2) *Erratic groups* – cohesive with centralised leadership, which may swing suddenly to violent pro-union or pro-management activity, seem to have deep-seated grievances; found among men doing identical jobs. (3) *Strategic groups* – highly cohesive, high union activity and con-tinuous pressure about grievances; found among highly skilled and paid workers doing individual jobs. (4) *Conservative groups* – moderately cohesive, few grievances, high output; found among men in highest-status jobs. If they have a sufficiently cooperative attitude, cohesive groups are more productive, especially at tasks requiring cooperation (Schutz, 1958), presumably because coordination over the joint task is more easily accomplished.

What form does interaction take in work-groups? In the first place the task performance may partly consist of interaction. If A passes a brick to B this is both task behaviour and interaction; if A likes B, more bricks will be passed (Van Zelst, op. cit.). He will pass them with accom-panying verbal and non-verbal signals, not strictly necessary for the task, but which sustain the social relationship. If A talks to B, where B is his supervisor, or colleague, it is impossible to disentangle the task and the informal interaction elements of the conversation. Much work in fact consists almost entirely of social interaction – the work of supervisors, interviewers, teachers and many others. In addition to interaction linked to the task, interaction may take place during coffee-breaks, in the lunch hour, after hours, and during unauthorised pauses from work. Non-verbal communication, such as gestures, may occur during the work process. Social interaction of the usual kind is perhaps more limited in work-groups than in groups of other kinds. The relationships established may only operate in the work situation – as when good working relations exist between members of different racial and social class groups. Only part of the personality is involved, but it is an important part, and work-relations can be very important to people. Friendships are made at work, especially between people of equal status in the organisation; many of the links joining family members to the outside world are made in the work situation. Relationships at work may also, on occasion, resemble the relaxed informality of the family. This is most common among young people, who know each other very well, and have shared emotional experiences. Life in the services has something of this quality. There is often considerable intensity of feeling in work-groups, because the economic position, the career, the self-image and sometimes the safety of members is at stake.

Work-groups show many of the same principles of social organisation as laboratory groups, which have often been replicas of work-groups. They usually have an appointed leader, but in addition to him, one or more informal leaders may emerge as well. If the foreman is ineffective, a 'straw boss' may do part of his job; a second kind of informal structure may be associated with trade union activities, or there may be a spokesman, chosen for his skill in dealing with management (Sayles, 1958). This is a kind of leader not encountered in the other kinds of group we have discussed – a leader of the opposition.

The sociometric structure is greatly affected by ecological considerations. Numerous studies show that sociometric choice depends on the proximity of seating at work. The norms established by work-groups are of course about work – how much to do, how it should be done, attitudes to management and so on. Severe sanctions may be brought to bear on those who fail to these norms, including physical violence and 'sending to Coventry'. The reason for this intensity of feeling is easy to understand – the level of pay of the rest of the group is thought to be threatened by such deviation.

What special interaction processes are found in work-groups? (1) Interaction arises out of cooperation and communication over task activity, and can be regarded as a secondary or informal system that sustains working relationships and satisfies interpersonal needs. (2)

Social relationships at work differ from those in the family or in adolescent groups in that they are based on concern for the task, tend to be less permanent and less intimate, and often do not operate outside the work situation. (3) The boundaries of work-groups are vague, and these groups may in fact consist of networks. (4) In addition to one or more informal leaders, there may be a leader of the opposition.

Committees, problem-solving and creative groups

This kind of group does its work entirely by talking, and consequently is not found in any species apart from man. Committees are concerned with taking decisions and solving problems; there are other kinds of working group, for example groups of research workers, who are more concerned with the creative solution of problems. There is no sharp division between the two kinds of group.

Committees are small groups of a rather special kind; while their devotion to problem-solving and their degree of formality make them different from other groups, these features are found to some extent in most other groups too. Committees normally consist of 3–20 members, though essentially similar processes are found in larger public meetings, like the Annual General Meetings of Societies. The members are usually in the 30–60 age-group, and as in work-groups are typically male rather than female. They are motivated by the usual interpersonal motivations – dominance, affiliation, sex, etc. They are also to varying degrees concerned about the task, which consists of solving problems and arriving at decisions. They may stand to gain or lose personally; they may have their own ideas about the policy the committee should pursue, and may be committed to the success of the enterprise; they may be representatives of other bodies which elected them to the committee, and feel under obligation or pressure to defend their views.

Committees always have a chairman, who is empowered to control the discussion, and is able to influence the decisions taken in various ways. There may also be other officers, such as secretary, or treasurer. Committees usually exist in an organisational setting, so that tasks are assigned to them; if these are not done the committee may be abolished or its membership changed. Meetings usually follow a formal agenda, and there are certain rules of procedure – all remarks must be addressed to the chairman, voting is taken on an amendment before voting on the original motion; particular committees may have their own rules – no member may speak more than twice on any one item in the agenda, meetings end by 11.00 p.m., etc.

Interaction in committees is unlike interaction in most other groups. It is primarily verbal; furthermore it consists of a number of carefully delivered utterances, in the formal mode of speech. The 12 categories of the Bales system (see p. 116) were devised to record interaction in groups of this kind. As well as pure task categories – asking for and giving opinions and suggestions, it includes socioemotional categories – agreeing and disagreeing, showing tension, showing antagonism and solidarity. As with work-groups interpersonal relations are established and maintained during the execution of the task. There is considerable use of non-verbal signals. To speak it may be necessary to catch the chairman's eye, and the regulation of who speaks and for how long is achieved by eye-movements, head-nods and smiles. Comments on what A is saying may be indicated by B's facial and gestural signals; these may be directed to A, or to another listener C. When the non-verbal channel proves inadequate, written messages may be passed along the table. To be an effective committee member requires special skills. These include squaring other people before the meeting, studying the papers before the meeting, and the usual social skills of persuasion and handling groups. There also appear to be skills unique to committees: a member should not seem to be emotionally involved with an issue, but be concerned with what will be acceptable to the others. A chairman should do his best to come to solutions which are acceptable to all members, rather than coming to majority decisions.

The activity of a committee is problem-solving and decision-taking. These terms refer to two different elements – arriving at new solutions to problems, and coming to agreements. These are rather different matters, which are however closely bound up together in committee work. Coming to an agreement has already been considered in connection with conformity; each agenda item produces in miniature a norm-formation situation. The item will be more or less closely related to more general norms held by the group, and to issues on which subgroups have their own views. The problem-solving process can be divided into two stages – information exchange and the study of hypotheses. Thibaut and Kelley (1969) discuss the conditions under which information is offered and accepted in groups, and what happens when the information is complementary, conflicting or simply heterogeneous. A number of experiments have been carried out in which the task of the group consists in putting together information related in these ways. In real committees this is certainly part of the story, but information exchange is usually followed by the study of suggestions and is affected by conformity processes. There is a great deal of experimental work in this area, of which one sample will be given. Freedman and Sears (1965), reviewing experiments by themselves and others, show that people do *not* just seek information that supports their existing views, as dissonance theory would seem to predict, but actually want to find out the facts. Thibaut and Kelley (op. cit.) argue that both individuals and groups start to engage in problem-solving activity when they think that they may be able to deal with the external world to better advantage.

The problem-solving process proper is performed by the identification of the problem and its elements, the putting forward of relevant information and hypotheses, and the examination of these. No doubt committees go through the phases of group development described earlier. On any particular problem a faster cycle is observed. At first there is information exchange, and discussion of the problem; solutions are suggested and discussed; finally there is agreement over a solution (cf. Bales, 1950). But do groups in fact do any better than individuals would have done?

Groups may do worse than some of the individuals could have done. This has been found with a certain type of problem – where it is difficult to demonstrate the solution to others (Davis and Restle, 1963). Groups may also be hindered by the normal social processes of groups – presence of a status hierarchy and conformity pressures, as will be shown below. In addition groups are certainly very much slower than individuals, as well as taking up more man-hours.

Groups are found to do better than most individuals for reasons which have nothing to do with interaction or discussion. The averaged judgements of a number of people who do not interact are found to be more correct than those of many individuals – simply because averaging removes error (Stroop, 1932). Groups are also more likely to contain one member who can solve a given problem. Both of these are usually known as 'pseudo group effects'.

A number of studies have found that when interaction takes place, a more accurate or qualitatively superior solution is arrived at compared with the solutions arrived at by a similar number of individuals working alone. Interaction seems to affect the outcome in three main ways.

(1) Perhaps the main advantage of interacting groups over individuals is that the problem can be divided up, and each part dealt with by the member best able to do it. When members have different and complementary skills, or information, and this can be coordinated, the group has an advantage over individuals. Lorge and Solomon (1955) proposed a model of group problem-solving simply in terms of the combination

of abilities in this way; Thibaut and Kelley (1969) conclude that there is no clear evidence that anything further happens, as a result of inter-action in the group.

(2) It seems very possible however that interaction can have further benefits – individuals may be able to correct errors, though this would only affect the weaker members; and the ideas produced by one member may stimulate associations in the minds of others, so that new ideas can emerge from the discussion (Jones and Gerard, 1967).

(3) As in other groups there is greater motivational arousal; group members put more effort into their contributions, and formulate their suggestions more carefully (Bos, 1937); on the other hand there is evidence that the presence of others inhibits the production of new responses and restrains creativity (Zajonc, 1965); it would be expected that conformity pressures would have a similar effect.

Committees show the same structural principles as other groups. Status in the group is often based on status in the surrounding organ-isation, and in the other bodies which members represent, and their security of tenure on the committee, in addition to the usual factors of personality and expertise. This is rather important, as the power structure affects the interaction and the solution: the group spends more time discussing the ideas of a high-status person, status differences inhibit discussion, and constitute barriers to problem-solving (Hoffman, 1965). Those members with more status or power will carry most weight in the final decision; but will this make it more or less accurate? If their position reflects their ability to deal with the problem – as is often the case in an informal group, this should help to produce a better answer. If their position does *not* reflect their relevant abilities, the solution will be worse – as was found in a study of air-crews where the commander was less well informed about survival techniques than the instructor in that subject (Torrance, 1955). Similarly Maier (1952) found that a hint about the solution to a problem led to its being used and adopted by the group only when it had been given to a talkative member of the group.

Since the normal processes of interaction may prevent the most useful answer appearing, it is important to have a good chairman. He should follow the usual principles of democratic control expounded in the next chapter. He should see that minority views are expressed; it has been found that this leads to a more accurate group solution (Maier and Solem, 1952). He should see that the right people deal with each prob-lem and sub-problem. Maier has devised a number of leadership skills for committees, and has obtained evidence of their value. These are (1) identify the problem, consider the available facts, ask each member for his views about the important factors; (2) focus on disagreements in the group, and try to arrive at a creative solution; (3) evaluate different solutions in relation to criteria if these can be agreed upon; (4) ask stimulating questions to make the group question its approach or consider other aspects; (5) divide a problem into sub-problems, which are taken in turn; (6) get the group to consider two possible solutions – it has been found that the second one is often superior to the first (Hoffman, 1965).

Committee members are usually elected by others outside the group (apart from those co-opted), so members may not know one another initially, and sociometric choices and rejections develop during the life of the committee. Often these bonds are very weak compared with those in other groups. There may however be sub-groups and coalitions, though there may be rapid realignments as different topics are discussed. It is well known that a determined minority group can carry a committee, especially if the others have no firm views, or have not done their homework. The problem becomes more difficult if there are opposed interests in the group, as when there are limited goods to be divided. Such cases of mixed cooperation–competition or of pure bargaining may be discussed quite calmly, often in a disguised form, as when impersonal arguments are brought forward.

Committees have norms, especially about the general policies to be pursued. They must also come to agreement on particular items, when this is purely a question of opinion, taste or values. But do conformity pressures help the members to come to the right answer? When the majority view is correct, or if the correct judgement lies within the range of individual judgements, convergence improves the average accuracy. When the majority are wrong the reverse can be the case. However, those perceived to be most competent will usually be allowed to carry most weight with the decision, as described above, and others will hold back (Guernee, 1937).

A feature of decision-taking which has attracted a lot of experimental interest is that of risk-taking. When solutions varying in riskiness have to be decided between, groups often come to riskier decisions than individuals, as many studies have now shown (Kogan and Wallach, 1967). The experimental procedure used in these studies is to ask individual subjects to say what level of risk, in probability terms, they would advise a number of people in hypothetical situations to accept – such as taking risky moves at chess, or investing money in unreliable companies. Subjects are then assembled into groups, asked to discuss the problems one by one, and make a second set of judgements about them. The general finding is there is a 'risky shift' in the second set of judgements. Wallach, Kogan and Bem (1964) obtained a similar result with a rather different task in which subjects stood to win different amounts of money. There is some conflict between the findings about the conditions in which the risky shift will occur. While Wallach and Kogan (1967) consider that group discussion is an essential ingredient, Bateson (1966) found a risky shift for *individuals* who spent as long thinking about the problems as the groups spent talking about them, and Teger and Pruitt (1967) found a risky shift when subjects merely revealed their previous decisions to one another (though discussion produced a greater shift).

There are three main theories about the risky shift. (1) Kogan and Wallach (op. cit.) maintain that it is due to the diffusion of responsibility among group members. This is supported by an experiment in which there was a shift towards choosing a less risky problem if one member was to be chosen at random to solve it and the winnings of all members would depend on this (Wallach, Kogan and Bem, 1968). Further support for this theory was obtained by Hilary Nicholson and the present author in an experiment in which some groups were 'de-individuated' by wearing uniform white coats. As predicted there was a greater risky shift for the de-individuated groups (where there would be more diffusion of responsibility) for females only (who would be more de-individuated by the concealing of their distinctive clothing). (2) Brown (1965) suggests that people take greater risks in groups because of a cultural norm in favour of taking risks. This is supported by the finding that most subjects think they are taking a greater than average risk in their initial decisions, and that the shift occurs as soon as they hear the judgements of the other subjects (Teger and Pruitt, 1967). It has also been found that there are certain problems which produce a non-risky shift; Brown argues that these problems arouse the opposite cultural value of caution, and that group processes simply accentuate the impact of whichever cultural value is salient. (3) Study of the behaviour of individual group members shows that some are more risky in the first place – those who are higher in extraversion and achievement motivation (Rim, 1966). Several studies have found that these people are regarded as more influential especially in female groups (Kogan and Wallach, 1967); Brown (op. cit.) suggests that the pro-risk position can be argued in a richer and more dramatic manner. Bateson's finding (1966) that individual familiarisation leads to a risky shift could be accounted for by supposing that an individual dramatises the risky arguments to himself.

Committees differ from other groups in several important ways. (1) Their main task is problem-solving and decision-taking; the task is achieved by verbal interaction. (2) The meetings are often formal, in that an agenda is followed and there are more or less elaborate rules of procedure. (3) Interpersonal attitudes and relationships arise directly out of the work of the group; there may be rapid changes of coalition during a single meeting, and there may be no social contact apart from the meetings.

We will now review briefly the main conditions under which it has been found that committees are most effective – in arriving at accurate or qualitatively good decisions, and in working quickly.

(1) *Ability of members.* The more able the members the better the group will solve problems; often the group can do no better than the ablest member. The problem may have component parts which require skills possessed by different people. Similarly members may be able to contribute complementary pieces of information. Problem-solving groups should therefore contain members who between them possess the knowledge and skills for the job.

(2) *Motivation of members.* Groups which are cooperative do better at problem-solving as with other tasks (cf. p. 223). Indeed this is the kind of group task where it is most useful to have cooperative attitudes, and several studies have shown that cooperative problem-solving groups do better than competitive ones (Deutsch, 1949; Marquis, Guetztkow and Heyns, 1950). Taking part in group activities often elicits altruistic striving for the group's goals, especially when members feel that they are fully consulted and are responsible for what happens.

(3) *Stimulating new ideas.* We saw above that groups may on the one hand stimulate new ideas through one member reacting to another, but may also inhibit creative thinking. Osborn (1957) developed the method of 'brainstorming', in which there is complete suspension of critical judgement while group members throw off as many ideas as they can, useful or not, and develop one another's suggestions, leaving critical evaluation until later. This method has been widely used, for example in advertising firms. However, Taylor, Berry and Block (1958) found that 'nominal groups' of four working independently produced more and better solutions to problems than did brainstorming groups. Dunnette et al. (1963) obtained similar results, and found that groups tended to follow the same line of thought for too long, though individual

members were found to be very productive *after* taking part in brainstorming. Cohen *et al.* (1960) on the other hand found brainstorming groups were superior to individuals when the members were able to choose one another.

(4) *Leadership skills*. We have shown that groups require coordination, or they become slow and inefficient. We have shown that the chairman should restrain the operation of the informal status hierarchy and allow the expression of minority opinions; similarly he should reduce the inhibiting effects of differences in formal status. He should prevent conformity pressures producing premature and inferior decisions. He should help the group to arrive at solutions which as far as possible are acceptable to all members. The social skills of handling the group to the greatest effect were discussed above (p. 256 f).

(5) *Size*. A number of experiments have compared the effectiveness of groups of different sizes over the range 3–12; there are conflicting results, though when more complex tasks are used the larger groups do better (Thomas and Fink, 1963). It has been suggested that there is an optimum size of group for each kind of problem – when the group contains all the different skills needed to solve it (Krech, Crutchfield and Ballachey, 1962). Other studies show that in larger discussion groups there is less shared distribution of participation, that they are slower, and members are less satisfied – 5 to 6 is the preferred number.

T-groups and therapy groups

Finally we turn to a kind of group which did not exist until psychologists invented it. Just as physicists study particles created by special experimental techniques so it is of interest to study the forms social interaction *can* take under quite new conditions. In fact the processes of feedback and analysis of the group found in this setting also take place, although with less intensity, in other groups too. On the other hand these groups are very different from natural groups in a number of ways, so that the findings cannot simply be generalised to other kinds of group. There has been a certain shift of interest away from laboratory groups towards T-groups (cf. Mann *et al.*, 1967), simply because the latter last longer and can be studied in greater detail. Apart from the limited generality of the findings it should be pointed out that most of these studies are essentially clinical investigations of a rather small number of groups (cf. Stock, 1964).

In most T-groups, about 12 trainees meet with a trainer for a number of 2-hour sessions; they may meet once a week, or more frequently for up to two weeks. The Harvard version has 20–30 members. The leader introduces himself, explains that he is there to help the members study the group, and then takes a passive role and leaves the group to get on with this task as best it can. From time to time he will intervene in various ways – (1) he shows how to make constructive and non-evaluative comments on the behaviour of members, (2) he shows how to receive such comments non-defensively, and learn from them, (3) he makes interpretations, i.e. explains what he thinks is happening, interpersonally, in the group, (4) he discusses the relevance and application of the group experiences to behaviour in real-life situations, (5) he tries to teach the members a more cooperative and less authoritarian attitude to people in authority. In addition to the T-group sessions proper there are sometimes lectures, role-playing and other ancillary training experiences (cf. Bradford, Gibb and Renne, 1964).

Therapy groups consist of a psychiatrist and usually 6–9 mental patients. The main differences from T-groups are that: (1) the members are emotionally disturbed and at a lower level of social competence, often suffering from real interpersonal difficulties; (2) the content of conversation is the actual symptoms or difficulties of group members; (3) the therapist creates an atmosphere of acceptance for sexual and aggressive material, but makes sure that the tension level does not get too high; (4) there is a greater gap between leader and group members – the former is not simply a more experienced member of the group; (5) the behaviour of members in the group situation is used to diagnose basic personality disturbances, rather than indicating their level of social competence (Powdermaker and Frank, 1953; Foulkes and Anthony, 1957).

The members of T-groups are usually managers, social workers, clergymen or others whose work involves dealing with people. In practice they are often middle-aged men. Therapy groups consist typically of neurotics, of both sexes, and of varied ages, though group counselling is also used with prisoners and has been found successful with schizophrenics. Members of T-groups are motivated to improve their sensitivity and social skill, perhaps in the hope of promotion, though the initiative may have come from their organisation rather than themselves. Members of therapy groups want to get better, to obtain relief from symptoms and distress. Thus in both kinds of group the members may be quite strongly motivated, and are therefore prepared to put up with unpleasant experiences.

The environmental setting of these groups resembles that of laboratory experimental groups in that the groups meet in training centres, laboratories or clinics, and are removed from the culture of the outside world. They are unlike other groups in that the rules and procedures are novel and unexpected. The leader behaves as no other leaders behave, and appears to have largely abdicated from the role of leader. The task – to study the group – is very odd, again unlike the tasks of other groups.

The 'task' of T-groups, like that of committees, consists of conversation, and is difficult to separate from 'interaction'. However, some kinds of conversation are regarded as more relevant to the task – conversation which is concerned with the interaction and relationships of members of the group, and about the symptoms of members of therapy groups. The goal to be attained is insight and understanding of group processes and emotional problems respectively. An important sub-goal is the formation of a sufficiently cohesive group for this understanding to develop in the group setting – i.e. the internal and external goals are closely intertwined (Tuckman, 1965). Unlike committees however these groups have no agenda, and proceed in a largely undirected and rambling manner, the leader taking whatever opportunities he can for explaining various phenomena. The content of the conversation is most unusual; language in the natural world is usually about external matters, and other people, rather than about relations between speaker and hearer, or about embarrassing personal matters. This kind of task is emotionally arousing and awkward, and for these reasons is often avoided in periods of 'flight' from the task – by making jokes, talking about other matters, and silence.

The flavour of T-group meetings can be conveyed by this extract from one of Mann's groups (op. cit.).

AUDREY: I think if you wouldn't push at people all the time they might relax and reveal themselves in a more natural way.

DR DAWES: I think people are afraid that I don't like them or care about them when I try to point out some of the things that they are expressing through their actions, and that isn't the case.

DON: I think he's got us cornered and boxed up and we're just going to have to squirm around until he's finished with us.

MABEL: I hate his guts.

BERT: I have more respect for him now that I see how hard his job really is.

MABEL: He gets paid for it.

FAITH: It's like being in the dentist's chair for an hour a day. It's not the course I thought it was going to be.

ROSS: I think we're going to have to admit that what Dr Dawes says is right, even though it hurts.

DON: Does a human guinea pig have any choice?

DR DAWES: Are parents too cruel and vengeful to be trusted? (from Mann *et al.*, 1967, p. 140.)

This is very different from the conversation of most natural groups, though it can happen in groups of adolescents and in families. In group and individual therapy it is accepted that the therapist is allowed to talk in this way – and he is also very skilled at commenting on a patient's behaviour in a way that is not upsetting and preserves the latter's self-esteem. The intention is that control of impulses and resolution of conflicts can be brought about by attaching verbal labels to emotional processes (Dollard and Miller, 1950).

The social interaction in T-groups can be thought of as including the task activity. Various classification schemes have been devised to deal with it, which between them provide some account of the forms interaction takes. The character of the interaction can be gathered from the excerpt given above, and from the account of common styles of individual behaviour given below. It should be added that the general atmosphere and flow of interaction are very different in these groups from those in the other groups which we have considered. While committees are formal, and groups of adolescents are relaxed and intimate, T-groups and therapy groups are tense and awkward. Both T-group and therapy group practitioners maintain that some degree of emotionality is necessary for any fundamental changes of behaviour to occur. Interaction sequences are reported in these groups which may be unique to them, for example: (a) an intensification of the process of becoming aware of the self-image from the reactions of others – which are here unusually frank and uninhibited; (b) obtaining insight into oneself through the close observation and study of another person with similar attributes or problems; (c) the 'condenser' phenomenon, in which interaction loosens group resistances, and common emotions, normally repressed, are suddenly released (Foulkes and Anthony, 1957).

We come now to the internal structure of these groups. They have their hierarchies, in terms of who speaks most, and who has most influence – and there is usually a struggle for dominance, and competition for the leader's approval, especially in therapy groups. Some members are silent, until drawn into the conversation by the leader or other members.

Role-differentiation appears which is more complex than that reported in laboratory groups, though perhaps no more so than that in natural groups. Mann *et al.* (1967) carried out a statistical analysis of four Harvard-style T-groups of 20–30 members. Seven roles, i.e. styles of interaction in the group, emerged in each group, and these will be reported in some detail as they give the clearest account yet available of the processes taking place in this kind of group.

(1) *Hero*. One male member of the group takes over the effective leadership of the group, from which the trainer has abdicated, in the early stages. While accepting the trainer's suggestion that the group should study itself, he rebels against the trainer's authority and resists accepting a dependent role. The rest of the group is hostile to the hero and asks the trainer to suppress him, which is refused. Eventually he is integrated into a cooperative and working group.

(2) *Moralistic resister*. Another male member rejects the tasks of seeking personal change through analysis of the group. He is anxious and rebellious, and acts as spokesman for the group in favour of 'balanced, sane discussion', and seeks a type of group interaction which is characterised by more nurturance and control.

(3) *Paranoid resister*. A similar pattern to the last was found in all groups, in a more rebellious and paranoid reaction to the unexpected and incomprehensible behaviour of the trainer. The paranoid resister is not popular, becomes hostile to the group, but is the main spokesman against T-group procedures in the group.

(4) *Distressed females*. Most females in these groups are less active than the males; they are passive and dependent on the leader, and do not accept responsibility to get on with the defined task. Towards the trainer they tend to be loyal and flirtatious.

(5) *Sexual scapegoat*. An inconspicuous male member becomes the centre of attention at one point in the group's development. He is uncertain of his masculinity and asks the group to study him. He is loyal and dependent towards the trainer, while finding the latter rather frightening. He seeks the company of the distressed females and may become their spokesman.

(6) *Male enactors.* Some of the male members accept the T-group task, and work together with the trainer, treating him as a colleague. Their initial rebellion gives way to loyalty.

(7) *Female enactors.* Some female members similarly accept the group task, but with a more dependent attitude to the trainer and show greater anxiety and depression than the males. They are more sensitive and help to prevent members of the group being hurt.

Role-differentiation has also been found in therapy groups. Bion (1948–51) classified the main states of these groups and their members as work, pairing, fight (i.e. with the therapist), flight (i.e. from the task) and dependency. Powdermaker and Frank (1953) add a few others including clowning.

T-groups and therapy groups, like other groups, have a sociometric structure. In addition to the choice of similar people, it has been found that members may choose others who have what the chooser wants; for example dependent people choose hostile ones, and vice versa (Browne and Crowe, 1953). Where similars are chosen, they are people who have similar symptoms or who are similar in orientations towards intimacy and authority – the two main issues to be resolved in a group (Bennis and Peabody, 1962). It is common in therapy groups for a sub-group of two or more people to cut itself off for a time from the life of the group, and these sub-groups may meet outside the normal hours of the group (Foulkes and Anthony, 1957). While some groups break up into pairs, others may form cohesive work-groups. In therapy groups, members usually meet only in the group, and have little opportunity for building up pair-relationships. There may also be hostilities in these groups; in the case of therapy groups A may be hostile to B, if B has a characteristic which A also possesses and rejects, or has repressed (Powdermaker and Frank, 1953).

There are certainly norms in T-groups and therapy groups – consisting mainly of the rules of interpersonal behaviour imposed by trainer or therapist. These rules, as we have seen, are at first rejected by most members but are later accepted by a proportion of the group. Different groups have different atmospheres, reflecting the personalities of the members. It is found that homogeneous groups 'seem to reinforce and permit expression of the individual tendencies of the members, at least initially' (Stock, 1964, p. 406). Groups may become preoccupied with certain themes which are a matter of common interest to the members. Powdermaker and Frank (op. cit.) report that these are often such topics as – feelings of inferiority and desire to be average, inability to handle emotional situations and emotional dependence, hostility, distrust and fear of people; blaming others versus accepting responsibility.

What special processes occur in T-groups and therapy groups? At first sight these groups look very different from other groups but it is possible that they produce in more concentrated form what also occurs less obviously elsewhere. (1) Members are confronted by a totally unfamiliar group situation and a person in charge who refuses to give much help. This is responsible for the initial rebellion of the group, and the permanent refusal of some members to cooperate. (2) The task and topic of conversation are very unusual – comments on the behaviour and problems of individuals and the interaction in the group. Something of this kind occurs in all groups, though usually at a non-verbal level. We shall discuss further in Chapter X how far this is a useful training experience. (3) There is considerable self-disclosure, especially in therapy groups, of matters normally concealed. In natural groups the amount of self-disclosure grows slowly to an upper limit – which is reached after nine weeks of sharing a room in college for example (Taylor, 1965). Self-disclosure at a much earlier stage is required in therapy groups, and this is one cause of the great emotional tension generated. In T-groups it is caused by the experience of receiving comments on one's own behaviour in the group. (4) The pattern of role-differentiation, some of the interaction sequences, and some of the bases of liking and disliking, have not been reported in other groups. (5) Lastly the motivation of members is to be cured or trained, not through instruction, but from direct social experiences in the group. The only other groups of which this may be true are groups of adolescents, and they are not aware that it is happening.

VII

Social Organisations

CONCEPTS AND METHODS

When two apes or monkeys meet, they classify one another as members or non-members of the same group, in terms of age and sex, and may have some idea of each other's standing in the troop. A more or less standard pattern of interaction results. In human societies the social structure is more complex; in all societies family relationships are important, and there is some degree of social stratification. One of the marks of an advanced civilisation is the development of large-scale social organisations for industrial, governmental, military, educational, religious and other purposes. Such organizational structures probably do not have any very direct biological origins, but are more the product of slowly developing ideas about the administration of large groups of people. In previous chapters we have overlooked the fact that social interactors occupy positions in social structures, and play social roles. All social interaction is to some degree *pre-programmed*: it has been worked out by previous occupants of the same positions, and it is expected that similar behaviour will occur again. In extreme cases interaction can depend almost entirely on the formal relations between people – for example at church services, Army drill parades, hospital operations and so on. In less extreme cases the relations between A and B will be different if A is B's boss, doctor, wife, psychoanalyst, priest, etc. It is not only a matter of power and status, but of the way the positions of A and B are related in the organisation.

In moving to consideration of the effects of organisation, a number of new concepts have to be introduced. *Position* refers to rank or office within the organisation; it may be associated with power and status, and with norms or duties which apply only to occupants of that position. It may place its occupants at a certain point in a communication structure or work-flow system. *Role behaviour* is the normal, i.e. statistically modal, pattern of behaviour for occupants of a position. This is partly the result of *role-expectations* on the part of occupants of other positions.

267

When different people or groups of people hold different role-expectations about a given position, the occupant is said to be in a state of *role conflict*. Two roles are said to be *interlocking* when there is a regular complementary or cooperative pattern of interaction between the position holders; in some cases one role cannot be performed unless the complementary role is performed too – for example a doctor can't act as a doctor without a patient.

Power and *status* have been introduced earlier (p. 232 ff), but in organisations an individual's power or status derives mainly from his position; power and status also depend on his personality, and on the kind of relationships he establishes with other people. Positions may be linked by power relationships, as where A is the supervisor of B and C. They may be linked by *communication structures*, which restrict who can communicate with whom. They may be linked by the *work-flow* which may entail that A passes the materials to B when he has finished his part of the work, or that B and C shall cooperate over the task.

The above factors are features of the *formal organisation* and might appear on a management organisation chart. In addition there is communication, friendship and cooperation which grows up and which is not on such charts – this is known as the *informal organisation*, and refers to interaction which is extra to the strictly formal structure. Oeser and Harary (1962) devised a method of representing various aspects of both formal and informal organisation on the same chart. An example of their method is shown in Fig. 7.1.

Special research methods are used in the study of social organisations. The more sociological questions are very hard to tackle; to decide for example whether organisations should be flat or hierarchical, large or small, for greater effectiveness, can only be done by comparing a considerable number of organisations, though this can be done (Porter and Lawlor, 1965). It is very difficult to hold other factors constant. The study of interaction is easier, since the units being compared are smaller; this means that a reasonable number can be compared statistically, and that the phenomena can be reproduced in the lab.

Social surveys have been used with some success in this field. They are not very good for finding out how those surveyed interact, but can find out how they are affected by the social organisation. For example Kahn *et al.* (1964) were able to study the effects of role conflict on tension and on attitudes to those producing the conflict. *Statistical field studies* consist of the comparison of individuals or groups which have been carefully selected for the purposes of the investigation. The design of such studies can be quasi-experimental, in that it is possible to hold constant everything except the variable being studied; for example in studies of industrial supervision comparisons are made of the product-ivity of a large number of departments differing as far as possible only in the style of supervision; the main drawback is the usual one with statistical designs – the direction of causation may be unclear. If there is more output in departments with democratic supervisors this may be because (a) democratic supervision produces more output, or (b) when men work harder their supervisors are more democratic, or (c) under some conditions, to do with the nature of the work for example, men work harder *and* supervisors become more democratic.

Laboratory experiments have the great advantage that the direction of causation is unambiguous and that further variables can be controlled

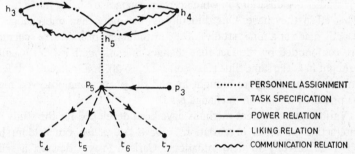

·········	PERSONNEL ASSIGNMENT
– – – –	TASK SPECIFICATION
―――――	POWER RELATION
–·–·–	LIKING RELATION
∿∿∿∿	COMMUNICATION RELATION

Figure 7.1. Relationship in a formal organisation (from Oeser and Harary, 1962)

with greater rigour. The difficulty with laboratory experiments here is that it is doubtful whether organisational variables can really be repro-duced in a laboratory setting. When power differences are set up in the course of a 40-minute experiment are these at all similar to power differences that affect a person's life? Mulder (1966) found that legiti-macy versus illegitimacy of experimentally imposed power relations had no effect on subjects. Such a negative result may simply be due to sub-jects not being sufficiently involved in the organisational structure created. Again, people in real organisations spend a number of years during which training and other kinds of influence help them to adjust to their positions. This is not the case in laboratory studies; on the other hand it is hopeful if during a fairly long series of trials the behaviour of subjects moves towards an asymptotic steady state, as in Mohanna and Argyle's study of communication structures with popular and un-popular central members (1960).

Field experiments avoid the disadvantages of statistical field studies – that direction of causation is unclear, and the snag of laboratory experiments – that they do not effectively reproduce organisational variables. Unfortunately field experiments are extremely hard to arrange, though one or two have been done. Morse and Reimer (1956) altered the amount of delegation of authority in opposite directions in two firms. It is often found in such experiments that output goes up in all experimental conditions: the main variable is the fact of being experimented upon. This is often called the 'Hawthorne effect' following the famous study in the Hawthorne plant of the Western Electric Company, in which various manipulations of lighting conditions and rest periods all led to increased output (Roethlisberger and Dickson, 1939).

Natural experiments are a solution to this problem; here the investigator studies organisations in which certain changes are being made to see what effect they have. One difficulty is that more than one change is usually made at a time; studies of the introduction of incentive schemes are confounded by the fact that changes in work methods are usually brought in at the same time (Davison *et al.*, 1958). It also makes a difference how the change is brought in, and the phenomena observed may be primarily a reaction to change *per se*.

Various measurement methods have been developed for the study of interaction in social organisations. *Social interaction* can seldom be observed directly in field situations. Carlson (1951) devised a self-recording device in which a manager fills in a form after each encounter or communication, showing the place, the persons involved, the mode of communication, the issues discussed and the action taken. The general pattern of interaction a person has with another can be studied by asking each to perform Q-sorts; Block (1953) asked each member of a department to report the kind of interactions he had with every other member in this way. The style of supervision or other behaviour of a member of an organisation can be studied by asking others to make ratings along a number of dimensions; it may be found that different ratings are made by those who are senior, equal or junior in rank to the person concerned. *Communication patterns* and *friendship choices* can be studied by interview or questionnaire methods. The Carlson method, described above, can be used to plot frequencies of contact between different members. Other methods can be used to trace the history of particular communications, upwards or downwards, and may reveal delays, distortions and blockages (Davis, 1953). Ordinary sociometry can be used to analyse the pattern of choices and rejections, on criteria both of friendship and leadership. *Subjective feelings*, for example of job satisfaction or role conflict (Kahn *et al.*, 1964), can be obtained by means of questionnaires usually including factor analysis of a number of items, all with some *a priori* validity. *Organisational effectiveness* is usually the main dependent variable in organisation research. It may include measures of output, accidents, absenteeism and labour turnover (cf. Argyle, 1957). *Morale* is a concept which is used in a variety of different ways; we shall use it, as we have already defined it, to refer to the extent to which an individual or group shares (is committed to) the goals of the organisation (Argyle, 1964c).

THE GROWTH OF SOCIAL ORGANISATIONS

From group to organisation

We saw, in the last chapter, how small social groups develop patterns of interaction which vary with the group task and with the personalities and needs of members. The social system provides a way of dealing with the external and internal tasks of the group. The social system can be analysed into the norms, the hierarchical and role-structures, and the affective and communication structure. When a small social group becomes larger, and its activities more complex, the group gradually becomes an organisation. An organisation develops when 'collective effort is explicitly organised for specific ends' (Blau and Scott, 1963, p. 223). Its characteristic features are (a) hierarchical structure, (b) division of labour, (c) incentives and contracts for working, and (d) rules.

(a) We saw in the last chapter how small groups spontaneously develop a hierarchical leadership structure; in problem-solving groups there are advantages in having a leader, since he can coordinate different contributions, and allow minority views to be expressed; Heinecke and Bales (1953) found that groups of four which developed a clear status hierarchy were more successful at problem-solving. In primitive societies a simple hierarchical structure develops in connection with production, and is based on the ascribed status system of the community (Udy, 1959). Since only a certain number of men can be effectively controlled by a leader, it follows that the larger the total organisation, the more levels there will be in the hierarchy.

(b) Small social groups develop role-differentiation and division of labour (p. 235f); the larger the group the more division of labour there is (Thomas and Fink, 1963). In primitive societies division of labour only occurs after a hierarchy has formed (Udy, op. cit.). When the organisation carries out specialised professional or technical activities there is more division of labour. The more complex the activities of an organisation the more levels of authority there are: Joan Woodward (1958), in a study of 92 British firms, found that with unit production the typical number of levels of authority was 3, with mass production it was 4, while with process production (e.g. chemical works) it was 6.

(c) In small groups the members all gain directly by the performance of task activities. In primitive societies there is a fairly simple system of cooperation based on family obligation and exchange of gifts. In large-scale organisations the product of the organisation's work is usually a product or service for others, so that members have to be rewarded in other ways for their work. Most organisations pay their members, and draw up contracts with them.

(d) Small groups have norms, though not all members conform to them. In organisations norms are replaced by organisational rules and methods of working, which are mainly laid down by the senior administrators, with or without consulting more junior members. As organisations become larger, increasing use is made of rules (Rushing, 1966). 'The formal rules make it possible to train, control, coordinate and integrate the work of all despite the fact that the various employees within the organisation are quite diverse in their interests, potential and training' (Bass, 1965, p. 253).

Social organisations are simply large social groups in which the leadership hierarchy and role-differentiation have become formalised into fixed ranks and offices, norms have become rules, and in which methods of communication and work are prescribed. Without organisation, the group will be chaotic and ineffective – like a guerrilla band compared with a trained and disciplined army. While a group of workmen could function quite effectively in a simple workshop, a modern factory is unthinkable without a very elaborate formal structure – consider the thousands of work activities that have to be coordinated to manufacture a modern car, for example. The growth of social organisation can be seen to some extent as a response to the task, and to the personalities and needs of the members. The particular form of the organisation can be looked at in the same way. It is found that small groups give more power to leaders when faced by crisis (p. 303); similarly military organisations are highly authoritarian, and little power is delegated to lower level members.

Some recent theorists have portrayed the social organisation as a social system which responds as a whole to external demands and stresses (e.g. Katz and Kahn, 1966). It may be objected however that the form of social organisation is largely determined by the senior administrators, often with little regard for the feelings of those lower down the hierarchy. Some consideration has to be paid to their needs and welfare, but it is possible to run a very effective organisation where most of the members are extremely discontented – if the administrators have enough power. The way the organisation is structured depends to a large extent on theories held by administrators, rather than on an adaptive response of the organisation. Recent research has put us in a position now to consider what are the best ways of designing organisations, ways that will meet human needs as well as performing the task effectively.

What is the difference between behaviour in a formal organisation and in an informal group? (a) The main difference is that the relationships and interaction patterns are there already in an organisation – two people can slip quite quickly into a standard role-relationship without spending a lot of time wondering whether they like one another. On the other hand if an individual has a personality that is different from that of those who built up the original pattern, he won't like it. (b) A formal leader differs from an informal leader – he is appointed usually by people outside the group, while an informal leader emerges from the group in the course of interaction, and is always chosen by the group. There is also a difference of power – a formal leader is able to deliver definite rewards and punishments, while an informal leader has to rely on his own powers of persuasion.

Social organisations are not completely frozen; change does take place; it is the job of people in innovating positions to ensure that the organisation keeps up to date with external and technological changes. Individuals also change their positions in organisations; there are career patterns and promotion, and the selection, training and assignment of personnel to positions is the main work of personnel managers and their equivalents in other organisations.

Changing ideas about organisational structure

It is very difficult to discover which kind of organisation does the job best. Organisations are designed according to theories, and their development can be traced historically. During the last 150 years the dominant theory has been classical organisation theory, which 'is actually a collection of hortatory rules based on nineteenth-century military formulas modified for the purposes of industry' (Bass, 1965, p. 239). Some of the basic assumptions of this theory are

1. A division of labour based on functional specialisation
2. A well-defined hierarchy of authority

3. A system of rules covering the rights and duties of employees
4. A system of procedures for dealing with work situations
5. Impersonality of interpersonal relations
6. Promotion and selection based on technical competence (Hall, 1963, p. 33).

This theory was put into practice in industry with the assistance of 'scientific management', using wage incentives and work-study. It was assumed that human beings are mainly motivated by economic self-interest, that they are inherently lazy and need to be motivated by incentives, that because of their irrational feelings they are incapable of self-discipline, with the exception of managers who are self-motivated, self-controlled and less dominated by their feelings (McGregor, 1960).

Classical organisation theory contains a highly inadequate theory of human motivation and social behaviour. Men have other needs besides money – affiliative and achievement needs for example. And members of organisations do not confine their social interaction to the receiving and giving of instructions – in particular they form informal groups with others at the same level in the hierarchy. As a result bureaucratic organisations do not produce much job satisfaction in their members. The hierarchical structure results in a high degree of conformity and the production of grey 'organisation men' who are unable to innovate, while communications in the hierarchy are inhibited and formal. Subordinates are controlled by economic rewards and coercion, not by persuasion or their involvement with the work. The organisational structure is fixed and frozen, and it is very difficult to make the changes which are increasingly needed for technological and other reasons.

There has been a rebellion against these assumptions and methods in the form of the 'human relations movement'. It began with the Hawthorne experiment (Roethlisberger and Dickson, 1939), which seemed to show that output is more dependent on interpersonal factors than on wage-incentives. (We believe that this conclusion was mistaken, p. 250, but the experiment was nevertheless extremely influential.) It was found that the style of supervision affected output and job satisfaction (p. 299 ff); this led to a great increase in supervisory and management training. Research on the working group showed that the size, cohesiveness and composition of groups also affected output and job satisfaction (p. 251 f). Changed economic conditions after World War II led to an increased concern with the welfare of workers; research workers turned their attention to the study of job satisfaction, partly in the belief that this would be related to output as well as to labour turnover and absenteeism.

The model of man and his motivation was revised to take account of social needs; less emphasis was placed on rational processes (Viteles, 1954). The Tavistock Institute of Human Relations showed that the effectiveness of work-flow systems depended on the patterns of interaction in them (p. 307 f).

Since about 1960 there has been something of a synthesis between production-centred scientific management and the human relations approach, between 'organisation without people' and 'people without organisation' (Quinn and Kahn, 1967). (1) It has been recognised that output and efficiency on the one hand, and interpersonal relations and job satisfaction on the other, are two organisational goals, both of which need to be promoted; it is possible to pursue them simultaneously, and to some extent the second leads to the first; the extent to which job satisfaction in fact leads to productivity is discussed below (p. 295). Blake and Mouton (1964) use a two-dimensional scheme for assessing a manager's 'concern for productivity' and 'concern for people', each on a 9-point scale. (2) The model of man and his motivation has been revised again, this time to take account of achievement and other work-related motivations. It has been found that job satisfaction depends on work success as well as on social factors (p. 295 f). (3) There has been a renewed interest in the organisational structure, as a source both of efficiency and satisfaction. Suggestions have been put forward for new kinds of organisations which may be more effective (p. 296 ff).

Types of organisation

There is no agreed way of classifying organisations. We will give two examples of classification, and then mention some of the main dimensions.

Etzioni (1961) suggested a division into three basic types of structure, which differ in the type of authority used and in the motivation appealed to in the members.

(1) *Coercive*, e.g. prisons and mental hospitals. Authority rests on the power of punishment; members do not want to be there at all, and are primarily motivated to get out and to avoid being punished; they are alienated.

(2) *Utilitarian*, e.g. industry. Authority rests on legal and reward power; members are motivated to earn as much money as possible and will work in exchange for such rewards.

(3) *Normative*, e.g. universities, hospitals, churches, voluntary and professional organisations. Authority rests on the ability to appeal to the motivation of members, who are committed to the organisational goals.

Etzioni also allows for mixed structures, for example the army is a mixture of coercive and normative. Some current trends in industrial organisation can be seen as attempts to change industry from Utilitarian to mixed Utilitarian–Normative.

Blau and Scott (1963) suggest a quite different typology, based on who is the prime beneficiary of the organisation's activities. It may be (1) the members, as in mutual benefit associations, such as professional organisations and unions, (2) the owners or managers, as in industrial and commercial concerns, (3) clients, as with service organisations such as hospitals and schools, (4) the public at large, as with government departments, the police and army, and research organisations.

The above typologies introduce some basic dimensions: Etzioni's scheme classifies organisations by the degree of commitment *v.* alienation of rank-and-file members, and by the degree of coerciveness in the controls used. Blau and Scott's scheme divides organisations according to who benefits from its work, and its relationships with the public.

Size is an important dimension; it is directly linked with the number of levels in the hierarchy. The relevant measure is probably the number of members in a relatively autonomous unit of the organisation. It has been found for example that the absenteeism rate increases with size, but in the case of coalmines absenteeism is a function of the size of the underground community, where there may be more than one of these at a single 'mine' (Acton Society Trust, 1953).

Delegation and democracy. Organisations designed along the lines of classical scientific management were highly authoritarian. Other firms have introduced a greater degree of delegation of authority to lower-line supervisors; some firms have taken steps towards 'industrial democracy', so that rank-and-file members also have a voice in decision-making (p. 297 f).

Type of structure. The classical structure consisted of a simple pyramid of authority, but this is commonly augmented in various ways. (a) A second hierarchy of 'staff' personnel is created in parallel to the 'line' hierarchy. Staff managers deal with technical matters, selection and training, etc., rather than with the direct supervision of production.

(b) Decisions are taken not by individuals but by committees, which allows junior personnel to take part. (c) There may be barriers to promotion at certain points in the hierarchy, creating a large social gap between adjacent levels – officers and men, executive and administrative class civil servants in Britain, inmates and staff in prisons.

INTERACTION AS A FUNCTION OF ORGANISATIONAL STRUCTURE

Social roles

Social organisations consist of a number, often a large number, of individuals interacting in a regular manner. The description of this regular pattern is made possible by means of the concept of *role*, which was defined above as the modal behaviour of occupants of a position. It does not require very sophisticated techniques of measurement to see that in a hospital, for example, the doctors, sisters, nurses, orderlies, patients and visitors differ in their behaviour; indeed in this case there is almost no overlap between the behaviour of occupants of these different positions. The behaviour of the occupants of a position shows a high degree of conformity: F. H. Allport (1934) found that in a number of instances it had a J-shaped distribution. In many organisations a high degree of role-conformity is essential or the organisation will break down – for example if one worker on a production line is absent or fails to function properly the final product will be unfinished.

There are several different aspects of roles. (a) In many organisations the main feature of the role is the work a person does, which may not be social in character, though it affects the way in which he relates to other members. (b) Much role behaviour is interpersonal and consists of ways of interacting with other members of the organisation. The role often includes patterns of non-verbal communication – a judge is dignified while a mother is warm (Sarbin and Allen, 1969). (c) Roles may entail attitudes and beliefs – managers usually hold different attitudes from trade unionists, for example. (d) People in different positions may wear special clothes, either as uniforms or as unofficial uniforms, both of which enable their positions to be perceived easily. (e) Individuals in a particular position may have other common attributes – age, sex, ability and so on; these are not very usefully regarded as part of the role since they do not consist of behaviour which can be modified.

The same role, e.g. that of doctor, includes a number of interaction styles – to nurses, patients, etc – so that the other person must be categorised before the appropriate role behaviour can be selected. This problem was discussed earlier in connection with person perception

(p. 154 f). In addition, the same person may at different times play the roles of e.g. doctor, father, teacher in the medical school, chairman of a committee, secretary of another committee, a member of the audience at the theatre, and a male, middle-aged, middle-class member of the public. He may encounter another person in different settings, and the situation will determine which role is appropriate. Having selected the appropriate roles of self and other, there may still be a number of different environmental settings, for which the rules, i.e. the role-expectations, are different.

Of course the different occupants of a position do not behave identically; there is variation between personalities, and there is gradual development and change in the organisation through innovation. However, if a person deviates too far he will be regarded as eccentric or mad, and he ultimately will not be accepted as a proper occupant of the position in question. This is the organisational equivalent of conformity and deviation in small social groups. There are a number of social pressures and sanctions producing conformity to roles, and to these we now turn.

One of the main pressures towards conformity to role behaviour arises from the interlocking of roles. A doctor can't act as a doctor unless the patient acts like a patient, so the doctor's role behaviour tends to elicit the complementary patient behaviour, otherwise synchronising will not take place. The interlocking of roles may take various forms. (1) There may be a synchronising pattern of interaction based on role-differentiation. Haythorn (1956) found that authoritarian leaders got on well with authoritarian followers, but that neither got on well with democratic opposite numbers. (2) Roles may be linked through cooperation over the task. An example of this is assembly-line work, where one person has to finish his part of the work before the next man can do his. (3) Interlocking may be in terms of one person supervising or having power over another.

Members of an organisation may bring various social pressures to bear on each other to conform to role-expectations. A patient may think that a doctor's primary duty should be to make him (and other patients) better, while the doctor's medical research colleagues may think that he should be contributing to the longer-term goals of research, for instance by trying out new treatments. Thus A may want B to conform to a role because this role meets A's needs, or because it fits A's less personal long-term goals.

Members have expectations about the role behaviour of other members, will communicate them in various ways, and may be able to deliver sanctions for deviation. Role-expectations are cognitions about the behaviour of others, and they can be assessed by means of survey methods. Sarbin and Jones (1956) for example studied expectations about the role of daughter in American society and found considerable agreement among their respondents. Pressures to conform to role-expectations take various forms, corresponding to the different sources of power (p. 286 ff). Another source of conformity to roles is the fact that the role represents a kind of consensus about the best way of doing a job, or of occupying a position. Teachers may find out by a long period of trial and error that they have to adopt a loud, clear and didactic voice, together with a firm and genial manner. Alternatively they may take a short cut to finding this out by being told by other teachers, or by imitating experienced teachers. We will return to these learning processes shortly.

One reason why people in a similar position display similar role behaviour is that there is selection for the position – only certain kinds of people can become bishops, hospital sisters or psychoanalysts. Often organisations perpetuate themselves by looking for people of 'the right type' among recruits. On the other hand one of the most effective ways to change an organisation is to select a different kind of person. There is also self-selection: only certain kinds of people want to be bishops, hospital sisters or psychoanalysts. People are attracted towards positions which will suit their particular personalities; for example students high in authoritarianism find their way towards military academies (Stern, Stein and Bloom, 1956).

We come now to the processes whereby role behaviour is learnt. During childhood there is basic socialisation, in the course of which sex-roles are acquired, and there is considerable exposure to models illustrating adult roles, on TV and elsewhere; children's play often consists of trying out adult roles, such as those of teacher or doctor. In later life there are further processes of social learning, sometimes called 'adult socialisation'; this consists of several kinds of learning experience which teach a person how to perform various adult roles. Several different learning processes seem to be involved (Argyle, 1964b; Sarbin and Allen, 1969). (a) Imitation of models is a very effective method of learning, and the new entrant to an organisation is likely to look on the more successful and prestigeful members as suitable models. He will also be anxious to please them, and for both these reasons will become more like them. The Cambridge research student, it has been observed, immediately after graduation becomes an 'embryo-don' and gets out the chess and madeira. (b) Role-playing practice. Role-playing followed by feedback is the best-known method of teaching a social skill (p. 402 ff),

and something like this happens in everyday life too. It is important that there should be a trainer to comment on the performance, and on training courses for new entrants there are such trainers. When a person first takes up a new position he is in much the same position as an actor – he 'role-plays', i.e. produces a rather carefully managed version of the role. When he is more experienced however the behaviour will come quite naturally to him, and is a part of his normal repertoire of behaviour. Experience of the role also teaches the performer how the people in complementary roles are likely to perform – in a sense he learns their roles too. Playing the role affects the way a person sees himself – if he is treated as a doctor he comes to perceive himself as a doctor (p. 367 f).
(c) Initiation rites, or their equivalent, are found in many organisations, both for new members and for changes of position.

Emotional arousal plays a role here, both in the shared emotional experiences during training, and in the effects of initiation ceremonies. New members of organisations often undergo a series of emotionally arousing experiences. They may encounter situations which are new and perplexing, or which arouse great anxiety. A group of new members who share these experiences tend to become very closely knit together, as well as dependent on the senior members who help them through. The result is a very strong tie of loyalty to the organisation. Initiation ceremonies are similar, and are perhaps unwittingly created where other sources of emotional arousal are lacking. One effect of such ceremonies is to celebrate publicly the new member's change of social position – he is now accepted and regards himself as a member of the group: a change of ego-identity is brought about. Adolescents in African tribes are subjected to

'the solemn, even frightening and unforgettable experience of pre-initiation training and the final climax of initiation. . . . Its whole aim was to strike deep into the minds and hearts the traditions of the community, the wisdom of the elders and the continuity with ancestors' (Hunter, 1962).

It has also been shown experimentally that subjects who have been exposed to an unpleasant initiation ceremony are later more attracted to the group. We suggest that initiation ceremonies may be linked with other cases of learning via emotional arousal: changes of ego-identity and group membership are facilitated by the experience. It is interesting that medicine, the Church and the army all involve group emotional experiences during training and that each of these professions has a strongly-felt mystique and a sense of apartness from ordinary people –

compared for example with management and the civil service (Argyle, 1964b, pp. 132-3).

Despite the processes of social learning, selection, and demands of the job, there is still a considerable variation in the role performances of different occupants of a position – a point which was overlooked in older views of organisations. Differences in background or personality lead people to positions that suit them, but this is a fallible process since often they have little idea of what the position will be like. Individual differences may be due to a carry-over of previous organisational experience – as when an army officer becomes a manager, or a hospital sister becomes a nun. More important are personality dimensions – their needs for affiliation and dominance, their social competence, authoritarianism and so on. The interaction of organisational and personality variables can be seen in a study by Berkowitz (1956). In an experiment using a restricted set of communication channels it was found that the central person in a star pattern became most influential and dominated the group. If the central person had an unassertive personality it took a number of trials before he would accept the position of leadership, and he never became as influential as an assertive person in the same position. Such subjects experienced conflict between role and personality. In real organisations they would become very discontented and probably leave. Stern, Stein and Bloom (1956) found that 20% of students who were very high in authoritarianism withdrew from a college by the end of the first year, whereas none of the low authoritarians did. Stogdill (1953) studied the relative weights of position and personality in a statistical field study of naval officers who had been promoted. He compared their behaviour in the new position with their behaviour in previous positions and the behaviour of the previous occupant of the new position. Some aspects of interaction were more determined by position, including popularity, while others were more determined by personality, including style of leadership. We have said that an organisation is a social group whose interaction patterns have been frozen. Presumably these ways of interacting were satisfying to their originators, but they may not be satisfying to all of the later occupants, despite the attempts of selectors to pick people who will fit in. Furthermore, slow changes in the organisation may render it increasingly unsatisfactory to numbers of its members. In these cases there is a failure of congruence between role and personality.

The role may on the other hand constitute a very important part of the personality. We shall show in Chapter IX how identity is partly based on roles played. When the role is all-absorbing, as in the case of some politicians, film stars, headmistresses and others, there is little to the personality apart from the role. In addition, at a given point in time while taking the role, the performer's degree of involvement may vary from very casual enactment to extreme degrees of intensity, as Sarbin and Allen (1969) point out. As an example of the latter they quote Basedowe's account of how an Australian aboriginal may take the role of the victim when a sorcerer has pointed a bone at him:

> The man who discovers that he is being boned by an enemy is, indeed, a pitiable sight. He stands aghast, with his eyes staring at the treacherous pointer, and with his hands lifted as though to ward off the lethal medium, which he imagines is pouring into his body. His cheeks blanch and his eyes become glassy and the expression of his face becomes horribly distorted. . . . He attempts to shriek but usually the sounds choke in his throat, and all that one might see is froth at his mouth. From this time onwards he sickens and frets, refusing to eat and keeping aloof from the daily affairs of the tribe. Unless help is forthcoming in the shape of a countercharm administered by the hands of the Nangarri, or medicine-man, his death is only a matter of comparatively short time (Sarbin and Allen, 1969).

The phenomenon above is an extreme example of what has been termed 'altercasting', i.e. forcing a role on another person. Where there are a number of roles which the other could occupy, taking up a complementary role acts as a pressure on him to select one of them (Weinstein and Deutschberger, 1963).

Role conflict and ambiguity

Behaviour in social organisations might be expected to flow smoothly because the performers have been pre-programmed – they have learnt a set of synchronising roles. However, they may not all have quite the same ideas about what the roles should be, in which case there is *role conflict*. Or they may have very vague ideas about what the roles should be, in which case there is *role ambiguity*.

Conflict between roles. The same person will occupy a number of different roles – as with the case of a man who is a doctor, father, etc. Often these roles can be kept apart so that behaviour in any one situation is governed by only one role. Attention was first drawn to the phenomenon of role conflict by Burchard's study (1954) of the military chaplain – who has to perform simultaneously the conflicting roles of clergyman and military officer. A person may be confronted by another person in more than one role-relationship, as when a lawyer has a friend as a client. The two roles may lead to different kinds of behaviour, and a performer may signal which role is uppermost by saying 'as your friend I would suggest . . .' This is another example of 'altercasting'.

Conflicting pressures about the same role. Conflict may arise because other members of the organisation have different expectations and exercise different pressures about the performance of a person's role. This kind of conflict was first reported in the role of the female student. While her teachers expect her to be hard-working and intellectual, the male students prefer her to be unintellectual and non-competitive (Komarovsky, 1946). School superintendents have been found to be under conflicting pressures concerning the decisions they should make: teachers and taxpayers for example exert different pressures on such matters as salary increases for teachers (Gross, Mason and McEachern, 1958). Such conflicts are extremely common in industry: Kahn *et al.* (1964) in a survey of American industrial employees found that 48% were sometimes confronted by conflicts of this kind, for example between pressures from representatives of management and of the unions, or from company and clients. The different pressures may come from people in interlocking positions, as in the cases given above, or there may be disagreement among the occupants of the position in question. In the study of school superintendents it was found that there was more agreement in role-expectations the longer the people in question had interacted; this is an example of the growth of conformity. Interaction between people in different positions however did *not* lead to similarity of role expectations (Gross *et al.*, op. cit.).

Personality–role conflict. There may be conflict between an individual's role-expectations and those of others in the organisation. This happens in T-groups, since trainees are often surprised and disturbed at the behaviour of the trainer and the behaviour that is expected of them (p. 411). Unfamiliar roles like this can be learnt; it is more serious when there is conflict between a person's personality and the role. Smelser (1961) created such a conflict experimentally by giving subjects with high scores on dominance the more submissive role in a laboratory task and vice versa. Another familiar kind of conflict is when an authoritarian personality takes a position in a non-authoritarian organisation, or vice versa. A person with strong affiliative needs may find a bureaucratic organisation too impersonal; the result may be the development of informal friendships independent of the formal structure.

Role ambiguity. There is role ambiguity if there is no clear consensus of role-expectations. This means that the performer doesn't know what he should be doing, and has no clear expectations about how others will behave towards him. In their survey of industrial employees Kahn *et al.* (1964) found that 35% of their sample were disturbed by lack of clarity about the scope and responsibilities of their jobs. They conclude that this was due to the complexity of modern industrial organisation, to the rate of organisational change, and to the failure of management to put employees fully in the picture. There are particular problems about role ambiguity in the case of completely new roles: Schwartz (1957) reports that mental nurses are sometimes at a loss as to how to behave for this reason, and that they would like more definite rules to follow. Individuals in unfamiliar roles may have to be taught the role before progress can be made with the task: Lennard and Bernstein (1964) found that in the early stages of psychotherapy quite a lot of time was spent by therapists teaching patients the role of patient. It may even be necessary to reassure those in unfamiliar situations that there is a tradition of role behaviour and that what they are being asked to do is quite normal.

When a person experiences role conflict or ambiguity he tends to be tense and unhappy. Kahn *et al.* (1964) in an intensive study of 53 managers found that those exposed to role conflict or ambiguity were higher on experienced conflict and job-related tensions, as assessed by interview. This may take the form of somatic complaints. Role conflict also results in lower job satisfaction, as was found in the studies by Kahn *et al.* (op. cit.), and Gross *et al.* (1958).

A second effect of role conflict is for the person concerned to reduce his rate of interaction and closeness of relationship with the role-senders who are creating the conflict. Kahn *et al.* (op. cit.) found that individuals in role conflict trusted the senders less, had less respect for them, liked them less, communicated with them less often, and attributed less power to them. For some this withdrawal was successful in solving the problem – their job satisfaction was not much lower than that of similar people in low role conflict. However, there were two situations in which it was not possible to withdraw from interaction. One was that of role-senders who were dependent on the focal person's performance – who 'are usually unrelenting in their pressures because diminishing the pressures would jeopardise their own job efficiency' (p. 212). The other is when the role-senders had power over the focal person. Such inescapable pressures create intense conflict and depression and a 'kind of hopeless psychological disengagement from [his] co-workers' (p. 219). On the other hand when there is agreement between the role-expectations of people in different roles there are easy social relations between those concerned. This was found in a study of relations between foreman and shop stewards (Jacobson, Charters and Lieberman, 1951).

A third effect of role conflict is ineffectiveness on the part of those exposed to the conflict. Finally, role conflict or ambiguity can lead to attempts to resolve the conflict or to clarify what is ambiguous. This is the organisational equivalent of attention to socio-emotional problems in small social groups. Role ambiguity is usually resolved by seeking more direct instructions or rulings, such as producing books of instructions. Role conflict is resolved in more complex ways, as described below.

Different kinds of personality are affected by role conflict differently; Kahn *et al.* (op. cit) obtained information about this from their intensive study of 53 managers. Neurotic and anxious people experience greater tension, but are less likely to withdraw from the role-senders, perhaps because of greater dependency. Introverts with role conflict withdraw from close personal relationships and are regarded as unsociable and independent. Flexible personalities are more receptive to role-demands and thus experience more role conflict than rigid people, who do exactly what their superiors say and reject role-demands that cause conflict. Achievement-oriented people are more involved with their jobs and are therefore more affected by role conflict than security-oriented people. The role-senders also treat different personalities differently: flexible people for example receive stronger pressures than rigid people, since it is found that the latter do not respond.

The individual confronted by role conflict is likely to resolve the conflict by giving one role-expectation precedence over another. This solves the problem when one is generally agreed to have precedence – attending to a sick wife would have precedence over attending a seminar. Individuals have their own private hierarchies for deciding between role-expectations, based on their needs and values. Gross *et al.* (1958) in their study of school superintendents found that some decided mainly on grounds of legitimacy – i.e. the extent to which others have a right to hold these role-expectations – while some decided mainly on the basis of the negative sanctions which those exerting the pressures were able to deliver. In other words their subjects varied along a moral-expedient dimension in their manner of choosing between conflicting role-expectations. Stouffer and Toby (1951) asked subjects how they would act if confronted by various situations in which the demands of friendship conflicted with ethical or legal considerations, or the public interest.

In this and other similar studies a relation was found between authoritarianism and choosing the universalistic (i.e. ethical) alternative. An individual may also arrive at the solution via a process of 'role bargaining', in which he tries out various compromise solutions to see how far these are acceptable to those in interlocking roles (Goode, 1960).

Individuals may deal with role conflicts by means of various kinds of distortion and withdrawal. Kahn *et al.* (1964) as reported above found that members of industrial organisations exposed to role conflict tended to withdraw from those exerting the conflicting pressures. People exposed to role conflict may compartmentalise the two roles, only attending to one at a time; this was found to be common in the case of military chaplains (Burchard, 1954). Those exposed to role conflict may change their beliefs for example about the importance or legitimacy of one of the roles. They may withdraw from the situation and resort to drugs, food, sleep or tranquillisers (Sarbin and Allen, 1969).

Role conflicts may also be resolved by changes in the social structure; such changes may be initiated by administrators, but may be partly brought about by the individuals involved in the conflict. One such measure is to prevent people getting into situations which may involve role conflict – such as preventing doctors from doing research on their own patients, or preventing members of organisations from employing their own relatives. Another solution is the gradual merging of two roles to form a more harmonious single role. Perry and Wynne (1959) found that some therapist-researchers in a mental hospital had managed to create a new dual role in which the other two were combined. Another way in which changes in social structure can help is in protecting from sanctions those who are likely to be exposed to role conflict, such as diplomats and lawyers (Secord and Backman, 1964).

Power

A is said to have *power* over B if he is able to influence B's behaviour in one way or another – he may not actually use this power. We described earlier the hierarchy of power and influence in small social groups (p. 229 ff); power there is based mainly on control of affiliative rewards, and the possession of expertise at the group task. As we shall see, power in organisations often has other bases – the control of rewards and punishments, a belief that it is legitimate for some people to wield power, and the internalisation of organisational goals by members. The social structure thus creates power relations between members of an organisation.

In many organisations, the goals will not be attained unless there is sufficient collective effort and conformity to roles. Organisational structures grow up mainly in order to ensure that this occurs. Part of every role includes accepting the authority of someone in a supervisory capacity; the rules make it clear who is responsible for each part of the work; thus the power of supervisory staff is *legitimated* by acceptance of the organisational structure, and the awareness of the need for coordination of effort (Katz and Kahn, 1966). In small social groups legitimation is brought about by demonstrating expertise at the job; in a formal organisation this is not so necessary. In organisations the extent to which members do accept the authority of others varies; it depends mainly on the skills of supervision and the arousal of motivation, which will both be discussed later.

Etzioni's classification of organisations into coercive, utilitarian or normative was based on whether the main form of power used is punishment, reward or appeal to internalised motivations (p. 275 f). A number of other sources of power have been described by French and Raven (1959) and others.

Coercive power is where A is able to punish B, or where B believes that he can. Kahn *et al.* (1964) found that the following coercive techniques were commonly used by industrial managers – threatening with transfer or dismissal, threatening to block salary increase or promotion, and withholding help, information or cooperation. The last three were used on peers and superiors as well as subordinates. Evidence was obtained that such coercive techniques were highly correlated with effective power; even though they were not often used they were there in the background to back up other methods of influence. A number of laboratory experiments have been carried out to study the processes involved. It is clear that coercive power requires close surveillance, and that it arouses resistance and dislike for the source of power; it can however produce the required behaviour, and may be more effective than reward power under some conditions (Schopler, 1965). Coercive power is the main form of power used in prisons, and is important in military organisations. When power is primarily coercive, members of the organisation tend to feel alienated from the organisation, and only do what they are told because they have to (Etzioni, 1961).

Reward power. A has reward power when he is able to influence B's behaviour by offering rewards which are conditional on B's acting as required. The most familiar example is the use of wage incentives – where B's pay depends on how much work he has done. A may be able to increase B's pay or promote him, or recommend such increases and promotions. Or he may simply provide satisfaction for B's needs for dependence or affiliation; informal leaders can do this too, but interpersonal gratifications are greater when they come from a prestigeful person. Katz and Kahn (1966) point out that reward power only works if (a) the rewards are seen as large enough to justify the additional effort needed, (b) the rewards are seen as being directly related to the required performance and follow directly on its accomplishment, (c) the rewards are seen as fair by most members of the organisation. Any aspect of performance can be controlled by reward power – in addition to rate of work, quality of work, absenteeism or cooperativeness can be influenced in this way. Economic rewards are certainly effective in motivating industrial workers: when there is a change from payment by the day to payment by results, an increase in the rate of work of 60% commonly occurs (Davison *et al.*, 1958). On the other hand the quality of work tends to deteriorate, more inspectors and accountants are needed, and the same results can be achieved by the introduction of machine-paced or automated working methods. When reward is the main type of power used, there is a 'rational' or calculated amount of cooperation, but there may be little commitment to its goals (Etzioni, 1961).

A has *legitimate* power over B if B thinks that A has a right to exert influence, and that he, B, has an obligation to accept it. Katz and Kahn (op. cit.) regard such acceptance of legitimate power as a central feature of organisations, as explained above. Gross *et al.* (1958) found that some school superintendents resolved conflicting role-expectation on the basis of which seemed the most legitimate. On the other hand experimental attempts to create differences of legitimacy in the laboratory, e.g. Mulder *et al.* (1966), have not been very successful. This may be because legitimacy cannot be created quickly, but is the result of years of socialization in the organisation. An experiment which could be interpreted in terms of the legitimate power of the *experimenter* in relation to experimental subjects is Milgram's study of obedience (1965): subjects were ordered by the experimenter to give large, possibly fatal, electric shocks to a confederate; 27% of subjects complied with these orders. To make use of legitimate power, a member of an organisation can 'use his authority', i.e. give orders reminding those to whom they are directed of the relationship between them. He may also use coercive and reward power, which are probably more effective if they are seen as legitimate. Non-legitimate rewards are seen as 'bribes'. One kind of legitimate power is that found in feudal and military organisations, where members respect 'authority' as such. Another source of legitimate power is expertise at the work of the organisation. In small social groups the person best at the group task usually emerges as the informal leader. In research and technological organisations it is important for power to be legitimised in this way.

Power can be based on *internalised goals* in other members of the organisation. The others may be committed to the goals of the organisations, as doctors share the goals of hospitals for example. To influence a person who is committed in this way all that needs to be done is to remind him or to appeal to him to help promote the goals in question. Etzioni (1961) observes that some organisations work predominantly in this way. The more senior members of industrial and administrative organisations become committed to organisational goals, though less senior members have to be influenced in other ways. A second kind of internalised goal is the pursuit of self-expression or 'self-actualisation' by doing work that is sufficiently interesting, challenging or meaningful. To influence people here what has to be done is to arrange the conditions of work so that it satisfies needs for self-expression, and individual goals are integrated with those of the organisation. Herzberg *et al.* (1959) found that positive satisfaction, for engineers and accountants, was linked with successful achievement in connection with the job. McGregor (1960) has outlined an approach to supervision based on the integration of subordinates' goals with those of the organisation. This factor is most important for craftsmen, research workers and highly skilled personnel; if social skills come to be seen as a kind of expertise, these too may come to be regarded as a medium for self-expression.

Referent power. Two rather different kinds of influence have been given this name. (i) If A identifies with B, i.e. takes B as a model for imitation, A can now influence B merely by allowing his performance to be observed. Zander and Curtis (1962) compared this kind of influence with coercion, and found that referent power led to a higher standard of performance, and less satisfaction with it. A great advantage of this form of influence is that no surveillance is needed. (ii) If A likes B, then B can influence A, since he can withhold social rewards. French (1956) suggested that lines of influence follow sociometric choices *in reverse*. A superior can influence his subordinates if they like him more than he likes them.

Much modern thinking about organisations has been concerned with replacing coercive and reward power by other kinds. Coercive power needs close surveillance, and arouses resistance and hostility. Reward power also needs surveillance and is a kind of rational bargain; organisations however need a considerable surplus of cooperation and goodwill over and above what people have to do or are paid to do – as is seen by the complete breakdown which occurs when they 'work-to-rule'. Kahn *et al.* (1964) found that effective power was highly correlated with coercive and reward power, but had low correlations with referent power (appeal to friendship, asking personal favours, etc.), and expert power. We shall show below, however, that the most effective leadership is based on techniques that produce internalised commitment to goals and align motivation with organisational goals.

What effects does power have on the behaviour of those involved? By definition if A has power over B, he will be able to influence B's behaviour. The relative effectiveness of different kinds of power has been considered above. In addition it is found that powerful people are imitated. This was shown in an experiment by Bandura *et al.* (1963) in which it was found that children imitated the person who controlled resources; the explanation given was that a child will envy the controller of resources and identify with him. A number of studies have shown that communication and liking are directed towards powerful people except when the power is solely coercive. Mulder *et al.* (1964) found that this tendency was greater if the power differences were small.

When A has power over B this may affect interaction in a number of ways, as Emerson (1962) and others have shown. Emerson points out that B may balance the power relationship by manipulating the situation so that A's power is reduced and B's increased. Firstly B can withdraw from the relationship so that his dependence on A is equal to A's dependence on B; we have seen that withdrawal commonly occurs when there is role conflict. Secondly B may develop alternative relationships so that he is less dependent on A. Thirdly B may form a coalition with other low-power people; not only can they out-vote, or in other ways overpower A, they can also create group norms to which A has to conform. For example they can refuse to cooperate unless A makes more reasonable demands. Fourthly B can make A dependent on him by flattery, ingratiation or similar social rewards. Finally it is probable that differences of power will decrease if two people continue to interact, since both become increasingly dependent on each other (Secord and Backman, 1964); in a formal organisation this would probably not proceed as far as equality.

Communication patterns

Just as small social groups develop stable patterns of interaction, so do social organisations. Some of the interaction is officially recognised, and embodied in organisation charts. Some is unofficial. The official or formal organisation of positions, lines of authority, and channels of communication, describes only part of the actual pattern of communication. It deals with only some of the task-related interactions between people, and not with socioemotional exchanges. We shall in this section attempt to describe the total set of communications that occur without regard to whether they are 'formal' or 'informal'. There is a great deal of communication within organisations, and this is particularly true in the centres of administration and decision-taking. Zajonc and Wolfe (1963) found that there was nearly as much informal as formal communication between the members of a company.

Communications within an organisation can be divided into task and socio-emotional. A lot of communication is however hard to classify: coffee-breaks and other regular social events are the occasion for a good deal of social interaction of various kinds, both task and socio-emotional, both in formal channels and outside them. The regular informal patterns of interaction may change from time to time, but are usually replaced by others of the same kind. For the organisation to deal with its tasks effectively and satisfy the interpersonal needs of its members, it is necessary for networks of communication to be established. For task purposes it is necessary to have fairly definite and limited channels, rather than everyone communicating with everyone else, though the formal channels may not be sufficient for this purpose.

Other links are created because of the interpersonal needs of members, which cannot be satisfied within the bureaucratic and hierarchical structure of the formal organisation. It is for all these reasons that the classical theory of bureaucracy does not describe how organisations work; managers need to understand how the whole interpersonal system functions, and not just the part described by the organisation chart.

Horizontal communication. Organisation charts often allow only for vertical communication, yet for the majority of members of organisations most interaction is in fact with equals, both those in the immediate working unit, and those in other departments. (*a*) *Cooperation and help* in the working group. We saw earlier that groups do better than individuals at tasks. One reason for this is that errors can be corrected and members can help one another. Blau (1955) carried out a study of interaction between colleagues in a government department. They tended not to ask their supervisors for help for fear that this would reveal their incompetence, and affect their career prospects. Instead they consulted each other; they approached their friends, rather

than those with the greatest expertise – this too would show up their incompetence. Reciprocity developed between pairs of colleagues who
helped one another. (*b*) *Communication with other groups or departments*.
Coordination of different departments in a large organisation is difficult
unless there are informal links between members. Landsberger (1961–2)
found that in one factory 41% of messages sent by the line production
manager were to other managers at the same level, and 40% of messages
received were also from this level. At Oxford University links between
university departments are created by the college system – a second
formal structure which operates as the informal background of the
university formal structure. Some individuals come to play an important
part in the communication flow because they belong to two overlapping
groups, and are willing to pass information on. (*c*) *Friendship and social
support*. Sociometric linkages and small social groups emerge inside social
organisations. These may grow out of formal linkages and within departments – what Homans (1951) called the 'secondary system' arising
out of the work-group. They may also emerge quite outside the formal
organisation, either through such semi-formal contacts as coffee-breaks,
or for extra-organisational reasons such as people living near to each
other. Relations between immediate colleagues may become difficult if
they are competing for promotion, and relationships may be easier if
they are less closely linked in the organisation – their association is useful to them and to the organisation by providing the links described in
(b).

Communication downwards. (a) Instructions, orders and information.
According to classical theory and the organisation chart this is the main
line of communication in organisations. In fact a complex two-way
pattern of interaction is involved. Superiors may have different amounts,
and also different kinds of power they may use a variety of styles of
supervision (p. 299 ff). Thus the instructions may be persuasive,
may give reasons or explanation, and may carry offers of reward or
punishment. Tactfully given instructions may be seen as information or
advice by the recipient (Burns, 1954). Information may be about the
job, about a person's performance, or about impending changes in the
organisation. Supervisors also give subordinates feedback about their
performance: there are often complaints by subordinates that they do
not know where they stand (Kahn *et al.*, 1964), but the process of giving
this information is found difficult and embarrassing by both parties.
McGregor (1960) devised the technique of asking subordinates to set
their own goals and appraise themselves in relation to these goals; if the

supervisor's appraisal differs, a personnel interview is held along the lines described on p. 304 f.

(b) Communications from experts. We saw above that members of work-groups seek help from others in the same group. Experts may or may not have formal positions commensurate with their expertise. Burns and Stalker (1961) found that young engineering graduates in electronics factories sometimes had more influence than more senior men because of their expertise in electronics. There are special lines of communication connected with expertise: 'opinion leaders' become accepted as sources of reliable information in their field of expertise; they in turn are in contact with even better-informed people; doctors who are regarded as experts in new drugs provide an example of this process (Coleman, Katz and Menzel, 1957).

(c) Two-step and indirect communication. If a senior manager wants to communicate with those two or more levels below him in the hierarchy he has three ways of doing so. (1) He can issue one-way messages over a tannoy, via notices or by letter. Such one-way communications may be felt to be frustrating to the recipients, since they are unable to comment or express their views, and they may not understand them or understand the background. (2) He can make direct contact with the lower-level people, going 'over the heads' of the first-line supervisors, which will upset the latter. (3) He can go through the normal hierarchical channels. This is the standard procedure, but it takes time. The message may have to be translated into more specific terms at each stage, it may become distorted on the way. It is difficult to receive any feedback, and it may make the first-line supervisor a 'man in the middle' who is under pressure from both sides, and has to implement someone else's instructions. Donald (1959) found that in larger branches of the League of Women Voters there were more downward and fewer upward communications, and that intermediate levels were sometimes skipped.

Upward communications. (a) Seeking help. It would be expected that a normal pattern of communication in a hierarchy would be for junior personnel to seek the help of senior, more experienced and knowledgeable members. We saw how in the government department studied by Blau (1955) there were barriers to asking for help. This is not necessarily the case in all organisations. Shepard (1954) in a similar study of a university engineering research group found that formal status did not act as a barrier to communication; in this group however the junior members were not dependent on their superiors for promotion.

(b) Reporting progress. It is essential for senior staff to have accurate information about progress with the work, difficulties encountered, etc. It is not always easy for them to get it. Information about progress with the job is liable to result in the use of sanctions, therefore such information tends to be delayed and distorted – the supervisor is told what he wants to hear and when he is thought to be in a receptive mood. Read (1962) found that upward communications in industrial organisations were less accurate if the senders were keen to be promoted. In brief, upward messages are often delayed, distorted or not sent at all.

(c) Suggestions and other upward communications. Although those at lower levels may be reluctant to report difficulties or lack of progress, they are more forthcoming about other matters. They like to be consulted, to get their grievances corrected and have their ideas heard at higher levels. In authoritarian organisations it is very difficult for this to happen, but in newer kinds of organisation upward communication is achieved by suggestion schemes, consultative styles of supervision, and representation on committees. Laboratory experiments show that low-status subjects communicate a lot upwards, including material irrelevant to the task (Kelley, 1951). In organisations they work hard presenting a favourable impression to their superiors, who of course are too concerned with presenting a favourable impression to *their* superiors to notice.

(d) Relationships between individuals at different levels. Social relations are easier between two individuals of the same rank. If A is B's immediate superior there is always a certain strain in the relationship, and friendship choice is unlikely. If A is of higher rank, but not B's superior, sociometric choice is more likely.

DETERMINANTS OF ORGANISATIONAL EFFECTIVENESS

The hierarchical structure

The practical application of research on social organisations is to find ways of increasing their effectiveness. The latter can be measured by various indices based on the goals of the organisation. Examples are measures of productivity (industry), known re-conviction percentage (prisons), research papers published or cited (research organisations), and performance in exercises (military units). Sometimes there will be several goals, e.g. costs *and* quality of output, re-conviction percentage *and* number of prisoners escaping, which would have to be weighted and combined in some way. Katz and Kahn (1966) suggest that the following types of individual behaviour are needed to produce organisational effectiveness:

1. Joining and staying in system
   (a) Recruitment
   (b) Low absenteeism
   (c) Low turnover.
2. Dependable behaviour: role performance in system
   (a) Meeting or exceeding quantitative standards of performance
   (b) Meeting or exceeding qualitative standards of performance.
3. Innovative and spontaneous behaviour: performance beyond role requirements for accomplishment of organisational functions
   (a) Cooperative activities with fellow members
   (b) Actions protective of system or subsystem
   (c) Creative suggestions for organisational improvement
   (d) Self-training for additional organisational responsibility
   (e) Creation of favourable climate for organisation in the external environment.

A further variable is individual job satisfaction: since people spend so much of their lives in working and other organisations it is important that the experience should be a satisfying one. Considerable research interest has been taken in the relationship between job satisfaction and other measures of individual behaviour related to organisational effectiveness. The results can be summarised as follows:

(1) When job satisfaction is high, labour turnover and absenteeism are low, especially if indices of voluntary absenteeism are used. This has been found in a number of studies, and the typical correlation is in the region of ·30 (Vroom, 1964).

(2) Job satisfaction has very little correlation with rate of manual work, whether individuals or departments are used as the units for statistical comparison (Brayfield and Crockett, 1955; Vroom, op. cit.). Factors accounting for this rather surprising result are: workers with high job involvement and high output are more upset by obstacles to progress; in very routine repetitive work there is little opportunity to obtain intrinsic satisfaction from achievement on the job; some people are happiest when taking it easy, others work hard to forget their sorrows.

(3) Cohesive groups produce high satisfaction and low turnover and absence; they also produce conformity to norms of productivity, but these may be for high or low levels of output, as shown in a study by Seashore (1954) – see Fig. 7.2.

Again it seems that there are two partly separate goals in organisations

– task performance and welfare of members. Both output and variables like absenteeism and turnover would be affected if members could be motivated to pursue organisational goals. The term 'morale' has sometimes been used to mean 'acceptance of organisational goals' and attitude scales have been devised to assess it. The problem is that in many organisations morale in this sense is very low for large numbers of members – they are 'alienated' from the organisation. This is particularly true of organisations like prisons which are both coercive and

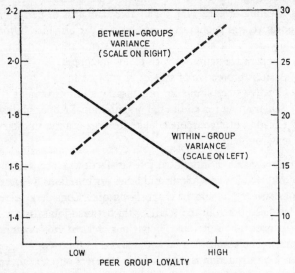

Figure 7.2. Relationship of peer-group loyalty to variance on productivity (from Seashore, 1954, redrawn by Likert, 1961)

'total' in that the life of the inmates is totally controlled by the staff. It is often true of the lower ranks of military organisations, especially when they are conscripts. It is true of many manual workers in industry, who are only there because they are paid to be, and may feel extremely hostile to the organisation. The author has known industrial concerns in which alienation has spread as far up as middle management. Research on organisations suggests a number of ways in which this and other problems might be resolved.

(1) *Making the organisation less hierarchical.* The adoption of democratic leadership makes an organisation less hierarchical in one sense; the effects of this style of leadership are discussed below; we are concerned here however with changes in the formal structure. We showed

above that the hierarchy creates barriers to upward communication, and that the more levels there are the more difficult communication is. Porter and Lawlor (1965) conclude from a review of the evidence that flat organisations are more effective than tall ones, when the organisation is small; that the larger the organisation the lower the job satisfaction, and the greater the absenteeism and labour turnover; and that there is an advantage in decentralisation when sections are not interdependent. Blau and Scott (1963) favour increasing the span of control on the grounds that in addition to reducing the number of levels, subordinates become more independent, supervision is less close and dependence on subordinates less likely.

The organisation can be 'flattened' by increasing the autonomy of lower levels by generally delegating greater powers to them, for example by increasing the amount of money they can spend without higher authority. Morse and Reimer (1956) carried out a field experiment in which the power given to lower levels in a company was increased. Junior leaders can be allowed to participate in decision-taking by making them members of committees, where all have an equal vote, at least in theory. Committees are widely used in British universities and the civil service. In industry they provide a means of bringing line managers and different technical specialists together.

The hierarchy can be reduced by more radical measures still – abolishing leaders. There have been experiments with 'autonomous work groups' which have no appointed first-line leader, and favourable results have been reported in a coal mine (Herbst, 1962). In fact workers in certain positions in the work-flow became informal leaders and did the work of formally appointed supervisors. This idea has not been developed, and it is probable that a formal leader using the recommended style of supervision would do the job better in view of his experience, formal power, and influence at higher levels. More plausible is the abolition of second or third line leaders. Their job is supposed to be coordinating the work of departments under first-line leaders. But some of these departments are not interdependent and do not need coordinating, while a great deal of coordination is in any case achieved by horizontal communication between first-line leaders (Simpson, 1959).

(2) *Steps towards industrial democracy.* The forms of 'flattening' and delegation discussed so far do not extend any more power to the rank and file members, except in so far as democratic supervision gives them a greater say in day-to-day matters. Full 'industrial democracy' would give every man an equal vote and the power to elect representatives

who would control the organisation, including the technical aspects of it. Something like this happens in voluntary and professional bodies, though even here it is common for an oligarchy to do most of the work, and for the majority of members to be apathetic (Blau and Scott, 1963). Degrees of industrial democracy have been tried out in some industrial firms.

(a) *Group decision* methods in working groups appear to extend democratic powers to the rank and file (Coch and French, 1948). In practice the area of problems over which group decisions may be taken is very limited – matters of the detailed implementation of decisions taken at more senior levels, rather than taking the decisions themselves.

(b) *Joint consultation* between management and representatives of workers has been widely tried; this has had rather varied success, the main difficulty being that the committees tend to concentrate on the discussion of workers' complaints (N.I.I.P., 1952). Works councils with rather wider powers have also been tried. The Glacier Metal Company was re-structured with the help of the Tavistock Institute. Workers were represented on the Works Council, and were able to exert influence within certain limits, but the management still ran the company (Brown, 1967). The hierarchy defeats democracy: managers are more senior and more expert at technical matters, and carry more weight on committees; the workers' representatives become estranged from those who elected them (Foster, 1968).

(c) *The Scanlon plan* involves setting up departmental production committees, with elected workers' representatives, as well as a company-wide committee, to decide on changes in production methods and payment (Scanlon, 1948). This entails moving quite a long way towards industrial democracy. Workers are paid 75–100% of the direct gains as bonus, and an attempt is made to create a feeling of mutual trust and partnership. This plan has been very successful in a number of industrial concerns, especially in fairly small ones. The effect is partly that individuals work harder, but they are also more cooperative and have more suggestions.

(d) *Shared responsibility*. A key feature of therapeutic communities, for mental patients, is the free discussion of each patient's problems by the community, and encouraging inmates to care for each other, and take some responsibility for each other's welfare (Rapoport, 1960). While discussions in these communities give the impression that technical decisions on medical matters are being handed over to patients, the main point is that taking part in decisions is therapeutic, and creates positive relations within the group.

(e) *Suggestions schemes.* We have seen that rank-and-file members like to communicate their ideas upwards, and that there are barriers to such communication. Suggestions schemes are one solution, and they are widely used. There should be rewards related to the profits to the company resulting from the use of the suggestions.

*   *   *   *   *

We have discussed some of the more important changes in social organisation which have been suggested by research, and tried out in a number of places. There is no simple solution to an organisation's problems: each one is unique, and a unique and imaginative solution is required. However, the principles suggested in this and the following sections provide a starting point.

Leadership

In most organisations there are first-line leaders, or supervisors, who direct the activities of those who do most of the work. There are second- and third-line leaders, or managers, who direct and coordinate the supervisors. It may be asked why leaders are necessary at all, since the organisational rules might be sufficient to keep things running. In fact considerable use is made of impersonal mechanisms of control in the form of automated and machine-paced equipment, and incentive schemes. Katz and Kahn (1966) suggest that leaders are necessary because the organisational plan is incomplete and does not provide for all contingencies, because there are changing environmental conditions to be responded to, because of the need for coordination and avoidance of conflicts inside the organisation, and because of the necessity to deal with individuals with their particular motivations and problems.

Leaders always have some formal powers to reward and punish, varying with the type of organisation. Apart from total institutions like prisons, leaders cannot depend on their formal powers alone, but must obtain a surplus of willing cooperation from their subordinates. Leaders also want their men to be sufficiently happy in their work to turn up regularly and to stay with the organisation. They may want them to be happy as an end in itself.

Leaders in organisations vary in their style of leadership. This section is concerned with the question of which styles are the most effective. The problem has been extensively studied and is perhaps the best instance of a social skill being defined by research on its effectiveness. Most of this research has consisted of the statistical comparison of leaders whose units differ in productivity, or other measures of effectiveness. The main weakness of this method is that such statistical results can be given more than one causal interpretation. When it is found for example that productivity is higher in departments where supervisors exercise *less* pressure for better performance (Seashore and Georgopoulos, cited by Likert, 1961, p. 8) this could be because high output results in less pressure rather than vice versa. There have been one or two experimental studies, in which style of leadership has been experimentally manipulated. Feldman (1937) found that when supervisors of clerks were moved round, the rank order of output of sections by supervisors remained the same, with departments changing 6–18%. Jackson (1953) found that when supervisors moved to groups of different output their styles of supervision did not change. There is a certain amount of evidence, then, that supervisors affect groups, rather than vice versa.

A number of rather different dimensions have been used for comparing supervisory behaviour. Halpin and Winer (1952), in studies of military leaders, obtained two main orthogonal dimensions by factor analysis, and in a number of later studies these have been found to be the two main dimensions along which industrial, military and other leaders vary. They are:

(i) *Initiating structure:* the extent to which the leader maintains standards of performance and follows routines, makes sure his position and functions are understood, and distributes tasks.

(ii) *Consideration:* the degree to which the leader shows warmth in personal relationships, trust, readiness to explain actions, and listens to subordinates.

It will be noted that these two dimensions correspond to the two kinds of behaviour and two kinds of leader found in small informal groups – the task and socio-emotional leaders respectively. We shall discuss other dimensions of leadership in relation to these two dimensions.

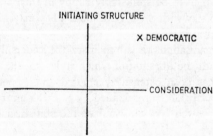

Blake and Mouton (1964) put forward a 'management grid' in which managers are rated from 1 to 9 on two dimensions of concern for production and concern for people; their two dimensions correspond closely to Initiating Structure and Consideration. 'Democratic' leadership can be looked at as a combination of the two dimensions. It involves special social techniques – persuasion, explanation and holding group discussions. Autocratic leadership is the polar opposite – orders are issued without explanation, and coercive, punitive methods of discipline are used. A considerable number of comparisons have been carried out on the effects of these two styles of leadership, in a variety of industrial and administrative organisations in the USA (Likert, 1961), in British firms (Argyle, Gardner and Cioffi, 1958) and elsewhere. The main finding is that democratic leaders, those fairly high both on Initiating Structure and on Consideration, are more effective. They are more effective both in terms of productivity or effectiveness variables, and in terms of high job satisfaction, low labour turnover and low absenteeism. It may be suggested that these studies between them define the optimum style of leadership in social organisations in contemporary American and European society. It is true that there are situations in which this result does not apply, and these are discussed below.

How far can the same leadership style simultaneously result in maximum productivity and job satisfaction? It is probably true in general that a supervisory style that is high on initiating structure will lead to increased productivity, possibly at the expense of job satisfaction. However, rate of work is not the only source of total productivity; absenteeism and labour turnover must also be kept low, and this entails keeping up job satisfaction. Furthermore, workers want to achieve good results at their work, either because of wage incentives, achievement motivation or motivational involvement in the work. Consequently the two goals of productivity and satisfaction are closely linked, and can be realised by the same leadership style.

There are probably three reasons why the democratic-persuasive style is effective. (a) It combines the task and socio-emotional aspects of leadership; using persuasion and consultation makes it possible to combine the two – to exert influence without arousing hostility, and to look after welfare and be on good terms with the men without losing influence. However, unlike an informal leader, a formal leader cannot necessarily rely on the desire of group members to attain the group goals; Blau and Scott (1963) suggest that the rewards produced by the leader create social obligations for reciprocation by complying with his requests – a case of social exchange. (b) The fact that subordinates participate in decisions has the result that they become committed to the plan of action decided, and there is internalisation of task motivation. In the study by Lippitt (1940) of boys' clubs, the democratically led group worked just as hard when the leader was out of the room whereas the autocratically led groups stopped work. (c) The democratic style encourages group discussion and communication between members: this increases cohesiveness and cooperation within the group; not only is better cooperation obtained, but fuller use is made of the ideas and skills of individual members.

Likert (1961) asks why, if democratic leadership is more effective, so many leaders continue to be authoritarian. He suggests that since there is no correlation between variables such as job satisfaction and output in the case of manual workers, supervisors learn to disregard the feelings of workers and concentrate on production. In the case of research workers, engineers, accountants and other highly skilled people there *is* a correlation between job satisfaction and output (see Herzberg *et al.*, 1959), and democratic supervision is more common. Authoritarian leadership can certainly result in high productivity, in industry or elsewhere, but job satisfaction is low. In addition absenteeism and labour turnover are high, and there is a high rate of psychosomatic illness. Selvin (1960) found that authoritarian leadership in the army led to a high rate of going AWOL, eating between meals, drunkenness, seeing the chaplain, blowing one's top, fighting, and sexual intercourse.

There are however conditions under which democratic leadership is not the most effective, where a higher degree of initiating structure is needed, with less consultation and discussion. Fiedler (1964) has presented a general scheme showing the conditions under which permissive leadership does and does not work. We think that it is better to look at the negative cases as exceptions to the general rule, where special circumstances favour the non-permissive approach. These conditions are as follows: (a) When group members have authoritarian personalities, they get on better with an authoritarian leader (Haythorn, 1956). Such members prefer being told what to do rather than sharing responsibility for decisions. It follows that training leaders in the new style may not be enough – the subordinates, or some of them, may have to be trained as well to take the proper complementary role. This consists of taking an active part in decision-taking, being helpful and cooperative towards the leader, and not treating him with undue deference. (b) When the group members have negative attitudes towards the leader, but when he also has high power over them, non-permissive methods of leadership are most effective (Fiedler, op. cit.). Here the leader has to fall back on coercive and reward power. (c) When the task is highly structured, all the leader has to do is to make sure it is carried out correctly, and non-permissive methods of leadership are again success-ful (Fiedler, op. cit.). This is more a question of surveillance, or inspec-tion, rather than leadership proper. As Fiedler points out, a leader might have to change his style with different phases of a group's work: the leader of a research group should be more permissive while the research plan is being discussed than when it is being carried out. Normally a research group needs very permissive leadership. Pelz (1956) found that greatest scientific productivity was achieved when there was a combina-tion of daily contact and maximum independence. (d) When decisions have to be taken very quickly, and in times of crisis, more authoritarian leadership is needed. Hamblin (1958) found that experimental groups rejected and replaced a leader if he did not deal with a crisis quickly and decisively. (e) In a larger group there is more need for central control: Hemphill (1950), in a questionnaire study, found that there was greater tolerance for leader-centred direction in groups with over 30 members. Maier and Solem (1952) found that problem-solving groups were more successful when the leader suppressed the more vocal members and allowed minority views to be heard.

Both first- and second-line leaders have the problem of facing both upwards and downwards, of being 'men in the middle'. They have to carry out instructions from their supervisors, and promote the goals of the organisation; they also have to deal with and look after the variety of individuals in their charge. They are very liable to be in role conflict and have to represent each side to the other. Leaders are thought by their subordinates to be effective if they are high on Consideration; but their supervisors judge them in terms of Initiating Structure (Gibb, 1969). A number of studies have shown that to be effective a first-line leader should be somewhat detached from his men. Fiedler (1958) found, in a variety of groups from basketball teams to steel workers, that leaders were more effective who discriminated clearly between the most and least preferred co-workers; Fiedler considers that this shows detachment from the group and a readiness to put task considerations before social ones. Leaders should also be independent of their own superiors: Pelz (1952) found that employee-centred supervision led to high job satisfaction only when supervisors were powerful and able to exert influence at higher levels. It is however very difficult to be sufficiently detached from both subordinates and superiors, and to be able to influence both parties. Blau and Scott (1963) found that supervisors who were loyal to their superiors were less likely to command the loyalty of their own subordinates.

At higher levels in the organisation it is found that the character of leadership changes, and one of the main jobs is actually changing and creating social structures. From this it follows that while junior leaders need skills of leadership, senior leaders need to understand how organisations work. It has been suggested by sociologists that senior leaders should have the magical aura known as 'charisma'; since they are only seen at a distance by most members of the organisation, visible qualities may become important. There are few empirical studies of second-line leaders and above. Stogdill *et al.* (1953) found that if second-line leaders delegated responsibility, this style was adopted by the first-line leaders; Fleishman (1953) found that the most important determinant of leadership style was the 'leadership climate' created from above.

All leaders have to hold periodic interviews with individual subordinates. We mentioned above McGregor's techniques (1960) for giving orders and setting targets, and for holding appraisal interviews. This approach can be applied to the 'personnel interview', where a leader has to talk to a subordinate whose performance is believed to be unsatisfactory. This is often found difficult and embarrassing and may be avoided. The personnel interview can take a very different form within the democratic-persuasive relationship, and is indeed a good example of the way this kind of leadership functions. The following account incorporates ideas from Sidney and Brown (1961) and Maier (1952).

1. The supervisor (S) finds out as much as he can about the performance and relevant circumstances of the client (C). He also decides on a strategy, what goals he will try to achieve, and what kinds of persuasion he will use. This strategy is provisional, as new facts may come to light during the interview.

2. S establishes rapport with C, who may be very nervous about the interview. This will be easier if S maintains good day-to-day contacts with C. They may chat briefly about common interests, so that status barriers are reduced, and C is ready to talk freely.

3. It may be necessary for S to explain that there is a problem – C has been persistently late so that production has fallen, C has been getting very low marks, etc. This should be done by stating objective facts, not by passing judgement, and should be done in a manner that is pleasant rather than cross.

4. S now invites C to say what he thinks about the situation, what he thinks the reason for it is. This may involve a certain amount of probing for fuller information, if C is reluctant to open up. S is sympathetic, and shows that he wants to understand C's position. S may ask C whether he thinks the situation is satisfactory; in an evaluation interview he can ask C to evaluate his own performance.

5. There now follows a period of joint problem-solving, in which C and S try between them to work out a solution to the problem. This may involve actions on S's side as well as on C's – such as giving C a different job, or making some other change in the situation. It may involve a trial period after which S and C will meet again to review the situation.

6. If some change of behaviour on C's part is indicated, and if C proves uncooperative, further steps may be necessary. The first of these is persuasion. S may be able to point out that C will not reach his own goals by his present line of action – as with a student who will fail his exams if he doesn't work harder. Such social influence is a subtle skill in itself, and depends on being able to appeal realistically to the right needs in a particular individual.

7. If this fails, and if further interviews become necessary, sterner means of influence may have to be resorted to. Most S's are in a position to control material sanctions, such as bonuses, promotions, and finally dismissal. S will not usually want to sack C – what he wants is to keep him but behaving differently. The possible use of such sanctions should first be mentioned reluctantly as a rather remote possibility – for example by the quite objective statement 'there are several other people who would like this job', or 'I may have to tell the people who pay your grant about your progress'.

8. The interview should end with a review of what has been agreed, the constructive steps that have been decided upon, when S and C will meet again to discuss progress, and so on. The meeting should end on as friendly a note as possible (Argyle, 1967, pp. 169–71).

If the democratic-persuasive style is adopted throughout an organisation this will constitute a major change in the nature of the organisation. (a) Consultation of subordinates, and delegation of authority, create greater autonomy at lower levels and freer upward communication. One of the main sources of low satisfaction and high turnover is the feeling of not being consulted. (b) The persuasive handling of individuals, and attempts to relate their motivation to organisational goals, as stressed by McGregor (1960), make maximum use of the motivation available. (c) Holding group discussions and making group decisions makes small groups cohesive and cooperative, and ensures that output norms are in the direction of high rather than low output. Likert (1961) sees this as a change in structure, in which the supervisor is himself a member both of the group he supervises, and of the group supervised by his own immediate superior, as shown in Fig. 7.3.

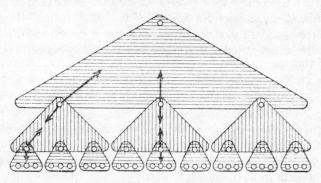

Figure 7.3. Likert's 'linking-pin' structure. The arrows indicate the linking-pin function (from Likert, 1961)

Work-flow and interaction

Most social organisations have a collective task. The activities of individual members are combined and coordinated so as to perform the task. The way in which this is done is known as the work-flow system. In industry it may take the form of assembly lines, automated plant, etc. The work-flow creates a certain pattern of interaction between those working on it, and can be regarded as one of the components of the organisation. The work-flow is designed by technologists, but it has to be operated by people, and people who cooperate.

The work-flow arrangements can create role-relationships along the two main dimensions of liking and status. If two or more people are brought together in a small group, and are closely dependent on each other, powerful positive bonds will be formed. Small group experiments show that cooperative attitudes are brought about by interdependent division of labour and incentives based on group performance (see p. 222 f.). On the other hand if men rarely interact, or interact in such a way as to frustrate or impede each other, negative attitudes will develop. The work-flow also creates status differences – when one person is paid more than another, or when one person has power to inspect, direct or otherwise control the activities of another.

The role-relationships are part of the total system; Trist and his colleagues at the Tavistock Institute of Human Relations have termed the whole organisation the 'socio-technical system'. Clearly attention should be paid to the design of the human and social part of the system, as well as to the technical. The main failure is that sometimes not enough cooperation is generated for the interpersonal links in the system to work properly. Van Zelst (1952) found that the performance of brick-layers was greater in cohesive versus non-cohesive work-groups; the difference is greater when the degree of cooperation demanded by the task is greater (Schutz, 1953). The main signs of failure in the social sphere are however labour turnover, absenteeism, accidents, and loss of production due to failure of cooperation. The solution requires imagination and ingenuity.

Most of the research in this area has been of the case-study variety, carried out in connection with industrial consulting, by the Tavistock Institute and others. We will give some examples of these case studies, with the principles which they suggest, and then describe some laboratory experiments.

(1) Whyte (1949) found that there were great tensions in Chicago restaurants between the waitresses and the cooks, which resulted in waitresses crying. The reason, he diagnosed, was that the cooks had to take orders from the lower-status waitresses. His solution was for the waitresses to place orders on a 'spindle', so that the cooks could attend to them at their convenience.

(2) Chapple and Sayles (1961) found that there was hostility and lack of cooperation between the sales and credit departments of a sales organisation. What happened, he found, was that customers went first to the sales department and then to the credit department where the lengthy efforts of the sales department were often wiped out by credit being refused. A very simple solution was suggested – customers were re-routed to the credit department first, as this was a much shorter operation than sales.

(3) Trist *et al.* (1963) from the Tavistock Institute of Human Relations studied the Longwall system of mechanical coal-mining. In this system, groups of 41 men under a single supervisor were divided into three shifts, each doing a different job – cutting, filling and stonework, but each shift was highly dependent on the others. Since the teams never met, it was impossible for cohesiveness and cooperation to develop, especially as different prestige was attached to the different jobs. It was

extremely difficult to supervise shifts working at different times; in addition these working groups were larger than those in earlier arrangements, and were more spread out spatially in the dark, so that the old cohesiveness, which served to reduce the anxieties of mining, was lost. There was a high level of absenteeism and discontent. It was possible to compare this arrangement with a modified version, in which the men were regrouped into composite groups, so that all three tasks were carried out on each shift. The result was an output of 5·3 tons per man-shift compared with 3·5 in the conventional Longwall design; absenteeism was 40% of the rate in the other groups. The reasons are probably that (a) better relations were established between those doing the three different jobs, and tensions between shifts were removed, (b) there was less division of labour and more variety of work, (c) status differences between those on different shifts and using different skills were abolished. This study shows that the same technological arrangements can be operated by quite different kinds of social organisation. This is not always the case – it would be difficult to operate an assembly line differently for example (Brown, 1967).

(4) Rice (1958), also of the Tavistock, was able to take a step further, and design a new structure for working groups in the Ahmedabad Textile mills in India. Automatic looms had been introduced, but production had not increased. Two hundred and twenty-four looms were looked after by 29 men, divided into 12 different task roles, and with a very confused pattern of relations between them. Rice's solution was to create 4 groups of 7, 3 on weaving, and 1 on maintenance, the groups being formed by mutual choice. Each group was collectively responsible for 64 looms, each group performing its own ancillary services. The result was an increase of 21% in productivity and a drop of 59% in damaged cloth; the new organisation was rapidly applied to other weaving sheds. The reasons for the success of this arrangement were probably that (a) workers belonged to small cohesive groups working on a cooperative task; (b) the task was more varied and added up to a meaningful total performance.

(5) Other case studies of automated systems have drawn attention to further aspects of the work-flow though the effects vary in different systems. Isolation and difficulties of communication between men at remote dials and control points has sometimes been reported (Walker, 1957). On the other hand men may have considerable physical mobility and there is often good teamwork between them. Status differences between supervisors and men may be increased and promotion prospects made worse if supervisors need to have higher technical qualifications

than before. The supervisors in turn may have little power since the process is controlled by even more skilled technologists. On the other hand frictions within the work-group may be reduced because differences of pay and status attached to different jobs are removed. There are also radical changes in the nature of the work which men do: repetitive and assembly-line work is replaced by work that is 'easier physically, harder mentally', and generally more interesting and responsible (Mann and Hoffman, 1960; D.S.I.R., 1956).

We turn now to laboratory experiments in which analogues of work-flow systems have been created. While these experiments are more rigorous than case studies in the field, they are also rather unrealistic. Leavitt (1951) compared 5-man groups with various communication arrangements for their ability to solve problems – the problem being

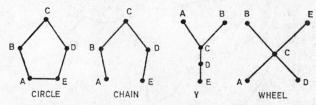

Figure 7.4. Leavitt's communication patterns (from Leavitt, 1951)

simply to find out which of a number of symbols given to each member was held by all 5 members. The communication patterns were as in Fig. 7.4. He found that the circle pattern was slowest, made most mistakes and needed the most messages; the Y pattern made the fewest errors. As Collins and Raven (1969) point out, the Leavitt task is one that can be carried out better by an individual than by a group. It follows that the most suitable group structure will be one where all the information can be given to one person as easily as possible. Guetzkow and Simon (1955) suggest that restriction of communication channels affects group performance mainly by making it more difficult for the group members to organise themselves for efficient performance. The differences in times between different structures is very small after 20 trials (cf. Fig. 7.5). Mulder (1960) devised an index of the extent to which a group actually achieves a centralised structure, and found that the most centralised groups within any given structure were fastest, but that the wheel groups achieved such a structure most often. Later experiments by Shaw (1964), using a more complex problem-solving task, found that here the circle pattern was faster than the wheel – the reverse of Leavitt's result. Other investigations have confirmed this result, and it is now clear that the best structure varies with the type of task. Experiments by Lanzetta and Roby (1956) have shown that in 3-man work-groups accuracy is reduced if subjects are dependent on others for information, if information is dispersed so that more than one source has to be used, if there is a high task load, and if the load is unevenly balanced between members (cf. Glanzer and Glaser, 1961). Shaw (1964) has suggested two general principles to account for the results in this area: (1) individuals perform more effectively if they have greater independence or autonomy, for example if they are not restricted

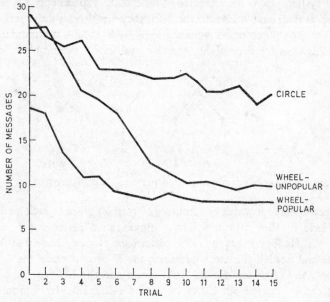

Figure 7.5. The efficiency of groups with popular and un-popular central members

by inaccessibility of information or the actions of others; (2) groups function better if the communication channels and the members are not saturated with more information than can be dealt with.

The effectiveness of a communication system also depends on the personalities of those concerned and the relations between them. Mohanna and Argyle (1960) compared wheel groups with popular and unpopular central members and circle groups. The groups with unpopular central members were initially even slower than circle groups, but after about seven trials overtook them, though never catching up the groups with popular central members (Fig. 7.5). Shaw (1968) found that, with an authoritarian central member, wheel groups were more efficient, since the number of messages used was less and saturation reduced.

Communication patterns also affect the relations between people. The people in more central positions assume informal leadership of the group. In the Berkowitz study (1956), subjects low in ascendance when placed in the central position gradually become more dominant on later trials. In the Lanzetta and Roby experiments, subjects became dependent on other subjects for information needed for their own task. In the Mohanna and Argyle experiment unpopular subjects rapidly became accepted as informal leaders, since the communication structure required this. The communication structure also affects the satisfaction of members. It has usually been found that satisfaction is greater for subjects in positions that are more central as opposed to peripheral; Shaw suggests that this is because of their greater autonomy. Satisfaction is reduced however when there is saturation, as the Lanzetta and Roby experiments show.

Producing organisational change

There is great resistance to change: small groups have norms and informal structures that resist change, and this is even more true of social organisations. In addition to genuine fears of loss of income or status, there are the largely unverbalised fears of a changed set of social relationships: the thought of relating to the same people in a different way can be so disturbing that members may choose the even greater change of leaving the organisation entirely; labour turnover is in fact a common result of changes. Change may be motivated by technological developments, by an awareness of ineffectiveness, or by general discontent, and may be initiated internally or externally, for example by social science consultants. It may be a matter of persuading members to accept formal changes of structure or to adopt different kinds of social relationship, such as new ways of handling subordinates.

Members need to be taught, and persuaded to accept, the new arrangements. Usually it is not enough for an administrator to send out instructions; special management techniques are required.

(1) *Training* is important, especially when new social skills will be required – such as a new style of supervision, or new ways of handling mental patients. We discuss the different methods of training in social skills in Chapter X, where we conclude that the most effective method

is role-playing supplemented by the use of films and sensitivity training (*not* T-groups). There is a further problem about training members of organisations – how to ensure that the skills learnt on the course are used on the job. Fleishman (1953) found that supervisors at the end of a two-week course emphasising the importance of consideration actually used this method only if they returned to an organisational climate in which their superior was in favour of consideration. When an individual is extracted from the organisation, sent to a remote training centre, and then returns to the firm, the effects of training are likely to be washed out by social pressures on the job. There are several ways of overcoming this problem. (i) Groups of colleagues are sent on the course, and give each other social support on their return. (ii) The course is run within the organisation, by consultants who remain as a source of influence. (iii) Senior members of the organisation are involved in the training, preferably acting as trainers.

(2) *Group methods of influence.* As indicated above it is possible to influence an individual during training, but once he returns to his group, group pressures are likely to outweigh the previous influence. This is a particular source of difficulty when group norms are opposed to the proposed change. One way of dealing with the problem is to tackle the group as a whole, try to persuade the group of the advantages of the new ideas, work out acceptable ways of implementing them, and bring the group to the point of deciding in favour of them. A number of field experiments have been carried out with this technique in industrial settings. Attempts to increase the productivity of shop-floor workers have not always been successful (Katz and Kahn, 1966), though the amount of skill of the leader is a crucial ingredient (Maier, 1953). It is still not entirely understood what the processes involved are: Bennett (1955) found that discussion and public commitment made no difference, but bringing the individual to the point of decision and perceiving a high degree of group agreement did affect the amount of change. An extension of this method can be used in changing whole organisations, i.e. there are a series of group discussions and larger meetings in which the changes are discussed. This method was used by Morse and Riemer (1956) in their experimental modification of the amount of delegation of authority.

Another application of group methods to organisational change was used by Jaques (1951) at the Glacier Metal Company. An attempt was made to overcome resistance to change by means of interpretative group therapy. It was assumed that resistance was due to unconscious fears, rather than to realistic fears of loss of economic or social advantages. A somewhat related approach is the use of T-groups in the hope that this will induce a general increase in interpersonal competence, and a resulting increase in the effectiveness of the organisation (Argyris, 1962).

(3) *Persuasion* is an important part of the process of several change, either via public meetings, or through other channels of communication. Change is easier if it can be made clear that there will be gains of salary and status, rather than the reverse, but it is more difficult to demonstrate the advantages of a different set of role-relations. Even this can be encouraged by incentives: in some British prisons, the officers are paid a bonus for doing group counselling and the latter inevitably brings about a different relationship with the prisoners. Such persuasion must be carried out by the most senior officials in the organisation – it is they who have the legitimate power. The governor of an American prison experienced great difficulty in converting it from a traditional authoritarian organisation to a more liberal, therapeutic one. He was finally successful as a result of importing a number of young assistant governors who were in favour of the new approach (McCleery, 1957).

(4) *Combined strategies*. Blake and Mouton (1964, 1965) developed a plan for organisational change which has been widely used. There are six stages: (i) Group laboratory sessions are used to demonstrate interpersonal phenomena and skills such as the use of power in supervision and ways of dealing with conflicting ideas about how work should be done. (ii) Trainees are helped to analyse the working of their own work teams. (iii) Horizontal links between colleagues are strengthened. (iv) Diagonal slice groups are used to discuss the setting of improved organisational goals. (v) Help is given with the detailed implementation of the changes. (vi) There is consideration of further areas where changes are needed. Blake *et al.* (1964) describe the application of this approach to a firm of 4,000 employees, including 800 managerial and technical staff, over a five-month period. Increases in productivity and profits are reported, together with improvements in ratings by subordinates of managers' performance: there appeared to be an improvement in supervisory skills and in relations with subordinates. Blake *et al.*, stress that line managers played a central role in the training, and that members were particularly helped by peer-group support.

Mann (1957) has developed a combination of group discussion and feedback from social surveys of the organisation. Often when consultants present social survey or similar material, the forces for resistance to change get the upper hand and the data is quietly filed and forgotten. Mann's method is to arrange for feedback sessions in which 'organisational families' of executives discuss the findings with a view to doing something about them. Each group tries to deal with the problems at its own level, and receives reports of discussions of more detailed problems at the level immediately below it in the hierarchy. In an application of this method to four branches of the accounting branch of a company, Mann found that there were changes in employee attitudes, and there were reported to be improvements in the effectiveness of supervisory behaviour.

VIII

Personality and Social Interaction

Behaviour is a function of personality as well as a function of the situation: $B = f(P.E.)$. In other areas of psychology individuals have been found to behave consistently across groups of situations. Correlational and factorial studies of performance at cognitive tasks led to the discovery of the factors of intelligence; similar studies of performance at laboratory tasks led to the discovery of further factors, such as extroversion and neuroticism (Eysenck, 1947, 1952). However, this kind of research has not yet been done for social behaviour, and it is not known what its dimensions are. Some of the familiar dimensions of 'personality' appear to have some connection with social performance – extroversion–introversion for example. However, the precise relationship of extroversion with the elements of social interaction turn out to be both complex and quite small. There are great individual differences in all aspects of social interaction: proximity for example is far more a function of personality than of any situational variables studied so far (Porter, Argyle and Salter, 1969). Meanwhile, the study of individual differences at the level of the elements of interaction enables us to describe personalities as they are experienced by others. The unique flavour of a particular person can be analysed into his particular pattern of interaction elements.

It is important to discover the dimensions of social performance for two reasons. Firstly it will enable us to understand more about the processes of interaction and how they are linked to personality mechanisms. Secondly it will make possible the prediction of behaviour by means of tests which could be used in personnel selection.

INDIVIDUAL DIFFERENCES IN THE ELEMENTS OF SOCIAL INTERACTION

Bodily contact. There are great cultural variations in the extent and form of bodily contact, and there are probably similar variations between

315

individuals within cultures, though little is known about them. Possible dimensions are the number of times per hour a person will touch another in a standard situation (Jourard, 1966) – though it would be difficult to find a standard partner. Another is the number of areas of the body which have been touched by various people; this can be assessed by a questionnaire method using a diagram (Jourard, op. cit.; and p. 93 f).

Proximity is highly consistent for a given person so is easily measured. Porter, Argyle and Salter (1969) asked subjects to hold an interview with a confederate, and measured the eye-to-eye distance selected. Williams (1963) applied the psychophysical 'method of limits' for measuring proximity: the tester moves slowly towards the subject, who says which distances are 'maximal', 'optimal' and 'minimal'; the tester then repeats the process starting toe-to-toe and moving slowly away. Mehrabian (1968) asked subjects to go and talk to a hat-stand, and to suppose that it was a person of specified age and sex. This might be a more convenient way of measuring an individual's preferred proximity.

Orientation can be studied by asking a person to sit at one of a number of chairs round a table, to talk to a confederate. Alternatively he can be asked to mark on a diagram where two people would sit under given conversational conditions. The alternative orientations are (a) side-by-side, (b) at right angles, (c) facing (closer distance, e.g. across a table), (d) facing (longer distance, e.g. at ends of a table). The same measure can be taken for a number of situations – friend of same sex, friend of opposite sex, cooperation, competition, etc. (Sommer, 1965; Cook, 1968b; and p. 96 f).

Posture varies with a person's emotional state, his attitude to the others present, and with the culture. Individual differences within the culture have not been studied. Variations of posture which affect others most could be used as dimensions of individual differences. The three most important aspects are (a) Friendly v. hostile postures, (b) superior v. inferior, and (c) tense v. relaxed, which indicates level of emotional arousal (see p. 97 f).

Physical appearance, of face, hair, hands and clothes. (a) An overall rating of physical attractiveness is highly predictive of reactions of others to a person, not only for young women, but also for young men (Walster *et al.*, 1966; Singer, 1964). (b) Physical appearance varies with and communicates a person's social status and position in society; perhaps status is a second dimension of appearance. (c) People also vary in the care they take over their appearance, through being more or less concerned with self-presentation; certain mental patients come at one extreme. This variable is difficult to assess, since some people deliberately cultivate a bedraggled bohemian appearance.

Facial and gestural movements primarily convey emotion and play a central part in interaction. (a) Allport and Vernon (1932) found consistency between expressive movements during walking, drawing, etc., and obtained factors of expansiveness, outward *v.* centrifugal tendency, and emphasis. (b) Facial expression conveys emotion, but people have a typical expression which could be classified in the same way as temporary expressions (p. 101 f). There would be difficulties in obtaining a standard situation and some kind of sampling would be necessary. (c) Hand movements are especially associated with nervousness, e.g. clasping them tightly together and hand–face contact, and are less carefully controlled than facial expression.

Direction of gaze. (a) The percentage of time spent looking at another can be standardised by using a confederate with a fixed looking pattern, e.g. looking all the time. The conditions must also be standardised, e.g. distance between them, intimacy and difficulty of topic. (b) The average length of a person's gazes is closely connected with percentage of total gaze, and is inversely correlated with frequency of gazes (Kendon and Cook, 1969).(c) Dominance of looking can be assessed by the proportion of times an individual breaks eye-contact first with a series of partners (Strongman and Champness, 1968). A more standard method would be to use a programmed interviewer who looked for a number of regular periods. (d) People also vary in whether they look while speaking or listening (Exline and Winters, 1965), and in other aspects of their pattern of looking.

Timing of speech has been more extensively studied in terms of individual differences than have the other elements. Goldman-Eisler (1952) showed that individuals are consistent in the timing of their speech when interacting with a series of other people. Chapple (1956) devised the standard interview which yields a large number of measures of individual response patterns. Kendon (1963) carried out a factor analysis of the behaviour of 39 subjects in the standard interview, and obtained four main factors: (a) average length of utterances, (b) readiness to initiate utterances,

(c) adjustment, i.e. few interruptions and silences, (d) resistance to interruption.

Emotional tone of speech. A person can be asked to read a neutral passage in a 'normal' tone of voice, and judges then rate a tape-recording along suitable dimensions. Lalljee (1967) produced profiles of the voices of four speakers, as shown in Fig. 8.1. Another approach would be to

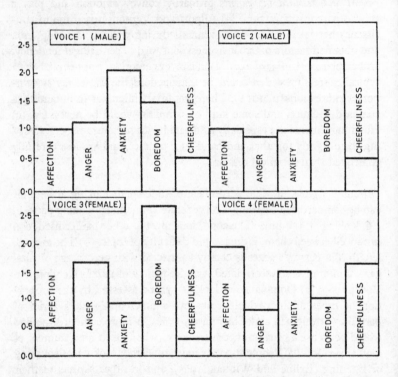

Figure 8.1. Ratings of the emotions expressed by four voices (Lalljee, 1967)

analyse a person's speech into its physical dimensions – speed, loudness, breathiness, pitch, etc. It is possible to analyse the frequency distribution of sounds by means of a speech spectrometer, as has been done for mental patients by Ostwald (1965).

Speech errors. It is easy to count speech errors, but difficult to find a standard situation, since they are very sensitive to audience effects and the difficulty of the content. Subjects can be asked to tell a story, describe a series of cartoons, or summarise the point or moral of such a series (Paivio, 1965; Goldman-Eisler, 1967). It is important to measure separately the rates of ah and non-ah speech errors (Cook, 1968a; and p. 112 f).

Verbal contents of speech have not as yet been studied in terms of individual differences. Possible dimensions are (a) formal – informal, (b) rewardingness, (c) skill and persuasiveness, (d) egocentricity, as measured by frequency of personal references for example, etc. There are also more nebulous variations in individual style (p. 119). Again there is the problem of obtaining typical samples of an individual's speech. He could be asked to initiate some encounters, such as teaching or interviewing someone.

SOME SUGGESTED DIMENSIONS OF SOCIAL PERFORMANCE

In the last section we described individual differences at the level of the elements of interaction, and ways of assessing them. Behaviour can be analysed at more than one level of abstraction and we showed earlier how interaction can be described at the level of the elements of behaviour and also at the level of more global patterns of behaviour such as 'dominance' (p. 200 f). We showed that individuals establish relationships in dyads by simultaneous moves at both levels, the more global patterns being reducible to the smaller components (p. 121 f). A number of dimensions describing the relationship between two people at this second level were proposed (p. 200 ff). We now consider whether there are global patterns of behaviour that are characteristic of individual personalities.

There are several research strategies which might lead to the establishment of broader dimensions of individual social behaviour. (1) Factor analyses could be carried out, using the elements as items to be intercorrelated. A number of factorial studies have been carried out, based on ratings of different aspects of social performance, and have commonly arrived at the two dimensions dominant–submissive and warm–cold (Leary, 1957; Foa, 1961; Lorr and McNair, 1965). A factor analysis based on elements of timing was performed by Kendon (1963) which suggested 'meshing' as one of the factors. (2) Styles of interaction could be studied in relation to their effects or effectiveness – a parallel to Eysenck's criterion group method (1952). Research on the styles of interaction which makes people popular, or successful leaders, is reviewed later (p. 330 ff). This research suggests further dimensions such as 'rewardingness' and 'poise'. (3) Another strategy is to start with mechanisms postulated by theoretical models of interaction. Whatever dimensions are arrived at, it is hoped that it will be possible to interpret them in terms of the operation of such mechanisms; perhaps we can start at this end. The social skill model suggests that 'perceptual sensitivity', and the 'capacity to control another by having a repertoire of techniques', are necessary in interaction; the extension of the model suggests that 'taking the role of the other' is also necessary.

This gives us a provisional list of seven patterns, dimensions, mechanisms or areas of performance. These dimensions appear repeatedly in very different studies, which gives us some confidence in them. However, it is very likely that some are intercorrelated (e.g. affiliation and rewardingness) so that they may be reducible to a smaller number of dimensions. On the other hand, as we shall see, in some of these areas there is in fact a rich diversity of performance, not reducible to a single dimension. Some of these dimensions are reducible to patterns of elements (e.g. dominance), while others are components of competence, representing psychological mechanisms (e.g. perceptual sensitivity). Some are more or less measurable along a single dimension (e.g introversion–extroversion), while others are really areas of performance (e.g. interaction skills). There may be more than seven, or there may turn out to be a smaller number of more general dimensions. There is also an eighth area which will be presented in the next chapter – self-presentation.

In terms of the model of social behaviour presented earlier, the dimensions can be classified as follows:

Motivation
  1. Extroversion and affiliation
  2. Dominance–submission
  3. Poise – social anxiety.
Translation and skill
  4. Rewardingness
  5. Interaction skills (meshing, control and repertoire).
Perception and feedback
  6. Perceptual sensitivity
  7. Role-taking ability.

(1) *Extroversion and affiliation.* Factor analytic studies show that a dimension of 'extroversion' or 'sociability' commonly emerges. The study

by Lorr and McNair (1965) is a good example: 16 categories of social behaviour were used and judges made ratings on 5-point scales of 250 subjects. The results were expressed in a circular, two-dimensional system as shown in Fig. 8.2. Foa (1961) has shown that this pattern emerges in studies of several kinds of social interaction – child-rearing and group behaviour for example. Schutz (1958) concluded that individual differences in behaviour in groups could be accounted for by three factors, of which one was a need for affection. The factors can be assessed by the FIRO questionnaire scales. Shipley and Veroff (1952)

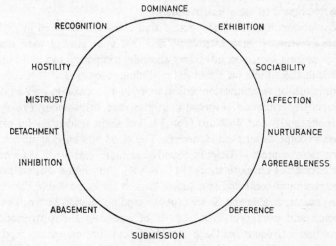

Figure 8.2. The interpersonal behaviour cycle (from Lorr and McNair, 1965)

developed a projective test measure of need for affiliation, which was found to be correlated with measures of amount of time spent with others, making telephone calls and writing letters. In the studies of Eysenck (1947, 1957), in which performance at various laboratory tasks was factor analysed, extroversion again emerged as a main dimension. Measures of social behaviour were not included, but the factor correlated highly with a questionnaire scale of extroversion – the MPI E-scale (Eysenck, 1959). Later research by Eysenck and Eysenck (1963) showed that the E-scale contains two partly independent components – social extroversion and behavioural extroversion (or impulsiveness).

From these studies a general picture of the extroverted pattern of social behaviour emerges. The extrovert spends a lot of time with other people, he is warm and affectionate and likes to establish intimate

L

relationships, would rather be popular than be a leader, and is more concerned with socio-emotional aspects of group life than with the task. This pattern can be assessed by one of the FIRO scales, or by part of the MPI E-scale. Another basic drive also results in a person wanting to be liked, and seeking out intimate relationships – sexual motivation. We discussed earlier the similarities and differences between affiliation and sex (p. 50).

We shall now consider the elements of interaction which comprise extroverted behaviour. Most of the relationships which have been found are rather small; this may be because the measures used are not very closely aligned to social extroversion.

Eye-contact. Mobbs (1967) found that extroverts engaged in slightly more eye-contact than introverts, and that their glances were almost twice as long – 3·1 seconds *v.* 1·7 seconds, comparing top and bottom thirds of the sample on extroversion. Exline (1963) found that subjects high in affiliative motivation looked more in a cooperative and less in a competitive situation, especially in the case of women. *Proximity.* Leipold (1963) and Williams (1963) found slight tendencies for extroverts to come closer than introverts. The effect was only significant for very close contact – Leipold found that more extroverts claimed to prefer dancing cheek to cheek (85% *v.* 50%), and found a difference in the minimum comfortable distance chosen for comfortable conversation. Porter, Argyle and Salter (1969) found no relation between extroversion and proximity in a number of interview and conversational conditions. *Orientation.* Cook (1968b) found that extroverts reported that they would sit opposite another person, in a variety of situations; introverts chose a 90° arrangement more often. Cook concludes from his data that extroverts want to be able to observe the other's reactions. *Speech.* Carment, Cervin and Miles (1965) found that extroverts spoke sooner and more than introverts. Leipold (op. cit.) found that subjects high in extroversion and need for approval talked more. Bass and Dunteman (1960) found that T-group members high in interaction-orientation avoided giving critical comments about other members. Tuckman (1966) found that other-directed subjects revealed more about themselves; they probed their friends less and acquaintances more than did other subjects.

What is the mechanism underlying extroversion that produces this pattern of behaviour? We think that the most useful approach is to postulate an affiliative drive, which takes different strengths in different people as a result of child-rearing experiences (p. 50 ff). However, an introvert could fail to take an active part in social activities for two reasons – lack of affiliative motivation or lack of social skill. In the second case he would like to but can't, or has been so unsuccessful in the past that avoidance forces have built up.

Another theory has been put forward by Eysenck (1967). He postulates that extroverts and introverts differ at the level of the physiology of the central nervous system. It is maintained that extroverts are at a lower level of cortical arousal than introverts; it follows that extroverts can tolerate more social activity, more intimacy, etc., than introverts. High degrees of arousal also result in disruption of skilled patterns of response; it follows that extroverts will perform more competently in many social situations – i.e. those where introverts are past the peak of the inverted–U arousal curve.

(2) *Dominance–submission.* A number of factorial studies have produced a second general factor of social performance – dominance–submission (see Fig. 3.8, p. 122). One of the FIRO scales is concerned with the need to control others in group situations (Schutz, 1958). There is a difference between wanting to control other people and being able to do so; here more than in the case of extroversion a factor of social skill is involved. The person who succeeds in controlling people operates in the NE sector of Fig. 3.8 – he advises, persuades, coordinates, explains and suggests rather than ordering and criticising. In addition to controlling he is affiliative and rewarding.

A distinction must be made between dominance and authoritarianism. An authoritarian, when he is in charge, tries to dominate; he is sensitive to differences of power and status, and will be submissive and deferential to more important people. His method of controlling, or attempting to control, consists of ordering and criticising in a rather punitive and unrewarding way; he assumes that he has the right to give orders and that others ought to obey (Adorno *et al.*, 1950; Titus and Hollander, 1957). When in a subordinate position an authoritarian is submissive, and entirely accepts his position in the hierarchy; a dominant person will be less content, and may be rebellious and anti-authority. Weitman (1962) found three types of person in a factorial study – those who are pro-authority, anti-authority and independent of authority; the third group scored low on prejudice and did better at cognitive tasks than the other two groups.

In general, it is agreed that a dominant person wants to control or influence the behaviour of others in a situation, he would rather be accepted as a leader and be admired than be popular, and is more concerned with the task than with social relations in a group. A submissive person wants to be told what to do, to be dependent on others, prefers to be a junior partner in decision-taking, will admire and respect the other members, and do what he is told.

Something is known about the detailed elements of behaviour, of which these styles consist. A dominant person follows the pattern of behaviour corresponding to high status: relaxed *posture* with raised head, unsmiling *facial expression* as opposed to the nervous appeasing smile of the submissive person. *Eye-movements*. A dominant person stares the other person down, forcing him to break eye-contact first (Strongman and Champness, 1968). He takes the role of the observer, studying the other coolly and critically (Argyle and Williams, 1969). *Speech*. He interrupts more, and succeeds in holding the floor for more of the time, thus controlling the flow of interaction (Chapple, 1956). He speaks louder and more decisively than other people; the reverse is the case with submissive people. *Perception*. Authoritarians (but not necessarily other dominant people) classify others primarily in terms of power and status variables. Wilkins (1962) found that they were more affected by 'external' power – such as ascribed social status, than by 'internal' power – such as forcefulness and decisiveness of speech. *Controlling behaviour*. Dominant people attempt to control the behaviour of others, dependent people want to be controlled (Schutz, 1958). Several studies show that people higher in needs for dependence or approval are more strongly influenced in operant verbal conditioning and other kinds of social influence situation (e.g. Crowne and Marlowe, 1964). *Aggression*. Dominant people are more aggressive, dependent people less so, while the aggressiveness of authoritarians varies with the status of the frustrating agent (Thibaut and Riecken, 1955).

What personality mechanism is responsible for this dimension of social performance? Our preference is for the postulation of a social drive whose strength is affected by childhood experience (p. 50 ff). There is an element of social skill as well – which distinguishes between authoritarian and more successful dominators. Dependence is another drive, with origins in early infancy, whose effects are the reverse of dominance.

(3) *Poise–social anxiety*. A number of investigators have located a factor of social anxiety and have developed questionnaire measures for it. Bjerstedt (1966) obtained such a factor in a questionnaire study of 415 American high-school children. The main loadings were on such items as not liking to be watched at work, being troubled with shyness, finding it difficult to speak in public, and feeling self-conscious. This

study suggests that anxiety in a variety of social situations is a general factor. Willoughby (1932) produced a questionnaire for various kinds of social anxiety, which has been used by Wolpe (1958) as a basis for the behaviour therapy of patients with this form of anxiety (p. 421 f).

Paivio (1965) devised an 'audience anxiety' scale for this particular form of social anxiety, and scores on this scale were found to be correlated with speech errors and other aspects of social performance (cf. p. 113). The opposite pole from social anxiety is 'poise' – being perfectly relaxed and happy in social situations. A particular group of people who are low in social anxiety are so-called 'Machiavellian' personalities – who engage in the calculating manipulation of others to their own advantage (Christie, 1962). Neuroticism has been found to be a general factor of personality (Eysenck, 1952), and no doubt social anxiety is part of it. However, we are specifically concerned here with the disruption by anxiety of *social* performance, and are therefore dealing with a rather narrower dimension than neuroticism.

Social anxiety can be measured in particular situations by physiological methods (Paul, 1966), or over a range of situations by one of the questionnaires mentioned above. The general pattern of social behaviour of an anxious person is that he is ill at ease, flustered and embarrassed, tense and awkward, and generally unable to cope. The poised person is thoroughly at home and enjoys himself in social situations, is confident and relaxed, and is able to control situations smoothly.

We can relate this dimension to some of the elements of interaction. *Bodily posture and gestures.* The anxious person adopts a tense and awkward posture and makes jerky movements. *Facial expression* is tense and flushed. *Eye-contact* is often low for anxious people; Exline *et al.* (1961) found that while most people reduce their eye-contact when implicated in deceit, this was not the case with Machiavellians. An anxious person takes the role of the observed, a poised person the observer. *Speech.* Anxious people talk fast, with many speech errors, in a breathy tone of voice, but with rather short utterances (Mahl and Schulze, 1964). In more extreme cases of neuroticism various disturbing and socially destructive techniques may be adopted (p. 348).

What psychological processes underlie this dimension? It could simply be a manifestation of the more general personality factor of neuroticism – the tendency to be anxious, to be easily upset by stress, etc. It is however a rather special kind of neuroticism – the tendency to be anxious in social situations, and this may exist in individuals who are not otherwise neurotic. Such anxiety could be acquired as a result of punishing experiences in social situations during childhood; this would lead to increased arousal and impaired skill on later occasions. Another approach to this dimension is via the concept of 'insecurity' – defined as the extent to which a person is uncertain about his self-image, and thus concerned about the reactions of others. This is probably related to concealment, i.e. unwillingness to reveal much about the self to others (Jourard, 1964). This approach will be developed later in connection with the self.

One source of social anxiety is probably sheer lack of social skills with which to deal with situations. This sets off a circular reaction since the heightened anxiety reduces effectiveness still further. Self-confidence in social situations may be based on an ability to cope with them, and part of the cure for social anxiety may be training in social skills.

(4) *Rewardingness*. This dimension has never before been suggested, and there are no tests for it, though factorial studies have sometimes produced dimensions in this area. Norman (1963) found a dimension of 'agreeableness', and Farber (1962) one of 'cooperation and support', for example. However, experiments in the 'exchange theory' tradition suggest that rewardingness should be a fundamental dimension of social performance. Helen Jennings (1950) found that the popular girls in a reformatory were the girls who were helpful and kind, while the unpopular girls tried to extract help or attention from others (p. 209 f). In another study using ratings, Lemann and Solomon (1952) found that popular people were described as generous, affectionate and enthusiastic. We referred earlier to studies showing that popularity was also a function of position in social structure – depending on whether a job provided rewards or punishments for others. Such findings have been interpreted in terms of the rewards given by the popular people and sought by the unpopular ones (e.g. Homans, 1960). Blau (1955) interpreted his data in a similar way; supervisors were able to influence their subordinates because they were rewarding to them. We shall cite data later in this chapter which show that mental patients are very low in rewardingness, and suggest that this is a source of their troubles.

Aspects of rewardingness have been assessed from performance in laboratory situations. Harteshorne, May and Shuttleworth (1930) devised five tests of 'service' in children (various kinds of helpfulness), and there are the more recent studies of helping behaviour (p. 192 f). Ratings have also been used. Loban (1953) obtained ratings on being 'sympathetic and sensitive', which correlated with scores on the Hawthorne (1932) test of cruelty–compassion. Sorokin (1950) obtained nominations for 'good neighbours' – who mostly turned out to be middle-aged married women who originally came from large families. Females have been found to score higher than males in numerous studies (e.g. Bennett and Cohen, 1959). Rewardingness can take a number of forms – warm and affiliative behaviour, submissive and admiring behaviour, helping with tasks, giving advice, taking an interest in another and endorsing his self-image, and sexual responsiveness. There is clearly some overlap between this dimension and affiliation; however, rewardingness includes components of other kinds, and not all affiliative behaviour is rewarding. Some of the elements of rewardingness may be suggested in the light of related research. A rewarding person is attentive to another, in terms of proximity, orientation and gaze; he adopts a friendly bodily posture, and smiles; he nods his head to indicate approval and agreement; he has a friendly tone of voice and does not interrupt; his utterances mesh smoothly; the content of his speech is rewarding in one of the ways indicated above.

Why are some people more rewarding than others? If a person is rewarding he evidently becomes both popular and influential, so that it is rewarding to be rewarding. It might therefore be expected that everyone would become increasingly rewarding. Many people do, in particular those whose jobs constantly require them to make friends and influence people – salesmen, politicians, air hostesses and others. A person could fail to be rewarding for one of several reasons. (1) He is not aware of his own non-verbal behaviour; trainees on social skills courses are often horrified to see and hear video-tapes of themselves. (2) The link between behaviour and its consequences is not sufficiently clear for them to connect one event with another; and they may fail to discover the right social techniques by trial and error. (3) The costs of being rewarding may be too great, as for example if a person is very high in dominance. In this case he could, by better social skills, become more influential through being rewarding.

(5) *Interaction skills.* The social skill model suggests that in addition to variations in motivation and perception there may also be individual differences at the level of motor responses and their organisation. A person may want to ride a bicycle and perceive correctly that he is about to fall off, but not be able to make the necessary responses in order to stay on.

(a) Kendon (1963) found that smoothness of meshing was a dimension of the timing of utterances and we shall see that this is a crucial type of failure of competence in schizophrenia. An essential part of social performance appears to be the ability to establish and sustain a smooth and easy pattern of interaction. Where new clients are constantly being encountered, it is mainly a matter of establishing rapport quickly. This is essential in the case of interviewers, salesmen and lecturers. It is also necessary to be able to interact with a wide range of different personalities. Such meshing involves rapid accommodation to the timing and emotional state of the other. Meshing can be reduced to the elements of interaction. The usual index is absence of pauses or interruptions. Other aspects are harmony of emotional state with another interactor, presence of gestural dance, and effective verbal communication.

(b) To be effective in most social situations it is essential to be able to control the social interaction. This does not always mean being the 'dominant' person in the ordinary sense, but keeping the initiative, and exercising influence over the relationship, the emotional tone, and the content of interaction. Control without dominance can be seen in an experienced salesman, or waiter. It is partly a question of responding in accordance with an internal plan, rather than simply reacting to the other's behaviour. Farber (1962) found a factor of 'autonomy' in his factorial study of competence in marriage.

(c) In any class of social situations particular skills are needed. In everyday situations this includes establishing a friendly relationship, cooperation, persuasion, explanation, etc. There are more difficult situations which require 'tact'. We describe below a test for performance in a sample of such situations (p. 353 f). In professional social skills there are a number of special techniques that have to be mastered; the selection interviewer for example should be able to ask awkward questions without causing embarrassment, the salesman must be able to find out what price the customer is prepared to pay. In all skills where the performer is of higher status than the client, the former should have mastered the skills of exerting influence by persuasive and consultative methods. An interviewer should be able to cope with a wide range of personalities, including several varieties of difficult person. People who are popular can interact easily with a wide range of personalities.

(6) *Perceptual sensitivity*. A number of studies have shown that perceptual accuracy or sensitivity is greater in individuals who are popular (p. 332 f), and who become leaders of groups (p. 333 f), while it is low in certain kinds of mental patient (pp. 338–50). There are several aspects to this area of social performance. (i) There is sensitivity to small verbal and non-verbal cues, such as tones of voice and bodily posture, and the ability to interpret them correctly. Davitz (1964) constructed a test of sensitivity to non-verbal aspects of speech: subjects are asked to identify

the emotion being expressed in a series of tape-recorded passages of neutral content. He found that there was a high correlation between sensitivity to non-verbal aspects of speech and to emotions expressed in music and art, and that both correlated with ability to express emotions, suggesting a general factor of sensitivity. (ii) There is the richness and complexity of data used and inferences made. Campbell and Yarrow (1961) found that popular children at a summer camp produced more highly organised and more inferential descriptions of other children. This is the dimension of 'cognitive complexity' which was introduced earlier (p. 159f). (iii) There is the absence of subjective distortions caused either by incorrect implicit personality theories or by strong motivations.

Perceptual sensitivity is a dimension of the efficiency of part of the social skill mechanism, and is not reducible to elements of interaction. It is probably related to one element however – the direction of gaze. An interactor who, like many schizophrenics, looks very little at another, will have little opportunity for gathering perceptual data. It probably depends too on the pattern of scanning, since useful data can be collected from other areas as well as the face, and there are certain crucial times at which it is most useful to look – e.g. at the ends of utterances.

Part of the basis for perceptual sensitivity is experience with people, especially with people like the person being judged or interacted with. On the other hand Jecker *et al.* (1964) found that experienced teachers were little better than novices in judging whether schoolchildren had 'understood' on the basis of facial and gestural cues alone. It is found that people can judge better those who are similar to themselves in age, sex, social class and cultural background. This is probably because they have more experience with people like themselves, are sensitive to the relevant cues, and interpret them correctly. Members of an unfamiliar group seem to be all alike, and it is hard to discriminate between them. It is also easier to empathise with members of one's own group.

(7) *Role-taking ability*. We suggested, in our analysis of dyadic interaction, that interactors take the role of the other, to a greater or lesser degree, and that this may be essential for effective interaction. Sarbin suggests that individuals differ in role-taking ability, which enables them both to take different roles themselves, and to put themselves in the position of a person with whom they are interacting (Sarbin and Allen, 1969). The 'as-if' test (p. 190) was devised to measure this capacity; Sarbin and Jones (1956) found that students who did well on this test were also good at role-playing the role of 'daughter' with a stooge.

Sarbin and Lim (1963) found that subjects who were easily hypnotisable were good at dramatic role-taking; Sarbin maintains that hypnotism is a case of role-taking.

Other studies have been concerned with the development of role-playing skills with age. Bowers and London (1965) found that role-playing ability correlated with age and social maturity as well as with intelligence and perceptual ability. According to Piaget (1950) children go through a series of developmental stages of conceptual ability; one such stage is the ability to decentre, i.e. to consider a physical object from more than one perceptual point of view. Feffer's role-taking test (p. 190) was found to show increasing scores with age as well as correlating with performance at a communication task.

Argyle and Williams (1969), in a series of experiments to be described later, found that individuals differ in the extent to which they feel that they are the 'observer' or the 'observed' in social situations (p. 379). Those who feel observed focus their attention on the other's reactions to them, they imagine the other's point of view. This is partly a function of the situation, but there are also consistent individual differences. Females feel observed by males. Males feel observed if they are submissive and insecure.

We have described three approaches to taking the role of the other; the first two see it as a kind of ability necessary for effective interaction, the third regards it as descriptive of a person's cognitive set during interaction; the optimum division of attention would depend on the situation (p. 191). This dimension is related to the elements of interaction less directly than the previous ones are; it summarises kinds of effective social performance in the same way that factors of intelligence summarise successful areas of problem-solving.

SOCIAL COMPETENCE
Social skills in different situations
The term 'social competence' or 'social skill' is often used, carrying with it the assumption that some people are better at dealing with social situations in general than others are. We do not know however whether social competence is a general trait. Will a person who is good at doing personnel selection interviews also be good at giving lectures or giving psychotherapy? Will a person who is good at making friends also be good at influencing people? If we were to follow the methods used in the study of cognitive abilities we would devise a large number of different social tasks, assess the competence of a large number of people in these

tasks, and study the matrix of inter-task correlations. Nothing like this has ever been done, and it seems likely that the correlations would not be very high, since for professional social skills at least competence depends very much on special experience and training. For the moment all that we can do is to leave open the possibility that there may be a general factor of social competence and look at competence in terms of a profile of specific abilities.

How can social competence be assessed? This is rather more straight-forward in the case of specific professional social skills, such as inter-viewing, teaching or conducting psychotherapy, where a person's work consists mainly of dealing with people in face-to-face situations. For all of these skills it is fairly clear what the criteria of successful performance are – an interviewer should select the best people, a teacher should teach his pupils a lot, and so on. There may be more than one such criterion – a salesman should not only sell a lot of goods, he should satisfy the customers so that they will be likely to go to that shop again, and to tell their friends about it. Measurement may not be easy, and indeed may be impossible without setting up elaborate follow-up pro-cedures, for example of the future career of psychotherapy patients. However, criteria have been agreed upon, and measurements made in the cases of a number of professional social skills. It has been possible to compare the personalities or social performance of successful and unsuccessful performers, and some of the results will be reviewed below.

Assessing competence in everyday social situations is more difficult. Is an extrovert more competent than an introvert, a dominant person more skilled than a submissive person? It would depend on his motiva-tion – a person with a very low need for affiliation would not want to be popular; on the other hand an apparent introvert might have strong affiliation needs but not possess the social skills to establish the relation-ship he wants. However, there are a fairly common set of social situations which a person of a particular age and sex would commonly meet, and where the same goals would be sought, so that competence at them could be assessed. N. Armistead devised a test of such social skills: a series of tape-recorded problems in everyday situations are presented to subjects, who have to say as quickly as they can what they would do. The prob-lems are given in the Appendix to this chapter. Armistead scored the answers by asking judges to rate the tape-recorded answers. He found positive correlations between items, suggesting that there is a general factor of competence in everyday situations.

The components of social competence

A number of workers have drawn up more or less *a priori* lists of the elements of which social competence may be composed. Tests have also been devised to measure the elements. An early test of 'social intelligence', the George Washington test, consisted of seven sub-scales, measuring various aspects of sensitivity and social insight. However, it turned out that this test correlated ·57 with verbal IQ, and that apart from IQ there was nothing in common between the sub-scales (Thorndike and Stein, 1937). Such paper-and-pencil measures, as is found with tests of honesty, correlate highly with IQ, but are not so clearly related to actual performance. Another approach is to study correlations between ratings of various aspects of social performance. Farber (1962) collected ratings by wives on 104 items about 495 husbands, and factor analysed the ratings. He found five factors, of which the first three were orthogonal – empathy, autonomy, resourcefulness, cooperation and support, and accuracy of perception. These results are necessarily limited by the fact that only one kind of social relationship was involved

In the previous section we drew up a list of seven components of social performance, which may also be related to social competence. One of them, 'Interaction skills', includes a series of alternative social techniques corresponding to different situations. There is an eighth, to be considered in Chapter IX, 'Appropriate self-presentation'. We will consider here which of these components lead to social competence in a number of situations, both everyday and professional.

Popularity. Not everyone wants to be popular, but many people do, so it is worth studying the properties of individuals that lead to their becoming popular. First we will consider the seven dimensions introduced above. (1) *Extroversion* correlates on average ·10 with popularity, according to a review of a large number of studies by Mann (1959). (2) *Dominance*. No relation. (3) *Social anxiety* leads to unpopularity (r = ·10), though more extreme degrees of anxiety probably have a more marked effect, because of the self-centredness and peculiar behaviour of people with anxiety neurosis (p. 347 ff). (4) *Rewardingness* is probably the most important source of popularity (p. 209f). (5) *Skills* are probably relevant, for example skills of easy meshing, cooperation, etc. (6) *Perceptual sensitivity*. A number of studies have shown that popular people are more accurate at person perception. There are however a number of methodological difficulties here – for example they may be able to perceive more accurately because they know people better (Mann, op. cit.). (7) *Taking the role of the other* would be expected to contribute to popularity, though this has not been demonstrated.

Are there any other personal qualities which produce popularity, not included in our seven dimensions? There is a small correlation with IQ (Mann, op. cit.). People are most popular in a group if they are of the same social status or slightly higher than the other, if they are of the same race, and if they are high in qualities valued by the group. They should be good at bowling in bowling groups, fighting in military groups, and work in work-groups (Hare, 1962).

The correlation between popularity and personality traits like extroversion and intelligence is very small. Better results are obtained with new dimensions such as rewardingness. It is important to note that a person's popularity does vary considerably between different groups – depending on whether or not he possesses the attributes valued by the group. Even within a group whether A is chosen by B depends on B as well as on A, and properties of A are only one source of variance.

Informal leadership. Not everyone wants to be influential, though many would like to be. We will review factors resulting in an individual becoming an informal leader. (1) *Extroversion* correlates with leadership status, on average $r = \cdot 15$ though it varies widely between different studies (Mann, op. cit.). Carment, Cervin and Miles (1965) found that extroverts influenced others by talking first and more. (2) *Dominance*. People don't exercise influence and dominance unless they have some motivation to do so; questionnaire measures of dominance correlate $\cdot 20$ with leadership (Mann, op. cit.). However, leadership correlates negatively with authoritarianism – if influence is to be exerted it must be done by subtler and more persuasive methods, as is also found in most formal leadership situations. (3) *Social anxiety*. The median correlation of leadership with adjustment is $\cdot 15$, though the highest reported is $\cdot 53$ (Mann, op. cit.). One interpretation is that the trait of integration or adjustment is valued by other people (Gibb, 1969). It has commonly been found that self-confident people become leaders; perhaps their self-confidence is taken as non-verbal evidence of their ability at the task. (4) *Rewardingness*. Blau (1955) provided evidence for a correlation between influence and rewardingness. (5) *Skills*. As indicated above, successful influence requires rather special social skills of persuasion (p. 299f). (6) *Perceptual sensitivity*. Several studies have found that leaders have more accurate social perceptions of other members of the group. This may be due to their being in a better position to perceive or because they create opinions themselves (Gibb, op. cit.). It seems likely that there is a fairly strong relationship here, and that its strength varies with such factors as the relevance for the task of being able to perceive particular aspects of group functioning (Exline, 1960). (7) *Taking the role of the other*. No evidence.

Does informal leadership depend on other attributes apart from those in the above list? Numerous studies have shown that people are allowed to become influential who are best at doing what the group is concerned with. Thus there are said to be 'families of situations' within which leadership may rotate (p. 233). Intelligence has often been found to be correlated with leadership, at $r = \cdot 15$ in groups of children and students: the strength of this correlation varies from $\cdot 50$ in problem-solving groups to o in groups of delinquents (Mann, op. cit.; Gibb, op. cit.). People whose influence is accepted are often taller, heavier and more energetic – bishops are taller than clergymen, sales managers than salesmen, for instance (Gowin, 1915). This relationship varies with the activity of the group, and is particularly found where physical activity is required. Singer (1964) found that more attractive girls were given better grades (a form of social influence), with intelligence held constant; $r = \cdot 40$ for first-borns. On the other hand leaders of delinquent gangs exceeded their followers in slovenliness (Ackerson, 1942).

The findings for leadership and influence are in striking contrast to those for popularity. On average leadership correlates with intelligence $\cdot 25$, dominance $\cdot 20$, extroversion $\cdot 15$ and adjustment $\cdot 15$. Since these dimensions are almost independent, they could provide a strong multiple correlation. In other words, capacity for leadership and influence is to some extent a general trait. On the other hand it is a familiar experience that the same person can lead in one group and not be allowed to speak in another. We mentioned above the numerous studies showing how different situations require different kinds of leader, in particular leaders who have the specific skills required for the task in hand.

Professional social skills – supervision of groups. We discussed the skills of leadership and supervision earlier (p. 299f). What are the attributes of an effective formally appointed leader? He should be high in *dominance*, in the sense of doing the leader's job – planning and coordinating the work, telling each man what to do, showing him how to do it if necessary, and checking that it has been properly done. He should be *rewarding*, he should look after the needs and interests of the group members, and be powerful enough to be able to do things for them. He needs the *skills* of exercising influence in a democratic, persuasive and consultative manner. He *takes the role of the other*; for example in matters of discipline he tries to find out the causes of the offending behaviour, and works out a solution by collaborative discussion with the person in question.

The selection interview. An interviewer must above all be high in *perceptual sensitivity*, be free from the various kinds of error of judgement and be high in cognitive complexity. An interviewer should be low in *social anxiety*, because this puts the candidate at ease, and makes gross biases of judgement less likely (Ulrich and Trumbo, 1965). He needs a number of special *social skills*, such as establishing rapport quickly, controlling different kinds of candidate, and extracting unfavourable information (Sidney and Brown, 1961). He needs to be able to *take the role of the other*, in order to understand the candidate's background and problems. There is some evidence that *introverts* do better, probably because they can remain more detached. Interviewers should, in addition, be similar to the candidates in age, sex and social background – probably because they can interact more easily with them, and are less liable to misinterpret their behaviour.

Psychotherapy. Although there are many different schools of psychotherapy, there is some evidence that what is important for curing patients is the adoption of the right social techniques and the establishment of a certain kind of relationship. Fiedler (1953) found that successful therapists belonged to diverse schools, but that they shared certain personality attributes and social skills; this has been confirmed by later studies. The successful therapist is poised and low in *social anxiety*, and has the ability to inspire confidence on the part of his patients and to create the expectation that they will recover (Frank, 1961). He is *rewarding*, in being warm, and interested in the patient, and can *take the role of the other* by empathising and coming to understand his point of view. He has particular *social skills* of treating the patient as an equal, getting him to talk freely about his emotional problems, and using techniques such as 'reflection' and 'interpretation'.

Public speaking and teaching. Public speakers, lecturers and teachers vary widely in effectiveness. The most effective ones probably have certain characteristics (cf. Argyle, 1967). A public speaker should have *dominance* in that he is prepared to control his audience or class; he also needs the *social skills* to do so; young women sometimes find it difficult to keep order because they have never acquired dominant social skills. A public speaker should be *poised*, and able to present himself appropriately. He should put on a performance and have presence, and not mutter feebly or chat in a relaxed familial manner – he will not be heard, and no one will take any notice. He should *take the role of the other* in that he establishes common links with the audience, and gains its confidence, and can relate his message to the interests and needs of his hearers. He should have sufficient *perceptual sensitivity* to be able to judge the audience's response accurately. He should also have prestige and be regarded as an expert in his subject.

SOCIAL INTERACTION AND MENTAL DISORDER

Detailed clinical studies of mental patients have made a very important contribution to many branches of psychology, and the same may be true in the study of social behaviour. The study of disturbed behaviour can provide valuable information about the mechanisms producing normal behaviour. For example it is difficult to appreciate the extent to which verbal utterances are normally synchronised without seeing the absence of synchronising in schizophrenia.

It may also be hoped that the detailed analysis of interaction in mental patients can make a contribution to understanding their psychopathology. The social performance of all patients is disturbed in one way or another, they are unsuccessful interactors and in some cases the main symptoms are in this area. The causes of disorders may be partly in failures of social behaviour; for example if a person has not acquired the skills of interacting with the opposite sex he is more likely to become a homosexual. In other cases social performance may be disturbed as a result of more general failures in the system – of thought processes for example. The social failure in this case would add to the patient's problems, by making everyday life more difficult.

It follows that, whether the social deficit is causal or not, it may be possible to help mental patients by training in the area of social skills. Attempts at doing so are reviewed in Chapter X.

Description of the main syndromes of mental disorder have been agreed by psychiatrists, and may be found in the appropriate textbooks. This includes some account of styles of interaction, in terms of rather global categories such as 'withdrawal'. We shall try to add to these descriptions more detailed analyses of the social performance of patients, as obtained in studies using special techniques to record eye-movements, emotional tone of speech, and other elements of interaction. We will then look at each disorder in terms of our dimensions, and see how far the characteristic social performance can be summarised in this way.

Schizophrenia

This is the most disabling and widespread form of psychosis. Onset is most common between 20 and 34, and is rather earlier in males than females. The basic syndrome can be defined as withdrawal from social relationships, disturbance of thought and speech, failure of persistent goal-directed behaviour, and flattening of emotions. Two main forms of the disorder have been distinguished by Zigler and Phillips (1962). *Process* schizophrenics are those with a poor history of adjustment before the onset of the disorder. *Reactive* schizophrenics on the other hand have a good history before breakdown, and for them the outlook is better. Phillips constructed a rating scale based on premorbid history, for making the distinction. In some ways this distinction has proved more valuable in research than the old classification into catatonic, hebephrenic, paranoid and simple schizophrenia. We turn now to details of the social performance of these patients.

Appearance. They look odd and untidy, do not wear their clothes well, and are totally unconcerned about their personal appearance. *Proximity.* It is found that they adopt quite unsuitable distances – too near or too far, and Sommer (1959) found that schizophrenics either chose very distant seats or sat side-by-side, but avoided a 90° situation. *Orientation* is often away from other people. In mental hospitals they spend 45% of their time doing nothing, and much of this time turned against the wall (Schooler and Parkel, 1966). *Posture and gestures* are often weird and are used not to communicate with others, but to symbolise various private fantasies. *Facial expression.* Some kinds of schizophrenic produce strange grimaces, but more commonly there is a blank facial expression. *Gaze-direction.* A number of studies have found partial or complete aversion of gaze among schizophrenics. In studies by the author and Adam Kendon it was found that chronic schizophrenics engaged in very little eye-contact, tended to gaze at 90° to the line of regard, and used very short glances. *Speech.* Schizophrenics speak little, and sometimes not at all; the content is rambling, incoherent and emotionally flat. They are unable to synchronise with another speaker, so that there are both interruptions and long silences (Matarazzo and Saslow, 1961; Chapple and Lindemann, 1942). Speech is difficult for them because they lack shared patterns of association and frameworks of ideas with other people, and because they have difficulty in establishing a relationship.

These are some of the elements of social interaction in schizophrenics. We now turn to the broader patterns of behaviour covered by our seven dimensions. *Introversion* is one of the main components. Schizophrenics are socially isolated and engage in the minimum amount of social activity. Unlike inmates of prisons, or of any other closed community, they do not engage in any cooperative activity, such as revolts or escapes or mutual aid against the staff; there are no status symbols or leadership, no financial transactions, no formation or enforcement of norms, and no evolution of common ideas or language (Sommer and Osmond, 1962). Schizophrenics do not establish relationships with one another, but it is possible to get into contact with them if enough patience and sympathy are used. Attempts to establish intimacy are rejected for a long time; Feldstein (1962) found that when interviewed in a personally involving manner, schizophrenics made more irrelevant remarks. Alternatively they may simply fail to perceive the relevant cues. *Rewardingness*. Longabaugh *et al.* (1966) suggest that schizophrenics are 'socially bankrupt' in that they have zero reward value for others, so are perceived as being of no value; the only relationships they can take part in are with the staff – who provide the rewards on a one-way basis. *Social anxiety*. Schizophrenics are very disturbed by social situations, and are particularly upset by criticism. Rodnick (1963) and Garmezy and their colleagues at Ohio confirmed this experimentally, and found that schizophrenics react sharply both to actual criticism, and to projective representations of it. Johannsen (1961) found that schizophrenics performed a task as well as normals under non-social feedback; however, with social feedback the normals did better, the schizophrenics worse. Lerner and Fairweather (1963) found that schizophrenics did more work in unsupervised work-groups; under supervision they became passive, hostile and withdrawn. Rodnick (op. cit.) found that process schizophrenics were particularly upset by criticism and were most upset by censure from females. Lefcourt and Steffy (1966) found that process patients were uncooperative with a female tester, reactives with a male tester. *Social skills*. Schizophrenics, as noted above, are poor at synchronising their utterances, perhaps because they look so little, and have difficulty in getting into rapport or establishing a relationship. It is however possible to establish asymmetrical relationships with schizophrenics, and this is the normal staff–patient relationship. They are able to carry out instructions, but are totally passive and have no goals of their own; this may be the effect of institutionalisation. *Perceptual sensitivity* is poor, especially to non-verbal communications. Schizophrenics are unable to detect emotions from photographs (Vandenberg, 1960), from tones of voice (Davitz, 1964), or from posture shown in stick-figures (Sarbin and Hardyck, 1953). Cumming and Cumming

(1962) report that it is necessary to put emotion into words, e.g. 'I am angry', in order to communicate emotion to schizophrenics. Donovan and Webb (1965) found that process schizophrenics had a high threshold for the recognition of words spoken by a female voice. *Taking the role of the other*. Milgram (1960) found that schizophrenics were worse than normals and brain-damaged patients at giving male and female word-associations; his evidence suggests that this is due to a failure of empathic ability rather than of cognitive ability.

What psychological processes are responsible for schizophrenic social behaviour? There is evidence from twin studies for a strong genetic component in the aetiology of schizophrenia. However, there is also an environmental contribution – as is shown by the different concordance rates of identical twins reared together and apart – 91·5% *v.* 77·6% (Kallmann, 1950). There is evidence that the genetic component is stronger for chronic (process) schizophrenics, and is stronger for males (Gottesman and Shields, 1966). It seems that the mixture of genetic and environmental components varies between the two main forms of the disorder.

There is a great deal of rather inconclusive evidence about bio-chemistry and arousal levels in different kinds of schizophrenic; these are presumably the intervening links between genes and symptoms (see Jackson, 1960). Apart from the breakdown of social performance, the most striking feature of schizophrenia is the failure of symbolic processes, and this may explain some of the social failure. To become a human being involves assimilating a cultural heritage as well as a biological one; it involves the acquisition of secondary drives, attitudes and some understanding of the world; it involves the integration of all this into a more or less unitary self. This is all made possible by the symbolic operations of the brain, which enable us to engage in learning from the past, problem-solving, and the formulation of plans for the future. In schizophrenics these symbolic processes have failed, with the result that there are no secondary drives and no ego-identity (Lidz and Fleck, 1964). If this theory is correct, there should be a correlation between cognitive disorganisation and social failure. Schooler and Parkel (1966) found a strong correlation between these variables for males, but almost none for females, in a study of 73 male and 75 female schizophrenics. Biochemical processes, in turn produced genetically, could produce such cognitive disorganisation. A variant of this approach is to stress the failure of identity-formation in schizophrenics: this may be described as ego-diffusion (Erikson, p. 371), or the separation of a false self from the true self (Laing, p 379). Several socialisation studies show that schizophrenics have been exposed to contradictory demands or communications (e.g. Bateson *et al.*, 1956). It has also been reported that schizophrenics break down when first exposed to the need to accept adult responsibility (Lu, 1962). Alternatively we could suppose that cognitive failure leads to a failure of the social skill mechanism at the 'translation' stage, including the ability to take the role of the other.

We showed above that there is room for some environmental causation of schizophrenia, especially for the less severe, reactive type, and perhaps for females. Schizophrenics are found to come from particular kinds of families, so it is possible that socialisation experiences in the family are of some aetiological importance. It is also of course possible that the families become like this as the result of having a schizophrenic, or schizophrenic-prone child, and that the parents of patients may themselves have some schizoid traits, which are passed on genetically rather than environmentally. The child-parent sequence is given some support from a study of Klebanoff (1959), who found that the parents of schizophrenics were no different from the parents of children with brain injuries – both sets were lacking in warmth and were over-possessive.

A number of groups of investigators have been studying schizophrenic parents and families, and interpreted the results in terms of causation by family experiences. However much of this research consists of studies of a few schizophrenic families, without a control group. At the present time these theories must be looked at as very interesting hypotheses than as established causes of schizophrenia (Mishler and Waxler, 1966).

(1) It is a fairly well established finding that schizophrenics often have dominant, rejecting and overprotecting parents (Ciccheti, 1967); numerous studies show this, though there is doubt about causality as shown above.

(2) Other studies are concerned, not with dyadic relations, but with the whole family constellation (Handel, 1965). It has often been found that there is more conflict between the parents of schizophrenics than between other parents (e.g. Farina, 1960); Lidz (1963) and his colleagues find that this is particularly the case with female patients. One interpretation is that the parents are competing for the child, another that the child internalises two conflicting social objects.

(3) Another finding is that the family structure is peculiar in certain ways. Lidz *et al.* (op. cit.) report a 'marital skew' pattern, particularly for male patients, where there is an incestuous relation with the mother. Wynne *et al.* (1958) maintain that the whole role-structure of the family is not sufficiently clear for identity-formation to take place.

(4) The style of communication in schizophrenics' families has been reported to be peculiar. Wynne *et al.* (op. cit.) describe it as fragmented, blurred and meaningless. Bateson *et al.* (1956) suggested that schizophrenics' parents engage in double-binds, i.e. emit communications where the verbal content is contradicted by the non-verbal (cf. p. 120). Berger (1965) found that schizophrenics reported greater frequency of double-bind communication from their parents, as assessed on a 'double-bind questionnaire', as compared with other groups of people. Such reports may be the result of selective or distorted memories, so do not provide very conclusive evidence.

Some very interesting new ideas about schizophrenia have come from sociologists in recent years; in view of the failure to find a biological basis for schizophrenia, and the inconclusive socialisation evidence, these must be taken seriously. It is also notable that schizophrenic symptoms are extremely heterogeneous; this casts some doubt on biological explanations; perhaps the common element is a common meaning for the symptoms – all are 'eccentric' or instances of 'rule-breaking'.

(1) Schizophrenics are also found to be socially isolated – they live alone in areas of social disorganisation and little family life, and work in solitary jobs; again this is probably because they seek these situations rather than because isolation produces schizophrenia. In addition schizophrenics are less likely to marry – partly because they don't want to and others don't want to marry them.

(2) Schizophrenics are about five times as common among working-class people – though this is partly due to downward mobility among those affected (Wardle, 1962). Again social class is more an effect than a cause, an effect of failure to deal with social and other aspects of the work situation.

(3) Sarbin (1967a) has suggested that schizophrenia is brought about through society locking up its eccentrics, and forcing them into the passive role of patients. Studies of institutionalisation do indeed show that the longer a patient has been inside the hospital the more dependent on it he becomes, and the better adjusted to his passive, dependent role (Wing, 1962). Studies of mental hospitals show that these pressures really do operate (Goffman, 1961).

(4) The reverse of the last theory has also been put forward, and may well be true of a different kind of hospital. It has been suggested that eccentric behaviour may be adopted deliberately in order to get an easy life with no work in hospital. Braginsky *et al.* (1969) found that patients presented more symptoms during an interview if they thought they

were going to be released, fewer symptoms if they thought they might be put in a closed ward.

However, despite these sociological contributions there is solid evidence for a genetic basis for schizophrenia, and the schizophrenia rate is just as high in primitive areas with no mental hospitals as it is in civilised countries (Demarath, 1956).

Autism in children is a rare condition, in some ways a more extreme version of schizophrenia in adults. These children are totally unresponsive to other people, and act as if other people do not exist, even in a crowded playroom (Hutt and Vaizey, 1966). They talk, but only to themselves, and engage in repetitive motor activity in relation to mechanical objects; they seem to see themselves as pieces of machinery and may draw diagrams to that effect (Bettelheim, 1959). They avoid looking at eyes and faces: Hutt and Ounsted (1966) found that they avoided masks of human faces in an experimental room, and were more interested in masks of animal faces and in the furniture. When together they looked briefly at each other, but in such a way as to avoid mutual gaze; brief mutual gaze was possible for very short periods if two autists were a sufficient distance apart. Hutt and Hutt (1965) suggest that autistic children are in a state of high cortical arousal and that eye-contact is very arousing for them. The parents of autistic children are often found to be cold and withdrawn (Rimland, 1962). Singer and Wynne (1963) compared the parents of autistic children with the parents of young adult schizophrenics on the TAT. The former had greater passivity and apathy about interaction, and gave evidence of an intellectualised distance from people. The authors deduce that the difference is that adult schizophrenics have at least had an early relationship with their parents which has later become impaired, through the processes discussed above.

Depression

This is the next most common form of psychosis and the most common form of hospitalisation after schizophrenia, but it has attracted far less attention from research workers. Depressive states are closely linked with manic ones, to be considered below: both are primarily disturbances of mood, and they can occur episodically at different times in the same people. There is more than one kind of depressed patient. In a factor analysis of the symptoms of 92 depressed patients Kiloh and Garside (1963) found two main types – endogenous and reactive. Endogenous depressives are older, fatter, more deeply depressed, have had a series of attacks, and can be regarded as psychotic. Reactive depressives have had a sudden onset, are more irritable, and are neurotic. In the same study however a general factor of depression was also found. We shall deal with this common pattern.

The elements of behaviour generally reflect the depressed emotional state. In *appearance* they look miserable and crushed, wear clothes that are sombre and drab, but they do not neglect their personal appearance, and are clean, neat and appropriately dressed. Their *posture* is generally drooping, with lowered head. *Gestures* are slow and feeble, *facial expression* is flat and mask-like; the *gaze* has a 'dull' quality (Riemer, 1955). *Speech*. Depressives speak little, do not initiate anything, and there are long silences (Chapple and Lindemann, 1942). Their voices are low-pitched, monotonous, of reduced volume, and slow. The contents of their conversation are pessimistic.

The main feature of depression, the emotional state, does not appear in our list of dimensions of social performance, but depressives have a characteristic style of social behaviour which can be described in these terms. *Introversion*. Depressives largely cut themselves off from interpersonal relations, and spend most of their time sitting and brooding quietly by themselves. They behave in a distant and guarded way. On the other hand they are able to interact, and will sit with other patients at meals (Grinker *et al.*, 1961). They have no interest in the opposite sex, and may lose interest in friends and members of their family (Mayer-Gross *et al.*, 1960). *Dependence*. Depressives relate to others mainly in a passive and dependent manner. Some however can be demanding or provocative. The *rewardingness* of depressives is extremely small. They are not so much suffering from *social anxiety* as lack of self-confidence; they have a very low opinion of themselves, and are obsessed with their own failure and guilt; 75% have suicidal ideas, and 10–15% try to commit suicide (Arieti, 1959). They are preoccupied with the past and have no hope for the future.

As with schizophrenia there is evidence for a strong genetic factor in the aetiology of depression, though this is weaker for reactive depression. There is also evidence of social factors in the aetiology, and as with schizophrenia some of the main symptoms concern relations with people. The precipitation of a depressive attack is usually of a social character, as will be shown below. This all suggests that depression can be accounted for at least partly in terms of interpersonal processes.

Socialisation studies show that manic-depressives come from families which were very critical and put great pressure on them to conform, to be conventional and respectable and to obtain prestige (Cohen *et al.*,

1954). It has also been found that manic-depressives as children showed
promise but became the object of envy on the part of siblings – leading
to a tendency to undersell themselves (Gibson, 1958). The personality
of depressives before breakdown is reported to be competitive and
dependent (Wittenborn, 1965). Another socialisation experience associated with later depression is the death of parents during childhood. It is
found that about 21% of depressives have lost their mother before the
age of 14 (6% in the general population), and 21% have lost their father
between 5 and 14 (5·7% in the general population), (Bowlby, 1962).
It is not known how this early event has an effect 30 years later; one
possibility is that the patient becomes depressed when he comes to the
age at which his parent died – a kind of role-taking.

Depression may be precipitated by known stresses, or take place
without any known external stress. However, in the majority of cases it
is brought about by the failure of a social relationship – a bereavement,
a sudden separation from a spouse or other close relation, or a career
failure in connection with an organisation (Arieti, 1959). It is not known
why separation results in depression. Possible mechanisms are frustration through loss of social rewards, loss of the possibility of anxiety-
reduction through social contact, loss of self-esteem or other aspects of
self-image through loss of supportive responses.

Sociological studies show a considerable decline in the prevalence
of the illness in the USA during this century, though in some countries
such as New Zealand it is more common than schizophrenia. It has
been suggested that the disorder is associated with inner-directed
societies, with their stress on individual achievement (Arieti, 1959).
Depression, unlike schizophrenia, occurs almost equally in all social
classes, and is if anything more common among middle-class people.
Suicide is considerably more common among people of higher status;
Henry and Short (1954) suggest that suicide is restrained when people
are under external restraints and belong to close relational systems. It is
found that people who attempt suicide are depressed and are socially
isolated. Does depression lead to social isolation, or isolation to depression? Depression may affect social behaviour in two ways. (1) The
low level of arousal reduces all activity, social included. (2) The loss of
self-esteem leads to loss of confidence with other people, and avoidance
of interaction.

Manic states

Manic states are in many ways the opposite of depressive ones, and may
occur in the same people at different times; in rare cases there is a

regular alternation between the two. Manic states however are much rarer than depressive ones, although the milder version, hypomania, is quite common among non-patients – particularly among entertainers, politicians, salesmen and people in similar professions.

The chief symptom of those in a state of mania and hypomania is an extreme elation of mood, a general state of excitement and jollity, enormous energy, and an inflated idea of themselves, sometimes amounting to delusions of grandeur. Otherwise they are more in touch than other psychotics and happier than any other patients.

Some of the elements of manic social behaviour are as follows. *Appearance.* Manics seem to enjoy robust and perfect health; they wear smart, striking and rather loud clothes; they look extremely happy. Their bodily *posture* is erect and they make vigorous *gestural* movements. Their *facial expression* is smiling and alert, and they may adopt a 'dramatic *gaze*'. *Speech.* They talk incessantly and at high speed, are easily distractable and move rapidly from topic to topic, with no particular purpose except to enjoy the conversation; they make ceaseless jokes and tell outrageous stories, based on puns or clang associations, and often in bad taste. Lorenz and Cobb (1952) found that they use more verbs and fewer adjectives than other people, and deduce the presence of anxiety; they found no disorganisation of speech.

In terms of our dimensions of social performance, manics are in many ways the opposite of depressives. *Extroversion.* They spend a lot of their time in social activity, making speeches, being the life and soul of the party, writing letters to and ringing up important people, and so on. *Dominance.* Manics tend to be dominating and overbearing, and they will not take criticism from others. They like to be the centre of attention and to be in charge of things. They like to make people laugh, and their own hilarity is infectious. *Poise.* Manics are often good at making speeches and putting on public performances – which they greatly enjoy. Their striking appearance suggests that they want to present an impressive image to others. *Social skills.* They often have many friends, are successful at handling people, as well as being good at public performances. Their *perceptual sensitivity* is poor – they fail to see when their dominance and jokes are annoying people, and they have a very inaccurate view of themselves. They probably fail to *take the role of the other.*

Since manic states often occur in the same people who have depression, the same social and environmental conditions apply. The same factors precipitate both. Where depressives are at a low level of motivation and self-esteem, manics for some reason are at a high level of both.

It has been said that manics are trying to distract themselves from other anxieties – as a girl might plunge herself into a round of parties, or a man travel to the Antipodes, to forget an unhappy love affair.

Paranoia and paranoid schizophrenia

We will consider these two conditions together: both are characterised by organised delusions, often of grandeur and persecution. Paranoid schizophrenics resemble other schizophrenics in their withdrawal and thought disorder. In a study of 400 patients with paranoid symptoms, Miller (1942) found that 38% were diagnosed as having paranoid schizophrenia, 16% were senile, 10% had straight paranoia, and the remainder were divided among a number of other conditions. Paranoid symptoms, in varying degree, are widespread, and may be found in many cranks and eccentrics.

Not much is known about the elements of social interaction of paranoids. Their *appearance* is often strange, as they may dress to fit their delusions. They have a 'guarded *gaze*' which is over-alert and suspicious (Riemer, 1955). In other respects they resemble schizophrenics.

In terms of our dimensions there is a characteristic paranoid profile. *Introversion.* Paranoids are secretive and seclusive, they do not trust people or confide in them; they are able to make social contact with others, but become excluded from social contact because of the way they behave. Their *rewardingness* is very low: their arrogance, touchiness and absurd ideas annoy others, and they gradually become rejected (Lemmert, 1962). Their *interaction skills* are better than those of schizophrenics, and they can interact quite well; however they are unable to profit from feedback from others and at the first hint of criticism or disagreement they become rigid and hostile (Cameron, 1959). Paranoids' *perception* can be greatly distorted in line with their delusions – white-coated nurses may be seen as courtiers for example. They may go further and interact with people who are not there at all. They think that behaviour is directed towards them when it is not, and they see imaginary slights and insults in perfectly normal behaviour. They are quite unable to *take the role of the other*. A central feature of paranoid social behaviour falls in the field of *self-presentation*: paranoids have an inflated idea of their importance, and this makes them touchy and sensitive to slights. They are arrogant and superior in manner, and think that they are being persecuted. They are apt to write letters to or otherwise approach important people about their grievances. They may believe that they have some important mission, message, discovery or position.

They are insecure and are very upset when other people fail to accept their ideas.

Although paranoid schizophrenia probably has a strong genetic component, this appears to be less true of other kinds of paranoia, so that we must look for environmental factors in the aetiology. While paranoia is usually regarded as being primarily a thought disorder, it is notable that it is mainly thoughts about identity and relations with other people that are disturbed, and social behaviour as a result is very disordered. Socialisation studies show that the parents of paranoids were often cruel, violent and frightening (Klein and Horwitz, 1949), or created a tense and suspicious atmosphere. The disorder is precipitated by stresses such as failure, competition, or a loss of a supporting social relationship as in divorce or separation (Cameron, op. cit.). It is most commonly found in people over 40, who are educated, and who are members of immigrant minority groups.

What processes are responsible for paranoid social behaviour? One factor is the growth of an identity which is unrealistic, made possible by isolation from others. This may be through language difficulties, through being protected by parents from peer-group criticism, or simply through being deaf. At the same time there is a failure to develop skills of person perception and of taking the role of the other. Basically the social performance of paranoids is disrupted by the formation of a false system of beliefs, which in turn is generated by internal forces in the personality (Tyhurst, 1957). It can be looked at as a defence mechanism – accepting the belief enables the patient to reduce anxiety; for example failure in an examination can be reacted to by believing that the examiners were unfair, or had a grudge against the candidate. One lesson for normal interaction is that for a person to be able to engage in social interaction he must to a large extent share the cognitions of the people with whom he is interacting – including ideas about himself.

Anxiety neurosis

The neuroses are widely spread in the population. Like intelligence and height, neuroticism is a matter of degree, though about 5% of people are found to have fairly severe symptoms, and a much larger percentage have lesser symptoms. There is nevertheless a discontinuity in individual histories – the point at which their 'nervous breakdown' occurs. We shall deal with the two main divisions of neurosis – hysteria and anxiety neurosis.

In anxiety neurosis the patient suffers from 'free-floating' anxiety about nothing in particular, and in addition may have specific phobias for such things as travel, height, animals, etc. In the closely related condition of obsessional neurosis he may be greatly worried by dirt and disorder.

The elements of interaction in anxiety neurosis reflect the state of anxiety. *Bodily posture* is tense and awkward, often with hands clasped tightly together; *gestural movements* are jerky and poorly controlled, with a lot of uncommunicative fiddling. *Facial expression* is tense. The *speech* of anxious people is very fast, though irregular, with many interruptions and speech errors; they respond rapidly and initiate interaction (Chapple and Lindemann, 1942; Matarazzo, 1958). Their tone of voice is breathy (Ostwald, 1965).

In terms of our dimensions, they may be introverted or extroverted, dominant or submissive. The main feature of their interaction style is their *social anxiety* and lack of poise: they are anxious about social situations – that others will not like them, that they are doing the wrong thing, wearing the wrong clothes, and so on; they do not like being watched or being the centre of attention, and do not enjoy social interaction. Their *social skills* may include complex patterns of behaviour which appear destructive and meaningless until the symbolic character has been disentangled. These patterns of behaviour are very varied, and Berne (1966) has given an amusing account of some of them. In what he calls 'Rapo': a woman at a party leads a man on until he responds, whereupon she slaps his face. While pointless and annoying to others, such behaviour relieves conflicts and tensions for the performer. Like paranoids their person *perception* is over-sensitive, in this case to suggestions of rejection or displeasure on the part of others. There is a characteristic form of *self-presentation;* they want to be and be seen as unselfish, saintly, loving and lovable (Portnoy, 1959).

Inheritance accounts for some of the aetiology, in much the same way as it does for intelligence – people are born with different degrees of anxiety and tendency to be easily upset by frustration. Inheritance is less important than it is in the psychoses. A number of socialisation studies show that these patients had close relations with their parents, especially their mothers, and were brought up very strictly with withdrawal of love discipline (O'Connor and Franks, 1960; Funkenstein *et al.*, 1957). Other studies provide evidence for neurotic, guilty and worrying behaviour on the part of the parents (Block *et al.*, 1958), and for traumatic events of various kinds during childhood (Portnoy, op. cit.). A breakdown into anxiety neurosis is precipitated by increased stress, either of a realistic kind, or of a kind which is made stressful by the sensitivity of the patient to certain kinds of event. Much of the social behaviour of anxious people can be ascribed to anxiety about social situations – in many of the cases treated by behaviour therapy the dominant symptoms have been in the social area (p. 421 ff). The destructive social techniques are more complicated: they result from inner conflicts about attitudes to others.

Hysteria

Hysteria is a form of neurosis which often involves bodily complaints such as paralyses and anaesthesias, or other psychosomatic troubles, as well as amnesias, and in extreme cases fugues and multiple personality. There is a characteristic style of social performance.

The elements of hysterical social behaviour include considerable attention to *appearance*: apart from great care with clothes, which may indicate their identity in an exaggerated way, they may also display their bodily ailments prominently. *Gestural* and *facial* movements too are over-dramatised. Excessive blinking of the eyes has been reported (Riemer, 1955). Patients produce a lot of *speech*, which is less nervous and more earnest than that of anxiety neurotics.

In terms of our dimensions, hysterics are clearly *extroverts*, though their extroversion takes a neurotic form (Eysenck, 1957). They have a great need to be the centre of attention, and are very demanding of attention and admiration, and dependent on other people for it. They are flirtatious but sexually frigid (Chodoff and Lyons, 1958; Blinder, 1966). Their vain behaviour, and demands for attention, make hysterics as *unrewarding* as most other mental patients, though like manics they can be quite entertaining. Much of their social performance may be summarised as a concern with *self-presentation* linked with uncertainty about identity. They over-dramatise themselves, exaggerating their emotional states, and making themselves out to be more interesting and exciting than they really are. They are egoistic and vain, but uncertain of themselves, needing constant confirmation of their identity. They take the role of the observed rather than the observer – and may do well as actresses, politicians or public speakers. Some become impostors and take on new and prestigeful identities; Helene Deutsch (1955) describes a juvenile delinquent who made a rapid transition to 'country gentleman'. Rather different from impostors are people in fugue states, in which a person suddenly takes on a new identity, and completely forgets his previous one. Hysterical bodily symptoms may also be looked at as pieces of self-presentation. There is a difference between malingerers, and people with uncontrollable bodily symptoms, though the first can develop into the second.

Hysterics, who are often women, are found to have been over-protected by their mothers (Spiegel and Bell, 1959). An interpretation of this is that as children these patients found that they were rewarded for minor illnesses – both by maternal attention, and by being able to avoid undesirable engagements. Szasz (1961) has developed the view that hysterical bodily symptoms are a kind of non-verbal communication which is resorted to when words have failed. The message may be about guilt and self-punishment, or it may seek attention, sympathy and help. It is a less precise language than that of words; this has the advantages that it doesn't commit the communicator, it insures against disappointment, and it avoids the embarrassment of admitting to the needs in question. In using bodily language, the hysteric is taking the role of the sick person, pretending to be ill, and being an impostor, in order to control other people as she previously discovered that she could influence her mother. This is an interesting extension of the normal use of non-verbal communication to control social relationships and to mediate normal self-presentation (p. 75). All this does not entirely explain the concern of hysterics with self-presentation. Perhaps another part of the aetiology is the development of an insecure personality, needing constant confirmation and attention (cf. Chap. IX).

Delinquency

There are several kinds of delinquent personality, of which we will consider two. The 'pseudo-social' delinquent (Hewitt and Jenkins, 1946) is so called because he behaves quite normally, indeed with loyalty, to members of his own gang, but with a blank wall of rejection to all others. There is little unusual about these delinquents at the level of the elements of interaction, except that in *appearance* they conform very strictly to the conventions of their group. In terms of our dimensions, they are somewhat *extroverted* in the sense that they spend a lot of time with a gang and show great loyalty to it. There is a failure of *social skill* in that they are unable to form a relationship with older people or those in authority. With borstal and prison officers they may pretend to be model inmates, in order to get out quickly, but refuse to form any real social relationships (Topping, 1943). There is some evidence of a failure of *perceptual sensitivity*: McDavid and Schroder (1957) found that delinquents had a high threshold for perceiving approval.

There is no evidence for inheritance, or physiological abnormality. The origins of pseudo-social delinquency probably lie in the process of identity-formation during adolescence. It is normal for adolescents to seek social support and an independent identity in groups outside the family (p. 246 ff). When there is a bad relationship with the family this process is strengthened; when the local groups are delinquent they form norms of delinquent behaviour and hostility to parents and other adults (Hewitt and Jenkins, op. cit.; Argyle, 1964b).

A second group of offenders are known as 'psychopaths', a rather mixed group of individuals who have in common a basic hostility and lack of concern for others, together with lack of shame or conscience, and high impulsiveness, especially for aggression and sex. Psychopaths are not clearly distinguishable from normals at the level of the elements of social performance, though a 'shifty, constantly moving' *gaze* has been reported (Feldman, 1959), and they may be rather smartly dressed, in the case of confidence men for example. Their most striking trait is an inability to *take the role of the other*: they simply cannot see another person's point of view, or have any understanding of another's emotional reactions (Cleckley, 1955), though they may take calculated account of another's point of view when manipulating him. Gough (1948) reports that psychopaths cannot understand disapproval or punishment, as they are unable to look at themselves from another point of view; they have no concern for another's feelings and cannot predict another's behaviour. Gough and Petersen (1952) constructed a test for psychopaths made up of items reflecting these notions, and the test was found to discriminate very well between delinquents and non-delinquents.

There is evidence for neurological origins for psychopathy – early brain injury or disease, abnormal EEG; twin studies suggest a strong genetic element (Shields and Slater, 1960). There is also evidence for socialisation origins – extreme childhood neglect, ill-treatment, no stable home (McCord and McCord, 1956). There is probably more than one type of psychopath; Craft (1961) arrived at the conclusion that there are three kinds: (1) brain-damaged, (2) affectionless, (3) emotionally unstable and impulsive. It is the social performance of the second group which is of most interest to us – and which fits Cleckley's description of a 'mask of sanity'. It is in this group that affiliative motivation and role-taking ability are lowest, presumably as a result of abnormal home-life during childhood.

Concluding remarks on mental disorder

Several points about the social behaviour of patients are worth noting. Among the elements the one most commonly disturbed is the pattern of eye-movements; we showed earlier that eye-movements play an essential part in the process of interaction; for example if a person does not look enough he will not receive feedback, and if he looks at the wrong time synchronising will be affected. Mental patients also display peculiarities of posture, gesture, facial expression and tone of voice – the non-verbal signalling system. The most interesting case is hysteria, where the main symptoms can be regarded as non-verbal communications intended to control the behaviour of others.

At the level of our dimensions, it is clear that the richness and diversity of abnormal behaviour cannot be summarised in terms of simple unitary dimensions. However, the dimensions are useful in drawing attention to some of the main features of abnormal social performance. The dimension in which nearly all mental patients are similar is rewardingness; however, the precise way in which they are unrewarding is very variable, though it might be correct to describe most patients as 'egocentric'. Meldman (1967) found that psychiatric patients talked about themselves more than controls did. One reason for their unrewardingness may be inability to take the role of the other, which is common to psychotics and psychopaths. This is associated in many cases with a basic failure to communicate or interact properly. Further disturbances are associated with peculiarities of self-image and resulting eccentricities of self-presentation. These failures of performance on the part of the mentally ill set off a vicious circle, in which other people withdraw from them and cease to provide rewards, so that patients are under greater stress in social situations and produce increasingly ineffective kinds of social interaction.

Studies of social interaction throw a new light on mental disorder. Previous research has shown that these disorders are partly inherited and involve physiological and cognitive disturbances. However, in most cases there is also evidence of abnormal interaction in the family (though this has not been shown to be causal), and precipitation by social events. Furthermore some of the main symptoms are in the field of interaction and interpersonal relations. It is behaviour in this area which often leads to a person becoming incompetent or a nuisance and therefore defined as a patient.

Techniques of training in social skill are now being experimented with in various quarters as means of treating mental patients. These

methods are discussed in Chapter X. Meanwhile here are some suggestions about how a patient's position on each of our seven dimensions
might be modified; these methods are described in the next chapter.

1. *Low affiliation.* Little is known about how to increase affiliative drive.
Some success has been obtained with operant conditioning.
2. *Low dominance.* It is possible to teach the social skills needed for
successful influence and leadership – for example by role-playing. It is
probably undesirable to modify the drive-state.
3. *Social anxiety* can be reduced by desensitisation methods; it is
possible that teaching the skills needed to handle social situations would
also be helpful.
4. *Low rewardingness.* One method would be to show patients video-
tapes of themselves being unrewarding. Another would be to use
role-reversal methods so that the patient is exposed to rewarding and
unrewarding styles of behaviour in the same way that leader trainees
are sometimes exposed to different styles of leadership.
5. *Inadequate interaction skills.* Patients can be trained by instruction
and demonstration, followed by role-playing practice with stooges,
using video-tape playback and verbal commentary. This method can
also be used for correcting elements of the patient's behaviour,
e.g. facial expression, posture, aspects of speech, eye-movements,
etc.
6. *Low perceptual sensitivity.* Various methods of training are available
for increasing sensitivity to tones of voice, facial expression, etc.
7. *Inability to take the role of the other.* It may be possible to improve
this ability by role-reversal training in which the patient tries to enact
the role of others, with whom he normally interacts.

The author, with Bridget Bryant and Barbara Lalljee, has been using
these techniques on neurotic out-patients whose difficulties are mainly
interpersonal. The results so far suggest that improvement can be
brought about in six sessions in many cases.

Appendix to Chapter VIII
    N. Armistead's test of social skill in everyday situations
Instructions:
    We would like to see what you would have to say for yourself in certain
situations. Below we describe a few situations to you. Whatever you think

of the circumstances and whether or not you would ever find yourself in such a position, we would like you to write down what you would actually say, going on the evidence given. As you will see, it's very important for you to say something appropriate or else you're in trouble. There is no time limit.

1. You have been late for work several times, using all the usual excuses and your boss is fed up with this. He tells you that you are slack and that any more such transparent excuses are not acceptable. Three days later you oversleep because you have been at a party and you are half-an-hour late. What do you say to the boss?

2. At a cocktail party you meet someone you don't like and don't want to be seen with, so you want to get away immediately. What do you say to the person?

3. You are sitting idly on a park bench by yourself, when this girl sits down with her shopping bag at the other end. You find her attractive, and would like to talk to her. Then she glances your way and smiles. What do you say to her?

4. Your parents want you to go on holiday with them, but you have already made plans to go with some friends. Then your parents ask you what date term finishes and where you would like to go. Without hurting their feelings, what do you say to them?

5. You go for an interview for a manager's job with the GPO. You have carefully prepared to answer the question 'Why do you want to work for the GPO?' But the interviewer sits you down and says in a firm voice: 'I have just one question to ask you. What do you think is wrong with the GPO?' What do you say to him?

6. You take a girl to a smart restaurant although you are casually dressed and eat £2 worth of food between you. Then you discover that neither of you has money or cheque book within striking distance. What do you say to the waiter?

7. You are with a male friend of yours having a heart-to-heart talk about friends in general and girls in particular. He says to you, 'I don't know why I have so much trouble making friends. Do you think it could be something like bad breath?' In fact, he does have bad breath. How would you inform him of this?

8. A girl you like very much but have only just met, phones up on Friday to invite you to a party the next night, but you are with

another girl whom you have promised to take to the coast for the week-end. She is actually in the room with you and you don't want to give either girl the impression that you prefer the other. What do you say on the phone to the first girl?

9. You are asked at the last minute to introduce the speaker at a seminar, although you don't know anything about him, not even his name and title. What do you say for an introduction?

10. You are at a party with a girl you really care for, but have only just met. She likes you and has dressed rather dramatically to please you and be in the fashion. Soon after you arrive, an acquaintance comes up to you and says, just loud enough so that your girl friend can over-hear, 'How long have you been going out with this tart?' Punching him would be out of place so what do you say to him?

IX

The Self and Interaction

INTRODUCTION AND MEASUREMENT

A number of interaction phenomena are closely connected with the self and are treated separately in this chapter. The self is used in two main senses in psychology: (1) there is the 'I', the conscious subject and active agent in behaviour, that takes decisions. (2) There is the 'me' that is reacted to by others as being a particular sort of person, of a given degree of esteem; these reactions are gradually accepted and become self-image and self-esteem. It is with the second aspect of the self that we are concerned in this chapter. It has two main components – the *self-image* is the descriptive part, what sort of person P thinks he is; and *self-esteem* – how favourably P regards himself. Between them they form a cognitive system which like other cognitive systems exerts a controlling effect on behaviour. There is a cognitive task, similar to concept-formation, to arrive at a unified conceptualisation of the self.

Perhaps the basic process is that people categorise each other in various ways, and use different styles of interaction as a result, as we saw in Chapter IV. The categorisation may be in terms of positions and roles, or of personality traits; in a given cultural group certain kinds of categorisation are common, though different dimensions may be salient for particular individuals – e.g. social class and religious affiliation (positions), intelligence and neuroticism (traits). As a result each person is constantly being categorised by others, learns to anticipate how he will be categorised, and eventually sees himself in these terms: this is *self-image*. People are also categorised as more or less rewarding, and more or less prestigeful; this is anticipated too and becomes *self-esteem*. Self-image and self-esteem are in addition affected by forces inside the personality – to generate a more or less integrated self-image, with a content that meets other needs, and that is sufficiently favourable. This gives rise to imagination and fantasy about the self, and to the growth of an *ideal self*. These cognitive processes affect social interaction,

356

because a self-image can only be sustained if others accept it, and react accordingly. There is often an element of *self-presentation* in behaviour whereby people try to induce others to classify them in the desired manner.

The self does not affect all behaviour: it influences behaviour in situations which are 'ego-involving', which bring the self-esteem system into operation. We shall discuss below the various conditions that do this. Goffman (1956a) gave an account of social behaviour in terms of drama – i.e. putting on a performance for others; he recognised however that some situations were 'off-stage'. We now know more about which situations are on-stage, and this chapter is primarily about behaviour in those situations. To analyse these phenomena it is necessary to analyse events at the level of conscious experiences and subjective meanings, rather than in terms of motor responses (McCall and Simmons, 1966). These higher-level fantasies and plans are however able to direct and organise the motor responses. Self-presentation can be interpreted in terms of the social skill model (p. 179 ff); the goal is to affect the perception of the self by others. It is on the other hand a special aspect of behaviour in that attention is focused on the imagined conscious experiences of others (Argyle and Williams, 1969).

The self-image is how a person perceives himself. The simplest way to find out how P perceives himself is to ask him, and this can be done in a number of ways. As with the perception of others, it is possible to learn which attributes are most salient by using an unstructured approach. Kuhn and McPartland (1954) devised the Twenty-Statements Test, or TST, in which subjects are asked to give 20 answers to the question 'Who am I?' About half the answers are found to be in terms of objective roles or other properties (e.g. female, married), and the rest in terms of personality traits or evaluations (e.g. happy, good). The first kind are written down first and may be more salient. Mulford and Salisbury (1964) gave the test to a sample of 1,213 adult residents of Iowa, and analysed the role answers. The four most frequent answers were in terms of family relationship (70%), occupation (68%), marital status (34%), religious identity (30%). Women used family categories more than men, who mentioned their occupation and sex more often. Age was mentioned most by old and young people. Kahn and McPartland (op. cit.) found that religious affiliation was mentioned most often by Roman Catholics, Lutherans, Sect members and Jews. McCall and Simmons (1966) recommend following up the TST with an interview to find out more about the roles and traits listed. They use a list of broad categories of roles – racial, sexual, family, occupational, religious, recreational, social, etc. They also ask questions of the kind 'How important is it to you personally to be a ——?' Another way of finding which parts of the self-image are most central, or form the 'core' of the self, is Hinkle's 'laddering' technique: concepts are elicited by the Rep. Grid method (p. 130), the subject being included in the triads; the subject is then asked why he prefers one end of each construct, thus producing a further construct, and so on up a ladder of 8–12 superordinate constructs (Bannister and Mair, 1968).

Subjective ratings of personality traits can be obtained in several ways. LaForge and Suczek (1955) constructed an Interpersonal Check List, which has 128 items, 8 for each of the 16 variables listed by Leary (1957); subjects say which adjectives apply to them. A convenient way of obtaining self-ratings is by means of the Semantic Differential (Osgood *et al.*, 1957). The three dimensions which normally underly this measuring system do not necessarily apply to self-ratings, and Smith (1962) reports the results of factor analysing a number of semantic scales which were administered to two samples of 96 psychiatric and other patients. The six most invariant dimensions were: (1) Self-confidence, (2) Social Worth, (3) Size, (4) Potency, (5) Intelligence and Leadership, and (6) Tension. These methods are free of acquiescence response set, but are they free of social desirability? Favourability of self-evaluation is one dimension that is usually measured, so there is no point in trying to eliminate it. On the other hand such questionnaire measures may encourage subjects to exaggerate this factor, thus giving an inaccurate measure of self-image. A method which to some extent evades this is the Q-sort, in which subjects sort a number of cards, with descriptive phrases or adjectives on them, into heaps which are more and less characteristic of him (Stephenson, 1953).

An important part of the self-image is the body image, which is perhaps the first part of it to be formed in young children. According to the study by Smith (1962), size is an important dimension of self-image. For females, it seems likely that physical attractiveness and its main components are of great importance. Jourard and Secord (1955) found that males were most satisfied with their bodies when they were large; females were more satisfied if their bodies were smaller than normal – but when their busts were larger than average. This and other studies suggest that people learn a cultural ideal of what the body should be like, and this results in varying degrees of satisfaction with the body – particularly during adolescence.

A number of investigators have devised unconscious measures of the body image or other aspects of the self, thinking that phenomenal, conscious measures are distorted. Wolff (1943) and others have done this by asking subjects to rate specimens of their own voices, hand-writing, pictures of their hands, etc., sometimes disguised by aniseikonic lenses, or by being shown in a mirror. It is found that subjects usually give very favourable judgements of samples of their own behaviour or body, but that some people gave very unfavourable judgements, while few are neutral. It is assumed that subjects recognise these samples unconsciously. It seems more probable that they are simply judging others who are seen as similar to themselves – it has been shown that people prefer those who are similar to themselves (cf. p. 212 f), but that a few individuals engage in 'projection' and reject their own characteristics as seen in others. Another way of assessing the unconscious self-image is by means of projection tests: Rogers and Dymond (1954) for example rated TAT protocols on self-concept, ideal self, etc. Fisher and Cleveland (1958) studied a dimension of the unconscious body image by means of the Rorschach test: their 'barrier score' is intended to be an index of how far people experience their body boundaries as definite and firm versus indefinite and vague. They found that individuals with high barrier scores were more likely to have psychosomatic symptoms on the body surface than inside it, and they had low interior reactivity, e.g. for heart-rate. The authors maintain that those with high barrier scores also have a firmer and clearer identity, are more extrapunitive and less suggestible. There is however no clear evidence that unconscious self-images really do affect behaviour independently of conscious self-perceptions, and we shall confine ourselves to the latter (cf. Wylie, 1961).

In addition to perceiving themselves more or less as they actually are at present, people build up in imagination an *ideal self*, which is what they would like to become. This is a future goal, to be striven for. It need not be unattainable; for some people it is just a little better than the actual self; when it is attained, the ideal self is then revised upwards a little. It may refer to positions and roles to be occupied, or to personality traits. It can be measured in much the same way as the actual self-image; for example the Semantic Differential can be used, with instructions to describe 'the kind of person I would most like to be'. An important and curious feature of the ideal self is that when the desired standard is attained, people do not sit back enjoying their self-esteem, but re-set their goals. This does not appear to reduce self-esteem, and it seems that satisfaction is derived from accepting the new goal, which in some sense is part of the self-image. To travel hopefully is better than to arrive.

We have now reviewed the elements which make up the self-image.

There are a series of roles that are played, of which some are more important to the individual than others; there are more pervasive personality traits, which operate in all or most of these roles – they describe the way the roles are played; there is also the body image, and there is the ideal self, which may consist of a number of different elements.

Self-esteem is the extent to which a person has favourable attitudes towards himself, i.e. there is a favourable attitude of 'I' towards 'me'. These favourable attitudes are generally assessed along a dimension of status or superiority. However, if self-esteem is based on the reactions of others, we should note that people respond to one another socially in terms of *two* main dimensions – (1) status and power, and (2) warmth and friendliness. Self-attitudes could be assessed along the second dimension too – the extent to which individuals like themselves or see themselves as 'nice' or 'friendly' – as persons to whom others will normally react positively, but not necessarily by regarding them as superior.

The evaluation dimension on the Semantic Differential gives an overall measure of positive self-attitudes, probably including both of the above components, depending on which scales are included. Self-esteem has often been assessed from the discrepancy between ratings or Q-sorts for 'self' and 'ideal self'. However, high discrepancy can be due to unrealistically high aspirations as well as to low evaluation of the self. Studies of changes in these ratings following therapy show that it is the self-ratings which change most, so that most of the variance in discrepancy scores is probably due to evaluations of self (Wylie, 1961). In Gough's adjective check list (1950), subjects check those of the 284 adjectives which they feel apply to themselves; 71 were originally rated by judges as being favourable; an index of self-acceptance is calculated by dividing the number of favourable adjectives checked by the total number checked. Another method of measuring self-esteem is by the use of questions or rating scales which enquire directly about self-evaluation; Rosenberg (1965) constructed an attitude scale for self-esteem which is mainly in the status and superiority area. It was found to agree quite well with free self-descriptions, and with ratings by nurses in the case of mental patients.

Self-consciousness is the extent to which a person is shy, easily embarrassed, and anxious when watched by other people. This can be measured on particular occasions by physiological measures of anxiety. Some people are very anxious in most social situations, and the personality dimension poise – social anxiety was introduced earlier (p. 324f).

Self-consciousness also has a purely cognitive component – the extent to which a person focuses his attention on how (he thinks) others see him, rather than on how he sees them. A measure of this was devised by Argyle and Williams (1969): subjects were asked, 'To what extent (in a particular situation) did you feel mainly the observer or observed?'

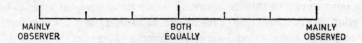

MAINLY OBSERVER   BOTH EQUALLY   MAINLY OBSERVED

This scale can be given in relation to a series of situations, e.g. 'With an older person of the opposite sex'; such scales correlate together and an average score for each subject can be calculated. The above authors found that feeling observed depended partly on the situation, e.g. being interviewed as opposed to interviewing; it was also partly a function of personality.

Integration–diffusion refers to the extent to which an individual has successfully integrated the different elements of his self-image into a unitary identity. This conception comes from the work of Erikson (1956), whose clinical studies with adolescents and others led him to postulate the occurrence of an 'identity crisis' in late adolescence; this is discussed later (p. 370 f). A person is said to be in a state of ego-diffusion if he does not know who he is or where he is going, i.e. if he has not chosen between or reconciled the diverse elements of motivation and self-image acquired in childhood; one extreme case of ego-diffusion is schizophrenia, where there is no central identity, and no long-term goals or persistent striving; another case, Marcia (1966) suggests, is the playboy. According to Erikson people pass through a number of stages, at each of which a particular crisis has to be overcome: the adolescent identity crisis is the fifth and most important of these.

Erikson (op. cit.) distinguishes two other states intermediate between integration and diffusion. One is where a 'moratorium' has been declared – i.e. the decisions involved in achieving integration have been postponed for a time, as in the case of a student who goes to India for a year 'to think things over'. The second is where there has been 'foreclosure', i.e. where a premature integration has occurred, but without taking an independent adult role; this corresponds to a dependent and obedient kind of personality. The ego-ideal also needs to be integrated, rather than containing inconsistent ambitions – as with a student who wants to be both a judge and a fighter pilot. In addition the goals must be realistic in relation to the present self and the individual's abilities and opportunities. Erikson assessed this variable from clinical interviews, and others such as Marcia (1966) used structured interview, the inter-viewer being instructed in the Erikson concepts.

Accessibility and disclosure refer to the extent to which a person reveals things about himself to others. Jourard (1964) constructed a 40-item scale covering 6 main areas, and he reports the disclosure scores of various samples of subjects, showing which areas are most accessible. Taylor and Altman (1966) present 671 items in 13 areas, which have been placed along an equi-appearing interval Thurstone scale by 16 judges. Two of the least accessible items are 'How old I was the first time I had sexual relations', and 'Things I dislike about my mother'. It is possible with either of these scales to arrive at an average score for a particular person, and his profile across different areas. It is usually found in these studies that the following areas are the least accessible: the person's sex-life and body, followed by his own family, his financial situation, his personality and emotions. How much is disclosed also depends on the other person. Rickers-Ovsiankina (1956) and Rickers-Ovsiankina and Kusmin (1958) found that most was disclosed to a close friend, less to an acquaintance, and least to a stranger. Jourard (op. cit.) found that students disclosed most to mother, followed by female friend, male friend and father; there was more disclosure to parents when there were positive feelings towards them.

Another aspect of accessibility is the physical closeness a person will permit. Felipe and Sommer (1966) carried out studies in which per-sonal space was violated by an experimenter sitting down next to a subject on a bench or seat in a public place. A high percentage of the victims left in a few minutes, others turned away, created barriers and avoided eye-contact. Jourard (1966) studied the areas of the body that were touched by others in different social relationships, again showing that accessibility varies systematically with the role of the other (p. 93). It is not known how far psychological and physical accessibility are related.

Unique and shared identities. The role and position aspects of self-image are shared with other occupants of the same role, and members of the same group. The trait components describe the more or less unique ways in which the roles are played, as well as affecting the roles that are selected. Some people share a group identity, with little stress on their own individuality. This is often found among the children in a family, who share the family identity; it is deliberately encouraged among recruits to the army, where individuality is suppressed and numbers are used instead of names; it happens among members of a crowd, where 'de-individuation' is likely to occur (p. 376f). Adolescents try to throw off their family identity by joining new groups, where they have a new identity – of 'mod', 'rocker', etc.; this is still a shared identity, but it gives them a new status in society (p. 246 ff). Middle-class intellectuals, artists and others prefer to emphasise the unique features of their identity. In extreme cases people feel apart from society, and do not share the common goals or norms of the surrounding culture. This has sometimes been looked at as 'anomie'; Srole (1956) devised a 5-item questionnaire for this; high scores were found among those who reject minority groups, isolated old people, and adolescent drug-takers. Perhaps the normal condition is a combination of shared and unique elements, where the individual takes a particular role in a group, is accepted for what he is, and makes his own distinctive contribution to group life (Ziller, 1964).

Realism and the self-image. Perception of the self is subject to motivational distortion: people see themselves as bigger and better than is justified in terms of their actual performance – as closer to the ideal self. It is reality in the form of others' reactions which usually prevents these inflated self-perceptions from getting too far out of line. It is no good thinking that you are the king of France if no one else shares this belief – in other words self-perceptions must be accepted for satisfactory interaction to be possible. Individuals engage in various strategies to create the right reactions on the part of others, and to protect themselves from meeting disconfirming responses. One strategy is to ignore the actual responses of others completely, either by distorting them (paranoia), or by withdrawing from interpersonal behaviour altogether into a world of fantasy (schizophrenia). An important dimension therefore of the self-image is the degree to which it is realistic.

ORIGINS OF THE SELF

Reactions of others

The main origin of self-image and self-esteem is probably the reactions of others. Cooley (1902) first put forward the 'looking-glass theory of the self' – we look at the reactions of others to find out what we are like. A number of studies have found that self-reports correlate with the reactions of others, though the self-reports tend to be more favourable (Wylie, 1961). However, this does not show that one set of reactions is the cause of the other – both could be based on objective features of an individual's performance. Several experiments have been carried out to study the effect of others' reactions upon self-perceptions. Videbeck

(1960) asked 30 subjects to read poems, after which they were evaluated by a supposed speech expert, half favourably and half unfavourably. It was found that self-ratings on aspects of poetry reading shifted accordingly; self-ratings on related scales shifted less, and self-ratings on scales concerning unrelated social skills did not change at all. The results are shown in Fig. 9.1. Adults often tell children how clever, tall or beautiful they are – or the reverse; adolescents and students commonly give one another fairly direct feedback of a similar sort; in adult

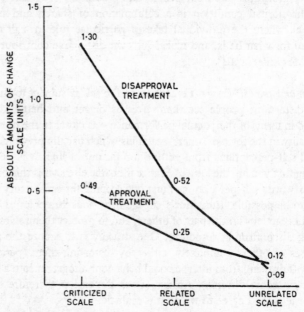

Figure 9.1. Effects of criticism on self-rating (from Videbeck, 1960)

life this is much more rare, except in specialised training situations like T-groups and role-playing (p. 260 ff). The changes in self-image may lead to change of behaviour and become self-reinforcing. Guthrie (1938) describes an instance of this; a group of male students played what was intended to be a practical joke on a rather dull, unattractive female student – they treated her for a time as if she was tremendously attractive and popular. The unexpected result was that 'before the year was over, she had developed an easy manner and a confident assumption that she was popular'. Such a confident and rewarding manner would elicit positive and reinforcing reactions from others; it is an example of a positive feedback cycle.

There is evidence that children have higher self-esteem if they have a good relation with their parents and their parents have positive attitudes towards them (e.g. Rosenberg, 1965). Self-reactions are probably learnt more readily if there is a close relationship with the person concerned – such as parents and psychotherapists. The latter are found to be more effective if they have a warm and accepting attitude to their patients (p. 335) – partly because this attitude is a source of new self-reactions.

Changes of self-image are more likely to occur if the other person is regarded as a valid source of information – e.g. teachers. It is sometimes necessary to deal with students whose self-images are out of touch with their abilities, and direct them towards alternative careers. This process of 'cooling out' is handled with skill by counsellors in some American colleges: the student is shown his academic record, helped to evaluate himself correctly, and to choose a different vocation (Clark, 1956). Another condition under which the reactions of others may be particularly effective in changing the self-image is a *rite de passage* – a ceremony marking a change of state, such as graduation or marriage. At such ceremonies the persons concerned are the focus of attention, and there is a lot of excitement. The combination of social pressure and emotional arousal is found to be a very powerful means of changing personality in other settings, such as religious conversion, and healing, and in Chinese thought reform (Sargant, 1957; Argyle, 1964b).

It was suggested by Argyle (1964a) that this process of learning – internalising the reactions of others – is a special type of learning, for which he used the term 'introjection'. Evidence was presented that the conscience is acquired in this way in some children who were found to feel guilty for those acts for which withdrawal of love had been used, they felt silly about what had been laughed at, and felt as if they could kick themselves for what they had been physically punished for. Two possible explanations of this process are offered. One is that X learns to anticipate the reactions of Y which are later aroused in fantasy in the absence of Y; X is then, in a sense, reacting to himself – though it is not clear why he should associate himself with Y's reactions. The other is that self-reactions are established by means of instrumental learning; if a child seems to be sufficiently guilty he may avoid further punishment; in addition persuasive methods may be used – 'aren't you ashamed of yourself for doing that?' It has been found that self-reactions can be modified by operant conditioning procedures. Merbaum (1963) and Gergen (1965) found that both positive and negative affective self-references were influenced by reflections of feeling and mild approval, such as 'good' and 'Yes, I think you are' in the course of experimental interviews.

Comparison with others

Another origin of self-image and self-esteem is comparison with other people. Although self-perceptions may include objective measures such as 'height', these only become meaningful when they can be compared with those of others – giving perceptions of being 'short' or 'tall'. Festinger (1954) postulated that there is a need for self-evaluation which is met by comparison with others who are similar. In the case of abilities he suggested that there was also a unidirectional drive upwards, since in Western society people are expected to do better and better. A number of experiments have been carried out to test these hypotheses. It has been found that subjects want to have information about the relative performance of those who are similar to themselves, and that this makes their self-evaluations more accurate; in the case of abilities they prefer information about others who are slightly better rather than those who are slightly worse, but they only choose the high person for comparison if highly motivated; if they are going to play games with the comparison person on the other hand they may choose a weaker person in order not to lose money (Latané, 1966; Rabbie et al., 1967). In other studies it has been found that people compare themselves with reference groups in order to make judgements on their good fortune or otherwise. American soldiers in World War II who were married compared their lot with that of married civilians or unmarried soldiers (Stouffer et al., 1949). It is familiar that such comparisons play an important part in wage negotiations. The performance of others provides a frame of reference, and anchoring points, which gives meaning to 'good' or 'poor' performance. A tennis player will feel that his tennis is quite good or improving, if he beats someone who is usually a little better than himself; he will not compare himself with Wimbledon champions, or with small children, in comparison with whom he is far worse and far better respectively.

Brookover, Thomas and Paterson (1964) found that self-evaluation of ability correlated with average grade among 13-year-old schoolchildren, while the correlation was higher for estimations of specific abilities and grades in particular courses. It is found that girls who are taller than other girls at the age of 13, for ever after see themselves as 'tall', even though at maturity they may be no taller than other people. This shows that self-comparisons can become a permanent feature of the self-image. It seems likely that children compare themselves with the other children who are most readily available for comparison purposes – siblings and members of the same class at school. This can result in a child thinking of himself as tall, intelligent, rich, etc.; indeed it can be observed that a child's self-image may change rapidly as a result of changing schools to one where he is, for example, richer rather than poorer than most of the other children. Rosenberg (1965) studied the origins of self-esteem in adolescents, and some of his results can be interpreted in terms of social comparison; self-esteem was greater for those who did well at school, were leaders of clubs and were of higher social class. A number of experiments have been performed to study the effects of experimental success or failure on self-esteem; these should perhaps be regarded as instances of comparison with others, since success and failure are defined in terms of such comparisons. The experiments generally show the expected effect, but there is more change of self-reports upwards following unexpected success than downwards following unexpected failure, on intelligence or other tests (Wylie, 1961).

The effects of roles played

This is a third source of self-image. Being of a particular age and sex, and acting in accordance with this role, creates corresponding self-perceptions. Couch (1962) gave the Twenty Statements Test to 60 students, and found that the salience of gender was greater when there had been more sex-role specialisation in the family for teenagers; this result held for males only. Playing occupational roles affects self-image in a similar way. Medical students come to see themselves as like doctors during the course of their training – 31% in their first year, 83% in their fourth year (Merton, 1957). It is difficult to disentangle the effects of playing the role from the effects of the reactions of others in these studies: 75% of these medical students, even in their first year saw themselves as doctors when dealing with patients especially when the patients treated them as doctors, rather than when dealing with nurses or with real doctors. The same is true of the study by Lieberman (1956), who found that when some workers were promoted to be foreman and others to be shop stewards, each group changed its attitudes in a direction congruent with their new position. Possibly the crucial experience is playing the role *and* having others respond accordingly.

There is some evidence that role-playing alone may affect the self-image. Clifford and Clifford (1967) studied the effects of Outward Bound training on 36 boys between 16 and 21 years of age. After the course, self-ratings were found to be more favourable, especially on such items as 'skilful', 'interesting', 'success', 'health', 'frail' and 'boring' (ratings on the last two concepts were lower). Other studies have shown how personality and attitudes are affected by playing a role; for example Janis and Mann (1965) found that heavy smokers became more anti-smoking after playing the role of a lung cancer patient, than those who listened to a tape-recording.

As described earlier (p. 278 f), there are individual differences in role performance, since people with different personalities take the same role differently. A person may come to see himself as a *progressive* clergyman, or an *intelligent* juvenile delinquent. The self-image consists of both roles and traits, and the combination would be manifested in role performance.

Goffman (1956a) suggested that in order to perform effectively in a new role the occupant has to put on a mask, to give the impression of possessing the qualities ideally required for the position. When he has given this impression for long enough, the role becomes an integral part of the personality, and is no longer a mask. It is in this way that people become moulded to occupational roles, or become members of a new social class.

Identification with models

A fourth source of self-image and self-esteem is the process of identification with models. When a follower identifies with a model he forms a strong emotional attachment to the latter, he wants to become like the model, his ideal self becomes like the model, and he feels that to some extent he already possesses some of the model's attributes. Stotland, Zander *et al.* (1964) found some of the conditions under which this takes place in an experiment in which boys heard a talk from someone who claimed to be a deep-sea diver. If he emphasised in his talk certain attributes which he and the boys had in common, the boys felt that they shared other of the deep-sea diver's attributes as well. Stotland *et al.*, found that followers with low self-esteem thought that they shared more of the model's attributes: one motive for identification is the raising of self-esteem by ascribing to oneself some of the model's properties. Helper (1955) found that if one parent rewarded a child for resembling the other parent, both the ideal self and the self-image of the child were more similar to the parent taken as model. Both of these studies show that not only the ideal self but also the self-image are affected by identification. Kipnis (1961) studied the self-ratings of students in relation to their ratings of others in the same dormitory; when friends were seen as different, self-ratings were found to shift in the following six weeks in such a way as to close the gap. This shows a shift of self-image in a real-life situation.

Other studies show that identification is more likely to occur under the following additional conditions: when the model rewards the follower, when the model is seen to be rewarded, and when the model is powerful, or prestigeful (Bandura, 1962). Children form a series of identifications as they grow up – first with parents, later with other young adults, teachers, film stars and so on. The ideal self is largely composed of a series of these identifications, which finally become integrated into a coherent unity; however the self-image is affected too – it is felt that the ideal self is in some sense part of the self, and the attributes are experienced as partly belonging to the self already.

An important kind of identification is with the parent of the same sex, producing amongst other things the appropriate sexual identity. Several studies show that masculine behaviour develops more when there is more contact with the father, and a warm relationship with him (e.g. Mussen and Distler, 1964). It was found by W. C. Bronson (1959) that, with boys aged 9–13, if there was a stressful relation with father the boys either rejected the masculine role or became masculine in a very exaggerated way – which the investigator interpreted in terms of 'defensive identification'. The male identity is developed further in male company with its emphasis on rough games and, later, economic achievement (Miller, 1963). There is evidence that homosexuality develops where there is no father to act as a model, and a close relation is formed with the mother (West, 1959).

Adolescent identity-formation

By about the age of 10–12 a child has acquired a number of elements of self-image; he has a body image, age, sex and other roles, has introjected the reactions of other, made comparisons with peers and siblings and formed identifications with parents and other models. These elements have no particular unity, and may be highly inconsistent – trigonometry and teddy-bears, soldiers and Sunday school, and so on. However, there is no very firm commitment to any of these elements, and there is no intention that they represent long-term goals or a permanent way of life; to a large extent the roles are games that have been played. With the onset of adolescence all this is changed, and during the next few years there is increasing pressure to develop a unified identity, which represents basic values and permanent commitments.

As Gesell and Ames (1956) observe, the 10-year-old seems to be 'a finished product of nature's handiwork'; but with the onset of adolescence 'new growth forces assert their creative energy'. The growth spurt and development of sexual maturity are probably responsible for the changes in identity; the body image is changed, and this creates a heightened concern with the reactions of others. At the same time, though it is not known why, the adolescent now has a strong desire to break away from a dependent relationship with parents, and wants to establish himself or herself as an independent person on equal terms with adults (cf. Muuss, 1962). The pressures to achieve a unified identity are of two main kinds. (1) During adolescence a number of important, and relatively final, decisions have to be taken. The most important of these is vocation, but there are also decisions about political and religious attitudes, which are decided at the same time. Society provides a fairly limited choice, and once this has been made, role-expectations from others create pressures to fit into the standard identity in question. (2) Lecky (1945) first put forward the hypothesis that there is a striving for 'consistency in the personality', and this has been supported by a number of clinicians. The main support for the hypothesis comes from studies of attitudes: many studies now support the idea that attitudes change towards a more consistent or balanced structure (Brown, 1964). However, it is not clear why these forces should be unleashed during adolescence.

Erikson (1956) put forward the theory that there is an 'identity crisis' during late adolescence, on the basis of clinical work with adolescents, and literary case studies. He postulates that the main developmental task of late adolescence is to establish this ego-identity. While children play at roles, adolescents experiment with them, and finally adopt them permanently. The process of experimentation is made possible by a period of 'moratorium', during which young people are allowed to experiment without commitment – a familiar feature of student life. While adolescence is a particularly important period for identity-formation, it does not stop there, and there is continued revision during later years. The identity has links with past and future – it has continuity with past experience, and points to future goals and commitments, which are linked to basic values; it should consist of an 'alignment of the individual's *basic drives* with his *endowment* and his *opportunities*' (Erikson, 1950b). To achieve this involves emphasising some elements, de-emphasising others, and synthesising different elements. In one of

Stephen Leacock's stories a student was asked what he was studying and said, 'Music, theology and Turkish'; his questioner replied, 'I suppose you are going to be a choir-master in a mosque in Constantinople', but was told that these were the only subjects not clashing with baseball times. An alternative to this rather imaginative synthesis would have been to emphasise one of the three and suppress the others, or to relegate them to hobbies. The conscious experience of a person who has achieved ego-identity is 'a feeling of being at home in one's body, a sense of knowing where one is going, and an inner assuredness of anticipated recognition from those who count' (Erikson, 1956). If identity is not achieved, a state of 'ego-diffusion' results – of not knowing who one is or where one is going; schizophrenia and the 'playboy' syndrome are two versions of this. Other possibilities are (1) a conflict between two alternative identities which cannot be reconciled, (2) being an impostor and claiming a bogus identity, (3) becoming paranoid and clinging to an unrealistic identity, and (4) forming a precarious identity that requires continual confirmation from others.

When a person becomes ill or mentally ill there is a point at which he 'takes the sick role'. Szasz (1961) and Sarbin (1967a) have argued that much mental illness is due to people being persuaded to adopt this role and the corresponding self-image. Goffman (1961) has shown how the identity changes that result include working out a revised version of the patient's past history, in a way that provides an acceptable explanation of how he became a mental patient. Sarbin (1967b) suggests that the position of the prisoner is even worse – he is defined by the institution as a 'non-person', a person of no value with no place in society; the possible reactions to this are developing an artificial prison society, violence, and psychosis. Whether or not these hypotheses are correct, it is clear that sudden changes in identity can be brought about in patients and prisoners, and it is important for their rehabilitation to allow for further identity changes to be possible.

The need for self-esteem

Many psychologists have thought it necessary to postulate a need for self-esteem, i.e. to have a favourable evaluation of the self (e.g. Rogers, 1942). As we have seen, self-evaluation is partly based on the reactions of others, and comparison with the performance of others. Both depend on successful performances of kinds valued by the group; as well as intellectual or physical achievement these may include having the approved clothes or accent, being of the right anatomical size or shape, and having the correct attitudes or beliefs. It would be possible to postulate a drive to be esteemed by others, but it is more economical to suppose that this is sought in order to justify favourable self-evaluations; when others react negatively, giving insufficient esteem, this is a source of anxiety and stress. It is for this reason that a variety of interpersonal strategies are used to evoke positive responses and to avoid negative responses from others. These are documented later in this chapter.

Secord and Backman (1964, 1965) offer an explanation of these phenomena in terms of the consistency principle found in the fields of attitudes and perception. Parents usually evaluate their children very favourably, with the result that the children form favourable self-evaluations and for ever after try to elicit congruent responses from others. Most investigations in this area have been concerned with the situation where the reactions of others are less favourable than self-reactions, and here the Secord and Backman hypothesis makes the same predictions as the theory of a need for self-esteem. The crucial test is when the reactions of others are *more* favourable than self-reactions. On the Secord and Backman hypothesis this would be just as uncomfortable as the other kind of incongruence, and people making such reactions would be disliked and avoided. Deutsch and Solomon (1959) have tested this hypothesis: subjects were caused to succeed or fail at an experimental task and were then given favourable or unfavourable evaluations by an observer. The results supported both the congruency hypothesis *and* the need for self-esteem hypothesis, neither alone being sufficient.

There are probably differences between cultures in the extent to which self-esteem is important. In the East 'loss of face' is a very serious matter. For some reasons, not yet understood, the immediate reactions of others have a greater impact on self-evaluation than in Western countries. This might be an example of Riesman's 'other-directedness' (1950): there are no internalised or permanent attitudes, and the views of others are the only criterion. There is extensive evidence that self-esteem is lower in mental patients (Wylie, 1961), and it is probably a major factor in unhappiness. A number of studies have found that counselling or psychotherapy have some effect on it. Rogers and Dymond (1954), and a number of other workers, have found that self/ideal self congruence increases as a result of therapy, and that self-esteem increases: these changes are correlated with other criteria of recovery.

CONDITIONS UNDER WHICH THE SELF BECOMES SALIENT

Only some behaviour is affected by processes connected with the self. Before considering *how* the self affects behaviour we shall consider *when* it affects it. The extent to which the self is active on particular occasions has been conceptualised in different ways. The earliest was the notion of 'ego-involvement', usually described as the extent to which status is felt to be at stake (Sherif and Cantril, 1947). The author and Marylin Williams have used a different definition – the extent to which a person feels that he is 'observed' rather than 'observer' in a situation (Argyle and Williams, 1969). Another version is the concept of 'individuation' – the extent to which people feel that they are seen or paid attention to as distinct individuals, as opposed to being submerged in the group or lost in the crowd.

Presence of an audience

The most familiar source of self-consciousness is appearing and performing in front of an audience. Paivio (1965) and his colleagues have carried out a number of studies of the anxiety produced by audiences; this is for example greater the larger the audience (Levin *et al.*, 1960). Zajonc and Sales (1966) showed that the sheer presence of other people produces an increased flow of adrenalin, and the other signs and effects of physiological arousal. It also makes a difference whether an audience gives positive responses, no response or negative responses, in that order (cf. Sarbin and Allen, 1969). An audience may have the same effects if it is not physically present, as with the audience of a TV performer; the absence of any direct feedback is a problem here, sometimes overcome by the use of a studio audience. The author (1967) found some evidence that inexperienced performers preferred to be *behind* an audience, or at a distance from the front of it. It is common experience too that the effects of an audience depend on the importance to the performer of its members, and on what he is doing in front of it.

When a salesman deals with a customer, or a waiter with a diner, he can be said to be putting on a professional performance for an audience. Goffman (1956a) has argued that much everyday behaviour is like that of actors on a stage, in that individuals and groups are constantly putting on performances for each other – performances intended to create certain impressions about the efficiency or other attributes of the performers. He distinguishes between the front and back regions of establishments: in the front regions of shops, hotels, hospitals or business offices the public are received, and appropriate impressions created for them. The public are kept out of the back regions where the performances are prepared. The setting of the front regions is usually expensive and impressive, while the back regions are dirty and chaotic; the behaviour of the performers, their clothes and their manners, are quite different – in the back regions they are more vulgar, dishevelled and informal. The same is true of the home; guests may be received in certain rooms, and are not supposed to see others; the host does not usually receive visitors while he is sitting in the lavatory, or having a bath – the stage is inappropriate for suitable impression-formation. This general theory will be discussed later (p. 380 ff); its importance for the moment is in drawing attention to an important variable creating salience of self.

Being assessed by others

The early experiments on 'ego-involvement' created this condition by making subjects feel that they were performing an important intelligence or personality test, for which the results would be made known. In the control condition subjects were simply told that they were helping to standardise a test (Iverson and Reuder, 1956). It was found by Argyle and Williams (1969) that an interviewee feels he is being observed while an interviewer feels that he is the observer; the interview is an assessment situation, but it is interesting that the interviewer feels *unobserved*. In the same study it was found that people felt more observed when interacting with an older person; the effect was much greater for adolescents than for adults. The results of this part of the study are shown in Fig. 9.2. It looks as if the relationship between older and younger resembles that between interviewer and interviewee, superior and subordinate, in that the older person is expected to observe and perhaps assess the younger. The same relationship probably exists between a teacher and pupil, in that it is the teacher's job to assess and comment on the pupil's behaviour. The teacher of social behaviour comments on parts of the pupil's behaviour which are not normally discussed in this way, and which are perhaps more closely linked with the self, compared with progress at academic studies; hence the anxiety generated by such training.

The self-presentation of human females to males may be similar. Goffman (1956a) quotes Simone de Beauvoir: 'with other women, a woman is behind the scenes, she is polishing her equipment, but not in battle'. She is preparing her presentation for a male audience. Argyle and Williams (op. cit.) found that among adolescents females felt observed, males felt themselves observers during cross-sex social contacts. Among peacocks and other birds, it is the male of the species that has the fine feathers, and puts on a display for the females, in order to attract a mate. Among humans the reverse seems to be the case, as far as visual appearance is concerned – females usually wear more vivid and interesting clothes and take more trouble about the appearance of

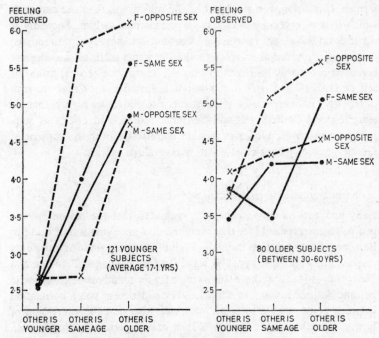

Figure 9.2. Effect of age and sex of the other on feeling observed

face and hair. On the other hand males could be said to put on the display in the fields of physical and verbal prowess. It may be suggested that the true reason for the phenomenon described by Goffman is a sex difference in instinctive biological mating roles.

Argyle and Williams (loc. cit.) carried out an experiment to find out how far feeling observed was due to a realistic perception of how much another person was actually looking at P. Subjects held conversations with stooges who looked them in the eye 20% or 80% of the time. There was no greater feeling of being observed in the 80% gaze condition, and a number of subjects showed a 'paradoxical' pattern of feeling more observed in the 20% condition. This experiment suggests that feeling observed is, in part at least, a kind of cognitive set induced by the situation and the prevailing role-relations. H. Nicholson and R. McHenry, at Oxford, found similar results for triads, but it is possible that amount of gaze has more effect when more people are present.

The extent to which being in front of an audience and being assessed by others arouses self-awareness depends on two main factors. Firstly it depends on the importance of the variable being assessed to the performer. If it belongs in the heart of the self-image, then the extent to which it is accepted by others is very important to him. Secondly it depends on the extent to which audience or assessors accept the image presented. Provided they react to P as he wants them to, i.e. slightly better than the way he reacts to himself, he will not become aware of self or bother about self-presentation. If however they react to him differently, and especially if they evaluate him less highly than is expected and desired, self-consciousness results, and efforts at self-presentation ensue. Under-evaluation or mistakes over the content of identity probably have most effect, over-evaluation least.

Individuation and de-individuation

Early accounts of crowd behaviour suggested that the reason crowds can behave irresponsibly is that members feel anonymous and cease to be aware of themselves as individuals, thus losing any sense of individual responsibility (Brown, 1954). It was found by Festinger, Pepitone and Newcomb (1952) that there was a tendency for members of groups who became de-individuated to show less restraint: there was a correlation between being unable to recall who said what and the expression of hostile attitudes towards parents. In a later experiment, Singer *et al.* (1965) created a feeling of individuation by asking girls to dress up for the experiment, and giving them name-tags; de-individuation was produced by dressing subjects in identical white lab. coats. These manipulations did not affect the memory of subjects for who said what, but under de-individuation there was greater use of obscene words during discussion of a passage from D. H. Lawrence. The authors suggest that loss of restraint can occur without loss of identity – as among old friends, who would not bother about impression management, and who would use taboo words, but who would not necessarily forget who was who.

If de-individuation can be brought about by wearing the same clothes, it follows that de-individuation should take place among soldiers and others in uniform. Vidich and Stein (1960) give an account of induction into the US Marines; they suggest that many of the procedures used have the effects, whether intended or not, of destroying individual identity and making the men see themselves merely as marines with numbers. Other experiments have used the technique of concealing or disguising subjects. Pollaczek and Homefield (1954) found that wearing masks had a favourable effect on stuttering boys – they ceased to stutter and were more active and relaxed. A person may become socially invisible and no attention may be paid to him if he has no role relevant to a situation, such as a workman engaged in repairs during a seminar – he is a 'non-person' (P. Ekman, personal communication).

These experiments do suggest another source of self-consciousness – the extent to which a person is in some way seen as different from others in a social situation. It is interesting that women's clothes are not only brighter and more striking than those of men – they are also more varied; women dislike other women to wear the same clothes, while men's clothes are relatively homogeneous. This suggests that women are seeking to be the object of attention and to be seen as individuals. Nicholson and Argyle obtained some support for this hypothesis in an experiment in which wearing uniform white lab. coats had a greater effect on females than males, in increasing risk-taking (p. 258).

Something like individuation occurs when a person is the odd man out in a social situation – by being the only female, the only non-teenager, the only non-Negro, etc. This is slightly different from the previous kind of individuation, since attention is focused on a person not as an individual but as an occupant of a position. Another case is that of the person who is stigmatised – by having some medical condition, or being inferior in some way (Goffman, 1963b). These cases are particularly difficult because the attention which is focused on the individual is of an unfavourable or hostile kind.

Self-confrontation

When a person sees himself in a mirror or sees a photograph of himself, it makes him think about himself. When he hears a tape-recording of his voice the effect is much stronger, partly because his voice sounds different from the way he usually hears it – which is through the bones of the head rather than through the air. In addition, while speaking there is continuous monitoring and correction of the noises made, while a tape-recording is heard from outside as one would hear another person. Traces of regional and class accent are also more clearly recognisable on a tape-recording, for reasons which are not entirely understood. Experience of seeing a film or video-tape recording of oneself has the same effect but in a more intense form; it draws attention particularly to the pattern of facial and gestural movements. The viewer is able to see himself as others must see (and hear) him, and again not while he is producing and able to control the visible behaviour; it focuses attention very sharply on the self which is now seen as an object; it adds to self-knowledge and can provide the basis for modifying the self as presented (Nielson, 1962; and Chapter X).

Penetration

Animals react with aggression if their territory is invaded; humans are more likely to withdraw if others come too close (p. 362). People do not like to be seen by the wrong people with too few clothes on, or when they have not been able to arrange their appearance. There is resistance to revealing certain areas of personality to others. As shown below (p. 385 f), a certain amount of deception is involved in impression management; keeping people at a distance is an important means of maintaining the illusion. Social accidents may happen, and others may see the truth behind the scenes. When any of these forms of penetration occur there is heightened awareness of the self and its boundaries.

Individual differences in self-consciousness

We could introduce self-consciousness in a theoretical way – it is the extent to which the self-system is readily activated, so that an interactor becomes concerned with the reactions of others to himself. Some of the measures which have been used are really measures of social anxiety, our Dimension 3 of social performance. Social anxiety is particularly associated with appearing in public, being the centre of attention, and being watched at work (but also with being criticised). Paivio (1965) and his co-workers found a second factor, orthogonal to their Audience Anxiety, which they call Exhibitionism, with items such as 'I like to recite poems in front of other people'. Those high on Exhibitionism seek to appear in public, while those high in Audience Anxiety avoid it. Since the two dimensions are uncorrelated it is possible to find subjects who both seek and avoid exposure; Levin et al. (1960) found that such children when speaking in public made the greatest number of speech errors, a result which was interpreted in terms of approach-avoidance conflict theory.

Self-consciousness is also related to our Dimension 7 – role-taking ability. Argyle and Williams (1969) studied the extent to which people felt that they were being observed, as opposed to being observers. While this varied greatly between different social situations as described above, there were also consistent individual differences between people – some people felt more observed than others in all situations. No correlation was found between this variable and neuroticism, so that it is probably quite distinct from audience anxiety. It did however have some correlation, for males only, with Maslow's insecurity scale ($r = \cdot35$), and with dominance ($r = -\cdot32$). We concluded, on the basis of other evidence, that feeling observed was a cognitive set, to perceive the situation in a particular way; an interviewer looks for different things than an interviewee, a male from a female, and it appears that there are some people who usually adopt the 'observed' set as opposed to the 'observer' set.

Laing (1960a and b) reports that schizoid patients are often very upset by being looked at; they feel depersonalised, turned to stone, engulfed by relationships, even by being looked at. They create a dead, mechanical, false self that is shown to the world, behind which the true-self is hidden, though in a disembodied form. Ring *et al.* (1967) have suggested an interesting typology for this area of behaviour and constructed a questionnaire. Their P type is inept and unpolished, feels awkward playing different roles; R's are poised, skilled and machiavellian, and perform different roles easily; C's are conformist and conventional and like to keep to the rules. There is a high negative correlation between the P and R scales, and it is the P's who are awkward and self-conscious. Self-consciousness is also related to low self-esteem. Rosenberg (1965) carried out a study of the correlates of self-esteem in 5,077 adolescents between the ages of 15 and 18. Those who were low in self-esteem reported themselves as shy (62% *v.* 33% – comparing points 1 and 7 on the 7-point scale of self-esteem), easily embarrassed (17% *v.* 4%), bothered very much if others had a poor opinion of them (63% *v.* 39%), eager to be approved of (40% *v.* 17%), and as putting up a façade (39% *v.* 8%). Those with low self-esteem also had more psychosomatic symptoms (40% *v.* 11% had 5 or more).

There are interesting age differences in self-consciousness. Young children are not at all self-conscious, and will often perform on the stage without anxiety up to the age of 10 or 12. Perhaps they are not able to take the role of the other sufficiently, as Feffer and Gourevitch (1960) suggest. According to Erikson's theory of identity-formation adolescents should be concerned about the reactions of others when they have not formed an identity or if they are not quite sure of it, and this would presumably make them anxious about being watched by others. Adolescents are notoriously self-conscious and easily embarrassed, and this may be the reason.

THE EFFECTS OF THE SELF-SYSTEM ON INTERACTION

Goffman's theory of self-presentation

Goffman's book *The Presentation of Self in Everyday Life* (1956a) has rightly been very influential in the study of the effect of self on social interaction. His theory is that interactors need information about one another for a number of reasons; this information is not directly available but must be inferred from gestures and other minor cues; the impressions formed are however deliberately manipulated in order to create perceptions that are more favourable than is warranted; there is a considerable element of conscious deception. Interactors try to establish a 'working consensus' in which certain perceptions of each other are agreed and there is a common definition of the situation. This deception is often necessary for the maintenance of a working social system, and is in the interests of both parties. Impression formation is achieved in the course of quasi-theatrical performances by individuals and groups, in the 'front' regions of homes and places of work, for the relevant 'audiences'; there is collusion between team-members, e.g. the members of a family receiving guests; they interact informally in the back regions and do not manipulate impressions for each other; in the absence of the audience they discuss the secrets of their performance, and express attitudes towards the audience different from those expressed in the presence of the audience. There is a constant danger of mistakes, in which the performance is discredited and reality shows through; this completely disrupts interaction and causes embarrassment; the audience cooperates to prevent this happening by being tactful, and not going into the back regions.

This constitutes a theory about social behaviour; it postulates that social behaviour is like the behaviour of actors, in that behaviour is enacted to generate impressions for an audience. It is presented very persuasively by evidence from literary sources such as George Orwell on waiters and Simone de Beauvoir on women, and from sociological case studies and books about professional groups such as house-detectives and undertakers. For example he cites Orwell's book *Down and Out in Paris and London*.

It is an instructive sight to see a waiter going into a hotel dining-room. As he passes the door a sudden change comes over him. The set of his shoulders alters; all the dirt and hurry and irritation have dropped off in an instant. He glides over the carpet, with a solemn priest-like air. I remember our assistant 'maitre d'hotel', a fiery Italian, pausing at the dining-room door to address his apprentice who had broken a bottle of wine. Shaking his fist above his head he yelled (luckily the door was more or less soundproof), 'Do you call yourself a waiter, you young bastard? You a waiter! You're not fit to scrub floors in the brothel your mother came from.'

Words failing him, he turned to the door, and as he opened it he delivered a final insult in the same manner as Squire Western in *Tom Jones*.

Then he entered the dining-room and sailed across it dish in hand, gracefully as a swan. Ten seconds later he was bowing reverently to a customer. And you could not help thinking, as you saw him bow and smile, with that benign smile of the trained waiter, that the customer was put to shame by having such an aristocrat to serve him (Orwell, 1951).

Goffman did not produce any evidence in the form of experiments or sociological field studies to support his thesis, nor did he present the elements of it in the form of clear, testable hypotheses. It may help to focus attention on the empirical predictions from the theory if we consider some possible lines of criticism, which could be settled by evidence. (a) Does social interaction involve as great an element of deliberate, conscious deception as is postulated? It is in fact people like waiters and undertakers who fit the model best, and there is no doubt that there is an element of window-dressing in most professional performances. This need not however be conscious, and Goffman admits that after a time the personality adjusts to fit the mask. Self-enhancement on the other hand is based more on self-deception than on deception of others. It may be suggested that the dramaturgical model applies quite well to confidence men, has some application to some aspects of professional performances, and very little application to everyday life.
(b) Are there really front and back regions in most establishments? Visitors to factories are usually shown over the entire establishment; hospitals and university departments have no obvious division between front and back. There are areas where people live their private lives and don't want to be disturbed, and there are comfortable board rooms for long meetings, but this is not a matter of front and back.
Private houses are an intermediate case. Visitors are shown into the sitting-room and perhaps the dining-room and are allowed to use a

lavatory; they are not usually (except in the middle West) so welcome in the kitchen, or the bedrooms. It may be suggested that the distinction between front and back applies well to institutions offering a service to the public, such as hotels and shops, but not so much to other places.

(c) Is the difference in behaviour to other members of the 'team' and to the 'audience' correctly interpreted in terms of collusion over impression management? It is often the case that P behaves differently to persons A and B, but this does not necessarily indicate that he is being bogus to one of them. He relates to each by developing a synchronising social system (a 'working consensus', as Goffman would say), and these will be different in each case depending on the personality and position of the other. Impression management is involved in each. The waiter behaves with skill, in order to elicit the desired reactions from the customers; his behaviour with the cooks is managed also, as they too have to be controlled. Goffman is probably right however in postulating an on-stage–off-stage dimension, in which behaviour in the more off-stage situations is more spontaneous and relaxed, more vulgar and intimate than behaviour on-stage.

(d) Does the acting model fit ordinary social behaviour? The actor follows a script which he has learnt; in everyday life behaviour is more spontaneous. Again, professional performers such as salesmen are like actors, in that they do have a script, but even they have to improvise to some extent. Actors only respond to one another in respect of timing. All social situations have rules, but they do not have a script; indeed it is one of the unspoken assumptions of social interaction that what is taking place is entirely new and spontaneous.

Other aspects of the theory, while being generally accepted, have subsequently been extended and elaborated by later research. We have discussed the origins of the self and the conditions under which the self becomes active; we shall now deal with aspects of the effect of self on interaction where it is now possible to go beyond Goffman's very suggestive formulations.

The motivation for self-presentation

There is more than one motivational basis for self-presentation, though the basic principle is that the way others treat P can be rewarding or otherwise in a number of ways, and this will depend on the way they perceive and categorise him. If P wants to be treated like a member of the upper classes, he will have to persuade other people to categorise him this way. In what ways will the categorisation and reactions of others be rewarding?

Firstly if P is categorised by others in a way that is different from the way he categorises himself, this will be experienced as disconcerting and dissonant, and it will give rise to difficulties of communication. It is necessary to achieve a 'working consensus' (Goffman) on such matters for interaction to be possible. This discomfort will be particularly acute in a person who is insecure, uncertain of his identity, and therefore dependent on confirmation from others. The same is true of a person with a strong need for self-esteem. Self-esteem can best be enhanced by receiving approving responses from others. This would be very important to a person who is trying to improve his or her standing, in the social class system for example.

Further, if P is performing a professional role – as a teacher, salesman, etc. – he will have to persuade others to see him in this way, in order for the right working consensus definition of the situation to be brought about. In addition, if the clients can be persuaded to have confidence in him, i.e. to see him as an expert, he will be more effective – and thus receive rewards of money and status connected with effective professional performance. Studies of teachers and psychotherapists show that their respective patients learn more and recover faster if they have confidence in the performer (Frank, 1961). Confidence is partly built up by the kind of professional deception emphasised by Goffman, but this is probably less important than actually being efficient.

In addition, there is something like a need for self-esteem, and self-perceptions are partly based on the reactions of others as we have seen. It follows that self-esteem can best be enhanced or confirmed by receiving approving responses from others. Self-presentation may focus on different aspects of self-image. In some situations, it may focus on position – in the example given below the speaker is establishing that he is a Member of Parliament. In other situations, for example where all those present are M.P.s, self-presentation might focus on individual personality traits, which differentiate him from the others. A person may also communicate 'role-distance', like a child who rides on a roundabout holding with only one hand – showing that there is more to him than the role he is currently playing (Goffman, 1961). If a person has been inappropriately treated in some respect, self-presentation will focus on making the necessary corrections. If his behaviour or personality have been criticised in some way, self-presentation will concentrate on providing an explanation or exposition which is acceptable and comprehensible to those involved. This process is often seen during personnel selection interviews: the experienced interviewee is able to provide a smooth cover-up story for black spots in his record.

Methods of self-presentation

Self-presentation is achieved by a variety of social techniques, including actual behaviour, and verbal and non-verbal communications. The most effective way is to give a performance which displays the roles or traits in question, but this is often impossible in a given social situation. Personality traits can be presented by acting in accordance with them – for example by acting in an intelligent, thoughtful or extroverted manner during the interaction. Abilities are difficult to demonstrate however, and roles are usually impossible.

The obvious alternative to actual performance is the use of words – to tell other people what one wants them to know about the self. However, in the West, and particularly in Britain, there is a taboo on this kind of talk, except with the most intimate friends and relations. To announce 'I am an extremely clever and important person' would simply produce mirth and disbelief. As a result people often resort to indirect means of verbal self-presentation, like 'name-dropping'. Stephen Potter (1952) has given a satirical account of indirect ways of claiming a prestigeful identity in his book *One-Upmanship* (1952). For example:

LAYMAN: Thank you, Doctor. I was coming home rather late last night from the House of Commons . . .

M.D.-MAN: Thank you . . . now if you'll just let me put these . . . hair brushes and things off the bed for you . . . that's right . . .

LAYMAN: I was coming home rather late. Army Act, really . . .

M.D.-MAN: Now just undo the top button of your shirt or whatever it is you're wearing . . .

LAYMAN: I say I was coming . . .

M.D.-MAN: Now if you've got some hot water – really hot – and a clean towel.

LAYMAN: Yes, just outside. The Postmaster General . . .

M.D.-MAN: Open your mouth please.

It is however quite common for people to engage in self-presentation by indirect verbal methods. This can be done with subtlety, as when the self-references are a minor and apparently unintentional part of an anecdote which is primarily directed towards something else.

Self-presentation is perhaps most effectively done by non-verbal behaviour. Goffman (1956a) describes the impressive settings which are sometimes arranged, for example in London clubs and main offices. More widely used are clothes, whose main purpose, apart from keeping out the cold, appears to be proclaiming the identity of the wearer. Uniforms are useful in identifying the rank, and clothes are one of the main indicators of social class in many societies; this cue has been weakened in the USA as a result of mass-production and general prosperity, and the same thing is happening in Britain. Medical students are made to dress like doctors when doing their clinical work, for otherwise the patients would not take them seriously. Ellis and Keedy (1960) report that academics who are judged as looking like professors are also judged as more successful. Clothes can also portray personality traits, by their smartness or untidiness, colourfulness or drabness, conformity or eccentricity, or approximation to various well-known types or models – hippy, county, city, etc. Clothes are also used to present an improved version of the body image. A large proportion of adolescents are worried about their body images, partly because of the sudden changes in size, shape and hair at the onset of adolescence, partly because of the new importance of appearance for sexual selection. An acceptable version of the body image can be presented by wearing suitable clothes (Fleming, 1963).

G. H. Mead (1934) emphasised the role of 'gesture' in social interaction, and Goffman (op. cit.) supposed that gestures are used in the place of actual performance to create impressions of the self. The general non-verbal style is clearly an important way of communicating this kind of information. It is possible to indicate social class by adopting the appropriate manner and, in Britain, accent. Seniority in an organisation can be indicated by an 'authoritative' manner. People with high self-esteem have a different style from those with low self-esteem. The deceptions of confidence men cited by Goffman are done by means of gesture – adopting the style of behaviour usually associated with solid and reliable middle-class friends.

We have argued that self-presentation does not usually involve much deception (p. 381). It does however involve quite a lot of *concealment*. We showed earlier that there are a number of topics, like money and sex, which are only discussed with close friends and relations (p. 362). Some psychologists, like Jourard (1964), have argued in favour of 'authenticity'; they maintain that people should 'be themselves' and conceal nothing. The opposite view is put by McCall and Simmons (1966) who say: 'Owing to the very peculiar nature of knowledge about persons, relationships necessarily turn on somewhat misguided and

N

misleading premises about the other parties, social order rests partly upon error, lies, deception, and secrets, as well as upon accurate know-ledge' (pp. 195–6).

There are for example a number of embarrassing episodes in any person's past history that he would prefer to forget about – and often does forget about. It is certainly not felt necessary to tell everyone about them, and they have no wish for him to do so. Perhaps people should be helped to move towards their ideal selves; eventually the mask will become true. The less deception has to be used however the better, since it causes anxiety, and the danger of embarrassment. Others help with the process of concealment and deception: they avoid referring to embarrassing matters, as they have no desire to cause unpleasantness (Goffman, 1955). Perhaps at the same time they are acting therapeutic-ally and helping people to overcome their problems. Another case where concealment, and possibly deception, is valuable, is where a person has a low evaluation of a colleague, relation or friend: nothing is to be gained by revealing this opinion. Instead he can be most helpful and constructive by quite different lines of action.

A person who is stigmatised has problems of self-presentation which are often solved by concealment. Many people are stigmatised in some way at some time – members of racial and religious minority groups, of certain occupations and social classes, as well as those who are deformed, or who are homosexuals, criminals, alcoholics, drug-addicts, etc. To reveal such stigmas in many situations may result in rejection and make social interaction impossible. Consequently those involved, when out-side the in-group, keep the stigma out of salience, and may conceal it entirely and pass as normal (Goffman, 1963b).

In dyadic encounters an interactor may by his manner of behaviour indicate the role or properties he wants the other person to have; this process of 'altercasting' is discussed elsewhere (p. 282). In order for there to be a working consensus it is necessary for the two identities to interlock properly, e.g. teacher and pupil rather than teacher and mis-tress, doctor and patient rather than doctor and income-tax collector. To achieve such a consensus involves an interaction process called role-bargaining, or the negotiation of identities.

Other methods of preserving the self-image

There is a certain gap between the way a person sees himself and the way many other people see him. This is partly because the need for self-esteem produces a favourable perception of the self; perceptions of others are likely to err on the side of generosity towards people who are liked, but in the other direction for those who are disliked (p. 150). Discrepancies may arise also because different social groups have different levels of performance; an individual's high self-esteem may be justified in relation to one group, but not in relation to a second. For each of these reasons individuals are liable to encounter people who do *not* react to them in the desired way. Secord and Backman (1964, 1965) have drawn attention to certain 'stabilising processes' that help to preserve the self-image.

One of these is selective interaction. Broxton (1963) found that college women who asked to change their room-mates chose new partners with a more congruent view of themselves. On the other hand people often aspire to membership of superior groups where they will not be much respected, and avoid inferior groups in which they would be; presumably status is gained by sheer membership of a group. A second protective process is changing the groups used for comparison purposes. Secord and Backman (1965) interpret several experiments in terms of the choice of suitable groups for self-comparison. When discussing self-comparison processes before (p. 366 f) we noted that people avoided comparing themselves with others greatly superior to themselves – but they do not compare themselves with those greatly inferior either. They compare themselves with others of about the same standing; perhaps stabilisation is achieved by small shifts in the range of others used for comparison.

Both selective interaction and shifting of comparison groups entail leaving one group for another, and this is not always possible. If there is discrepancy, a strong motivation is created for changing actual behaviour in a way to produce more favourable reactions from the group. One way of doing this is by conforming to group norms in respect of attitudes, beliefs, clothes or other aspects of behaviour. Awareness of discrepancy may create strong pressures to try harder, and do better, in directions of achievement approved by the group, though this is more difficult.

Another way of preserving the self-image in the face of disconfirmation by others, is to form a lower opinion of the people in question so that their opinion no longer matters. Harvey (1962) presented subjects with judgements by another at five degrees of discrepancy in a negative direction; liking for the evaluator was found to fall accordingly, particularly if he was a stranger. Deutsch and Solomon (1959) found evidence that people are disliked both if their judgements are *unfavourable* and also if they are discrepant or *incongruent*, as reported earlier.

Lombard (1955) found the same process operating in a study of sales-girls. He found that they preserved their image of competence when confronted by customers whom they couldn't please by categorising them as 'nasty' or in some other unfavourable way.

A more extreme protective device is simply to disbelieve or ignore the evidence for disconfirming responses from others. In the experiment cited above, Harvey (1962) found that subjects lowered their degree of belief in the responses, particularly if the evaluator was a friend. Such distortions of perception or belief can evidently occur in normals, under laboratory conditions at least. Further degrees of the same process how-ever lead to psychotic states of paranoia and schizophrenia. The lunatic who thinks he is the King of France is not at all disturbed by the fact that no one else shares this view. Such people use a further protective mechanism – withdrawal from real persons and events into a private world of fantasy. When others impinge on them at all the former are systematically misperceived and their unsatisfactory behaviour ration-alised to preserve the self-image.

If these protective devices fail to preserve the self-image, the only thing left to do is to change it. While this is painful, it is one of the main ways in which the self-image is formed and modified.

Embarrassment

We deal with embarrassment at this point because the recent study of this phenomenon began with Goffman's theory that it results from dis-confirmation of the self-image presented in an encounter. First however we will describe the phenomenon itself. Embarrassment is really a form of social anxiety, but is usually restricted to instances of sudden anxiety precipitated by events during interaction. We shall therefore refer to people who are self-conscious in an audience or interview situa-tion as being socially anxious, but not as embarrassed. Embarrassment may be brought about during interaction, or at the beginning of it, in several ways. When this happens, the victim is liable to lose poise, he blushes, stutters, fumbles, sweats, avoids eye-contact, may withdraw from the situation entirely, and even (mainly in the East) commit suicide. His state of discomposure spreads to the others, and interaction between them temporarily comes to a halt. Embarrassment is of considerable theoretical interest, since study of it can tell us something about the conditions necessary for interaction to proceed smoothly. It is also of practical importance, since the possibility of and fear of social en-counters being disrupted by embarrassment sometimes hovers over them as a constant threat; it may be possible to prescribe ways of avoiding embarrassment.

Goffman's theory (1955, 1956b) is that people present themselves in a particular way in encounters; this presentation is partly bogus; if the image presented is invalidated in the course of the encounter, embarrassment ensues. Interaction temporarily ceases because the working consensus has been destroyed, and it takes time for a new one to be worked out. Another related source is when one of the 'audience' sees into the 'back regions' and learns some of the secrets about how impression management is being done. This theory applies to cases of professional deception – though it may be doubted whether such practitioners would actually be embarrassed, and there is no evidence on this point. It would cover instances of strangers who indicate that their knowledge, social class or abilities are better than turns out to be the case. Gross and Stone (1964) collected instances of embarrassment as described by 880 students and others, and decided that a proportion of them could be classified as due to discrediting of self-presentation. Examples are making mistakes in public, exposure of false front, being caught out in cover story, and invasion of other's back regions. However, many of their cases could not be classified quite so well in this way. It seems doubtful whether embarrassment can be accounted for in terms of any single unitary process. We will suggest two other causes, which are related to two of the basic interaction processes – meshing and social skill.

Failure of meshing may be due to disagreement over the definition of the situation, or failure to agree on the roles played by those present. This may be a more inclusive principle than Goffman's; here we are concerned with the cases not contained by his theory. Garfinkel (1963) carried out a number of demonstrations in which he deliberately created disagreements about the situation or the roles of performers. Investigators entered shops and tried to buy things from other customers, behaved in their own homes as if they were lodgers, or flagrantly broke the rules of games, such as by moving the opponent's pieces. This kind of behaviour in fact created rather more than embarrassment – there was consternation, anger and withdrawal from the situation. Examples of this kind of embarrassment in more normal situations would be an interactor suddenly becoming aware of deformity or other stigmata in another person, becoming aware that X was present as well as Y, where he normally treats X in a quite different way from Y, discovering that the establishment or its rules are not what was thought – it is a religious place and a different style of behaviour is expected, or finding that another interactor is more important than was previously believed. In each of these cases the pattern of interaction established on the basis of earlier assumptions suddenly becomes inappropriate and must be considerably revised. Interaction is brought to a sudden stop and time is needed to construct a new pattern.

Motor skills may be disrupted by accidents, which are partly due to unexpected events, partly to lack of skill. Social skills may be disrupted by social accidents and lead to embarrassment. These may be of several kinds. (a) Some accidents are really failures of motor skill – tripping over the carpet, failing to control equipment, catching tablecloths or other people's dresses in trouser-zips, and so forth. The nervous person tends to be jerky and awkward in his movements on social occasions and is more likely to get into these kinds of difficulty. (b) Some accidents are due to failure to control bodily behaviour – uncontrollable laughter, drunkenness, undue display of emotion. Gross and Stone (1964) suggest that the body must be kept under control and in a state of readiness. (c) An interactor may forget another's name, introduce him with the wrong name, forget important facts about him, e.g. that he is divorced, a Roman Catholic, etc. (d) A harmless question or line of conversation may unexpectedly embarrass another – if for example it is something about which he feels guilty or worried. (e) In common to some of these though it includes further cases is the situation in which an interactor simply does not know how to proceed, when there is no social technique in his repertoire to deal with the problem.

Embarrassment is a form of social anxiety, and for this reason is more likely and more acute when people are anxious already. If any of the above things happens when in front of a large audience, or on an important occasion, or to a person who is normally self-conscious or anxious, the embarrassment will be greater. Embarrassment is particularly acute when things go wrong on formal occasions like weddings and banquets, partly because a lot of important people may be watching, but also perhaps because the proper responses are very narrowly defined, and nothing is prescribed for when they do not take place as planned. One of Garfinkel's examples shows how embarrassment can be multiply determined, and fall into more than one of our categories: a man at a banquet was told his zip-fastener was undone, on doing it up he caught the tablecloth in it, and on standing up to make his speech he pulled everything off the table. This could be seen as a case of discrediting of self-presentation, as failure to control equipment, as lack of social techniques to handle the situation, all of this taking place at a public and formal occasion.

Is it possible to avoid embarrassment? In the first place, other inter-actors are usually very helpful in saving each other's faces, and thus preventing embarrassment; it is quite easy to embarrass friends, rela-tions or colleagues by mentioning things they would rather forget; this is usually avoided because embarrassment will spread to others present and cause general unpleasantness. 'Tact' is the name given to this social skill; it includes such behaviour as coughing outside doors when a couple is likely to be making love on the other side of it. The rules of etiquette do the same thing, often in a more complicated and formalised way; for example don't issue invitations more than three weeks ahead as it makes them difficult to refuse (Goffman, 1963b). On the other hand etiquette can add to embarrassment for those who are not quite sure what the rules are, or who manage to break them. Adolescents often tease and insult one another, deliberately causing embarrassment. Gross and Stone (op. cit.) interpret this exception to the usual process of collusion as a process of training in poise, so that members of the group can deal with awkward situations in the future. This may be the result, but it may be doubted whether this is really the intention behind such be-haviour; in any case it is not a very effective form of training, as it does not teach young people how to avoid or deal with embarrassment. To this topic we now turn.

Discrediting of self-presentation can be overcome by greater authen-ticity of presentation. This creates a problem for anyone who has to perform in public or give any kind of performance; it is not sufficient to give a modest, informal performance – this would be inaudible, dull and quite ineffective. Once he puts on a performance however he is im-plicitly claiming that he is worth watching or listening to – a claim that is in danger of being discredited. This may explain the unwillingness of some Americans to take the performer role with 'presence', and a prefer-ence for the informal 'familial' style, noted by Riesman, Potter and Watson (1960). The solution may be to carry out the performer role with due modesty, and to try to interest and generally meet the needs of the audience.

Changes in the perceived nature of the situation can to some extent be avoided by careful study of the situation and the participants in the early stages of the encounter. When the new element is perceived, the solution is to retain poise and self-control, and perhaps to acknowledge the new situation by non-verbal signals, for example of the presence of an unnoticed person, or of the changed status of one already there; then a suitably modified style of behaviour can be adopted without an awk-ward pause.

Accidents in the case of motor skills like driving can to some extent be avoided by greater care and greater skill, but they may still occur on rare occasions. Social accidents can be avoided by maintaining motor and emotional control – by not becoming too emotionally aroused. When another person is unintentionally embarrassed there is no need for the person who upset him to feel embarrassed if his own utterance was made in good faith; instead he should express sympathy and help the other back into interaction.

Individual differences in self-presentation

Persons with low self-esteem are shy, easily embarrassed, and eager to be approved of (Rosenberg, 1965). They are more concerned with what people think of them, and they are less effective in social situations. Perhaps the balance between concern with self and concern with others is tipped too far towards concern with self (cf. p. 191). In a number of studies it has been found that people who accept themselves also accept others, though the processes involved are not yet known (e.g. Berger, 1952). One possibility is that low rewardingness or low social skill result in negative reactions from others, which in turn produce negative self-reactions and negative reactions *to* others. It has been found that therapy leads both to greater acceptance of self and greater acceptance of others; if the above hypothesis is correct, social skill training would have similar effects. However, it was found that if the self-esteem of females was experimentally reduced, they preferred a male who asked them for a date (Walster, 1965). Individuals with low self-esteem are found to use some of the techniques for stabilising the self-image. They are more easily influenced by social pressures (Hovland and Janis, 1959), and imitate more readily (Rosenbaum *et al.*, 1962).

It follows from Erikson's theory (p. 370) that those with a greater degree of 'identity achievement' would be less vulnerable to unfavourable information about themselves or reactions from others; Marcia (1966) found this to be the case. He also found that those in a state of 'foreclosure' were more authoritarian and had the greatest discrepancy between self and ideal self. It would be expected that those with the most recently formed or precarious identities would dramatise themselves, and be very careful about clothes and appearance, in the way that hysterics are (p. 349). Those in a state of ego-diffusion on the other hand would be more like schizophrenics and present no clear picture of themselves (p. 338). Maslow (1954) suggested that there should be characteristic behaviour for those with different combinations of 'security' (roughly corresponding to ego-integration) and self-esteem. A person with low esteem and high security would be quiet, sweet and dependent; high esteem and low security on the other hand produces an aggressive boastfulness and hostility to others.

X

Training for Social Competence

INTRODUCTION AND METHODS

Much research on social interaction is carried out in the hope that it may be possible to make social interaction more effective and more enjoyable. One of the main applications of this research is in training people to interact better. Many people are ineffective and unsuccessful in their jobs through lack of social competence. Candidates fail to get jobs and interviewers select the wrong people through lack of competence on either side. The 'normal' human condition so far in the history of mankind has been that many people are lonely and unhappy or mentally ill, simply because they cannot establish and sustain social relationships with others. Conflicts between different social classes and cultural groups are partly due to difficulties of interaction.

Extensive research data has now been gathered on interaction, and the processes involved are far better understood than they have ever been before. We shall now consider the various techniques of training that have been tried out in this field. These have been used in a number of different contexts with little cross-fertilisation, so that it may prove possible to bring them together, and recommend the application of techniques found to be successful in one field in others. We shall not be concerned with methods of changing the social structure of whole groups or organisations, which is discussed on p. 311 ff. Some of the same methods, for example T-groups, have been used for this purpose.

Training for professional social skills such as interviewing, teaching, supervision and psychotherapy, is one of the main areas of interest. It is curious that while manual workers often receive extensive and carefully planned courses of training, their more responsible and more highly paid supervisors and managers receive so little. It has been realised for some time that traditional methods of instruction – lectures, discussion and reading – are probably insufficient to affect social performance, just as riding a bicycle or swimming cannot be taught in these ways. As a result there has been a slow growth of role-playing, and of various group methods of training.

The treatment of mental patients is another field where attempts are made to modify social behaviour. It has become increasingly realised that it is primarily inadequacies in the sphere of social interaction that make life difficult for many patients; these inadequacies were documented in Chapter VIII. Psychotherapy and behaviour therapy have both been used to influence interpersonal skills, but as yet little use has been made of the techniques used to teach social skills in other contexts.

Rather less attention has been given to training normal people to deal with everyday social situations. This has always been one of the aims of education, but no systematic tuition has ever been given. We shall discuss current attempts to apply in the school situation those methods which have been found effective elsewhere, and consider how these might be extended. This might be one of the most important applications of knowledge about social behaviour. The 'normal' state of mankind in which there is so much loneliness, unhappiness, misunderstanding and conflict, might be radically changed if education included training in social behaviour among the other, probably less important, subjects in the curriculum.

We shall consider in this chapter nine main methods of training in social skill, including a number of variations. How can it be decided whether a particular method is or is not effective? Experience shows that any method of training or treatment is reacted to with enthusiasm by many of those who have been trained or treated. Their response is probably due in part to reduction of dissonance – they are not prepared to admit to themselves that they have been wasting their time (and often money). It is necessary to show that there have been changes in performance when performance before and after the training is compared. Ideally there should be a control group of people who are also assessed twice, but who receive no training; this eliminates the effects of external changes in conditions with the passage of time, and the effects of practice in taking tests where these are used. The measurements should not just consist of paper-and-pencil tests; Fleishman *et al.* (1955) found that the attitudes of foremen were influenced by a training course but that their behaviour was not. Ratings by colleagues are often used in follow-up studies. The main weakness of these is that they may be affected by whether the raters expect the course to have positive results or not; in theory this could be avoided by using 'blind' ratings – i.e. where the raters do not know whether those rated are being trained or are members of the control group – but in practice this is very difficult.

Another approach is to use behavioural tests of social skill, and role-playing performance has been used in this way (e.g Maier, 1953). If reliable tests of social skill come to be developed along the lines described earlier (p. 353 f), these could be used as criteria. In the case of professional social skills perhaps the most valid criterion is effectiveness at the job – productivity, absenteeism, labour turnover, etc. for foreman, sales for salesman, and so on. To follow up more therapeutic kinds of treatment the subjective state of those treated would be one of the main areas to be studied; here popularity, or other aspects of the reactions of others, should be assessed as well. To sum up, in order to demonstrate that a training method is effective it is necessary to show that there is improvement if before and after measures are compared, that change is greater than for an untrained control group, and when objective assessments of performance or effectiveness are used.

What are the areas of social competence that need to be trained? In Chapter VIII we concluded that social competence had a number of components; which might be trained:

(1) *Motivational.* People vary in extraversion and dominance, and this will affect their popularity and the influence they are able to exert. It is probably not possible or desirable to modify a person's position along these dimensions, but it is certainly possible to give him the social skills which make successful dominance possible. Social anxiety is different – it is highly incapacitating and techniques have been discovered which can successfully modify it. For professional social skills, training may modify the goals which are being sought; for example salesmen may be persuaded to aim at meeting the needs of customers, rather than selling a lot of goods.

(2) *Perceptual.* Training may be directed towards making people more aware of the non-verbal and verbal elements of interaction, teaching them the best strategy of scanning, and teaching them to interpret the cues correctly. They can also be trained to take the role of the other during interaction.

(3) *Response patterns.* Several components of social skill can be distinguished. One of the recurring features of the socially effective person in a number of contexts is that he is highly rewarding to other people. One of the most common features of mental patients is that they are not. The effective social performer must be able to synchronise his inter-

actions with others both in terms of floor apportionment and of other dimensions such as emotional mood and intimacy. He is able to control the course of interaction and the relationships that develop, though he does not necessarily dominate. For each professional social skill there are a number of special response patterns to be mastered. For everyday life there is a similar repertoire corresponding to the most common everyday social encounters.

(4) *Self-confidence and self-presentation.* As well as being poised the competent performer should be able to present himself clearly to others, without too much concealment or exaggeration, and without embarrassment.

Some kinds of training affect one area of social competence more than others; it will be useful to keep this list in mind while considering the usefulness of the various approaches.

It is of theoretical importance to consider the nature of the learning process involved when social skills are learnt. Some of the training methods have developed out of a particular theory of learning – for example behaviour therapy from instrumental learning. Other methods have developed without regard for the kind of learning taking place. Study of the effects of different training methods may provide valuable information about the kinds of learning which underlie social behaviour.

LEARNING ON THE JOB

The commonest way of learning social skills is through repeated performance in the relevant social situations over a period of time. Since formal training in social skills is rare, and since most people have some degree of social competence, clearly this method can be successful. On the other hand, since many people are incompetent, and persist in the use of ineffective social techniques, it is equally clear that this method has serious limitations. The acquisition of everyday social skills takes place in this way during childhood and adolescence, with very little assistance from other forms of training. The process of learning involved is primarily trial and error with feedback. No doubt the imitation of models plays some part here, and this process will be discussed later. Professional social skills are mainly learnt in similar ways, though there is usually some instruction and coaching by the supervisor, and sometimes feedback is given.

The effect of sheer repetition has been studied in a number of laboratory and field studies. Argyle, Lalljee and Lydall (1969) studied the learning curve for sales for newly appointed sales staff in three departmental stores, where there was very little training. An index of individual sales performance was devised – the beginner's monthly sales were expressed as a percentage of the average of 2–3 experienced salesmen in the same department; this eliminates the effects of seasonal fluctuations and departmental differences. The results are shown in Fig. 10.1. This shows that there is an *average* improvement over time, and suggests that this may be faster under an individual incentive scheme – though the shops were not matched for other variables. However, there were very considerable individual variations – while some

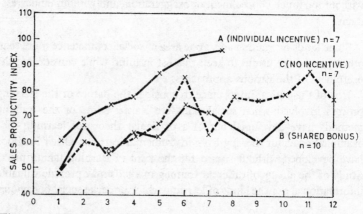

Figure 10.1. Learning curves for selling (from Argyle, Lalljee and Lydall, 1968)

girls improved, others became steadily worse, fluctuated wildly, or failed to improve at all (see Argyle, 1967, p. 186 for figure). The feedback in the sales situation is of two kinds: firstly whether or not a sale is made – which has direct financial consequences when there is a bonus scheme, and secondly there may be verbal comments by other members of staff.

McPhail (1969) has studied the process of acquiring social competence during adolescence. He gave problem situations to 100 males and females aged 12–18. Alternative solutions were offered, corresponding to a number of theoretically possible modes of response. An example of one of the problems, with the coding scheme, is given below:

Situation: A boy or girl of your own age, with whom you are friendly, appears to be very upset for some reason unknown to you.
Question: What would you do?

Possible courses of action	*Classification*
You would:	
1. Do nothing	Passive
2. Feel disturbed but don't know what to do.	Passive-emotional
3. Point the situation out to some adult.	Dependent-adult
4. Talk to your friends about the situation.	Dependent-peer
5. Tell the person concerned to pull himself/ herself together.	Aggressive
6. Jeer at that boy or girl.	Very aggressive (Psychopathic)
7. Avoid him/her.	Avoidance.
8. Ask your friend what is the matter	Experimental-crude
9. Try to talk to him/her as if you have not noticed anything is wrong.	Experimental-sophisticated
10. Comfort your friend.	Mature-conventional
11. Set about interesting the person concerned in something which is going on, at the same time being available to help if asked.	Mature-imaginative

McPhail found that the percentage who gave the 'mature' responses increased with age over this age-span, as shown in Fig. 10.2. This study shows that skill in everyday social situations can be acquired by practice, and in the absence of training.

The next problem is to find out more about the learning processes that are taking place; this may suggest the conditions under which sheer practice will be effective. Three main processes appear to be involved.

(1) *Feedback.* Laboratory experiments on the learning of motor skills have shown that practice is ineffective unless there is also feedback in the form of reward or punishment or of knowledge of how successful the performance has been. The selling situation probably supplies clearer feedback than most other kinds of social performance. The author conducted a classroom experiment in which students taught the game of Scrabble or the use of a slide-rule to a series of other students. Analysis of the lessons showed that the teachers retained in a stereotyped way those phrases and illustrations that seemed to work in earlier lessons. Feedback may also take the form of verbal comments.

Gage *et al.* (1960) asked 3,900 schoolchildren to fill in 12 rating scales about 176 teachers to describe their ideal teacher and their actual teachers. The results were shown to half of the teachers who subsequently improved on 10 of the 12 scales as shown by later ratings compared with the control group. More extensive use is made of verbal comments in the feedback given in connection with role-playing, as described below (p. 402 ff). Feedback can work below the conscious level, as in operant verbal conditioning, or can act through the formation of verbalised cognitive controls which direct later behaviour (p. 183 ff).

One reason for the failure of sheer repetition to teach may be that feedback is not accessible. Likert (1961) suggests that authoritarian

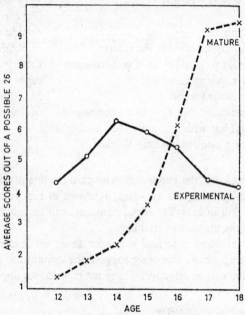

Figure 10.2. Experimental and mature solutions to social problems (from McPhail, 1967)

styles of supervision persist in industry because, although they clearly generate discontent among subordinates, it is realised that there is no connection between satisfaction and productivity for manual workers; authoritarian supervision is much less common when subordinates are more highly skilled, where there *is* a connection between satisfaction and productivity. When feedback or coaching is given, it is rarely about interpersonal aspects of a trainee's behaviour.

(2) *Generation of new responses.* Practice involves trial and error; if feedback has shown a response to be ineffective, new responses are devised

to replace it. Imitation plays an important role in producing such new behaviour, though there may also be an element of genuine creativity. McPhail (op. cit.) in his study of adolescents found evidence for what he calls 'experimental behaviour', i.e. social behaviour which is being tried out, in many cases with the intention of controlling social situations, or of getting on terms of equality with adults – which adolescents are strongly motivated to do – but in a crude and usually unsuccessful way. An example is given on p. 398 f above, and the relation of this kind of behaviour to age is shown in Fig. 10.2. It looks as if this kind of behaviour gradually gives way to more mature behaviour, but that a process of trial and error learning is involved. Adolescents often explain their strange behaviour by saying they were finding out what would happen or were just trying it out.

(3) *Integration of a series of responses.* In the learning of a motor skill the integration of smaller parts of larger units is an important process. The morse performer learns to send 'words' rather than a series of single letters. A similar integration probably occurs with social skills. In the Scrabble experiment described above it was found that the teachers' utterances became longer, smoother and contained fewer speech errors. It was also observed that these sequences became fixed – a lesser version of the stereotyped behaviour of museum guides. The integration of responses into longer units probably results in the performer becoming less receptive to feedback, at any rate during each unit.

These may be motivational changes as a result of practice, though these are not usually regarded as part of the 'learning'. Initial enthusiasm may decline, as the social task becomes familiar, possibly boring, and hence a weaker source of arousal. In social situations this may include reduced social anxiety, and lend to increased poise.

We saw earlier that social roles can be acquired through the influence of people in related positions (p. 278). Those in interlocking roles will behave in a complementary style, and thus help to elicit the expected role behaviour. Other members of the organisation will have role-expectations about how an individual will behave, and will exert various kinds of social influence to get him to act in this way. His self-image will be changed as a result of others treating him as a doctor, an officer, or whatever his position is. These principles can be made use of to teach a person new social skills – he is simply placed in a position which requires them; this is done in a number of training courses. An extension of this process is to control the behaviour of other members so as to produce changes in behaviour. We have seen that changes in self-image can be engineered in this way (p. 364). Mental nurses, especially those in therapeutic communities, behave in a warm, cooperative way, giving responsibility to inmates (Rapoport, 1960); they may also deliberately reinforce or punish particular patterns of behaviour and this has been found to be effective in modifying social behaviour (Ayllon and Michael, 1959).

Learning on the job can be accelerated if efforts are made to provide coaching and feedback, and it has the great advantage that there is no problem of transferring to the job skills which have been learnt at a remote training centre; on the other hand the pressure of work makes it difficult to devote much time to the trainee and his problems. The success of such coaching depends on there being a good relation between the trainee and his supervisor (Bass and Vaughan, 1966). The trainee should be allocated to someone who acts as his tutor; the latter should regularly observe the trainee in action and hold frequent feedback sessions; the coach should be an expert on the social skills in question and should be sensitised to the elements and processes of which social interaction consists.

Conclusion. There is no doubt that people can acquire and improve social skills by sheer repetition. They may not succeed however in learning the most effective style of performance, and long-term results of practice tend to be a smooth, stereotyped, poised and bored performance, and with little sensitivity to feedback. The amount of improvement that takes place with practice is largely a function of the availability of feedback, and the performer's sensitivity to it. It is possible that the shortcomings of learning social skills in the real-life situation itself can be partly overcome if there is someone who can act as an effective coach.

ROLE-PLAYING AND SIMULATION

In role-playing, trainees practise the part they are going to play in a classroom situation, and are given some kind of feedback on their performance. This method was first developed for training industrial supervisors, though it has also been used for some time in the training of interviewers, salesmen and teachers. More recently the availability of the video-tape recorder has added considerably to the power of this method. Role-playing is also used in training actors in the method proposed by Stanislavsky: trainees improvise how they would behave in various situations – 'walk to pass time: walk to annoy the people who live in an apartment below' (Moore, 1960).

Before role-playing can be used, it is necessary to draw up a list of the social problems to be faced by the trainee, and to discover the most effective social techniques for dealing with them. The list of problems can be arrived at by a 'critical incident' survey, in which practitioners are asked to give examples of awkward situations encountered. Flanagan (1961) collected 40 critical incidents which he used for training industrial managers in leadership skills. Stolurow and Santhai (1966) constructed an elaborate classification for critical incidents relevant to the skills of behaviour in another culture.

The author and Elizabeth Sidney have devised a three-day training course for personnel selection interviewing, which is organised by the Careers Research and Advisory Centre at Cambridge. Two sets of problem situations are used. The first set consists of the most common kinds of awkward candidate:

> talks too much
> talks too little
> asks too many questions
> very nervous
> over self-presentation
> class or cultural difference
> unrewarding
> female
> not very interested in job
> neurotic

Trainees conduct short interviews with trained confederates who act these parts; amateur actors have been found to be the most successful in these roles. If the trainee is quite unable to cope with a confederate, the interview is interrupted, and he is given further instructions. The second set consists of asking trainees to assess, one at a time, a number of the most relevant personality traits – intelligence, judgement, creativity, authoritarianism, neuroticism, self-image, social competence, and achievement motivation. After each interview a discussion is held about what rating (on a 7-point scale) the 'candidate' should be given in the trait in question. When a complete profile has been obtained for a candidate, a discussion is held on his overall suitability for various kinds of job. We shall describe feedback procedure later.

The second preliminary is that research should have been conducted to find out the most effective social techniques for the task in question, as well as the best ways of handling the problem situations. Such research has been done for some skills, such as leadership (p. 299 ff); for

other skills, such as interviewing, use can be made of the views of experienced informants, combined with knowledge of the general principles of social interaction. Learning to behave in other cultures requires
anthropological information.

The role-playing procedure is typically as follows:

1. The trainer gives a lecture and holds a discussion about the social
skills being taught. There may be a demonstration or a film may be
shown to provide models for imitation.

2. A series of situations or problems are role-played by the trainees in
turn. Each should be carefully prepared. For interviewer training the
person to be interviewed fills in a complete application form, and a job
specification is provided. The interviewee may be instructed to behave
in a special way, as described above. For supervisor training a small case
study is presented to the trainee and those playing the complementary
roles (examples are given in Corsini *et al.*, 1961, and Maier *et al.*, 1964).
They may be given different sections of the background information;
for example in a personnel interview the supervisor is not told the cause
of the worker's unsatisfactory behaviour. The role-playing can proceed
for any time between 5 and 30 minutes, depending on the time available
and the skill being taught.

3. After each role-playing performance, a feedback session is held,
along lines described below.

Role-playing requires role partners or stooges, to play the counter
role or roles. Other members of the course are often used in this way,
but they may be of the wrong age, sex or cultural background, in which
case outside stooges can be brought in. Argyle and Sidney use Cambridge undergraduates to play the role of candidates to be interviewed.
When training is being given in the handling of particular kinds of
personality, the stooges have to be instructed in these parts.

While role-playing is primarily directed towards the skills of the performer, trainees benefit in other ways too. Those who play the counter
role may come to see the other point of view, for example foremen who
take the role of shop stewards, and probation officers who take the role
of juvenile delinquents. Johnson (1966) found that role-reversal led to
greater understanding of the other's position, in laboratory studies of
negotiation. A widely used role-reversal technique is the 'power-
spectrum' role play introduced by Blake and Mouton (1961): trainees
meet in pairs in the role of supervisor and subordinate; a third of those
acting as supervisors take this role in a coercive authoritarian way, a
third are permissive or democratic, and a third give all the power to
the subordinate. Observers of the role-playing may also benefit from

observing and discussing it; Rosenberg (1952) found that some observers became actively involved, were critical and analytic, and made a lot of useful suggestions about alternative ways of behaving.

The feedback following role-playing can be given in two main ways – verbal comments by trainer and group, and playback of audio- and video-tape recordings.

Verbal comments can be given by the trainer, who can correct errors, for example interruptions, sounding and looking unfriendly; he can suggest better social techniques, such as ways of dealing with situations that arose during the role-playing; he can increase sensitivity to what was happening during the encounter. This has to be done with great skill, or the trainee will be upset and fail to receive the message. The trainer should be objective but warm and helpful in manner, and phrase his comments as positive suggestions. Trainees are ambivalent about the feedback – they know they need it, but they dislike it. The group of observing trainees is usually drawn into the discussion too: this is valuable to them and it is valuable to the performer if good suggestions are made. They may need to be taught the gentle art of giving feedback, the group should not be larger than eight, and they should have had time to get to know each other. It is possible to define the situation as a cooperative group task, rather than a role-playing competition (cf. Corsini, Shaw and Blake, 1961).

A number of follow-up studies have been made of role-playing for industrial supervisors, though many of the courses studied included other elements such as group discussion. Speroff (1959) for example found that role-playing combined with group therapy over a six-month period made supervisors better able to deal with grievances. Lawshe *et al.* (1959) found that role-playing courses for 120 supervisors resulted in greater sensitivity and more favourable attitudes to employees, as measured by tests. Miles (1958) and Smith and Kight (1959) found that there was more change when strong negative feedback was given, though trainees did not enjoy this. The experience of T-groups suggests that very great care must be taken with these anxiety-arousing experiences.

Audio and video-tape playback. Training by playing back audio-tape recordings is now familiar as part of the technique of language laboratories, and it has been found that this considerably shortens the time needed to learn a language (Carroll, 1963). The tape-recorder can also be used to play back role-playing sessions, for example in interviewer training. This is a valuable supplement to verbal commentary, since it focuses attention on verbal and non-verbal aspects of speech, for example pauses, interruptions, tone of voice, unclear questions, failure to follow up, and so on. It is also possible to measure such things as the proportion of time each person spoke.

In about 1965 the author and others became aware of the possibilities of the video-tape recorder for the same purpose. The author carried out a small-scale experiment in interviewer training at the University of Delaware in 1965, which showed much more rapid improvement when VTR feedback was added to verbal feedback. Haines and Eachus (1965) found that subjects learnt the skills of interacting in an imaginary new culture more rapidly if VTR playback was added to the feedback. Nielsen (1962) in Copenhagen had found that 'self-confrontation' of this kind made subjects very interested in their bodily movements, and gave them new information about themselves. When shown the film again after an interval of a year and a half they were able to view themselves in a more objective and detached way – more as representing a class of people of a certain age than as a unique person different from others. Stoller (1968) made use of VTR feedback in connection with group therapy: video-tapes are played back to groups immediately after they have been taken, the attention of the group is focused on aspects of the interaction, a verbal commentary is added by the therapist, and patients are helped to find alternative ways of dealing with situations. A follow-up study of this technique was carried out by Jacobs and Robinson (1968) for 40 mental hospital patients who had six one-hour sessions of this kind; ratings were made of the audio-tapes, and these patients improved more than others receiving group therapy followed by discussion sessions – but only for ratings made by judges and not for self-ratings.

Since audio-tapes focus attention on the voice, and video-tapes focus on bodily movements and facial expression, the ideal arrangement may be to use both methods. Both kinds of playback provide feedback in the absence of verbal comments, since trainees become aware of aspects of their performance which they did not know about before. A further refinement of role-playing technique is to use an earphone through which the trainer can communicate with the trainee during the role-playing (Flanagan, 1961). The author has found this very useful; an alternative is to interrupt the role-playing if serious mistakes are being made, or if the trainee is incapable of dealing with the problem presented; the other performer or performers are asked to leave, and a discussion is held about how the trainee could handle the situation better.

The ideal laboratory arrangements for role-playing an interview would be as shown in Fig. 10.3. The other trainees watch the role-playing through a one-way screen; the television camera simultaneously films the interviewer and candidate by the use of a mirror; the trainer communicates with the trainee interviewer through an earphone.

A useful adjunct to role-playing is the use of demonstrations. This can be provided by means of films (p. 418 f) or by the trainer on the spot.

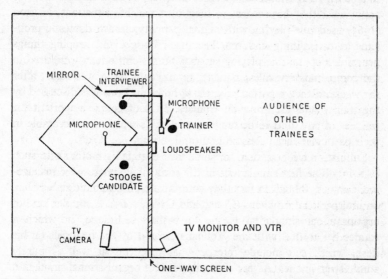

Figure 10.3. Laboratory arrangements for interviewer training

Sarason (1968) found that role-playing combined with demonstrations was effective in training juvenile delinquents in skills like applying for a job. Such demonstrations would be particularly useful when the skills are unfamiliar to the trainees.

A number of learning processes are probably involved in role-playing. Trial and error with feedback is one. The feedback takes the form mainly of verbalisation of social responses, and bringing the usually spontaneous non-verbal aspects of behaviour under conscious control. The combination of verbal commentary with playback methods helps with the verbal labelling of behaviour. Increased sensitivity to inter-personal behaviour and interaction processes is produced by the careful study of audio- and video-tapes. The finding that strong negative feedback produces the best results suggests that some degree of emotional arousal may help the learning process, as has been found in other contexts. There are also changes of self-perception, especially when playback methods are used.

One difficulty with role-playing is that trainees may think it is silly, or not take it seriously, or over-dramatise their performances, or play to the gallery of the other trainees. This can be dealt with by making introductory remarks, which orientate trainees appropriately, and increase their faith in the method. Another difficulty is that trainees have to apply what they have learnt to their own real-life situations. Morton (1965) used role-playing with mental patients of such domestic problems as disciplining children, keeping a budget and keeping things peaceful. For the role-playing sessions nurses and others were used in the complementary roles; patients returned home at weekends; after the weekend they reported progress at home and this was discussed by the trainer and the group of trainees. It is of course important for trainees of any kind to be taught social skills which are acceptable in their particular social class and cultural setting.

Simulation has been used for some time in training motor skills, such as flying. The first simulations in the social skill sphere were management games, though in fact they concentrate on economic rather than on interpersonal problems (Cohen and Cyert, 1965). A simpler kind of organisational simulation is the 'in-basket' technique, in which a trainee has to deal with the problems created by the materials on his desk, which can include interpersonal problems as well as purely administrative ones. A very elaborate form of organisational simulation has been developed in connection with Conflict Research, partly in order to give participants some experience of the problems facing those in different positions in international politics.

Conclusions. Role-playing is one of the most effective methods of training in social skills and is particularly useful for teaching rather specific skills such as interviewing and supervision, though success has also been obtained with mental patients. It requires research into what the main problems are, and how they should be dealt with, and the trainer should be able to spot mistakes and correct them tactfully; trainees need to be orientated carefully, and attention must be paid to applying the new skills in their real-life situation.

T-GROUPS

T(training)-groups were first developed in the National Training Laboratories at Bethel, Maine, in 1947; they grew in popularity during the next 15 years, but have been subjected to considerable criticism in recent years. The procedure was described on p. 260 ff, above: trainees meet in groups of about 12 for a series of two-hour sessions, and their sole task is to study the processes of interaction in the group itself; the leader explains that he is there to help them to do this, and occasionally intervenes to comment on what is happening. The group goes through a series of stages of group-formation as described previously.

The standard Bethel procedure is for 30–150 trainees to meet at a residential conference centre for 2–3 weeks. The central activity is attending the T-groups themselves, which meet for 30–40 hours. In addition to the T-groups proper there are also lectures and discussions about the social psychology of groups and organisations, role-playing especially of problems faced by trainees in their work, and group exercises and demonstrations. In addition to verbal interventions by the trainer, tape-recordings of earlier sessions are studied and members may take turns as observers, and report back to the group later. An alternative procedure is for a T-group to meet once a week over a period, and for the other activities to be omitted. In the Harvard T-groups described by Mann (1967) 20–30 students meet once a day for an hour for 32 sessions. Most of the follow-up studies have been concerned with the Bethel procedure. T-group training is very expensive and for this reason has mainly been given to industrial managers, though social workers, clergymen and interested psychologists have also experienced it. The most extensive discussions of T-groups are to be found in Bradford, Gibb and Benne (1964) and Schein and Bennis (1965).

It is important to consider what the goals of T-group training are, as they are rather different from those of the other training methods discussed in this chapter. The following are most frequently mentioned in the writings of T-group practitioners (e.g. Benne, Bradford and Lippitt, 1964; Argyris, 1962):

1. Sensitivity to emotional reactions in others, and to interpersonal phenomena, in groups and organisations.
2. Clearer self-perception, awareness of how the trainee is seen by others, and greater self-understanding and self-acceptance.
3. Learning to behave as a member of a democratic group, becoming less dependent on leaders, and more accepting of others.
4. Better understanding of interpersonal behaviour in groups and organisations.
5. Greater effectiveness in the work situation.
6. Learning how to learn, by making use of feedback and seeking the help of others.

This is an extremely comprehensive and sophisticated list of goals for training; the question is how far are they attained? There have been a number of follow-up studies, using both ratings by colleagues, and tests of social skill (reviewed by Stock, 1964; Smith, 1966). Perhaps the most extensive study is that by Bunker (1965) of 200 people who attended the Bethel laboratories, and an equal number of controls who did not; open-ended comments by colleagues were obtained before the T-groups and 12 months later, and analysed by content analysis. The follow-up results of this and other studies can be summarised in relation to the six goals listed above:

1. *Sensitivity*. It is found that trainees describe people and situations in more interpersonal terms; however, there have been generally negative results when measures of accuracy in person perception have been used (Campbell and Dunnette, 1968).

2. *Self-perception*. Improved self-understanding was found in the Bunker study, and in studies in which the trainees were interviewed.

3. *Democratic group behaviour*. Both ratings and questionnaire measures indicate better human relations skills.

4. *Understanding*. No evidence.

5. *Work effectiveness*. There is good evidence for improved inter-personal skills on the job.

6. *Learning to learn*. No evidence.

Follow-up studies report different degrees of success. Typical findings are that 30–40% of trainees improve to some extent compared to 10–20% of the control groups (Campbell and Dunnette, 1968). Furthermore, it has not been shown that the T-groups proper are responsible for the changes, since the courses which were followed up had numerous other activities, such as role-playing and lectures, in addition. It is interesting to note that Lippitt (1949) reported successful results in a follow-up of 32 social workers who had been on a two-week workshop with all the usual activities *except* T-groups. Bunker and Knowles (1967) found that there was more improvement for a 3-week course compared with a two-week course, the amount of T-group training being the same in each. Some of the follow-up results must be treated with caution since they are based on self-report by trainees (who, as noted above, tend to be enthusiastic about any course); others must be dis-counted since they treated *group development*, or changes in perception of other members of the group, as *learning* (cf. Smith, loc. cit); even where ratings by colleagues were used, the latter's attitudes to the course may have affected their ratings – the raters are selected by, and pre-sumably interact with, the trainees.

Although a proportion of trainees are often reported to have benefited by T-group training, a serious problem is created by the others. Underwood (1965) found that one trainee became less effective for every two that became more effective; in the control group the ratio was one to four. During the course some trainees fail to behave in the expected way, for example by refusing to participate, or show acute anxiety. Some are very seriously disturbed, and a few have had nervous breakdowns as a result of attending T-groups. The main cause of stress is the experience of direct critical comment from other members of the group. Stress is also created by the unexpected behaviour of the trainer, who (a) refuses to act like someone in charge, (b) does not become a member of the group on equal terms, and (c) is often annoyingly dominant, competent and self-confident (P. McPhail, personal communication). The level of stress could be reduced by screening out those liable to be upset, or by trainers being more watchful for signs of distress. Another solution would be to lower the level of emotional stress in T-groups. Some T-group trainers do these things but others believe that the emotional stress is necessary for changes in behaviour to take place. Indeed there seem to be wide variations in styles of T-group leadership and some trainers seem to be totally unfit for the task. It is the author's opinion that unless T-groups can meet the problems of creating serious emotional disturbance in a proportion of trainees, they should be discontinued.

We showed before that trainees react in a number of different ways to the T-group experience (p. 264 f). Among the regular patterns of response found by Mann (1967) in the Harvard T-groups, two types cooperated in the approved way (the male and female enactors), and five types did not (hero, paranoid and moralistic resisters, sexual scapegoat, distressed females). In the typology devised by Bion (1948–51), three types are now regarded as cooperating (work, pair and fight) and two as not doing so (dependency and flight). It is generally recognised that a considerable proportion do not behave in the intended way in T-groups, and it is now known that these people do not benefit from the training (Stock, 1964).

Several studies have been concerned with personality differences between those who benefit from T-groups and those who do not. These studies are reviewed by Stock (op. cit.): they do not provide very clear-cut results, but three factors seem to be important. (1) Trainees with some degree of internal conflict, and who are unsure of their self-image, change most. On the other hand they should not be too anxious; it is possible that the relationship is curvilinear. (2) They should be affiliative and outgoing; those who show a pairing or fight reaction benefit, which those reacting by dependency or flight do not. (3) They should be open, receptive to new ideas, flexible and not defensive. These personality differences were studied in relation to benefiting from T-group training; it would be important in addition to know which personalities are most emotionally disturbed. It seems likely that these will be the trainees who are high in anxiety and defensiveness.

On the other hand firms sometimes select for T-group courses managers whose interpersonal behaviour is unsatisfactory; how far are these going to be the very people who break down? It is likely that some of those whose behaviour is unsatisfactory would react badly. One group that is commonly sent for training that would be expected to be upset is the over-authoritarian manager, who will not have had any direct feedback on his behaviour for a long time (though families often fulfil this function). Glidewell (1956) studied the effects of T-groups on four kinds of unsatisfactory manager – the 'stepchild' (who is worried about how others treat him), the 'innocent bystander' (who sees problems as belonging to others), the manager with the 'service' syndrome (who thinks that problems are solved by serving others) and the 'do-it-yourself club' (who sees problems as human relations problems, and thinks that the outcome is determined by themselves). Between 50% and 67% of the members of these groups showed positive changes. In England the most difficult managers to train are probably those who are highly authoritarian. T-groups can make them see how other people really see them but the experience is likely to be very painful. A number of observers have felt that T-groups create more emotional disturbance in Britain than in the USA.

T-groups have mainly been used for managers and other administrators, but a kind of T-group training has been devised for use with mental patients by Morton (1965) and others. The procedure includes T-groups, but there is more emphasis on sensitisation by taking the observer's role, exercises, role-playing, and the invention of new social techniques. Johnson *et al.* (1965) report a follow-up of this procedure using 141 mainly neurotic mental hospital patients. They received an intensive four-weeks course, and were as well recovered as other patients treated by group therapy; the group therapy patients were in hospital 50% longer however.

What kinds of learning are involved in T-groups? The training situation is a strange one, though with some similarity to psychotherapy, especially group psychotherapy, with its emphasis on the verbal labelling and interpretation of here-and-now behaviour.

Trainees often learn the importance that is attached to seemingly trivial or harmless behavior. For example, people with high status do not always realize the effect their jokes, sarcasm, indifference, or modes of questioning may have on others; they may learn of this effect in the training group only when persons of lower status open up and reveal their feelings to them. People of high status, who usually have an inordinate amount of interpersonal influence because of their potential to reward and punish others around them, sometimes also learnt that they have unconsciously been blocking communication or that they have caused some of their staff unnecessary discomfort because of offhand remarks they have innocently made (Bass and Vaughan, 1966).

There is also increased sensitisation to interpersonal phenomena, obtained by taking the role of other, and as a result of the trainer's comments. There is feedback, as in role-playing, though only in respect of performance in the T-group, not a real task. Lastly there is a very high level of emotional arousal, which is known to be one of the conditions for major personality change in such fields as religious conversion and brainwashing (Sargant, 1957).

Conclusions. (a) T-group training has far-reaching and comprehensive goals – the overall improvement of social sensitivity, understanding and skill. Here it contrasts with role-playing, which is intended to teach specific social skills. (b) T-group training appears to benefit 30–40% of the trainees (though there are some doubts over which part of the course is responsible). Some of the others are seriously disturbed by the experience, and this constitutes the main objection to T-group methods. The solution could be either to reduce the emotional stress generated, or to screen out those liable to be disturbed – though the latter evidently include some who are thought to be in special need of training. (c) The American courses include role-playing and a variety of other exercises; these can be used without the T-group experiences proper, and it is possible that much of the success of these courses is a result of the other activities. (d) It is doubtful whether social competence in general can be taught: clearly the actual social skills needed by a manager, a clergyman or a social worker are different. Further, the social atmosphere of different organisations of the same type may be very different. Pugh (1965) has pointed out that the democratic styles of behaviour taught in T-groups may not be useful if trainees go back to a hierarchical and authoritarian organisation.

ALTERNATIVE KINDS OF SENSITIVITY TRAINING

In the training of manual workers in industry considerable attention is often paid to training in perception (Seymour, 1966). Trainees have to learn to discriminate fine cues, to interpret them correctly, and to acquire a pattern of perceptual activity that is integrated with the motor responses. Belbin, Belbin and Hill (1957) for example found that training to mend woollen fabrics was faster if attention was drawn to the correct perception of cues. While T-groups apparently improve sensitivity for a proportion of their members, it is possible to do this in other ways.

Finer discrimination and interpretation of physical cues is acquired by doctors – who are able to observe different states of a patient's skin, pupils and way of walking – and can make deductions about the state of his blood, whether he takes drugs, and the state of his joints. Similar discriminations and interpretations from cues are important to the interactor. He needs to be able to detect another person's emotional state, his interpersonal attitudes, whether he has understood or agrees with what has been said. For particular social skills there are particular perceptual needs: a salesman needs to know which goods a customer likes, an interviewer needs to know whether a candidate wants the job and is telling the truth.

Several early experiments showed that ability to identify emotions from photographs can be improved by training (e.g. Guilford, 1929), though as we have seen this skill is of dubious value in actual interaction (p. 128 f). Davitz (1964) found that accuracy of identifying emotions from tape-recorded speeches with neutral content could be improved by training. During the training, groups of 3–8 subjects listened to a practice tape in which letters of the alphabet were read with different emotional expressions, and they tried to identify the emotions; during a second playing they were told which emotions were to be expressed before each item; they later tried to express the emotions themselves, and their attempts were discussed by the group. The training occupied several 15-minute sessions. In another experiment Jecker *et al.* (1965) succeeded in improving the accuracy with which teachers could judge from short silent films whether or not children understood what they were being taught. A series of films each lasting 45 seconds were prepared, each showing a child being taught; interrogation of the child revealed whether he had in fact understood or not. Training consisted of four $1\frac{1}{2}$–2-hour sessions, during which the attention of trainees was drawn to the gestures and facial expressions which accompany understanding. Three different sets of film were used for the before and after tests and the training session; a control group showed no improvement.

Some kinds of T-group aim at increasing sensitivity by giving members practice at observing the group and recording what happens by means of rating scales or other instruments. Members may take it in turn to sit out from the group, or they may observe at the same time as they participate, and compare notes with each other (Blake and Mouton, 1962). The author makes use of another technique to sensitise trainees to the elements of social interaction, though no follow-up study has yet been made. The method is to arrange for groups of 2–5 people to interact for a few minutes in front of the rest of the group. Different members are asked to record an element each – for example length and number of gazes, length and number of utterances, interruptions and pauses, speech errors, questions, instructions and socio-emotional utterances, changes in posture and facial expression. The data are then assembled and the process of interaction is discussed in detail.

Interactors also need to be able to classify other people in terms of variables of individual difference. The visitor to Africa is sometimes disconcerted to find that he can't tell how old people are – because the cues for age are different for Africans. When he has learnt these he also has to learn how to tell which of the local tribal groups a person belongs to. In Western society social class is a relevant dimension – the main cues in Britain, but not in America, being clothes and accent. Personality traits are more difficult to recognise. In the interviewing course devised by the author and Elizabeth Sidney (see p. 403 f) instruction is given on the recognition of eight common personality traits from visible social behaviour, and on the lines of questioning which will establish a candidate's position on each dimension. Trainees are given practice in assessing each trait in turn with an unknown subject; the trainer asks further questions, other trainees make their estimates on a 7-point scale, and a discussion is held about the subject's score. Discussion is also held on processes of person perception and the main errors.

The second aspect of sensitivity training is teaching people the best pattern of perceptual activity in relation to the motor performance. In the case of manual skills this may entail collecting some information by touch, and other information by visual perception; it may be necessary to feel or look in a particular place at particular points in time during social interaction, as we have seen (p. 403); inputs are mainly through vision and hearing. The auditory inputs are intermittent, though a trainee can be taught to be sensitive to 'listening behaviour', i.e. the noises a person makes while listening. He should also attend very carefully to the emotional tone of speech, and to the latent messages contained in the choice of verbal expressions (p. 105 ff). The normal pattern of visual activity is also intermittent; it is particularly important to look the other in the eyes at grammatical pauses to see if he is willing for the speaker to continue, and at the ends of utterances to collect feedback. An interactor would also scan other visible parts of the other, to note his bodily posture for example, and to engage in regular scanning of all the others present, for example when making a speech.

Conclusion. While the follow-up evidence is small, it seems that it is possible to train people to discriminate and interpret cues, and it may be possible to teach them strategies of perceptual scanning.

EDUCATIONAL METHODS OF TRAINING

Lectures and discussion

This is of course the most extensively used method in many educational settings. It has also been applied to social skill training, particularly in the training of foremen and managers in supervisory skills, typically in about 12 sessions of $1\frac{1}{2}$ hours. A number of follow-up studies have been carried out, and these were reviewed by Argyle, Smith and Kirton (1962). There is no doubt that knowledge and understanding can be conveyed by lectures. A number of studies have failed to find much difference between lecture and discussion methods for young people (Wallen and Travers, 1963); discussion methods are favoured for older people since more motivation is aroused. Some of the foreman courses which have been followed up produced no changes at all, while others produced changes in paper-and-pencil test scores but not in behaviour. In some cases there was a change only when the 'leadership climate' set by senior managers was in support of the new style of behaviour (Hariton, 1951; Fleishman, *et al.*, 1955). It looks as if lectures and discussion of this kind can effect social skills, but only when combined with other social influences. Management courses sometimes include a number of other group methods, such as syndicate work and case studies. Some of these courses have been found to have positive effects on ratings of social performance, for example 'delegation' and 'cooperation' (Sorenson, 1958). Managers may however be better able than foremen to apply new principles on the job.

Several courses on human relations and mental hygiene have been developed for use in American schools. Ojemann (1955) devised a method of teaching classes in history, civics and social science, in such a way as to draw attention to psychodynamic principles, and the causes of human behaviour. In addition to classwork, a collection of readings was was prepared, and use made of plays and skits in which children dramatised ways of dealing with the problems which they met. Bullis (1952) prepared a course, complete with textbooks, which has been used in a number of schools in Delaware and New York State. There is one class each week: the teacher reads a stimulus story which illustrates an emotional problem, e.g. 'submitting to authority', 'emotional problems at home'. The class then discusses the problem freely, with examples from their own experience. The teachers help the class to arrive at appropriate conclusions. Elizabeth Force (cited by Williams, 1966) built up a classroom course on etiquette and everyday social skills. In the classes there is discussion of the rules and proper behaviour in different situations at school, at home, at work, etc. In addition to discussion, children are encouraged to observe adults and other children in different situations, ideas are discussed with parents and various professional people, who are encouraged to visit the class. The reading material consists of a large collection of books on etiquette, human relationships, etc. It should be emphasised that there is no follow-up material on the success of these courses, but it is reported that all three of them aroused great enthusiasm among those taking part (Williams, op. cit.).

Lectures and discussions can play a useful part in teaching social skills, but they are better if combined with demonstrations and exercises, such as films, role-playing and experiments.

Reading and self-instruction

Reading is the other traditional method of education, and there is little doubt of its effectiveness. Can social behaviour be taught this way? Dale Carnegie's book *How to make Friends and Influence People* (1936) has had very large sales, so there is clearly a demand for this kind of reading. An organisation called A. Thomas & Co. in Preston, England, sells various self-improvement books by mail-order; memory is the most popular, but there are also books on topics like *How to Cultivate Confidence and Promote Personality*. The Psychology Publishing Company in Marple, Cheshire, offer correspondence courses, including one on Conversation Studies, though again memory is most popular. The Conversation course gives advice on how to handle various kinds of conversation, with extracts from imaginary good and bad conversations.

The books and courses mentioned above are largely based on enlightened common sense, and make no use of research on social behaviour. There is no evidence about their effects on behaviour (cf. Barr, 1967).

It is possible to design more ingenious kinds of verbal material. An example is Stolurow's (1965) Culture Assimilator which is a programmed text to teach behaviour in another culture. The Arab Culture Assimilator consists of 55 problem episodes based on critical incidents, dealing mainly with the role of women, the importance of religion in the Middle East, and interaction skills. The trainee assesses the causes of misperception or conflict for each problem, and is then told of the significance of his choice in terms of cultural concepts. The training takes three hours. A follow-up study of 27 American ROTC members showed that this course had slightly more effect than a similar course on Middle East geography on skills of handling groups of Arabs, but the effects were mainly non-significant. However, this text did not include information about the elements of interaction – which are strikingly different in Arab culture (p. 87). Foa (1967) suggests that one of the most important areas of training for cross-cultural purposes is the social structure, i.e. relations between roles, in the second culture. He points out that a lot of cross-cultural misunderstanding is due to there being different relations in the status hierarchy, between the sexes, or between family members, in two cultures.

Programmed learning has been extensively developed for other kinds of instruction (Lumsdaine, 1963), but little use has been made of it for teaching social skills. It has been used for sales staff, but is thought to be more effective in teaching the knowledge and clerical procedures involved than in teaching selling skills (Retail Trades Training Council, 1966).

Since social behaviour is partly mediated by learnt, cognitive components, there is *a priori* a case for instruction of a cognitive kind either via lectures or reading. It has yet to be shown however that such instruction is effective in improving social behaviour. The main weaknesses, *a priori*, are that (1) it is difficult to teach people about non-verbal behaviour by verbal methods alone; (2) in addition it is not possible to learn a skill without practice at the skill itself.

Instructional films

Learning by experience and trial and error is usually speeded up by imitating successful performers. Training courses for interviewing, psychotherapy and other professional social skills often include demonstrations by the trainer. The trainees may observe through a one-way vision screen, so as not to affect the encounter, as for example with psychotherapy. In this section we shall be concerned with the rather more carefully prepared demonstrations, with accompanying comment-ary, that are possible with films, video-tapes and film-strips.

A certain amount of use is made of films and film-strips in training salesmen, supervisors and psychotherapists. These films have not how-ever been prepared with such sophistication and ingenuity as the films used in other kinds of education, and no research has been carried out on their effectiveness. We shall therefore turn to studies of films in other areas, and consider whether films could be used more widely in teaching social skills. Films and TV have been extensively studied as methods of teaching school subjects: Schramm (1962) reviewed 393 comparisons with convential teaching methods, and found that 21% of studies favoured TV, 65% showed no difference and 14% favoured conventional methods. Films have also been used to teach motor skills such as industrial assembly tasks, and follow-up studies suggest that this can be done successfully. Research has also provided valuable in-formation in the conditions under which films are most effective in teaching motor skills, and it is probable that the findings would apply to the training of social skills.

The research is reviewed by Lumsdaine (1963) and Zinser (1966). Some of the main results are as follows: (1) There is more learning if the learner has to make an active response after limited amounts of material have been presented – e.g. Maccoby and Sheffield (1957) with an assembly task. 'Mental practice', i.e. performing the skill in imagina-tion, is also useful (Richardson, 1967). (2) It is better if the film is taken from the learner's point of view, i.e. over the demonstrator's shoulder – as found by Roshal (1949) in a study of learning to tie knots. (3) It is better if various film techniques are used when appropriate, such as the use of slow motion, animation, and rapid sequences of stills showing successive steps; on the other hand music and humorous cartoons and comments have been found to have detrimental effects. (4) The verbal commentary is important; there should not be too much or too little of it; among other things it can draw attention to perceptual cues. (5) There should be discussion or lectures before or after the film.

Research on imitation is also relevant in suggesting the conditions under which films would be most effective. The model should therefore be prestigeful, but somewhat similar to the trainee, the model seen to be rewarded for his performance, and observers should anticipate that they will be rewarded for successful performances.

The learning process involved in watching films is partly imitation – though imitation is normally concerned with the development of the *motivation* to do something, not the ability – anyone can cross the road or wear a red tie, but do they do it? More important is the perceptual study of another's responses combined with verbal commentary, which produces cognitive learning about the task, which can later be converted into performance.

Films could make a very useful contribution to social skill training, and the full potentialities have not yet been used. They could act as a prelude to role-playing. They could be valuable in demonstrating unfamiliar techniques, such as psychotherapy. They could be constructed to demonstrate conveniently the main personalities and problem situations encountered in a skill, and show the right and wrong ways of dealing with them. They could display some of the main processes of social interaction.

Conclusion. Educational methods of teaching social skill have not been fully tried since the necessary materials have not been available. There are some books, and it is hoped that there will soon be films suitable for this purpose.

BEHAVIOUR THERAPY

Behaviour therapy includes a number of methods of treating mental patients which are based on learning theory. They differ from other kinds of psychotherapy in emphasising simple learning processes rather than verbal labelling and insight. Early methods of behaviour therapy were found to be effective in the treatment of relatively isolated symptoms, such as enuresis, tics and phobias. It has recently been found possible to treat more pervasive disturbances, both neurotic and psychotic (Eysenck and Rachman, 1965). We shall be particularly interested in the treatment of patients with interpersonal difficulties by behaviour therapy.

There are a number of special problems about the follow-up of any techniques of therapy. (1) Patients recover spontaneously, at the rate of about 70% in two years in the case of neurotics (Eysenck, 1952), so that it is important to have a control group. (2) Patients improve when treated with a placebo if they believe that they are being treated (Frank, 1961), so that it is necessary to have a control group who think that they are being attended to. (3) The effects of treatment may be only temporary, so that the follow-up should take place after an interval of, perhaps, a year. (4) There are problems about what constitutes a relevant criterion of the patient's state of health; in the studies in which we are interested, observed performance in social situations, questionnaire measures of anxiety or social anxiety, and estimates of improvement by the therapist have been the main criteria.

We shall discuss four varieties of behaviour therapy which have been used to improve social behaviour.

Desensitisation by relaxation. This method is used for patients with phobias, or who are made anxious by certain situations, such as death, illness and various kinds of social situation. The therapist discusses with the patient the things that upset him most, and they work out 'gradients' of related situations from the least to the most disturbing, for example:

1. Being at a burial
2. Being at a house of mourning
3. The word 'death'
4. Seeing a funeral procession. (The nearer, the more disturbing)
5. The sight of a dead animal, e.g. cat
6. Driving past a cemetery. (The nearer, the more disturbing)
   (from Wolpe, 1961)

The patient is then taught how to relax his whole body, taking each group of muscles in turn. He is now asked to imagine the various scenes in the hierarchy in turn, working upwards from the bottom. After each item the therapist says, 'Stop imagining the scene, and relax.' The patient is placed in a comfortable chair and is often put into a state of light hypnosis. At each session each scene is presented 3–8 times, and imagined for about 5 seconds, so that up to 50 presentations may be given in a session, and up to four separate hierarchies run through.

Carefully controlled studies have shown that this procedure is effective. Lang and Lazowik (1963) found that 13 subjects who were afraid of snakes improved more than a control group did, after five 45-minute sessions; a six-month follow-up period was used. Paul (1966) carried out a study of the treatment of anxiety over speaking in public. This study is of considerable interest, both because the condition treated was primarily a social one, and because comparisons were made with the effects of psychotherapy, placebo treatment and other controls. The desensitisation treatment had the greatest effect, on various measures of anxiety, as shown in Fig. 10.4. The relaxation treatment consisted of five sessions of one hour, during which subjects were presented an

8–20-item hierarchy (varying between individuals). The above studies did not use patients. Gelder, Marks and Wolff (1967) carried out a carefully controlled study of the response of patients with phobias to various forms of treatment. Desensitisation was somewhat more effective than psychotherapy or group therapy both on the phobias and on social adjustment, and it worked faster.

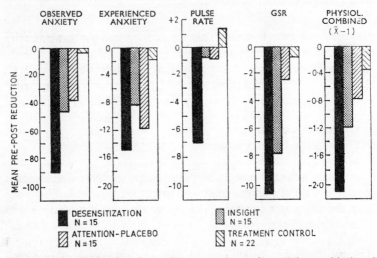

Figure 10.4. Reduction in audience anxiety after different kinds of therapy (from Paul 1966)

Reciprocal inhibition using assertion. Salter (1950) first practised the technique of getting patients to overcome their social anxiety and fear of people by adopting assertive behaviour in real-life situations; the theory is that assertion (which is thought to be related to anger) involves parasympathetic autonomic arousal, which inhibits the sympathetic arousal corresponding to anxiety. Salter recommends six techniques for these patients – expressing emotions clearly in words, and by facial expression; disagreeing with people; using the word 'I' as much as possible; accepting praise rather than disowning it; improvising and acting spontaneously. Wolpe (1958) has developed this method to deal with a variety of social difficulties, such as not being able to express affection or aggression, and being over-dependent with members of the opposite sex. During therapy sessions advice is given on becoming more assertive in particular situations which the patient will be meeting. There are no controlled studies of the effects of assertion treatment, but some conclusions can be drawn from 88 cases reported by Wolpe (op. cit.). Fifty-seven of these were treated by assertion *and* desensitisation, and 78% of them were reported as cured or much improved.

Wolpe (op. cit.) recommends the use of Stephen Potter's techniques in this connection, in that patients are able to control others in indirect ways. It may be suggested further that patients would benefit from training in the necessary social skills, for example by role-playing. The author has found that young women sometimes do not have these skills – they don't know how to interrupt and thus control another's amount of speech, and don't know how to direct another's behaviour in the warm and dominant style (p. 300 f).

Taken together, desensitisation and assertion treatment appear to be effective in improving neurotic disturbance when interpersonal difficulties are the main symptoms. In the Wolpe series of 88 cases, for 61 of them 'interpersonal anxiety' was the main symptom or one of them, and 92% were reported 'cured' or 'much improved' as against 70% for the whole group. Lazarus (1963) reports the treatment of 126 cases of severe and pervasive neurosis; 47 of them were diagnosed as having 'interpersonal problems' and 81% of these improved, the highest success rate among all the categories of problems treated. These two studies did not employ control groups, but suggest that interpersonal neuroses are somewhat more responsive to behaviour therapy than are other kinds of neurosis. It is interesting to note what these interpersonal difficulties consist of. Wolpe (1961) reports the topics of the main hierarchies of 39 patients. Social anxieties were by far the most common and included (a) criticism, disapproval, being devalued, 12; (b) being watched at work, 7; (c) rejection, 4; (d) being the centre of attention, 4; (e) authority figures, 2.

Aversion therapy has been used with some success for alcoholism, drug-addiction and fetishism. The application of greatest interest to us is homosexuality. Feldman and MacCulloch (1965) have reported success in weakening the sexual attachment of male homosexuals to men. They show slides of athletic men to patients, who receive a severe electric shock unless they switch the slide off immediately. They advise some of their patients to take lessons in one relevant social skill – dancing; Feldman has suggested that training in the skills of interacting with women would also be useful. Many male homosexuals are rather frightened of women, so some desensitisation and assertion treatment might be useful too.

Operant conditioning has been used mainly with psychotic patients, for whom verbal methods are often impossible. Lindsley (1956) first applied operant conditioning to schizophrenics : patients were immediately rewarded with sweets, money or cigarettes for carrying out the desired behaviour. Isaacs, Thomas and Goldiamond (1960) used a 'shaping' technique whereby mute schizophrenics were taught to say 'Gum, please' in order to receive chewing gum. Ayllon and Haughton (1962) managed to eliminate eating difficulties in psychotic patients by simply locking the dining-room if they failed to turn up, and withdrawing the social reinforcement normally given to patients with feeding problems. They then arranged an operant conditioning situation in which pairs of patients had to cooperate to press two buttons in order to be admitted to the dining-room. Lovaas *et al.* (1967) used reinforcement techniques of shaping to establish imitation in 11 psychotic children. Among other things they were taught to imitate social behaviour, such as playing games. O'Leary *et al.* (1967) used reward and punishment methods to stop two brothers of 3 and 6 from fighting; there was a considerable growth in helpful and cooperative behaviour which generalised to other social situations.

The learning processes taking place during behaviour therapy are maintained by most practitioners to be such elementary learning processes as instrumental and avoidance conditioning. The treatment of schizophrenics by reinforcement is clearly a case of this; it has been pointed out however that most kinds of behaviour therapy are similar to other kinds of psychotherapy in that they involve a close relationship with the therapist which provides reassurance, and conversation which is liable to convey understanding and insight.

Conclusion. (a) It is clear that a large proportion of neurotics are primarily troubled by interpersonal problems and anxieties, and that these people can be helped by desensitisation and assertion therapy. As yet little use has been made of the other ways of training social behaviour described in this chapter, and there is some evidence that patients with inter-personal difficulties can be helped by role-playing, sensitivity training and imitation methods. They can be taught to handle social situations generally as well as how to deal with people in authority, women, to make speeches, etc. As well as constructing gradients the therapist can draw up a list of situations which the patient finds difficult to handle. (b) Could behaviour therapy be made use of in other social skill training situations? Among those who come to be trained as interviewers, teachers, etc., there are a proportion who suffer from acute social anxiety. It is likely that teaching them the skills will reduce their anxiety, but this may not be enough, and some behaviour therapy would be useful.

PSYCHOTHERAPY

One of the common symptoms of neurosis is difficulty in getting on with people, so psychotherapy is partly concerned with modifying social behaviour. It is not at all clear what proportion of neurotic patients are primarily disturbed in this way: 70% of 88 cases treated by Wolpe (1958) were reported to be like this, but a more representative figure is perhaps the 21% of 345 who sought help because of interpersonal problems, in a survey by Gurin, Veroff and Field (1960) – though another 42% sought help with their marriages. It is important to note that a great deal of psychotherapy is concerned with relations between two or three people – husband and wife, parents and children. For this kind of problem there is as yet no alternative method of treatment. We shall not discuss the psychotherapy of the psychoses here, as there is no evidence that it is successful.

The methods of treatment used by therapists vary, but there are a number of common elements which are found in all varieties. (1) The therapist expresses a warm, accepting and uncritical attitude of interested concern towards the patient, and creates a strong interpersonal relationship; it is a kind of ideal friendship, in which the therapist participates emotionally, though it is restricted to the therapeutic hour. (2) The patient is encouraged to talk about his anxieties, conflicts and other bottled-up emotions; the cathartic expression of these feelings, and sharing them with another person who does not react critically, helps to relieve them, and enables the patient to think about painful problems. (3) The therapist tries to explore the patient's subjective world of feeling and thinking, tries to understand the patient's point of view, and to open up communication with him; this includes the use of non-verbal communication. (4) The therapist tries to bring about emotional or cognitive changes; he tries to give the patient insight into why he reacts as he does, and thus to change him. (5) The patient is encouraged to try out new ways of dealing with people and situations; he is asked to make positive efforts, to become committed, rather than indifferent and passive (Frank, 1961; Sundberg and Tyler, 1962; Schofield, 1964). Different therapists place different emphasis on these common elements, and they vary particularly in their handling of number (4), bringing about emotional or cognitive changes. Much psychotherapy is given in groups, and it is possible that group therapy is beneficial for patients with interpersonal problems; the procedure is described on p. 260 ff.

The above techniques can be applied to any kind of personal problem, including interpersonal ones. Some psychotherapists however maintain that interpersonal problems lie at the root of all or most neuroses, whether the symptoms are in the social sphere or not. These therapists focus attention on the patient's social behaviour and relationships. We shall give a brief account of the approaches of some of these therapists.

The first three are psychoanalysts who broke away from traditional Freudian thinking to emphasise the role of social relationships. Sullivan (1947) was probably the first to suggest that mental disorders are primarily disturbances of communication and interpersonal relations. In his psychotherapy he stressed sensitivity to what the patient is trying to communicate verbally or non-verbally, and tried to find out about the patient's relations with others and his social milieu. He worked mainly with schizophrenics and obsessionals. Sullivan's approach has been very influential in leading to research into the social behaviour of mental patients, which is reviewed on p. 336 ff (see Sundberg and Tyler, 1962).

Fairbairn (1952) was influenced by Melanie Klein, and maintained that motivation is primarily to establish various kinds of relationships between the self and others. Mental disorder is caused by early relations with the parents going wrong, with the result that 'bad objects' are internalised, and there is splitting of the ego, the patient becomes preoccupied with an inner world, and social relationships become distorted. He emphasised the transference relationship with the analyst, to whom the patient becomes attached, as a 'good object', so that bad objects can be abandoned (see Guntrip, 1961).

Berne (1961, 1966) put forward a revised Freudian model: instead of the Id, Ego and Super-ego, people are seen as playing Parent, Adult or Child roles. Relationships are analysed in these terms, for example one person may play a Child role to the other's Parent role. Neurotic social behaviour is analysed as a series of 'games', as described earlier (p. 348). Therapy, with individuals or groups, consists in making a 'transactional analysis' of the patient's relationships with others in terms of the roles and games involved. Most of Berne's patients appear to be middle-class, neurotic females, though he has also worked with psychotics. Each of these three psychoanalytic writers has put forward a theory of social behaviour and personality development, using his own terminology. They have made no use of systematic research on interpersonal behaviour, and their own formulations, while interesting, are extremely speculative.

Several American therapists have concentrated on bringing about cognitive changes. Ellis (1957) found that neurotics often hold certain mistaken ideas, some of them in the interpersonal sphere, for example 'it is necessary to be loved and approved by everyone', 'certain people are bad and should be punished', 'one should be dependent and rely on someone stronger', and 'one should get upset over others' problems'. In his method of rational psychotherapy, Ellis gets the patient to take action that will show him that these assumptions are wrong, shows the patient how they are causing his distress, and teaches him to re-think these assertions. A higher success rate is reported for 78 patients treated in this way than for others treated by psychoanalysis.

Rogers (1942) emphasised changes in the self, and his kind of therapy has been found to bring about greater self-acceptance, and reduced conflict between self and ego-ideal (Rogers and Dymond, 1954). This non-directive technique of therapy emphasises acceptance and reflection of the patient's feelings, and avoids interpretation and direction. It has the advantage that it is not very difficult to learn.

The cognitive approaches to therapy seem a little closer in touch with recent thinking and research in psychology than the psychoanalytic methods, and there is some evidence that they are more effective. They might be expected to correct disturbances of social behaviour which are due to failure in the cognitive sphere, rather than to peculiarities of motivation or lack of response skills.

Most therapists emphasise the establishment of a relationship with the patient, but they interpret it differently. Psychotics are out of touch with everyone, but it is possible to get into rapport if enough time patience and sympathy are used. Delinquents are out of contact with adults and efforts are made by young members of the staff of institutions to establish a relationship with them: when this is achieved it is found that the treatment is more successful (McCord and McCord, 1944). Perhaps similar processes are operating when racial prejudice is removed by the experience of living together in a youth-camp, or under similar conditions (Harding *et al.*, 1954).

There has been doubt over whether psychotherapy actually cures people since Eysenck's paper (1952a) showing that the rate of recovery for neurotics is about 70% in two years whether they are treated or not. Patients who are on waiting lists, and others who are untreated, recover 'spontaneously', perhaps because they discuss their problems with friends, or find some solution to them. Patients who are given 'placebo' treatment also recover, because they believe that the medicine will cure them: the element of faith is very important in therapy. The study by

Paul (1966), reported earlier, showed that psychotherapy produced improvement in social behaviour, as well as in subjective reports, compared with untreated and placebo groups – though behaviour therapy did even better. A number of recent studies with control groups have demonstrated that psychotherapy can be effective (Dittman, 1966), though clearly there are a proportion of unsuccessful cases. Some therapists are more successful than others, and this appears to be more a matter of social skills, rather than holding a particular theory. Fiedler (1953) found that the most effective therapists were those who were warm, permissive, interested in and liked the patient, and able to empathise with him. They should also be able to build up the patient's confidence in their therapeutic powers (Frank, 1961). Some patients do better than others – those who are middle-class, intelligent, anxious, have some motivation to recover, are submissive, and only moderately maladjusted (Frank, op. cit.).

Probably a number of forms of learning, and social influence are involved in psychotherapy – control of behaviour through labelling and verbalisation, imitation and persuasion, and anxiety-reduction through discussion and acceptance, for example.

Conclusions. The evidence that psychotherapy can improve social behaviour is not very impressive, and the evidence suggests that behaviour therapy can probably deal better with neurotic difficulties in this sphere. On the other hand behaviour therapy requires considerable training and expertise, and there are not enough practitioners to deal with the very large numbers of people who need help. Many psychotherapists are very highly trained and skilled too, but there is evidence that relatively untrained people can be successful as psychotherapists (Matarazzo, 1965); as we have seen it is the social skill rather than the particular kind of therapy that counts. Probably unskilled people would do better with the non-directive and cognitive approaches, which requires little understanding of psychopathology. Schofield (1964) suggests that psychotherapy should be much more widely practised by clergy, teachers and friends, since almost everyone is in need of help at some time. It is interesting to see that Gurin, Veroff and Field (1960) found that when the people in their sample were in need of help with emotional problems 42% went to clergymen, 29% to a doctor and only 18% to a psychiatrist or psychologist. A lot of psychotherapy is directed towards interpersonal problems in families, and as yet there is no other means of dealing with them.

CONCLUSIONS

We have reviewed the main techniques that have been used for improving social skills. Some have been used in particular settings but not made use of in others. In suggesting the most useful methods for particular purposes we should bear in mind both the evidence from follow-up studies, and in addition the convenience, cost and acceptability of these techniques.

(1) *Professional social skills*, such as interviewing, teaching, selling and supervision, are most often learnt on the job, which we have seen is not a very reliable method unless coaching and feedback are available. The single most effective method, it may be suggested, is role-playing, with the elaborations described above. It can be supplemented by lectures and discussions and instructional film on the skill in question where available. Sensitivity training, as described above, is useful, but T-groups are too dangerous. A trainer is needed, who is reasonably experienced and competent at the skill in question himself, and who is familiar with the use of these training methods.

(2) *Education*. Training in social skills has long been a goal of education, and it was hoped that it would be attained by the prefect system, team-games, and other group activities. Recently there has been a growth of interest in the development of more specific training. Methods of classroom work, making use of suitable reading materials and exercises have been described. These could be supplemented by the use of role-playing of the problems discussed, and the use of films as these become available. Some training will be needed for the teachers involved, and there is a need for suitable reading material.

(3) *Mental health*. A great deal is already being done for people with interpersonal difficulties by friends, family, doctors and clergy. This may consist of 'psychotherapy' of a non-technical kind, akin to the rational and non-directive approaches, and is probably quite successful. At this non-professional level it would also be perfectly feasible to do role-playing of the situations which the 'patient' finds difficult. Among more seriously disturbed people, neurotic social anxiety responds best to desensitisation therapy. Recent research by the author and his colleagues suggests that neurotic patients with interpersonal difficulties can be cured by social skill training (p. 353).

XI

Wider Implications

A REVISED MODEL OF MAN

Psychology has put forward some very strange models of what man is like. 'Thus psychoanalytic theories seem to suggest that man is basically a battlefield. He is in a dark cellar in which a well-bred spinster lady and a sex-crazed monkey are forever engaged in mortal combat, the struggle being refereed by a rather nervous bank clerk' (Bannister, 1966). Nevertheless the Freudian model includes some of the essential biological and cultural ingredients – it postulates instinctive needs which orient the individual towards others, and which are modified by family experiences. Learning theorists have produced a very different model in which man appears to be a kind of telephone headquarters operated by a rather low-grade computer; which has to be fed and watered. Cognitive theorists have tried to reinstate the role of conscious, rational processes, and suppose that the main human activity is pigeon-holing events, forming hypotheses and trying to understand the outside world.

The Freudian model gives an account of certain kinds of social relationships in the family, but does not deal with other kinds of interaction. Learning and cognitive theories say nothing about social behaviour. The latter has as a result remained somewhat mysterious, a fitting domain for theologians, moralists and novelists (not to mention the authors of pop songs and *Mad* magazine). These writers have indeed recognised that relations with others are the most important part of human life, and that most of the essential human characteristics cannot be manifested by a person in isolation. They have rightly been unconvinced of the relevance to human affairs of experiments with people (or rats) studied while they perform laboratory tasks in isolation.

What research on social interaction has done is to show how the model of man needs to be revised to take account of his social nature. We have seen that for the survival of the group, the satisfaction of biological needs and the continuation of the species, cooperation in groups is necessary in animals and men; that there are innate tendencies to respond to others, which in man in particular require experiences in the family for their completion; that there is a system of non-verbal signals for communicating interpersonal intentions and attitudes; that in man there is a second signalling system of language; that interaction is conducted by the two channels of vision and hearing, with the verbal and the non-verbal closely coordinated; and that patterns of communication and interaction are accumulated in each culture as part of the shared solution to the human situation. There is probably one more essential component: it seems likely that there is an innate moral sense, evolved to keep in-group aggression under control; we have seen that sympathy appears in young children, and that taking account of the point of view of the other is an essential ingredient in interaction. Concern with the views of another takes a second important form: the self-image is largely constructed out of the reactions of others, and leads to self-presentation behaviour to elicit appropriate reactions in later social situations. Social behaviour is produced as a stream of closely integrated responses, subject to continuous correction as a result of feedback, controlled by more or less conscious plans, and subject to partly verbalised rules derived from the culture. It is not supposed that this picture is complete. The full role of cognitive processes in social behaviour has yet to be delineated. For example there is presumably creativity in social behaviour, as in other kinds of behaviour, but nothing as yet is known about it.

This basic equipment, partly innate, partly acquired from the culture, leads to the formation of interpersonal bonds, small social groups and social structures. Relationships between pairs of people are an essential part of human life; they are built up through a gradual process of trial and error, resulting in a pattern of interaction which is synchronised and satisfying to both. People interact in small social groups, in the family, at work and with friends. Here the interaction patterns are more complex, and groups evolve a stable system with norms and differentiation of roles. In larger groups, the roles become formalised and the whole pattern of interaction follows a regular pattern, which is learnt by new members; this is called a social structure.

PROBLEMS CREATED BY THE NEW KNOWLEDGE

It is sometimes said that the new knowledge about, for example, the role of bodily posture and head-nods, will have the effect of making the behaviour of those who learn about it less natural and spontaneous. We observed earlier that some areas of behaviour are more under conscious control than others. For example the contents of speech are well controlled, the emotional tone of speech less so; facial expression is fairly well controlled, while posture, eye-movements and head-nods are not – for most people apart from actors and students of social interaction. It does seem very likely that more of the elements of interaction will now be brought under control.

There are some positive advantages to be gained. People will be able to indicate more clearly to one another what their feelings and attitudes to each other are. The non-human primates communicate clearly to one another, but human beings often fail to do so, as the result of cultural restraints on the expression of emotion, or other social learning experiences leading to modification of the natural use of non-verbal communication. A second advantage is that the perception of the emotions and attitudes of others becomes more accurate if the cues are known, as experiments in training for sensitivity have shown. It is not very clear why the non-verbal code should need to be learnt, as it is innately present in primates; possibly our focusing of attention on the verbal content of interaction has led to the non-verbal code falling partly into disuse.

It is objected that people will become self-conscious, awkward and anxious in their social behaviour. 'I shall never be able to look you in the eye again,' several people have said to the author. As we have seen, much social behaviour has the characteristics of a motor skill. When a person learns a new skill, such as learning the gears on a strange car, he goes through a period when the behaviour is awkward, requires full conscious attention and is accompanied by actual or silent speech. This phase rapidly comes to an end as the skill is learnt and becomes habitual, and is done 'without thinking'. Social behaviour is different from most other motor skills, in that part of what is learnt is simply the re-establishment of habits which had been lost by being overlaid by other learning.

It is possible that when people become trained to interact better their behaviour may become more contrived and insincere, become more like acting. This is a complex and controversial issue: while authenticity and sincerity are attractive, it may also be argued that civilisation depends on the restraint of many interpersonal feelings – aggressive, sexual and disapproving in particular. The most effective kind of behaviour does not necessarily consist of the direct outward expression of inner feelings, but of more skilful and complex strategies of behaviour. There are cultural rules governing this aspect of behaviour, some of which become moral principles.

If people become more knowledgeable about the non-verbal code, these signals may come to acquire a much more definite significance: raising the head 10° will be seen as an assertion of status, a shift in orientation as an expression of intimacy, and so on. If this happened the non-verbal code could lose its valuable property of vagueness whereby interactors are not committed to a particular relationship, and shifts in attitude can be made quite easily. There is no research to show whether this loss of vagueness is likely to happen, or how interaction would be affected by this.

It has been suggested that the discovery of better ways of performing in social situations creates a danger that people may be 'manipulated' by practitioners of the new skills. All scientific discoveries can be used for good or ill, and findings in the field of social interaction are no exception. Findings about mass persuasion could similarly be used to persuade people to love one another, to kill one another, or to become more resistant to mass persuasion. It is often assumed that the skilled performer will spend his time outwitting other people and controlling situations to his own disadvantage. Let us consider three classes of situations, involving different degrees of conflict of interests. (1) A is a professional social skill performer such as a teacher or psychotherapist. Here he is primarily concerned to attain certain goals for B, and clearly the more skilled A is the better. A could be said to be engaged in 'manipulation', but this is true whether he has been trained or not. (2) In many situations there is a partial conflict of interests, for example where A is trying to sell B something. There is also considerable overlap of interests. A should aim to discover B's needs and meet them; if A sells B things he doesn't really want, B may return them and will be likely to shop elsewhere in future. Unless A pays sufficient attention to B's needs, B will not continue the relationship. In everyday situations, at home, at work, and with friends, if one person is highly skilled, it is usually to the advantage of all concerned, since he can ease the whole process of interaction, to the mutual benefit of all present. Suppose A is interviewing B for a job; A wants to find out if B is the right person for the job, and B wants to find out if the job will suit him, so again there is a considerable alignment of interests, and the better each is at interacting the better. (3) In the last example there may also be some conflict of interests – if B could do the job and would like to have it, but where there are other, stronger candidates. If B is a skilled interviewee he could create a highly favourable impression on A and get the job; however if he indulges in bogus self-presentation he will be in danger of being caught out and embarrassed during the interview, and of not being able to do the job when he has got it. If A is a highly skilled interviewer, he will be able to see through B's presentation, and give the job to one of the other candidates. There is already a state of escalation about this kind of situation. All that can be said is that it is in everyone's interest to be as socially competent as possible. The same is of course true of other capacities: it is accepted that a person who can think faster and speak fluently has an advantage in many situations.

CONTRIBUTION TO SOCIAL PROBLEMS

Of any new scientific finding, the question is always asked, 'What use is it?' Like most research, work on social interaction has been carried out mainly for scientific motives – because investigators were fascinated by the phenomena and wanted to understand them and know more about them. Exactly how the results may be applied is usually not known while the research is being done. Although quite a lot of this research was done in the setting of psychotherapy, the pay-off has been much greater in certain other areas, such as industrial psychology, and a start has been made at applying it in a number of other areas.

(1) *Industrial problems.* There are three types of industrial problem to which interaction research is relevant – low job satisfaction (together with high absenteeism and labour turnover), low output, and conflict between groups. The most important contribution has been the discovery of the styles of supervision and management which are most effective in different situations – and this can help with all three problems (p. 299 ff). We also know the most effective methods for training people in social skills, once it is known what should be taught. Very little attention has been paid hitherto to training people in the social skills required for their work. Research has also provided some information about the design of social groups and social structures so that people will interact in them happily, effectively and without coming into conflict with one another (p. 307 f). A great deal remains to be discovered about the design of organisations, partly because the necessary research is very difficult to do.

We now turn to three types of social problems where the application of research in social interaction is just beginning, but where the results could be very important – mental health, delinquency and conflict between different races and classes.

(2) *Mental disorder* affects a very large proportion of the population – 1% are psychotic and about 8% neurotic – causing those affected to be

unhappy, a nuisance to others and wholly or partly incapacitated. Almost nothing has been done in the area of prevention, and treatment for the neuroses (by psychotherapy) is extremely slow and expensive, while treatment for the psychoses (mainly by drugs) has little permanent effect. Interaction research may be able to help in a number of ways. Mental disorders can be looked at, in part at least, as disturbances of interpersonal behaviour. Although there is a strong genetic and bio-chemical basis for schizophrenia, for example, it is often precipitated by social events, and the main symptoms are in the sphere of interaction. A contribution could be made to prevention by applying what has been discovered about the child-rearing styles of parents of patients (Chapter VIII). It is not known whether schizophrenia and the other psychoses are actually caused, in part, in this way, or whether the disturbed interaction in the family is a consequence; there is little doubt however that parental behaviour contributes to neurosis. We presented evidence to show that mental patients are poor interactors, and suggested that this may be a factor in some disorders. More general training in social skills, at school for example, could contribute to the prevention of mental disorder. On the treatment side, research is now in progress to find out if training in social skills can help patients whose main problems appear to be in this area.

(3) *Crime and delinquency*. All over the world the crime rate has been rising since 1945, especially in large cities, among young working-class males. In some places the situation is virtually out of control, and in many others it will become so if the increase continues at its present rate (Argyle, 1964b). The *rate* of increase in Britain has been checked, mainly through increased police efficiency, but the crime-rate continues to increase. Interaction research suggests steps that could be taken both for prevention and treatment. Parents of delinquents handle their children quite differently from other parents – they are less affectionate, use discipline that is too feeble or too harsh, and make little use of persuasion and explanation. Instruction or training for parents in the skills of child-rearing would be valuable here. Delinquency usually breaks out at adolescence, during the critical and difficult period of identity-formation and becoming independent of parents. Much research remains to be done to find out how parents, teachers and social workers should handle adolescents. Delinquency and crime also depend on the social structure of society, in at least two ways. Firstly there is most crime among the underprivileged members of highly stratified societies. Secondly delinquency has probably increased as a result of

the growth of teenage society, whose members are no longer responsive to adult influence. These are both matters of the social structure of society, and the province of sociology. However, social structure consists of regular patterns of interaction, and it would be possible to change these without any changes in the material conditions of those involved. Educating young people in the social skills needed to deal with those of other ages or classes might be very beneficial. Teenage society has appeared in Britain in the relatively short period since 1945. The author has argued elsewhere (1964b) that such social changes could be brought under the control of society in much the same way that economic changes have been, though rather different controls would be needed.

(4) *Racial, class and international conflicts.* It is generally agreed that these are the most important social problems of our time. They are partly due to inequalities of opportunity, wealth and all that goes with it, but this is not the whole story. There is no immediate prospect of all men being equally affluent (and within a given community some differentials may be a necessary part of the system in order to create incentives and leadership). It is still possible for patterns of interaction to be established so that people of unequal affluence (and status) can interact and cooperate happily. Feudalism is an example of such a system, and the interaction patterns of the American class system are another; neither is being commended here, they are simply given as examples of interaction patterns that bridge social differences. In fact the worst racial conflicts are between individuals of very similar affluence. Two factors have emerged from interaction research which may help to resolve these conflicts. Firstly there is evidence that styles of interaction in different cultural groups are sometimes different so that intercultural contacts are found difficult and confusing. Recent developments in language teaching are relevant here: pupils are taught not only the words, but the pattern of non-verbal communication that accompanies them (p. 86). Secondly, it is necessary to take the role of the other in order to interact effectively with him, and this is more difficult if he comes from another culture, and sees things differently. Training for interaction in other cultures has included anthropological materials about for example the role of religion, the position of women and the social structure (p. 418). Both of these kinds of instruction could be included in the school curriculum, though actual experience of interaction with members of the other cultural group is also needed (Harding *et al.* 1954).

We have suggested two main kinds of application of social interaction research – the discovery and training of social skills, and the discovery and implementation of kinds of group and social structure. It is interesting to reflect how far these applications might go. Compare the performance of a typical interviewer and a typical car-driver, both of whom are using motor skills. The driver has his car under finger-tip control. He can steer the car at high speed, missing other cars and the side of the road by inches, and responds to the unexpected at lightning speed. Compared to this the interviewer is a hopeless failure: he may not be able to control the amount of talk of the candidate, who may talk far too much or too little; he has great difficulty in controlling the candidate's emotional state, and often cannot make him less nervous; he has difficulty extracting the information he needs, and may be completely baffled if the candidate behaves in an unexpected way. It is possible to train an interviewer so that he is more like the driver (p. 403 f), but training is not pursued to the point where an interviewer is as skilled as a driver. If we consider totally new kinds of social skill and new designs for social organisation, the possibilities are unlimited. Engineering and technology provide a possible analogy: the enormous advances brought about by new ways of organising physical objects may be equalled by the consequences of new ways of organising people.

SOCIAL INTERACTION IN EVERYDAY LIFE

We have discussed the impact and potential impact of interaction research on work situations and various social problems. Perhaps the greatest impact of all however may be on behaviour in everyday life. As we said elsewhere

> relations with others can be the source of the deepest satisfaction and of the blackest misery. .... Many people are lonely and unhappy, some are mentally ill because they are unable to sustain social relationships with others. Many everyday encounters are unpleasant, embarrassing or fruitless, because of inept social behaviour. .... Many of those difficulties and frustrations could be eliminated by a wider understanding, and better training in the skills of social interaction (Argyle, 1967, p. 11).

Enough is known already to make people more effective in a number of ways, to make them more popular, more influential, or whatever it is they want to be. We suggested that the most useful place for the relevant training to take place is at school (p. 416 f). A great deal of emphasis is placed in education on understanding and dealing with the physical world, but very little is done about understanding and dealing with people. A lot of educational effort is put into verbal skills, but none at all into non-verbal skills. Sometimes people emerge from such an education with highly developed intellectual skills, but unable to play any useful part in the world because of their inability to cope with people and social situations.

Research on interaction can certainly help people to be better at their jobs and to make friends and influence people. It may also show people how to understand each other and how to help those who need it. Being 'rewarding' to others is an essential part of life, and leads to the popularity of the rewarder (p. 210). Being 'helpful' to another goes rather further, and may include helping them in a therapeutic way. We have argued that emotional distress is a normal part of life, that there are not enough psychiatrists to deal with it, and that the necessary 'therapy' can be given by laymen, if they have the necessary, rather simple social skills (p. 428). This is one example of the way in which greater knowledge of and education in social interaction may be able to raise the whole level of everyday social behaviour.

References

ACKERSON, L. (1942) *Children's Behavior Problems*. Univ. of Chicago Press.

ACTON SOCIETY TRUST (1953) *Size and Morale*. London: Acton Society Trust.

ADAMS, B. N. (1967) 'Interaction theory and the social network', *Sociometry*, **30**, 64–78.

ADORNO, T. W., FRENKEL-BRUNSWIK, E., LEVINSON, D. J., and SANFORD, R. N. (1950), *The Authoritarian Personality*. New York: Harper.

ALLEN, V. L. (1965) 'Situational factors in conformity', *Advances in Experimental Social Psychology*, **2**, 133–176.

ALLPORT, F. H. (1934) 'The J-curve hypothesis of conforming behavior', *J. Soc. Psychol.*, **5**, 141–183.

ALLPORT, G. W. (1961) *Pattern and Growth in Personality*. New York: Holt, Rinehart and Winston.

ALLPORT, G. W., and VERNON, P. E. (1932) *Studies in Expressive Movement*. New York: Macmillan.

ALTMAN, I., and HAYTHORN, W. (1967) 'The ecology of isolated groups', *Beh. Sci.*, **12**, 169–182.

AMBROSE, J. A. (1961) 'The development of the smiling response in early infancy', *in* B. M. Foss (ed.) *Determinants of Infant Behaviour*. London: Methuen, pp. 179–195.

AMBROSE, J. A. (1963) 'The concept of a critical period for the development of social responsiveness', *in* B. M. Foss (ed.) *Determinants of Infant Behaviour*, **2**. London: Methuen, pp. 201–225.

ANDERSON, H. H. (1939) 'Domination and social integration in the behaviour of kindergarten children and teachers', *Genet. Psychol. Monogr.*, **21**, 287–385.

ANDERSON, H. H., and ANDERSON, G. L. (1954) 'Social development', *in* L. Carmichael (ed.) *Manual of Child Psychology*. New York: Wiley.

ANDERSON, H. H., and ANDERSON, G. L. (1962) 'Social values of teachers in Rio de Janeiro, Mexico City, and Los Angeles County, California: a comparative study of teachers and children', *J. soc. Psychol.*, **58**, 207–226.

ANDERSON, N. H. (1965) 'Primacy effects in personality impression formation using a specialised order effect paradigm', *J. pers. soc. Psychol.*, **2**, 1–9.

APPELL, G., and DAVID, M. (1965) 'A study of mother–child interaction at thirteen months', *in* B. M. Foss (ed.) *Determinants of Infant Behaviour*, 3. London: Methuen, pp. 129–142.

ARDREY, R. (1967) *The Territorial Imperative*. London: Collins.

ARGYLE, M. (1953) 'The Relay Assembly Test Room in retrospect', *Occ. Psych.*, 27, 98–103.

ARGYLE, M. (1957a) *The Scientific Study of Social Behaviour*. London: Methuen.

ARGYLE, M. (1957b) 'Social pressures in public and private situations', *J. abnorm. soc. Psychol.*, 54, 172–175.

ARGYLE, M. (1964a) 'Introjection: a form of social learning', *Brit. J. Psychol.*, 55, 391–402.

ARGYLE, M. (1964b) *Psychology and Social Problems*. London: Methuen.

ARGYLE, M. (1964c) 'Morale', *in* J. Gould and W. L. Kolb (eds.) *A Dictionary of the Social Sciences*. London: Tavistock, pp. 443–445.

ARGYLE, M. (1967) *The Psychology of Interpersonal Behaviour*. Harmondsworth: Penguin Books.

ARGYLE, M., and DEAN, J. (1965) 'Eye-contact, distance and affiliation', *Sociometry*, 28, 289–304.

ARGYLE, M., GARDNER, G., and CIOFFI, F. (1958) 'Supervisory methods related to productivity, absenteeism and labour turnover', *Hum. Relat.*, 11, 23–45.

ARGYLE, M., and KENDON, A. (1967) 'The experimental analysis of social performance', *Advances in Experimental Social Psychology*, 3, 55–98.

ARGYLE, M., LALLJEE, M., and COOK, M. (1968) 'The effects of visibility on interaction in a dyad', *Hum. Relat.*, 21, 3–17.

ARGYLE, M., LALLJEE, M. G., and LYDALL, M. (1968) 'Selling as a social skill' (roneoed).

ARGYLE, M., SALTER, V., NICHOLSON, H., WILLIAMS, M., and BURGESS, P. (1970) 'The communication of inferior and superior attitudes by verbal and non-verbal signals', *Brit. J. soc. clin. Psychol.*, 9, 222–231.

ARGYLE, M., SMITH, T., and KIRTON, M. J. (1962) *Training Managers*. London: Acton Society Trust.

ARGYLE, M., and WILLIAMS, M. (1969) 'Observer or observed? A reversible perspective in person perception' *Sociometry*, 32, 396–492.

ARGYRIS, C. (1957) *Personality and Organization*. New York: Harper.

ARGYRIS, C. (1962) *Interpersonal Competence and Organisational Effectiveness*. London: Tavistock.

ARIETI, S. (1959) 'Manic-depressive psychosis', *in* Arieti, S. (ed.) *American Handbook of Psychiatry*, 1, 419–454. New York: Basic Books.

ARMISTEAD, N. (1968) 'A test of social skills' (roneoed). Oxford Institute of Experimental Psychology.

ARONSON, A., and CARLSMITH, J. M. (1968) 'Experimentation in social psychology', Chap. 9 in G. Lindzey and E. Aronson (eds) *The Handbook of Social Psychology*. Reading, Mass.: Addison-Wesley.

ARONSON, E., and LINDER, D. (1965) 'Gain and loss of esteem as determinants of interpersonal attractiveness', *J. exp. soc. Psychol.*, **1**, 150–172.

ASCH, S. E. (1946) 'Forming impressions of personality', *J. abnorm. soc. Psychol.*, **41**, 258–290.

ASCH, S. E. (1952) *Social Psychology*. New York: Prentice Hall.

ATKINSON, J. W. (1958) (ed.) *Motives in Fantasy, Action and Society*. New York: Van Nostrand.

AYLLON, T. and HAUGHTON, E. (1962) 'Control of the behavior of schizophrenics by food', *J. exp. anal. Behav.*, **5**, 343–352.

AYLLON, T., and MICHAEL, J. (1959) 'The psychiatric nurse as behavioral engineer', *J. exp. anal. Behav.*, **2**, 323–334.

AZRIN, N. H., HOLZ, W., ULRICH, R., and GOLDIAMOND, I. (1961) 'The control of the content of conversation through reinforcement', *J. exp. anal. Behav.*, **4**, 25–30.

BACK, K. W. (1951) 'Influence through social communication', *J. abnorm. soc. Psychol.*, **46**, 9–23.

BACK, K. W. (1961) 'Power, influence and pattern of communication', *in* L. Petrullo and B. Bass (eds.) *Leadership and Interpersonal Behavior*. New York: Holt, Rinehart and Winston.

BALES, R. F. (1950) *Interaction Process Analysis*. Cambridge, Mass.: Addison-Wesley.

BALES, R. F. (1952) 'Some uniformities of behaviour in small social systems', *in* G. E. Swanson, T. M. Newcomb and E. L. Hartley (eds.) *Readings in Social Psychology* (2nd ed.). New York: Holt.

BALES, R. F. (1953) 'The equilibrium problem in small groups', *in* *Working Papers in the Theory of Action* by T. Parsons, R. F. Bales and E. A. Shils. Glencoe, Ill.: Free Press.

BALES, R. F., STRODTBECK, F., MILLS, T., and ROSEBOROUGH, M. E. (1951) 'Channels of communication in small groups', *Amer. sociol. Rev.*, **16**, 461–468.

BANDURA, A. (1962) 'Social learning through imitation', *in* M. R. Jones (ed.) *Nebraska Symposium on Motivation*. Lincoln: University of Nebraska Press.

BANDURA, A., ROSS, O., and ROSS, S. A. (1963) 'A comparative test of the status envy, social power, and secondary reinforcement theories of identification', *J. abnorm. soc. Psychol.*, **67**, 527–534.

BANNISTER, D. (1966) 'Psychology as an exercise in paradox', *Bull B.P.S.*, **19**, No. 63, 21–26.

BANNISTER, D., and MAIR, J. M. M. (1968). *The Evaluation of Personal Constructs*. London and New York: Academic Press.

BANTA, T. J., and NELSON, C. (1964) 'Experimental analysis of resource location in problem-solving groups', *Sociometry*, **27**, 488–501.

BARKER, R. G., and WRIGHT, H. F. (1954) *Midwest and its children: the Psychological Ecology of an American Town*. Evanston, Ill.: Row, Peterson.

BARR, J. (1967) 'Improvement via the pillar box', *New Society*, May 4th, 637–638.

BARTLETT, F. C. (1932) *Remembering*. Cambridge U.P.

BARTLETT, F. C. (1943) 'Fatigue following highly skilled work', *Proc. Roy. Soc. B.*, **131**, 247–257.

BASS, B. M. (1949) 'An analysis of the leaderless group discussion', *J. appl. Psychol.*, **33**, 527–533.

BASS, B. M. (1965) *Organizational Psychology*. Boston: Allyn and Bacon.

BASS, B. M., and DUNTEMAN, G. (1960) 'Behavior in groups as a function of self, interaction, and task orientation', *J. abnorm. soc. Psychol.*, **66**, 419–28.

BASS, B. M., and VAUGHAN, J. A. (1966) *Training in Industry*, London: Tavistock.

BATESON, G. *et al.* (1956) 'Toward a theory of schizophrenia', *Beh. Sci.*, **1**, 251–264.

BATESON, N. (1966) 'Familiarization, group discussion and risk taking', *J. exp. soc. Psychol.*, **2**, 119–129.

BELBIN, E., BELBIN, R. M., and HILL, F. (1957) 'A comparison between the results of three different methods of operator training', *Ergonomics*, **1**, 39–50.

BELOFF, H. (1958) 'Two forms of social conformity: acquiescence and conventionality', *J. abnorm. soc. Psychol.*, **56**, 99–103.

BENDER, A., and MAHL, G. F. (1960) 'Stress, feelings of identification, and language usage' (cited by Mahl and Schulze, 1964).

BENNE, K. D., BRADFORD, L. P., and LIPPITT, R. (1964) 'The laboratory method', *in*, Bradford, Gibb, and Benne (1964), pp. 15–44.

BENNETT, E. B. (1955) 'Discussion, decision, commitment and consensus in "group decision" ', *Hum. Relat.*, **8**, 251–273.

BENNETT, E. M., and COHEN, L. R. (1959) 'Men and women: personality patterns and contrasts', *Genet. Psychol. Monogr.*, **59**, 101–155.

BENNIS, W., and PEABODY, D. (1962) 'The conceptualisation of two personality orientations and sociometric choice', *J. soc. Psychol.*, **57**, 203–215.

BENOIT-SMULLYAN, E. (1944) 'Status, status types and status interrelations', *Amer. sociol. Rev.*, **9**, 151–161.

BERGER, A. (1965) 'A test of the double-bind hypothesis of schizophrenia', *Family Process*, **4**, 198–205.

BERGER, E. M. (1952) 'The relation between expressed acceptance of self and expressed acceptance of others', *J. abnorm. soc. Psychol.*, **47**, 778–782.

BERKOWITZ, L. (1956) 'Personality and group position', *Sociometry*, **19**, 210–222.

BERKOWITZ, L. (1960) 'Repeated frustrations and expectations in hostility arousal', *J. abnorm. soc. Psychol.*, **60**, 422–429.

BERKOWITZ, L. (1962) *Aggression: A Social Psychological Study*. New York: McGraw-Hill.

BERKOWITZ, L. (1968a) 'Responsibility, reciprocity, and social distance in help-giving: an experimental investigation of English social class differences, *J. exp. soc. Psychol.*, 4, 46–63.

BERKOWITZ, L. (1968b) 'Beyond exchange: Ideals and other factors affecting helping and altruism' (roneoed). University of Winconsin.

BERKOWITZ, L., and DANIELS, L. R. (1964) 'Affecting the salience of the social responsibility norm: effects of past help on the response to dependency relationships', *J. abnorm. soc. Psychol.*, 68, 273–281.

BERKOWITZ, L., and FRIEDMAN, P. (1967) 'Some social class differences in helping behaviour', *J. pers. soc. Psychol.*, 5, 217–225.

BERKOWITZ, L., and LUNDY R. M. (1956) 'Personality characteristics related to susceptibility to influence by peers or authority figures', *J. pers. soc. Psychol.*, 25, 306–316.

BERKOWITZ, L., and LUTTERMAN, K. G. (1964) 'The Socially Responsible Personality, Culture, and Political Attitudes' (roneoed).

BERNE, E. (1961) *Transactional Analysis in Psychotherapy*. New York: Grove Press.

BERNE, E. (1966) *Games People Play*. London: Deutsch.

BERNSTEIN, B. (1959) 'A public language: some sociological implications of a linguistic form', *Brit. J. Sociol.*, 10, 311–326.

BERNSTEIN, B., and HENDERSON, D. (1969) 'Social class differences in the relevance of language to socialisation', *Sociology*, 3, 1–20.

BETTELHEIM, B. (1959) 'Joey: a "mechanical boy" ', *Scientific American*, March, 116–127.

BIERI, J. (1955) 'Cognitive complexity–simplicity and predictive behaviour', *J. abnorm. soc. Psychol.*, 51, 263–268.

BIERI, J. et al. (1966) *Clinical and Social Judgement*. New York: Wiley.

BION, W. R. (1948–51) 'Experiences in groups', *Hum. Relat.*, 1–7.

BIRDWHISTELL, R. L. (1952) *Introduction to Kinesics*. Louisville.

BIRDWHISTELL, R. L. (1963) 'Some relationships between American Kinesics and spoken American English', paper to Amer. Anthrop. Assoc.

BIRDWHISTELL, E. L. (1968) 'Kinesics', *International Encyclopedia of the Social Sciences*, 8, 379–385.

BIXENSTINE, V. E., and WILSON, K. V. (1963) 'Effects of level of co-operative choice by the other player on choices in a prisoner's dilemma game. Part II', *J. abnorm. soc. Psychol.*, 67, 139–148.

BJERSTEDT, A. (1966) 'Factor analyses of an inventory of behavior in social settings', *Educational and Psychological Interactions*, No. 9. Malmö, Sweden: School of Education.

BLAKE, R. R. (1958) 'The other person in the situation', *in Person Perception and Interpersonal Behavior*, ed. R. Tagiuri and L. Petrullo. Stanford U.P.

BLAKE, R. R., and MOUTON, J. S. (1961) *Power, People and Performance Reviews*. *Advanced Management*, **26**, 13–27.

BLAKE, R. R., and MOUTON, J. S. (1964) *The Managerial Grid*. Houston: Gulf Pub. Co.

BLAKE, R. R., and MOUTON, J. S. (1965) 'A 9·9 approach for increasing organizational productivity', *in* E. H. Schein and W. G. Bennis (eds.) *Personal and Organizational Change through Group Methods*. New York: Wiley.

BLAKE, R. R., ROSENBAUM, M., and DURYEA, R. (1955) 'Gift-giving as a function of group standards', *Hum. Relat.*, **8**, 61–73.

BLAKE, R. R. *et al.* (1964) 'Breakthrough in organization development', *Harv. Bus. Rev.*, **42**, Nov.–Dec., 133–155.

BLAU, P. M. (1955) *The Dynamics of Bureaucracy*. University of Chicago Press.

BLAU, P. M., and SCOTT, W. R. (1963) *Formal Organizations*. London: Routledge and Kegan Paul.

BLINDER, M. G. (1966) 'The hysterical personality', *Psychiatry*, **29**, 227–235.

BLOCK, J. (1953) 'The assessment of communication; role variation as a function of interactional content', *J. Pers.*, **21**, 272–286.

BLOCK, JEANNE *et al.* (1958) 'A study of the parents of schizophrenic and neurotic children', *Psychiatry*, **21**, 387–397.

BLOOD, R. O., and WOLFE, D. M. (1960) *Husbands and Wives*. New York: Free Press.

BLURTON-JONES, N. G. (1967) 'Some aspects of the social behaviour of children in a nursery', *in* D. Morris (ed.) *Primate Ethology*. London: Weidenfeld and Nicolson.

BONARIUS, J. C. J. (1965) 'Research in the personal construct theory of George A. Kelly: role construct repertory test and basic theory', *Progress in Experimental Personality Research*, **2**, 2–46.

BOND, J. R., and VINACKE, W. E. (1961) 'Coalitions in mixed-sex triads', *Sociometry*, **24**, 61–75.

BONNEY, M. E. (1943) 'Personality traits of socially successful and unsuccessful children', *J. educ. Psychol.*, **34**, 449–472.

BOOMER, D. S., and DITTMAN, A. T. (1964) 'Speech rate, filled pause, and body movement in interviews', *J. Nerv. Ment. Dis.*, **139**, 324–327.

BORGATTA, E. F. (1962) 'A systematic study of interaction process scores, peer and self-assessments, personality and other variables', *Genet. Psychol. Monogr.*, **65**, 219–291.

BOS, M. C. (1937) 'Experimental study of productive collaboration', *Acta Psychologica*, **3**, 315–426.

BOSSARD, J. H. S., and BOLL, E. S. (1950) *Ritual in Family Living*. Philadelphia: University of Pennsylvania Press.

BOSSARD, J. H. S., and BOLL, E. S. (1956) *The Large Family System*. Philadelphia: University of Pennsylvania Press.

BOTT, E. (1957) *Family and Social Network*. London: Tavistock.

BOWERS, P., and LONDON, P. (1965) 'Developmental correlates of role playing ability'. (Unpublished paper, cited by Sarbin and Allen 1969.)

BOWLBY, J. (1952) *Maternal Care and Child Health*. Geneva; WHO.

BOWLBY, J. (1962) 'Childhood bereavement and psychiatric illness', *in* D. Richter *et al.* (eds.) *Aspects of Psychiatric Illness*. London: OUP.

BOWLBY, J., *et al.* (1956) 'The effects of mother child separation: a follow-up study', *Brit. J. Med. Psychol.*, 29, 211–247.

BRACKMAN, J. (1967) 'The put-on', *New Yorker*, June 24th, 34–73.

BRADFORD, L. P., GIBB, J. R., and BENNE, K. D. (1964), *T-Group Theory and Laboratory Method*. New York: Wiley.

BRAGINSKÝ, B. M., BRAGINSKY, D. D., and RING, K. (1969) *Methods of Madness: The Mental Hospital as a Last Resort*. New York: Holt, Rinehart and Winston.

BRAYFIELD, A. H., and CROCKETT, W. H. (1955) 'Employee attitudes and employee performance', *Psychol. Bull*, 52, 396–424.

BREER, P. E. (1960) 'Predicting interpersonal behavior from personality and role'. Harvard Ph.D.

BRIDGES, K. M. B. (1932) 'Emotional development in early infancy', *Child Dev.*, 3, 324–341.

BRONFENBRENNER, U. (1962) 'Soviet methods of character education: some implications for research', *Amer. Psychol.*, 17, 550–564.

BRONFENBRENNER, U., HARDING, J., and GALLWEY, M. (1958) 'The measurement of skill in social perception', *in Talent and Society*, ed. D. C. McClelland *et al.* New York: Van Nostrand.

BRONSON, G. W. (1959) 'Identity diffusion in late adolescents', *J. abnorm. soc. Psychol.*, 59, 414–417.

BRONSON, W. C. (1959) 'Dimensions of ego and infantile identification', *J. Pers.*, 27, 532–545.

BRONSON, W. C., KATTEN, E. S. and LIVSON, N. (1959). 'Patterns of authority and affection in two generations', *J. abnorm. soc. Psychol.*, 38, 143–152.

BROOKOVER, W. B., THOMAS, S., and PATERSON, A. (1964) 'Self concept of ability and school achievement', *Sociol. Educ.*, 37, 271–278.

BROWN, R. (1954) 'Mass phenomena', *in* G. Lindzey, (ed.) *Handbook of Social Psychology*. Cambridge, Mass: Addison-Wesley, Chap. 23.

BROWN, R. (1958) *Words and Things*. Glencoe, Ill.: Free Press.

BROWN, R. (1965) *Social Psychology*. New York: Free Press.

BROWN, R., and LENNEBERG, E. H. (1954) 'A study in language and cognition', *J. abnorm. soc. Psychol.*, 49, 454–462.

BROWN, R. K. (1967) 'The Tavistock's industrial studies', *Sociology*, 1, 33–60.

BROWNE, S. A., and CROWE, M. (1953) 'Personality structure as a determinant of sociometric choice', cited by Stock, D. (1964).

BROXTON, J. A. (1963) 'A test of interpersonal attraction predictions derived from balance theory', *J. abnorm. soc. Psychol.*, 60, 394–397.

BRUN, T. (1969) *The International Dictionary of Sign Language*. London: Wolfe Publishing Ltd.

BRUNER, J. S., SHAPIRO, D., and TAGIURI, R. (1958) 'The meaning of traits in isolation and in combination', *in* R. Tagiuri and L. Petrullo (eds.) *Person Perception and Interpersonal Behavior*. Stanford U.P.

BRUNSWIK, E. (1945) 'Social perception of traits from photographs', *Psychol. Bull.*, **42**, 535–536.

BÜHLER, C. (1933) 'The social behavior of children', *in* C. Murchison (ed.) *A Handbook of Child Psychology*. Clark U.P.

BULLIS, H. E. (1952) 'An educational programme for the development of the "normal personality" '. *Amer. J. Psychiat.*, **109**, 375–377.

BUNKER, D. R. (1965) 'The effects of laboratory education upon individual behavior', *in* Schein, E. H., and Bennis, W. G. (1965).

BUNKER, D. R., and KNOWLES, E. S. (1967) 'Comparison of behavioral changes resulting from human relations training laboratories of different lengths, *J. appl. beh. sci.*, **2**, 505–524.

BURCHARD, W. W. (1954) 'Role conflicts of military chaplains', *Amer. sociol. Rev.*, **19**, 528–535.

BURNS, T. (1954) 'The directions of activity and communication in a departmental executive group: a quantitative study in a British engineering factory with a self-recording technique', *Hum. Relat.*, **7**, 73–97.

BURNS, T. (1964) 'Non-verbal communication', *Discovery*, **25** (10), 30–37.

BURNS, T., and STALKER, G. M. (1961) *The Management of Innovation*. London: Tavistock.

BUSS, A. H. (1961) *The Psychology of Aggression*. New York: Wiley.

BYRNE, D. (1962) 'Response to attitude similarity–dissimilarity as a function of affiliation need', *J. Pers.*, **30**, 164–177.

BYRNE, D., and NELSON, D. (1965) 'Attraction as a linear function of proportion of positive reinforcements', *J. pers. soc. Psychol.*, **1**, 659–663.

CAMERON, N. (1959) 'Paranoid conditions and paranoia', *in* Arieti, S. (ed.) *American Handbook of Psychiatry*. New York: Basic Books.

CAMPBELL, D. T., KRUSKAL, W. H., and WALLACE, W. (1966) 'Seating aggregation as an index of attitude', *Sociometry*, **29**, 1–15.

CAMPBELL, D. T., and STANLEY, J. C. (1963) *Experimental and Quasi-experimental Designs for Research*. Chicago: Rand McNally.

CAMPBELL, J. D. (1964) 'Peer relations in childhood', *in* M. L. Hoffmann and L. W. Hoffman (eds.) *Review of Child Development Research*, **1**, 289–322. New York: Russell Sage Foundation.

CAMPBELL, J. D., and YARROW, M. R. (1961) 'Perceptual and Behavioral correlates of social effectiveness', *Sociometry*, **24**, 1–20.

CAMPBELL, J. P., and DUNNETTE, M. D. (1968) 'Effectiveness of T-group experiences in managerial training', *Psychol. Bull.*, **70**, 73–104.

CARLSON, S. (1951) *Executive Behaviour*. Stockholm: Strömbergs.

CARMENT, D. W., MILES, C. S., and CERVIN, V. B. (1965) 'Persuasiveness and persuasibility as related to intelligence and extraversion', *Brit. J. soc. clin. Psychol.*, **4**, 1–7.

CARNEGIE, D. (1936) *How to Win Friends and Influence People*. New York: Simon and Schuster.

CARROLL, J. B. (1944) 'The analysis of verbal behavior', *Psychol. Rev.*, **51**, 102–119.

CARROLL, J. B. (1963) 'Research on teaching foreign languages', *in* N. L. Gage, (ed.) *Handbook of Research on Teaching*. New York: Rand McNally.

CARTER, L. F. and NIXON, M. (1949) 'An investigation of the relationship between four criteria of leadership ability for three different tasks', *J. Psychol.*, **27**, 245–261.

CARTWRIGHT, D., and ZANDER, A. eds. (1959) *Group Dynamics*. London: Tavistock.

CENTERS, R. (1963) 'A laboratory adaptation of the conversational procedure for the conditioning of verbal operants', *J. abnorm. soc. Psychol.*, **67**, 334–339.

CHANCE, M. R. A. (1955) 'The sociability of monkeys', *Man.* **55**, 162–165.

CHANCE, M. R. A. (1962) 'The interpretation of some agonistic postures: the role of "cut-off" acts and postures', *Symp. Zool. Soc. Lond.*, **8**, 71–89.

CHANCE, M. R. A. (1967) 'Attention structure as the basis of primate rank orders', *Man.*, **2**, 503–518.

CHAPPLE, E. D. (1953) 'The standard interview as used in interaction chronograph investigations', *Hum. Org.*, **12** (2), 23–32.

CHAPPLE, E. D. (1956) *The Interaction Chronograph Manual*. Moroton, Conn.: E. D. Chapple Co. Inc.

CHAPPLE, E. D., and DONALD, G. (1947) 'An evaluation of department store salespeople by the interaction chromograph', *J. Marketing*, **12**, 173–185.

CHAPPLE, E. D., and LINDEMANN, E. (1942) 'Clinical implications of measurements of interaction rates in psychiatric interviews', *Appl. Anth.*, **1** (2), 1–11.

CHAPPLE, E. D., and SAYLES, C. R. (1961) *The Measure of Management*. New York: MacMillan.

CHEEK, F. E. (1964) 'A serendipitus finding: sex roles and schizophrenia', *J. abnorm. soc. Psychol.*, **69**, 392–400.

CHELSEA, L. (1965) 'A study of implicit personality theories' (cited by Smith, 1967).

CHODOFF, P., and LYONS, H. (1958) 'Hysteria, the hysterical personality and "hysterical" conversion', *Amer. J. Psychiat.*, **114**, 734–740.

CHOMSKY, N. (1957) *Syntactic Structures*. S'Gravenhage, Netherlands: Mouton.

CHRISTIE, R. (1962) 'Impersonal interpersonal orientations and behaviour'. Unpublished.

CICCHETI, D. V. (1967) 'Reported family dynamics and psychopathology: I. The reactions of schizophrenics and normals to parental dialogues, *J. abnorm. Psychol.*, **72**, 282–289.

CLARK, K. B., and CLARK, M. K. (1940) 'Skin color as a factor in racial identification of negro preschool children', *J. soc. Psychol.*, **11**, 159–169.

CLARK, R. A., and SENSIBAR, M. R. (1955) 'The relationship between symbolic and manifest projections of sexuality with some incidental correlates', *J. abnorm. soc. Psychol.*, **50**, 327–334.

CLECKLEY, H. (1955) *The Mask of Sanity* (3rd ed.). St Louis: The C. V. Mosby Co.

CLIFFORD, E., and CLIFFORD, M. (1967) 'Self-concepts before and after survival training', *Brit. J. soc. clin. Psychol.*, **6**, 241–248.

CLINE, V. B. (1964) 'Interpersonal perception', *Progress in Experimental Personality Research*, **1**, 221–284.

COCH, L., and FRENCH, J. R. P. (1948) 'Overcoming resistance to change', *Hum. Relat.*, **1**, 512–532.

COFER, C. N., and APPLEY, M. H. (1964) *Motivation: Theory and Research*. New York: Wiley.

COHEN, A. K. (1955) *Delinquent Boys*, Glencoe, Ill.: Free Press.

COHEN, A. R. (1958) 'Upward communication in experimentally created hierarchies', *Hum. Relat.*, **11**, 41–53.

COHEN, D., WHITMYRE, J. W., and FUNK, W. H. (1960) 'Effect of group cohesiveness and training upon creative thinking', *J. appl. Psychol.*, **44**, 319–322.

COHEN, K. J., and CYERT, R. M. (1965) 'Simulation of organizational behavior', *in* J. G. March (ed.) *Handbook of Organizations*. Chicago: Rand McNally.

COHEN, M. B. *et al.* (1954) 'An intensive study of twelve cases of manic-depressive psychosis', *Psychiatry*, **17**, 103–137.

COLEMAN, J. C. (1949) 'Facial expressions of emotions', *Psychol. Monogr.* **63**, No. 296.

COLEMAN, J. S. (1963) *The Adolescent Society*, Glencoe, Ill.: Free Press.

COLEMAN, J. S., KATZ, E., and MENZEL, H. (1957) 'The diffusion of an innovation among physicians, *Sociometry*, **20**, 253–270.

COLLINS, B., and RAVEN, B. (1969) 'Psychological aspects of structure in the small group', *in* G. Lindzey and E. Aronson (eds.) *Handbook of Social Psychology*. Reading, Mass.: Addison-Wesley.

CONDON, W. S., and OGSTON, W. D. (1966) 'Sound film analysis of, normal and pathological behavior patterns', *J. Nerv. Ment. Dis.*, **143**, 338–347.

COOK, M. (1969) 'Anxiety, speech disturbances, and speech rate', *Brit. J. Soc. clin. Psychol.* **8**, 13–21.

COOK, M. (1968) 'Studies of orientation and proximity' (roneoed). Oxford Institute of Experimental Psychology.

COOLEY, C. H. (1902) *Human Nature and the Social Order*. New York: Scribner's.

CORSINI, R. J., SHAW, M. E., and BLAKE, R. R. (1961) *Role playing in Business and Industry*. Glencoe, Ill.: Free Press.

COSS, R. G. (1965) *Mood Provoking Visual Stimuli their Origins and Applications.* University of California, Los Angeles, Industrial Design Graduate program.

COUCH, C. J. (1962) 'Family role specialization and self-attitudes in children', *Sociol. Quart.*, **3**, 115–121.

CRAFT, M. (1961) 'Psychopathic personalities: a review of diagnosis, aetiology, prognosis and treatment', *Brit. J. Crim.*, **1**, 237–253.

CRISWELL, J. H. (1949) 'Sociometric methods in personnel administration, *Sociometry* **12**, 287–300.

CROCKETT, W. H. (1965) 'Cognitive complexity and impression formation', *Progress in Experimental Personality Research*, **2**, 47–90.

CRONBACH, L. J. (1955) 'Processes affecting scores on "understanding of others" and "assumed similarity",' *Psychol. Bull.*, **52**, 177–193.

CROSSMAN, E. R. F. W. (1964) 'Information processes in human skill', *Brit. med. Bull.*, **20**, 32–37.

CROWNE, D. P., and MARLOWE, D. (1964) *The Approval Motive.* New York: Wiley.

CRUTCHFIELD, R. S. (1955) 'Conformity and character', *Amer. Psychol.*, **10**, 191–198.

CUMMING, J., and CUMMING, E. (1962) *Ego and Milieu.* London: Prentice-Hall International.

DANIELS, L. R., and BERKOWITZ, L. (1963) 'Liking and response to dependency relationships', *Hum. Relat.*, **16**, 141–148.

DARWIN, C. R. (1872) *The Expression of the Emotions in Man and Animals.* London: Murray.

DAVIS, J. A. (1961) 'Compositional effects, role systems and the survival of small discussion groups', *in* A. P. Hare *et al.* (eds.) *Small Groups.* New York: Knopf.

DAVIS, J. H. and RESTLE, F. (1963) 'The analysis of problems and prediction of group problem-solving, *J. abnorm. soc. Psychol.*, **66**, 103–116.

DAVIS, K. (1953) 'A method of studying communication patterns in organisations', *Personnel Psychol.*, **6**, 301–312.

DAVIS, K., and MOORE, W. E. (1945) 'Some principles of stratification', *Amer. sociol. Rev.*, **10**, 242–249.

DAVISON, J. P. *et al.* (1958) *Productivity and Economic Incentives.* London: George Allen and Unwin.

DAVITZ, J. R. (1964) *The Communication of Emotional Meaning.* New York: McGraw-Hill.

DECHARMS, R., and ROSENBAUM, M. F. (1960) 'Status variables and matching behaviour', *J. Pers.*, **28**, 492–502.

DE HAAN, J. A. B. (1929) 'Animal language in relation to that of Man', *Biol. Rev.*, **4**, 249–268.

DEMARATH, N. J. (1956) 'Schizophrenia among primitives', *in* A. M. Rose (ed.), *Mental Health and Mental Disorder.* London: Routledge and Kegan Paul.

DEUTSCH, H. (1955) 'The impostor: contribution to ego psychology of a type of psychopath', *Psychoan. Quart.*, **24**, 483–505.

DEUTSCH, M. (1949) 'An experimental study of cooperation and competition', *Hum. Relat.*, **2**, 199–231.

DEUTSCH, M. (1958) 'Trust and suspicion', *J. Confl. Res.*, **2**, 265–279.

DEUTSCH, M. (1960) 'The effect of motivational orientation upon trust and suspicion', *Hum. Relat.*, **13**, 121–139.

DEUTSCH, M., and GERARD, H. B. (1955) 'A study of normative and informational social influences upon individual judgement', *J. abnorm. soc. Psychol.*, **51**, 629–636.

DEUTSCH, M., and KRAUSS, R. M. (1960) 'The effect of threat on interpersonal bargaining', *J. abnorm. soc. Psychol.*, **61**, 181–189.

DEUTSCH, M., and SOLOMON, L. (1959) 'Reactions to evaluations by others as influenced by self-evaluations', *Sociometry*, **22**, 93–111.

DEVORE, I. (ed.) (1965) *Primate Behavior*. New York: Holt, Rinehart and Winston.

DEVORE, I. (1968) 'Primate behavior', *International Encyclopaedia of the Social Sciences*, **14**, 351–360.

DIEBOLD, A. R. (1967) 'Anthropology and the comparative psychology of communicative behavior', *in* T. A. Sebeok (ed.) *Animal Communication – Techniques of Study and Results of Research*. Indiana University Press.

DITTES, J. E., and KELLEY, H. H. (1956) 'Effects of different conditions of acceptance on conformity to group norms', *J. abnorm. soc. Psychol.*, **53**, 100–107.

DITTMAN, A. T. (1962) 'The relationship between body movements and moods in interviews', *J. Consult, Psychol.*, **26**, p. 480.

DITTMAN, A. (1966) 'Psychotherapeutic processes', *Ann. Rev. Psychol.*, **17**, 51–78.

DOLLARD, J., and MILLER, N. E. (1950) *Personality and Psychotherapy*. New York: McGraw-Hill.

DONALD, M. N. (1959) 'Some concomitants of varying patterns of communication in a large organization'. Ph.D. thesis, Univ. of Michigan, cited by Guetzkow (1965).

DONOVAN, M. J., and WEBB, W. W. (1965) 'Meaning dimensions and male–female voice perception in schizophrenics with good and poor premorbid adjustment', *J. abnorm. soc., Psychol.*, **70**, 426–431.

D.S.I.R. (1956) *Automation*. London: HMSO.

DULANEY, D. E. (1961) 'Hypotheses and habits in verbal operant conditioning', *J. abnorm. soc. Psychol.*, **63**, 251–263.

DUNNETTE, M. D., CAMPBELL, J., and JAASTAD, K. (1963) 'The effect of group participation on brainstorming effectiveness for two industrial samples', *J. appl. Psychol.*, **47**, 30–37.

EFRAN, J. S. (1968) 'Looking for approval: effects on visual behavior of approbation from persons differing in importance', University of Rochester (roneoed).

EFRAN, J. S., and BROUGHTON, A. (1966) 'Effect of expectancies for social approval on visual behavior', *J. pers. soc. Psychol.*, **4**, 103–107.

EFRON, D. (1941) *Gesture and Environment*. New York: King's Crown Press.

EKMAN, P., and FRIESEN, W. V. (1967a) 'Non-verbal behavior in psychotherapy research', *Research on Psychotherapy*, 3.

EKMAN, P., and FRIESEN, W. V. (1967b) 'Origin, usage and coding: the basis for five categories of non-verbal behavior'. Paper at Symposium in Communication Theory and Linguistic Models in the Social Sciences, at Buenos Aires, Argentina (roneoed).

EKMAN, P., and FRIESEN, W. V. (1967c) 'Head and body cues in the judgement of emotion: a reformulation', *Perc. Mot. Skills*, **24**, 179–215, 711–724.

ELDRED, S. H., and PRICE, D. B. (1958) 'Linguistic evaluation of feeling states in psychotherapy', *Psychiatry*, **21**, 115–121.

ELKIN, F. (1946) 'The soldier's language', *Amer. J. Sociol.*, **51**, 414–422.

ELLIS, A. (1957) 'Rational psychotherapy and individual psychology', *J. indiv. Psychol.*, **13**, 38–44.

ELLIS, R. A., and KEEDY, T. C. (1960) 'Three dimensions of status: a study of academic prestige', *Pacif. Sociol. Rev.*, **3**, 23–28.

EMERSON, R. M. (1962) 'Power-dependence relations', *Amer. Sociol. Rev.*, **27**, 31–41.

EMMERICH, W. (1959) 'Parental identification in young children', *Genet. Psychol. Monogr.*, **60**, 257–258.

ERIKSON, E. H. (1950a) *Childhood and Society*. New York: Norton.

ERIKSON, E. H. (1950b) 'Growth and crises of the healthy personality: VI Identity versus self-diffusion', *in* M. J. E. Senn (ed.) *Symposium on the Healthy Personality. II Problems of Infancy and Childhood*. New York: Josiah Macy Foundation.

ERIKSON, E. H. (1956) 'The problem of ego identity', *Amer. J. Psychoanal.* **4**, 56–121.

ERVIN, S. M. (1961) 'Changes with age in the verbal determinants of word-association', *Amer. J. Psychol.*, **74**, 361–372.

ERVIN-TRIPP, S. (1966) 'Language development', *Review of Child Development Research*, **2**, 55–105.

ETZIONI, A. (1961) *A Comparative Analysis of Complex Organizations*. Glencoe, Ill.: Free Press.

EVERSTINE, L., and CROSSMAN, E. R. F. W. (1966) 'An experiment on the coding of messages in the formation of a private language'. University of California, Berkeley. Center for Research in Management Science (roneoed).

EXLINE, R. V. (1960) 'Effects of sex, norms, and affiliation motivation upon accuracy of perception of interpersonal preferences', *J. Pers.*, **28**, 397–412.

EXLINE, R. V. (1963) 'Explorations in the process of person perception:

visual interaction in relation to competition, sex and need for affiliation', *J. Pers.*, **31**, 1–20.

EXLINE, R. V. (1966) 'The effects of cognitive difficulty and cognitive style upon eye to eye contact in interviews' (roneoed).

EXLINE, R. V., GRAY, D., and SCHUETTE, D. (1965) 'Visual behavior in a dyad as affected by interview content and sex of respondent', *J. pers. soc. Psychol.*, **1**, 201–209.

EXLINE, R. V., and MESSICK, D. (1967) 'The effects of dependency and social reinforcement upon visual behaviour during an interview', *Brit. J. soc. clin. Psychol.*, **6**, 256–266.

EXLINE, R. V., and WINTERS, L. C. (1965) 'Affective relations and mutual gaze in dyads', *in* S. Tomkins and C. Izzard (eds.) *Affect, Cognition and Personality*. New York: Springer.

EXLINE, R.V., and ZILLER, R. C. (1959) 'Status congruency and interpersonal conflict in decision-making groups', *Hum. Relat.*, **12**, 147–162.

EXLINE, R. V. *et al.* (1961) 'Visual interaction in relation to machiavellianism and an unethical act', *Amer. Psychol.*, **16**, 396.

EYSENCK, H. J. (1947) *The Dimensions of Personality*. London: Kegan Paul.

EYSENCK, H. J. (1952a) 'The effects of psychotherapy: an evaluation', *J. consult. Psychol.*, **16**, 319–324.

EYSENCK, H. J. (1952b) *The Scientific Study of Personality*. London: Routledge and Kegan Paul.

EYSENCK, H. J. (1957) *The Dynamics of Anxiety and Hysteria*. London: Routledge and Kegan Paul.

EYSENCK, H. J. (1959) Manual of the *Maudsley Personality Inventory*. University of London Press.

EYSENCK, H. J. (ed.) (1960) *Behaviour Therapy and the Neuroses*. Oxford: Pergamon.

EYSENCK, H. J. (1968) *The Biological Basis of Personality*. Springfield, Ill.: Thomas.

EYSENCK, H. J., and RACHMAN, S. (1965) *The Causes and Cures of Neuroses*. London: Routledge and Kegan Paul.

EYSENCK, S. B. G., and EYSENCK, H. J. (1963) 'On the dual nature of extraversion', *Brit. J. soc. clin. Psychol.*, **2**, 46–55.

FABRICIUS, E., and JANSSON, A. -M. (1963) 'Laboratory observations on the reproductive behaviour of the pigeon (*Columbia livia*) during the pre-incubation phase of the breeding cycle', *Animal Behaviour*, **11**, 534–547.

FAIRBAIRN, W. R. D. (1952) *Psychoanalytic Studies of the Personality*. London: Tavistock.

FARBER, B. (1962) 'Elements of competence in interpersonal relations: a factor analysis', *Sociometry*, **25**, 30–47.

FARINA, A. (1960) 'Patterns of role dominance and conflict in parents of schizophrenic patients', *J. abnorm. soc. Psychol.*, **61**, 31–38.

FEFFER, M., and GOUREVITCH, V. (1960) 'Cognitive aspects of role-taking in children', *J. Pers.*, **28**, 383–396.

FEFFER, M., and SUCHOTLIFF, L. (1966) 'Decentering implications of social interactions', *J. pers. soc. Psychol.*, **4**, 415–422.

FELDMAN, H. (1937) *Problems in Labor Relations*. New York: Macmillan.

FELDMAN, M. P., and MACCULLOCH, M. J. (1965) 'The application of anticipatory avoidance learning to the treatment of homosexuality. I. Theory, technique and preliminary results', *Beh. Res. Ther.*, **2**, 165–183.

FELDMAN, R. E. (1968) 'The response to foreigner and compatriot who seek assistance', *J. pers. soc. Psychol.*, **10**, 202–214.

FELDMAN, S. S. (1959) *Mannerisms of Speech and Gestures in Everyday Life*. New York: International Universities Press.

FELDSTEIN, S. (1962) 'The relationship of interpersonal involvement and affectiveness of content to the verbal communication of schizophrenic patients', *J. abnorm. soc. Psychol.*, **64**, 39–45.

FELIPE, N. J., and SOMMER, R. (1966) 'Invasions of personal space,' *Social Problems*, **14**, 206–214.

FERNBERGER, S. W. (1928) 'False suggestion and the Piderit model', *Amer. J. Psychol.*, **40**, 562–568.

FESHBACH, S., and SINGER, R. D. (1957) 'The effects of fear arousal and suppression of fear upon social perception', *J. abnorm. soc. Psychol.*, **55**, 283–288.

FESTINGER, L. (1950) 'Informal social communication', *Psychol. Rev.*, **57**, 271–282.

FESTINGER, L. (1954) 'A theory of social comparison processes', *Hum. Relat.*, **7**, 117–140.

FESTINGER, L., PEPITONE, A., and NEWCOMB, T. M. (1952) 'Some consequences of deindividuation in a group', *J. abnorm. soc. Psychol.*, **47**, 382–389.

FESTINGER, L., RIECKEN, H. W., and SCHACHTER, S. (1956) *When Prophecy Fails*. University of Minnesota Press.

FESTINGER, L., SCHACHTER, S., and BACK, K. W. (1950) *Social Pressures in Informal Groups*. New York: Harper.

FIEDLER, F. E. (1953) 'Quantitative studies on the role of therapists' feelings towards their patients', *in* O. H. Mowrer (ed.) *Psychotherapy, Theory and Research*. New York: Ronald.

FIEDLER, F. E. (1958a) *Leader Attitudes and Group Effectiveness*. Urbana: Univ. of Illinois Press.

FIEDLER, F. E. (1958b) 'Interpersonal perception and group effectiveness', *in* R. Tagiuri and L. Petrullo (eds.) *Person Perception and Interpersonal Behavior*. Stanford U.P.

FIEDLER, F. E. (1964) 'A contingency model of leadership effectiveness', *Advances in Experimental Social Psychology*, **1**, 150–191.

FISHER, S., and CLEVELAND, S. E. (1958) *Body-Image and Personality*. Princeton: Van Nostrand.

FLANAGAN, J. C. (1961) 'Leadership skills: their identification, development and evaluation', *in* L. Petrullo and B. M. Bass (eds.) *Leadership and Interpersonal Behavior*. New York: Holt, Rinehart and Winston.

FLEISHMAN, E. A. (1953) 'Leadership climate, human relations training and supervisory behavior', *Personnel Psychol.*, **6**, 205–222.

FLEISHMAN, E. A. *et al.* (1955) *Leadership and Supervision in Industry*. Columbia U.P.

FLEISHMAN, E. A., and HARRIS, E. F. (1962) 'Patterns of leadership behavior related to employee grievances and turnover', *Personnel Psychol.*, **15**, 43–56.

FLEMING, C. M. (1963) *Adolescence*. London: Routledge and Kegan Paul.

FOA, U. G. (1958) 'Empathy or behavioral transparency?', *J. abnorm. soc. Psychol.*, **56**, 62–66.

FOA, U. G. (1961) 'Convergences in the analysis of the structure of inter-personal behavior', *Psychol. Rev.*, **68**, 341–353.

FOA, U. G. (1967) 'Differentiation in cross-cultural communication', *in* L. Thayer (ed.) *Communication, Concepts and Perspectives*. Washington: Spartan Books.

FORD, C. S., and BEACH, F. A. (1952) *Patterns of Sexual Behaviour*. London: Methuen.

FOSS, B. M. (ed.) (1961–5) *Determinants of Infant Behaviour*, vols. 1–3. London: Methuen.

FOSTER, M. (1968) 'Work involvement and alienation', *Manpower and Applied Psychology*, **2**, (1), 35–48.

FOULKES, S. H., and ANTHONY, E. J. (1957) *Group Psychotherapy. The Psychoanalytic Approach*. London: Penguin Books.

FOURIEZOS, H. T., HUTT, M. L., and GUETZKOW, H. (1950) 'Measurement of self-oriented needs in discussion groups', *J. abnorm. soc. Psychol.*, **45**, 682–690.

FRANK, J. D. (1961) *Persuasion and Healing*. Baltimore: Johns Hopkins Press.

FRANK, L. K. (1957) 'Tactile communication', *Genet. Psychol. Monogr.*, **56**, 209–225.

FRAYN, M. (1967) 'That groaning board', *Observer*, Feb. 12th, 1967.

FREEDMAN, J. L., and SEARS, D. O. (1965) 'Selective exposure', *Advances in Experimental Social Psychology*, **2**, 57–97.

FRENCH, J. R. P. (1956) 'A formal theory of social power', *Psychol. Rev.*, **63**, 181–194.

FRENCH, J. R. P., and RAVEN, B. H. (1959) 'The bases of social power', *in* D. Cartwright (ed.) *Studies in Social Power*. Ann. Arbor: Univ. of Michigan Press.

FRENKEL-BRUNSWIK, E. (1954) 'Further explorations by a contributor to *The Authoritarian Personality*', *in* R. Christie and M. Jahoda (eds.) *Studies in the Scope and Method of the Authoritarian Personality*. New York: Free Press.

FRIEDMAN, N. (1967) *The Social Nature of Psychological Research*. New York: Basic Books.

FRIEDMANN, G. (1961) *The Anatomy of Work*. Glencoe, Ill.: Free Press.

FUNKENSTEIN, D. H., KING, S. H., and DROLETTE, M. E. (1957) *Mastery of Stress*. Harvard U.P.

GAGE, N. L., RUNKEL, P. J., and CATTERJEE, B. B. (1960). *Equilibrium Theory and Behavior Change: an experiment in feedback from pupils to teachers*. Urbana: Bureau of Educ. Res.

GAMSON, W. A. (1964) 'Experimental studies of coalition formation', *Advances in Experimental Social Psychology*, **1**, 82–110.

GARFINKEL, H. (1963) 'Trust and stable actions', *in* O. J. Harvey (ed.) *Motivation and Social Interaction*. New York: Ronald

GARRISON, K. C. (1951) *Psychology of Adolescence*. New York: Prentice Hall.

GATES, G. S. (1923) 'An experimental study of the growth of social perception', *J. educ. Psychol.*, **14**, 449–461.

GELDER, M. G., MARKS, I. M., and WOLFF, H. H. (1967) 'Desensitization and psychotherapy in the treatment of phobic states: a controlled enquiry', *Brit. J. Psychiat.*, **113**, 53–73.

GERGEN, K. J. (1965) 'The effects of interaction goals and personalistic feedback on the presentation of self', *J. pers. soc. Psychol.*, **1**, 413–424.

GESELL, A., ILG, F. L., and AMES, L. B. (1956) *Youth*. London: Hamish Hamilton.

GESELL, A., and THOMPSON, H. (1934) *Infant Behavior: its Genesis and Growth*. New York: McGraw-Hill.

GEWIRTZ, J. L. (1961) 'A learning analysis of the effects of normal stimulation, privation and deprivation on the acquisition of social motivation and attachment', *in* B. M. Foss (ed.) *Determinants of Infant Behaviour*, **1**. London: Methuen, pp. 213–299.

GEWIRTZ, J. L. (1965) 'The course of infant smiling in four child-rearing environments in Israel', *in* B. M. Foss (ed.) *Determinants of Infant Behaviour*, **3**. London: Methuen, pp. 161–184.

GIBB, C. A. (1969) 'Leadership', *in* G. Lindzey and E. Aronson (eds.) *Handbook of Social Psychology*. Cambridge, Mass.: Addison-Wesley.

GIBSON, R. W. (1958) 'The family background and early life experience in the manic-depressive patient', *Psychiatry*, **21**, 71–90.

GILBERT, G. M. (1951) 'Stereotype persistence and change among college students', *J. abnorm. soc. Psychol.*, **46**, 245–254.

GLANZER, M., and GLASER, R. (1961) 'Techniques for the study of group structure and behavior: II Empirical studies of the effects of structure in small groups', *Psychol. Bull.*, **58**, 1–27.

GLIDEWELL, J. C. (1956) 'Changes in approaches to work problem analysis during management training', cited by Stock (1964).

GOFFMAN, E. (1955) 'On face-work', *Psychiatry*, **18**, 213–231.

GOFFMAN, E. (1956a) *The Presentation of Self in Everyday Life*. Edinburgh Univ. Press.

GOFFMAN, E. (1956b) 'Embarrassment and social organisation', *Amer. J. Sociol.*, **62**, 264–271.

GOFFMAN, E. (1957) 'Alienation from interaction', *Hum. Relat.*, **10**, 47–60.

GOFFMAN, E. (1961) *Asylums*. New York: Anchor Books.

GOFFMAN, E. (1963a) *Behavior in Public Places*. Glencoe, Ill.: Free Press.

GOFFMAN, E. (1963b) *Stigma*. Englewood Cliffs, N.J.: Prentice Hall.

GOLDFARB, W. (1955) 'Emotional and intellectual consequences of psychological deprivation in infancy: a revaluation', *in* P. H. Hock and J. Zubin (eds.) *Psychopathology of Childhood*. New York: Grune and Stratton. 105–119.

GOLDMAN-EISLER, F. (1952) 'Individual differences between interviewers and their effect on interviewees' conversational behaviour', *J. ment. Sci.*, **98**, 660–671.

GOLDMAN-EISLER, F. (1961) 'A comparative study of two hesitation phenomena', *Language and Speech*, **4**, 18–26.

GOLDTHORPE, J., and LOCKWOOD, D. (1962) 'Not so bourgeois after all', *New Society*, Oct. 18th, 18–19.

GOODALL, J. (1965) 'Chimpanzees of the Gombe stream reserve', *in* I. DeVore (ed.) *Primate Behavior*. New York: Holt, Rinehart and Winston.

GOODE, W. J. (1960) 'A theory of role strain', *Amer. sociol. Rev.*, **25**, 483–496.

GOODENOUGH, F. L. (1931) 'Anger in young children', *Inst. Child Welf. Monogr.* University of Minnesota Press.

GORANSON, R. E., and BERKOWITZ, L. (1966) 'Reciprocity and responsibility reactions to prior help', *J. pers. soc. Psychol.*, **3**, 227–232.

GORER, G. (1965) *Death, Grief and Mourning*. Garden City, New York: Doubleday.

GOTTESMAN, I. I., and SHIELDS, J. (1966) 'Contributions of twin studies to perspectives of schizophrenia', *Progress in Experimental Personality Research*, **3**, 1–84.

GOUGH, H.G. (1948) 'A sociological theory of psychopathy', *Amer. J. Sociol.*, **53**, 359–366.

GOUGH, H. G. (1950) 'Predicting success in Graduate Training', Berkeley: Institute in Personality Assessment and Research.

GOUGH, H. G. (1957) *Manual for the California Psychological Inventory*. Palo Alto, Calif.: Consulting Psychologists Press.

GOUGH, H. G. (1965) 'A validational study of the Chapin social insight test', *Psychol. Reports*, **17**, 355–368.

GOUGH, H. G., and PETERSEN, D. R. (1952) 'The identification and measurement of predispositional factors in crime and delinquency', *J. consult. Psychol.*, **16**, 207–212.

GOULDNER, A. W. (1960) 'The norm of reciprocity: a preliminary statement', *Amer. sociol. Rev.*, **25**, 161–178.

GOWIN, E. B. (1915) *The Executive and his Control of Men.* New York: Macmillan.

GREENBERG, P. J. (1932) 'Competition in children: an experimental study', *Amer. J. Psychol.*, **44**, 221–248.

GREENSPOON, J. (1955) 'The reinforcing effect of two sounds on the frequency of two responses', *Amer. J. Psychol.*, **68**, 409–417.

GRINKER, R. R. et al. (1961) *The Phenomena of Depressions.* New York: Hoeber.

GROSS, E., and STONE, S. P. (1964) 'Embarrassment and the analysis of role requirements', *Amer. J. Sociol.*, **70**, 1–15.

GROSS, N., MASON, W. S., and MCEACHERN, A. W. (1958) *Explorations in Role Analysis.* New York: Wiley.

GROSSMAN, B. A. (1963) 'The measurement and determinants of interpersonal sensitivity', M.A. thesis, Michigan State Univ., cited by Smith (1967).

GUERNEE, H. (1937) 'A comparison of collective and individual judgments of facts', *J. exp. Psychol.*, **21**, 106–112.

GUETZKOW, H. (1960) 'Differentiation of roles in task-oriented groups', *in* D. Cartwright and A. Zander (eds.) *Group Dynamics* (2nd ed.). London: Tavistock.

GUETZKOW, H. (1965) 'Communications in organizations', *in* J. G. March (ed.) *Handbook of Organizations.* Chicago: Rand McNally.

GUETZKOW, H., and SIMON, H. A. (1955) 'The impact of certain communication nets upon organization and performance in task-oriented groups', *Management Science*, **1**, 233–250.

GUILFORD, J. F. (1929) 'An experiment in learning to read facial expressions', *J. abnorm. soc. Psychol.*, **24**, 191–202.

GUNTRIP, H. (1961) *Personality Structure and Human Interaction.* London: Hogarth Press.

GURIN, G., VEROFF, J., and FIELD, S. (1960) *Americans View their Mental Health.* New York: Basic Books.

GUTHRIE, E. R. (1938) *The Psychology of Human Conflict.* New York: Harper.

HAGGARD, E. A., and ISAACS, K. S. (1966) 'Micromomentary facial expressions as indicators of ego mechanisms in psychotherapy', *in* L. A. Gottschalk and A. H. Auerback (eds.) *Methods of Research in Psychotherapy.* New York: Appleton-Century.

HAINES, D. B., and EACHUS, H. T. (1965) 'A preliminary study of acquiring cross-cultural interaction skills through self-confrontation'. Aerospace Medical Research Laboratories, Wright-Patterson Air Force Base, Ohio.

HAIRE, M., and GRUNES, W. F. (1950) 'Perceptual defences: processes protecting an organised perception of another personality', *Hum. Relat.*, **3**, 403–412.

HALL, E. T. (1963) 'A system for the notation of proxemic behavior', *Amer. Anthropol.*, **65**, 1003–1026.

HALL, E. T. (1966) *The Hidden Dimension*. Garden City, New York: Doubleday.

HALL, K. R. L. (1962) 'The sexual, agonistic and derived social behaviour patterns of the wild Chacma baboon, *Papiu ursinus*', *Proc. Zool. Soc. Lond.*, **139**, (II), 283–327.

HALL, R. H. (1963) 'The concept of bureaucracy: an empirical assessment', *Amer. J. Sociol.*, **69**, 32–40.

HALPERN, H. M. (1955) 'Empathy, similarity and self-satisfaction', *J. consult. Psychol.*, **19**, 449–452.

HALPIN, A. W., and WINER, B. J. (1952) *The Leadership Behavior of the Airplane Commander*. Columbus: Ohio State University.

HAMBLIN, R. L. (1958) 'Leadership and crisis', *Sociometry*, **21**, 322–335.

HANDEL, G. (1965) 'Psychological study of whole families', *Psychol. Bull.*, **63**, 19–41.

HANFMANN, E. (1935) 'Social structure of a group of kindergarten children', *Amer. J. Orthopsychiat.*, **5**, 407–410.

HARDING, J. et al. (1954) 'Prejudice and ethnic relations', *in* G. Lindzey (ed.) *Handbook of Social Psychology*. Cambridge, Mass.: Addison-Wesley.

HARE, A. P. (1953) 'A study of interaction and consensus in different sized groups', *Amer. sociol. Rev.*, **17**, 261–267.

HARE, A. P. (1962) *Handbook of Small Group Research*. Glencoe, Ill.: Free Press.

HARE, A. P., BORGATTA, E. F., and BALES, R. F. (1955) *Small Groups: Studies in Social Interaction*. New York: Knopf.

HARITON, T. (1951) 'Conditions influencing the training of foremen in human relations principles', Michigan Ph.D.

HARLOW, H. F., and HARLOW, M. K. (1962) 'Social deprivation in monkeys', *Sci. Amer.*, **207**, 136–146.

HARLOW, H. F., and HARLOW, M. K. (1965) 'The affectional systems', *in* A. M. Schrier et al. (eds.) *Behavior of Nonhuman Primates*. New York and London: Academic Press.

HARRISON, R. P. (1965) 'Pictic analysis: towards a vocabulary and syntax for the pictorial code: with research on facial communication', *Diss. Abstr.*, **26**, 519.

HARTESHORNE, H., MAY, M. A., and SHUTTLEWORTH, F. K. (1930) *Studies in the Organisation of Character*. New York: Macmillan.

HARVEY, O. J. (1962) 'Personality factors in resolution of conceptual incongruities', *Sociometry*, **25**, 336–352.

HASTORF, A. H., RICHARDSON, S. A., and DORNBUSCH, S. M. (1958) 'The problem of relevance in the study of person perception', *in*

R. Tagiuri and L. Petrullo. *Person Perception and Interpersonal Behavior*. Stanford U.P.

HAWTHORNE, J. W. (1932) 'A group test for the measurement of cruelty-comparison; a proposed means of recognizing potential criminality', *J. soc. Psychol.*, **3**, 189–211.

HAYES, A. S. (1964)'Paralinguistics and kinesics: pedagogical perspectives', *in* T. A. Sebeok (ed.) *Approaches to Semeotics*. The Hague: Mouton.

HAYES, C. (1952) *The Ape in our House*. London: Gollancz.

HAYTHORN, W. *et al*. (1956) 'The effects of varying combinations of authoritarian and equalitarian leaders and followers', *J. abnorm. soc. Psychol.*, **53**, 210–219.

HEBB, D. O. (1966) *A Textbook of Psychology*. Philadelphia: W. B. Saunders.

HEBB, D. O., and THOMPSON, W. R. (1954) 'The social significance of animal studies', *in* G. Lindzey (ed.) *Handbook of Social Psychology*. Cambridge, Mass.: Addison-Wesley.

HEDIGER, H. (1955) *Studies of the Psychology and Behaviour of Captive Animals in Zoos and Circuses*. New York: Criterion.

HEIDER, F. (1958) *The Psychology of Interpersonal Relations*. New York: Wiley.

HEINECKE, C., and BALES, R. F. (1953) 'Developmental trends in the structure of small groups', *Sociometry*, **16**, 7–38.

HEISS, J. S. (1962) 'Degree of intimacy and male–female interaction', *Sociometry*, **25**, 197–208.

HELPER, M. M. (1955) 'Learning theory and the self concept', *J. abnorm. soc. Psychol.*, **51**, 184–194.

HEMPHILL, J. K. (1950) 'Relations between the size of the group and the behavior of "superior" leaders', *J. soc. Psychol.*, **32**, 11–22.

HENRY, A. F., and SHORT, J. F. (1954) *Suicide and Homicide*. Glencoe, Ill.: Free Press.

HERBST, P. G. (1952) 'The measurement of family relationships', *Hum. Relat.*, **5**, 3–35.

HERBST, P. G. (1962) *Autonomous Group Functioning*. London: Tavistock.

HERZBERG, F., MAUSNER, B., and SNYDERMAN, B. B. (1959) *The Motivation to Work*. New York: Wiley.

HESS, E. H. (1965) 'Attitude and pupil size', *Sci. Amer.*, **212**, (4), 46–54.

HEWITT, L. F., and JENKINS, R. L. (1946) *Fundamental Patterns of Maladjustment the Dynamics of their Origin*. Illinois: D. H. Green.

HILDUM, D. C., and BROWN, R. W. (1956) 'Verbal reinforcement and interviewer bias', *J. abnorm. soc. Psychol.*, **53**, 108–111.

HOFFMANN, L. R. (1965) 'Group problem-solving', *Advances in Experimental Social Psychology*, **2**, 99–132.

HOFFMANN, L. R., HARBURG, E., and MAIER, N. R. F. (1962) 'Differences and disagreement as factors in creative group problem solving', *J. abnorm. soc. Psychol.*, **64**, 206–214.

HOFFMANN, L. R., and MAIER, N. R. F. (1966) 'An experimental re-examination of the similarity-attraction hypothesis', *J. pers. soc. Psychol.*, **3**, 145–152.

HOLLANDER, E. P. (1958) 'Conformity, status and idiosyncrasy credit', *Psychol. Rev.*, **65**, 117–127.

HOLLANDER, E.P. (1967) *Principles and Methods of Social Psychology*. New York: O.U.P.

HOLLANDER, E. P., and WEBB, W. B. (1955) 'Leadership, followership, and friendship: an analysis of peer nominations', *J. abnorm. soc. Psychol.*, **50**, 163–167.

HOLLANDER, E. P., and WILLIS, R. H. (1967) 'Some current issues in the psychology of conformity and non-conformity', *Psychol. Bull.*, **68**, 62–76.

HOMANS, G. C. (1951) *The Human Group*. London: Routledge and Kegan Paul.

HOMANS, G. C. (1961) *Social Behavior: the Elementary Forms*. New York: Harcourt Brace.

HOVLAND, C. I. (1959) 'Reconciling conflicting results derived from experimental and survey studies of attitude change', *Amer. Psychol.*, **14**, 8–17.

HOVLAND, C. I., and JANIS, I. L. (eds.) (1959) *Personality and Persuasibility*. Yale University Press.

HUMPHREY, G., and ARGYLE, M. (1962) *Social Psychology through Experiment*. London: Methuen.

HUNTER, G. (1962) *The New Societies of Tropical Africa*. London: OUP.

HUTT, C., and HUTT, S. J. (1965) 'Effects of environmental complexity on stereotyped behaviour of children', *Anim. Behav.*, **13**, 1–4.

HUTT, C., and OUNSTED, C. (1966) 'The biological significance of gaze aversion with particular reference to the syndrome of infantile autism', *Beh. Sci.*, **11**, 346–356.

HUTT, C., and VAIZEY, M. J. (1966) 'Differential effects of group density on social behaviour', *Nature*, **209**, 1371–1372.

IRWIN, O. C. (1960) 'Language and communication', *in* P. H. Mussen (ed.) *Handbook of Research Methods in Child Development*. New York: Wiley.

ISAACS, W., THOMAS, J., and GOLDIAMOND, I. (1960) 'Application of operant conditioning to reinstate verbal behavior in psychotics', *J. speech. hear. Disord.* **25**, 8–12.

ITTELSON, W. H., and SLACK, C. W. (1958) 'The perception of persons as visual objects', *in* R. Tagiuri and L. Petrullo. *Person Perception and Interpersonal Behavior*. Stanford U.P.

IVERSON, M. A. and RENDER, M. E. (1956) 'Ego-involvement as an experimental variable, *Psychol. Reports*, **2**, 147–181.

JACK, L. M. (1934) 'An experimental study of ascendant behavior in pre-school children', *Univ. Iowa Stud. Child Welf.*, **9**, No. 3.

JACKSON, D. D. (ed.) (1960) *The Aetiology of Schizophrenia*. New York: Basic Books.

JACKSON, J. M. (1953) 'The effect of changing the leadership of small work groups', *Hum. Relat.*, **6**, 25–44.

JACKSON, J. M. (1959) 'Reference group processes in a formal organization', *Sociometry*, **22**, 307–327.

JACOBS, A., and ROBINSON, M. (1968) 'A research study investigating the effects of video-tape feedback on group interaction, self-awareness, and behavioral change: methods, results, implications' (roneoed). Univ. Southern California.

JACOBSON, E., CHARTERS, W. W., and LIEBERMAN, S. (1951) 'The use of the role concept in the study of complex organizations', *J. Soc. Issues*, **7** (2), 18–27.

JAFFE, J. (1964) 'Verbal behavioral analysis in psychiatric interviews with the aid of digital computers', *in* D. McK. Rioch and E. A. Weinstein (eds.) *Disorders of Communication Res. Publ. Ass. Res. Nerv. Ment. Dis.*, **42**, Chap. 27.

JAHODA, G. (1962) 'Social class', *in* G. Humphrey and M. Argyle (eds.) *Social Psychology through Experiment*. London: Methuen.

JAHODA, G. (1963) 'Refractive errors, intelligence and social mobility', *Brit. J. soc. clin. Psychol.*, **1**, 96–106.

JANIS, I. L., and MANN, L. (1965) 'Effectiveness of emotional role-playing in modifying smoking habits and attitudes', *J. exp. res. Pers.*, **1**, 84–90.

JAQUES, E. (1951) *The Changing Culture of a Factory*. London: Tavistock.

JAY, P. (1965a) 'Field studies', *in* A. M. Schrier *et al.* (eds.) *Behavior of Non-human Primates*. New York and London: Academic Press.

JAY, P. (1965b) 'The common langur of North India', *in* I. DeVore (ed.) *Primate Behavior*. New York: Holt, Rinehart and Winston.

JECKER, J. D., MACCOBY, N. and BREITROSE, H. S. (1965) 'Improving accuracy in interpreting non-verbal cues of comprehension', *Psych. in the Schools*, **2**, 239–244.

JENNINGS, H. H. (1950) *Leadership and Isolation*. New York: Longmans, Green.

JERSILD, A. T., and MARKEY, F. V. (1935) 'Conflicts between preschool children', *Child Developm. Monogr.*, No. 21.

JOHANNSEN, W. J. (1961) 'Responsiveness of chronic schizophrenics and normals to social and nonsocial feedback', *J. abnorm. soc. Psychol.*, **62**, 106–113.

JOHNSON, D. W. (1966) 'The use of role-reversal in intergroup competition'. ONR Report.

JOHNSON, D. W. *et al.* (1965) 'Follow-up evaluation of human relation training for psychiatric patients', *in* E. H. Schein and W. G. Bennis (eds.) *Personal and Organizational Change through Group Methods*. New York: Wiley.

JONES, E. E. (1964) *Ingratiation*. New York: Appleton.

JONES, E. E., and DAVIS, K. E. (1966) 'From acts to dispositions', *Advances in Experimental Social Psychology*, **2**, 220–267.

JONES, E. E., DAVIS, K. E., and GERGEN, K. J. (1961) 'Role playing variations and their informational value for person perception', *J. abnorm. soc. Psychol.*, **63**, 302–310.

JONES, E. E., and DECHARMS, R. (1957) 'Changes in social perception as a function of the personal relevance of behavior', *Sociometry*, **20**, 75–85.

JONES, E. E., and GERARD, H. B. (1967) *Foundations of Social Psychology*. New York: Wiley.

JONES, E. E., and THIBAUT, J. W. (1958) 'Interaction goals as bases of inference in interpersonal perception', *in* R. Tagiuri and L. Petrullo *Person Perception and Interpersonal Behavior*. Stanford U.P.

JONES, E. E. *et al.* (1959) 'Reactions to unfavourable personal evaluation as a function of the evaluator's perceived adjustment', *J. abnorm. soc. Psychol.*, **59**, 363–370.

JOOS, M. (1962) 'The five clocks', *Int. J. Amer. Ling.*, **28** (2), Part V.

JOURARD, S. M. (1964) *The Transparent Self*. Princeton: Van Nostrand.

JOURARD, S. M. (1966) 'An exploratory study of body-accessibility', *Brit. J. soc. clin. Psychol.*, **5**, 221–231.

JOURARD, S. M., and SECORD, P. F. (1955) 'Body-cathexis and personality', *Brit. J. Psychol.*, **46**, 130–138.

KAGAN, J. (1964) 'Acquisition and significance of sex typing and sex role identity', *Review of Child Development Research*, **1**, 137–167.

KAGAN, J., and MOSS, H. H. (1962) *Birth to Maturity*. New York: Wiley.

KAHN, R. L., WOLFE, D. M., QUINN, R. P., and SNOEK, H. D. (1964) *Organizational Stress*. New York: Wiley.

KALLMANN, F. J. (1950) 'The genetics of psychoses: an analysis of 1,232 twin index families', *Cong. Int. Psychiat. Rapports*, **6**, 1–27. Paris: Herrmann.

KASL, S. V., and MAHL, G. F. (1965) 'The relationship of disturbances and hesitations in spontaneous speech to anxiety', *J. pers. soc. Psychol.*, **1**, 425–433.

KATZ, D., and BRALY, K. W. (1933) 'Racial prejudice and racial stereotypes', *J. abnorm. soc. Psychol.*, **30**, 175–193.

KATZ, D., and KAHN, R. L. (1966) *The Social Psychology of Organizations*. New York: Wiley.

KATZ, E., and LAZARSFELD, P. F. (1955) *Personal Influence*. Glencoe, Ill.: Free Press.

KELLEY, H. H. (1950) 'The warm–cold variable in first impressions of persons', *J. Pers.*, **18**, 431–439.

KELLEY, H. H. (1951) 'Communication in experimentally created hierarchies', *Hum. Relat.*, **4**, 39–56.

KELLEY, H. H., and THIBAUT, J. W. (1969) 'Group problem-solving', *in*

G. Lindzey and E. Aronson, *Handbook of Social Psychology.* (eds.) Reading, Mass.: Addison-Wesley.

KELLEY, H. H., THIBAUT, J. W., RADLOFF, R., and MUNDY, D. (1962) 'The development of cooperation in the "minimal social situation"', *Psychol. Monogr.,* **76,** No. 19.

KELLY, G. A. (1955) *The Psychology of Personal Constructs.* New York: Norton.

KELMAN, H. C. (1961) 'Processes of opinion change', *Pub. Opin. Quart.,* **25,** 57–78.

KENDON, A. (1963) Temporal aspects of the social performance in two person encounters, Oxford D.Phil. thesis.

KENDON, A. (1965) Progress report of an investigation into aspects of the structure and function of the social performance in two-person encounters. Roneoed report to DSIR.

KENDON, A. (1967) 'Some functions of gaze direction in social interaction', *Acta Psychologica,* **26** (1), 1–47.

KENDON, A. (1968) 'Some observations on interactional synchrony'. A preliminary report (roneoed). Cornell University.

KILOH, L. G., and GARSIDE, R. F. (1963) 'The independence of neurotic depression and endogenous depression'. *Brit. J. Psychiat.,* **109,** 451–463.

KING, D. L. (1966) 'A review and interpretation of some aspects of the infant–mother relationship in mammals and birds', *Psychol. Bull.,* **65,** 143–155.

KINSEY, A. C., POMEROY, W. B., and MARTIN, C. E. (1948) *Sexual Behavior in the Human Male.* Philadelphia: Saunders.

KIPNIS, D. M. (1961) 'Changes in self concepts in relation to perceptions of others', *J. Pers.,* **29,** 449–465.

KLEBANOFF, L. B. (1959) 'Parental attitudes of schizophrenic, brain-injured and retarded, and normal children', *Amer. J. Orthopsychiat.,* **29,** 445–454.

KLEIN, H. R., and HORWITZ, W. A. (1949) 'Psychosexual factors in the paranoid phenomena', *Amer. J. Psychiat.,* **105,** 697–701.

KLEIN, J. (1965) *Samples from English Cultures.* London: Routledge and Kegan Paul.

KLUCKHOHN, C. (1954) 'Culture and behavior', *in* G. Lindzey (ed.) *Handbook of Social Psychology.* Cambridge, Mass.: Addison-Wesley.

KOCH, H. L. (1956) 'Attitudes of young children toward their peers as related to certain characteristics of their siblings', *Psychol. Monogr.,* **70,** No. 19.

KOGAN, N., and WALLACH, M. A. (1967) 'Risk taking as a function of the situation, the person, and the group', *in New Directions in Psychology* **3.** New York: Holt, Rinehart and Winston.

KOMAROVSKY, M. (1946) 'Cultural contradictions and sex roles', *Amer. J. Sociol.,* **52,** 184–189.

KOOS, E. L. (1946) *Families in Trouble.* New York: King's Crown Press.

KRAMER, E. (1963) 'Judgement of personal characteristics and emotions from non-verbal properties of speech', *Psychol. Bull.*, **60**, 408–420.

KRASNER, L. (1958) 'Studies of the conditioning of verbal behavior', *Psychol. Bull.*, **55**, 148–170.

KRECH, D., CRUTCHFIELD, R. S., and BALLACHEY, E. L. (1962) *Individual in Society*. New York: McGraw-Hill.

KROUT, M. H. (1954a) 'An experimental attempt to produce unconscious manual symbolic movements', *J. general Psychol.*, **51**, 93–120.

KROUT, M. H. (1954b) 'An experimental attempt to determine the significance of unconscious manual symbolic movements', *J. general Psychol.*, **51**, 121–152.

KUHN, M. H., and MCPARTLAND, T. S. (1954) 'An empirical investigation of self-attitudes', *Amer. sociol. Rev.*, **19**, 68–76.

KUHN, T. S. (1962) *The Structure of Scientific Revolutions*. Univ. of Chicago Press.

LA BARRE, W. (1964) 'Paralinguistics, kinesics, and cultural anthropology', *in* T. A. Sebeok (ed.) *Approaches to Semiotics*. The Hague: Mouton.

LA FORGE, R., and SUCZEK, R. (1955) 'The interpersonal dimension of personality: III An interpersonal check list', *J. Pers.*, **24**, 94–112.

LAING, R. D. (1960a) *The Self and Others*. London: Tavistock.

LAING, R. D. (1960b) *The Divided Self*. London: Tavistock.

LAING, R. D., PHILLIPSON, H., and LEE, A. R. (1966) *Interpersonal Perception*. London: Tavistock.

LALLJEE, M. (1967) 'On the classification of voices', (roneoed). Oxford Institute of Experimental Psychology.

LAMBERT, W. E. *et al.* (1960) 'Evaluational reactions to spoken languages', *J. abnorm. soc. Psychol.*, **60**, 44–51.

LANCASTER, J. B., and LEE, R. B. (1965) 'The annual reproductive cycle in monkeys and apes', *in* I. DeVore (ed.) *Primate Behavior*. New York: Holt, Rinehart and Winston.

LANDIS, C. (1924) 'Studies of emotional reactions. II General behavior and facial expression', *J. comp. Psychol.*, **4**, 447–509.

LANDSBERGER, H. A. (1961–2) 'The horizontal dimension in bureaucracy', *Admin. Sci. Quart.*, **6**, 299–332.

LANG, P. J., and LAZOWIK, A. D. (1963) 'The experimental desensitization of a phobia', *J. abnorm. soc. Psychol.*, **66**, 519–525.

LANGNER, T. S., and MICHAEL, S. T. (1963) *Life Stress and Mental Health*. London: Collier-Macmillan.

LANZETTA, J. T., and ROBY, T. B. (1956) 'Effects of work-group structure and certain task variables on group performance', *J. abnorm. soc. Psychol.*, **53**, 307–314.

LASHLEY, K. S. (1951) 'The problem of serial order in behavior', *in* L. A. Jeffress (ed.) *Cerebral Mechanisms in Behavior*. New York: Wiley.

LATANÉ, B. (ed.) (1966) 'Studies in social comparison', *J. Exp. Soc. Psychol.*, Supplement 1.

LAWSHE, C. H. *et al.* (1959) 'Studies in management training evaluation. II The effects of exposure to role-playing', *J. appl. Psychol.*, **43,** 287–292.

LAZARUS, A. (1963) 'The results of behavior therapy in 126 cases of severe neurosis', *Beh. Ther. Res.*, **1,** 65–78.

LEARY, T. (1957) *Interpersonal Diagnosis of Personality*. New York: Ronald.

LEAVITT, H. J. (1951) 'Some effects of certain communication patterns', *J. abnorm. soc. Psychol.*, **46,** 38–50.

LEAVITT, H. J., and MUELLER, R. A. H. (1951) 'Some effects of feedback on communication', *Hum. Relat.*, **4,** 401–410.

LECKY, P. (1945) *Self-consistency, a Theory of Personality*. New York: Island Press.

LEFCOURT, H. M., and STEFFY, R. H. (1966) 'Sex-linked censure expectancies in process and reactive schizophrenics', *J. Pers.*, **34,** 366–380.

LEFCOURT, H. M. *et al.* (1967) 'Visual interaction and performance of process and reactive schizophrenics as a function of examiner's sex', *J. Pers.*, **35,** 535–546.

LEIPOLD, W. D. (1963) 'Psychological distance in a dyadic interview as a function of introversion–extraversion, anxiety, social desirability and stress', Ph.D. thesis, Univ. of N. Dakota.

LEMANN, T. B., and SOLOMON, R. L. (1952) 'Group characteristics as revealed in sociometric patterns and personality ratings', *Sociometry*, **15,** 7–90.

LEMMERT, E. M. (1962) 'Paranoia and the dynamics of exclusion', *Sociometry*, **25,** 2–20.

LENNARD, H. L., and BERNSTEIN, A. (1960) *The Anatomy of Psychotherapy*. Columbia U.P.

LENNEBERG, E. H. (1964) 'A biological perspective of language', *in* E. H. Lenneberg (ed.) *New Directions in the Study of Language*. Boston: MIT Press.

LENROW, P. D. (1965) 'Studies of sympathy', *in* S. S. Tomkins and C. E. Izard (eds.) *Affect, Cognition and Personality*. London: Tavistock.

LERNER, M. J. (1963) 'Responsiveness of chronic schizophrenics to social behavior of others in a meaningful task situation', *J. abnorm. soc. Psychol.*, **67,** 292–299.

LERNER, M. J., and FAIRWEATHER, G. W. (1963) 'Social behavior of chronic schizophrenics in supervised and unsupervised work groups', *J. abnorm. soc. Psychol.*, **67,** 219–225.

LEUBA, C., and LUCAS, C. (1945) 'The effects of attitudes on descriptions of pictures', *J. exp. Psychol.*, **35,** 517–524.

LEVIN, H., BALDWIN, A. L., GALLWEY, M., and PAIVIO, A. (1960) 'Audience stress, personality and speech', *J. abnorm. soc. Psychol.*, **61,** 469–473.

LEWIN, K. (1952) *Field Theory in Social Science*. London: Tavistock.

LEWIS, H. B. (1944) 'An experimental study of the role of the ego in work. I. The role of the ego in cooperative work'. *J. exp. Psychol.*, **34**, 113–126.

LEWIS, M. M. (1959) *How Children Learn to Speak*. New York: Basic Books.

LIDZ, T. (1963) *The Family and Human Adaptation*. New York: Int. Univ. Press.

LIDZ, T., and FLECK, S. (1964) 'Schizophrenia, human integration, and the role of the family', *in* D. D. Jackson (ed.) *The Etiology of Schizophrenia*. New York: Basic Books.

LIEBERMAN, S. (1956) 'The effects of changes in roles on the attitudes of role occupants', *Hum. Relat.*, **9**, 385–402.

LIFTON, R. J. (1961) *Thought Reform and the Psychology of Totalism*. New York: Norton.

LIGGETT, J. (1957) 'A non-verbal approach to the phenomenal self', *J. Psychol.*, **43**, 225–237.

LIKERT, R. (1961) *New Patterns of Management*. New York: McGraw-Hill.

LINDSLEY, O. R. (1956) 'Operant conditioning methods applied to research in chronic schizophrenia', *Psychiat. Res. Rpts*, **5**, 118–139.

LINDZEY, G., and BORGATTA, E. F. (1954) 'Sociometric measurement', *in* G. Lindzey (ed.) *Handbook of Social Psychology*. Cambridge, Mass.: Addison-Wesley.

LIPPITT, R. (1940) 'An experimental study of the effects of democratic and autocratic atmospheres', *Univ. Iowa Stud. Child Welf.*, **16**, 45–195.

LIPPITT, R. (1949) *Training in Community Relations*. New York: Harper.

LIPPITT, R., POLANSKY, N., and ROSEN, S. (1952) 'The dynamics of power: a field study of social influence in groups of children', *Hum. Relat.*, **5**, 37–64.

LIPPS, T. (1903) *Leitfaden der Psychologie*. Leipzig: Engelmann.

LIPPS, T. (1907) 'Das wissen von fremden Ichen', *Psychol. Untersuch.*, **1**, 694–722.

LIPSET, S. M. (1961) 'A changing American character?', *in* S. M. Lipset and L. Lowenthal (eds.) *Culture and Social Character*. New York: Free Press.

LITTLE, B. (1967) 'Age and sex differences in the use of psychological role and physicalistic constructs', paper to BPS (roneoed). Oxford Institute of Experimental Psychology.

LITTLE, B. (1969) 'Studies of psychospecialists', *Psych. Reports* (in press).

LITTLE, K. B. (1965) 'Personal space', *J. exp. soc. Psychol.*, **1**, 237–247.

LOBAN, W. (1953) 'A study of social sensitivity (sympathy) among adolescents', *J. educ. Psychol.*, **44**, 102–112.

LOEHLIN, J. C. (1965) ' "Interpersonal" experiments with a computer model of personality', *J. pers. soc. Psychol.*, **2**, 580–584.

LOIZOS, C. (1967) 'Play behaviour in higher primates: a review', *in* D. Morris (ed.) *Primate Ethology*. London: Weidenfeld and Nicolson.

LOMBARD, G. F. F. (1955) *Behavior in a Selling Group*. Harvard University Press.

LONGABAUGH, R. (1963) 'A category system for coding interpersonal behavior as social exchange', *Sociometry*, **26**, 319–344.

LONGABAUGH, R. *et al.* (1966) 'The interactional world of the chronic schizophrenic patient', *Psychiatry*, **29**, 78–99.

LOOMIS, C. R., and BEEGLE, J. A. (1950) *Rural Social Systems*. New York: Prentice Hall.

LOOMIS, J. L. (1959) 'Communication, the development of trust and cooperative behavior', *Hum. Relat.*, **12**, 305–315.

LORENZ, K. (1963) *On Aggression*. London: Methuen.

LORENZ, M., and COBB, L. (1952) 'Language behavior in manic patients', *Arch. Neurol. & Psychiat.*, **67**, 763–770.

LORGE, I., and SOLOMON, H. (1955) 'Two models of group behavior in the solution of eureka-type problems'. *Psychometrika*, **20**, 139–148.

LORR, M., and MCNAIR, D. M. (1965) 'Expansion of the interpersonal behavior circle'. *J. pers. soc. Psychol.*, **2**, 813–830.

LOTT, A. J., and LOTT, B. E. (1965) 'Group cohesiveness as interpersonal attraction: a review of relationships with antecedent and consequent variables', *Psychol. Bull.*, **64**, 259–309.

LOVAAS, O. I., FREITAS, L., NELSON, K., and WHALEN, C. (1967) 'The establishment of imitation and its use for the development of complex behavior in schizophrenic children', *Beh. Res. Ther.*, **5**, 171–181.

LU, Y-C. (1961) 'Contradictory parental expectations in schizophrenia', *Arch. Gen. Psychiat.*, **6**, 219–234.

LUCHINS, A. S. (1957a) 'Primacy-recency in impression formation', *in* C. I. Hovland *et al. The Order of Presentation in Persuasion*. New York: Yale U.P.

LUCHINS, A. S. (1957b) 'Experimental attempts to minimize the impact of first impressions', *in* C. I. Hovland *et al. The Order of Presentation in Persuasion*. New York: Yale U.P.

LUMSDAINE, A. A. (1963) 'Instruments and media of instruction', *in* N. L. Gage (ed.) *Handbook of Research on Teaching*. Chicago: Rand McNally.

LURIA, A. R. (1961) *The Role of Speech in the Regulation of Normal and Abnormal Behaviour*. New York: Liveright.

LURIA, A. R. (1963) *The Role of Speech in the Development of Normal and Abnormal Behaviour*. Oxford: Pergamon.

MCCALL, G. J., and SIMMONS, J. L. (1966) *Identities and Interactions*. New York: Free Press.

MCCANDLESS, B. R., and MARSHALL, H. R. (1957) 'Sex differences in social acceptance and participation of preschool children', *Child Develpm.*, **28**, 421–425.

MCCARTHY, D. (1929) 'A comparison of children's language in different situations', *J. genet. Psychol.*, **36**, 583–591.

MCCARTHY, D. (1954) 'Language development in children', *in* L. Carmichael (ed.) *Handbook of Child Psychology*. New York: Wiley.

MCCLEERY, R. H. (1957) *Policy Change in Prison Management*. Michigan State University.

MCCLELLAND, D. C. (1961) *The Achieving Society*. New York: Van Nostrand.

MCCLELLAND, D. C., ATKINSON, J. W., CLARK, R. A., and LOWELL E. L. (1953) *The Achievement Motive*. New York: Appleton-Century.

MCCORD, W., and MCCORD, J. (1944) 'Two approaches to the cure of delinquents', *J. Crim. L., Criminology and Police Science*, **44**, 442–467.

MCCORD, W., and MCCORD, J. (1956) *Psychopathy and Delinquency*. New York: Grune and Stratton.

MCDAVID, J. W. (1965) 'The sex variable in conforming behavior'. ONR Report. Univ. of Miami.

MCDAVID, J., and SCHRODER, H. M. (1957) 'The interpretation of approval and disapproval by delinquent and non-delinquent adolescents', *J. Pers.*, **25**, 539–549.

MCGINN, N. F., HARBURG, E., and GINSBURG, G. P. (1965) 'Dependency relations with parents and affiliative responses in Michigan and Guadalajara', *Sociometry*, **28**, 305–321.

MCGREGOR, D. (1960) *The Human Side of Enterprise*. New York: McGraw-Hill.

MCGREGOR, O. R., and ROWNTREE, G. (1962) 'The family', *in* A. T. Welford *et al.* (eds.) *Society*. London: Routledge and Kegan Paul.

MCNEIL, D. (1966) 'The creation of language', *Discovery*, **27**, No. 7, 34–38.

MCPHAIL, P. (1967) 'The development of social skill in adolescents', paper to BPS (roneoed). Oxford Department of Education.

MACANDREW, C., and EDGERTON, R. (1966) 'On the possibility of friendship', *Amer. J. ment. def.*, **70**, 612–621.

MACCOBY, N., and SHEFFIELD, F. D. (1957) *Theory and Experimental Research on the Teaching of Complex Sequential Procedures by Alternate Demonstration and Practice*. Maintenance Laboratory, Lowry Air Force Base, Colorado, cited by Zinser (1966).

MACDONALD, D. (1958) 'A caste, a culture, a market', *New Yorker*, Nov. 22nd and Nov. 24th.

MACLAY, H., and OSGOOD, C. E. (1959) 'Hesitation phenomena in spontaneous English speech, *Word*, **15**, 19–44.

MADARIAGA, S. DE (1928) *Englishmen, Frenchmen, Spaniards*. London: O.U.P.

MAHL, G. F., and SCHULZE, G. (1964) 'Psychological research in the extra-linguistic area', *in* T. A. Sebeok *et al.* (eds.) *Approaches to Semiotics*. The Hague: Mouton.

MAIER, N. R. F. (1952) *Principles of Human Relations*. New York: Wiley.

MAIER, N. R. F. (1953) 'An experimental test of the effect of training on discussion leadership', *Hum. Relat.*, **6**, 161–173.

MAIER, N. R. F., and SOLEM, A. R. (1952) 'The contribution of a discussion leader to the quality of group thinking: the effective use of minority opinions', *Hum. Relat.*, **5**, 277–288.

MAIER, N. R. F., SOLEM, A. R., and MAIER, A. A. (1964) *Supervisory and Executive Development*. New York: Wiley.

MANDRY, M., and NEKULA, M. (1939) 'Social relations between children of the same age during the first two years of life', *J. genet. Psychol.*, **54**, 193–215.

MANIS, J. G., and MELTZER, B. N. (eds.) (1961) *Symbolic Interaction*. Boston: Allyn and Bacon.

MANN, F. C. (1957), 'Studying and creating change: a means to understanding social organization', *Res. Indust. Hum. Relat.*, **17**, 146–167.

MANN, F. C., and HOFFMAN, L. R. (1960) *Automation and the Worker*. New York: Holt.

MANN, R. D. (1959) 'A review of the relationships between personality and performance in small groups', *Psychol. Bull.*, **56**, 241–270.

MANN, R. D. *et al.* (1967) *Interpersonal Styles and Group Development*. New York: Wiley.

MARCIA, J. E. (1966) 'Development and validation of ego-identity status', *J. pers. soc. Psychol.*, **3**, 551–558.

MARCUS, P. M. (1960) 'Expressive and instrumental groups: toward a theory of group structure', *Amer. J. Sociol.*, **66**, 54–59.

MARLER, P. (1965) 'Communication in monkeys and apes', *in* I. DeVore (ed.) *Primate Behavior*. New York: Holt, Rinehart and Winston.

MARLOWE, D., GERGEN, K. J., and DOOB, A. N. (1966) 'Opponent's personality, expectation of social interaction, and interpersonal bargaining', *J. pers. soc. Psychol.*, **3**, 206–213.

MARQUIS, D. G., GUETZKOW, H., and HEYNS, R. W. (1950) 'A social psychological study of the decision-making conference', *in* H. Guetzkow (ed.) *Groups, Leadership and Men*. Pittsburgh: Carnegie.

MASLOW, A. H., HIRSH, E., STEIN, M., and HONIGMANN, I. (1945) 'A clinically derived test for measuring psychological security–insecurity', *J. general Psychol.*, **33**, 21–41.

MASON, W. A. (1965a) 'Sociability and social organization in monkeys and apes', *Advances in Experimental Social Psychology*, **1**, 278–303.

MASON, W. A. (1965b) 'The social development of monkeys and apes', *in* I. DeVore (ed.) *Primate Behavior*. New York: Holt, Rinehart and Winston.

MATARAZZO, J. D. (1965) 'Psychotherapeutic processes', *Ann. Rev. Psychol.*, **16**, 181–224.

MATARAZZO, J. D., and SASLOW, G. (1961) 'Differences in interview interaction behavior among normal and deviant groups', *in* I. A. Berg and B. M. Bass (eds.) *Conformity and Deviation*. New York: Harper.

MATARAZZO, R. G. *et al.* (1958) 'Psychological test and organismic correlates of interview interaction patterns', *J. abnorm. soc. Psychol.*, **56**, 329–338.

MAUSNER, D. (1954) 'The effect of prior reinforcement on the interaction of observer pairs', *J. abnorm. soc. Psychol.*, **57**, 65–68.

MAYER-GROSS, W., SLATER, E., and ROTH, M. (1960) *Clinical Psychiatry*. London: Cassell.

MEAD, G. H. (1934) *Mind, Self and Society*. University of Chicago Press.

MEAD, M. (1937) *Co-operation and Competition among Primitive Peoples*. New York: McGraw-Hill.

MEHRABIAN, A. (1966a) 'Attitudes in relation to the forms of communicator–object relationship in spoken communications', *J. Pers.*, **34**, 80–93.

MEHRABIAN, A. (1966b) 'Immediacy: an indicator of attitudes in linguistic communication', *J. Pers.*, **34**, 26–34.

MEHRABIAN, A. (1966c) 'Orientation behaviors and non-verbal attitude communication', (roneoed). UCLA.

MEHRABIAN, A. (1968) 'The inference of attitudes from the posture, orientation, and distance of a communication', *J. Consult. Psychol.* **32**, 296–308.

MEHRABIAN, A., and FERRIS, S. R. (1967) 'Inference of attitudes from non-verbal communication in two channels', *J. Consult. Psychol.*, **31**, 248–252.

MEHRABIAN, A., and WIENER, M. (1967) 'Decoding of inconsistent communication', *J. pers. soc. Psychol.*, **6**, 109–114.

MELDMAN, M. J. (1967) 'Verbal behavior analysis of self-hyperattentionism', *Dis. Nerv. Syst.*, **28**, 469–473.

MELIKIAN, L. H. (1959) 'Authoritarianism and its correlates in the Egyptian culture and in the United States', *J. Soc. Issues*, **15**, No. 3.

MELLY, G. (1965) 'Gesture goes classless', *New Society*, June 17th, 26–27.

MERBAUM, M. (1963) 'The conditioning of affective self-references by three classes of generalised reinforcers', *J. Pers*, **31**, 179–191.

MERTON, R. K., READER, G. G., and KENDALL, P. L. (1957) *The Student-Physician*. Harvard UP.

MILES, M. B. (1958) 'Factors influencing response to feedback in human relations training', cited by Stock (1964).

MILGRAM, N. A. (1960) 'Cognitive and empathetic factors in role-taking by schizophrenic and brain-damaged patients', *J. abnorm. soc. Psychol.*, **60**, 219–224.

MILGRAM, S. (1961) 'Nationality and conformity', *Sci. Amer.*, **205** (6), 45–51.

MILGRAM, S. (1963) 'Behavioral study of obedience' *J. abnorm. soc. Psychol.*, **67**, 371–378.

MILGRAM, S. (1965) 'Liberating effects of group pressure', *J. pers. soc. Psychol.*, **1**, 127–134.

MILLER, C. W. (1941) 'The paranoid syndrome', *Arch. Neurol. & Psychiat.*, **45**, 953–963.

MILLER, D. R. (1963) 'The study of social relationships: situation, identity, and social interaction', *in* S. Koch (ed.) *Psychology: A Study of a Science*, **5**, 639–737. New York: McGraw-Hill.

MILLER, D. R. (1967) 'The matching of mates', seminar paper given at Oxford.

MILLER, D. R., and SWANSON, G. E. (1960) *Inner Conflict and Defense*. New York: Holt, Rinehart and Winston.

MILLER, G. A. (1965) 'Some preliminaries to psycholinguistics', *Amer. Psychol.*, **20**, 15–20.

MILLER, G. A., GALANTER, E., and PRIBRAM, K. H. (1960) *Plans and the Structure of Behavior*. New York: Holt.

MILLER, N. E. (1944) 'Experimental studies of conflict', *in* J. McV. Hunt (ed.) *Personality and the Behavior Disorders*. New York: Ronald.

MILLER, N. E. (1948) 'Theory and experiment relating psychoanalytic displacement to stimulus-response generalisation', *J. abnorm. soc. Psychol.*, **43**, 155–178.

MILLER, N. *et al.* (1966) 'Similarity, contrast and complementarity in friendship choice', *J. pers. soc. Psychol.*, **3**, 3–12.

MILLS, T. M. (1953) 'Power relations in three person groups', *Amer. sociol. Rev.*, **18**, 351–357.

MILLS, T. M. (1967) *The Sociology of Small Groups*. Englewood Cliffs, N.J.: Prentice Hall.

MINTZ, A. (1951) 'Non-adaptive group behavior', *J. abnorm. soc. Psychol.*, **46**, 150–159.

MISHLER, A. L. (1965) 'Personal contact in international exchanges', *in* H. C. Kelman (ed.) *International Behavior*. New York: Holt, Rinehart and Winston.

MISHLER, E. G., and WAXLER, N. E. (1966) 'Family interaction processes and schizophrenia: a review of current theories', *Int. J. Psychiat.*, **2**, 375–413.

MITFORD, N. (1956) *Noblesse Oblige* (with A. S. C. Ross). London: Hamish Hamilton.

MOBBS, N. A. (1967) 'Eye-contact and introversion-extroversion', Reading B.A. thesis.

MOHANNA, A. I., and ARGYLE, M. (1960) 'A cross-cultural study of structured groups with unpopular central members, *J. abnorm. soc. Psychol.*, **60**, 139–140.

MOORE, H. T. (1922) 'Further data concerning sex differences', *J. abnorm. soc. Psychol.*, **17**, 210–214.

MOORE, S. (1960) *An Actor's Training: the Stanislavski Method*. London: Gollancz.

MORENO, J. L. (1953) *Who Shall Survive?* (2nd ed.). Beacon, N.Y.: Beacon House Inc.

MORRIS, D. (1967) *The Naked Ape*. London: Cape.

MORRIS, R., and MORRIS, D. (1966) *Men and Apes*. London: Hutchinson.

MORSE, N., and REIMER, E. (1956) 'The experimental change of a major organizational variable, *J. abnorm. soc. Psychol.*, **52**, 120–129.

MORTON, R. B. (1965) 'The uses of the laboratory method in a psychiatric hospital', *in* E. H. Schein and W. G. Bennis (eds.) *Personal and Organizational Change through Group Methods*. New York: Wiley.

MOSCOVICI, S. (1967) 'Communication processes and the properties of language', *Advances in Experimental Social Psychology*, **3**, 226–270.

MOSCOVICI, S., and PLON, M. (1966) 'Les situations-colloques: observations théoriques et expérimentales', *Bulletin de Psychologie*, **247**, 702–722.

MPHAHLELE, E. (1962) *The African Image*. London: Faber and Faber.

MULDER, M. (1960) 'Communication structure, decision structure and group performance', *Sociometry*, **23**, 1–14.

MULDER, M. *et al.* (1964) 'Non-instrumental liking tendencies towards powerful group members, *Acta Psychologica*, **22**, 367–386.

MULDER, M. *et al.* (1966) 'Illegitimacy of power and positivity of attitudes towards the power person', *Hum. Relat.*, **19**, 21–38.

MULFORD, H. A., and SALISBURY, W. W. (1964) 'Self-conceptions in a general population', *Sociol. Quart.*, **5**, 35–46.

MUNN, N. L. (1965) *The Evolution and Growth of Human Behavior*. London: Harrap.

MURDOCK, G. P. (1949) *Social Structure*. New York: Macmillan.

MURPHY, L. B. (1937) *Social Behavior and Child Personality: the Exploratory Study of some Roots of Sympathy*. New York: Columbia U.P.

MUSGROVE, F. (1963) 'Inter-generation attitudes', *Brit. J. soc. clin. Psychol.*, **2**, 209–223.

MUSSEN, P. (1967) 'Early Socialization: learning and identification', *in* T. M. Newcomb (ed.) *New Directions in Psychology*, **3**, 51–110. New York: Holt, Rinehart and Winston.

MUSSEN, P. H., CONGER, J. J., and KAGAN, J. (1963) *Child Development and Personality*. London: Harper and Row.

MUSSEN, P., and DISTLER, L. (1964) 'Child-rearing antecedents of masculine identification in kindergarten boys', *Child Developm.*, **31**, 89–100.

MUUSS, R. E. (1962) *Theories of Adolescence*. New York: Random House.

NAEGELE, K. D. (1958) 'Friendship and acquaintance: an exploration of some social distinctions'. *Harvard. Educ. Rev.*, **28**, no. 3, 232–252.

NEWCOMB, T. M. (1943) *Personality and Social Change*. New York: Dryden.

NEWCOMB, T. M. (1961) *The Acquaintance Process*. New York: Holt, Rinehart and Winston.

NEWCOMB, T. M., TURNER, R. H., and CONVERSE, P. E. (1965) *Social Psychology*. New York: Holt, Rinehart and Winston.

NIELSEN, G. (1962) *Studies in Self Confrontation*. Copenhagen: Munksgaard.

N.I.I.P. (1952) *Joint Consultation in British Industry*. London: Staples.

NISSEN, H. W., and CRAWFORD, M. P. (1936) 'A preliminary study of food-sharing behavior in young chimpanzees', *J. Comp. Psychol.*, 22, 383–419.

NORMAN, W. T. (1963) 'Toward an adequate taxonomy of personality attributes', *J. abnorm. soc. Psychol.*, 66, 574–583.

NORTHWAY, M. L. (1944) 'Outsiders: a study of the personality patterns of children least acceptable to their age mates', *Sociometry*, 7, 10–25.

O'CONNOR, N., and FRANKS, C. M. (1960) 'Childhood upbringing and other environmental factors', *in* H. J. Eysenck (ed.) *Handbook of Abnormal Psychology*. London: Pitman.

OESER, O. A., and HARARY, F. (1962) 'A mathematical model for structural role theory. I, *Hum. Relat.*, 15, 89–109.

OJEMANN, R. H. (1955) 'The role of the community in the mental health programme of the school', *in* P. Witty (ed.) *Mental Health in Modern Education*. Univ. of Chicago Press.

O'LEARY, K. D., O'LEARY, S., and BECKER, W. C. (1967) 'Modification of a deviant sibling interaction pattern in the home', *Beh. Res. Ther.*, 5, 113–120.

ORWELL, G. (1951) *Down and Out in Paris and London*. London: Gollancz.

OSBORN, A. F. (1957) *Applied Imagination*. New York: Scribner.

OSGOOD, C. E. (1953) *Method and Theory in Experimental Psychology*. New York: OUP.

OSGOOD, C. E. (1966) 'Dimensionality of the semantic space for communication via facial expressions', *Scand. J. Psychol.*, 7, 1–30.

OSGOOD, C. E., SUCI, G. J., and TANNENBAUM, P. H. (1957) *The Measurement of Meaning*. Urbana: Univ. of Illinois Press.

OSTWALD, P. F. (1965) 'Acoustic methods in psychiatry', *Sci. Amer.*, 212, March, 82–91.

PAIVIO, A. (1963) 'Audience influence, social isolation and speech', *J. abnorm. soc. Psychol.*, 67, 247–253.

PAIVIO, A. (1965) 'Personality and audience influence', *Progress in Experimental Personality Research*, 2, 127–173.

PARSONS, T., and BALES, R. F. (1955) *Family, Socialization and Interaction Process*. Glencoe, Ill.: Free Press.

PARTEN, M. B. (1933) 'Social participation among pre-school children', *J. abnorm. soc. Psychol.*, 27, 430–440.

PASTORE, N. (1960) 'Attributed characteristics of liked and disliked persons. *J. soc. Psychol.*, 52, 157–163.

PAUL, G. L. (1966) *Insight v. Densensitization in Psychotherapy*. Stanford U. Press.

PAVLOV, I. P. (1927) *Conditioned Reflexes*. Oxford: Clarendon Press.

PELZ, D. C. (1952) 'Influence: a key to effective leadership in the first-line supervisor', *Personnel*, **3**, 209–217.

PELZ, D. C. (1956) 'Some social factors related to performance in a research organization', *Admin. Sci. Quart.*, **1**, 310–325.

PEPITONE, A. (1950) 'Motivational effects in social perception', *Hum. Relat.*, **3**, 57–76.

PEPITONE, A. (1958) 'Attributions of causality, social attitudes, and cognitive matching processes', *in* R. Tagiuri and L. Petrullo. *Person Perception and Interpersonal Behavior*. Stanford, U.P.

PERRY, S. E., and WYNNE, L. C. (1959) 'Role conflict, role definition, and social change in a clinical research organization, *Soc. Forces*, **38**, 62–65.

PFUNGST, A. (1911) *Clever Hans (the Horse of Mr von Osten): a contribution to Experimental, Animal and Human Psychology* (trans. C. L. Rahn). New York: Holt.

PHILLIPS, E. L., SHENKER, S., and REVITZ, P. (1951) 'The assimilation of the new child into the group', *Psychiatry*, **14**, 319–325.

PIAGET, J. (1934) *The Language and Thought of the Child*. London: Kegan Paul, Trench and Trubner.

PIAGET, J. (1950) *The Psychology of Intelligence*. New York: Harcourt Brace.

PITTENGER, R. E., HOCKETT, C. F., and DANEHY, J. J. (1960) *The First Five Minutes*. New York: Martineau.

POLLACZEK, P. P., and HOMEFIELD, H. D. (1954) 'The use of masks as an adjunct to role-playing', *Ment. Hyg. N.Y.*, **38**, 299–304.

PONDER, E., and KENNEDY, W. P. (1927) 'On the act of blinking', *Quart. J. exp. Physiol.*, **18**, 89–110.

PORTER, E., ARGYLE, M., and SALTER, V. (1970) 'What is signalled by proximity?' *Perceptual and Motor Skills*, **30**, 39–42.

PORTER, L. W., and LAWLOR, E. E. (1965) 'Properties of organization structure in relation to job attitudes and job behavior', *Psychol. Bull.*, **64**, 23–51.

PORTNOY, I. (1959) 'The anxiety states', *in* S. Arieti (ed.) *American Handbook of Psychiatry*, **1**, 307–323. New York: Basic Books.

POSTMAN, L., and SASSENRATH, J. (1961) 'The automatic action of verbal rewards and punishments', *J. gen. Psychol.*, **65**, 109–136.

POTTER, S. (1952) *One-Upmanship*. London: Hart-Davis.

POWDERMAKER, F. B. and FRANK, J. D. (1953) *Group Psychotherapy*. Harvard University Press.

PUGH, D. (1965) 'T-group training from the point of view of organization theory', *in* G. Whitaker (ed.) *T-Group Training. Group Dynamics in Management Education*. Oxford: Blackwell.

QUINN, R. P., and KAHN, R. L. (1967) 'Organizational psychology', *Ann. Rev. Psychol.*, **18**, 437–466.

RABBIE, J. (1965) 'A cross-cultural comparison of parent–child relationships in the United States and West Germany', *Brit. J. soc. clin. Psychol.*, **4**, 298–310.

RABBIE, J. *et al.* (1967) 'Social comparison, improvement and competition'. Working paper of the European Research Training Seminar in Experimental Social Psychology, Louvain.

RAPOPORT, A., and ORWANT, C. (1962) 'Experimental games: a review', *Beh. Sci.*, **7**, 1–37.

RAPOPORT, R., and RAPOPORT, R. H. (1964) 'New light on the honeymoon', *Hum. Relat.*, **17**, 33–56.

RAPOPORT, R. H. (1960) *Community as Doctor.* London: Tavistock.

RASMUSSEN, J. E. (1964) 'Relationship of ego identity to psychosocial effectiveness', *Psychol. Reports*, **15**, 815–825.

READ, W. H. (1962) 'Upward communication in industrial hierarchies', *Hum. Relat.*, **15**, 3–16.

RETAIL TRADES EDUCATION COUNCIL (1966) 'Enquiry into Training in the Distributive Trades' (roneoed).

RETTIG, S., and PASAMANICK, B. (1962) 'Invariance in factor structure of moral value judgements from American and Korean college students', *Sociometry*, **25**, 73–84.

REVANS, R. W. (1953) *Size and Morale.* London: Acton Society Trust.

RHEINGOLD, H. L. (1956) 'The modification of social responsiveness in institutional babies, *Monogr. Soc. Res. Child Develpm.*, **21**, No. 2.

RICE, A. K. (1958) *Productivity and Social Organization: the Ahmedabad Experiment.* London: Tavistock.

RICHARDSON, A. (1961) 'The assimilation of British immigrants in a Western Australian community – a psychological study', *Research Group for European Migration Problems*, **9**, Nos. 1–2.

RICHARDSON, A. (1967) 'Mental practice: a review and discussion', *Research Quarterly*, **38**, 95–107, 263–273.

RICKERS-OVSIANKINA, M. A. (1956) 'Social accessibility in three age groups', *Psychol. Reports*, **2**, 283–294.

RICKERS-OVSIANKINA, M. A., and KUSMIN, A. A. (1958) 'Individual differences in social accessibility', *Psychol. Reports*, **4**, 391–406.

RIECKEN, H. W., and HOMANS, G. C. (1954) 'Psychological aspects of social structure', *in* G. Lindey (ed.) *Handbook of Social Psychology.* Cambridge, Mass.: Addison-Wesley.

RIEMER, M. D. (1949) 'The averted gaze', *Psychiat. Quart.*, **23**, 108–115.

RIEMER, M. D. (1955) 'Abnormalities of the gaze. A classification', *Psychiat. Quart.*, **29**, 659–672.

RIESMAN, D., GLAZER, N., and DENNEY, R. (1950) *The Lonely Crowd*, Yale U.P.

RIESMAN, D., POTTER, R. J., and WATSON, J. (1960) 'Sociability, permissiveness and equality', *Psychiatry*, **23**, 323–340.

RILEY, M. W., RILEY, J. W., and MOORE, M. E. (1961) 'Adolescent values and the Riesman typology, *in* S. M. Lipset and L. Lowenthal (eds.) *Culture and Social Character*. New York: Free Press.

RIM, Y. (1966) 'Machiavellianism and decisions involving risk', *Brit. J. soc. clin. Psychol.*, **5**, 30–36.

RIMLAND, B. (1962) *Infantile Autism*. London: Methuen.

RING, K. *et al.* (1967) 'Performance styles in interpersonal behaviour: an experimental validation of a typology, *J. exp. soc. Psychol.*, **3**, 140–159.

ROBINSON, P., and RACKSTRAW, S. J. (1967) 'Variations in mothers' answers to children's questions as a function of social class, verbal intelligence test scores and sex', *Sociology*, **1**, 259–276.

ROBSON, K. S. (1967) 'The role of eye-to-eye contact in maternal–infant attachment', *J. Child Psychol. Psychiat.*, **8**, 13–25.

ROBSON, R. A. H. (1967) 'The effects of different group sex compositions on support rates and coalition formation, paper to Canad. Sociol. Anthrop. Assoc. (roneoed). Univ. Brit. Columbia.

RODNICK, E. H. (1963) 'Clinical psychology, psychopathology, and research on schizophrenia, *in* S. Koch (ed.) *Psychology: A Study of a Science*, Vol. V. New York: McGraw-Hill, pp. 738–779.

ROETHLISBERGER, F. J., and DICKSON, W. J. (1939) *Management and the Worker*. Cambridge, Mass.: Harvard University Press.

ROGERS, C. R. (1942) *Counseling and Psychotherapy*. Boston: Houghton Mifflin.

ROGERS, C. R., and DYMOND, R. (1954) *Psychotherapy and Personality Change*. Univ. of Chicago Press.

ROMMETVEIT, R. (1960) *Selectivity, Intuition and Halo Effects in Social Perception*. Oslo University Press.

ROSE, A. M., and STUB, H. R. (1956) 'Summary of studies on the incidence of mental disorders', *in* A. M. Rose (ed.) *Mental Health and Mental Disorder*. London: Routledge and Kegan Paul.

ROSEN, S., and BIELEFELD, R. J. (1967) 'Help received by a needy competitor as contingent upon the deference he shows', Paper to APA (roneoed). Marquette University, Wisconsin.

ROSENBAUM, M. E., HORNE, W. C., and CHALMERS, D. H. (1962) 'Level of self-esteem and the learning of imitation and nonimitation', *J. Pers.*, **30**, 147–156.

ROSENBERG, M. (1965) *Society and the Adolescent Self-Image*. Princeton University Press.

ROSENBERG, P. P. (1952) 'Experimental analysis of psychodrama', Harvard Ph.D. cited by Stock (1964).

ROSENFELD, H. M. (1966) 'Instrumental affiliative functions of facial and gestural expressions', *J. pers. soc. Psychol.*, **4**, 65–72.

ROSENFELD, H. M. (1967) 'Nonverbal reciprocation of approval: an experimental analysis', *J. exp. soc. Psychol.*, **3**, 102–111.

ROSENTHAL, R. (1966) *Experimenter Effects in Behavioral Research.* New York: Appleton-Century-Crofts.

ROSHAL, S. M. (1949) 'Film-mediated learning with varying representations of the task: viewing angle, portrayal of demonstration, motion and student participation', *in* A. A. Lumsdaine (ed.) (1961) *Student Response in Programmed Instruction: A Symposium.* Washington: Nat. Acad. of Sci. – Nat. Res. Co.

ROSS, A. S. C., MITFORD, N. *et al.* (1956) *Noblesse Oblige.* London: Hamish Hamilton.

ROSS, I. and ZANDER, A. (1957) 'Need satisfaction and employee turnover', *Personnel Psychol.*, **10**, 327–338.

RUESCH, J., and KEES, W. (1956) *Non-Verbal Communication.* Berkeley: University of California Press.

RUSHING, W. A. (1966) 'Organizational size, rules, and surveillance', *J. exp. soc. Psychol.*, **2**, 11–26.

RYCHLAK, J. F. (1965) 'The similarity, compatibility, or incompatibility of needs in interpersonal selection', *J. pers. soc. Psychol.*, **2**, 334–340.

SACKETT, G. P. (1965) 'Monkeys reared in isolation with pictures as visual input: evidence for an innate releasing mechanism', *Science*, **154**, 1468–1473.

SACKETT, G. P. (1967) 'Some effects of social and sensory deprivation during rearing on behavioral development of monkeys', *Revista Interamerica de Psicologia*, **1**, 55–80.

SAHLINS, M. D. (1965) 'On the sociology of primitive exchange', *in The Relevance of Models for Social Anthropology*, ASA monographs 1. London: Tavistock Publications.

SALTER, A. (1950) *Conditioned Reflex Therapy.* New York: Creative Age Press.

SAMPSON, E. E. (1965) 'The study of ordinal position: antecedents and outcomes', *Progress in Experimental Personality Research*, **2**, 175–228.

SANFORD, F. H. (1942) 'Speech and personality: a comparative case study', *Char. & Pers.*, **10**, 169–198.

SAPIR, E. (1921) *Language: An Introduction to the Study of Speech.* New York: Harcourt, Brace & Co.

SAPOLSKY, A. (1965) 'Relationship between patient–doctor compatibility, mutual perception, and outcome of treatment', *J. abnorm. Psychol.*, **70**, 70–76.

SARASON, I. G. (1968) 'Verbal learning, modeling, and juvenile delinquency', *Amer. Psychol.*, **23**, 254–266.

SARBIN, T. R. (1967a) 'Role theoretical analysis of schizophrenia', *in* J. H. Mann (ed.) *Reader in General Psychology.* New York: Rand McNally.

SARBIN, T. R. (1967b) 'The dangerous individual: an outcome of social identity transformations', *Brit. J. Crim.*, **7**, 285–295.

SARBIN, T. R., and ALLEN, V. L. (1969) 'Role theory', *in* G. Lindzey and E. Aronson (eds.) Mass.: Addison Wesley.

SARBIN, T. R., and HARDYCK, C. D. (1953) 'Contributions to role-taking theory: role-perception on the basis of postural cues'. Unpublished, cited by Sarbin, T.R. (1954) 'Role theory', *in* G. Lindzey (ed.) *Handbook of Social Psychology*. Cambridge, Mass.: Addison-Wesley.

SARBIN, T. R., and HARDYCK, C. D. (1955) 'Conformance in role perception as a personality variable, *J. consult. Psychol.*, **19**, 109–III.

SARBIN, T. R., and JONES, D. S. (1956) 'An experimental analysis of role behavior', *J. abnorm. soc. Psychol.*, **51**, 236–241.

SARBIN, T. R., and LIM, D. T. (1963) 'Some evidence in support of the role-taking hypothesis in hypnosis', *Intern. J. Clin. Exp. Hypnosis*, **11**, 98–103.

SARBIN, T. R., TAFT, R., and BAILEY, D. E. (1960) *Clinical Inference and Cognitive Theory*. New York: Holt, Rinehart and Winston.

SARGANT, W. (1957) *Battle for the Mind*. London: Heinemann.

SARNOFF, I., and ZIMBARDO, P. G. (1961) 'Anxiety, fear and social affiliation', *J. abnorm. soc. Psychol.*, **62**, 356–363.

SARTRE, J-P. (1943) *L'Être et le Néant;* (1956) *Being and Nothingness*, trans. H. Barnes. London: Methuen.

SAYLES, L. R. (1958) *Behavior of Industrial Work Groups*. New York: Wiley.

SCANLON, J. N. (1948) 'Profit sharing under collective bargaining: three case studies, *Ind. & Lab. Rels. Rev.*, **2**, 58–75.

SCHACHTER, S. (1951) 'Deviation, rejection and communication', *J. abnorm. soc. Psychol.*, **46**, 190–207.

SCHACHTER, S. (1959) *The Psychology of Affiliation*. Stanford University Press.

SCHACHTER, S. (1964) 'The interaction of cognitive and physiological determinants of emotional state', *Advances in Experimental Social Psychology*, **1**, 49–80.

SCHAEFER, E. S. (1959) 'A circumplex model for maternal behavior', *J. abnorm. soc. Psychol.*, **59**, 226–235.

SCHAEFER, E. S., and BAYLEY, N. (1963) 'Maternal behavior, child behavior, and their intercorrelations from infancy through adolescence', *Monogr. Soc. Res. Child Develpm.*, **82**, No. 3.

SCHAFFER, H. R. (1963) 'Some issues for research in the study of attachment behaviour, *in* B. M. Foss (ed.) *Determinants of Infant Behaviour*, **2**. London: Methuen, 179–196.

SCHAFFER, H. R., and EMERSON, P. E. (1964a) 'The development of social attachments in infancy, *Monogr. Soc. Res. Child Develpm.*, **29**, No. 3.

SCHAFFER, H. R., and EMERSON, P. E. (1964b) 'Patterns of response to physical contact in early human development', *J. Child Psychol. Psychiat.*, **5**, 1–13.

SCHEFF, J. J. (1966) *Being Mentally Ill: A Sociological Theory*. Chicago: Aldine.

SCHEFLEN, A. E. (1965) *Stream and Structure of Communicational Behavior*. Commonwealth of Pennsylvania: Eastern Pennsylvania Psychiatric Institute.

SCHEIN, E. H. (1965) *Organizational Psychology*. Englewood Cliffs, N.J.: Prentice Hall.

SCHEIN, E. H., and BENNIS, W. G. (1965) *Personal Learning and Organizational Change through Group Methods*. New York: Wiley.

SCHLOSBERG, H. (1952) 'The description of facial expressions in terms of two dimension', *J. exp. Psychol.*, **44**, 229–237.

SCHMUCK, R., and LOHMAN, A. (1965) 'Peer relations and personality development' (roneoed). University of Michigan: Institute for Social Research.

SCHOFIELD, W. (1964) *Psychotherapy. The Purchase of Friendship*. Englewood Cliffs, N.J.: Prentice Hall.

SCHOOLER, C., and PARKEL, D. (1966) 'The overt behaviour of chronic schizophrenics and its relationship to their internal state and personal history', *Psychiatry*, **29**, 67–77.

SCHOOLER, C., and SCARR, S. (1962) 'Affiliation among chronic schizophrenics: relation to intrapersonal and birth order factors', *J. Pers.*, **30**, 178–192.

SCHOPLER, J. (1965) 'Social power', *Advances in Experimental Social Psychology*, **2**, 177–219.

SCHOPLER, J., and BATESON, N. (1965) 'The power of dependence', *J. pers. soc. Psychol.*, **2**, 247–254.

SCHOPLER, J., and THOMPSON, V. D. (1968) 'Role of attribution processes in mediating amount of reciprocity for a favor', *J. pers. soc. Psychol.*, **10**, 243–250.

SCHRAMM, W. (1962) 'Mass communication', *Ann. Rev. Psychol.*, **13**, 251–284.

SCHRIER, A. M., HARLOW, H. F., and STOLLNITZ, F. (1965) *Behavior of Nonhuman Primates*. New York and London: Academic Press.

SCHUHAM, A. I. (1967) 'The double-bind hypothesis a decade later', *Psychol. Bull.*, **68**, 409–416.

SCHUTZ, W. C. (1953) 'Construction of high productivity groups'. Tufts College Dept. of Systems Analysis.

SCHUTZ, W. C. (1958) *FIRO: A Three-Dimensional Theory of Interpersonal Behavior*. New York: Holt, Rinehart and Winston.

SCHWARTZ, C. G. (1957) 'Problems for mental nurses in playing a new role on a mental hospital ward', *in* M. Greenberg *et al.* (eds.) *The Patient and the Mental Hospital*. New York: Free Press.

SEARS, R. R. (1936) 'Experimental studies of projection: I. Attribution of traits', *J. soc. Psychol.*, **7**, 151–163.

SEARS, R. R. (1961) 'Relation of early socialization experiences to aggression in middle childhood', *J. abnorm. soc. Psychol.*, **63**, 466–492.

SEARS, R. R. (1963) 'Dependency motivation', *in* M. R. Jones (ed.) *Nebraska Symposium on Motivation*. Lincoln: University of Nebraska Press.

SEARS, R. R., MACCOBY, E. E., and LEVIN, H. (1957) *Patterns of Child Rearing*. New York: Row, Peterson.

SEASHORE, S. E. (1954) *Group Cohesiveness in the Industrial Work Group*. Ann Arbor: Institute for Social Research.

SECORD, P. F. (1958) 'The role of facial features in interpersonal perception', *in* R. Tagiuri and L. Petrullo (eds.) *Person Perception and Interpersonal Behavior*, Stanford U.P.

SECORD, P. F., and BACKMAN, C. W. (1964) *Social Psychology*. New York: McGraw-Hill.

SECORD, P. F., and BACKMAN, C. W. (1965) 'An interpersonal approach to personality', *Progress in Experimental Personality Research*, **2**, 91–125.

SELVIN, H. C. (1960) *The Effects of Leadership*. New York: Free Press.

SEYMOUR, W. D. (1966) *Industrial Skills*. London: Pitman.

SHAW, M. E. (1968) 'Communications networks', *Advances in Experimental Social Psychology*, **1**, 111–147.

SHEPARD, H. A. (1954) 'The value system of a university research group', *Amer. sociol. Rev.*, **19**, 456–462.

SHERIF, M., and CANTRIL, H. (1947) *The Psychology of Ego-Involvements*. New York: Wiley.

SHERIF, M., and SHERIF, C. W. (1964) *Reference Groups*. New York: Harper.

SHIELDS, J., and SLATER, E. (1960) 'Heredity and psychological abnormality', *in* H. J. Eysenck (ed.) *Handbook of Abnormal Psychology*. London: Pitman.

SHIPLEY, T. E., and VEROFF, J. (1952) 'A projective measure of need for affiliation', *J. exp. Psychol.*, **43**, 349–356.

SHOUBY, E. (1951) 'The influence of the Arabic language on the psychology of the Arab', *Middle East J.*, **5**, 284–302.

SIDNEY, E., and BROWN, M. (1961), *The Skills of Interviewing*. London: Tavistock.

SIDOWSKI, J. B. (1957) 'Reward and punishment in a minimal social situation', *J. exp. Psychol.*, **54**, 318–326.

SIDOWSKI, J. B., WYCOFF, L. B., and TABORY, L. (1956) 'The influence of reinforcement and punishment in a minimal social situation', *J. abnorm. soc. Psychol.*, **52**, 115–119.

SIMPSON, R. L. (1959) 'Vertical and horizontal communication in formal organizations, *Admin. Sci. Quart.*, **4**, 188–196.

SINGER, J. E. (1964) 'The use of manipulation strategies: Machiavellianism and attractiveness, *Sociometry*, **27**, 138–150.

SINGER, J. E., BRUSH, C. A., and LUBLIN, S. C. (1965) 'Some aspects of deindividuation: identification and conformity, *J. exp. soc. Psychol.*, **1**, 356–378.

SINGER, M. T., and WYNNE, L. C. (1963) 'Differential characteristics of childhood schizophrenics, childhood neurotics, and young adult schizophrenics, *Amer. J. Psychiat.*, **120**, 234–243.

SLATER, P. E. (1955) 'Role differentiation in small groups', *in* A. P. Hare *et al.* (eds.) *Small Groups*. New York: Knopf.

SMELSER, W. T. (1961) 'Dominance as a factor in achievement and perception in co-operative problem solving interactions', *J. abnorm. soc. Psychol.*, **62**, 535–542.

SMITH, E. E., and KIGHT, S. S. (1959) 'Effects of feedback on insight and problem-solving efficiency in training groups', *J. appl. Psychol.*, **43**, 209–211.

SMITH, H. C. (1967) *Sensitivity to People*. New York: McGraw-Hill.

SMITH, M. E. (1926) 'An investigation of the development of the sentence and the extent of vocabulary in young children', *Univ. Iowa Stud. Child. Welf.*, **3**, No. 5.

SMITH, P. A. (1962) 'A comparison of three sets of rotated factor analytic solutions of self-concept data', *J. abnorm. soc. Psychol.*, **64**, 326–333.

SMITH, P. B. (1966) 'The effects of T-group training', *in* D. S. Whitaker and M. A. Lieberman (eds.) *Psychotherapy Through Group Processes*. New York: Atherton.

SOMMER, R. (1959) 'Studies in personal space', *Sociometry*, **22**, 247–260.

SOMMER, R. (1961) 'Leadership and group geography', *Sociometry*, **24**, 99–109.

SOMMER, R. (1962) 'The distance for comfortable conversation: a further study', *Sociometry*, **25**, 111–116.

SOMMER, R. (1965) 'Further studies of small group ecology', *Sociometry*, **28**, 337–348.

SOMMER, R. (1967) 'Small group ecology', *Psychol. Bull.*, **67**, 145–152.

SOMMER, R., and OSMOND, H. (1962) 'The schizophrenic in society', *Psychiatry*, **25**, 244–255.

SORENSON, O. (1958) *The Observed Changes Enquiry*. New York: GEC.

SOROKIN, P. A. (1950) *Altruistic Love*. Boston: Beacon Press.

SPARKS, J. (1967) 'Allogrooming in primates: a review', *in* D. Morris (ed.) *Primate Ethology*. London: Weidenfeld and Nicolson.

SPENCER, H. (1904) *The Principles of Ethics*. London: Williams and Norgate.

SPEROFF, B. J. (1959) 'Group psychotherapy as adjunct training in handling grievances, *Group Psychotherapy*, **12**, 169–174.

SPIEGEL, J. P. (1956) 'Interpersonal influences within the family', *in* B. Schaffner (ed.) *Group Processes*. New York: Josiah Macy Foundation.

SPIEGEL, J. P., and BELL, N. W. (1959) 'The family of the psychiatric patient', *in* S. Arieti (ed.) *American Handbook of Psychiatry*. New York: Basic Books.

SPIELBERGER, C. D. (1965) 'Theoretical and epistemological issues in verbal conditioning, *in* S. Rosenberg (ed.) *Directions in Psycholinguistics*. New York: Macmillan.

SPIRO, M. E. (1958) *Children of the Kibbutz*. Cambridge, Mass.: Harvard U.P.

SPITZ, R. A. (1946) 'The smiling response: a contribution to the ontogenesis of social relations, *Genet. Psychol. Monogr.*, **34**, 57–125.

SPITZ, R. A. (1965) *The First Year of Life*. New York: International Universities Press.

SROLE, L. (1956) 'Social integration and certain corollaries', *Amer. sociol. Rev.*, **21**, 709–716.

STEPHENSON, W. (1953) *The Study of Behavior: Q-technique and its Methodology*. University of Chicago Press.

STERN, G. G., STEIN, M. I., and BLOOM, B. S. (1956) *Methods in Personality Assessment: Human Behavior in Complex Social Situations*. New York: Free Press.

STOCK, D. (1964) 'A survey of research on T-groups', *in* L. P. Bradford, *et al.* (1964).

STOGDILL, R. M. (1953) *The Prediction of Navy Officer Performance*. Personnel Research Board. Ohio State University.

STOGDILL, R. M. *et al.* (1953) *Aspects of leadership and Organization*. Columbus: Ohio State University.

STOLLER, F. H. (1964) 'Closed circuit television and video tape for group psychotherapy with chronic mental patients', *Amer. Psychol.* (abstract), 525.

STOLLER, F. H. (1968) 'Focused feedback with video tape: extending the group's functions', *in* G. M. Gazda (ed.) *Innovations to Group Therapy*. Springfield, Ill.: Thomas.

STOLUROW, L. M. (1965) 'Idiographic programming', *Nat. Soc. Prog. Instruct. J.*, Oct., 10–12.

STOLUROW, L. M., and SANTHAI, S. (1966) 'Critical incidents with hetero-cultural interactions'. ONR Report.

STOLZ, H. R., and STOLZ, L. M. (1944) 'Adolescent problems related to somatic variations, *in* H. E. Jones (ed.) *Adolescence*. The 43rd yearbook. Nat. Soc. Study Educ. Univ. of Chicago.

STONE, G. C., LEAVITT, G. S., and GAGE, N. L. (1957) 'Two kinds of accuracy in predicting another's responses, *J. soc. Psychol.*, **45**, 245–254.

STOTLAND, E., and WALSH, J. A. (1963) 'Birth order and an experimental study of empathy', *J. abnorm. soc. Psychol.*, **66**, 610–614.

STOTLAND, E., ZANDER, A. *et al.* (1964) 'Studies of identification'. NIMH Report.

STRODTBECK, F. L. (1951) 'Husband–wife interaction over revealed differences', *Amer. sociol. Rev.*, **16**, 468–473.

STRONGMAN, K. T., and CHAMPNESS, B. G. (1968) 'Dominance hierarchies and conflict in eye contact', *Acta Psychologica*, **28**, 376–86.

STROOP, J. R. (1932) 'Is the judgment of the group better than that of the average member of the group?', *J. exp. Psychol.*, **15**, 550–562.

STOUFFER, S. A., and TOBY, J. (1951) 'Role conflict and personality', *Amer. J. Sociol.*, **56**, 395–406.

STOUFFER, S. A. et al. (1949) *The American Soldier*. Princeton University Press.

SULLIVAN, H. S. (1947) *Conceptions of Modern Psychiatry*. Washington: W. A. White Foundation.

SUMBY, W. H., and POLLACK, I. (1954) 'Visual contribution to speech intelligibility in noise', *J. acoust. soc. Amer.*, **26**, 212–215.

SUNDBERG, N. D., and TYLER, L. E. (1962) *Clinical Psychology*. New York: Appleton-Century-Crofts.

SUTHERLAND, E. H. (1937) *The Professional Thief*. University of Chicago Press.

SZASZ, T. S. (1961) *The Myth of Mental Illness*. London: Secker and Warburg.

TAGIURI, R. (1958) 'Social preference and its perception', *in* R. Tagiuri and L. Petrullo (eds.) *Person Perception and Interpersonal Behavior*. Stanford U.P.

TAGIURI, R. (1969) 'Person perception', *in* G. Lindzey and E. Aronson (eds.) *Handbook of Social Psychology*. Reading, Mass.: Addison-Wesley.

TAJFEL, H. (1969) 'Social and cultural factors in perception', *in* G. Lindzey and E. Aronson (eds.) *Handbook of Social Psychology*. Reading, Mass.: Addison-Wesley.

TAJFEL, H., and WILKES, A. L. (1964) 'Salience of attributes and commitment to extreme judgements in the perception of people', *Brit. J. soc. clin. Psychol.*, **3**, 40–49.

TAYLOR, D. A. (1965) 'Some aspects of the development of interpersonal relationship: social penetration processes', Naval Medical Research Inst., Washington.

TAYLOR, D. A., and ALTMAN, I. (1966) 'Intimacy-scaled stimuli for use in studies of interpersonal relations', *Psychol. Reports*, **19**, 729–730.

TAYLOR, D. W., BERRY, P. C., and BLOCK, C. H. (1958) 'Does group participation when using brainstorming facilitate or inhibit creative thinking?', *Admin. Sci. Quart.*, **3**, 23–47.

TEGER, A. I., and PRUITT, D. G. (1967) 'Components of group risk taking', *J. exp. soc. Psychol.*, **3**, 189–205.

TERMAN, L. M. (1938) *Psychological Factors in Marital Happiness*. New York: McGraw-Hill.

THAYER, S., and SCHIFF, W. (1967) 'Stimulus factors in observer judgement of social interaction. I. Facial expression and motion pattern' (roneoed). City College of the City University of New York.

THIBAUT, J. W., and FAUCHEUX, C. (1965) 'The development of contractual norms in a bargaining situation under two types of stress', *J. exp. soc. Psychol.*, **1**, 89–102.

THIBAUT, J. W., and KELLEY, H. H. (1959) *The Social Psychology of Groups*. New York: Wiley.

THIBAUT, J. W., and RIECKEN, H. W. (1955) 'Some determinants and consequences of the perception of social causality', *J. Pers.*, **24**, 113–133.

THOMAS, E. J. (1957) 'Effects of facilitative role interdependence on group functioning', *Hum. Relat.*, **10**, 347–366.

THOMAS, E. J., and FINK, C. F. (1963) 'Effects of group size', *Psychol. Bull.*, **60**, 371–384.

THOMPSON, G. G. (1962) *Child Psychology*. Boston: Houghton Mifflin Co.

THORNDIKE, R. L., and STEIN, S. (1937) 'An evaluation of the attempts to measure social intelligence', *Psychol. Bull.*, **34**, 275–285.

THORNTON, G. R. (1944) 'The effect of wearing glasses on judgements of personality traits of people seen briefly', *J. appl. Psychol.*, 28, 203–207.

THORPE, W. H. (1962) *Learning and Instinct in Animals*. London: Methuen.

TINBERGEN, N. (1951) *The Study of Instinct*. Oxford University Press.

TINBERGEN, N. (1953) *Social Behaviour in Animals*. London: Methuen.

TINBERGEN, N. (1968) 'On war and peace in animals and men', *Science*, **160**, 1411–1418.

TITUS, H. E., and HOLLANDER, E. P. (1957) 'The California F scale in psychological research 1950–1955', *Psychol. Bull.*, **54**, 47–65.

TOGNOLI, J. J. (1968) 'Reciprocity and reactance in game-playing behavior', *Bull. B.P.S.*, **21**, no. 70, p. 39.

TOPPING, R. (1943) 'Treatment of the pseudosocial boy', *Amer. J. Orthopsychiat.*, **13**, 353–360.

TORRANCE, E. P. (1955) 'Some consequences of power differences on decision making in permanent and temporary three-man groups', *in* A. P. Hare *et al.* (eds.) *Small Groups: Studies in Social Interaction*. New York: Knopf.

TRIANDIS, H. C. (1964) 'Cultural influences upon cognitive processes', *Advances in Experimental Social Psychology*, **1**, 2–48.

TRIST, E. L. *et al.* (1963) *Organizational Choice*. London: Tavistock.

TROW, D., and HERSCHDORFER, G. (1965) 'An experiment on the status incongruence phenomenon'. ONR Report.

TSUMORI, A. (1967) 'Newly acquired behavior and social interactions of Japanese monkeys', *in* S. A. Altmann (ed.) *Social Communication among Primates*. Univ. of Chicago Press.

TUCKMAN, B. W. (1965) 'Developmental sequence in small groups', *Psychol. Bull.*, **63**, 384–399.

TUCKMAN, B. W. (1966) 'Interpersonal probing and revealing and systems of integrative complexity', *J. pers. soc. Psychol.*, **3**, 655–664.

TURK, H. (1961) 'Instrumental and expressive ratings reconsidered', *Sociometry*, **24**, 76–81.

TURNER, R. H. (1956) 'Role-taking, role standpoint, and reference-group behavior', *Amer. J. Sociol.*, **61**, 316–328.

TYHURST, J. S. (1957) 'Paranoid patterns', *in* A. H. Leighton *et al.* (eds.) *Explorations in Social Psychiatry*. London: Tavistock.

UDY, S. H. (1959) *The Organization of Work*. New Haven: Human Relations Area Files.

ULRICH, L. and TRUMBO, D. (1965) 'The selection interview since 1949', *Psychol. Bull.*, **63**, 100–116.

UNDERWOOD, W. J. (1965) 'Evaluation of laboratory method training', *Train. Dir. J.*, **19**, (5), 34–40.

VANDENBERG, S. G. (1960) 'The interpretation of facial expressions by schizophrenics, other mental patients, normal adults and children', *Proc. Int. Cong. Psych. Bonn.*

VAN HOOFF, J. A. R. A. M. (1967) 'The facial displays of the Catarrhine monkeys and apes', *in* D. Morris (ed.) *Primate Ethology*. London: Weidenfeld and Nicolson.

VAN ZELST, R. H. (1952) 'Validation of a sociometric regrouping procedure', *J. abnorm. soc. Psychol.*, **47**, 299–301.

VAUGHAN, G. M. (1964) 'The trans-situational aspect of conformity behavior', *J. Pers.*, **32**, 335–354.

VEROFF, J. *et al.* (1960) 'The use of Thematic Apperception to assess motivation in a nationwide interview study', *Psychol. Monogr.*, **74**, No. 499.

VERPLANCK, W. S. (1955) 'The control of the content of conversation: reinforcement of statements of opinion', *J. abnorm. soc. Psychol.*, **51**, 668–676.

VIDEBECK, R. (1960) 'Self-conception and the reactions of others,' *Sociometry*, **23**, 351–359.

VIDICH, A. J. and STEIN, M. R. (1960) 'The dissolved identity in military life', *in* M. R. Stein (ed.) *The Eclipse of Community*. Princeton University Press.

VINACKE, W. E. and ARKOFF, A. (1957) 'An experimental study of coalitions in the triad', *Amer. sociol. Rev.*, **22**, 406–414.

VINE, I. (1969) 'Communication by facial-visual signals', *in* J. H. Crook (ed.) *Social Behaviour in Animals and Men*. London and New York: Academic Press.

VITELES, M. S. (1954) *Motivation and Morale in Industry*. London: Staples.

VON NEUMANN, J., and MORGENSTERN, O. (1944) *Theory of Games and Economic Behaviour*. Princeton University Press.

VROOM, V. (1964) *Work and Motivation*. New York: Wiley.

WALKER, C. R. (1957) *Toward the Automatic Factory*. New Haven: Yale U.P.

WALKER, E. L., and HEYNS, R. W. (1962) *An Anatomy for Conformity*. Englewood Cliffs, N.J.: Prentice Hall.

WALLACH, M. A., KOGAN, N., and BEM, D. J. (1964) 'Diffusion of responsibility and level of risk taking in groups', *J. abnorm. soc. Psychol.*, **68**, 263–274.

WALLEN, N. E., and TRAVERS, R. M. W. (1963) 'Analysis and investigation of teaching methods', *in* N. L. Gage (ed.) *Handbook of Research in Teaching*. Chicago: Rand McNally.

WALLER, W., and HILL, R. (1951) *The Family: A Dynamic Interpretation*. New York: Dryden.

WALSTER, E. (1965) 'The effect of self-esteem on romantic liking', *J. exp. soc. Psychol.*, **1**, 184–197.

WALSTER, E. *et al.* (1966) 'Importance of physical attractiveness in dating behaviour', *J. pers. soc. Psychol.*, **5**, 508–516.

WALTERS, R. H., and PARKE, R. D. (1964) 'Social motivation, dependency, and susceptibility to social influence', *Advances in Experimental Social Psychology*, **1**, 232–276.

WALTERS, R. H., and PARKE, R. D. (1965) 'The role of the distance receptors in the development of social responsiveness', *Advances in Child Development and Behavior*, **2**, 59–96.

WALTERS, R. H., and RAY, E. (1960) 'Anxiety, social isolation, and reinforcer effectiveness', *J. Pers.*, **28**, 358–367.

WARDLE, C. J. (1962) 'Social factors in the major functional psychoses', *in* A. T. Welford, *et al.* (eds.) *Society*. London: Routledge and Kegan Paul.

WARR, P. B. (1965) 'Proximity as a determinant of positive and negative sociometric choice', *Brit. J. soc. clin. Psychol.*, **4**, 104–109.

WATSON, O. M., and GRAVES, T. D. (1966) 'Quantitative research in proxemic behavior', *Amer. Anthrop.*, **68**, 971–985.

WEINSTEIN, E. A., and DEUTSCHBERGER, P. (1963) 'Some dimensions of altercasting', *Sociometry*, **26**, 454–466.

WEISBROD, R. M. (1965) 'Looking behavior in a discussion group', unpublished paper. Cornell. Cited by Argyle and Kendon (1967).

WEITMAN, M. (1962) 'More than one kind of authoritarian', *J. Pers.*, **30**, 193–208.

WEIZENBAUM, J. (1967) 'Contextual understanding by computers', *Communications of the A.C.M.*, **10**, 474–480.

WELFORD, A. T. (1958) *Ageing and Human Skill*. Oxford U.P.

WEST, D. J. (1959) 'Parental figures in the genesis of male homosexuality', *Int. J. soc. Psychiat.*, **5**, 85–97.

WHEELER, L., and ARROWOOD, A. J. (1966) 'Restraints against imitation and their reduction, *J. exp. soc. Psychol.*, **2**, 288–300.

WHITING, J. W. M., and CHILD, I. L. (1953) *Child Training and Personality: a Cross-Cultural Study*. New Haven: Yale U.P.

WHITTEMORE, I. C. (1925) 'Influence of competition on performance: an experimental study', *J. abnorm. soc. Psychol.*, **19**, 236–253.

WHORF, B. L. (1956) *Language, Thought and Reality* (ed. J. B. Carrol). Cambridge, Mass.: Technology Press.

WHYTE, W. F. (1949) 'The social structure of the restaurant', *Amer. J. Sociol.*, **54**, 302–308.

WICKLER, W. (1967) 'Socio-sexual signals and their intra-specific imitation among primates', *in* D. Morris (ed.) *Primate Ethology.* London: Weidenfeld and Nicolson.

WIENER, M., and MEHRABIAN, A. (1968) *Language within Language: Immediacy, a Channel in Verbal Communication.* New York: Appleton-Century-Croft.

WILKINS, E. J. (1962) 'Authoritarianism and response to power cues', *J. Pers.*, **30**, 439–457.

WILLIAMS, J. H. (1964) 'Conditioning of verbalization: a review', *Psychol. Bull.*, **62**, 383–393.

WILLIAMS, J. L. (1963) 'Personal space and its relation to extraversion-introversion', unpublished M. A. thesis. Univ. of Alberta.

WILLIAMS, N. (1966) 'Human relations in school: accounts of four projects' (roneoed). Farmington Foundation Research Unit., Oxford.

WILLIS, R. H. (1963) 'Two dimensions of conformity–nonconformity', *Sociometry*, **26**, 499–513.

WILLIS, R. H., and HOLLANDER, E. P. (1964) 'An experimental study of three response modes in social influence situations', *J. abnorm. soc. Psychol.*, **69**, 150–156.

WILLOUGHBY, R. R. (1932) 'Some properties of the Thurstone personality schedule and a suggested revision', *J. soc. Psychol.*, **3**, 401–424.

WINCH, R. F. (1958) *Mate-selection: A Study of Complementary Needs.* New York: Harper and Row.

WING, J. K. (1962) 'Institutionalism in mental hospitals', *Brit. J. soc. clin. Psychol.*, **1**, 38–51.

WISHNER, J. (1960) 'Reappraisal of "impressions of personality" ', *Psychol. Rev.*, **67**, 96–112.

WITTENBORN, J. R. (1965) 'Depression', *in* B. B. Wolman (ed.) *Handbook of Clinical Psychology.* New York: McGraw-Hill.

WOLFF, P. H. (1963) 'Observations on the early development of smiling', *in* B. M. Foss (ed.) *Determinants of Infant Behaviour*, **2.** London: Methuen, pp. 113–138.

WOLFF, W. (1943) *The Expression of Personality: Experimental Depth Psychology.* New York: Harper.

WOLFLE, D. L., and WOLFLE, H. M. (1939) 'The development of cooperative behaviour in monkeys and young children', *J. genet. Psychol.*, **55**, 137–175.

WOLPE, J. (1958) *Psychotherapy by Reciprocal Inhibition.* Stanford U.P.

WOLPE, J. (1961) 'The systematic desensitization treatment of neuroses', *J. Nerv. Ment. Dis.*, **132**, 189–203.

WOODWARD, J. (1958) *Management and Technology.* London: DSIR.

WYLIE, R. C. (1961) *The Self Concept.* Lincoln, Nebraska: Univ. of Nebraska Press.

WYNNE, L. *et al.* (1958) 'Pseudo-mutuality in the family relations of schizophrenics', *Psychiatry*, **21**, 205–220.

WYNNE-EDWARDS, V. C. (1962) *Animal Dispersion in Relation to Social Behaviour.* Edinburgh and London: Oliver and Boyd.

YARROW, L. J. (1964) 'Separation from parents during early childhood', *Review of Child Development Research*, **1**, 89–136.

YOUNG, M., and WILMOTT, P. (1957) *Family and Kinship in East London.* London: Routledge and Kegan Paul.

ZAJONC, R. B. (1965) 'Social facilitation', *Science*, **149**, 269–274.

ZAJONC, R. B., and SALES, S. M. (1966) 'Social facilitation of dominant and subordinate responses', *J. exp. soc. Psychol.*, **2**, 160–168.

ZAJONC, R. B., and WOLFE, D. M. (1963) 'Cognitive consequences of a person's position in a formal organization'. Univ. of Michigan: Institute for Social Research. Tech. Report 23.

ZANDER, A., and CURTIS, T. (1962) 'Effects of social power on aspiration setting and striving', *J. abnorm. soc. Psychol.*, **64**, 63–74.

ZANDER, A., and WOLFE, D. (1964) 'Administrative rewards and coordination among committee members', *Admin. Sci. Quart.*, **9**, 50–69.

ZAZZO, R. (1960) *Les Jumeaux, le Couple et la Personne.* Paris: Presses Univ. France (cited by Ervin-Tripp, 1966).

ZELDITCH, M. (1955) 'Role differentiation in the nuclear family: a comparative study', *in* T. Parsons *et al.* (eds.) *Family, Socialisation and Interaction Process.* Glencoe, Ill.: Free Press.

ZIGLER, E., and PHILLIPS, L. (1962) 'Social competence and the process-reactive distinction in psychopathology', *J. abnorm. soc. Psychol.*, **65**, 215–222.

ZILLER, R. C. (1964) 'Individuation and socialization', *Hum. Relat.*, **17**, 341–360.

ZINSER, O. (1966) 'Imitation, modeling and cross-cultural training'. Aerospace Medical Research Laboratories, Wright-Patterson Air Force Base, Ohio.

ZIPF, G. K. (1935) *The Psycho-biology of Language.* Boston: Houghton Mifflin.

Name Index

Ackerson, L., 334
Adams, B. N., 21, 245
Adorno, T. W., 56, 232
Allen, V. L., 189, 191, 224, 228–9, 277, 279, 282, 286, 329
Allport, F. H., 277, 317
Altman, I., 201, 217, 362
Ambrose, J. A., 48–9
Ames, L. B., 370
Anderson, G. L., 63, 88
Anderson, H. H., 53, 63, 88
Anderson, N. H., 157
Anthony, E. J., 261, 263, 265
Appell, G., 50
Appley, M. H., 45, 52
Ardrey, R., 28, 34
Argyle, M., 16, 20, 53, 56, 64, 78, 85, 95, 104, 107–9, 120, 135, 142–3, 145, 171, 180–1, 186–8, 201, 222, 226, 229, 246, 250–1, 269, 271, 279, 281, 301, 305, 310–11, 315–16, 322, 324, 330, 335, 357, 361, 365, 373–5, 377, 379, 397–8, 404, 416, 435, 437
Argyris, C., 250, 313, 409
Arieti, S., 343–4
Arkoff, A., 239
Armistead, N., 331, 353
Aronson, A., 20, 152
Arrowood, A. J., 173
Asch, S. E., 128, 152, 156
Atkinson, J. W., 65, 153
Ayllon, T., 402, 424
Azrin, N. H., 178

Back, K. W., 118, 206, 211, 228
Backman, C. W., 23, 224, 286, 290, 372, 387
Bailey, D. E., 145, 192

Bales, R. F., 14, 57, 115–16, 168, 171, 219, 229–31, 241, 245, 254–5, 271
Ballachey, E. L., 260
Bandura, A., 172, 178, 234, 290, 369
Bannister, D., 17, 23, 130, 358, 430
Banta, T. J., 230
Barker, R. G., 84
Barr, J., 418
Bartlett, F. C., 155, 180
Bass, B. M., 234, 272–3, 322, 402, 413
Bateson, G., 120, 340–1
Bateson, N., 198, 258
Bayley, N., 55
Beach, F. A., 31, 44
Beegle, J. A., 211
Belbin, E., 414
Belbin, R. M., 414
Bell, N. W., 350
Beloff, H., 225
Bem, D. J., 258
Bender, A., 114
Benne, K. D., 261, 409
Bennett, E. B., 312
Bennett, E. M., 327
Bennis, W., 265
Bennis, W. G., 409
Benoit-Smullyan, E., 234
Berger, A., 341
Berger, E. M., 392
Berkowitz, L., 46–7, 88, 152, 174–5, 193, 281, 311
Berne, E., 117, 207, 348, 426
Bernstein, A., 115, 166, 203, 208, 284
Bernstein, B., 80–1
Berry, P. C., 259

489

Subject Index

accent, 114
achievement motivation, 54
adolescent, groups, 248 ff
  identity-formation, 369 f
  social skills, 398 f
affiliation, behaviour pattern, 122
  cross-cultural differences, 82
  drive, 50 ff
  interaction dimension, 320
  primates, 31 ff
affiliative balance, 53, 107 f
aggression, 28 f, 45 f
anxiety, 324 ff, 420 ff
  neurosis, 347 f
Arabs, 83 f, 86 f
audience, anxiety, 325
  effects of, 373 f
authoritarian leaders, 302, 400
  personality, 53 f, 323
  cross-cultural differences, 82
autistic children, 342
aversion therapy, 413

Bales categories, 116, 168
behaviour therapy, 420 ff
body colouration, primate, 38
  contact, 92 ff, 315 f
  image, 358 ff

castes, 89 f
categorisation, 133 f, 144
channel control, 72, 86, 109, 202
children, social interaction, 55 ff
  friendship, 62 f
  language development, 67 ff
  peer group, 60 ff
class differences, 80 f, 89 f, 174
  conflict, 436 f
clothes, 99 f
coalition, 239

coding, 75 f
cognitive complexity, 159 f
  processes, interaction, 185
  perception, 128 f, 153 f
cohesiveness, 14, 220 f, 237 f
committees, 253 ff
communication, failure of, 76 f
  nets, 309 f
  in organisations, 290 ff
compatibility, 204 f
complementarity, 213
computer simulation, 168 f, 204
concealment, 385 f
conformity, 82 ff
consistency, 205
cooperation, 222 f
crime, 435 f
critical incidents, 403
cross-cultural differences, 81 ff,
  137 f, 139
culture, 78 ff
cut-off, 109

decentering, 190
deception, 381, 385 f
de-individuation, 376 f
delinquency, 350 f, 435 f
democratic leadership, 300 ff
dependency, 36 f, 47 ff, 323 f
depression, 342 ff
desensitisation, 421 f
deviates, 226 f
dimensions of social performance,
  319 ff
direction of gaze, *see* gaze
disclosure, 208 f
dominance, dimension, 323
  drive, 53
  elements, 122
  non-verbal signals, 141

501